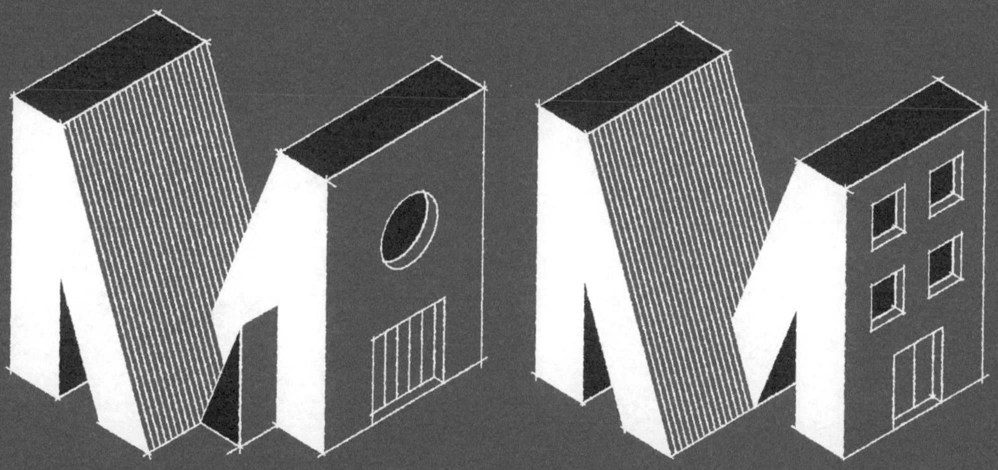

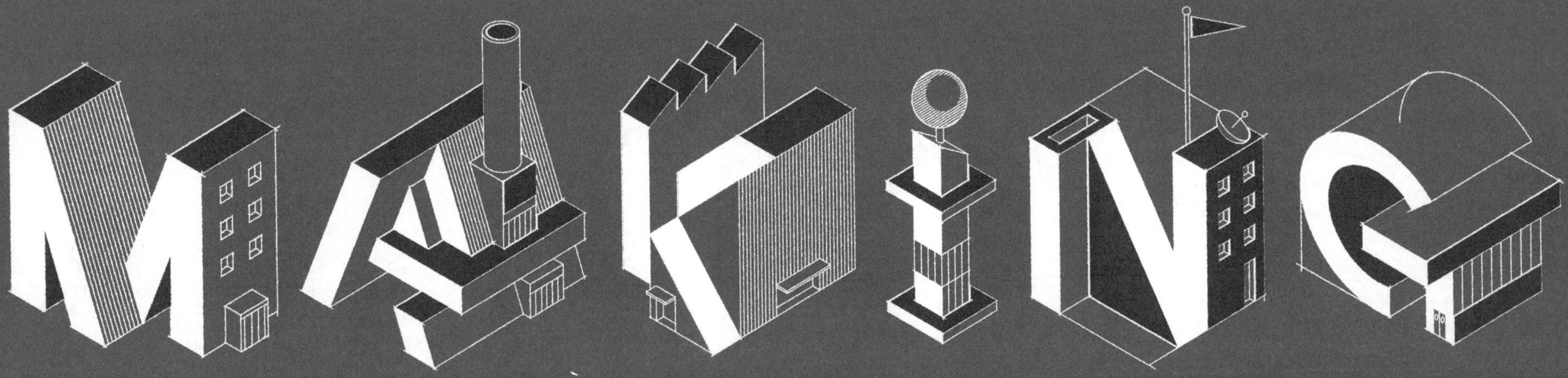

Thames & Hudson

with over 900 illustrations

WILL JONES

ARCHITECTS' SKETCHBOOKS – THE CREATIVE PROCESS

CONTENTS

FOREWORD • THE NEED TO SKETCH

BENEDICT O'LOONEY

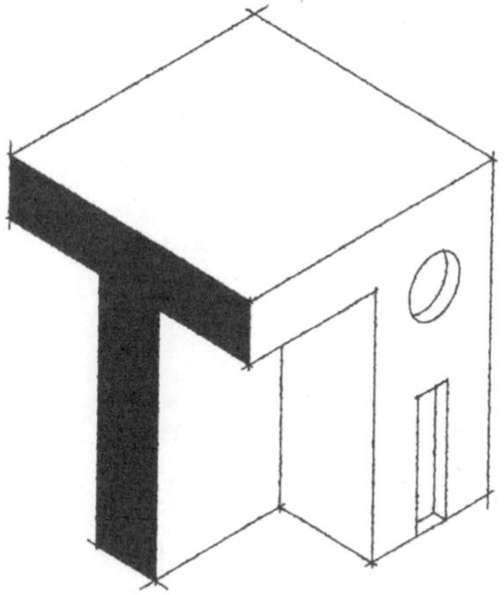

The best architects are both accomplished builders and visual artists. Sketching is our primary mode of communication, discovery and delight: it is central to our lives, developing throughout careers and shaping us as designers and people.

Most of us leave an expressive trail of drawings as children, but it was not until I was 21 that I began to energetically sketch. As an undergraduate at Hunter College in New York, I joined a study tour to Rome. I remember being so excited about the ancient and Baroque architecture I encountered – drawing seemed the only effective way to understand these incredible buildings.

In retrospect, it is clear that excitement was the core driver behind this passion and desire to connect, to feel the power and muscular monumentality of the city's iconic churches. By drawing, I began to learn about the architecture and the people who designed and built these amazing structures.

IN FOR A PENNY, IN FOR A POUND: DISCOVERING ARCHITECTURE

My parents were art historians, so sketching was fused with the joy of reading about the cities I found myself in. Back in New York, I began to seek out and sketch the city's best and most significant architecture and sculpture – starting with the early skyscrapers, and later exploring the blaze of modern and contemporary architecture in Manhattan. The laden shelves of the college and public libraries guided me through these journeys, my trusty bicycle making the architecture and sights so accessible.

In my idealistic, youthful naivety, I believed in the École des Beaux-Arts narrative that 'architecture is the mother of the arts'. Drawing seemed to link painting, architecture and sculpture wonderfully. New York is one of the great Beaux-Arts cities, and this romantic ideal of buildings adorned with sculpture and murals seemed to greet me at every turn. Happily, 30 years later, this architectural vision remains a guiding spirit.

LEARNING FROM THE MASTERS

This first stage of sketching was a powerful tool for learning and exploration, as well as developing an identity as a visual artist. I believe that one's character, visual outlook and understanding are shaped by what one sees and interacts with. I devoured the art and architecture of New York: it was my world.

Between college and graduate school, my emergent skills as a draughtsman landed me a job assisting an artist in Cologne. From there, I set out to explore Europe and a new horizon of architecture and urbanism began to open up – the organic, super-compact cities of the 'Old World', which I documented in my sketchbooks. By the age of 25 I had discovered many of the masters of townscape drawing: Hugh Ferriss's potent vision of Manhattan's skyscrapers from the 1920s and '30s; Canaletto's stunning command of perspective; and the beautiful drawings and paintings of Manet and Degas. This belief in the unity of architecture and the fine arts propelled me to museums to copy the works I found there.

Through my need to read about architecture and urban history, I evolved an approach to sketching that combined drawing with notes, and began to fill the pages of my sketchbooks with fields of words and sketches – a phase that culminated in a series of aerial views of midtown Manhattan, from the rooftops of Art Deco skyscrapers. These quirky drawings found me a place at Yale School of Architecture.

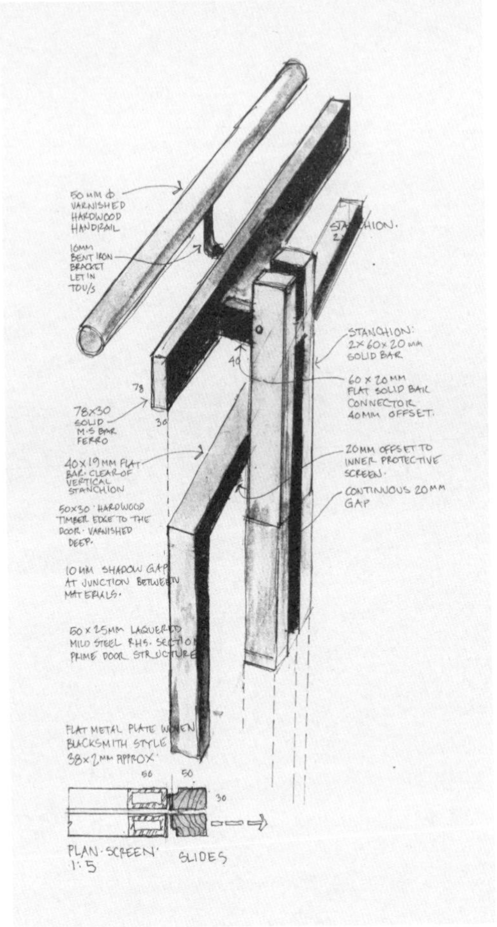

Scarpa, Benedict O'Looney

DISCOVERY FUELS DESIGN

Upon arrival at Yale, this period of discovery paid off handsomely. I found that the ideas always flowed, drawn from an incredibly rich mental library of great buildings and spaces that I could immediately deploy and reconfigure to meet diverse design briefs.

Although coming from a liberal-arts background, I soon found that I could compete with the more advanced students. I had this curious confidence as a designer, imbued with the swirl of the finest buildings and urban spaces in Europe and America, which I had been sketching and cycling my way through. My passion for drawing also made it easy to visualize spaces and details. In short, lively sketching skills helped make the challenge of studying architecture fun.

'EQUIPPED WITH NEW SKETCHES, I FELT SO MUCH MORE CONFIDENT ABOUT MY OWN WORK, KNOWING THAT IT WAS ROOTED IN THE DIRECT EXPERIENCE OF THE ARCHITECTURE DOCUMENTED IN MY SKETCHBOOK.'

After graduation in 1992, sketching took on a new dimension. I took a job at Nicholas Grimshaw & Partners in London, working on some seriously 'High Tech' buildings. There was a strong culture of drawing in that studio; the intricate detailing of the structures and skins was created with stacks of hand-drawn details, sometimes at 1:1.

Feeling cast into the deep end, I began to find that the answers to many of the questions I had as a junior architect were all around me in the city's buildings. After work, armed with a sketchbook, I would seek out the great contemporary examples, and sketch, measure and draw the details I was looking for. The following morning, equipped with new sketches, I felt so much more confident about my own work, knowing that it was rooted in the direct experience of the architecture documented in my sketchbook.

THE JOY OF KEEPING A SKETCHBOOK

The final strand to this drawing narrative is the joy of making interesting things to share with people. I usually work with a large landscape sketchbook, a format that allows quite long, horizontal views. For me, that is mostly cityscapes, often taken over a number of sessions. I have found that these large drawings can happily co-exist with smaller sketches on the same sheet of paper. By combining drawings, page by page, the sketchbooks begin to take on a narrative life, giving order to weekly discoveries. Some drawings succeed, some fail, but all show the interest in recording the important and inspiring things we encounter.

My work varies between pencil, pen and ink, watercolour and coloured pencils, with some drawings featuring all of these. With a big sketchbook, it is great fun to collage different sketches together, the different 'motifs' demanding different media. Sketching delivers so much: it is a playful way to learn, and a source of strength and wisdom for a designer and fulfilment for a visual artist. As you will discover over the following pages of this book, sketching unites us wonderfully in our pursuit of a more beautiful and refined world.

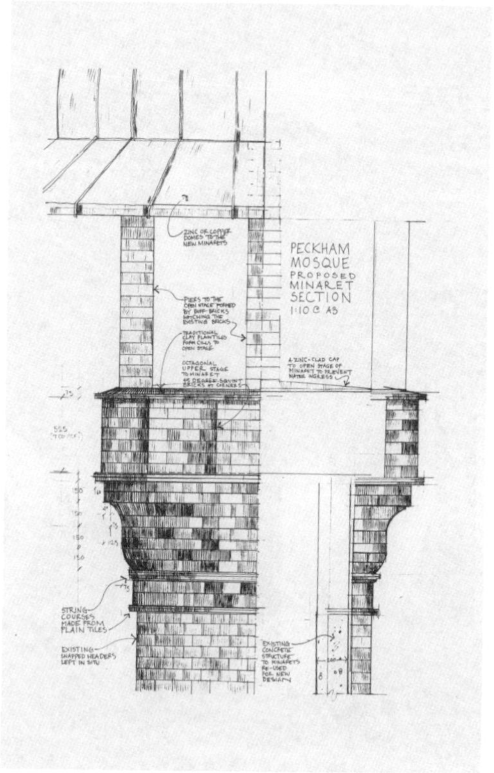

Peckham Mosque, Benedict O'Looney

INTRODUCTION • OF MICE AND MEN
WILL JONES

If you are reading these words, you are probably holding this book, and therefore already understand the value of physical versus digital. You are taking in much more than the information on the page, because you are experiencing the book on multiple levels: its weight, the texture and thickness of the pages and the way the light reflects from them, even the smell. You have an immediate and tactile response that is far more complete than you could ever hope to experience through a digital device. This is why the physical realm and our interaction with and immersion into it is so important, and why we will never truly succumb to a fully digital lifestyle.

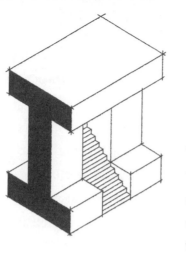

Now consider the role of the architect and the progression of a profession that has been swept along in our digital revolution, turning its practitioners from masters of the pen, pencil and slide rule into computer geeks and 3D-visualization specialists. Where once every line in the design for a new building was pored over by an individual for at least as long as it took to draw it by hand, now the majority of plans, elevations and sections are crafted by armies of plastic mice!

Architecture has changed, as was the need, to keep up with and push forward the boundaries of just what architects can create, and it has done so willingly and digitally – or so we've been led to believe. The proof: a cornucopia of fantastical buildings, of ever wilder and wackier forms, which look as if they have spawned directly from the bowels of some digital progenitor with little or no human help. But delve behind the scenes, root through the desk drawers of the rows of digitally crowned workstations at almost any architectural practice, and you'll discover a secret: notepads, stacks of paper, pencils, fine-point pens. These are the architect's tools, and all that is needed to get back to the heart of design: the sketch.

Canadian architect Rob Miners (p. 206) believes that sketching allows an intuitive, instant expression of ideas in physical form, and he knows

'WHERE ONCE EVERY LINE IN THE DESIGN FOR A NEW BUILDING WAS PORED OVER BY AN INDIVIDUAL FOR AT LEAST AS LONG AS IT TOOK TO DRAW IT BY HAND, NOW THE MAJORITY OF PLANS, ELEVATIONS AND SECTIONS ARE CRAFTED BY ARMIES OF PLASTIC MICE!'

'GOOD DESIGN CAN ONLY ARISE FROM QUIET OBSERVATION, MEDITATION, REFLECTION. IN A WAY, SKETCHING IS THE YOGA OF THE ARCHITECT, OPENING A GATE TO CHILDHOOD MEMORIES OF AFTERNOONS WITH PAPER AND COLOURED PENCILS ON THE FLOOR. HOW COULD THIS NOT IMPROVE OUR DESIGNS?'

where these instincts come from. 'I've been drawing since long before I knew my alphabet,' he says. 'I imagined a tree, and it appeared on paper. With each passing year, the drawing of the tree satisfied me more as my sketching abilities improved. Sketches allow flexibility, since they don't require the same level of precision as a computer, and something that you initially thought would be 15 cm (6 in.) wide can easily be reinterpreted as 20 cm (8 in.) wide. The best computer programs will allow room for imprecision, but they can't replicate an innate skill developed over a lifetime, so they present more barriers to expression and creativity.'

So architects do still sketch and, in fact, they have never stopped, because there is no better way in which to instantly express an idea. Much faster than fumbling with technology, this is the direct route: non-stop, no detours, no diversions. The architect pours out his or her thoughts onto paper and with each stroke of the pen, pencil or brush, there is more than an illustrative direction. The very weight of the line conveys emotion, whether a speculative stroke, a fanciful flourish of smudged charcoal or a thick line denoting a particularly important aspect of the design. So much more than the digital already – and these are just the first few doodles.

Carlos Gómez of Spanish firm InN Arquitectura (p. 120) embraces the value of physically orientated design and describe sketching as the 'most enjoyable' part of the process. He believes that the constant flow of sketched ideas releases inner tension and gives a sense of calm to their work, noting that 'architects must rebel against the frenetic production rhythm of our time'.

'Good design can only arise from quiet observation, meditation, reflection,' he explains. 'In a way, sketching is the yoga of the architect, opening a gate to childhood memories of afternoons with paper and coloured pencils on the floor. How could this not improve our designs? Blueprints are produced digitally, plans and sections are remastered, stored and sent electronically – but imagine trying

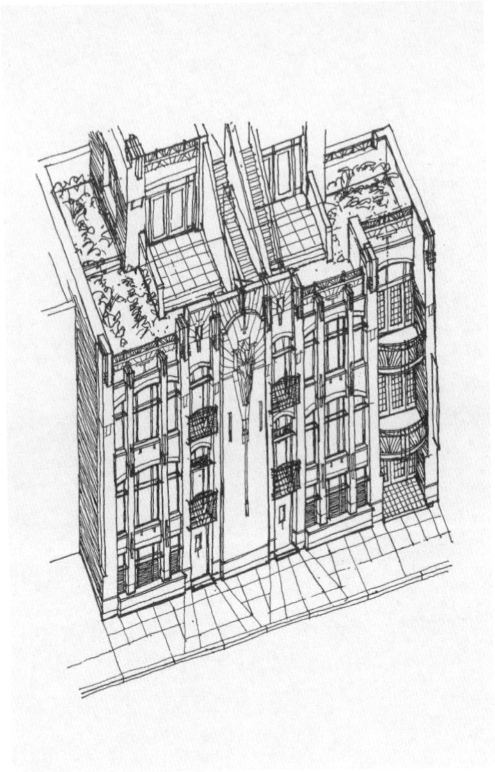

Above: Sybaris Condominiums, Rob Miners
Opposite: Composite of sketches, Eek en Dekkers

-600 = 4550
Binnenwerks!
OPLOSSING RAMEN BOVEN
WATER loop.
Bovendorpel
grote steen
(zoals dicht geschilderde
ramen in badkamer!)
Hoogte trappen meten!
3300
1400
2800
330.
P = 3300

'ARCHITECTS SKETCH BECAUSE THEY FIND IT TO BE ONE OF THE BEST METHODS OF COMMUNICATING THEIR IDEAS WITH OTHERS, AND BECAUSE THEY NEED TO DOWNLOAD THEIR IDEAS FROM BRAIN TO PAPER AND THERE IS NO MORE DIRECT WAY.'

to express the instinctive emotion of a sketch in digital format? It would be like pouring out your heart to your girlfriend in Morse code. Eventually, you would get the message across, but it would take a while. By the time you had finished, she'd have got bored and started dating the guy in the next seat, who was chatting to her face to face!'

The importance of the 'physical' cannot be overstated in all aspects of the architectural profession, especially when explaining designs to the people they are for. 'Clients absolutely love sketches,' says Indian architect Sanjay Puri (p. 266). 'There have been many instances when clients have asked me to just send my sketches to them, since they find the drawings easier to understand than a digital representation. This also saves time: making an entire set of drawings and a 3D visualization can take one to two weeks, whereas a sketch explaining the concept could be sent to a client within a few hours at most.'

Yes, architects sketch because they find it to be one of the best methods of communicating their ideas with others, and because they need to download ideas from brain to paper and there is no more direct way. They sketch because they need to relax, and for many other reasons besides. In this second volume of *Architects' Sketchbooks*, the architects explain in their own words how and why they still believe in physical design. We'll also see the work they produce, allowing us to fully appreciate why a sketch, drawing, model or painting is so much more exciting than any 3D fully rendered fly-through. We'll also be able to feel their emotions, because the sketches they have shared with us each contain within them a small part of the architect's soul.

Dive into this book with all of your senses as you explore some wonderful designs and magical pieces of artwork. Download a digital version of it, a review or a screengrab to show to a friend – but remember to impress upon them that the true beauty of this volume and everything inside it cannot be found on a screen, just as the true genius of the contributing architects must be experienced physically to be fully understood.

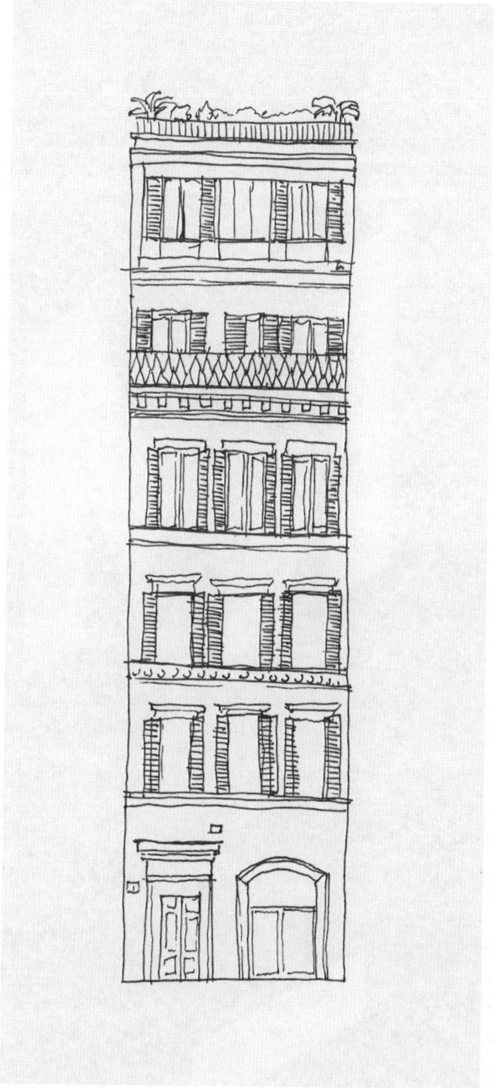

Above: Rome, InN Arquitectura
Opposite: Composite of sketches, InN Arquitectura

MAK
ING

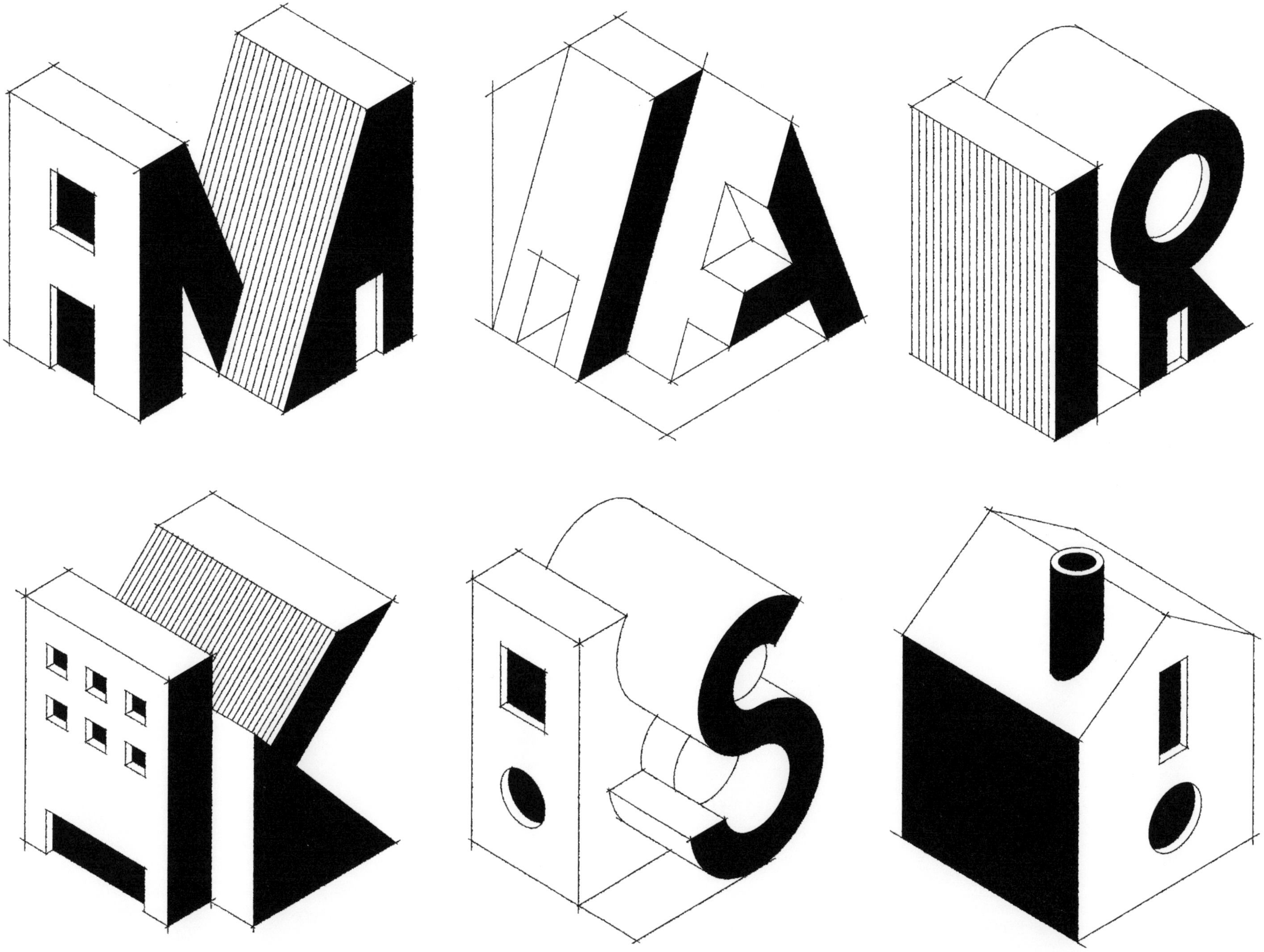

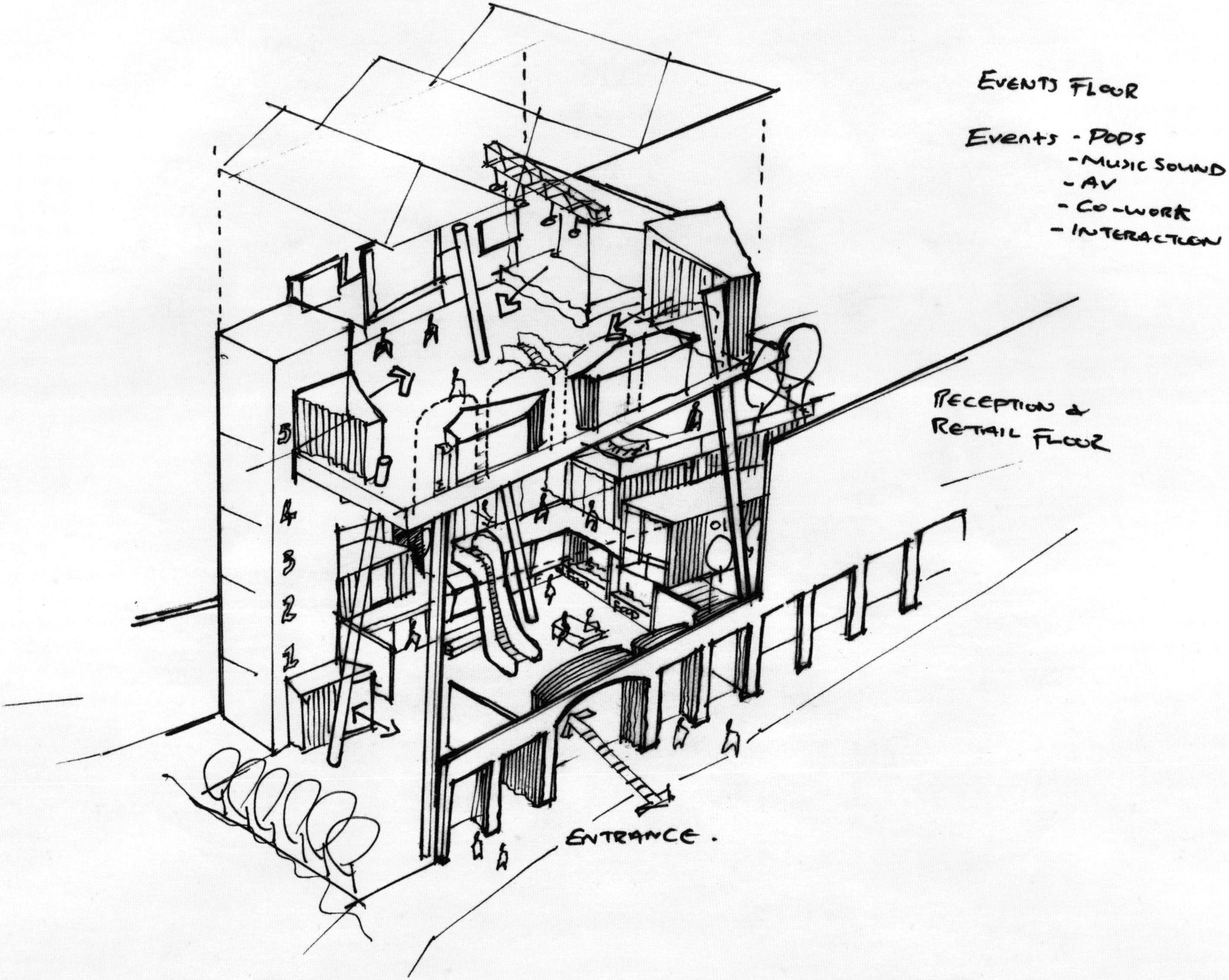
EVENTS FLOOR
EVENTS - PODS
-MUSIC SOUND
-AV
-CO-WORK
-INTERACTION
RECEPTION &
RETAIL FLOOR
5
4
3
2
1
ENTRANCE.

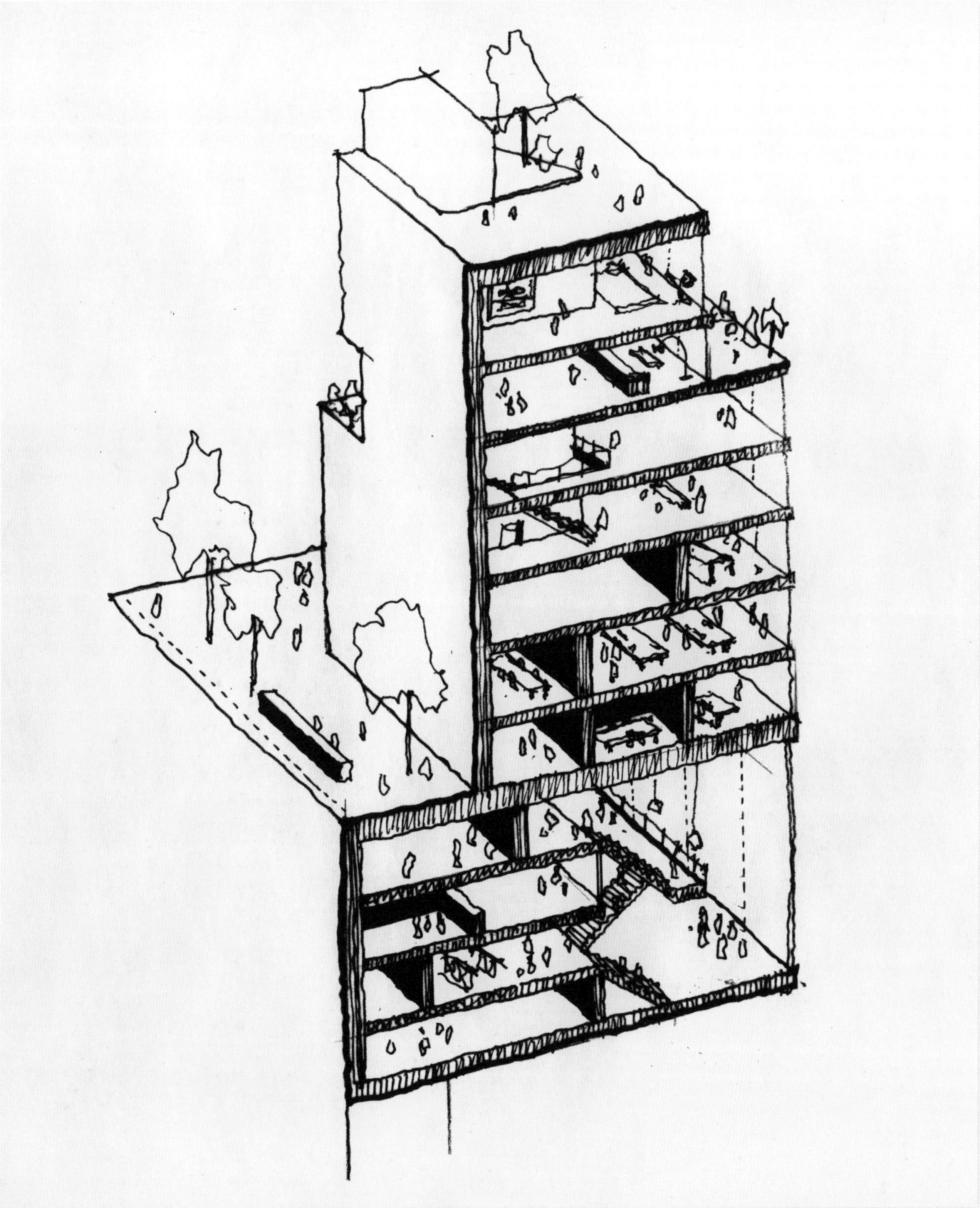

BEN ADAMS

Ben Adams Architects • UK

Featured projects: Guggenheim Helsinki [p. 18]
Future Workspace [p. 19] · Study of Metropol
Parasol, Seville [pp. 20–1] · Pointless City [p. 22–23]

'My aunt, who is an artist, was delighted to discover that all of the architects she knows reach for a pen or a pencil when trying to explain something,' says Ben Adams, an architect himself. 'It can be directions to a restaurant, an idea for a painting or a shopping list, but it will still end up as a sketch if an architect is involved.'

The first line of his company's design statement is: 'We like handmade buildings'. It is this tactile nature that the firm, founded in 2010 and located in London, brings to its designs, and physical design methods have always been part of this architect's arsenal.

'I learned to draw and paint as part of my education,' he says, 'so the urge to sketch when thinking about a problem is an immediate one. We have different tools now that let us see ideas in three dimensions via computer modelling, 3D-printing, virtual reality, and so on, yet the sketch remains an unmatched way of thinking architecturally and working out an idea.'

While Adams and many other architects note the importance of the immediacy of sketching, he also extols the benefits of its time-consuming nature. 'Space is tangibly four-dimensional, as the three spatial dimensions combine with time to allow architecture to emerge,' he explains. 'We design in the same way: the process of drawing and the time it takes allow the muse to take hold and ideas to emerge at their own pace. Other methods demand too much detail or precision up front, and too little slackness or vagueness, which are also necessary.'

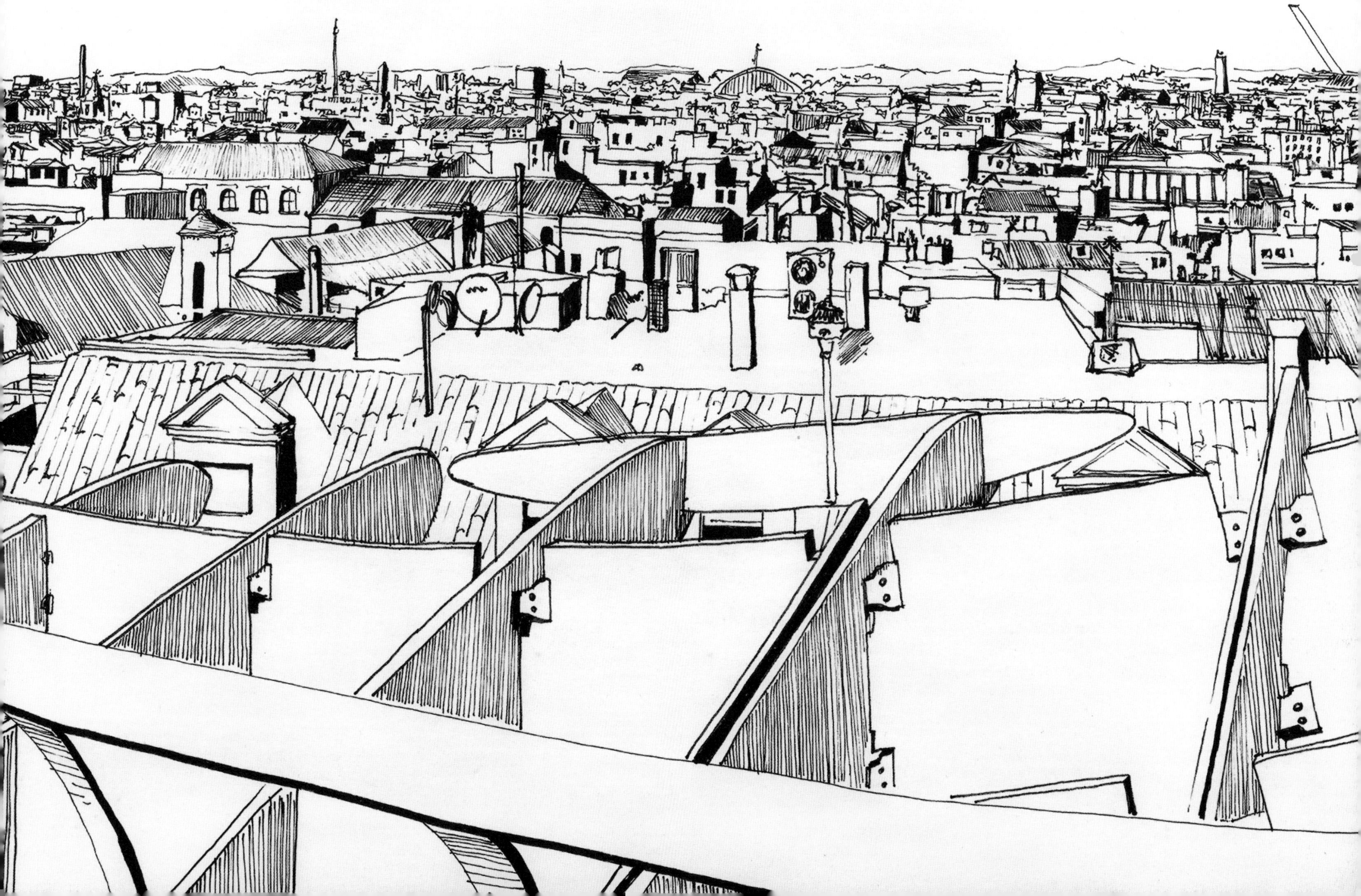

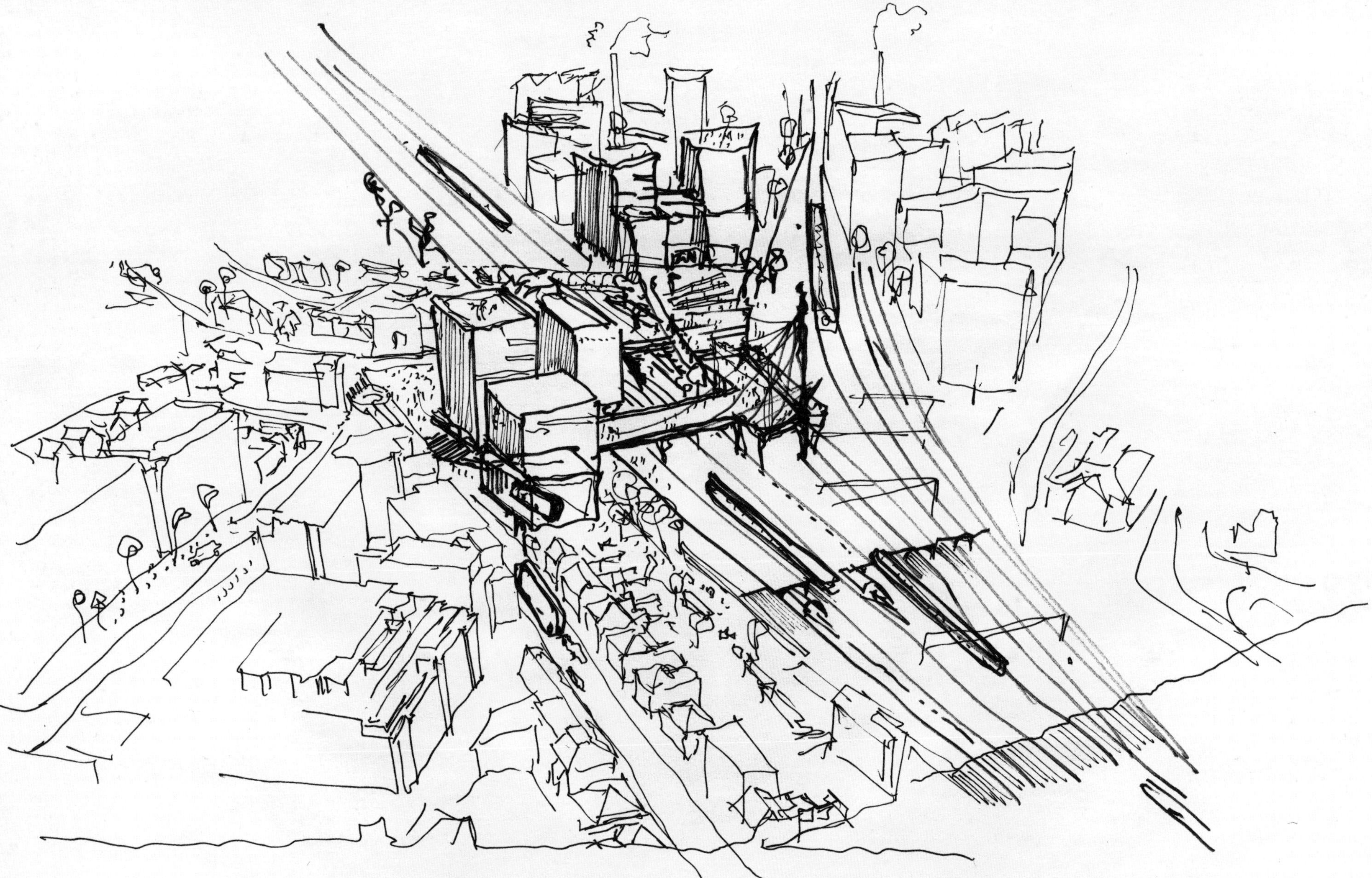

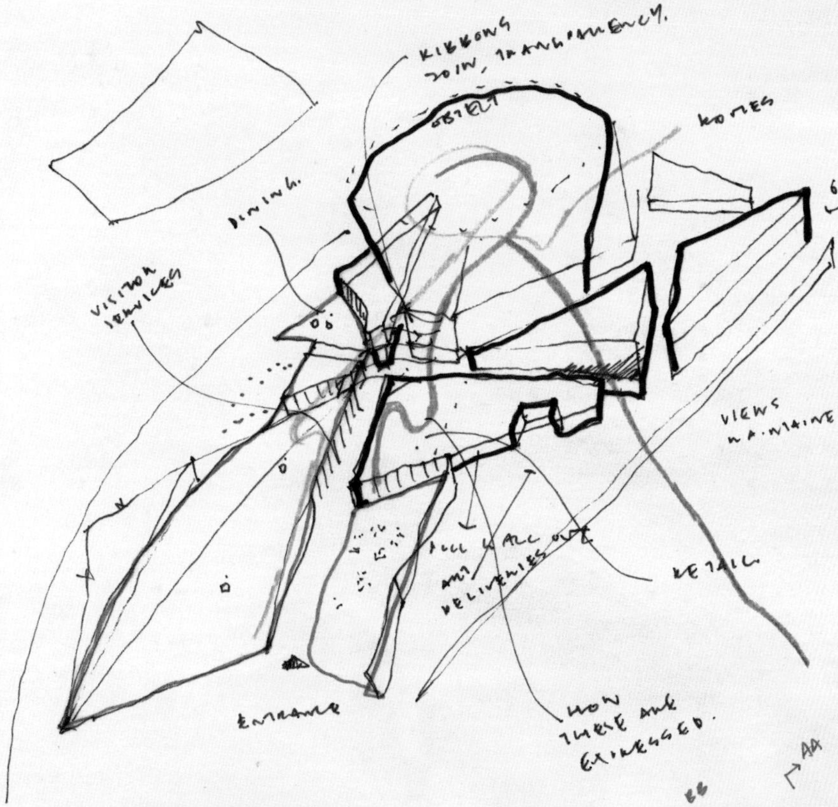
DINING
VISITOR SERVICES
HOMES
RETAIL
ENTRANCE
HOW THESE ARE EXPRESSED.

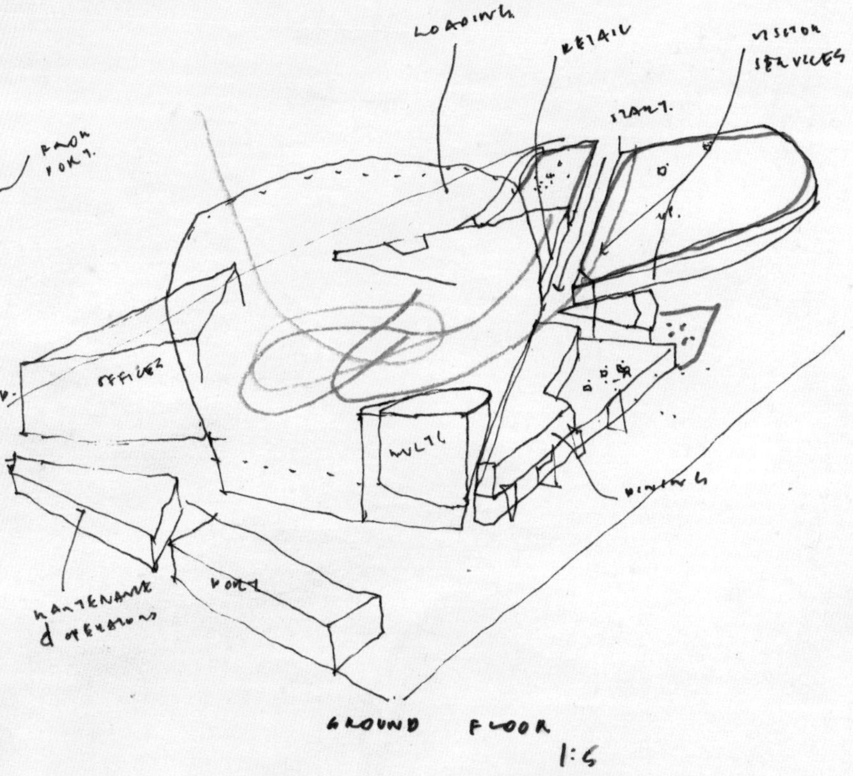
LOADING
RETAIL
VISITOR SERVICES
STAFF
VIEWS MAINTAINED.
OFFICES
MULTI
DINING
PORT
GROUND FLOOR

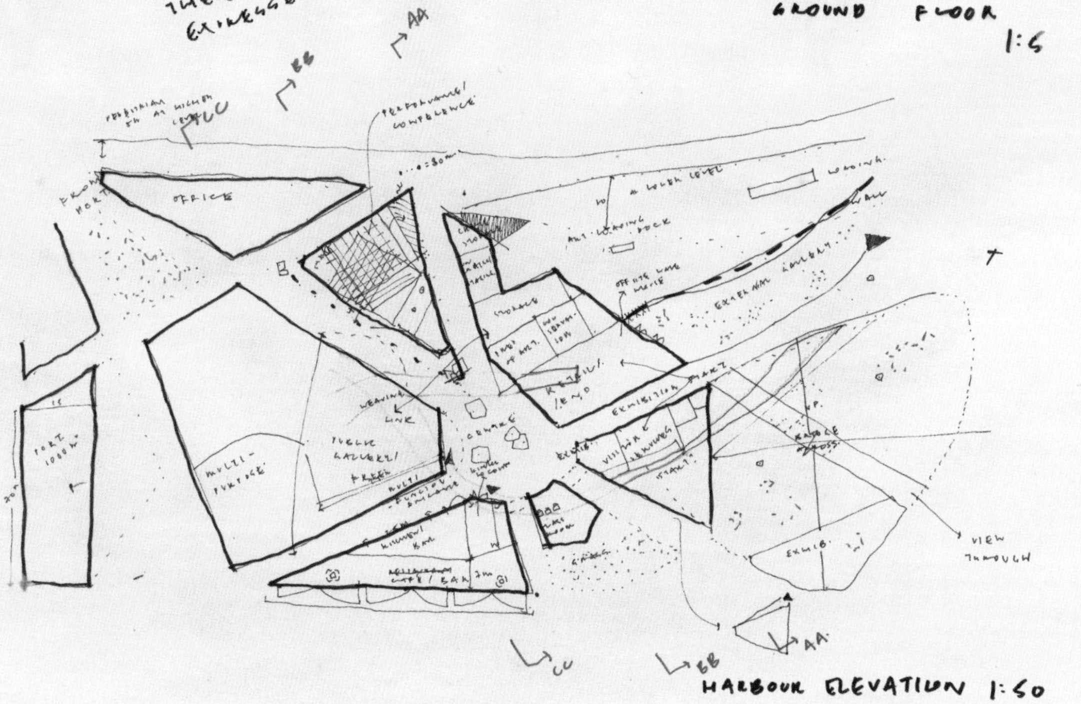
OFFICE
EXTERNAL GALLERY
EXHIBITION
VIEW THROUGH
HARBOUR ELEVATION 1:50

MANUEL AIRES MATEUS

Aires Mateus e Associados • Portugal

Featured project: Alhambra [pp. 24–5]

'Sketching establishes a swifter relationship between the representation and the brain than non-physical methods, allowing for a continuous dialogue,' says Manuel Aires Mateus, principal of the Lisbon-based Aires Mateus e Associados. 'It will continue to be the way to work with any subject in architecture.'

Since graduating in 1986, Aires Mateus has held academic positions in universities in Europe and the US, and has lectured around the world. Today, he uses sketches primarily as an internal design tool within the firm. He carries notepads and pens wherever he goes, and believes in sketching as a tool for forming ideas: its process exploring 'fringes of uncertainty' and enriching the final result, and its value increased with each iteration.

'We communicate with clients through scale models and more comprehensible, computer-generated drawings,' he explains, 'but we will often use sketches during meetings if there are any issues to be clarified.'

Aires Mateus sees the sketch as a critique of other forms of representation: a swift and tactile method of questioning designs; a format understood and interpreted by architects, more so than by clients. 'The sketch is a quick record that allows for constant questioning,' he says. 'It is also a skill that implies a manual capacity, which helps to clarify the ideas. In this sense, it comes closer to architecture than other forms of representation.'

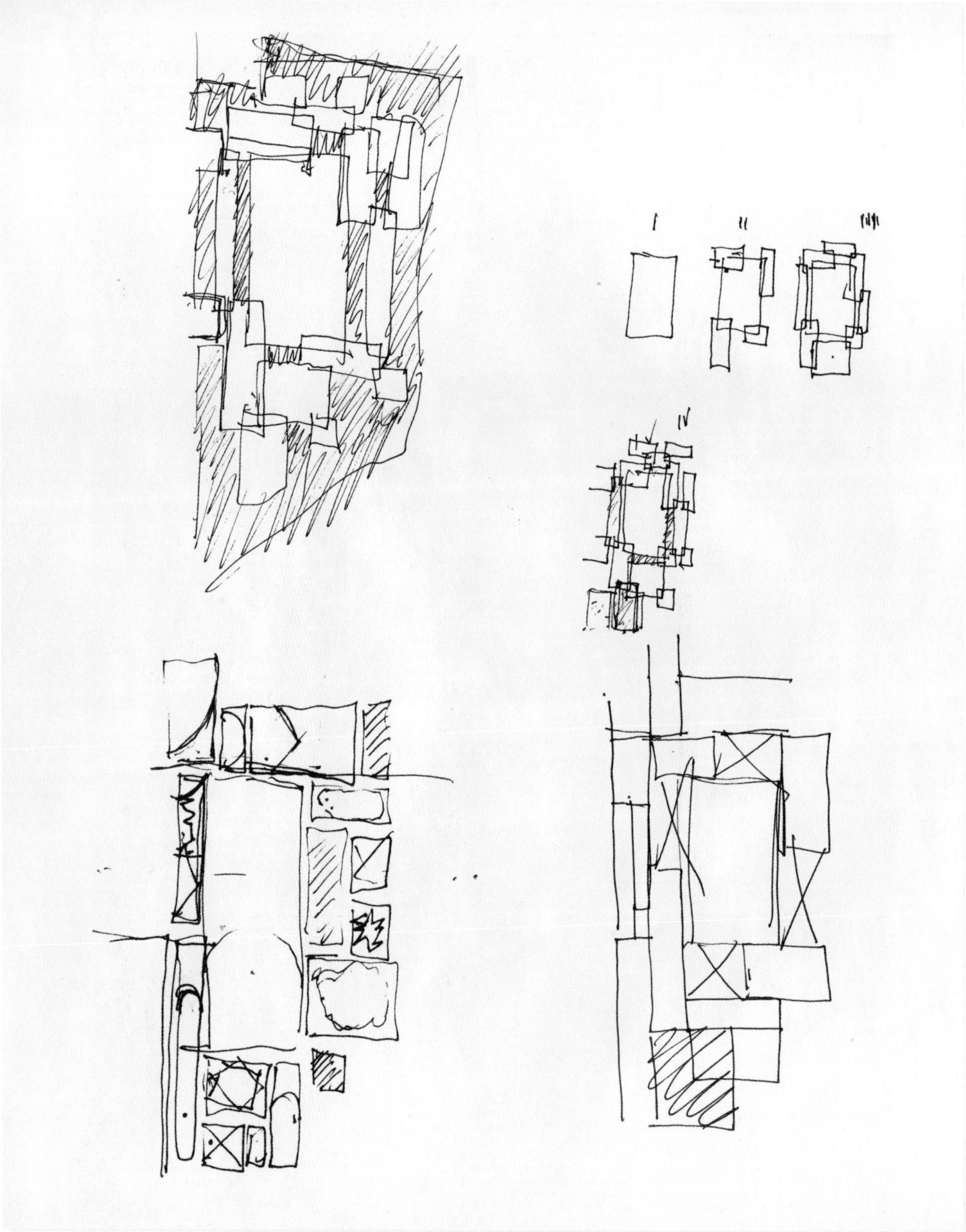

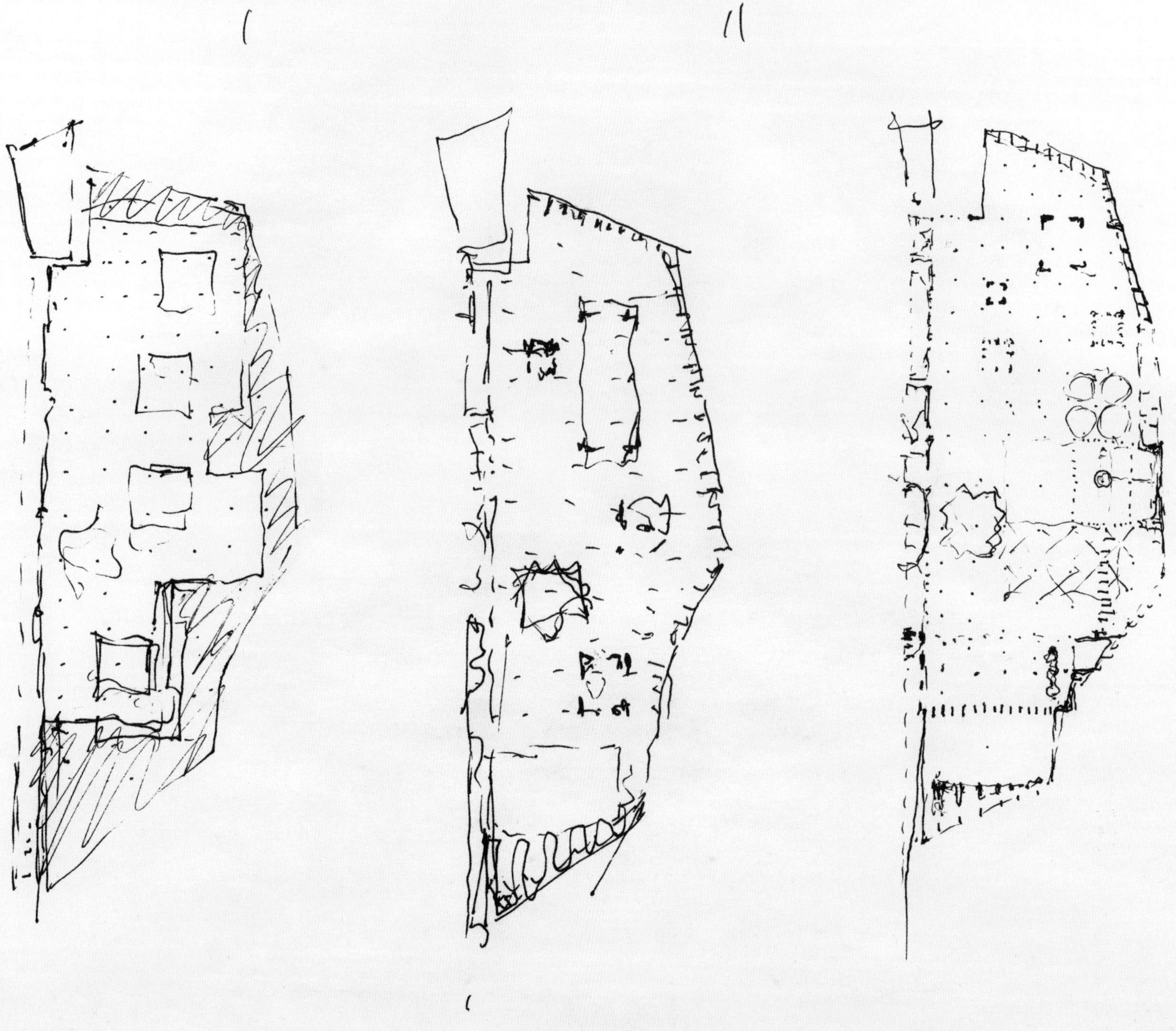

WIEL ARETS

Wiel Arets Architects • Netherlands

Featured projects: A' Tower [p. 26, left] · Campus Hoogvliet [p. 26, right]
B' Tower [p. 27, left] · Beltgens Fashion Shop [right]

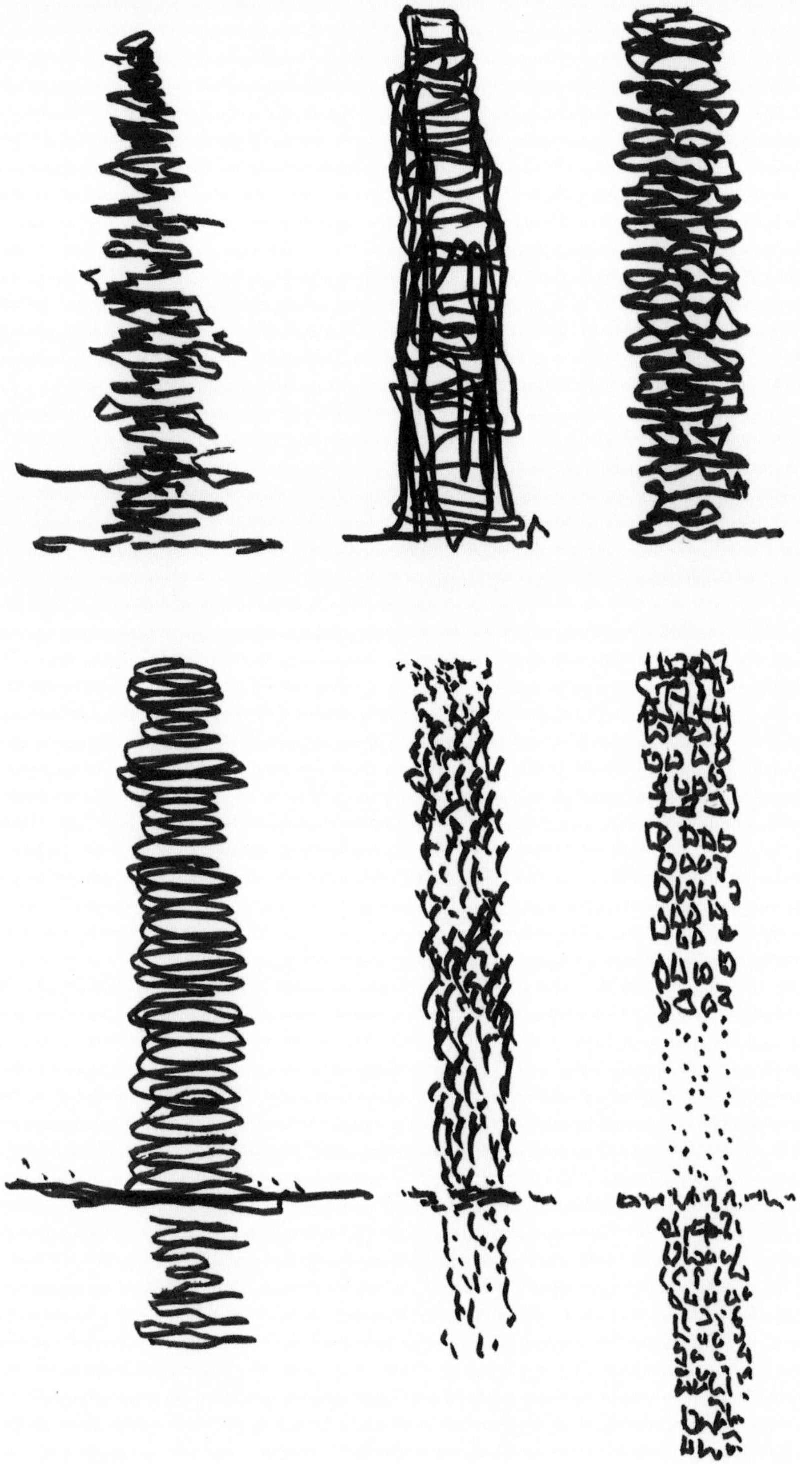

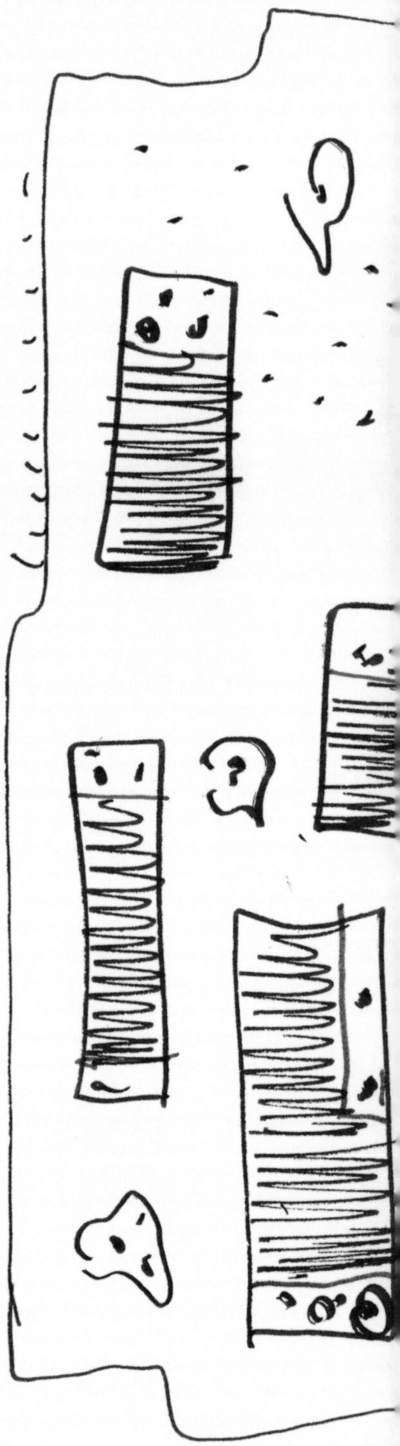

'It is the ideas behind objects that interest me, rather than the objects themselves,' says Dutch architect Wiel Arets. 'The difference between a work of art produced by an artist and a drawing made by an architect is that for the latter, the drawing is not the end product. In the office, I often sketch to help me work through my thoughts. More often than not, I will make a sketch and throw it away after a meeting. Drawings are not precious objects to save and cherish.'

Arets could be described as a theorist, industrial designer and urbanist, as well as an architect, such are his talents and breadth of knowledge. His firm has offices throughout Europe and the US, and he has held academic positions in Chicago, Berlin and Rotterdam.

'Why sketch?' he muses. 'Sketching is very useful for working out initial thoughts for a project, although it has become less important with the introduction of the computer. But it is critical when thinking conceptually about a new project, whether a design for a spoon, a house or a masterplan. Designing any of these things would be harder without sketching, but it is not essential to the design process. I rarely save my drawings. If I sketch during a meeting with clients, it is to help them visualize my ideas. In this sense, clients do not interact with my sketches, but observe the ideas within them.'

Rotterdam
2009

CECIL BALMOND

Balmond Studio • UK

Featured projects: Element [p. 28, top] · Broken Moon [p. 29, top]
Congrexpo [p. 29, bottom] · Mesquita [p. 30, top] · Untitled
[pp. 28, bottom; 30, bottom; 31]

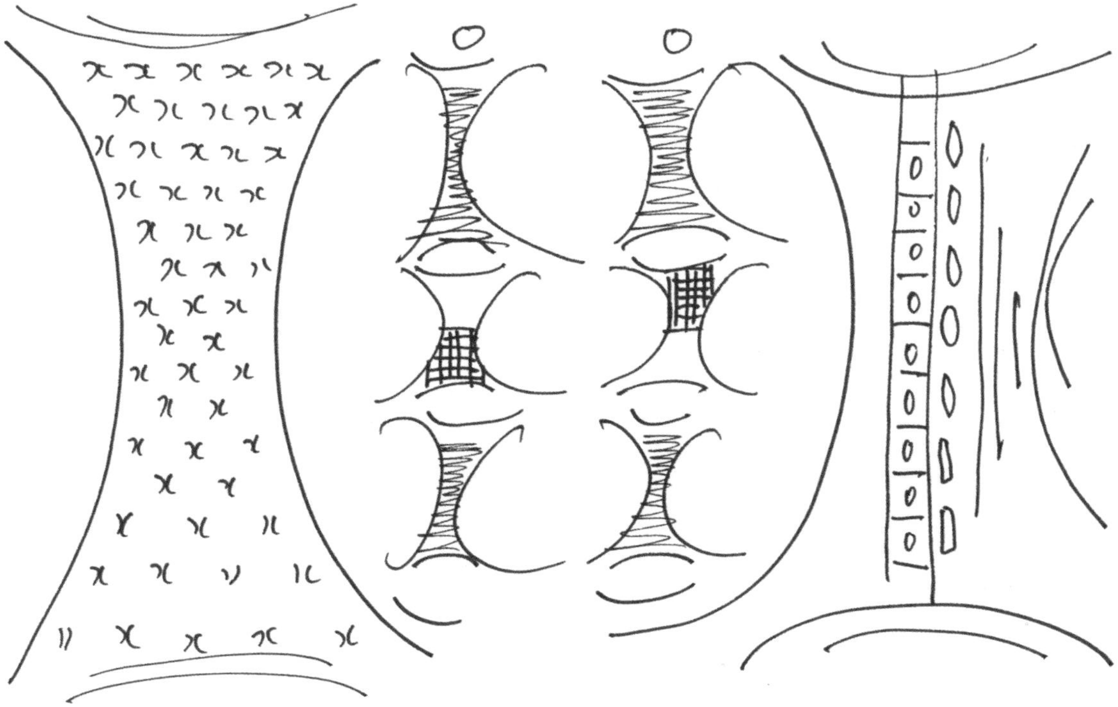

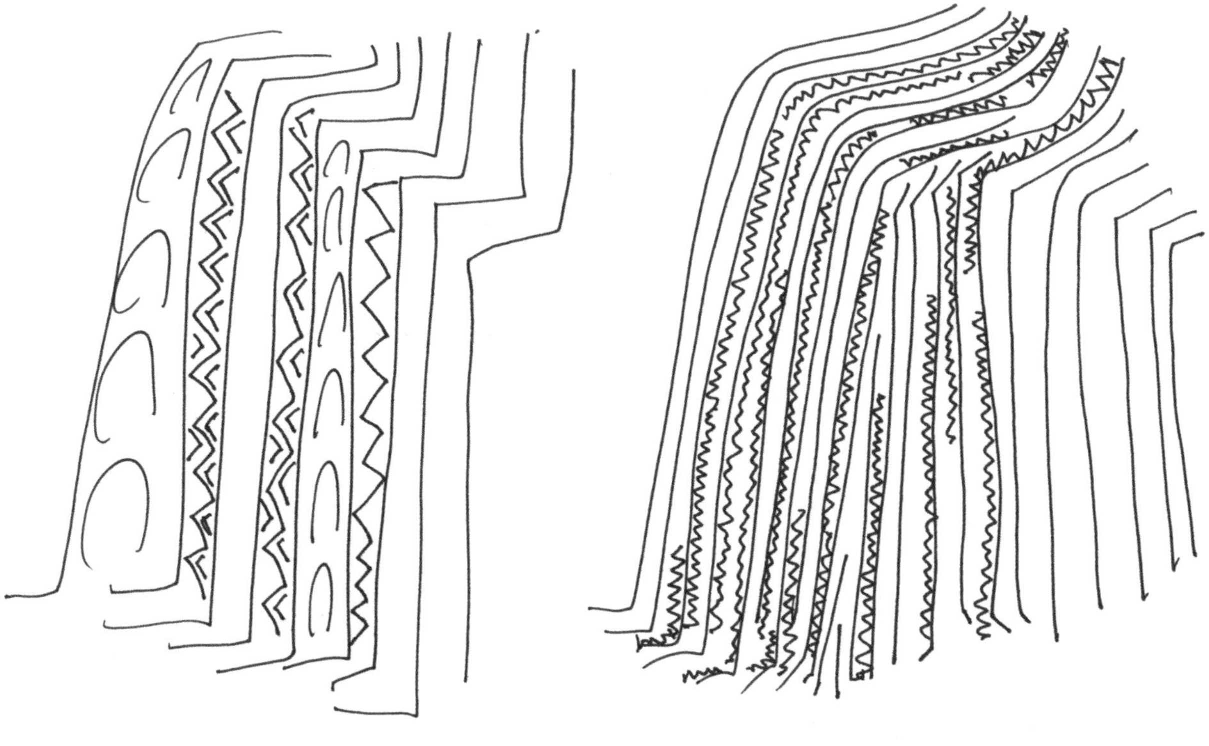

Architect Cecil Balmond's desk is awash with pieces of paper, layer upon layer of his 'thoughts' spread out before him. Iteration, the 'search for the convergence of the idea', is the foundation of his design methodology. It is a style that has seen successful collaborations with his peers and renowned artists, as well as standout works of his own.

During a distinguished career at Arup, including forming and heading the groundbreaking Advanced Geometry Unit, Balmond has explored the crossover between art and science. The result, he believes, is a reinvention of the very concept of space and transformation of the meaning of geometry, form and structure. Some might think that his background as an engineer would remove him somewhat from the artistic element of the architectural process, but this critical thinker says that he is compelled to sketch.

'I can't talk without a free line accompanying my thought,' he explains. 'The sketch keeps the concepts alive like no digital medium could, and refreshes the pragmatic journey towards our objective.'

While many other architects favour models or digital means to communicate designs with clients, Balmond often conveys his most radical ideas to clients in the medium he feels most at ease working in. 'My clients love sketches,' he explains. 'They feel involved: they feel like they are at the source.'

broken moon

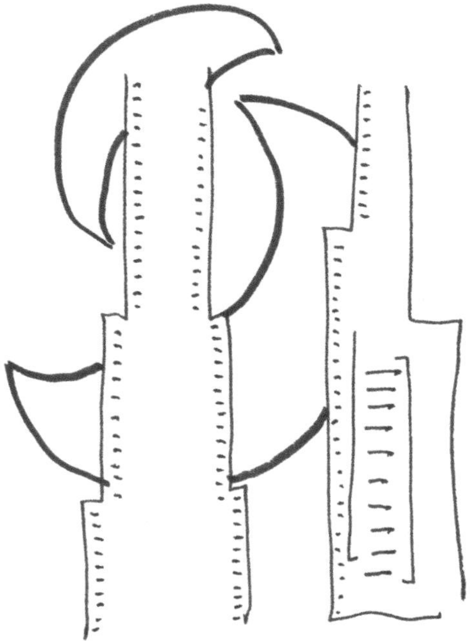

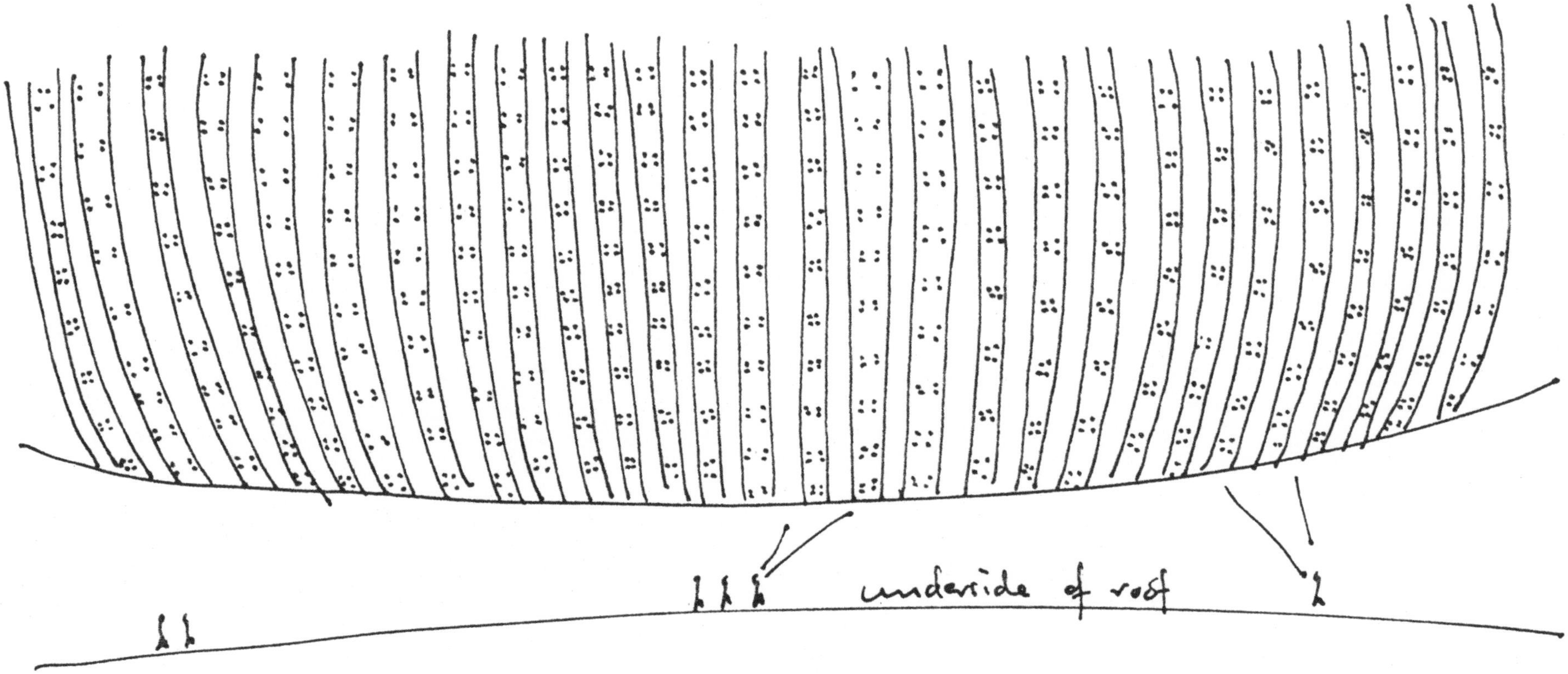

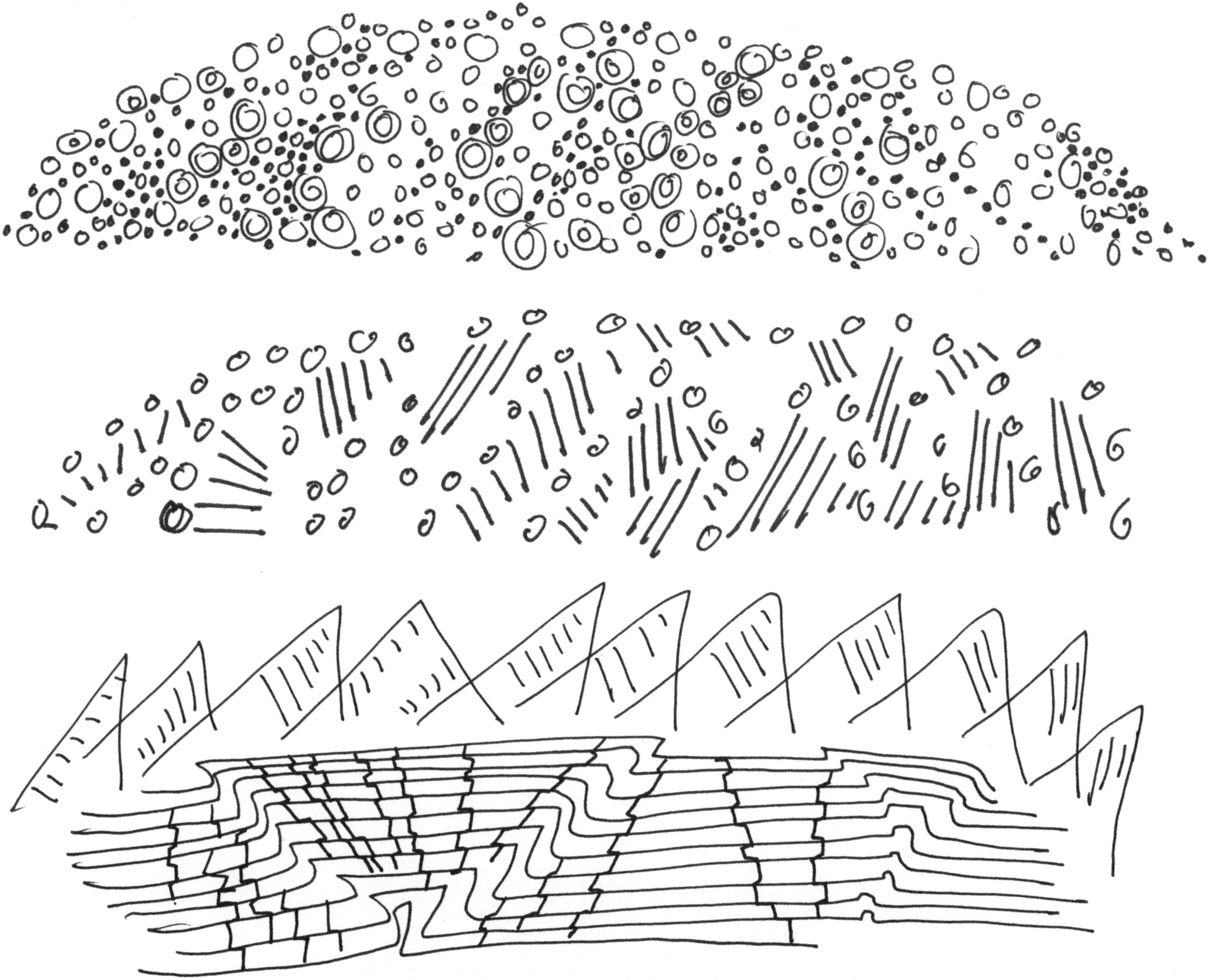

BEN VAN BERKEL

UNStudio • Netherlands

Featured projects: 5 Franklin Place [p. 32]
Scott's Tower [p. 33] · Office research facility [p. 34; bottom]
Untitled abstract sketches [pp. 34, top; 35]

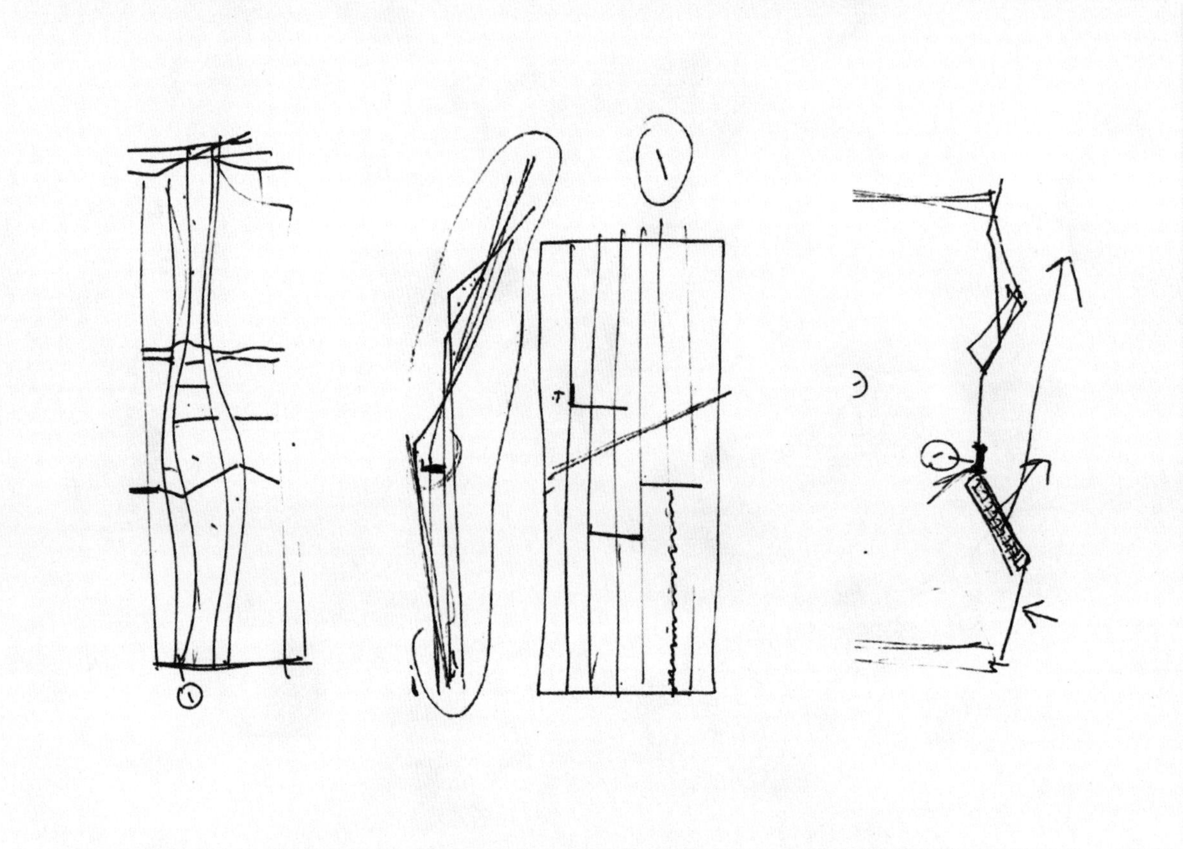

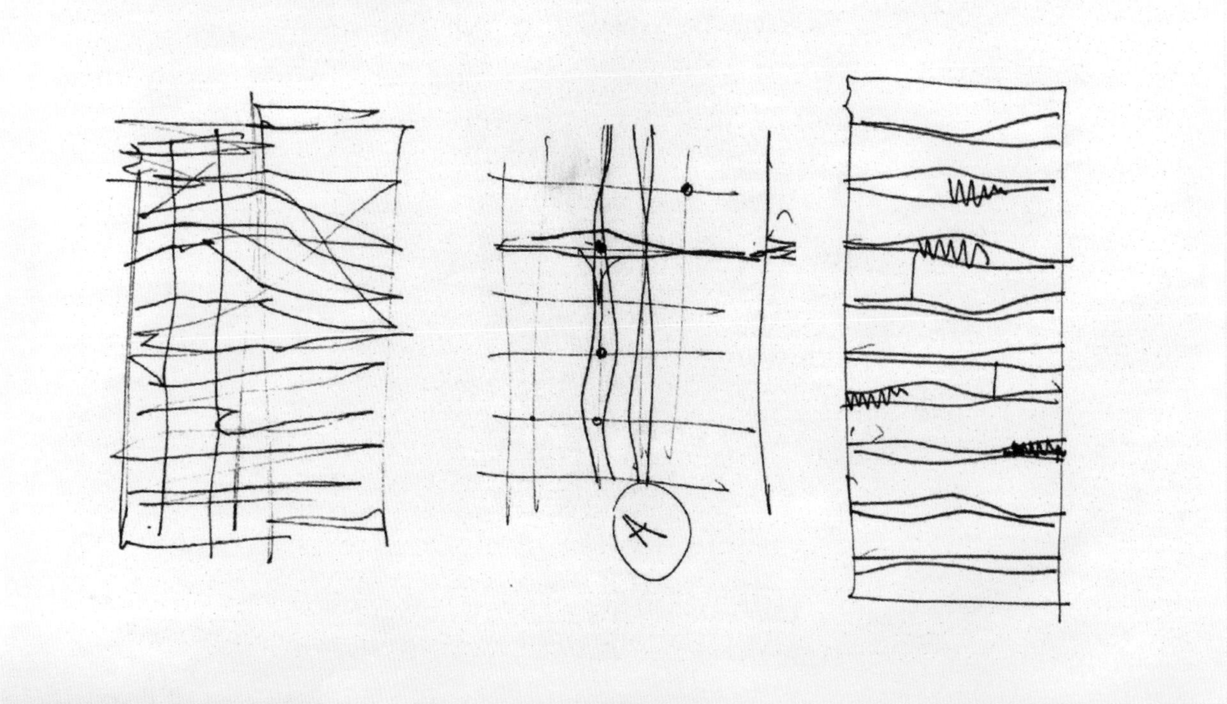

'Sketching is another form of training the mind,' says Ben van Berkel, co-founder – together with Caroline Bos – of UNStudio. 'I have always believed in an organic hand-to-mind learning process: while you sketch, you learn. Sketching is also closer to your own sensorial experiences, and how you physically connect with and touch something – not just when drawing, but also when making models. It is important to remain active and work with different materials, so that you keep on learning.'

Van Berkel and Bos set up Van Berkel & Bos Architectuurbureau in 1988, with UNStudio following a decade later; today, the duo are world renowned. Van Berkel has lectured at architectural schools around the world, and currently holds the Kenzo Tange Visiting Professor's Chair at the Harvard University Graduate School of Design.

'The ideas in my sketches are often speculative or suggestive, and can be about completely different things than my designs,' he says. 'I do a lot of personal sketching – observations, thoughts, ideas. My sketches don't make a logical, visual step from an idea to the form of a building; they are more like diagrams for potential variants of organizational strategies. We use the drawings in the designs, but they are more instrumental than representational. I see some of the sketches I make as idiograms, where words and ideas are expressed through graphic symbols that come together in a formal gesture. So it is an actualization of the two. From that, I can pick up an organizational idea for a potential building.'

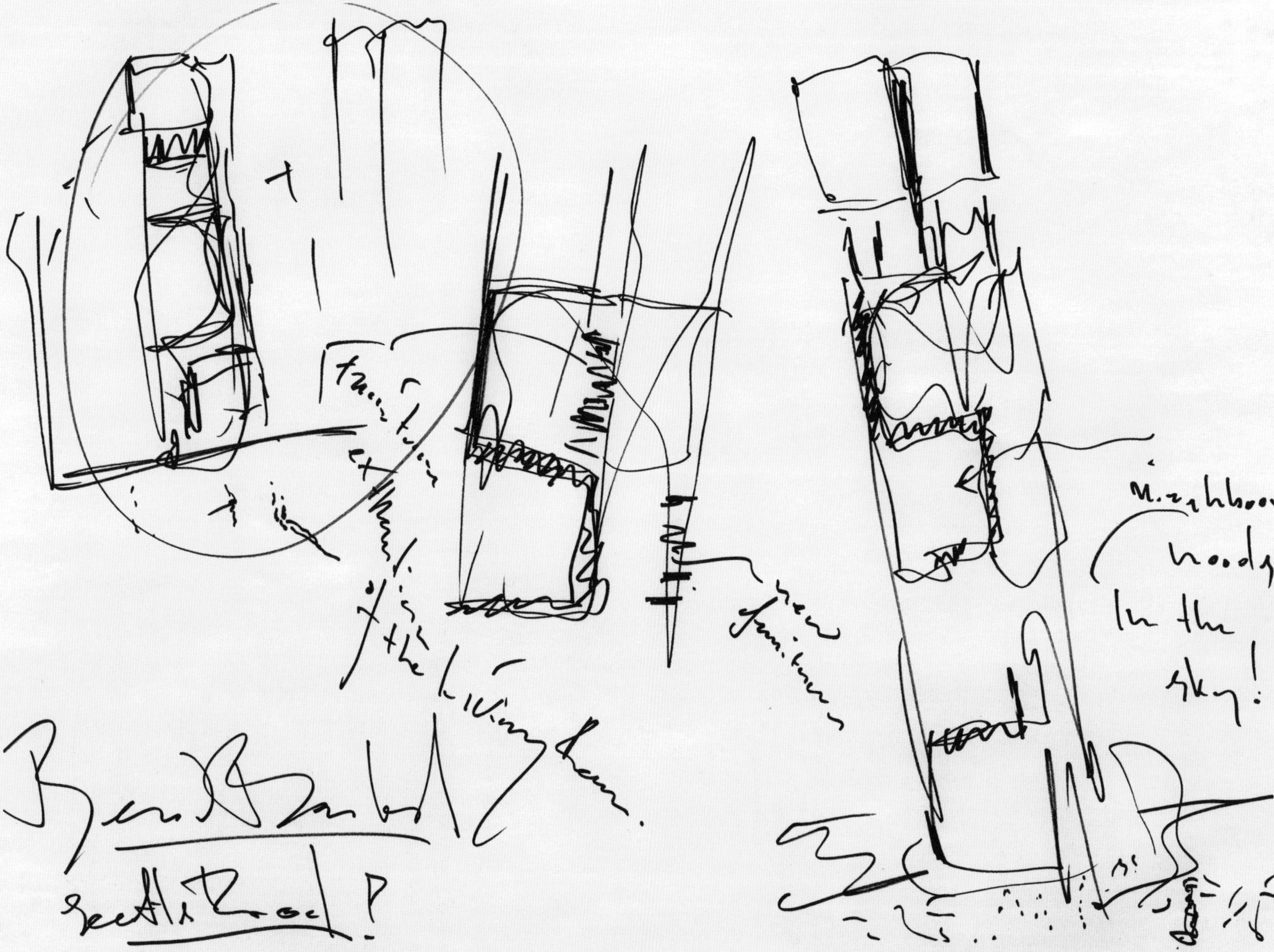
woods
in the
sky!

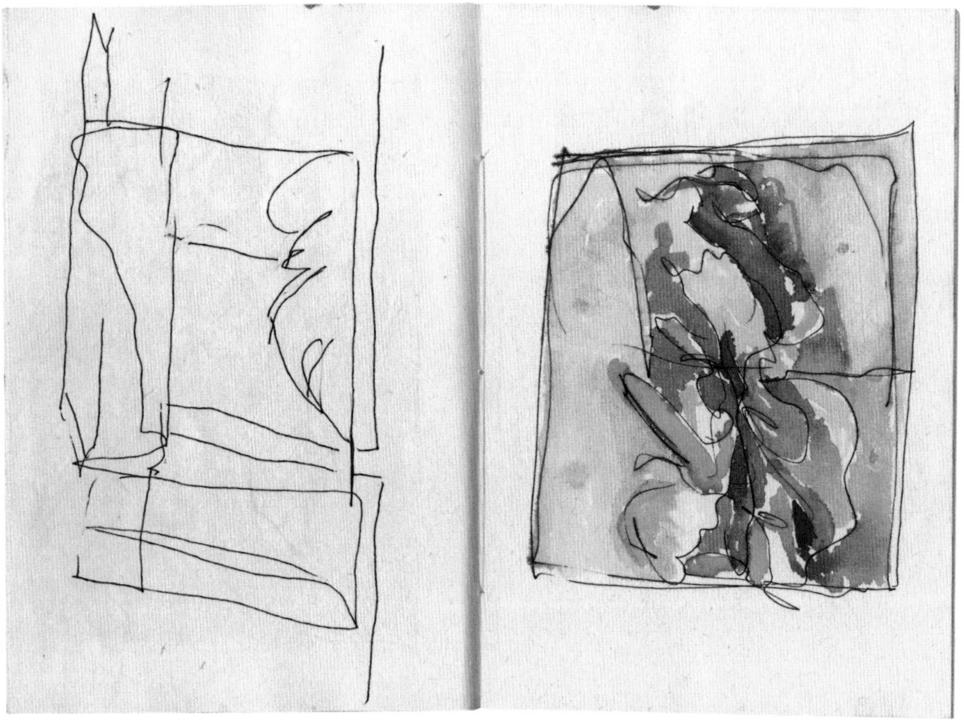

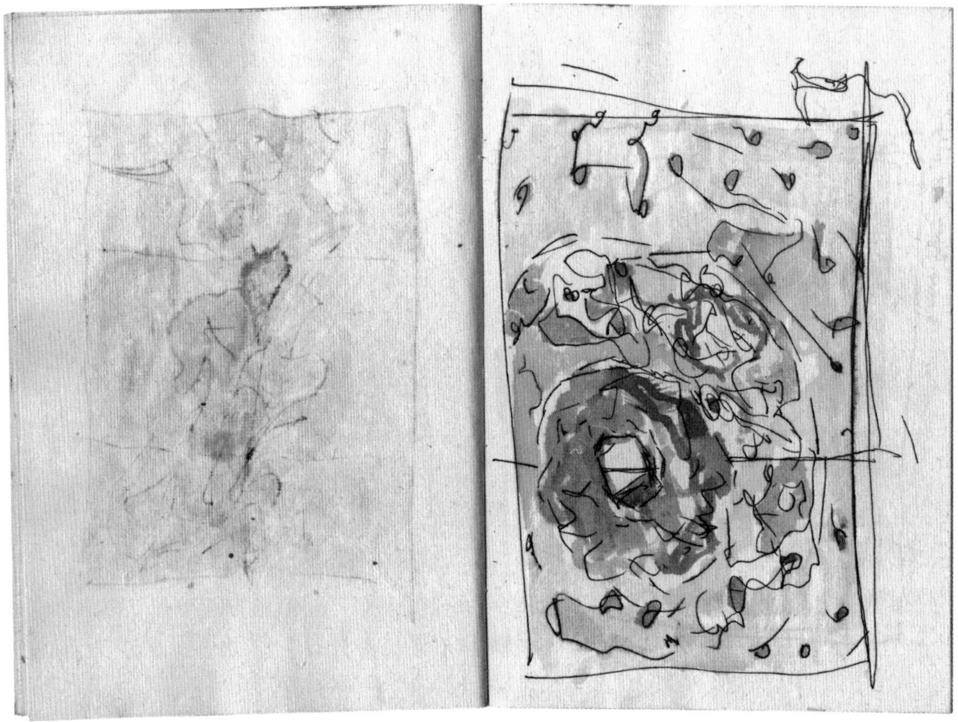

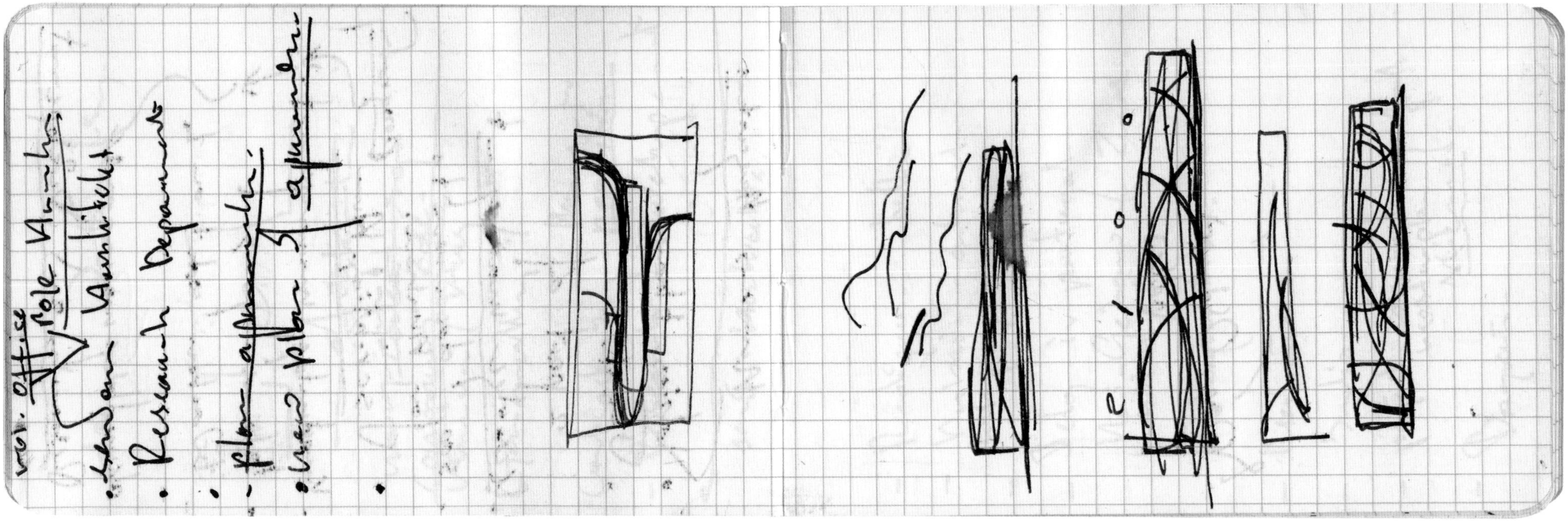

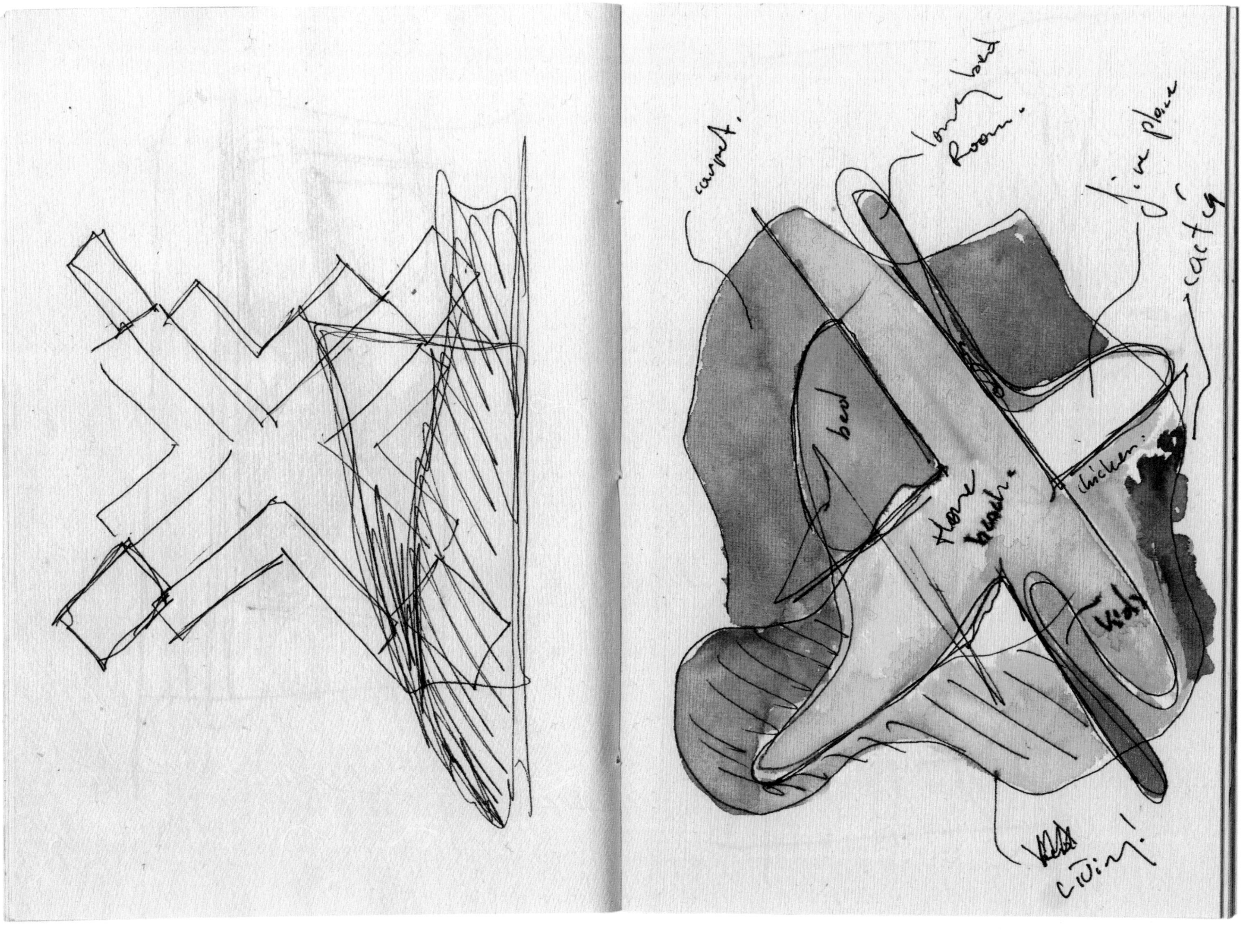
carpet.
Room.
bed
kitchen
kids
living

PETER BERTON

+VG Architects • Canada

Featured projects: Coffee table and end table [p. 36, top left]
Jewelry box with hidden compartments [p. 36, top right];
Dining-room credenza [p. 36, bottom] · Cottage in Muskoka [p. 37]

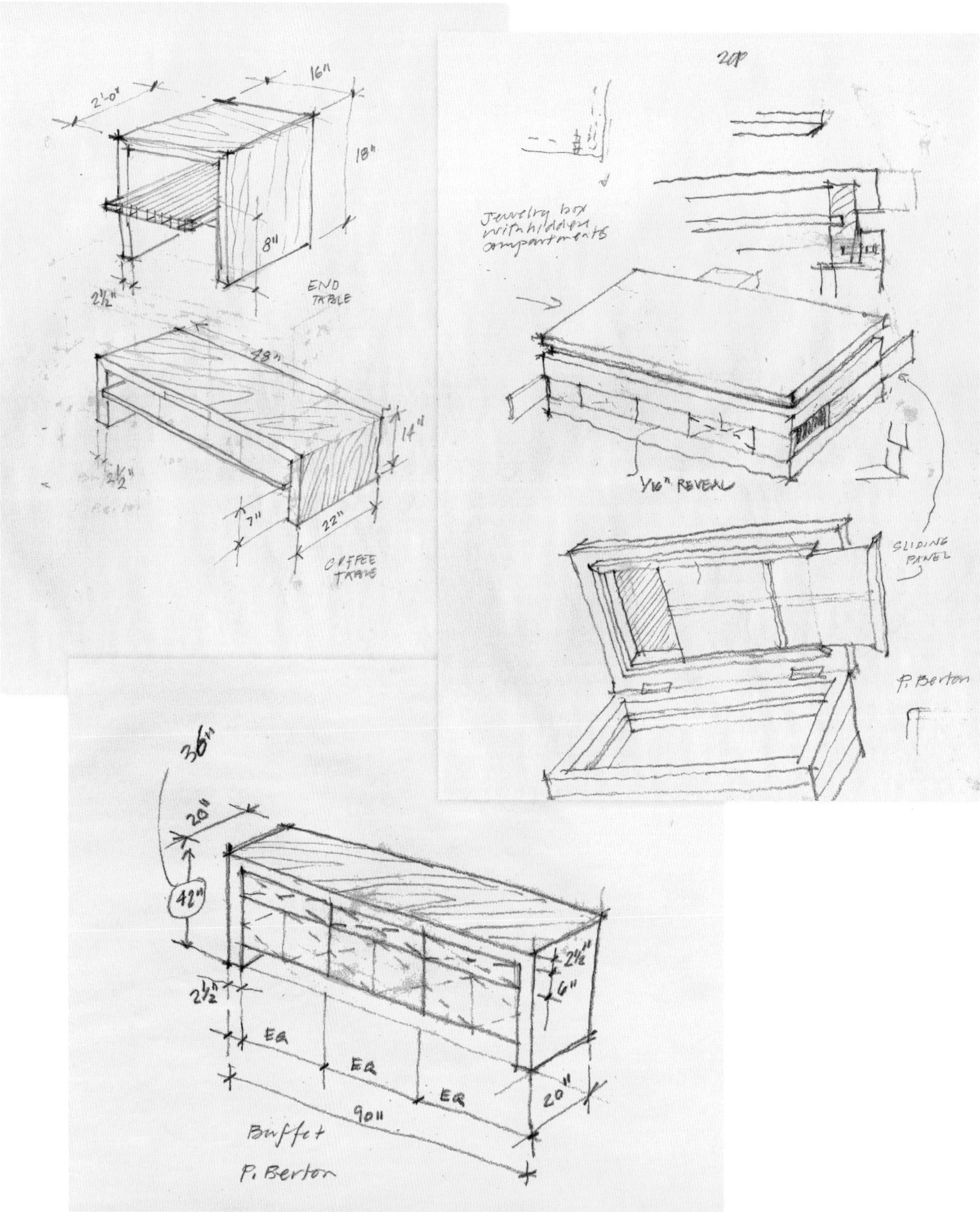

'Nowadays, many people think the computer does the design – definitely not the case,' says Peter Berton, partner-in-charge of the Toronto office of +VG Architects (see also p. 204). 'But there is a common perception that architects will become obsolete because of the digital world. For the vast majority, digital drawings are simply a tool to quickly confirm that a sketch has worked. I find it much more engaging to draw by hand than in CAD; the possibilities are more open and less rigid. There is a dialogue with the paper. When simply sketching what I see, it is exactly that. It is not about the ability to draw, but the ability to see.'

Berton is an expert in the design of educational buildings, courthouses and historic restorations. For many of his residential projects, he designs everything, from the building, furniture and lighting down to the fire tools and rugs.

'Many young architects today do not sketch by hand at all, and it is a shame,' he says. 'It is important to do freehand sketching, because it opens possibilities, and nothing is yet cast in stone. When doing a design sketch, versus just drawing something I see, I visualize the drawing before the sketch goes on paper. The sketch is a realization of what was in my mind's eye. Clients respond positively to the fact that a real person is behind the concept, and not a computer.'

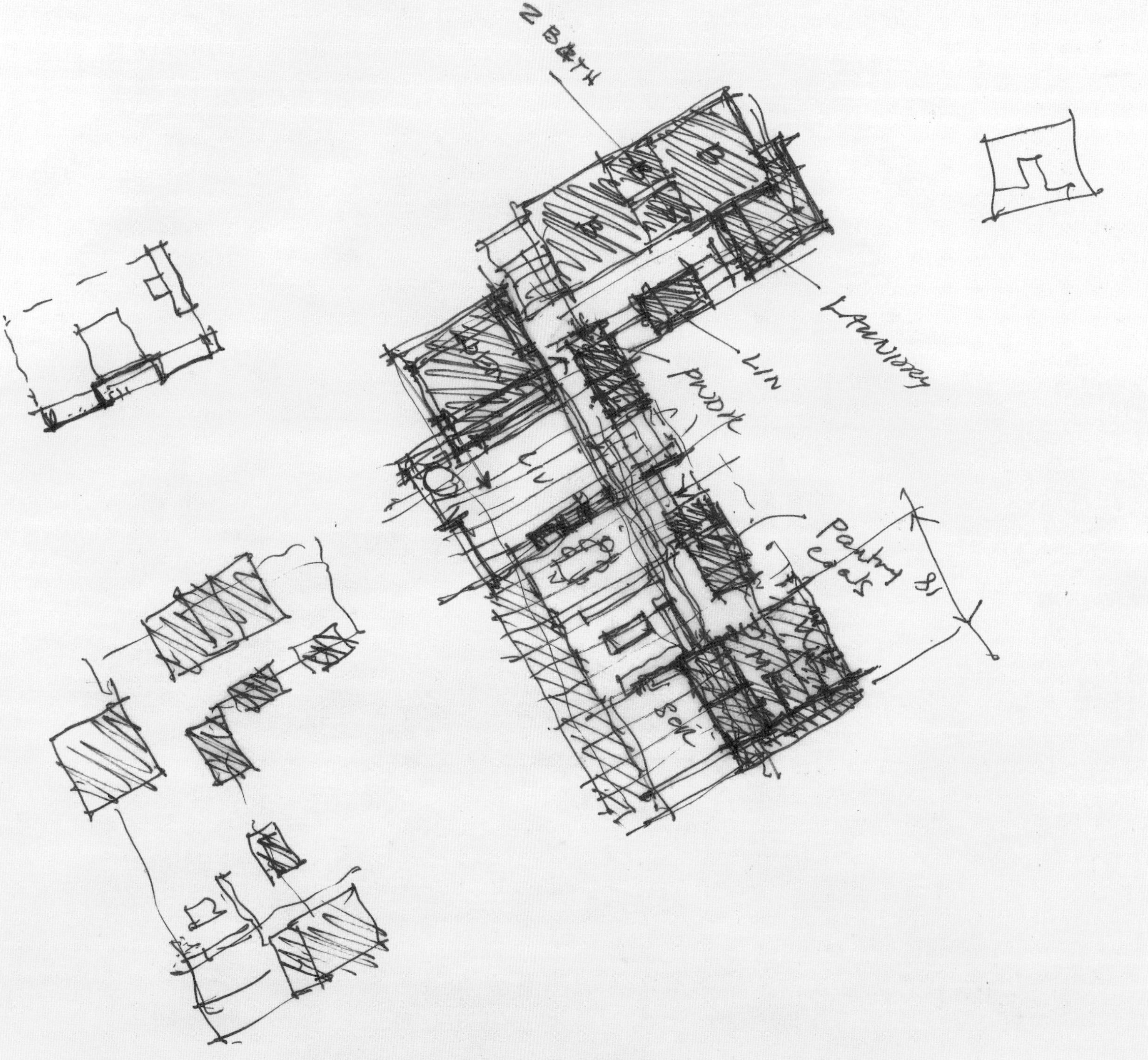
LAUNDRY
LIN
Pantry
coats

ADAM BRADY

Lett Architects • Canada

Featured projects: Bedoukian Barn [p. 38]
Dobbins House [p. 39, right]

'Sketching allows me to react to an on-site issue and convey an idea quickly and pragmatically, for the benefit of an audience,' says Adam Brady of Lett Architects, based in Peterborough, Ontario. 'Often I can be found standing in the middle of a construction site, sketching on the backs of all my pretty CAD drawings, resolving details on the fly.'

Brady's role within the firm is multifaceted. From day to day, he may be working on a new project proposal, or battling with the minutiae of design details on the site of a live project. He sees sketching as a release from the often 'muddied thoughts' that swim around inside his head.

'Working entirely within the digital plane can be difficult and mentally exhausting,' he explains. 'An entire site plan, room layout and wall section can exist within the same drawing file, and with a few clicks of the mouse can be perceived all at once or not at all. There is a loss of scale between the architect and the building when working only in the digital realm. I feel disconnected from a project when the computer is my sole means of production.'

Like architects the world over, Brady carries notebooks with him and sketches whenever and wherever inspiration strikes. 'I don't get ideas, I lose them,' he says, 'so putting them down on paper, in the moment, is vital. On most Sunday nights, I can find myself sitting at the kitchen table, listening to the loons or the spring peepers, letting my mind unwind and my muscles relax, with a glass of rye, a warm fire or a cool breeze. Then I get an incredible amount of design work done in a very short amount of time.'

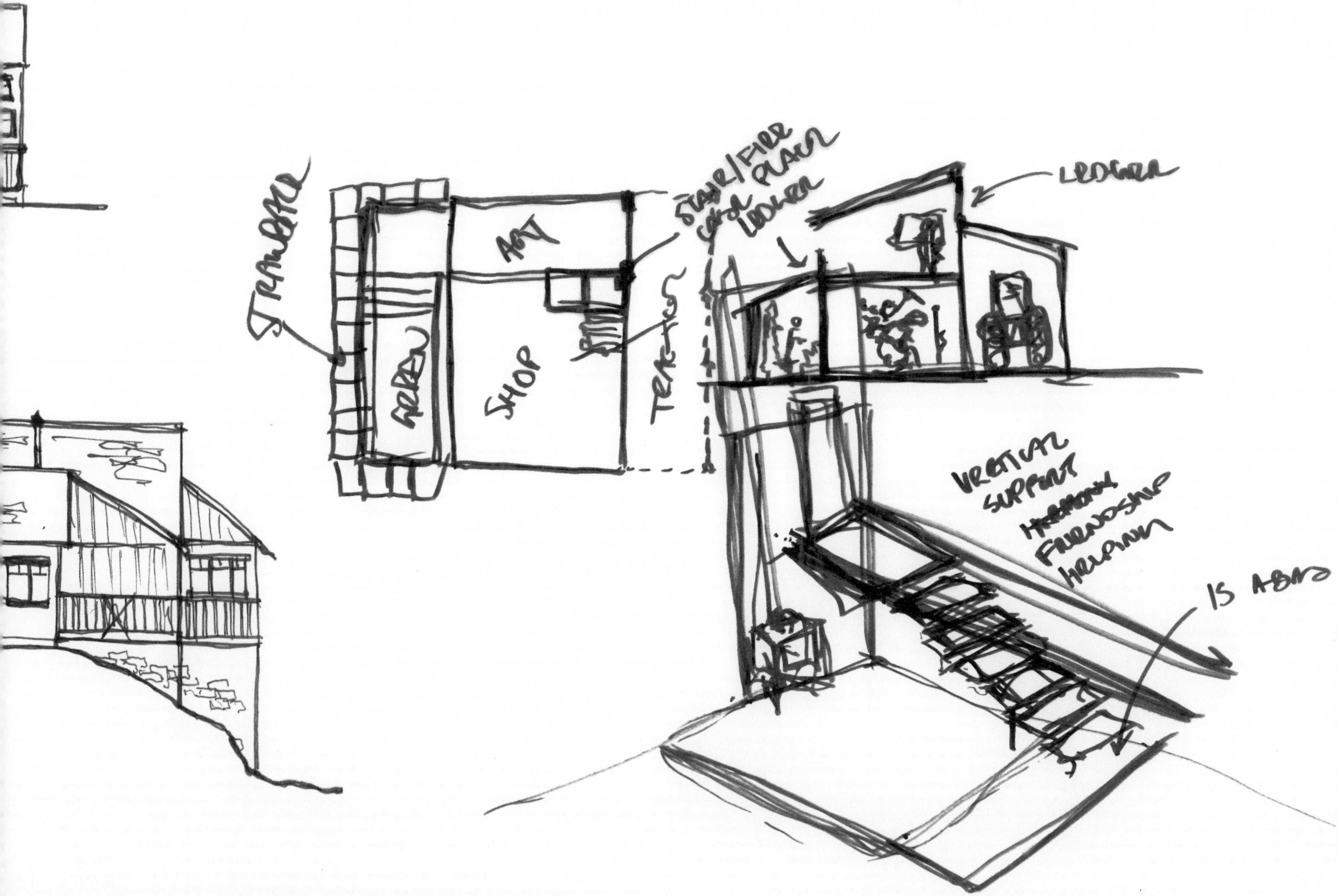
ART
SHOP
LEDGER
VERTICAL SUPPORT
FRIENDSHIP

The Parthenon, 447 BC - to - 3.26.08.
still a working job site.

3.19.08 Pza Coll. Romano.

DREAM
St. Pete Beach

JACOB BRILLHART

Brillhart Architecture • USA

Featured projects: Parthenon · Piazza Rome · Piazza del Popolo [top, left to right]
Santa Marinella · Foro Italico · Hat Schip [bottom, left to right]

'It is still essential to know how to draw,' says painter, author and architect Jacob Brillhart. 'Travel drawing, in particular, serves as a fundamental form of research and development for young architects. The experience of recording what we see enables us to bring back a new way of seeing, as well as sketchbooks full of information and an understanding of architectural principles: colour, light, and all the other elements that make architecture matter and affect the human condition. We return with the understanding of another culture, history and place, and the emotion, memories, sounds and smells of being in situ. This level of engagement allows us to see, and see again.'

Brillhart's fascination with Le Corbusier and the doctrines of the Modernist school has informed the work of his Miami-based firm. 'Each project is explored using a matrix of different media lenses, including painting, hand-drawing, physical models and mock-ups, as well as CAD, hyper-photorealistic renderings and 3D computer models, in which application and implication are prioritized,' he says.

'Most of our designs start out with sketches and small physical models,' Brillhart continues. 'From these studies, we begin to formulate a parti, or concept, which then goes into the computer, so that we can apply actual dimensions to it. With a working base, we go back and forth, printing out the 3D and planometric views and sketching over them to test alternative ideas and "feel" the project through our hands and eyes.'

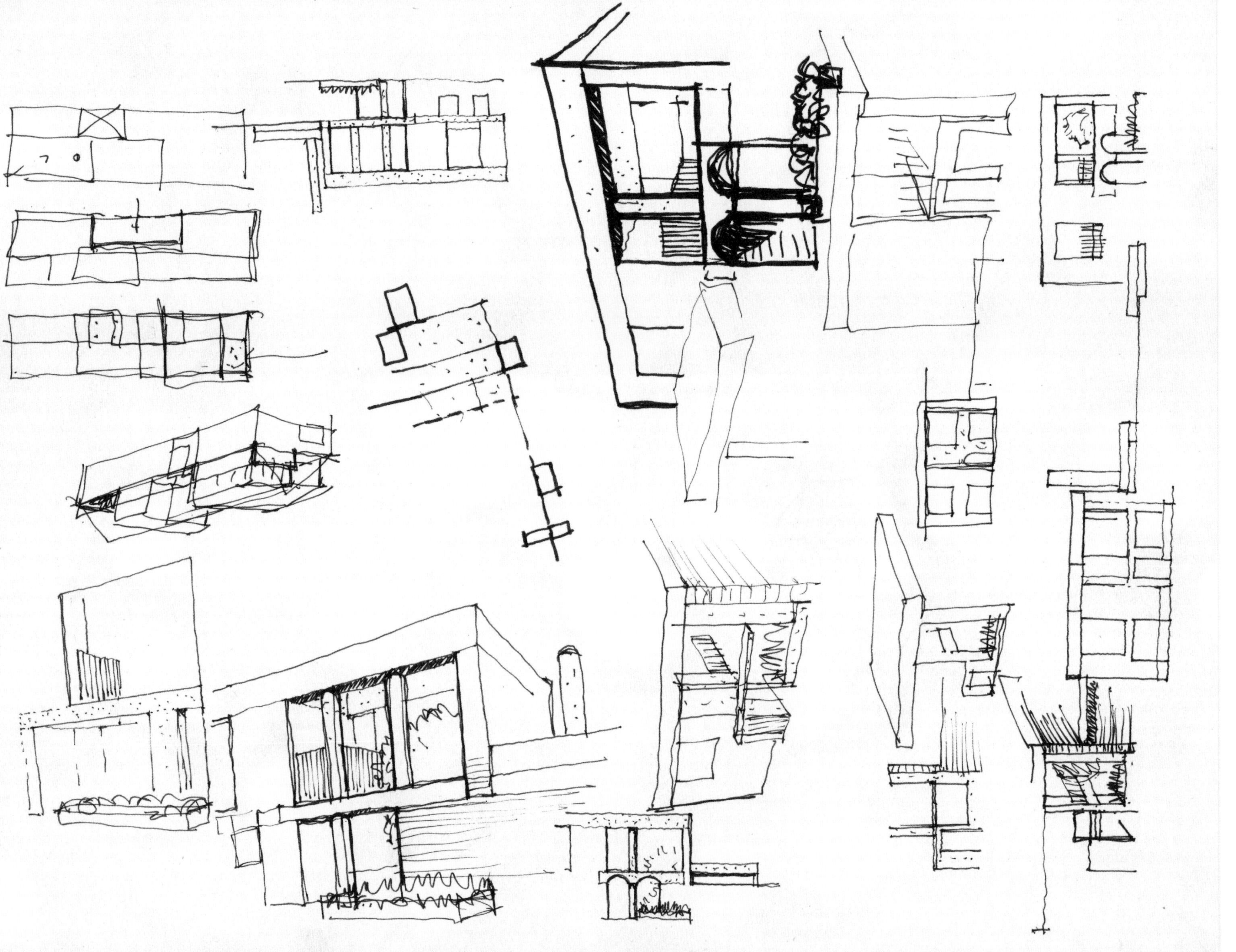

WILL BURGES

31/44 Architects • UK

Featured projects: Four Column Houses [pp. 42–5]
House in Oregon [pp. 46–7] · Redchurch and Whitby [pp. 48–9]

'Hand-sketches are much more exploratory than digital ones,' says Will Burges of 31/44 Architects. 'When you draw a line digitally, you know precisely where it starts, the direction of travel and where it will come to a halt. A line drawn by hand might start from a similar position, but its journey is looser, exploratory, even adventurous. The speed of placing the line allows your brain to adjust and quickly change direction. You'll discover at the end of the line that you've arrived somewhere you didn't necessarily expect.'

Burges is one-third of the trio – along with James Jeffries and Stephen Davies – who founded 31/44 in 2001 (its numerical name reflects the international dialling codes of the company's two studio locations: the Netherlands and the UK). All three directors currently teach at Kingston University in London.

'All of our projects are generally developed with hand-sketches, which are then refined and tested with CAD, as well as physical models and computer modelling,' Burges says. 'We tend to extract the digital information and then work over it by hand. We follow these ideas in our teaching roles, constantly drawing with our students to share our processes and hopefully help them find their own working methods. We use two thicknesses of pens, finding that this liberates the process further. A thicker pen moves faster and in some way feels looser and less constrained – we often swap pens when we feel the drawings, and design process, may be slowing down.'

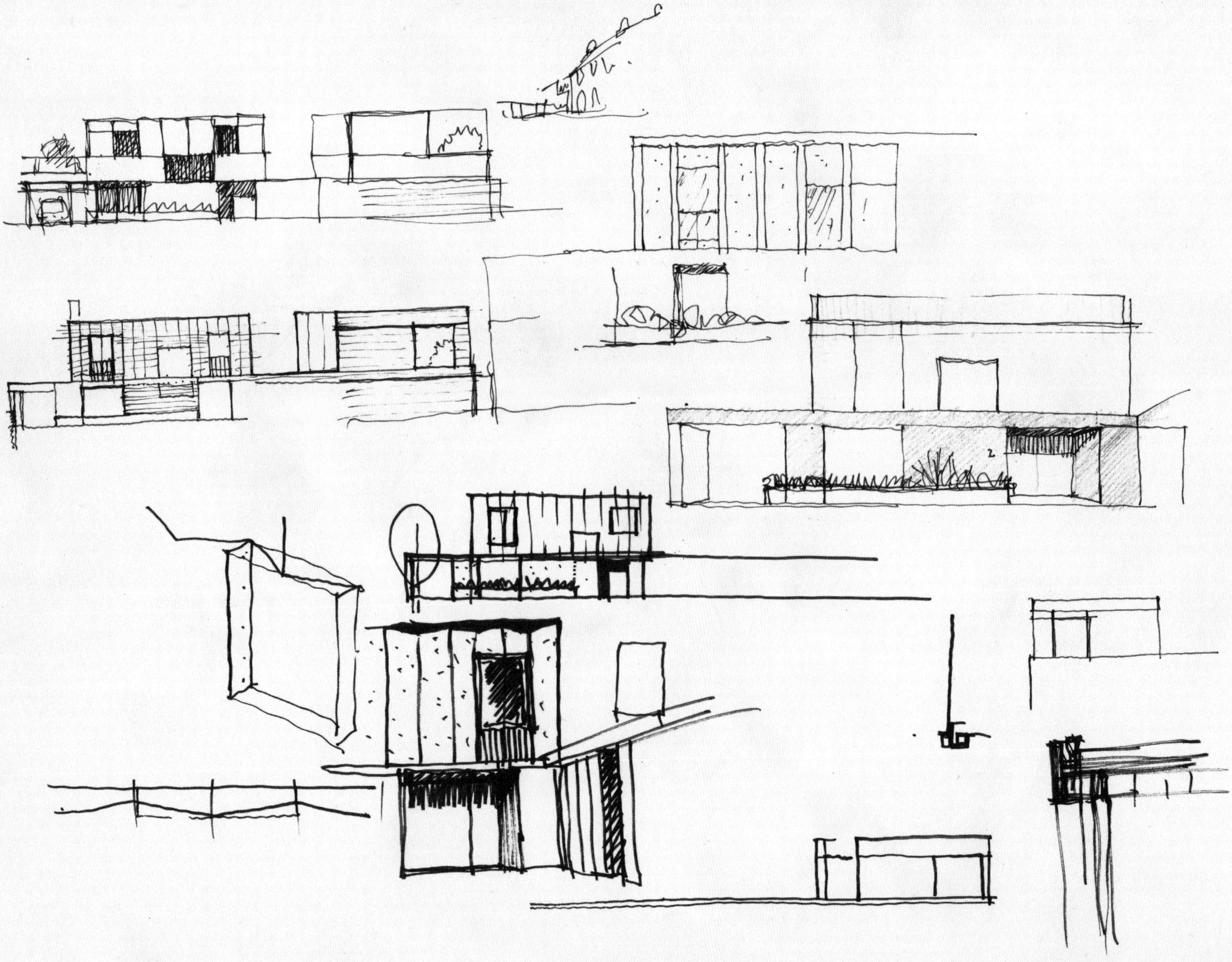

5

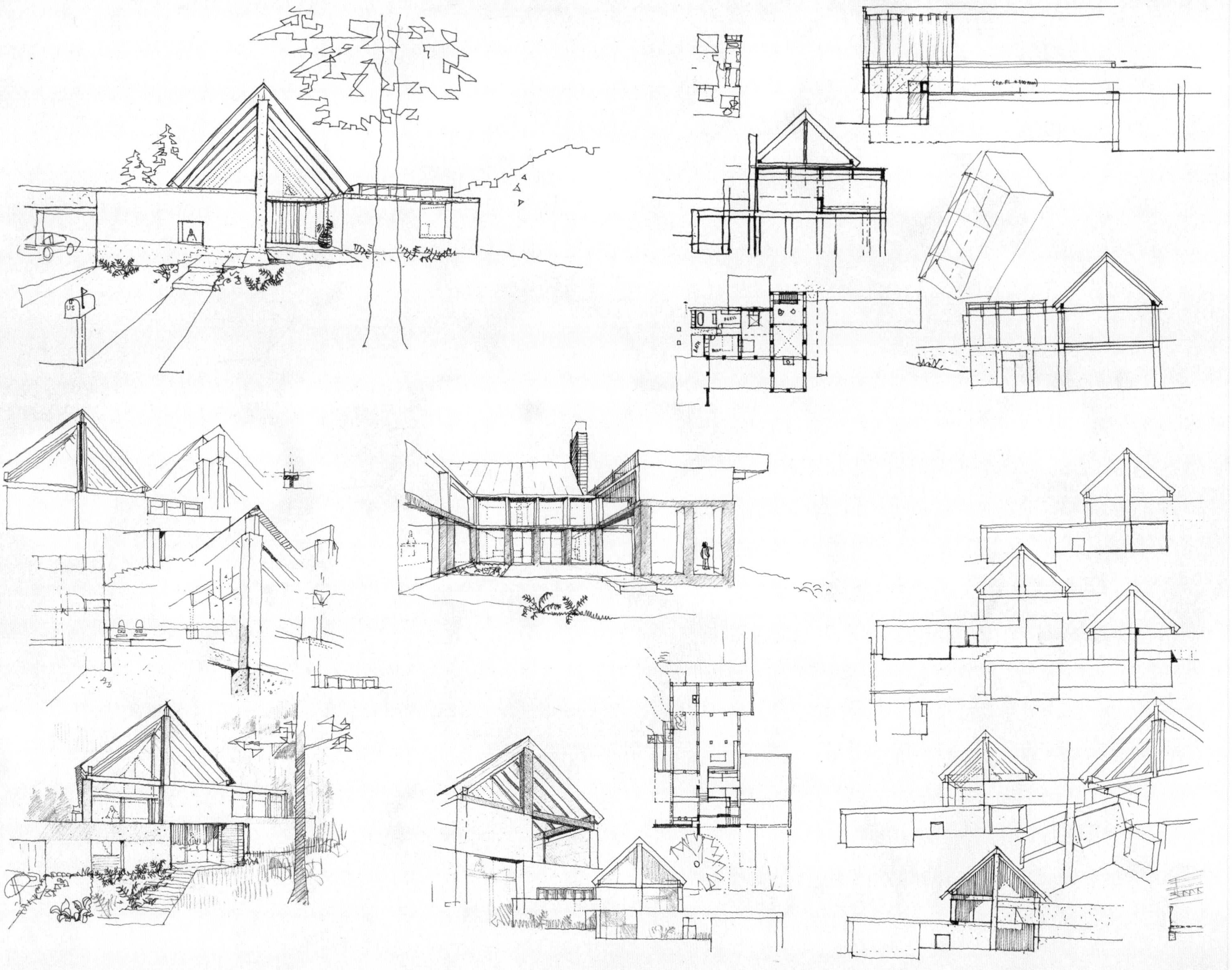
US

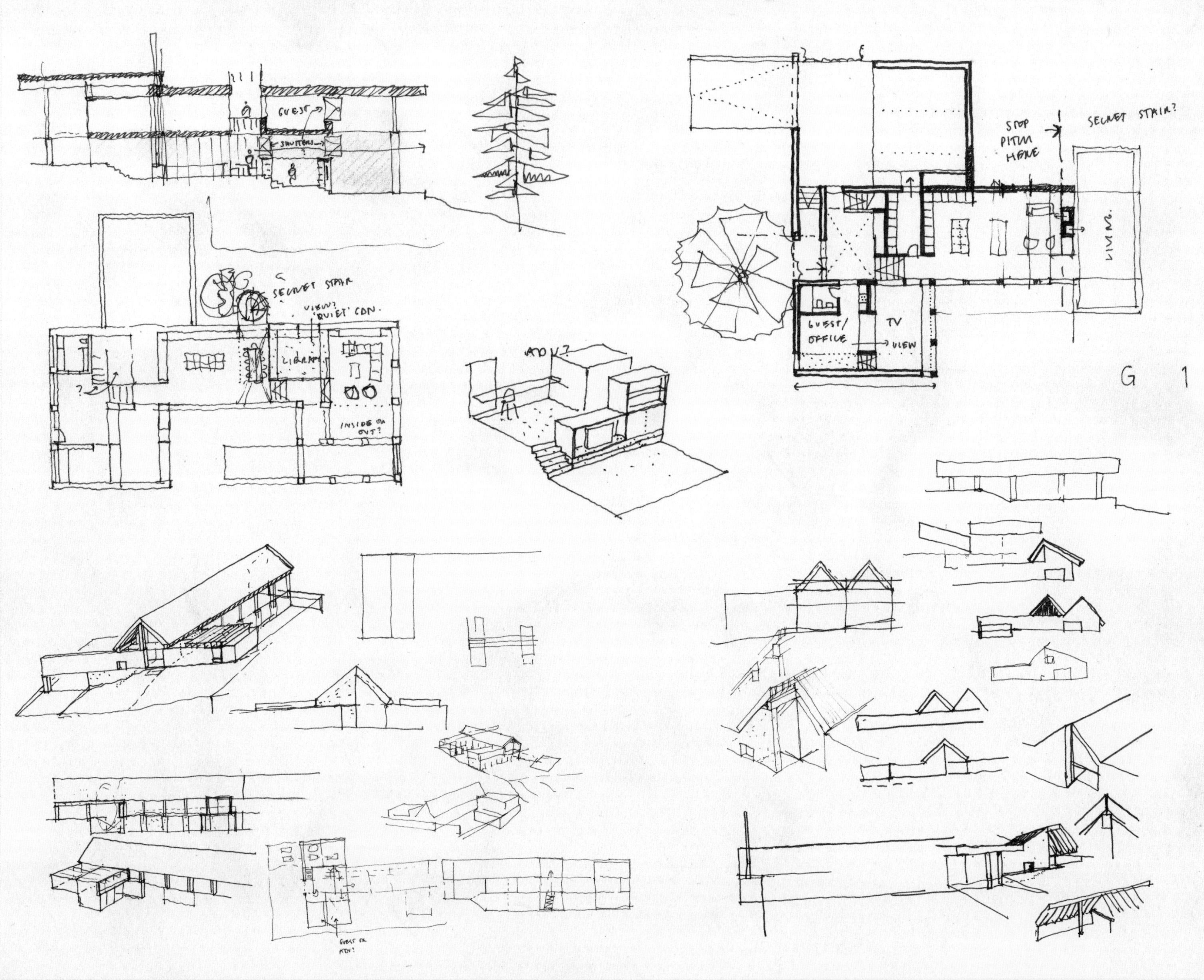
GUEST
SHUTTERS
SECRET STAIR?
STOP PITCH HERE
LIVING
GUEST/ OFFICE
TV
VIEW
G 1
SECRET STAIR
LIBRARY
ADU?

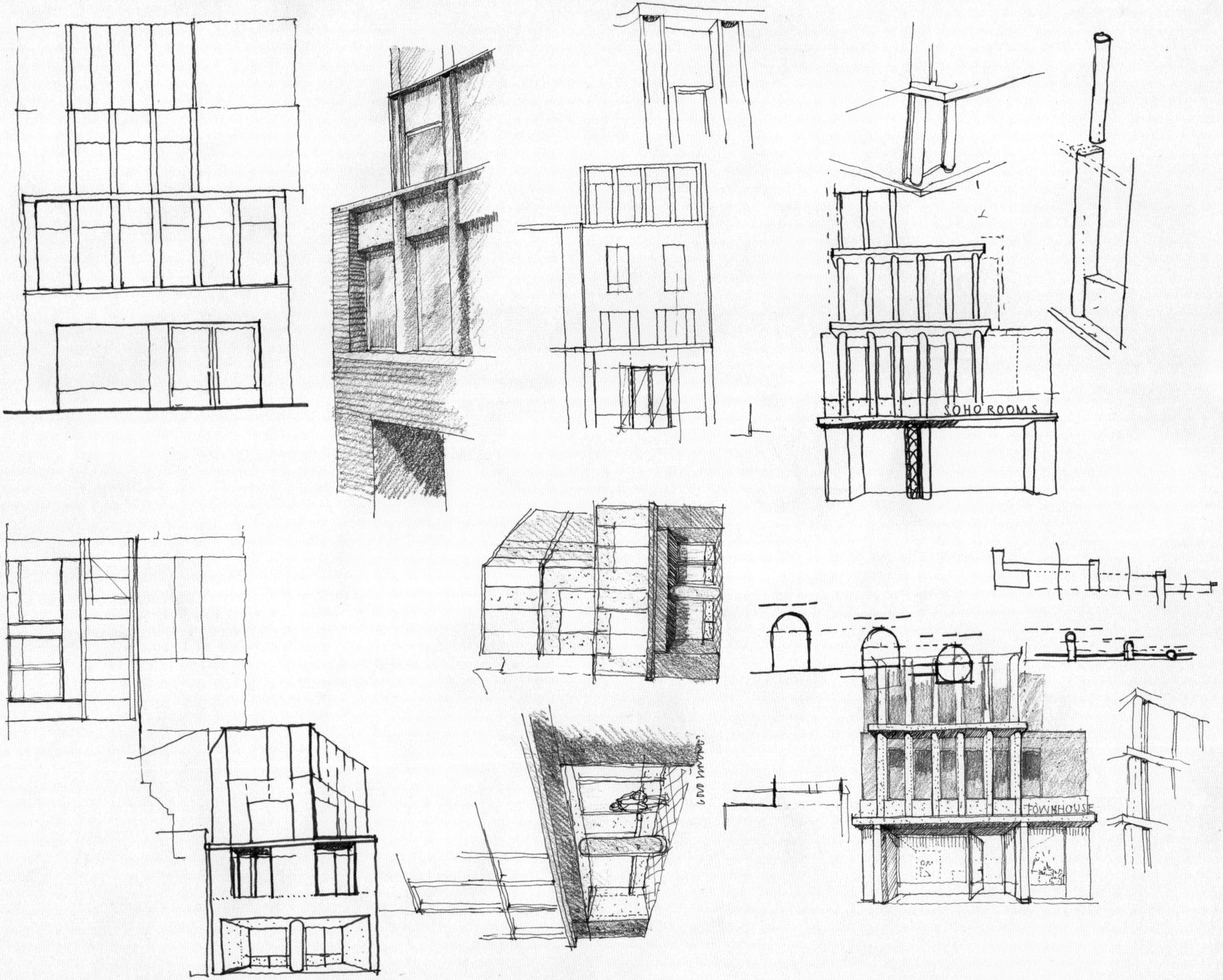
SOHO ROOMS
TOWNHOUSE

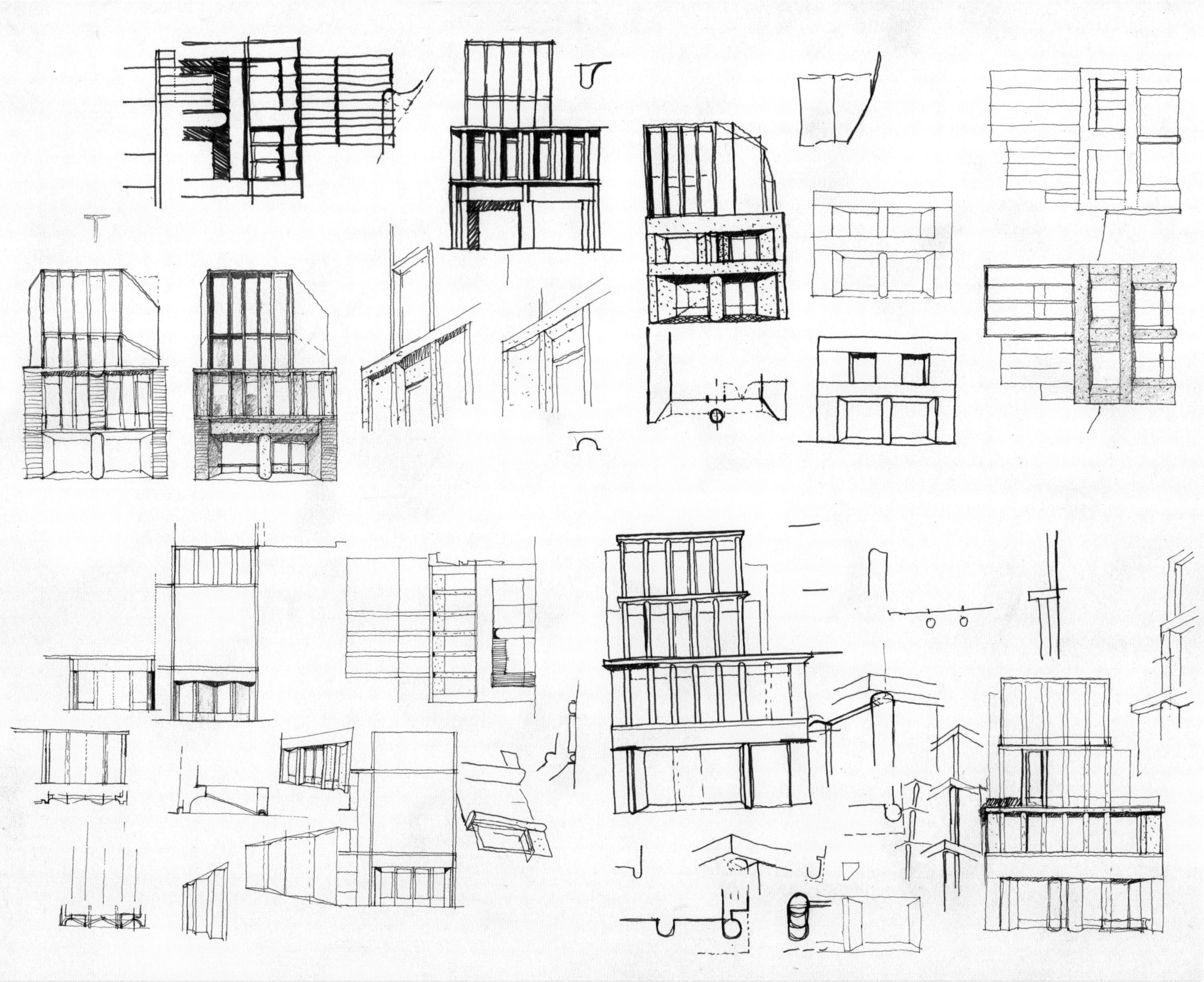

ALBERTO CAMPO BAEZA

Studio Alberto Campo Baeza • Spain

Featured projects: Infinite House [pp. 50–1]
Raumplan House [pp. 52–5]

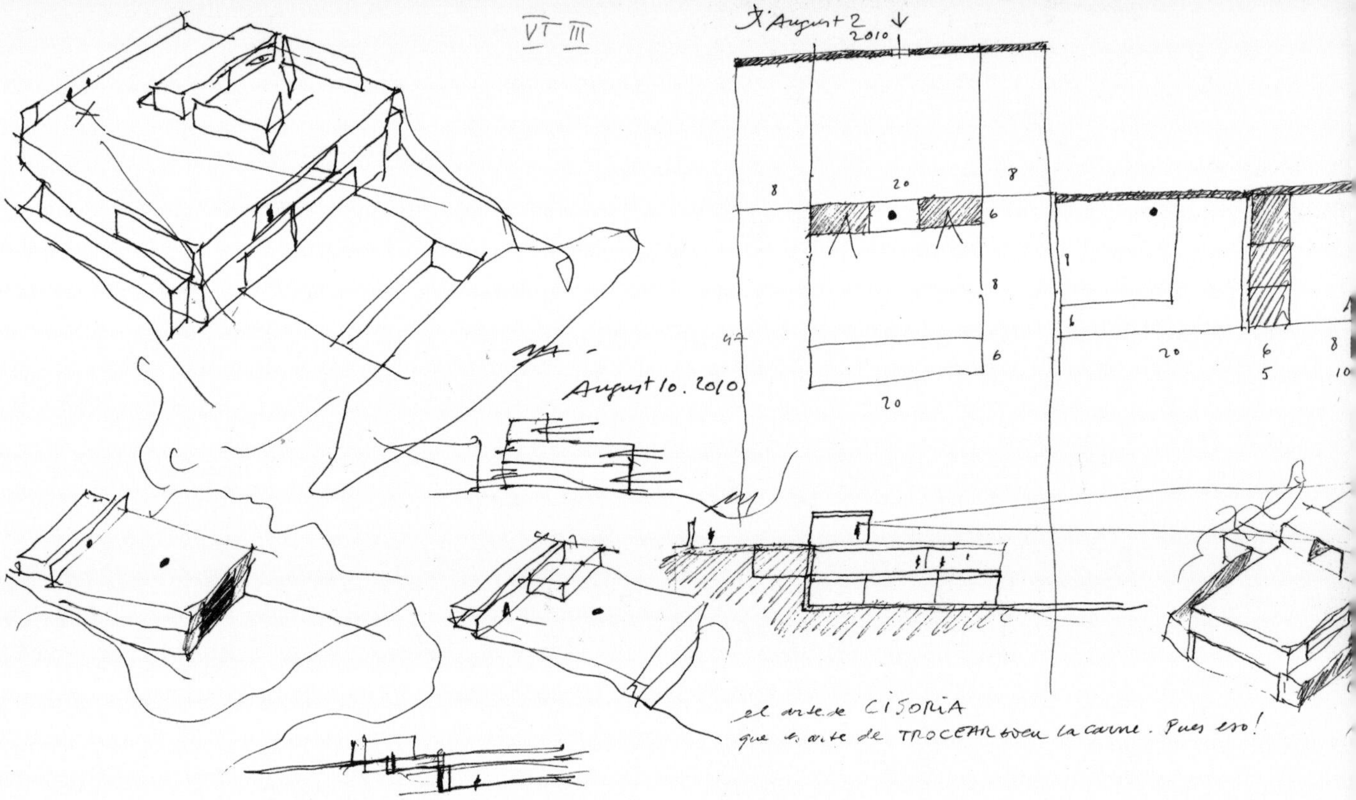

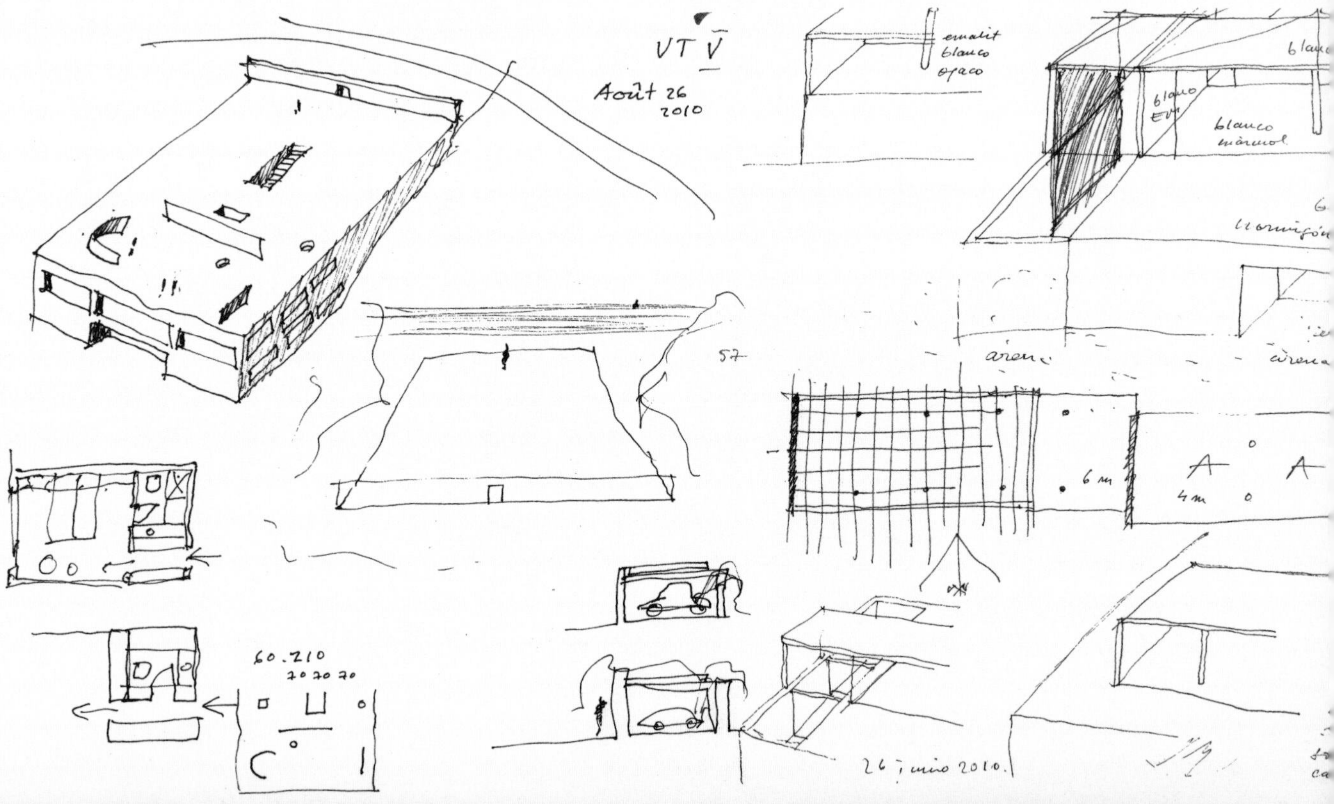

'The ability to reason is the architect's primary instrument, capable of generating the idea of a project,' says Alberto Campo Baeza. 'But it becomes immediately necessary to translate that thought, which is already spatial in our head, to a drawing capable of transmitting that spatial idea. The sketch, therefore, is a must; it is a drawn thought.'

Following in the footsteps of his architect grandfather, Campo Baeza, based in Madrid, has become globally renowned for his designs, winning awards in the US, UK and across Europe. His work has been exhibited around the world and included in numerous publications.

Campo Baeza believes that it is impossible to design without sketching. 'Sketches are the best way to transmit ideas to one's collaborators, so that they can develop the later phases of the project,' he says. 'An architect is not someone who chooses between the solutions proposed by others, but someone who, through sketches, proposes to them what needs to be done. Words are not enough; sketches are necessary.'

Architecture is not a process, he says, in which, once you have a clearly defined idea, you begin losing things along the way as it develops – quite the opposite. 'The idea goes in crescendo,' he continues. 'It begins taking shape and maturing in such a way that at the end, when the work is built, something wonderful happens. The architect recognizes the building, the materialization of his or her dream, which started out as a sketch.'

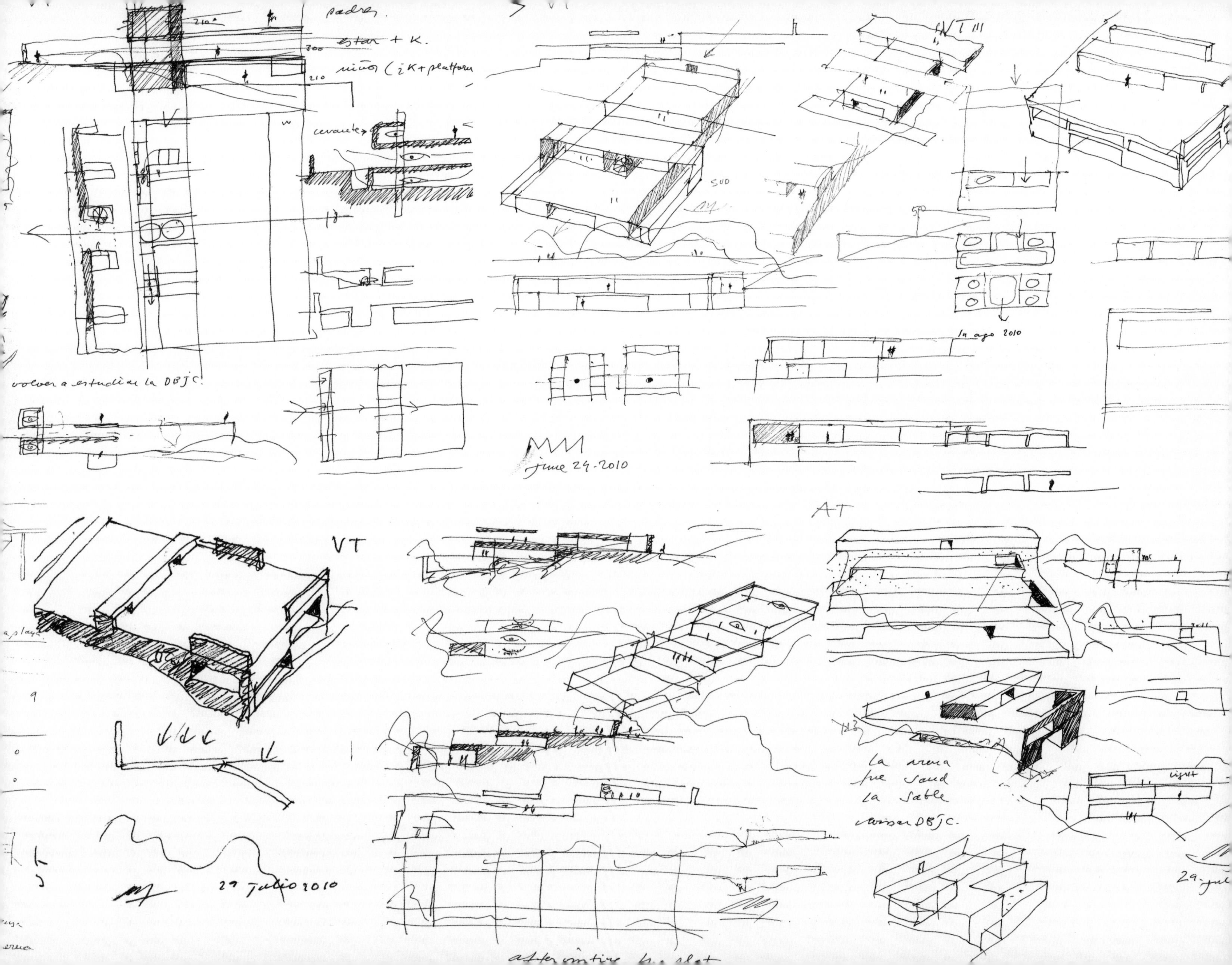

estar + K.
volver a estudiar la DBJC.
SUD
June 24-2010
14 ago 2010
AT
VT
La arena
fue sand
La sable
light
29 Julio 2010

CALA house

Feb. 7. 2013

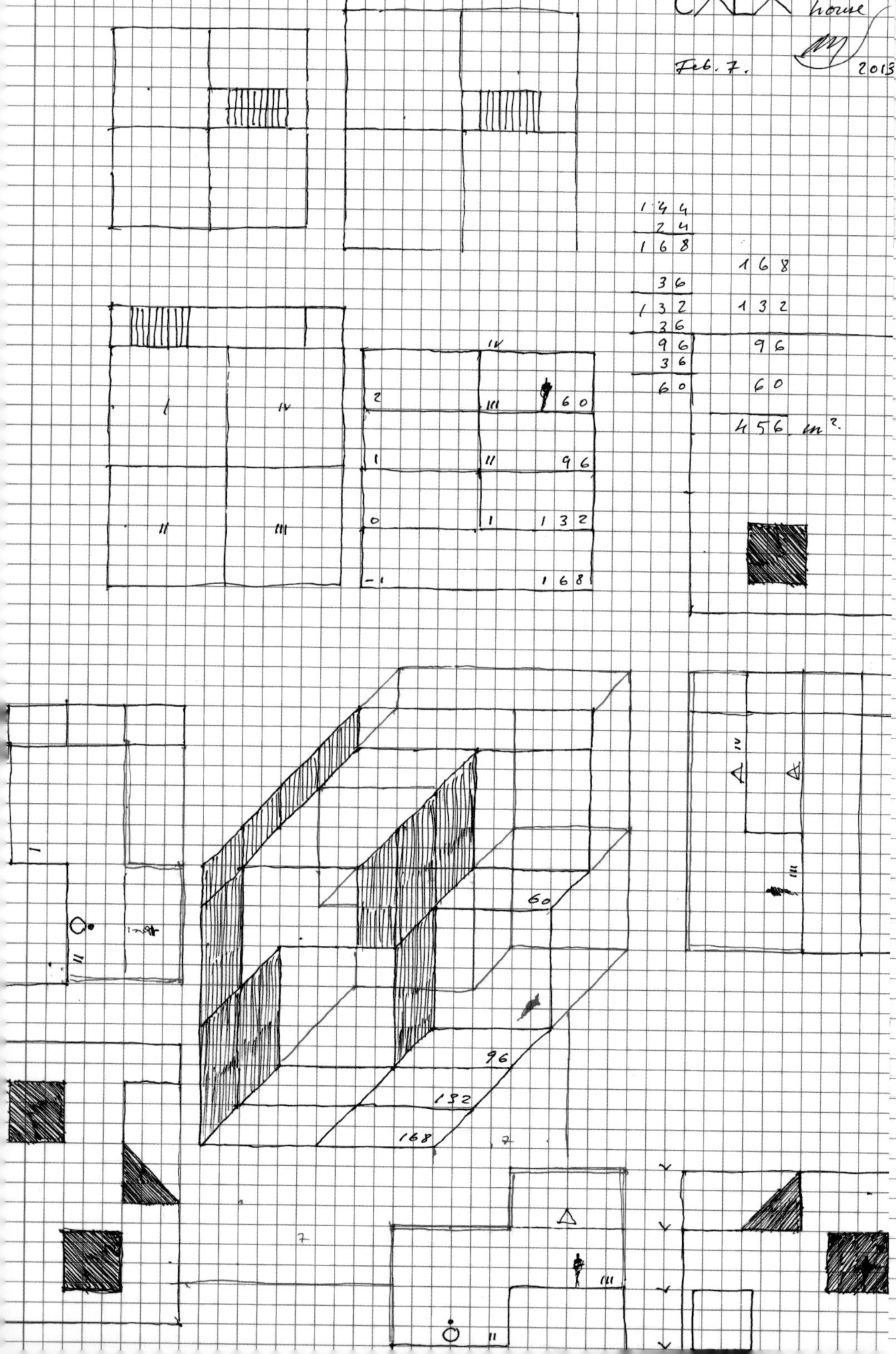

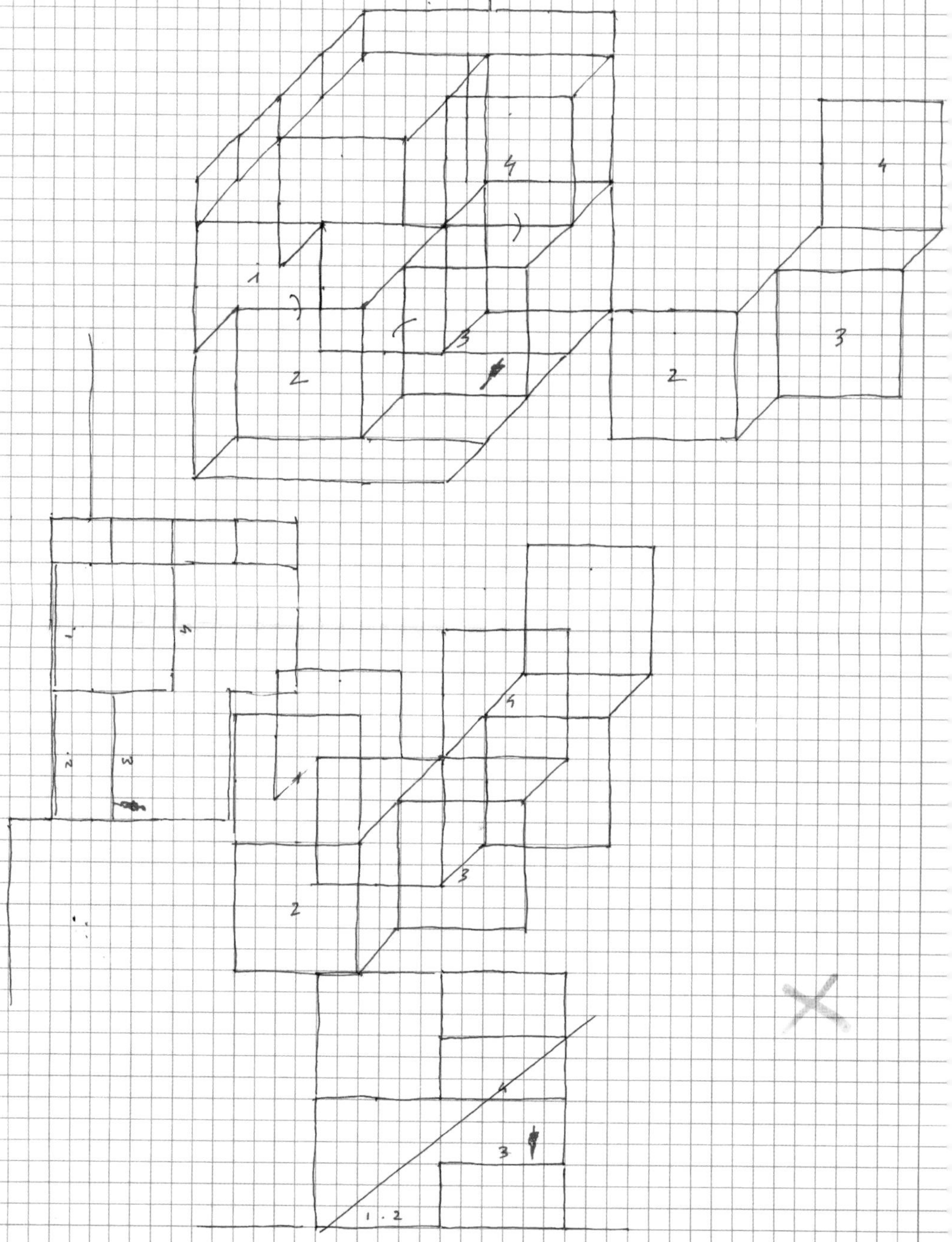

FACHADA SUR

CALA HOUSE

Feb. 8. 2013.

march 9. 2013

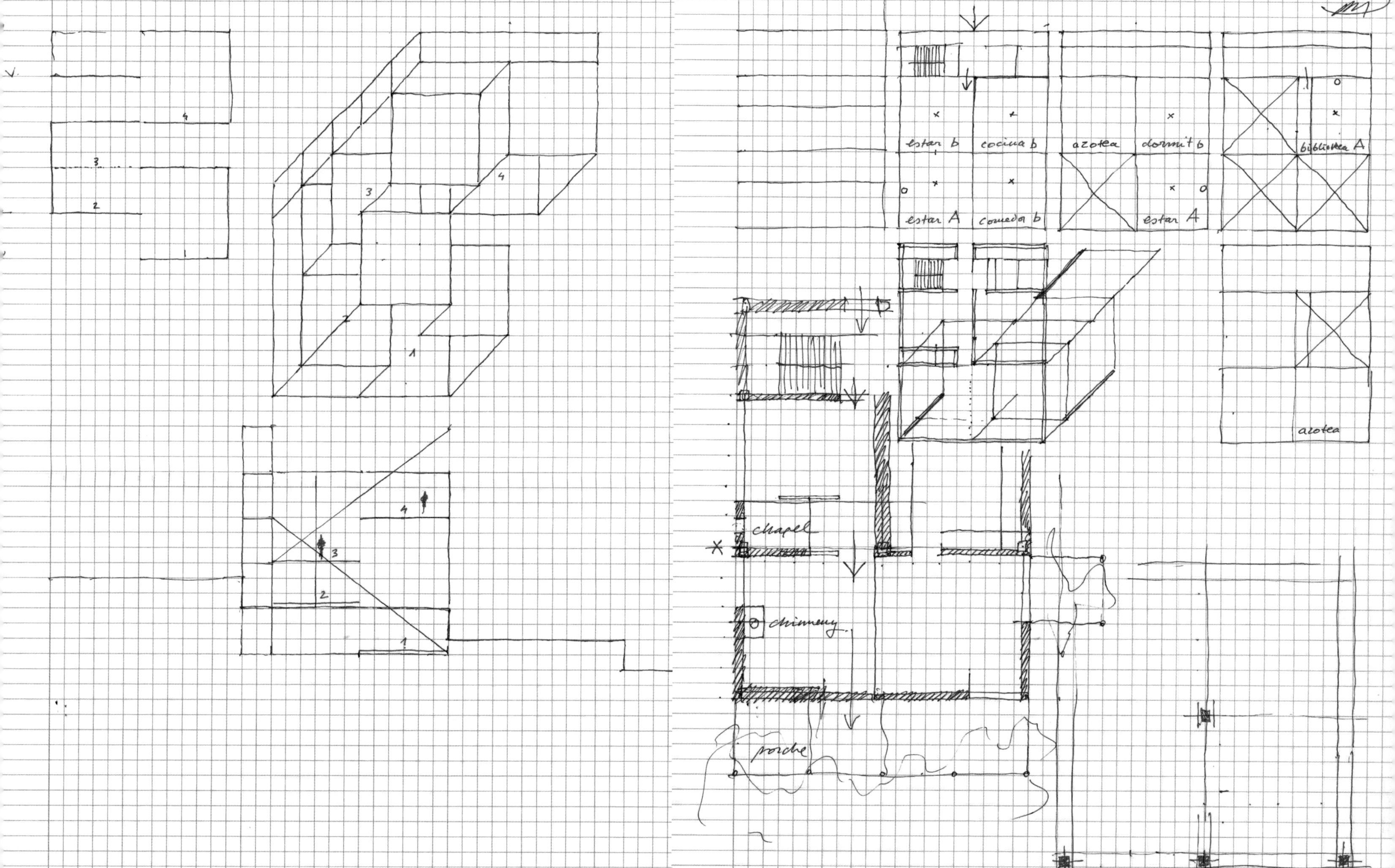

CALA HOUS

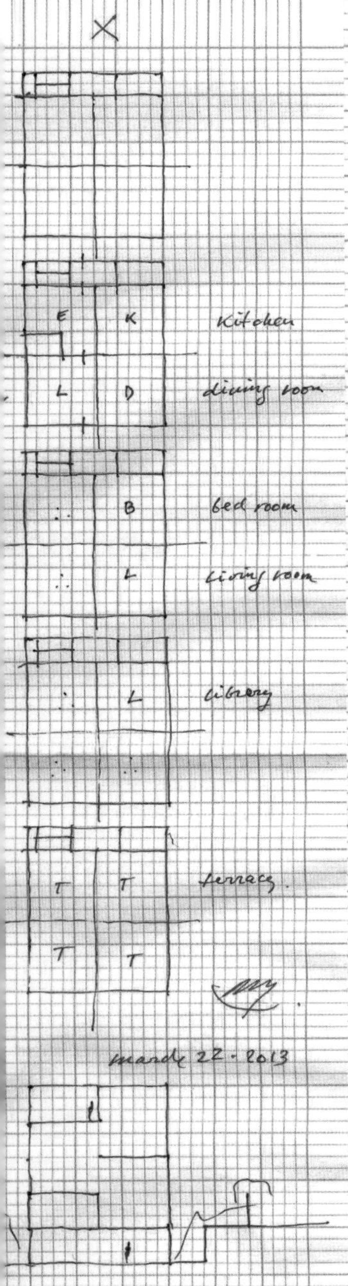
Kitchen
dining room
bed room
living room
library
terrace
marzo 22 · 2013

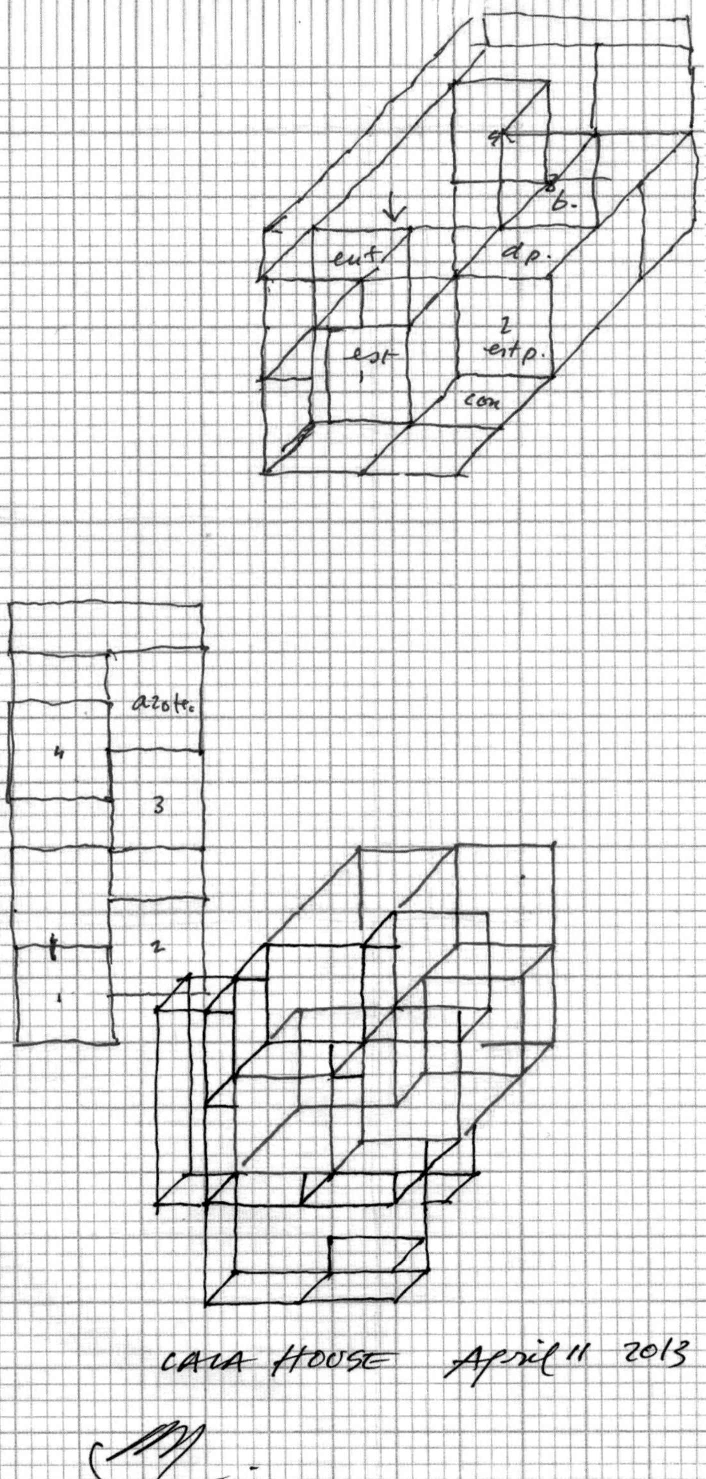
ent.
dp.
b.
est
entp.
con
azotea
CALA HOUSE April 11 2013

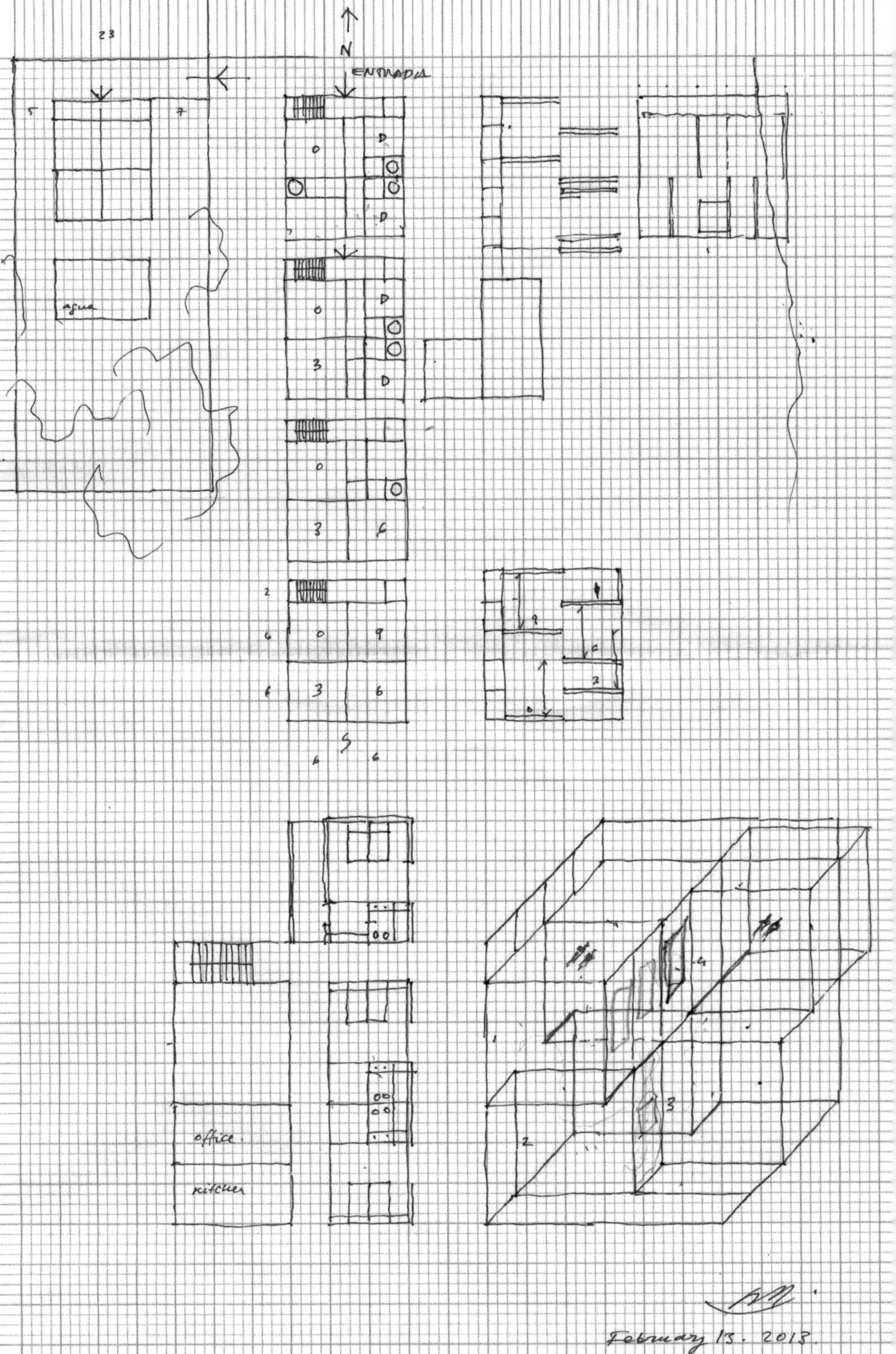
N
ENTRADA
agua
office
kitchen
February 13 · 2013

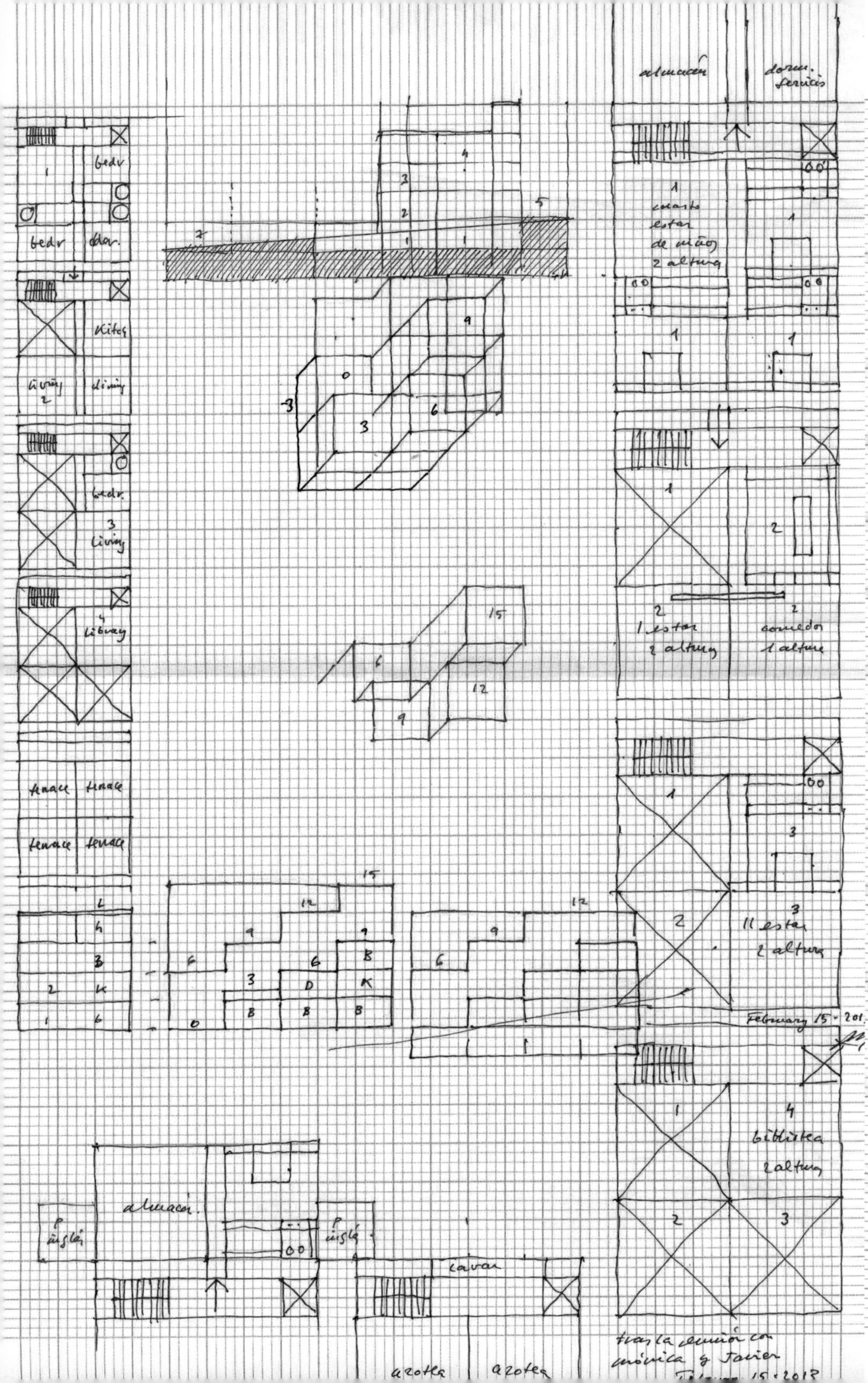
almacén
dorm. servicio
bedr
bedr
dber.
kitches
living
dining
bedr
living
library
terrace
terrace
terrace
terrace
cuarto estar de niños 2 altura
estar 2 altura
comedor 1 altura
estar 2 altura
February 15 · 2013
biblioteca 2 altura
almacén
inglés
inglés
cavar
azotea
azotea
tras la reunión con mónica y Javier
15 · 2013

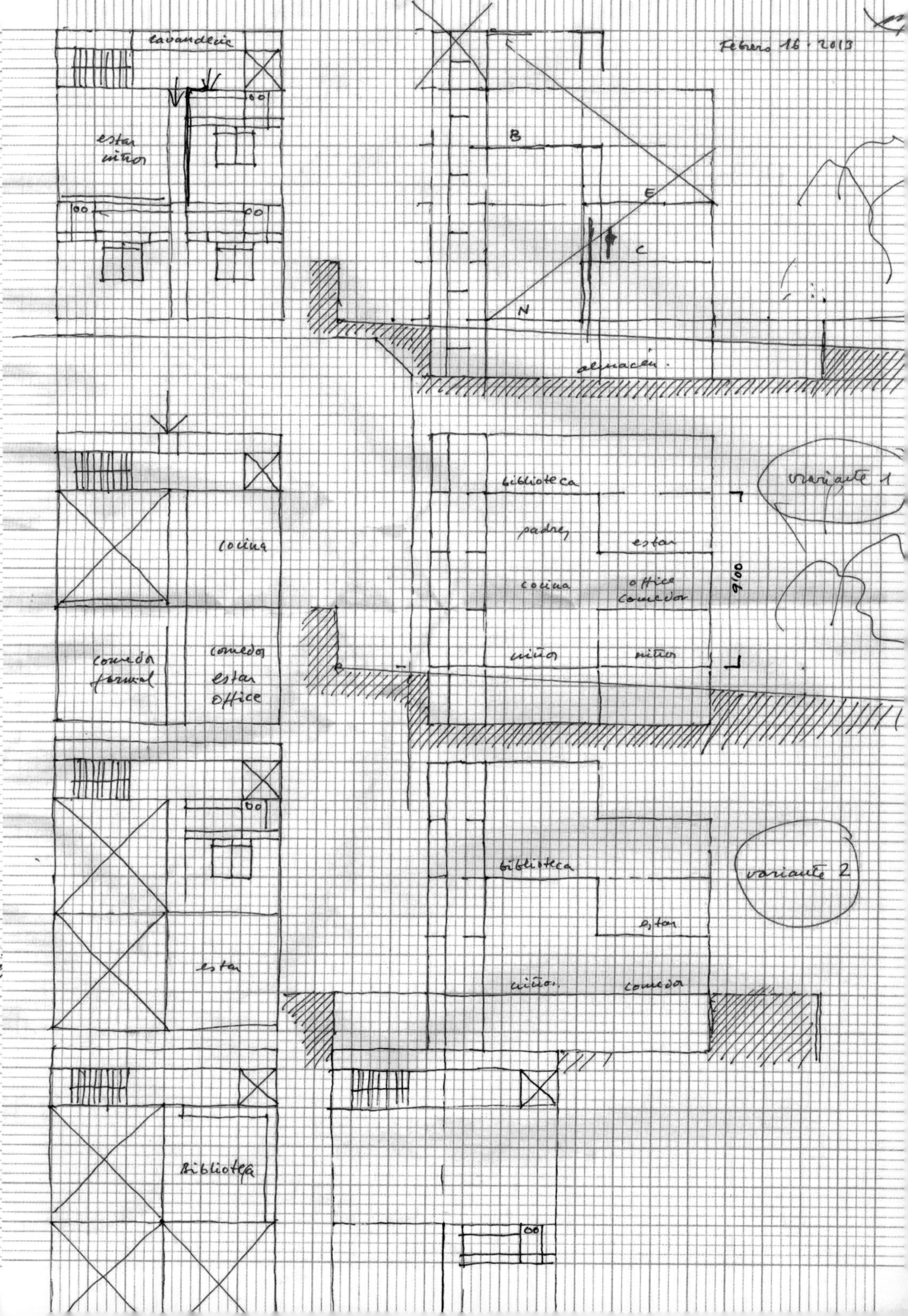
lavandería
Febrero 16 · 2013
estar niños
almacén
biblioteca
padres
estar
cocina
cocina
office comedor
niños
niños
variante 1
9.00
comedor formal
comedor estar office
biblioteca
variante 2
estar
estar
niños
comedor
biblioteca

JO COENEN

Netherlands

Featured projects: Tivoli Music Palace [p. 56]
Amsterdam Public Library [p. 57] · Stibbe Headquarters [pp. 58–9]

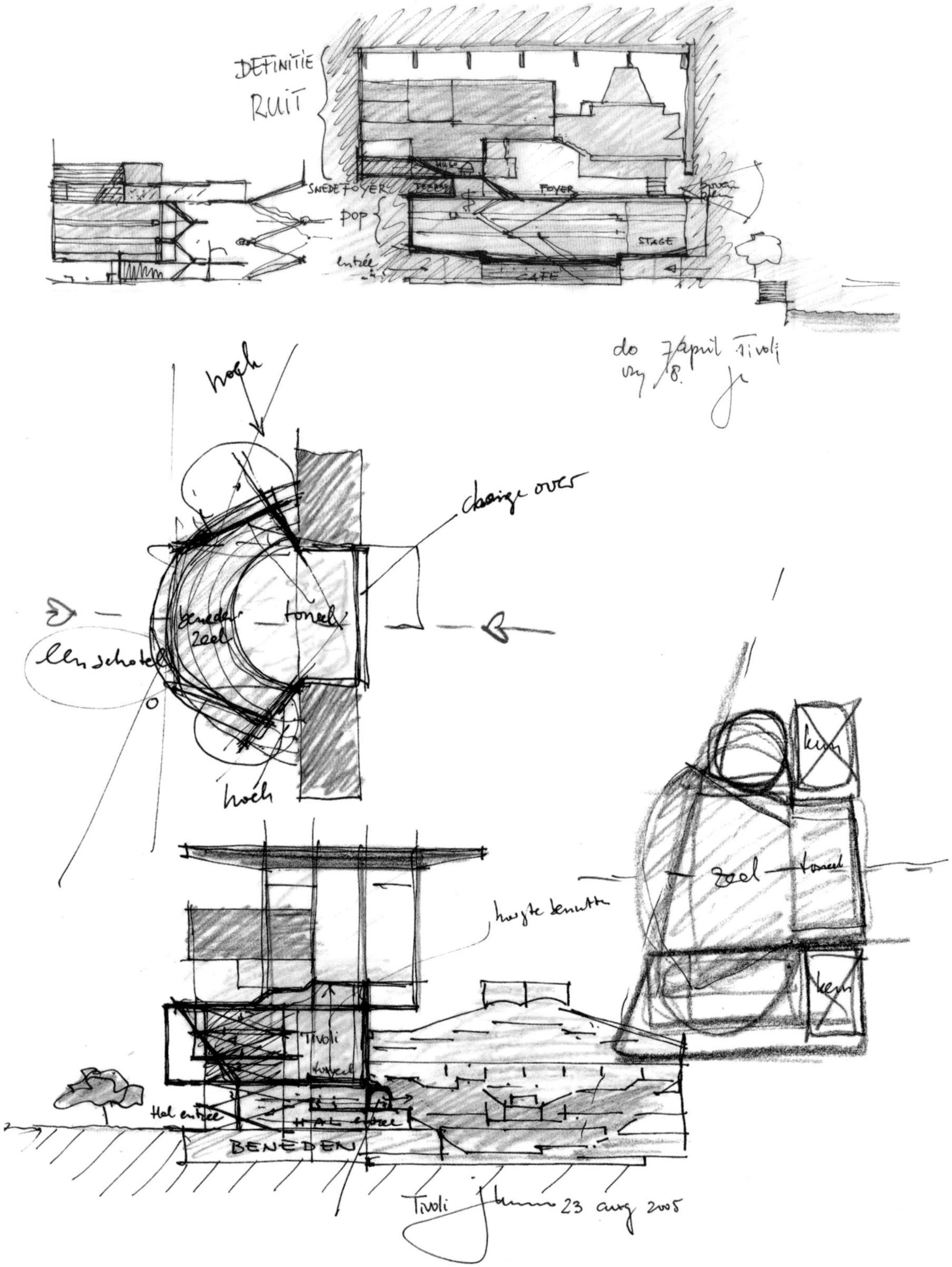

'When I sketch, I am three times quicker than when I draw on the computer,' says Jo Coenen, an 'architect and urbanist' with offices in Switzerland, Germany and Italy, as well as his native Holland. 'Since a sketch is, by definition, not a finished product, it allows me to focus on what is essential, rather than having to take into consideration other – sometimes superfluous – aspects. All of these things make sketching extremely practical; I can point someone in a certain direction just by using a bit of colour.'

A former Chief Government Architect of the Netherlands, in 2006 Coenen established the MIT Research Center for Modification, Intervention and Transformation at the Delft University of Technology, where he emphasized the 'art of interweaving past and present' into design.

'When I sketch, I evaluate different options in a search for what works best,' he explains. 'It is the ideal medium in which to investigate the various possibilities. The process ensures that I have a better memory of what I do. In my opinion, this physical working method should not be lacking in this century.'

Coenen believes that sketching assists the design process from start to finish. 'I can turn to it at unguarded moments and elaborate on the design of the entire building or masterplan,' he explains. 'I may take the computer drawing as a starting point – I place my sketching paper over the print and take it from there. It is something I prefer over digital drawing, because the computer will always keep a certain amount of control over your actions. I try to escape technology in order to be better able to search for the freedom within the existing situation.'

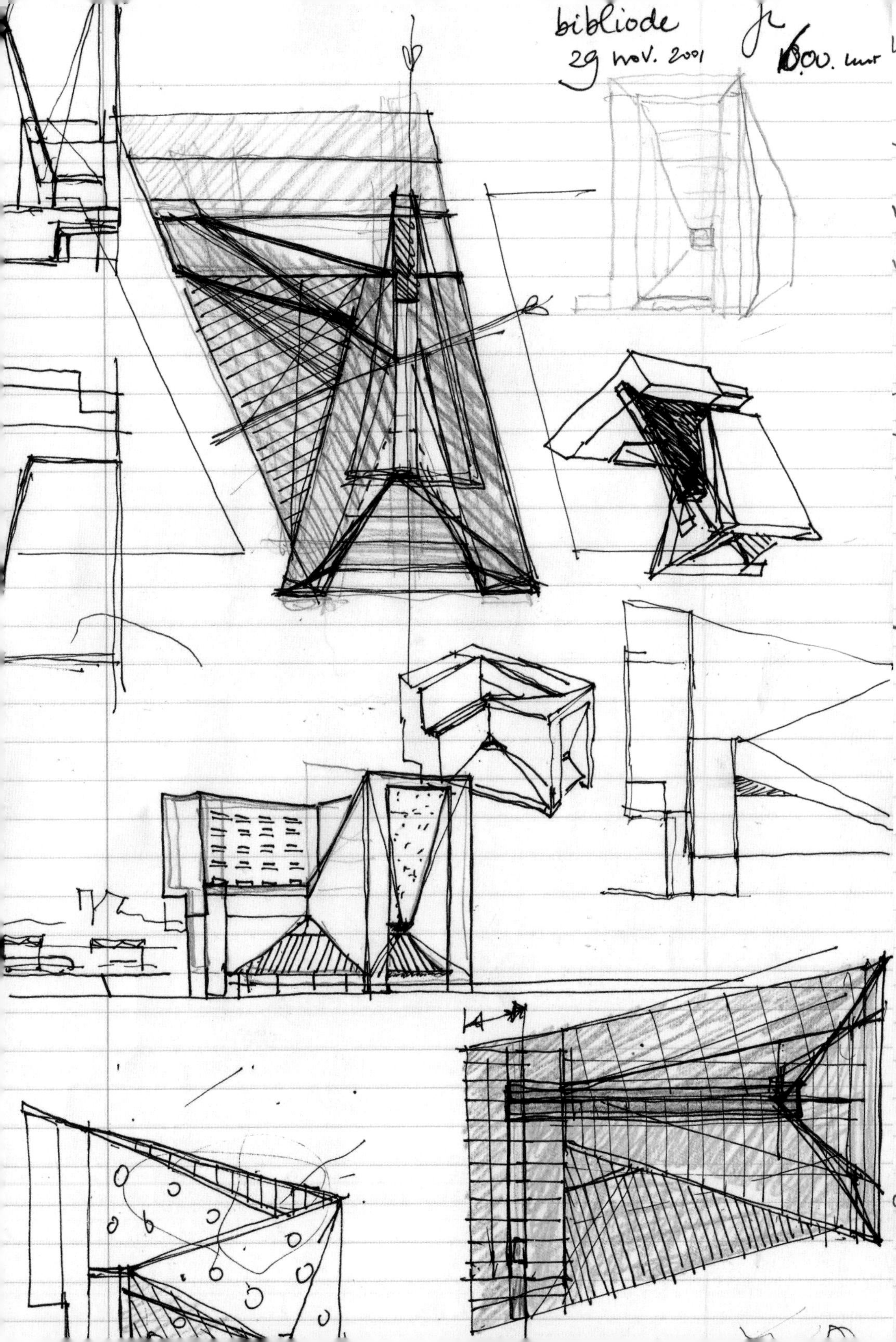

bibliode
29 nov. 2001

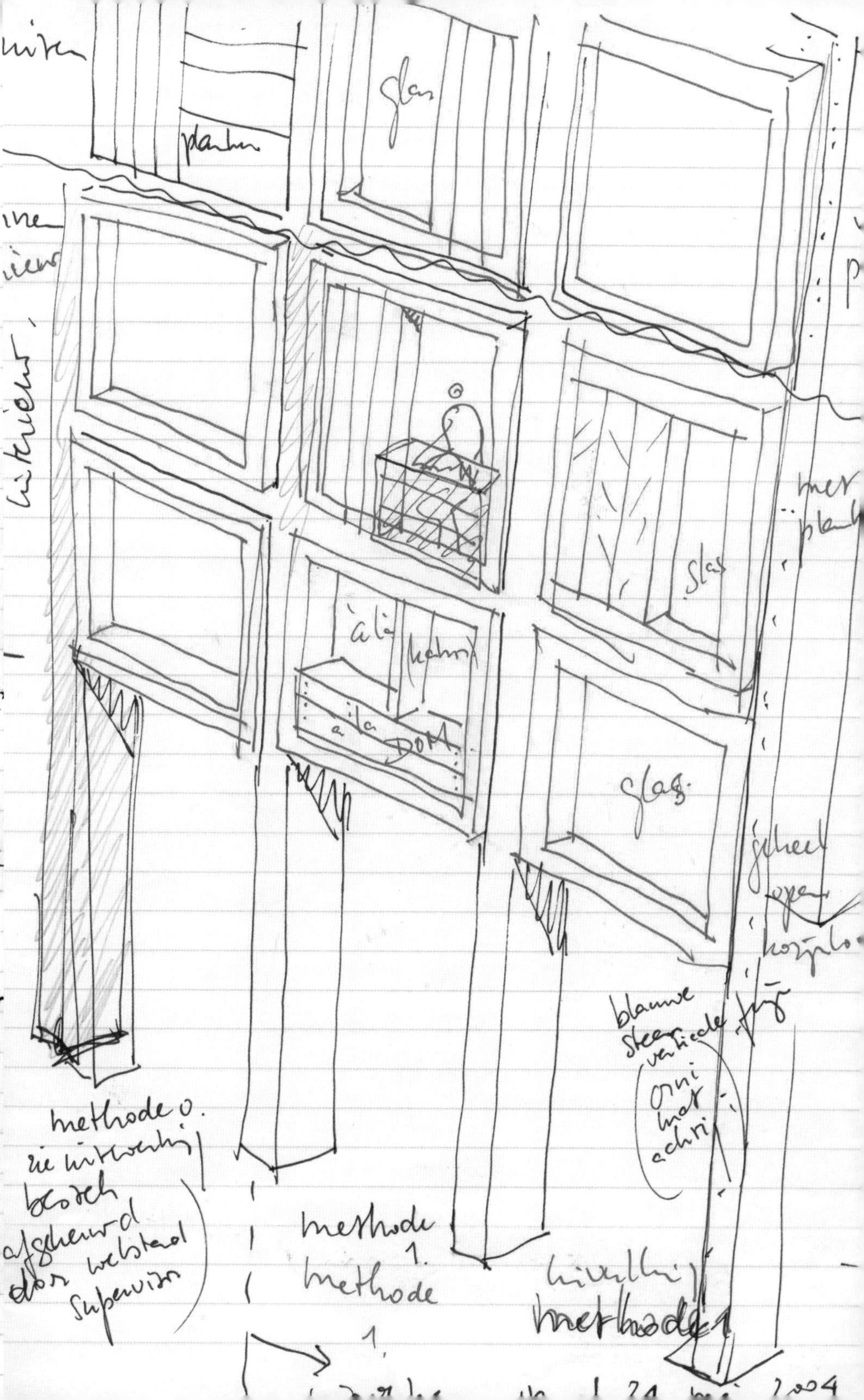

glas
planken
glas
glas
methode 0.
methode
1.
methode
methode 1

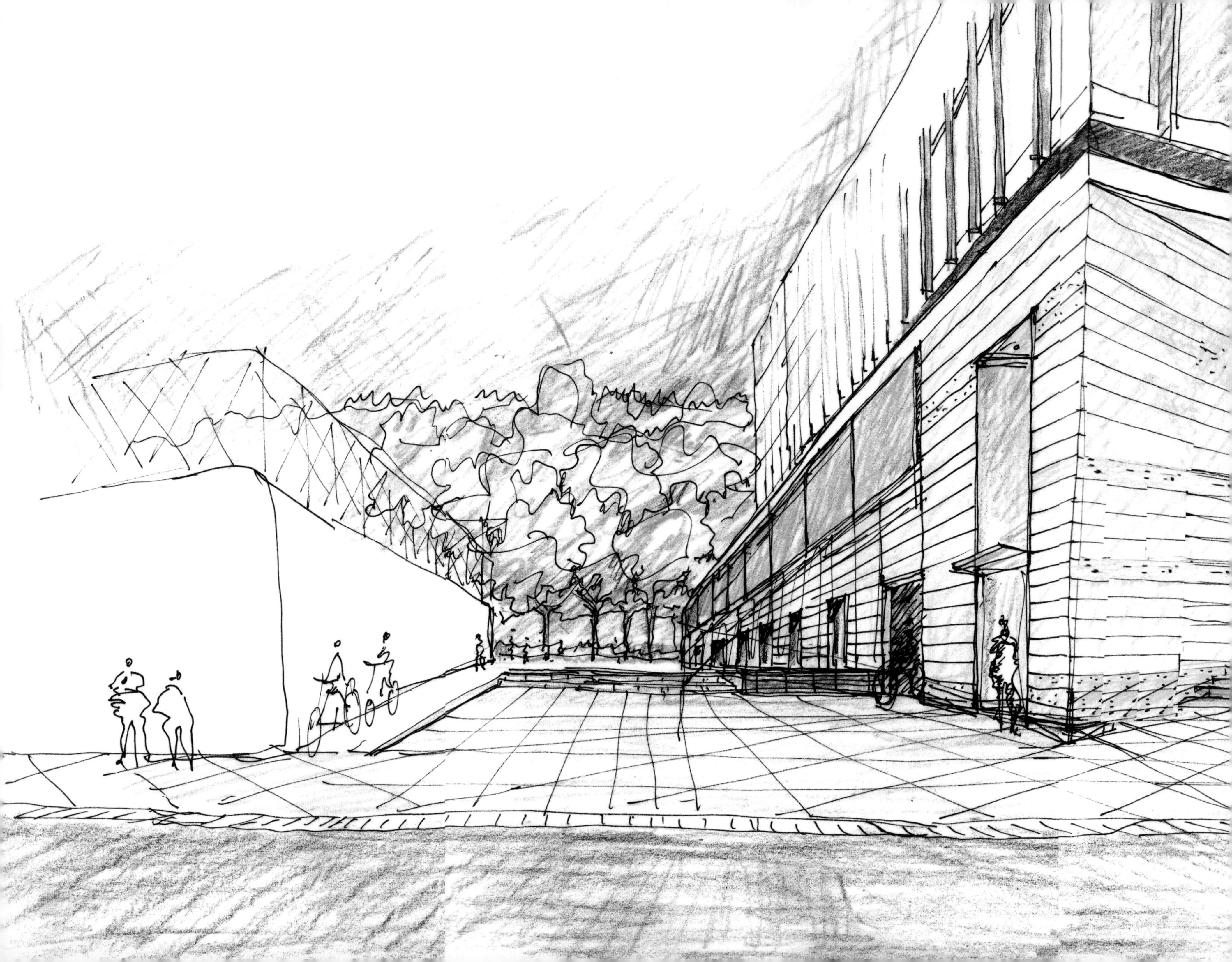

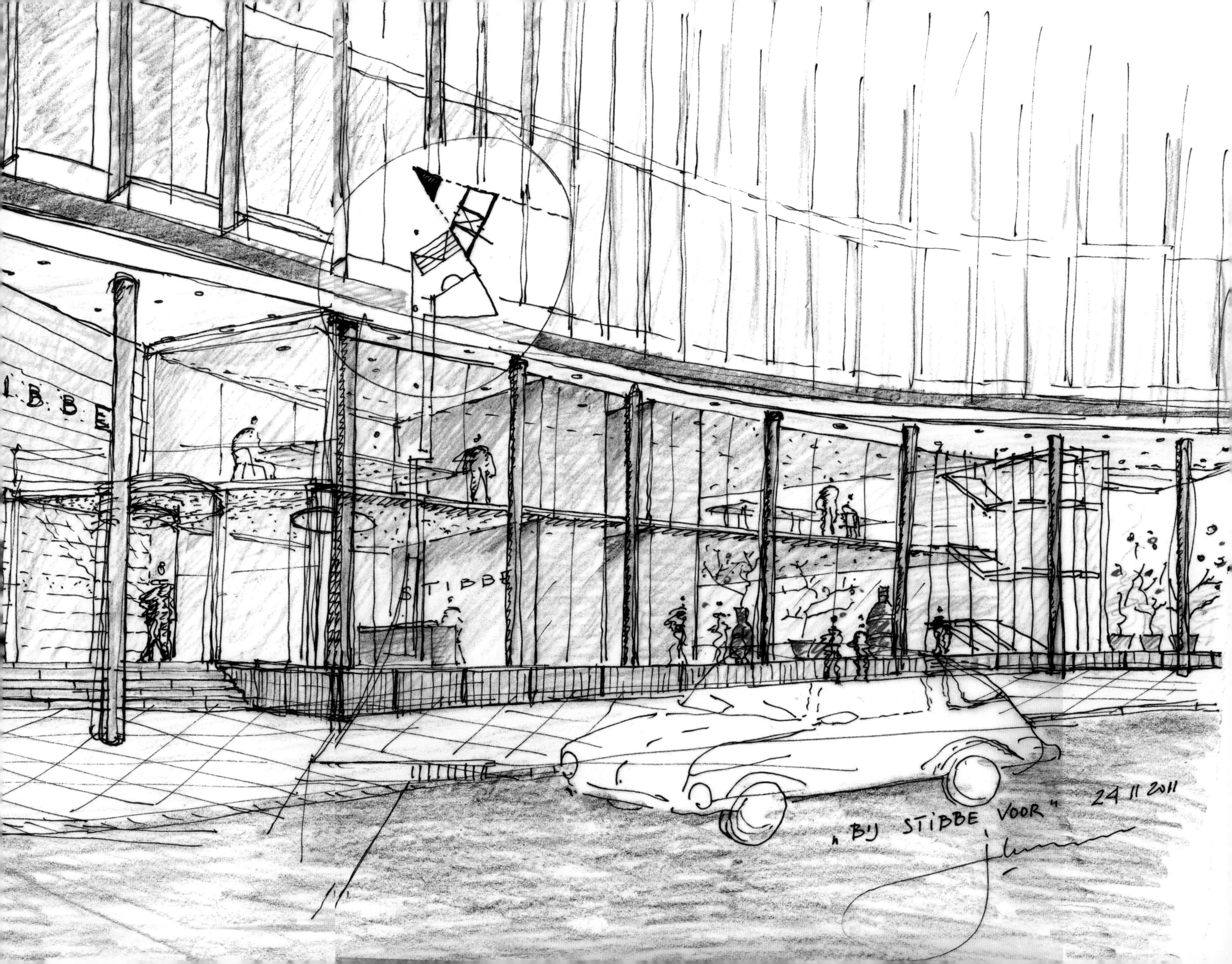
I.B.B.E
STIBBE
„BIJ STIBBE VOOR"
24 11 2011

JACK DIAMOND

Diamond Schmitt • Canada

Featured projects: Hearn Generating Station [pp. 60–65]

'There is no faster or more telling means of conveying conceptual approaches to design than sketching,' says Jack Diamond, principal partner at Toronto-based firm Diamond Schmitt (see also p. 284). 'It is the most expressive graphic shorthand possible. Computers don't come close.'

Diamond, a Royal Architectural Institute of Canada Gold Medallist, has been practising architecture for some 50 years, and is an Honorary Fellow of the American Institute of Architects, a member of the Order of Ontario, and Officer of the Order of Canada. Established in 1975, the globally renowned Diamond Schmitt has designed buildings that range from the Life Sciences Complex at McGill University in Montreal and the New Mariinsky Theatre in St Petersburg to private residences as far afield as Switzerland.

Diamond believes that digital means are ideal for testing design in sketch form. 'The computer's discipline is best for accuracy,' he explains. 'One cannot fudge proportion or dimension. But sketching is an exploratory process. It is one of discovery, sometimes of revelation. Sketches suggest ideas that are often not those originally portrayed.'

Using pen or soft pencil, Diamond communicates with clients via sketching. 'They react with greater understanding of the problem and its solution,' he says. 'Indeed, sketching can be an effective and rapid means of mutual exploration. And there is a further drawback to digital computation and graphics: it is a medium that appears as a resolved design, whether it is or not.'

AJD '16

AJD '16

AJD'16

AJD

AJD 1/16

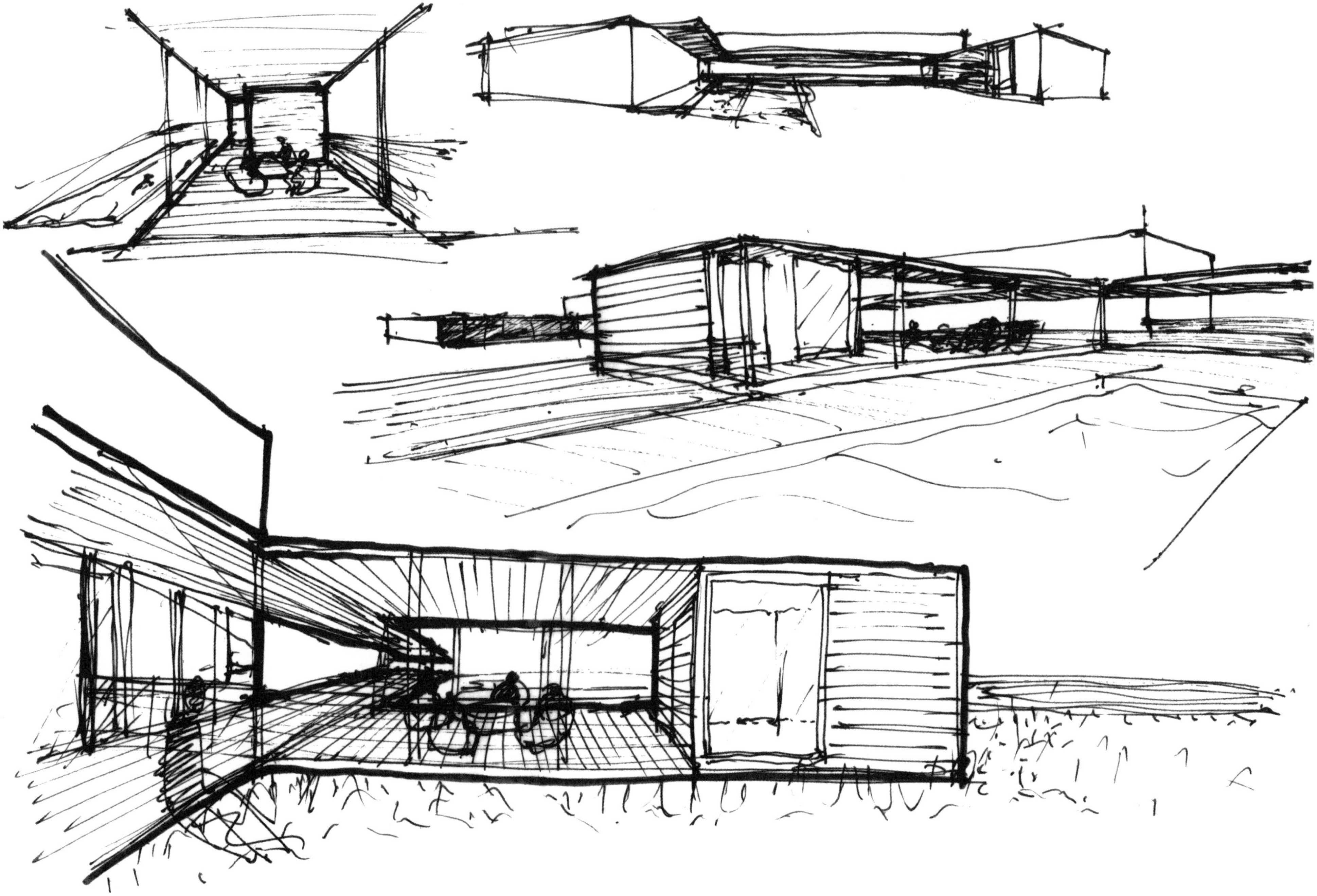

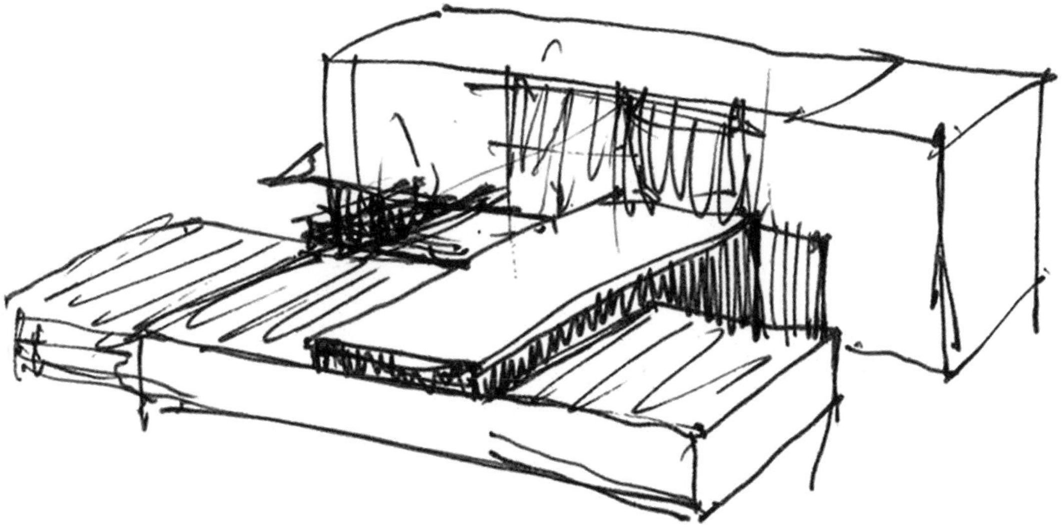

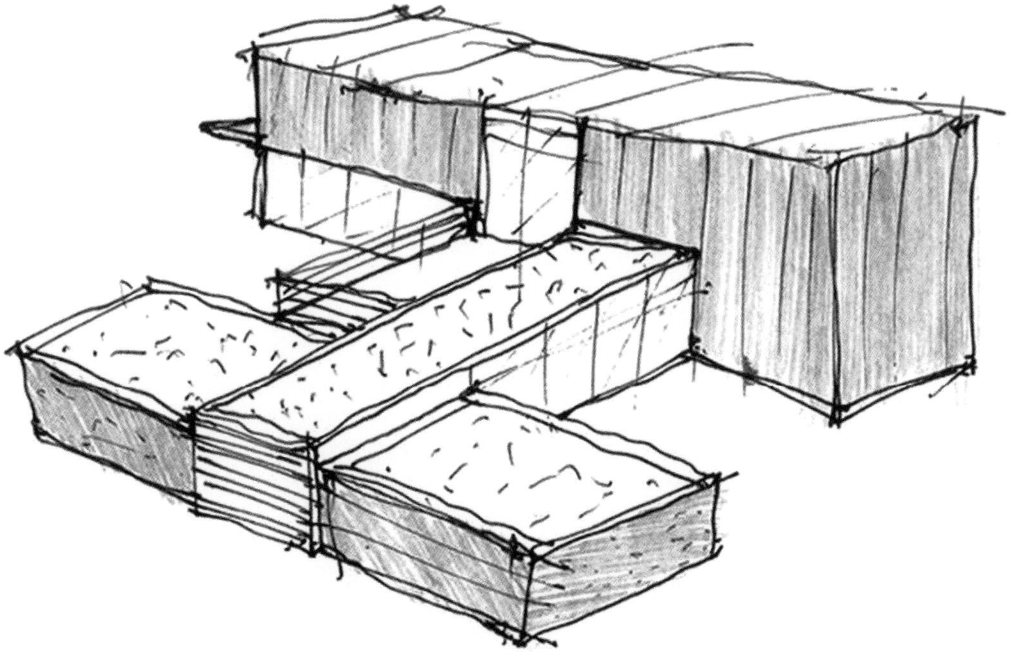

HEATHER DUBBELDAM

Dubbeldam Architecture & Design • Canada

Featured projects: Fourth Line House [pp. 66–9] · Slide House [p. 70]
Skygarden House [p. 71]

'Even though we have access to a variety of tools for representing our spatial ideas, drawing by hand is still the most poetic means of visually explaining a space,' says Heather Dubbeldam, founder of Dubbeldam Architecture & Design. 'It is also a skill that most people develop as children, so it feels more natural and comfortable, as opposed to any digital means.'

The 10-person firm, based in Toronto, was awarded the Professional Prix de Rome Award in 2017, and Dubbeldam herself has recently been named one of the '30 Must-Know Women Architects' by design journal *Azure*.

'Our ideas are rarely fully formulated, and that's the beauty of sketching,' she says. 'You don't know where it will lead you and what ideas you will uncover by formulating a drawing. The sketch is a process of discovery, so it is an iterative process, as it continually leads you in new directions.'

Dubbeldam and her team use sketching as a method of thinking through an idea. They will often draw together, during meetings or at their own desks. 'Sketching is a collaborative exercise,' she explains. 'Team members may sketch out ideas on their own, bring them to the table, combine them with other drawings, or come up with entirely new ideas. The act of sketching provides clarity and makes the ideas seem more tangible, so sketching can let you see multiple designs at once. Sketching also forces us to develop these initial thoughts, because we must think about what we want to depict.'

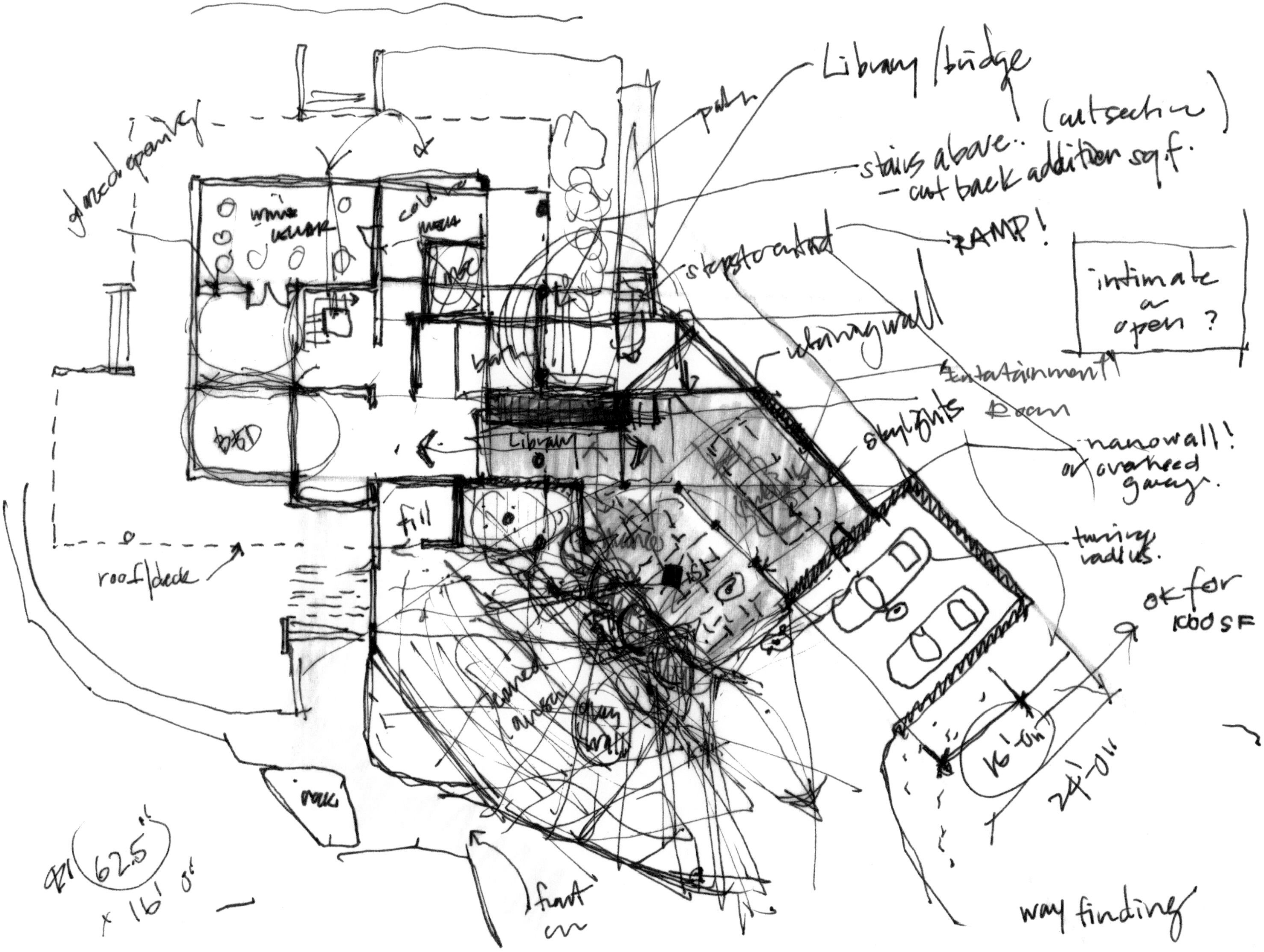
Library/bridge
path
(cut section)
stairs above..
- cut back addition sq.f.
RAMP!
intimate
or
open ?
Entertainment
Room
skylights
nanowall!
or overhead
garage.
turning
radius.
Library
roof/deck
fill
16'-0"
24'-0"
way finding
front

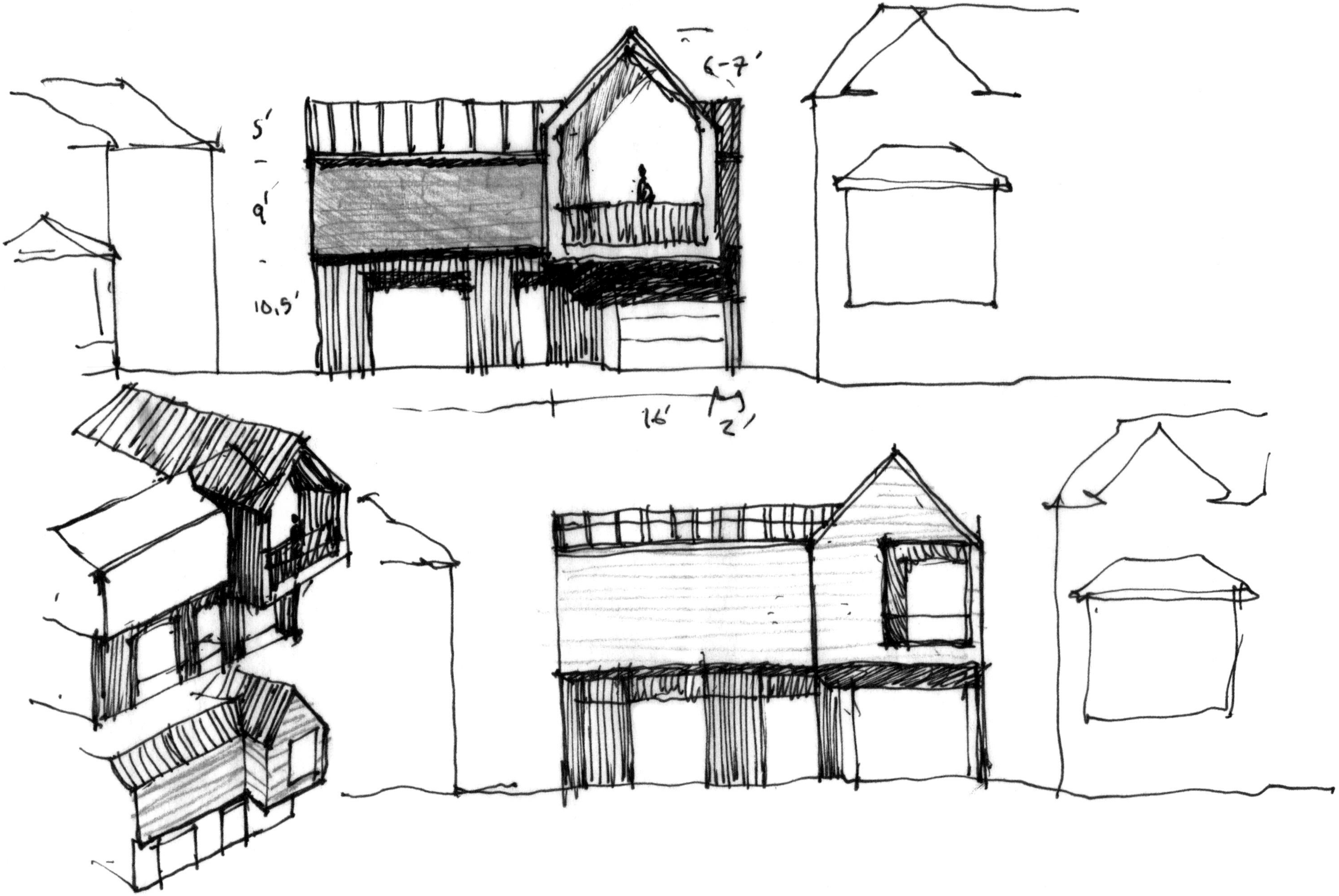
6-7'
5'
9'
10.5'
16'
2'

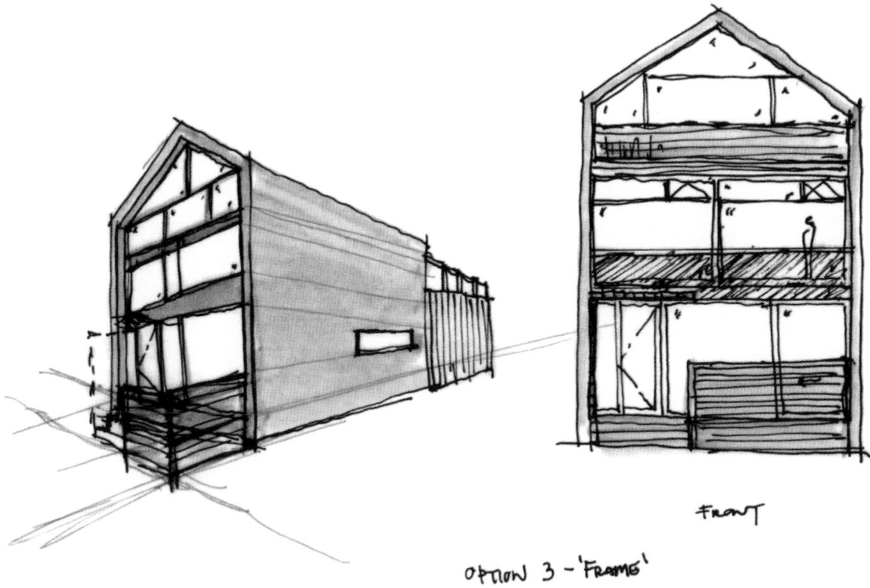
FRONT
OPTION 3 - 'FRAME'

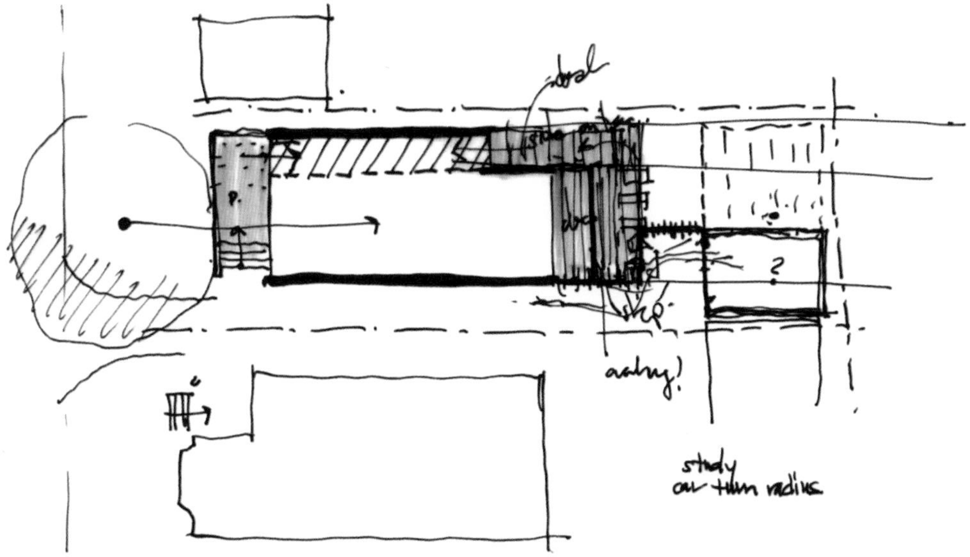
study
on turn radius

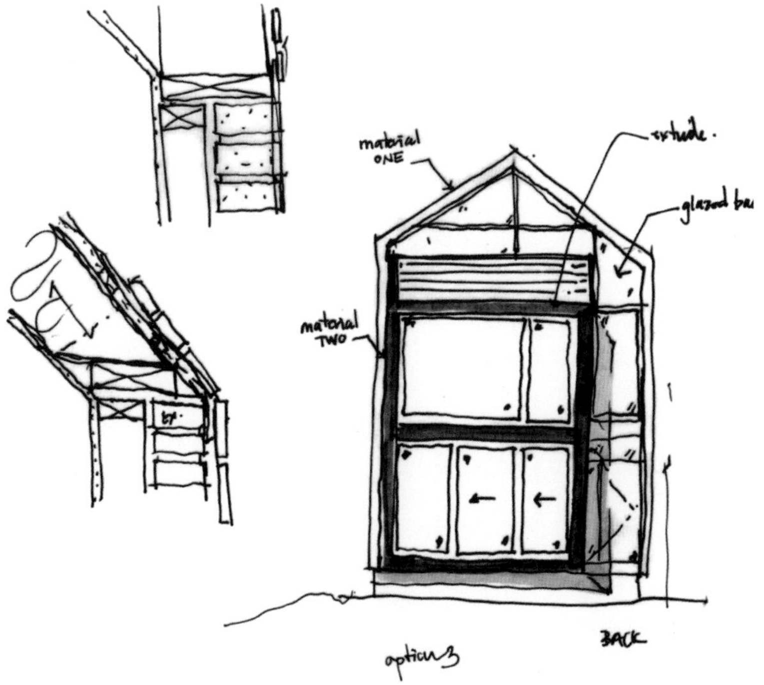
material ONE
material TWO
glazed bar
option 3
BACK

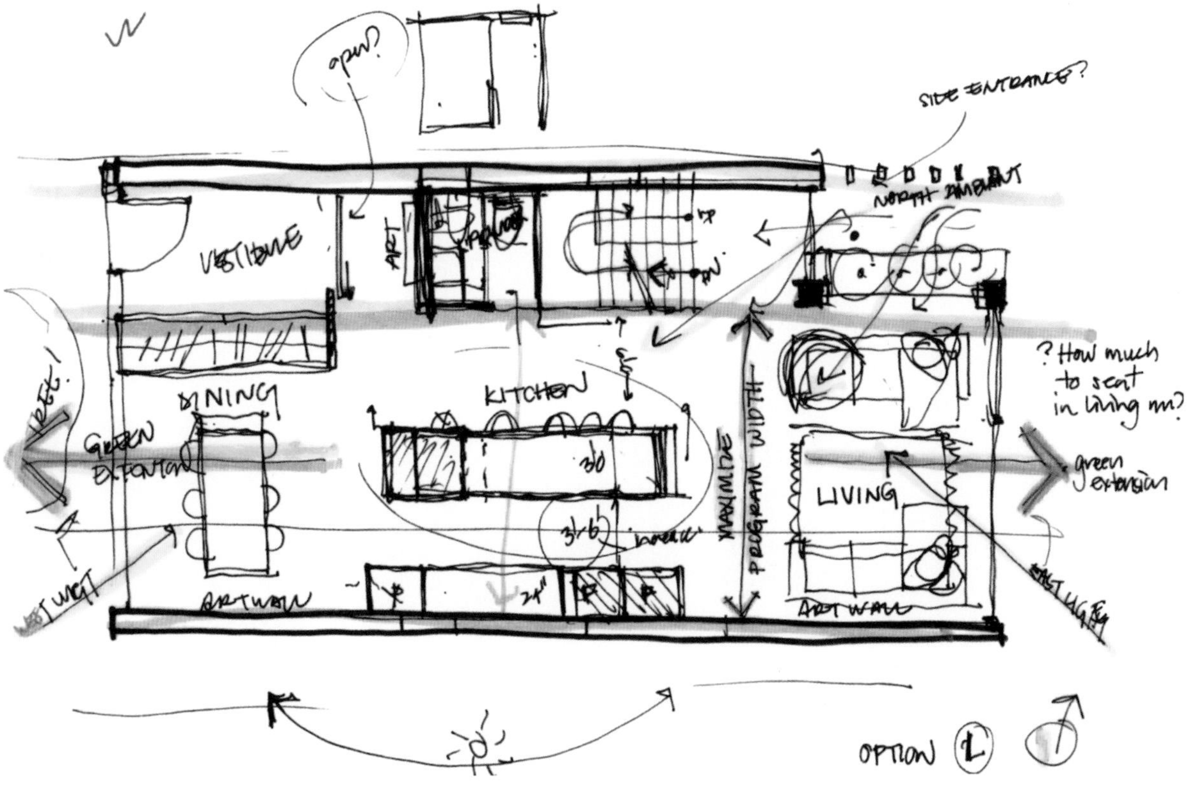
open?
SIDE ENTRANCE?
NORTH AMBIENT
VESTIBULE
ART
DINING
KITCHEN
GREEN EXTENSION
MAXIMIZE PROGRAM WIDTH
LIVING
? How much to seat in living rm?
green extension
ARTWALL
ART WALL
OPTION 1

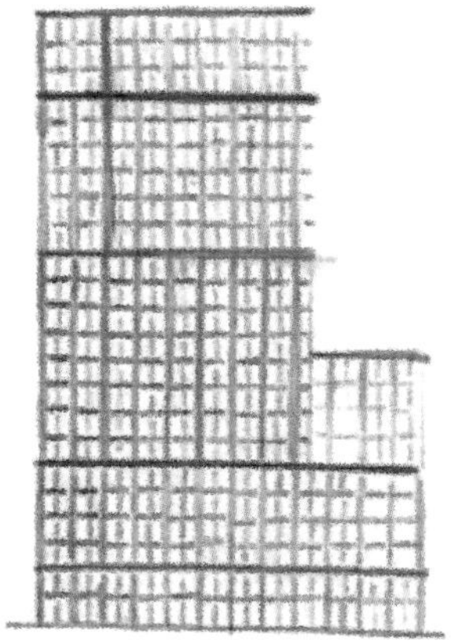

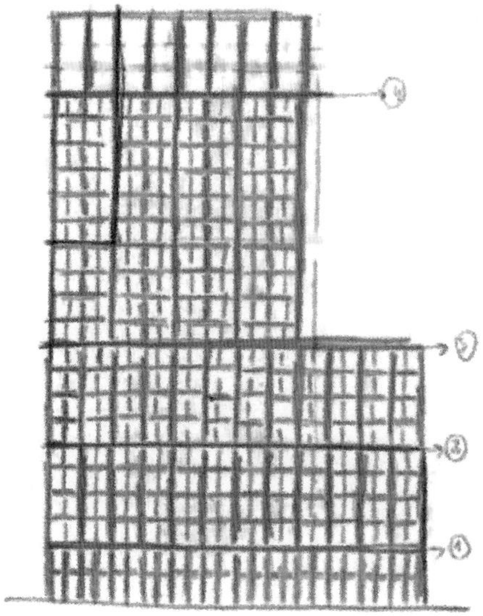
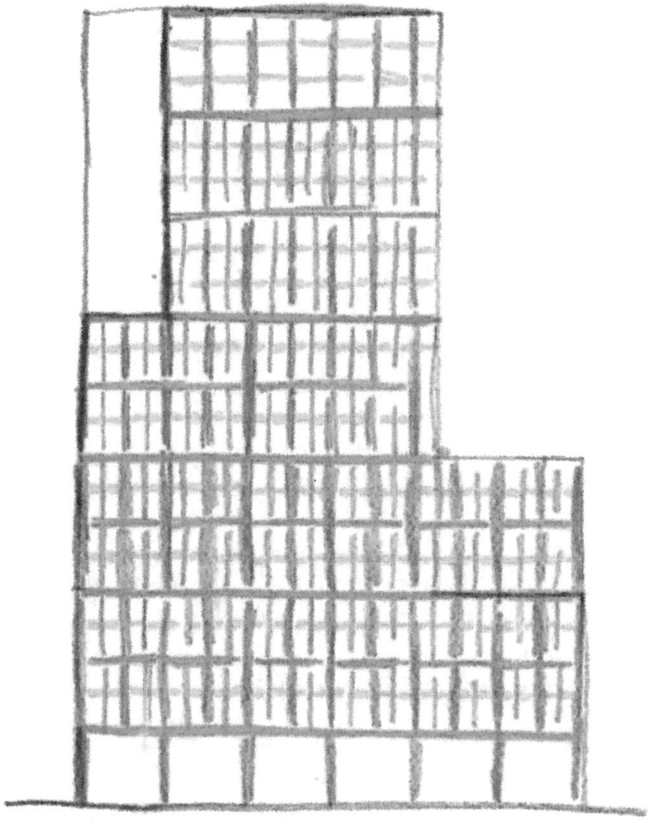
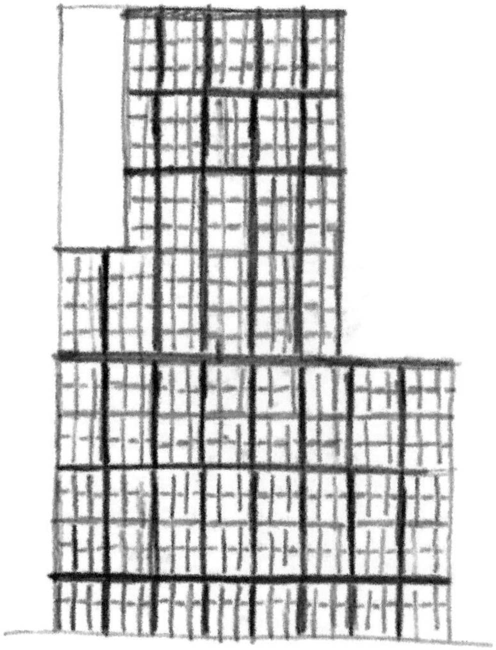

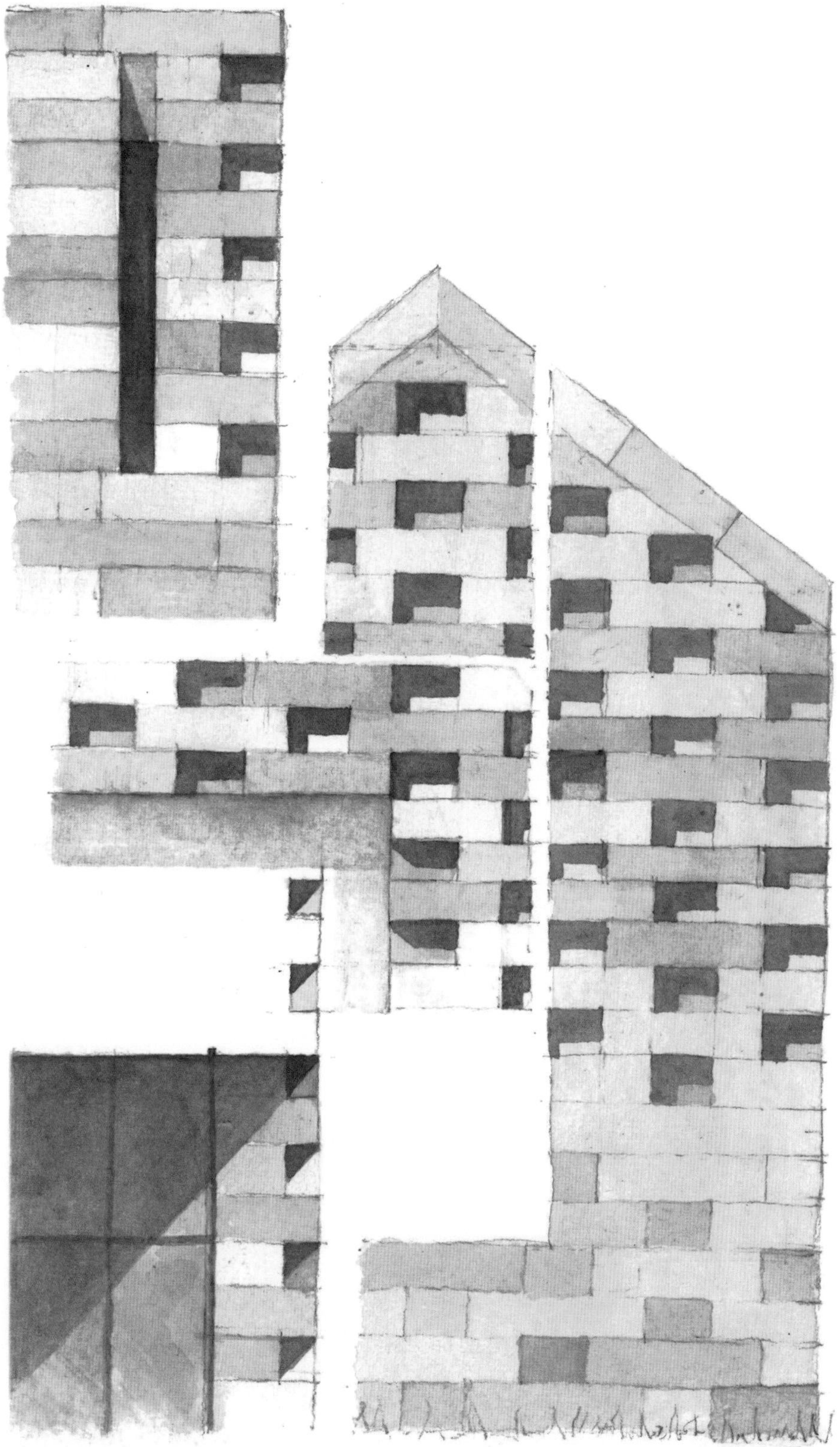

DUGGAN MORRIS ARCHITECTS

UK

Featured projects: Sylvan Heritage [pp. 73, 74–5]
Bartrams [p. 75, right] · Strand East [p. 76] · Bohemia [p. 78] · Models [p. 79]

'Sketching and model-making are fundamental to the design development process in our practice,' say the team at Duggan Morris Architects. 'They allow us to quickly and succinctly convey ideas on paper or in model form, and promote collective discussions within the office. In an industry where digital means of design development are constantly evolving, these skills remain crucial in facilitating an iterative and interrogative design process and to promote creative thinking at all levels.'

Duggan Morris, formed in 2004 by Joe Morris and Mary Duggan (who has since left the firm), has been honoured with eight RIBA awards, three Civic Trust Awards, the Manser Medal and the Stephen Lawrence Prize.

'We find that sketching and model-making regularly overlap and complement our digital-design work,' Morris and his colleagues note. 'We often produce sketches and models at an early stage, while the design is still fluid, to explore different ideas that then feed into a more resolved and digitalized output. This process is adopted at all stages, from concept to brief development and construction detailing. We even produce physical mock-ups during the construction stage to convey ideas and details to contractors and suppliers.'

The office thrives on the ability to design, develop and communicate ideas and designs through different mediums, and sketching and model-making are fundamental skills that, the team say, they can't do without. 'The physical and immediate nature of sketching allows us to develop designs as they are being discussed,' they add, 'and aids communication in design-team workshops and progress meetings with clients and contractors.'

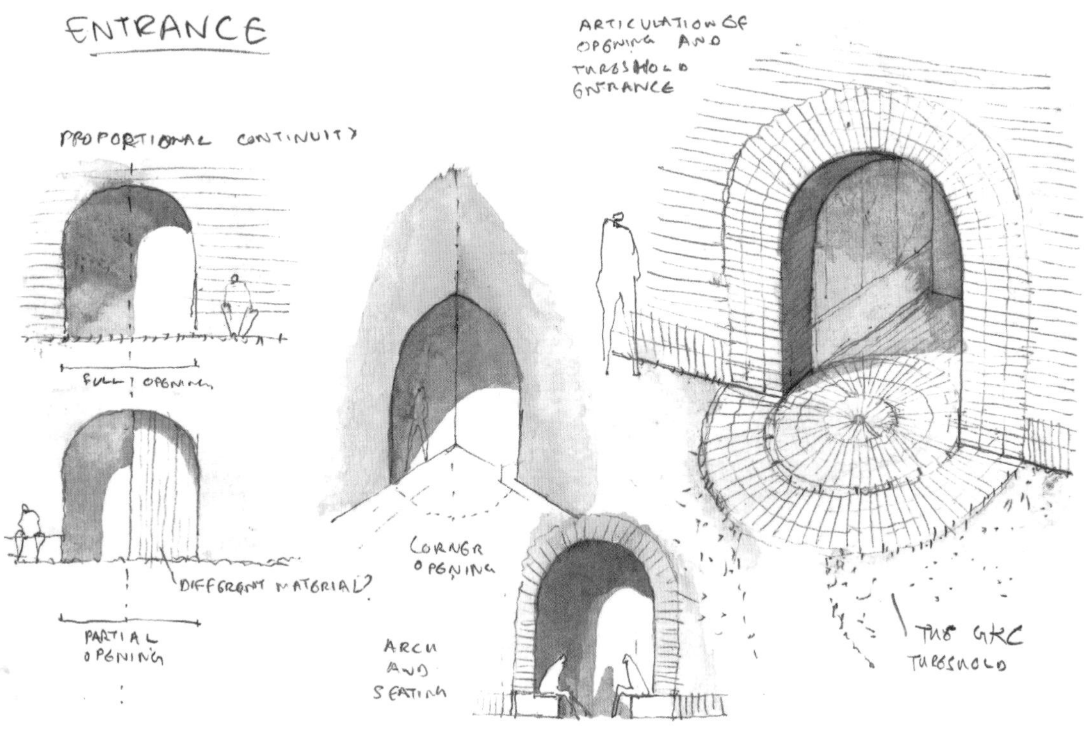
ENTRANCE
ARTICULATION OF OPENING AND THRESHOLD ENTRANCE
PROPORTIONAL CONTINUITY
FULL OPENING
DIFFERENT MATERIAL?
PARTIAL OPENING
CORNER OPENING
ARCH AND SEATING
THE GRC THRESHOLD

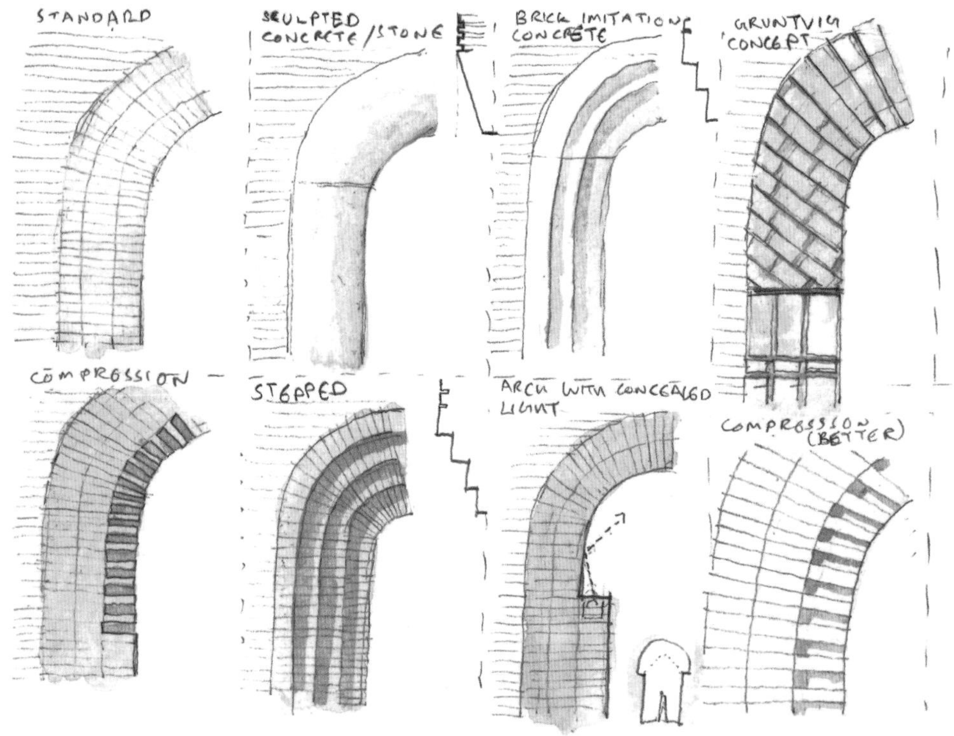
STANDARD
SCULPTED CONCRETE/STONE
BRICK IMITATION CONCRETE
GRUNTVIG CONCEPT
COMPRESSION
STEPPED
ARCH WITH CONCEALED LIGHT
COMPRESSION (BETTER)

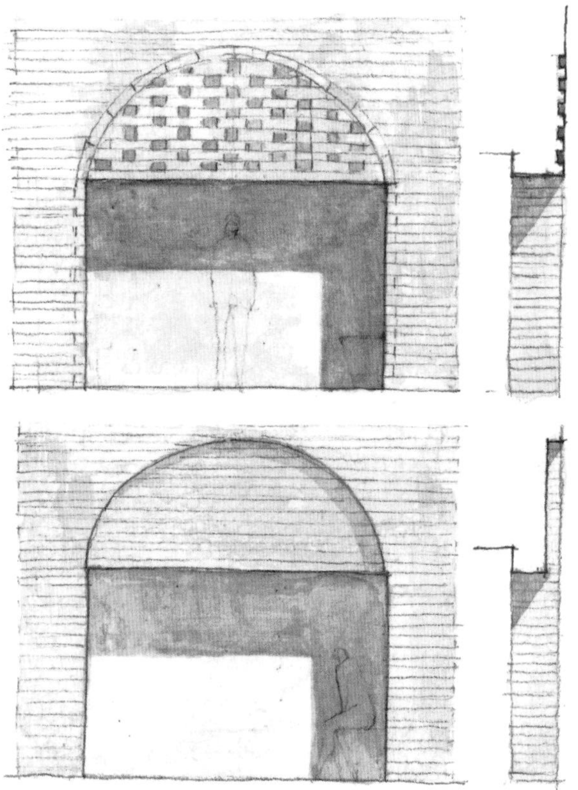

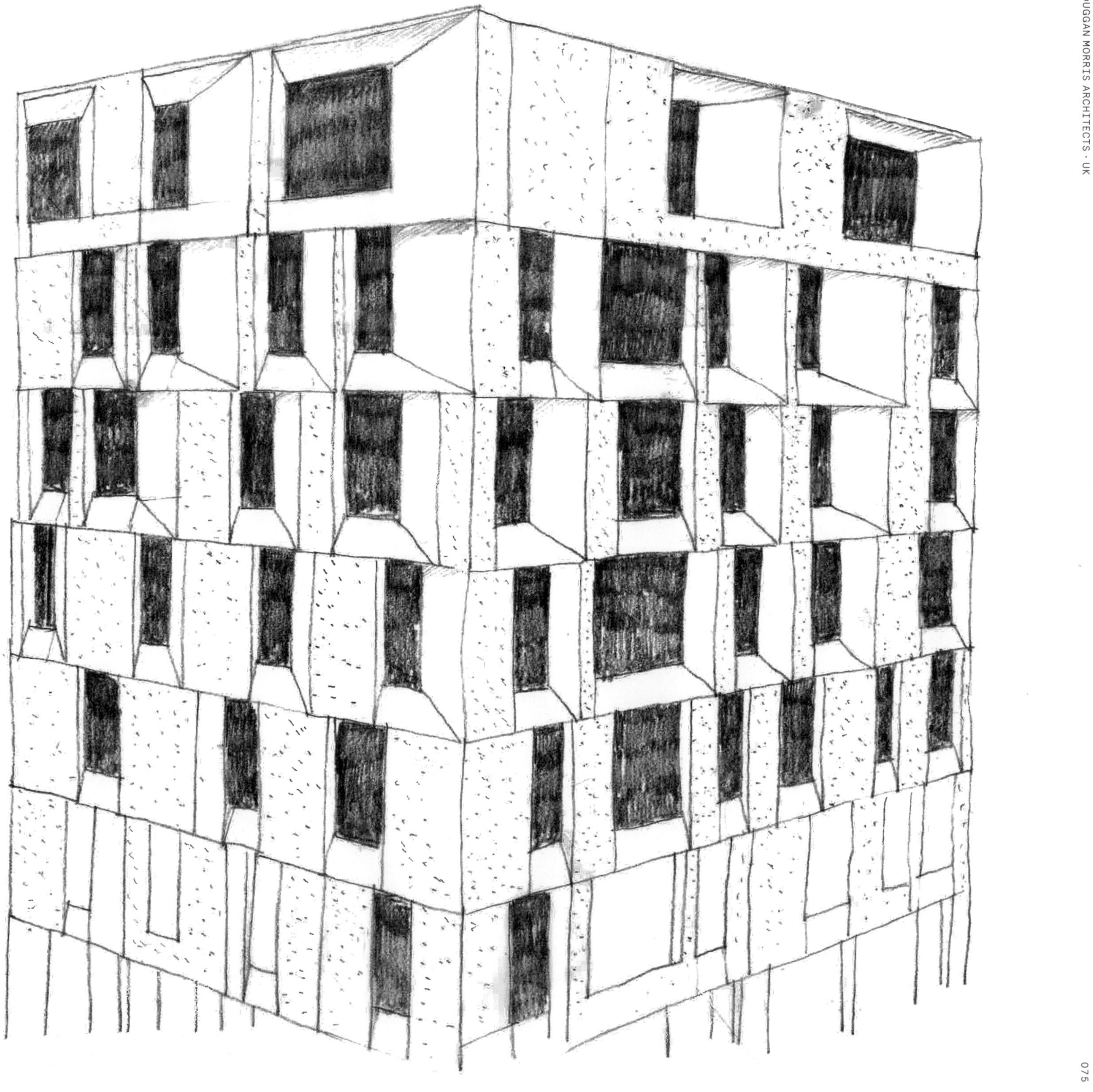

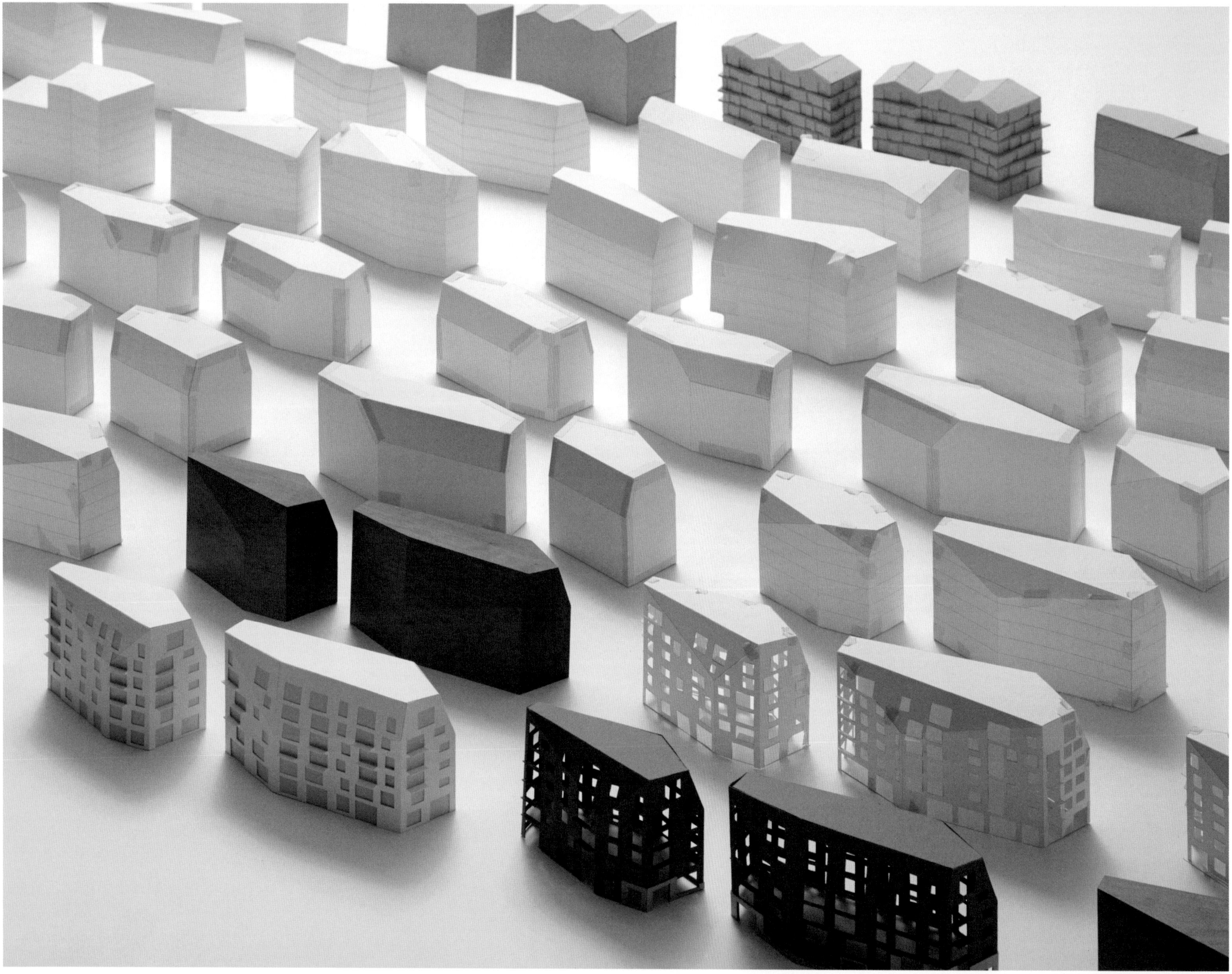

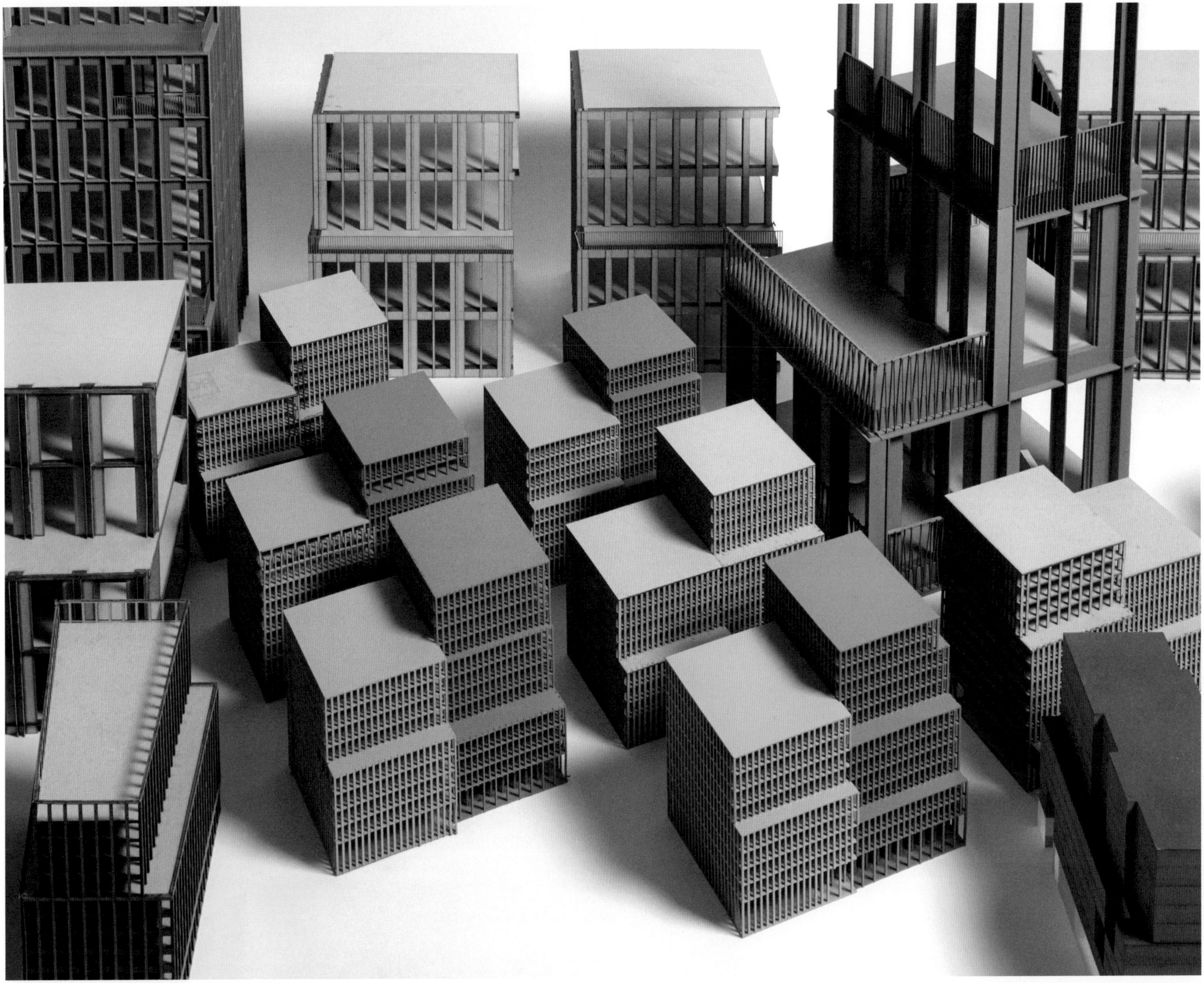

PIET HEIN EEK & IGGIE DEKKERS

Eek en Dekkers • Netherlands

Featured projects: Beach Pavilion Noord [p. 80]
TD Building [p. 81] · Drie Haringen [p. 82]
RF Building [p. 83] · Le Moulin [pp. 84–5]
Greenhouse [pp. 86–7] · Woudsend [pp. 88–9]

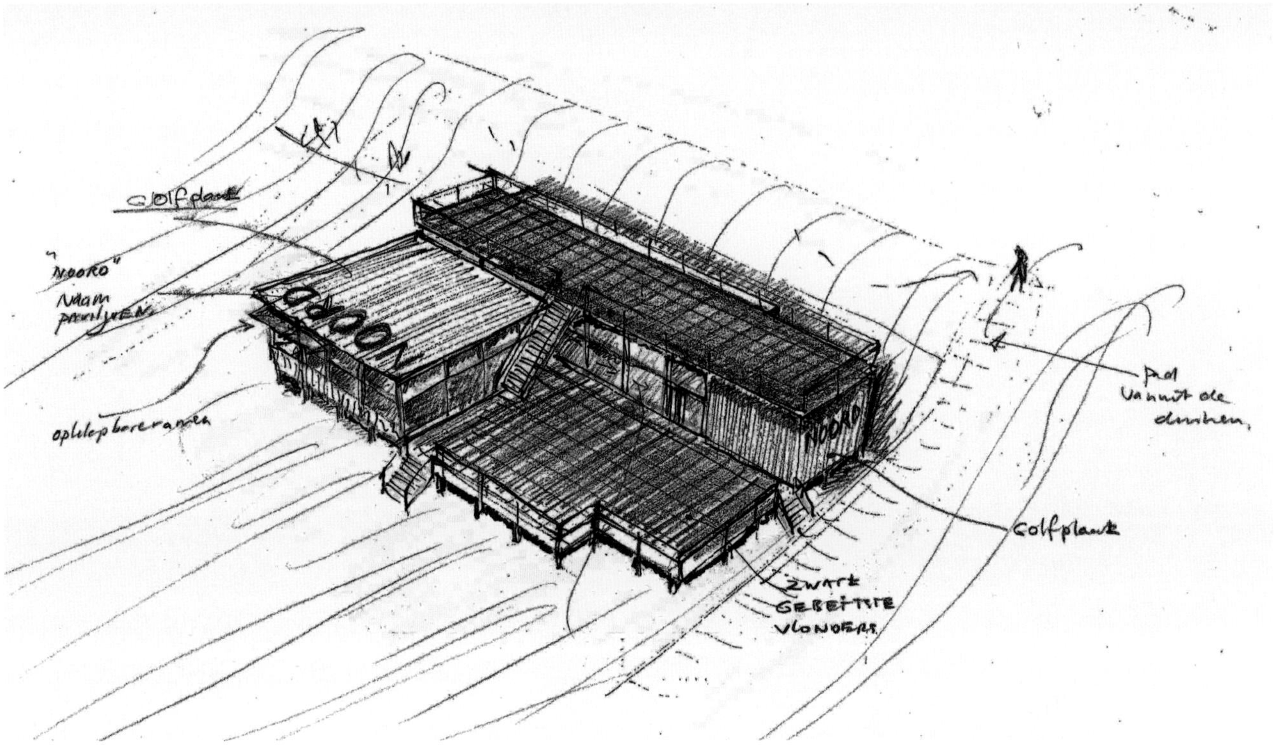

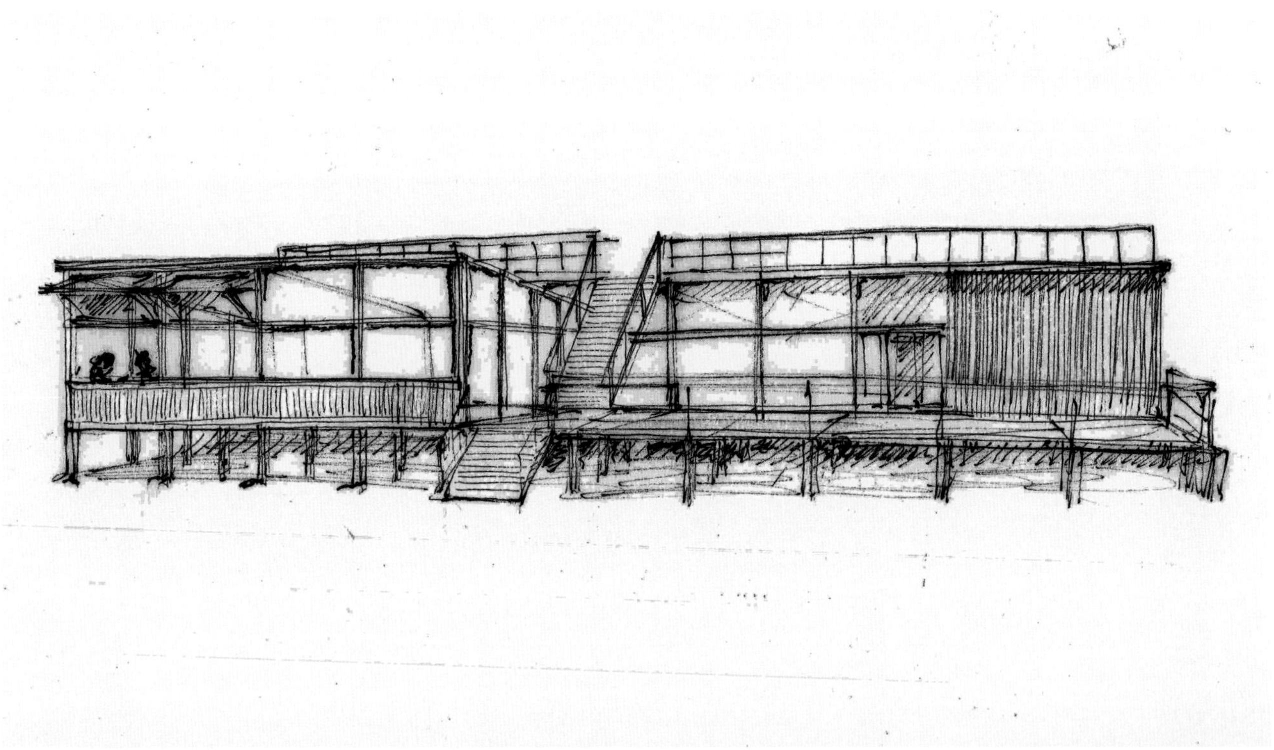

'A computer drawing fills in a lot of information, but each line of a sketch on a sheet of paper must be drawn by you,' note designer Piet Hein Eek and architect Iggie Dekkers, who work together as Eek en Dekkers. 'Computer drawings, programs and processes are fed by a standard library of existing details and solutions. If you are not aware of this, it kills creativity and encourages the repetition of bad choices and details.'

This collaborative team is renowned for their dual approach to design, which encompasses architecture, product and furniture design, a restaurant and a store. 'Each design starts with a sketch,' they say. 'Once we are satisfied with the concept, we begin making two- and three-dimensional plans on the computer. Issues will nearly always occur during this process, and we go back to sketching to see how they can be resolved. Afterwards, we translate the sketch into a digital drawing. The problem with these computer drawings is that they tend to have a sense of reality, because of the way they are presented, but an actual sketch is often more accurate.'

For both Eek and Dekkers, sketching is an iterative process, a quick way to see proportions, volumes and possible impossibilities, and to merge all aspects in one drawing in an instant. 'You might say that sketching to search and determine the concept is the only way to work from an holistic point of view,' they say. 'This is extremely important, because the process of architecture is cut into pieces and very specialized. This quality is important for both the creator and the client.'

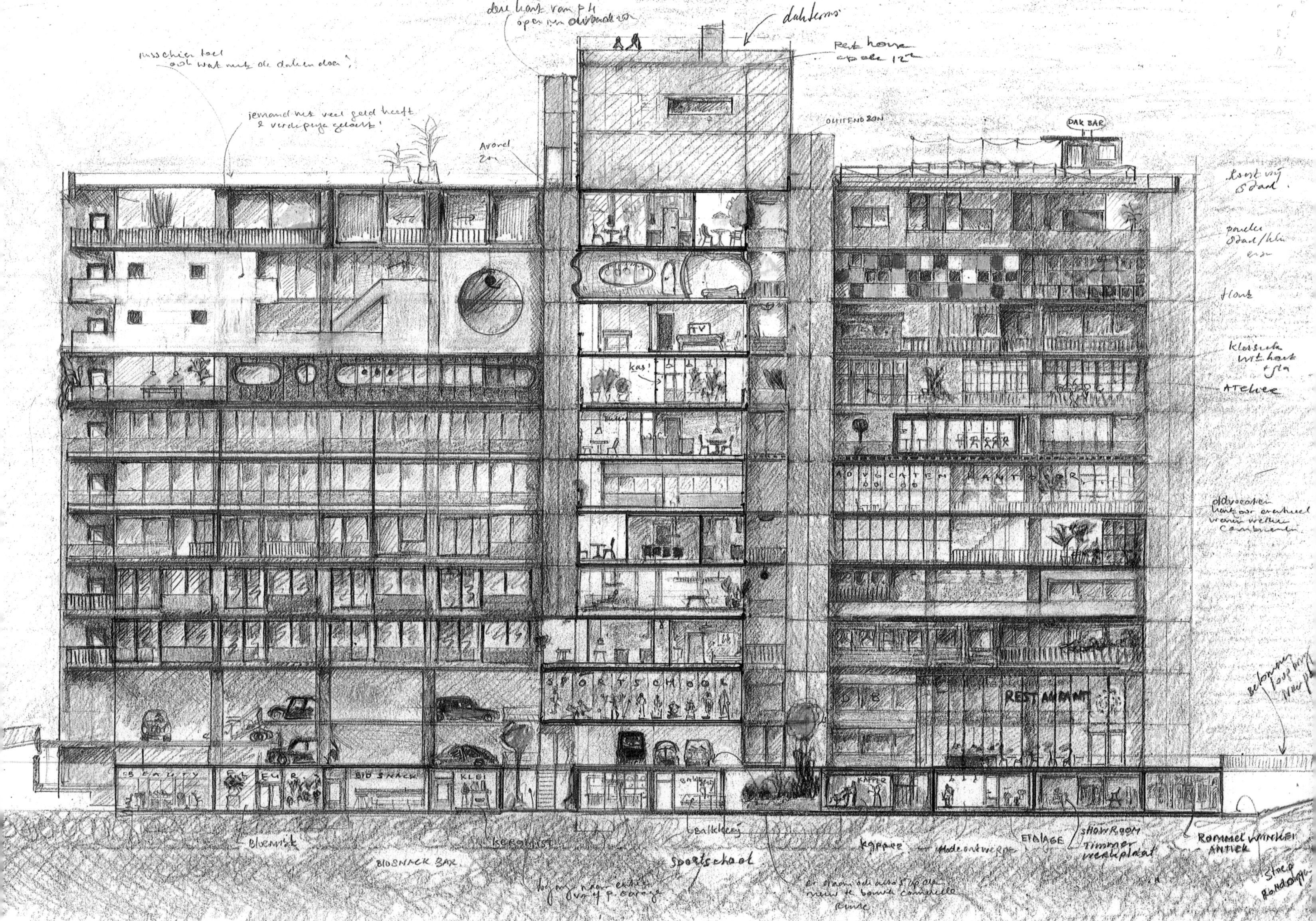

DAK BAR
OCHTEND ZON
Avond zon
kas!
TV
ATELIER
ADVOCATEN KANTOOR
SPORTSCHOOL
RESTAURANT
BIO SNACK
KLEI
KAPPER
Bloemist
Keramist
BIOSNACK BAR
Sportschool
Bakkerij
Kapper
Modeontwerper
ETALAGE
SHOWROOM
ROMMELWINKEL
ANTIEK

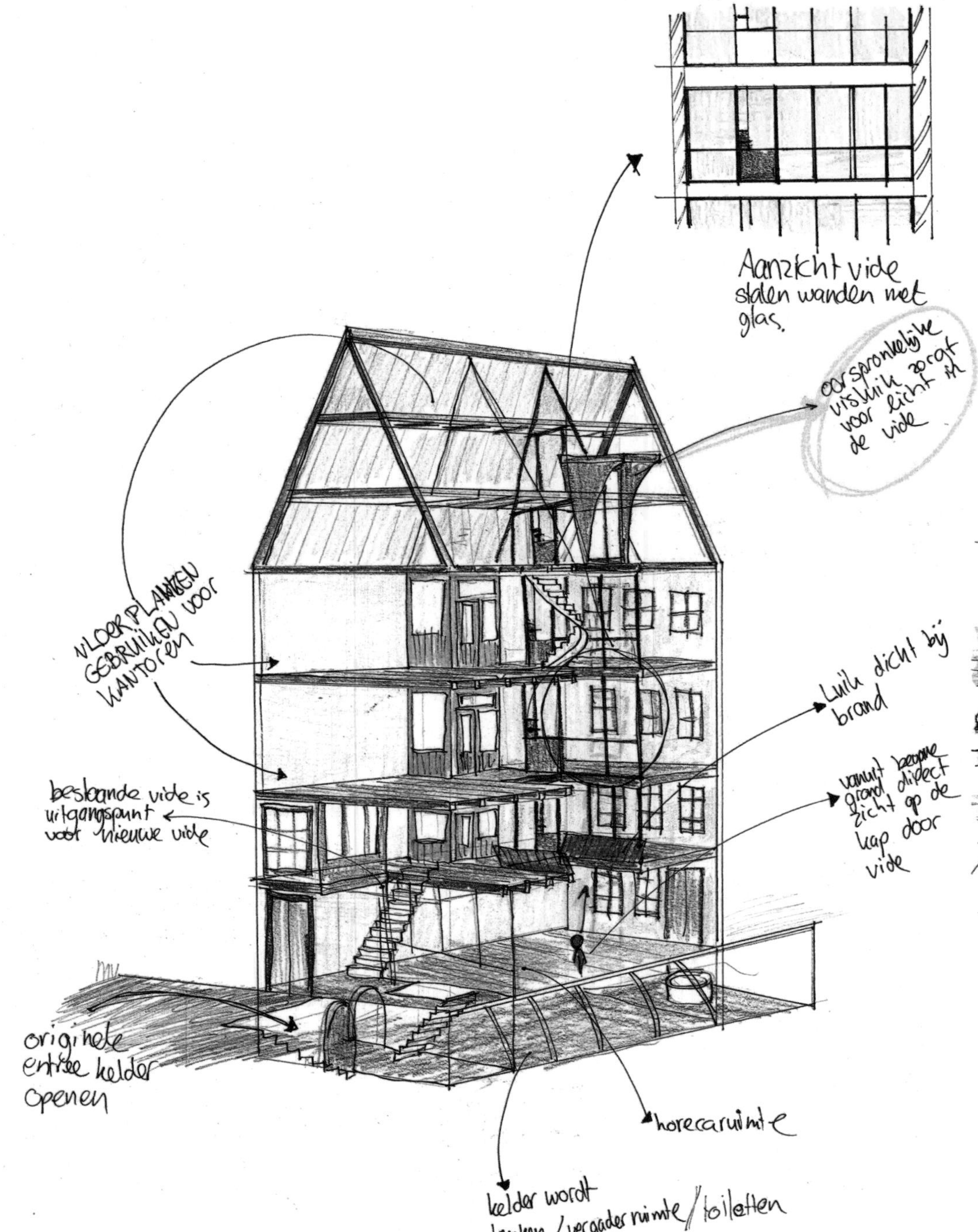

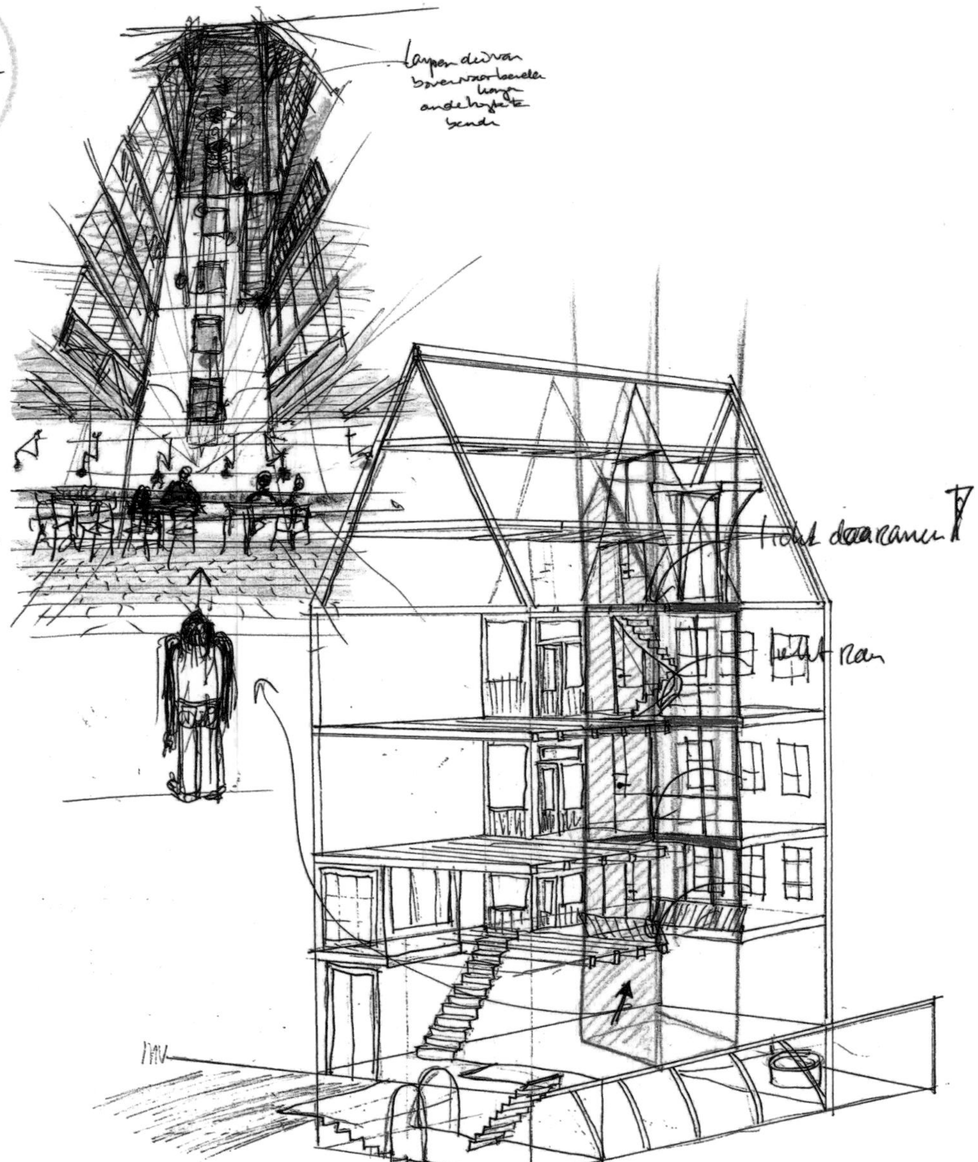

De Drie Haringen - Deventer.

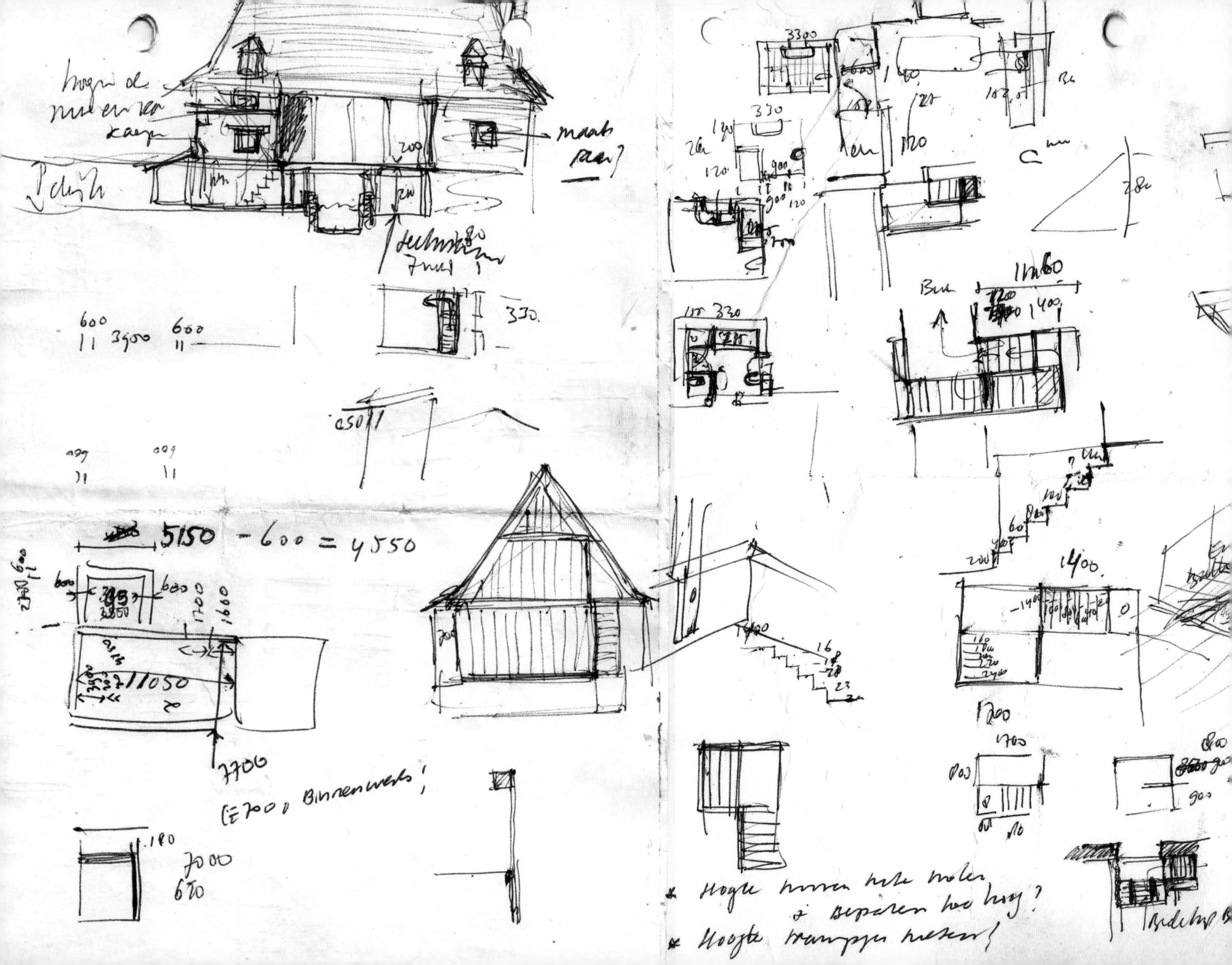
600
3900
5150 - 600 = 4550
11050
7700
(E700 Binnenwerks!
7000
330
3300
1400
1460

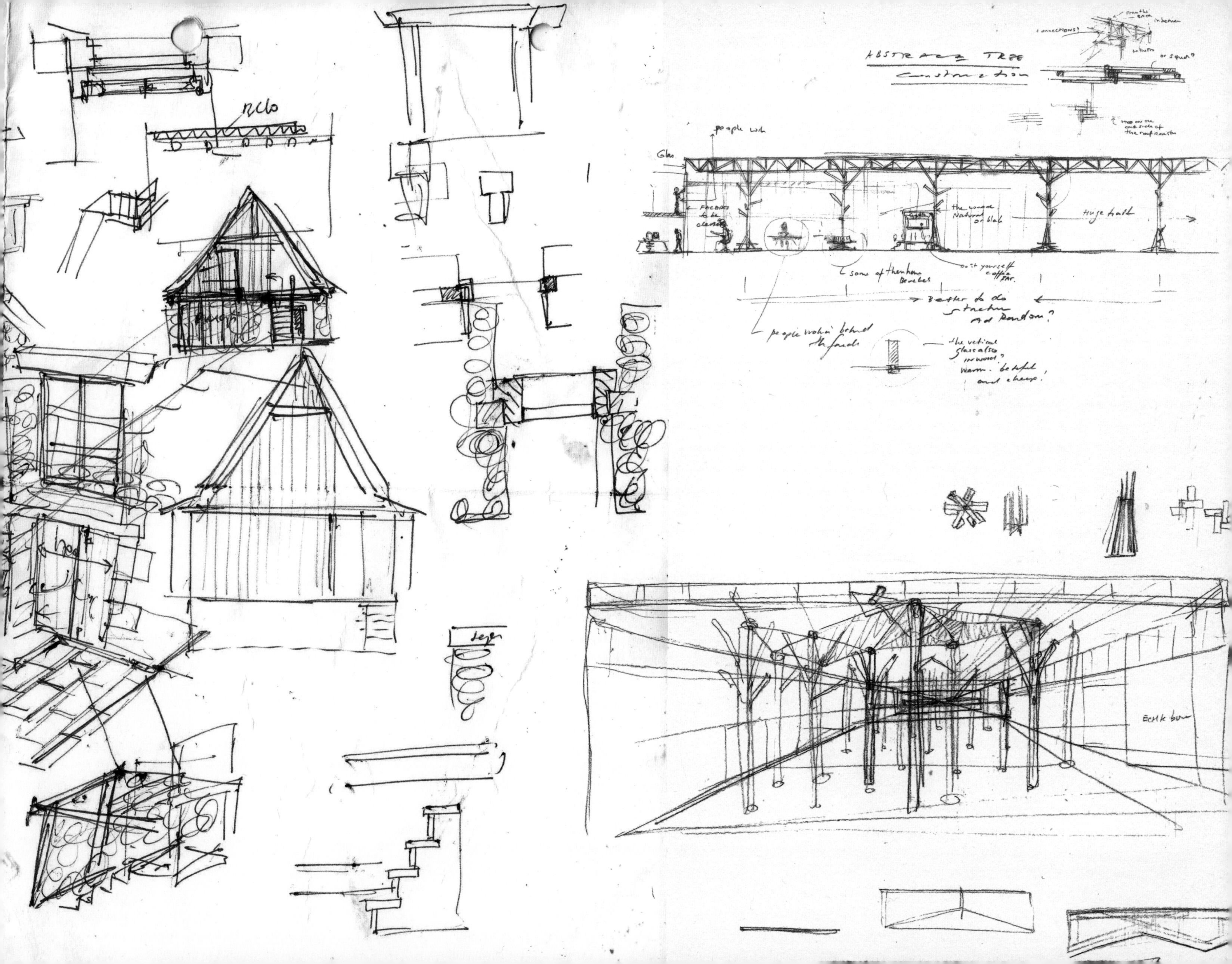
ABSTRACT TREE
Construction
connections?
or squar?
people walk
Glas
the wood
Natural
or blak
Huge hall
Do it yourself
coffee
BAR.
some of them have
Benches
Better to do
structure
AD Random?
people walkin behind
the facade
the vetical
glass also
in wood?
Warm. beautiful
and cheap!

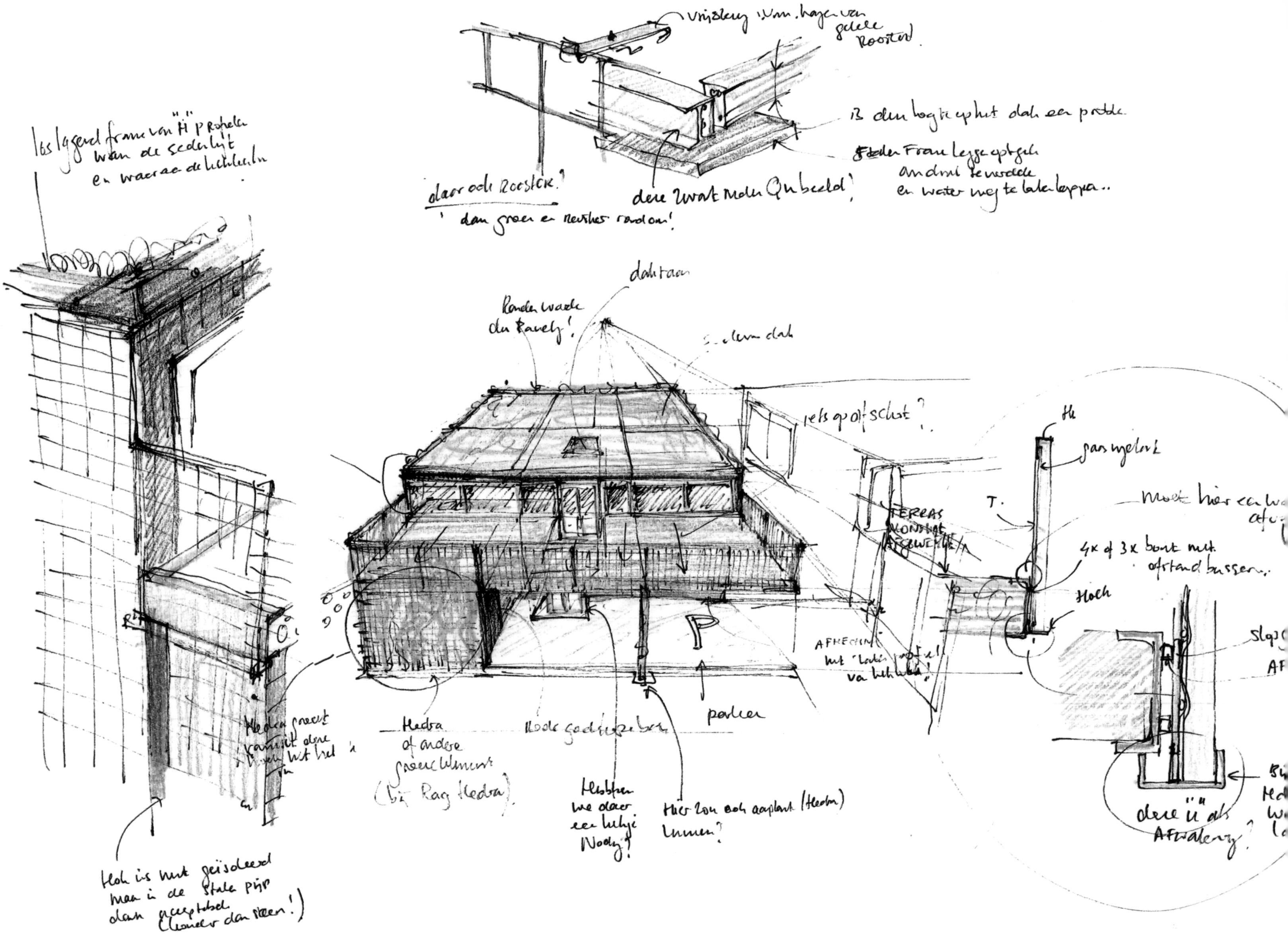

dakraam
TERRAS
Hedera
of andere
groenelement
parkeer
Hebben
we daar
een lichtje
Nodig?
Hier zou ook aanplant (Hedera)
kunnen?
en water weg te laten lopen..

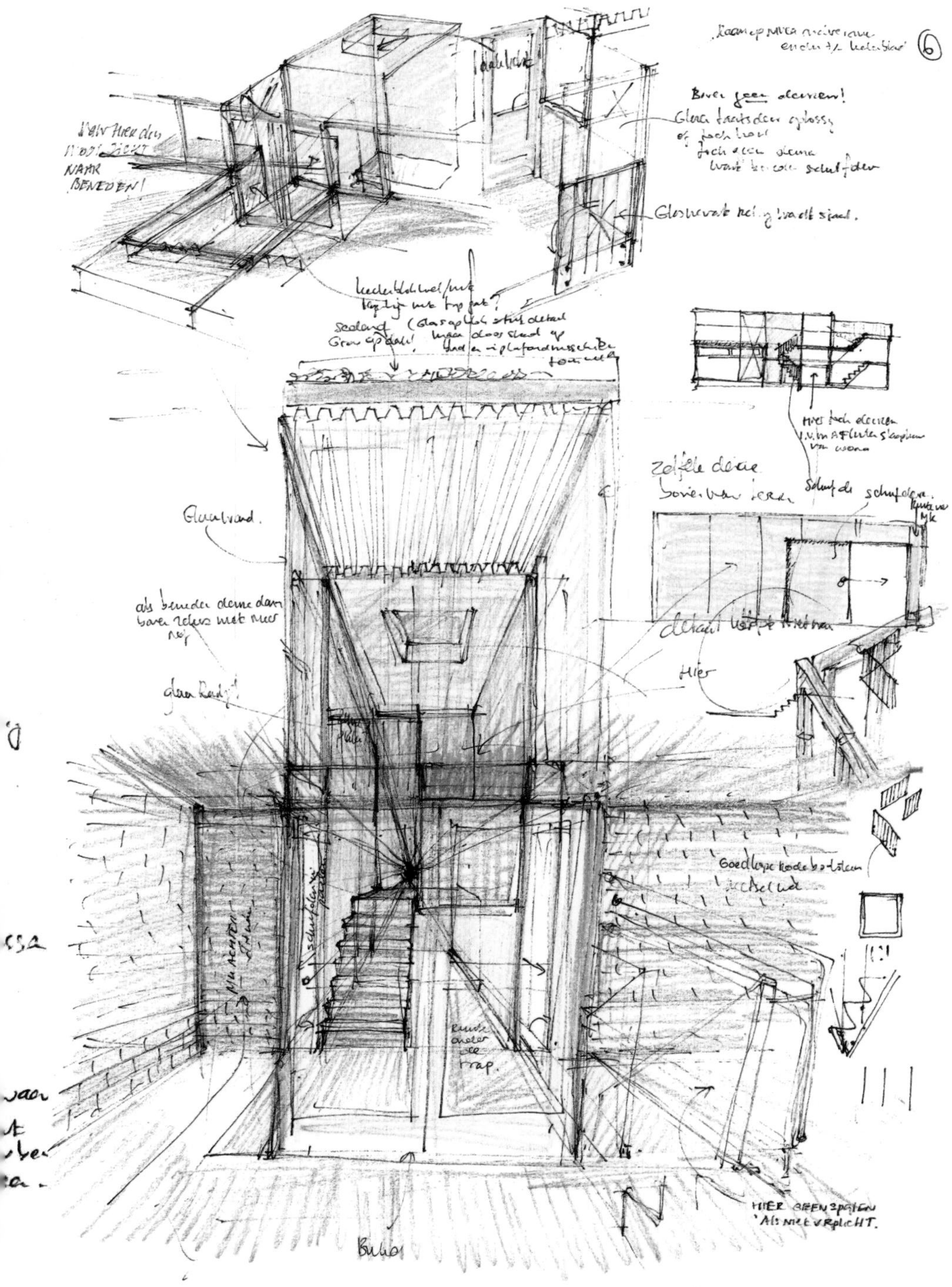

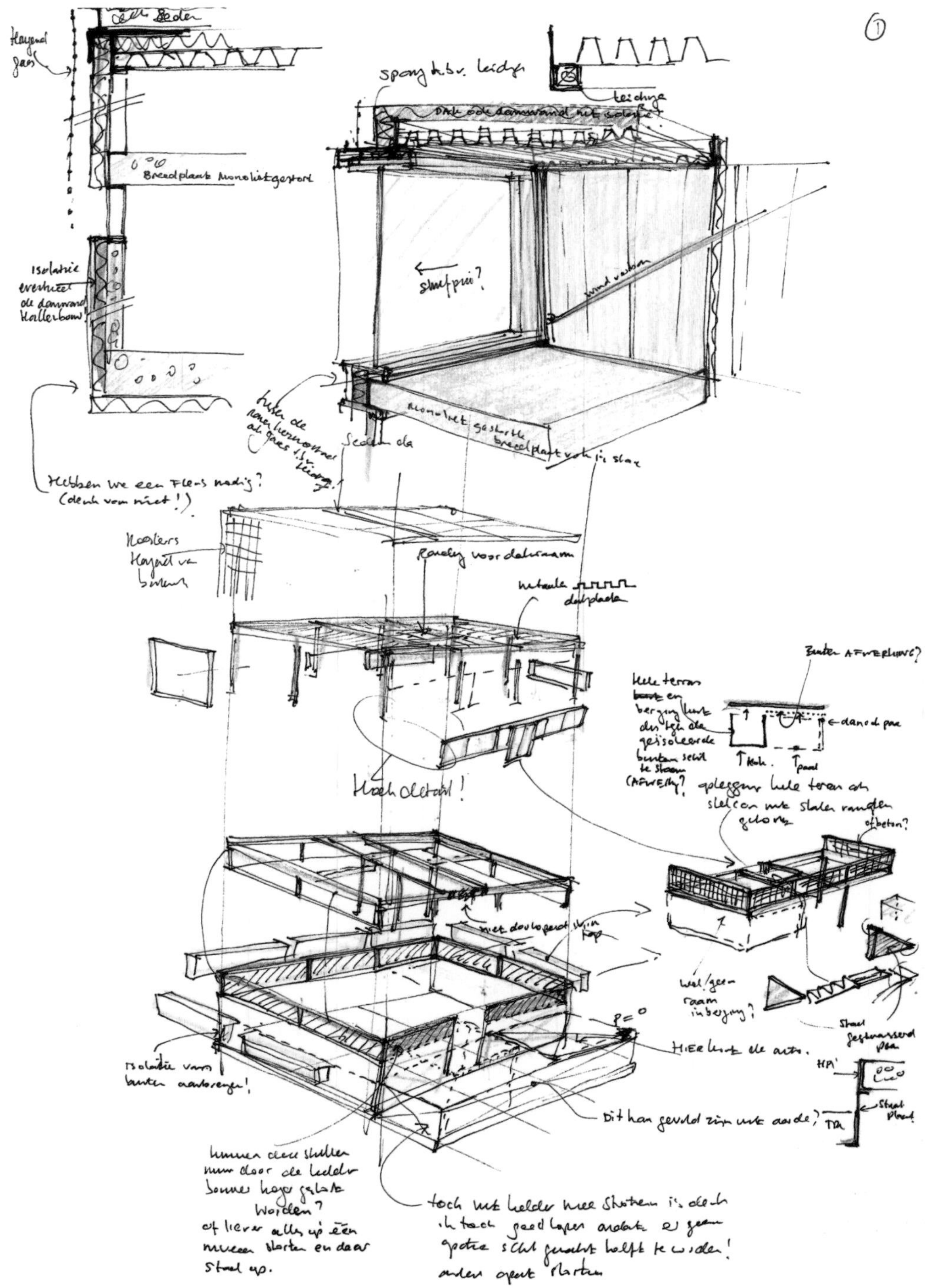
Hebben we een Flens nodig?
(denk van niet!)
Breedplaat Monolietgestort
Hier kunt de auto.

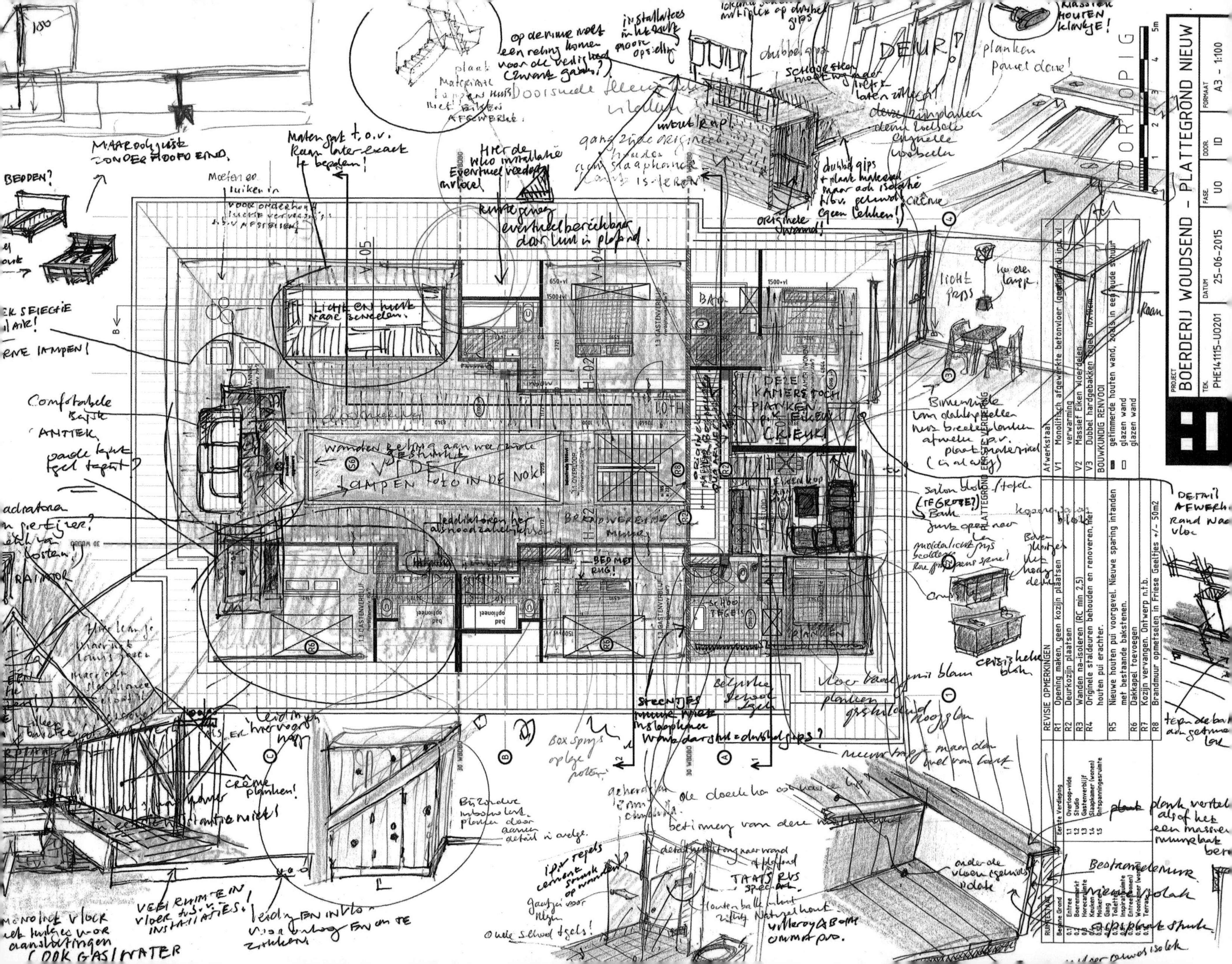
PROJECT BOERDERIJ WOUDSEND - PLATTEGROND NIEUW
TEK. PHE141115-U0201
DATUM 25-06-2015
FASE UO
DOOR ID
FORMAAT A3 - 1:100
VOORLOPIG
PLATTEGROND EERSTE VERDIEPING
Afwerkstaat
V1 Monolitisch afgewerkte betonvloer
V2 Massief Eiken vloerdelen
V3 Dubbel hardgebakken tegels 10x10cm
BOUWKUNDIG RENVOOI
getimmerde houten wand
glazen wand
glazen wand
REVISIE OPMERKINGEN
R1 Opening maken, geen kozijn plaatsen
R2 Deurkozijn plaatsen
R3 Wanden na-isoleren (RC min 2,5)
R4 Originele staldeuren behouden en renoveren, met houten pui erachter.
R5 Nieuwe houten pui voorgevel. Nieuwe sparing intanden met bestaande baksteen.
R6 Dakkapel toevoegen
R7 Kozijn vervangen. Ontwerp n.t.b.
R8 Brandmuur opmetselen in Friese Geeltjes +/- 50m2
RUIMTESTAAT
Begane Grond
0.1 Entree
0.2 Boerenmarkt
0.3 Horecaruimte
0.4 Keuken
0.5 Molkerei
0.6 Gang
0.7 Toiletten
0.8 Inspiratieruimte
0.9 Entree (wonen)
0.10 Woonkamer (wonen)
0.11 Terras
Eerste Verdieping
1.1 Overloop-vide
1.2 Studio
1.3 Gastenverblijf
1.4 Slaapkamer (wonen)
1.5 Ontspanningsruimte
1.3 GASTENVERBLIJF
1.1 OVERLOOP
1.2 STUDIO
bad optioneel
bad optioneel
BAD
650+vl
1500+vl
DEUR?
crème planken!
BED MET RUG!
SCHOOL TEGELS
PLANKEN

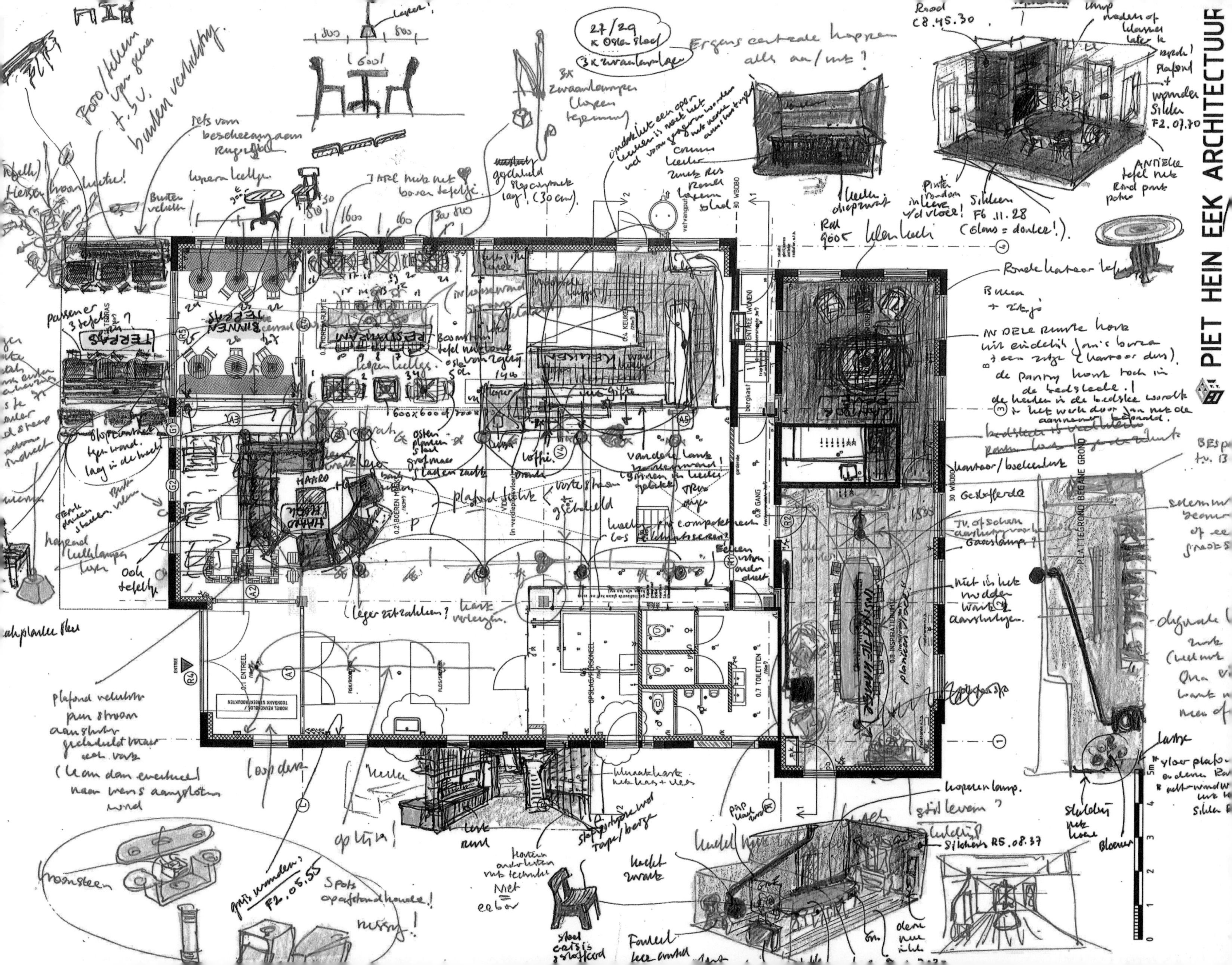

PIET HEIN EEK ARCHITECTUUR
PLATTEGROND BEGANE GROND
TERRAS
BINNEN TERRAS
RESTAURANT
KEUKEN
0.1 ENTREEL
0.4 KEUKEN
0.7 TOILETTEN
0.8 GANG
0.3 INSPIRATIERUIMTE
VIDE (in verdiepingsvloer)
ENTREE
garderobe
bergkast
30 WBDBO
Ergens centrale knoppen alle aan/uit?
Ronde kantoor tafel
kantoor/boekenkast
Gaaslamp?
koperen lamp.
stilleven?
Silikeen R5.08.37
Silikeen F6.11.28 (Glans = donker!).
Spots op afstandbediening!
600 x 600

RICARDO FLORES & EVA PRATS

Flores & Prats Arquitectes • Spain

Featured project: Casal Balaguer [pp. 90–7]

'We consider the act of observing as akin to design,' say Ricardo Flores and Eva Prats of Spanish firm Flores & Prats Arquitectes. 'For an architect, drawing while looking is an intense practice that questions reality. It is a way of seeing how reality is articulated. We also sketch for research, and use drawing as a way of thinking, making thoughts visible. These thoughts can then be critiqued to progress the design. In later stages, drawing is used to get into the building process, and later to register what has been built.'

The duo established their studio in 1998, after winning a competition for designing a masterplan for the renovation of the historic quarter of Vilanova i la Geltrú. They have served as visiting professors at universities in Spain, Argentina, Italy, Denmark, Norway, the US, UK and Australia, and are currently associate professors in design at the Barcelona School of Architecture.

'Regarding the education of young architects, what interests us is the instilling of confidence in drawing as a way of thinking,' Flores and Prats note. 'We draw with our students to observe old cartographies and the reality of the street; to document and exchange information. Drawing by hand is a language we use throughout the course. It works for us in terms of communication, and to have classroom sessions where one can clearly see what is happening – large sheets of paper are more public than any computer screen. We have discovered that students prefer to think with a pencil on paper. We accompany them in the process of thinking, to reflect and propose, each one with his or her own rhythm and attitude.'

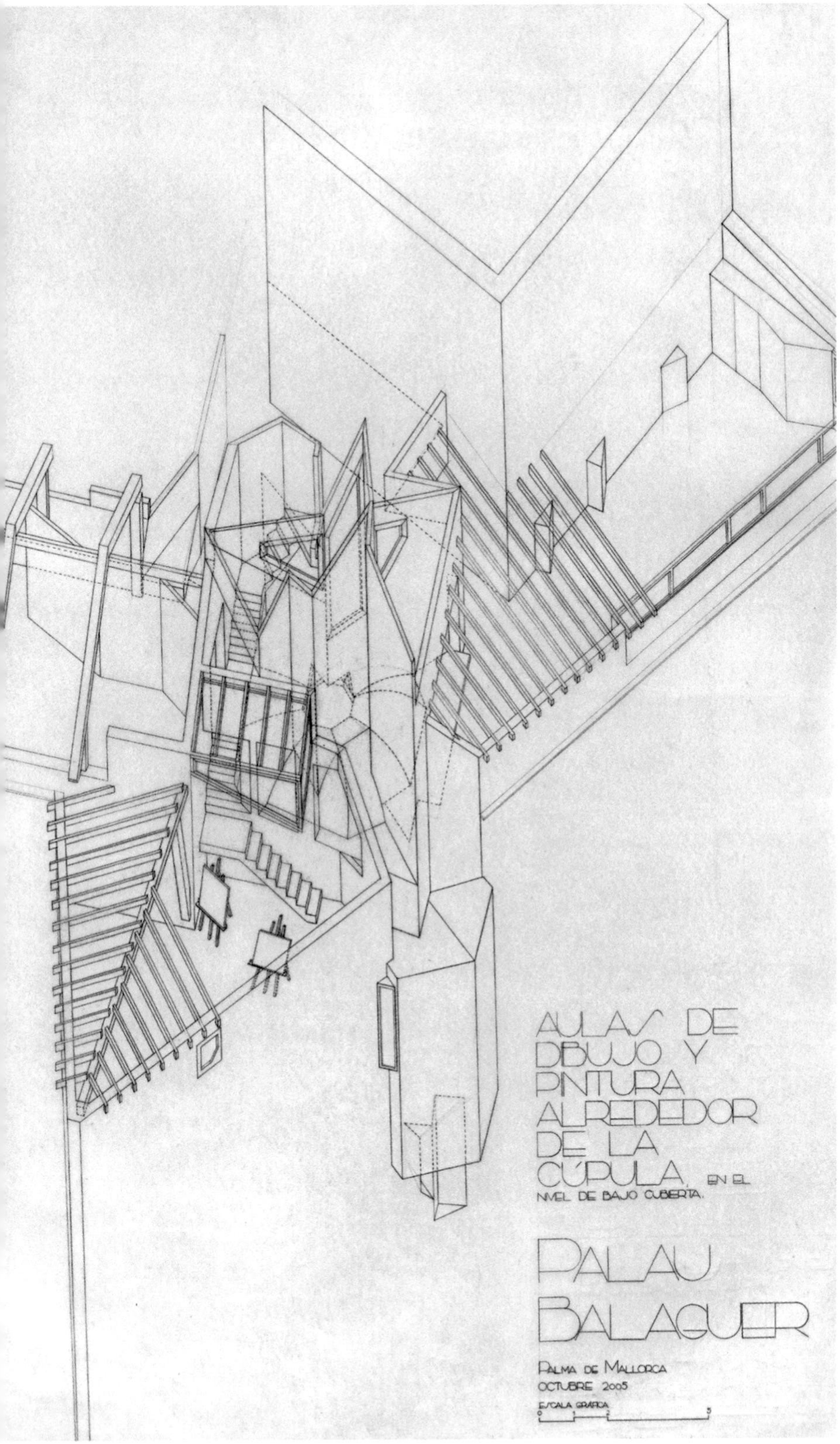
AULAS DE DIBUJO Y PINTURA ALREDEDOR DE LA CÚPULA, EN EL NIVEL DE BAJO CUBIERTA
PALAU BALAGUER
PALMA DE MALLORCA
OCTUBRE 2005
ESCALA GRÁFICA

CONEXIÓN DE AULAS Y TERRAZA A TRAVÉS DE LA CÚPULA
PALAU BALAGUER
PALMA DE MALLORCA
OCTUBRE 2005
ESCALA GRÁFICA

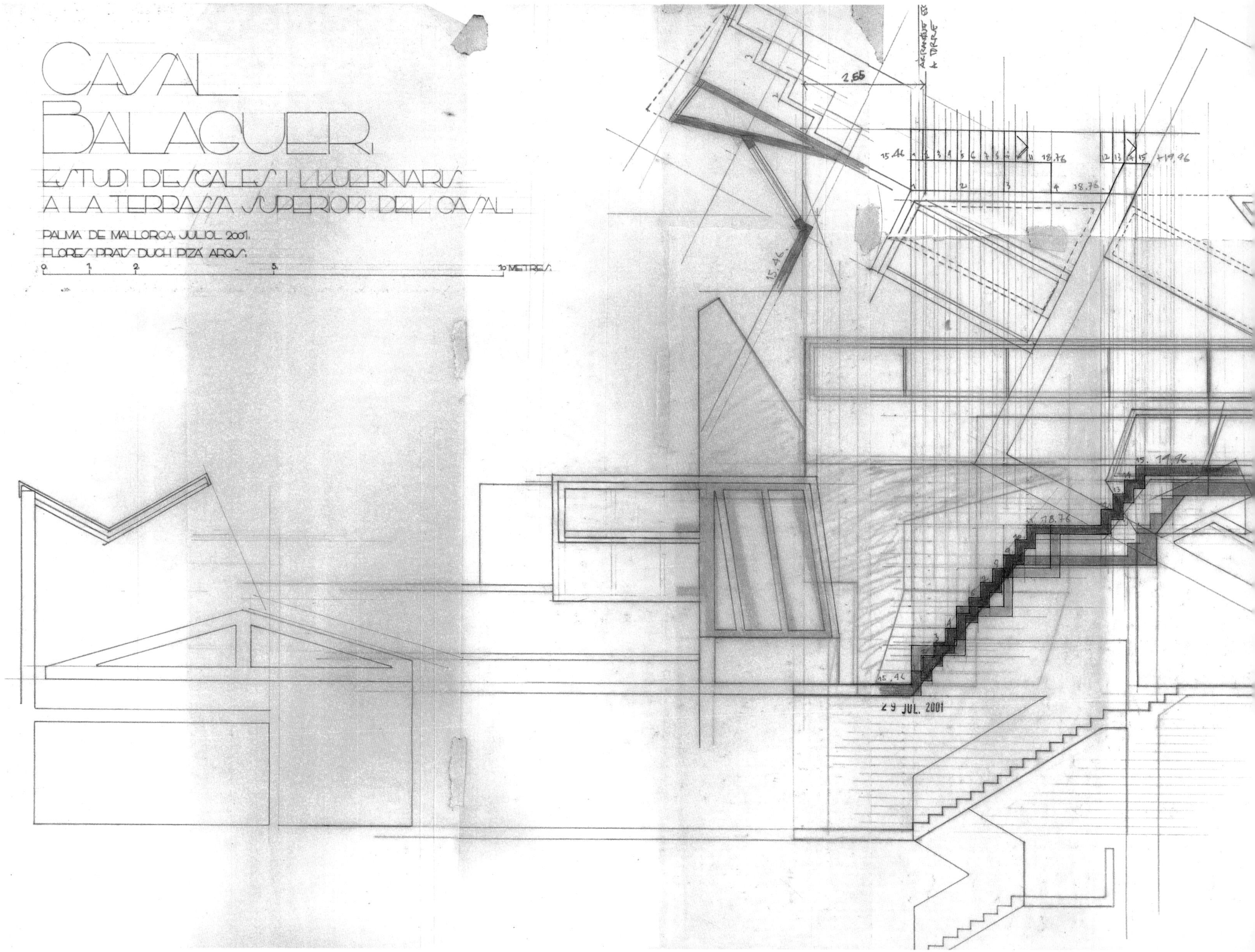
CASAL
BALAGUER.
ESTUDI D'ESCALES I LLUERNARIS
A LA TERRASSA SUPERIOR DEL CASAL.
PALMA DE MALLORCA, JULIOL 2001.
FLORES PRATS DUCH PIZÀ ARQS.
0 1 2 5 10 METRES
2,55
15,46
18,76
+19,96
15,46
18,76
15. 19,96
29 JUL. 2001

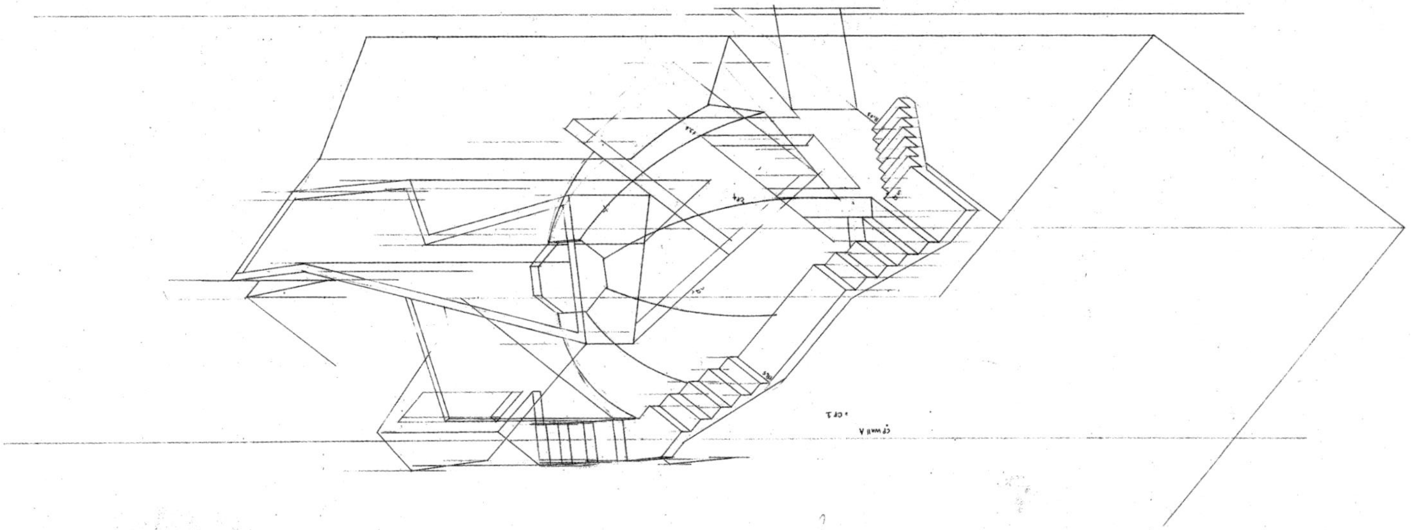

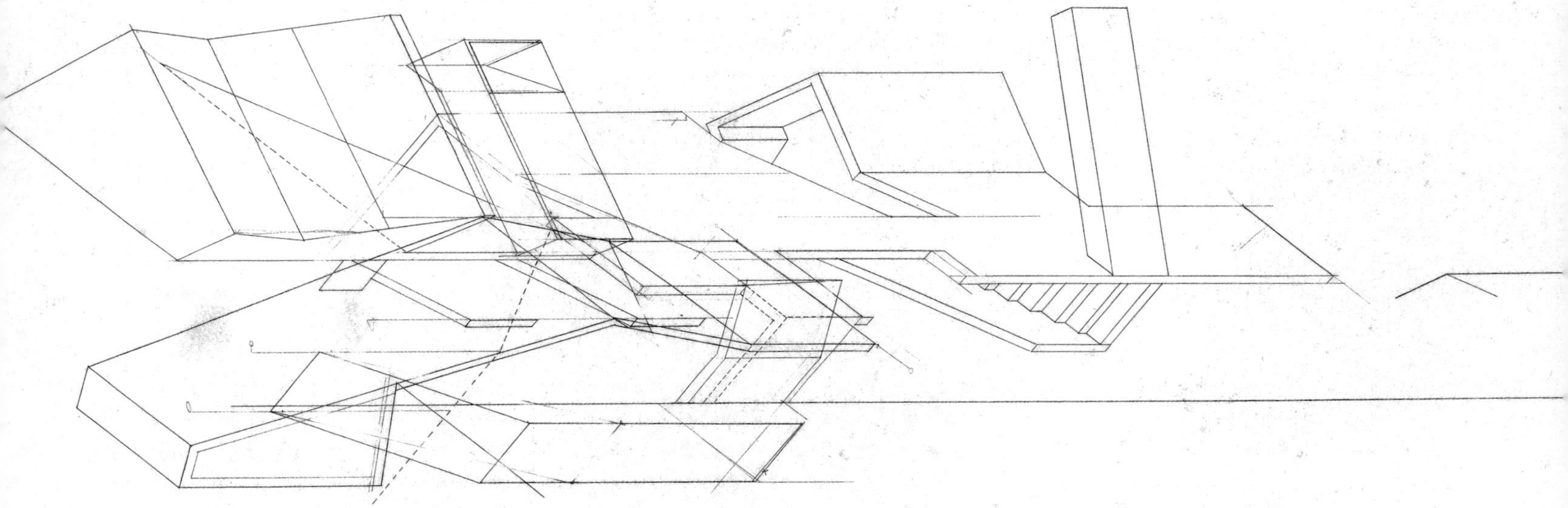

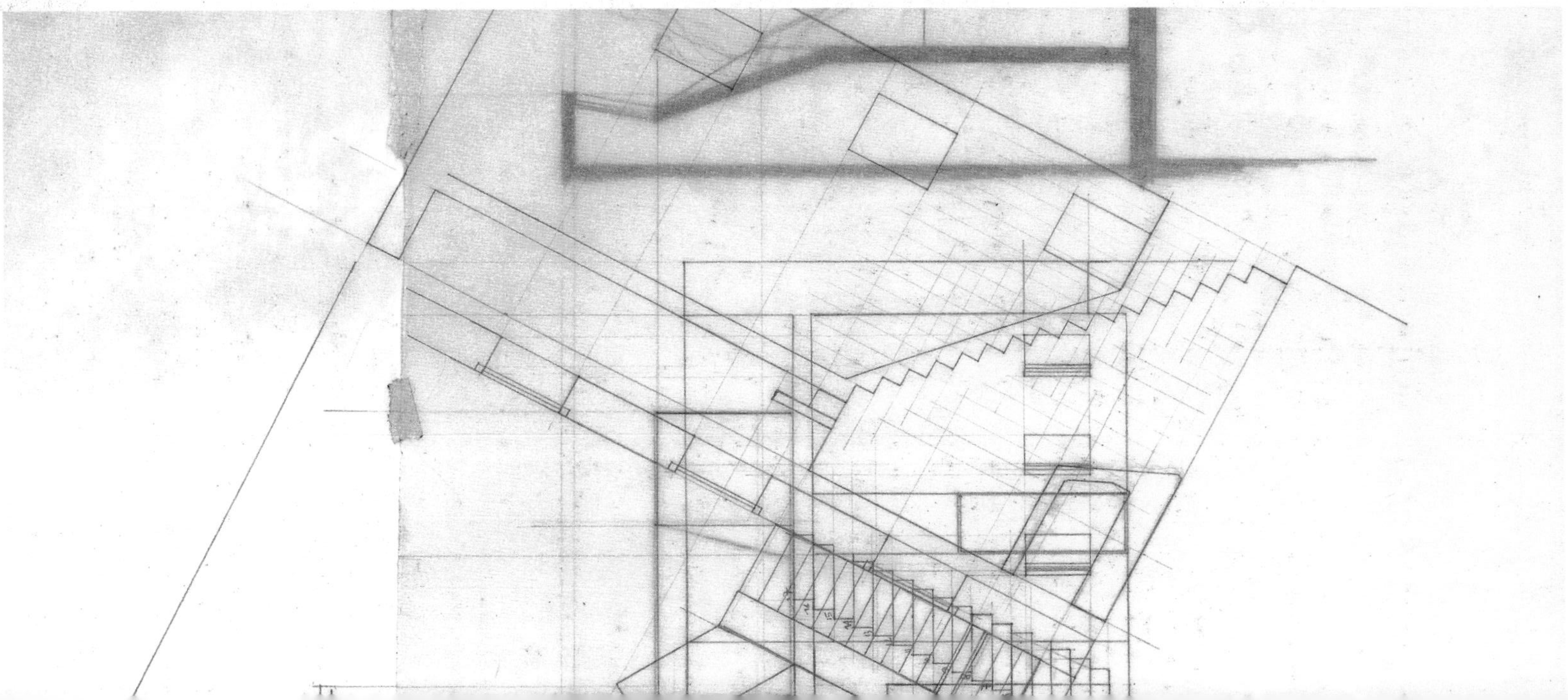

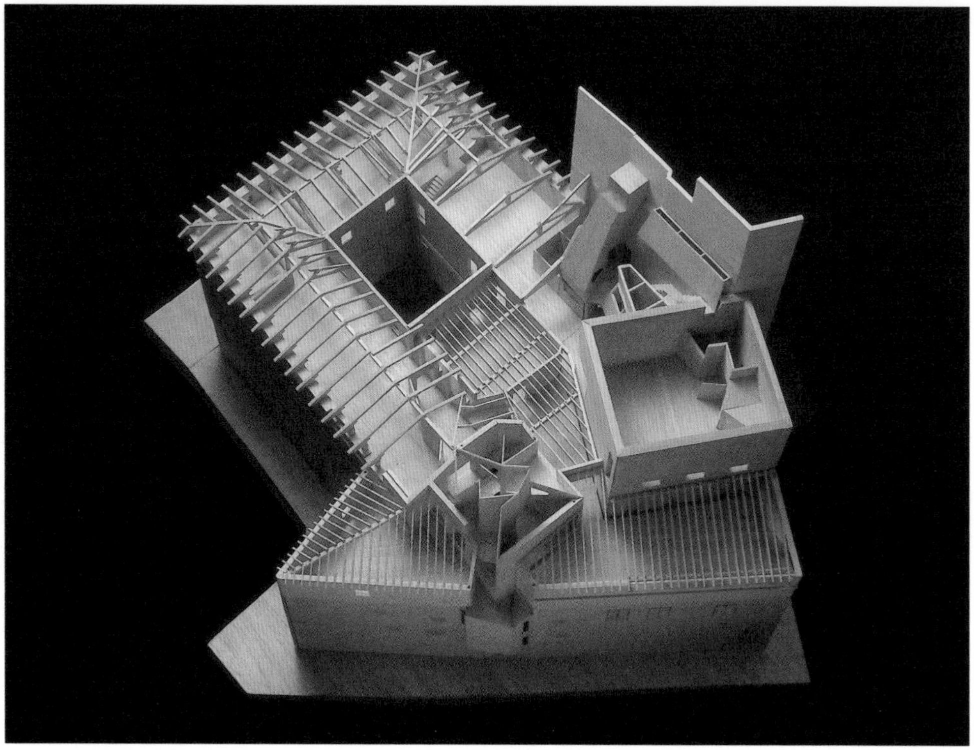

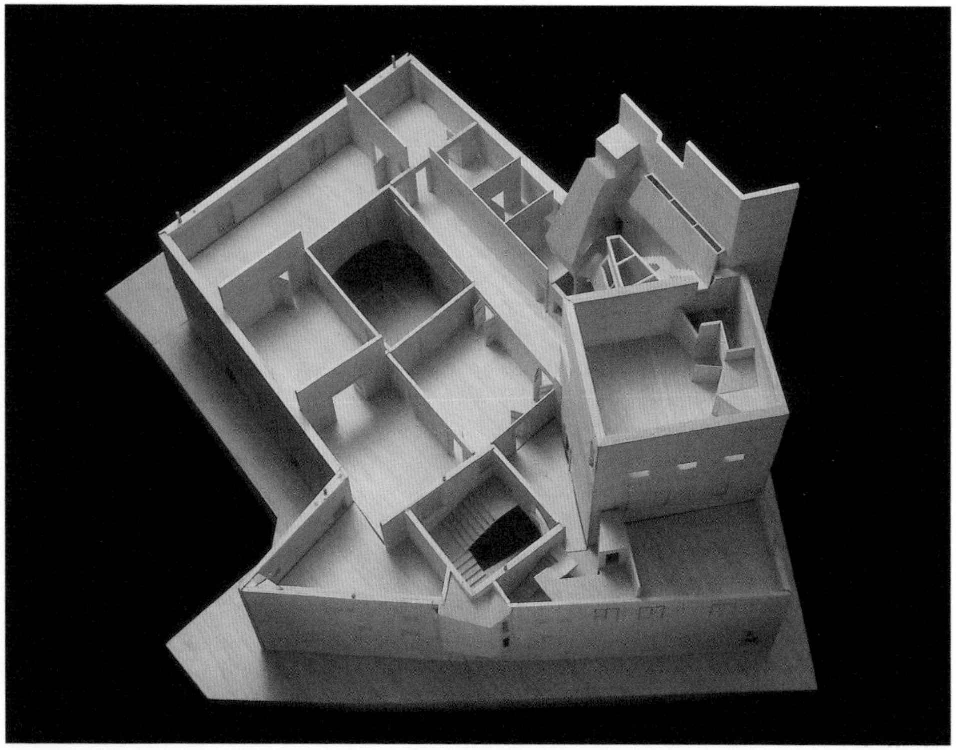

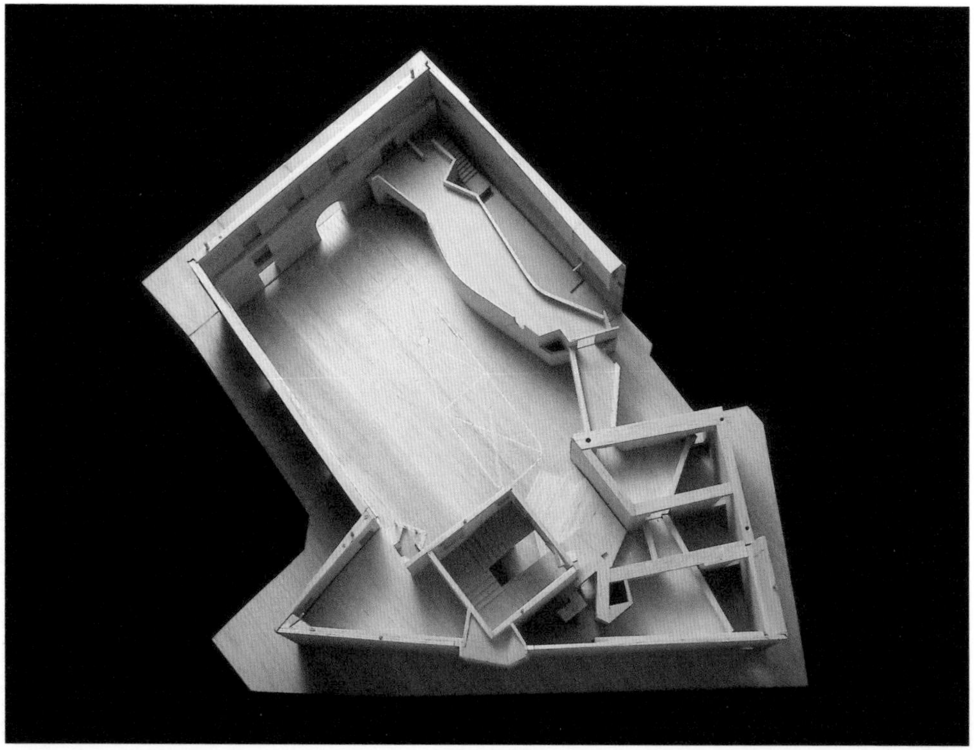

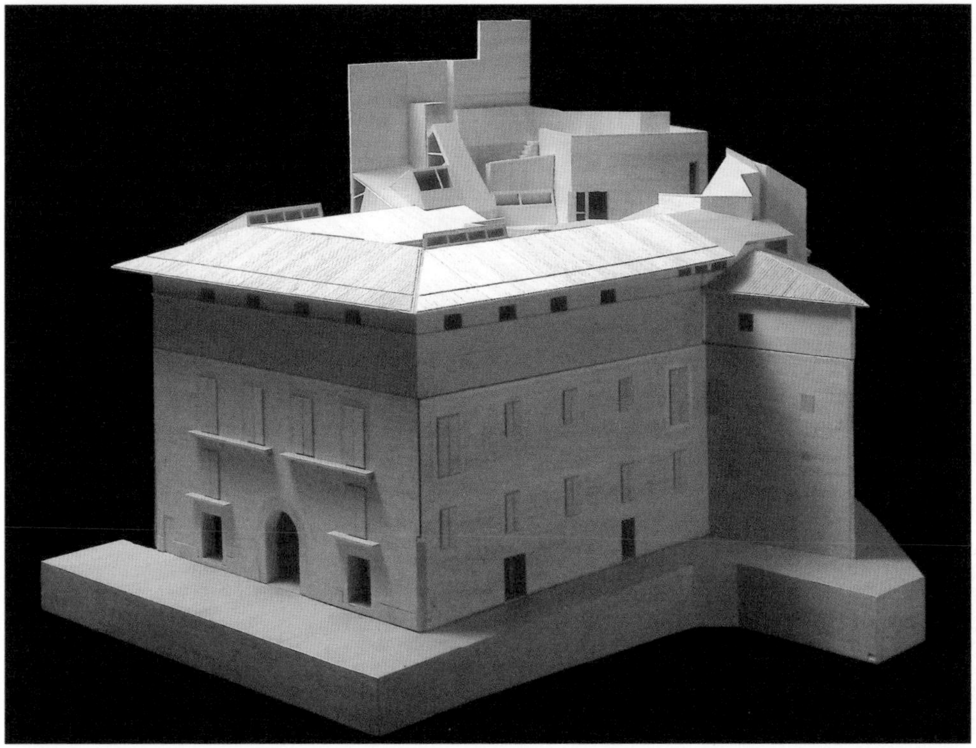

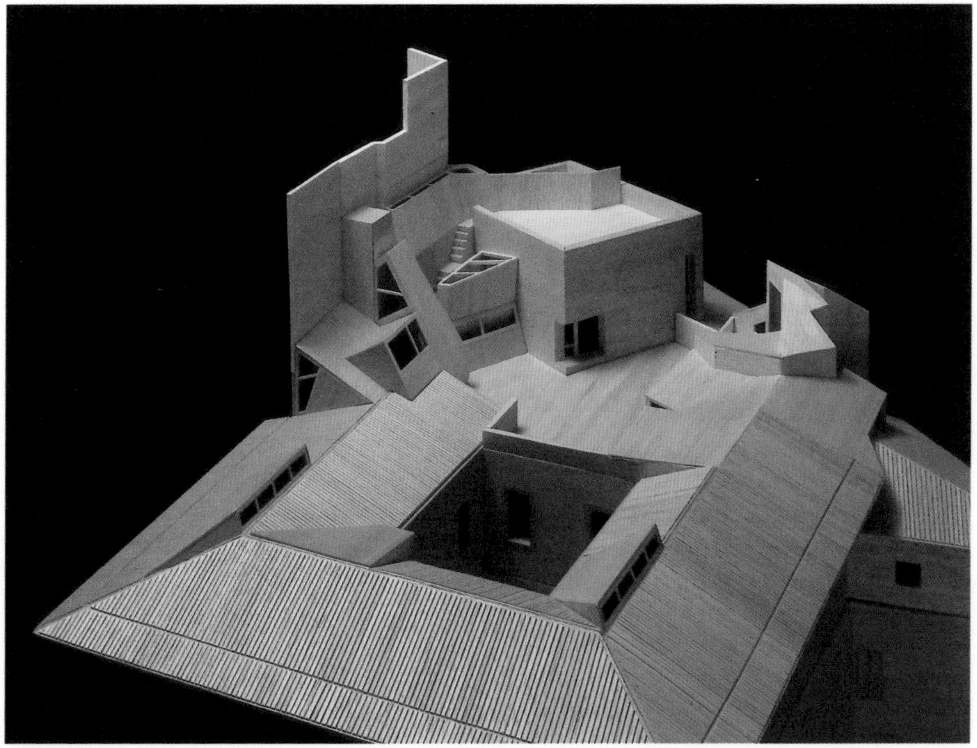

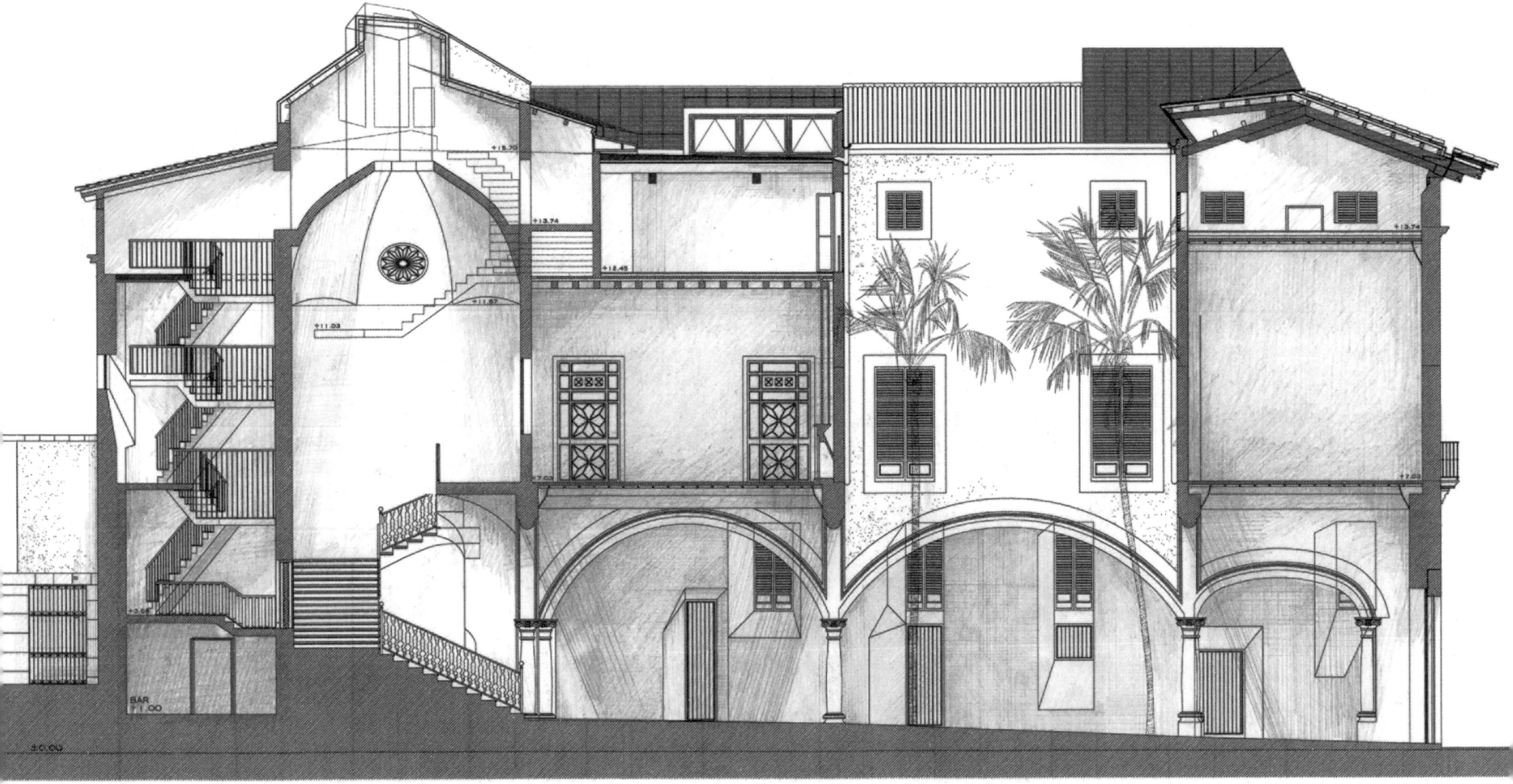
+15.70
+13.74
+12.45
+11.67
+11.03
+7.03
+13.74
+7.03
+3.56
BAR
+1.00
±0.00

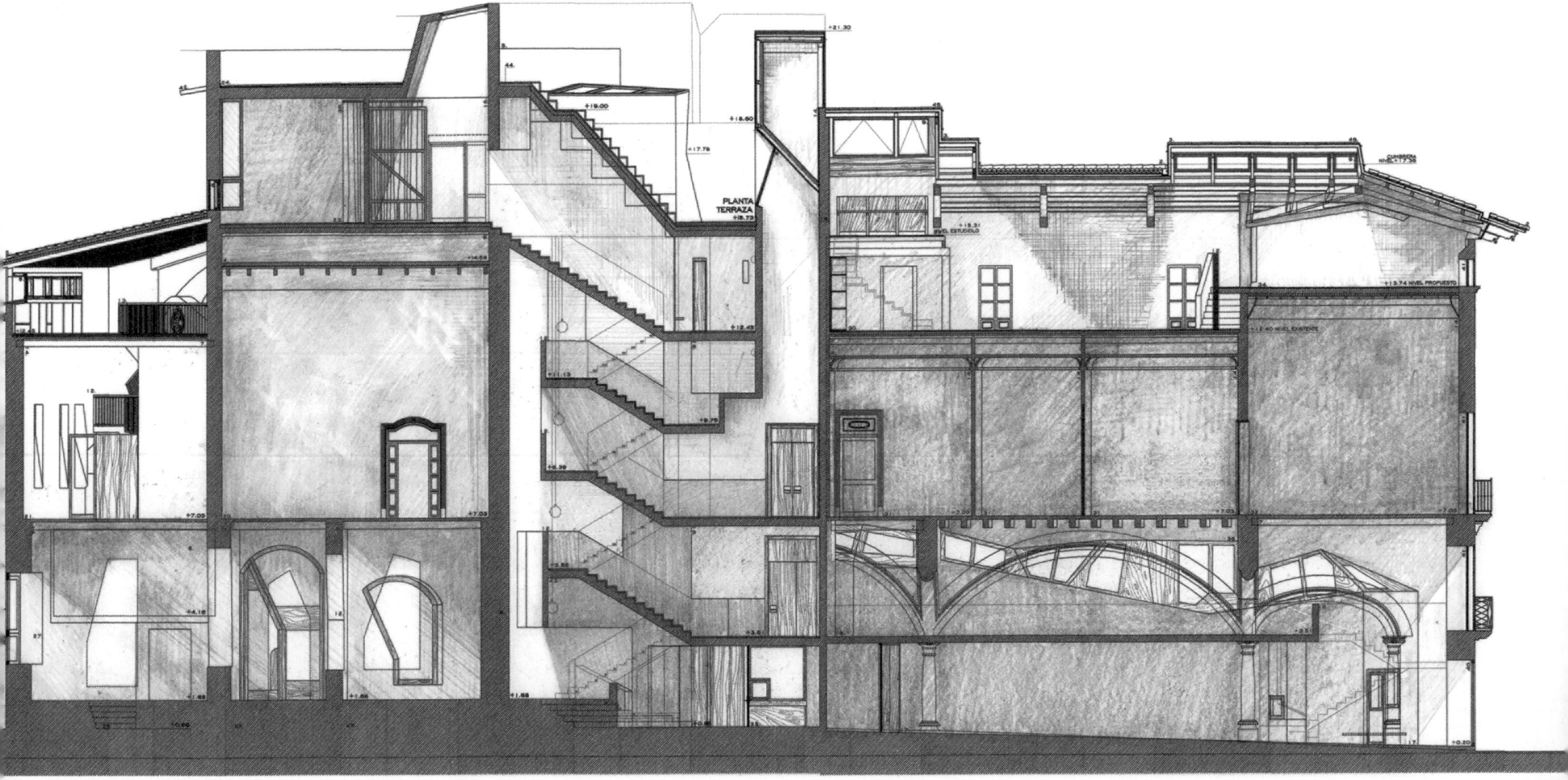
PLANTA
TERRAZA
+15.73
+21.30
+19.00
+18.60
+17.78
+12.45
+7.03

ALBERT FRANCE-LANORD

AF-LA • Sweden

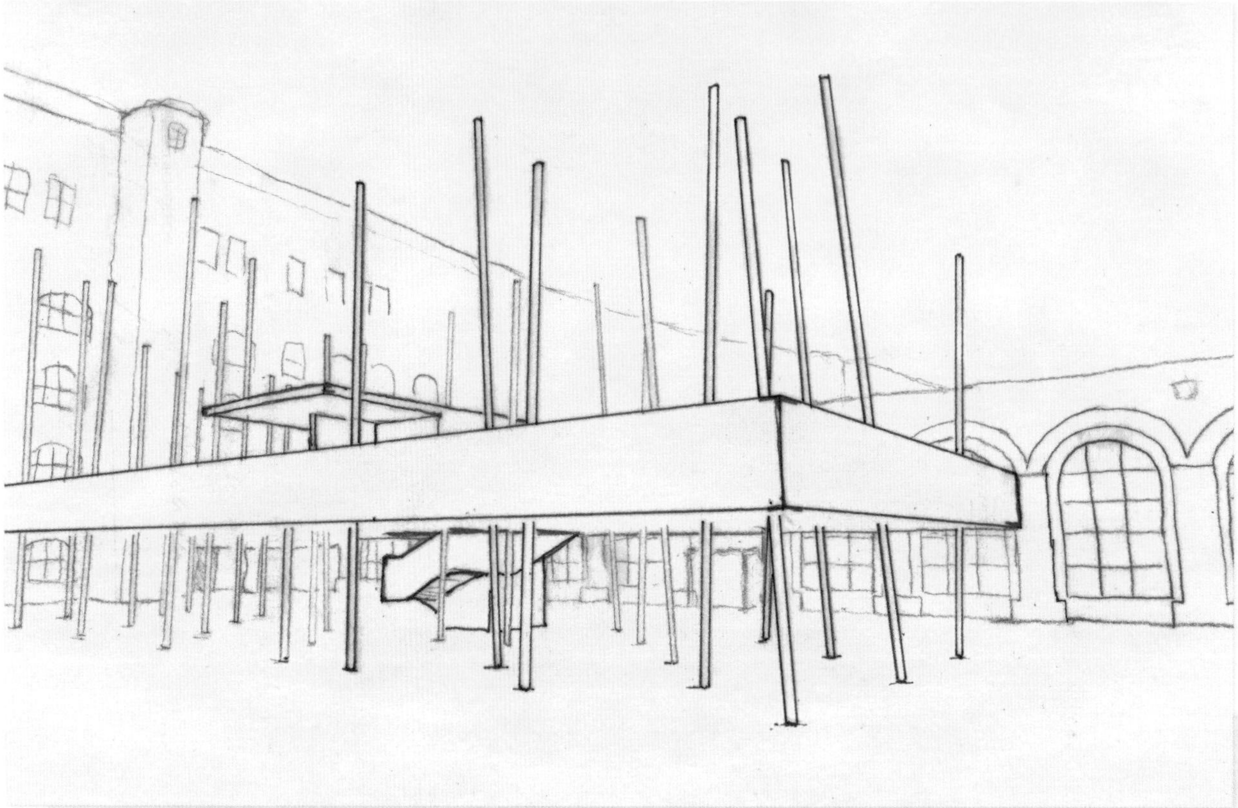

'The sketching process always begins with diagrams integrating the constraints, programme and site, which define shapes, angles and openings,' says Swedish architect Albert France-Lanord. 'When I taught at the School of Architecture in Stockholm, we would encourage students to sketch simultaneously from the inside to the outside (programme to volume), and vice versa (the building envelope to the internal organization). The essence of sketching is multi-layered, and tracing paper lets you see through five or six layers of lines.'

Together with his team, France-Lanord has designed all manner of projects, from high-end fashion shop interiors to modern villas and homes, even an underground facility for an Internet provider in an anti-atomic bunker.

'Lines on a computer are either straight or curved, but a line in a sketch can be both,' he explains. 'I need this flexibility at the beginning of the design process. It can be very effective to try a 3D volume in CAD, but I'll sketch directly on the perspectives by hand. As soon as we agree on an idea, we try it on the computer and often make physical models. CAD definitely takes over the process, but significant changes are always tried out by sketching first, because it is the quickest way to translate an idea from brain to paper. It allows you to try out various ideas at different scales without locking a form or an aesthetic.'

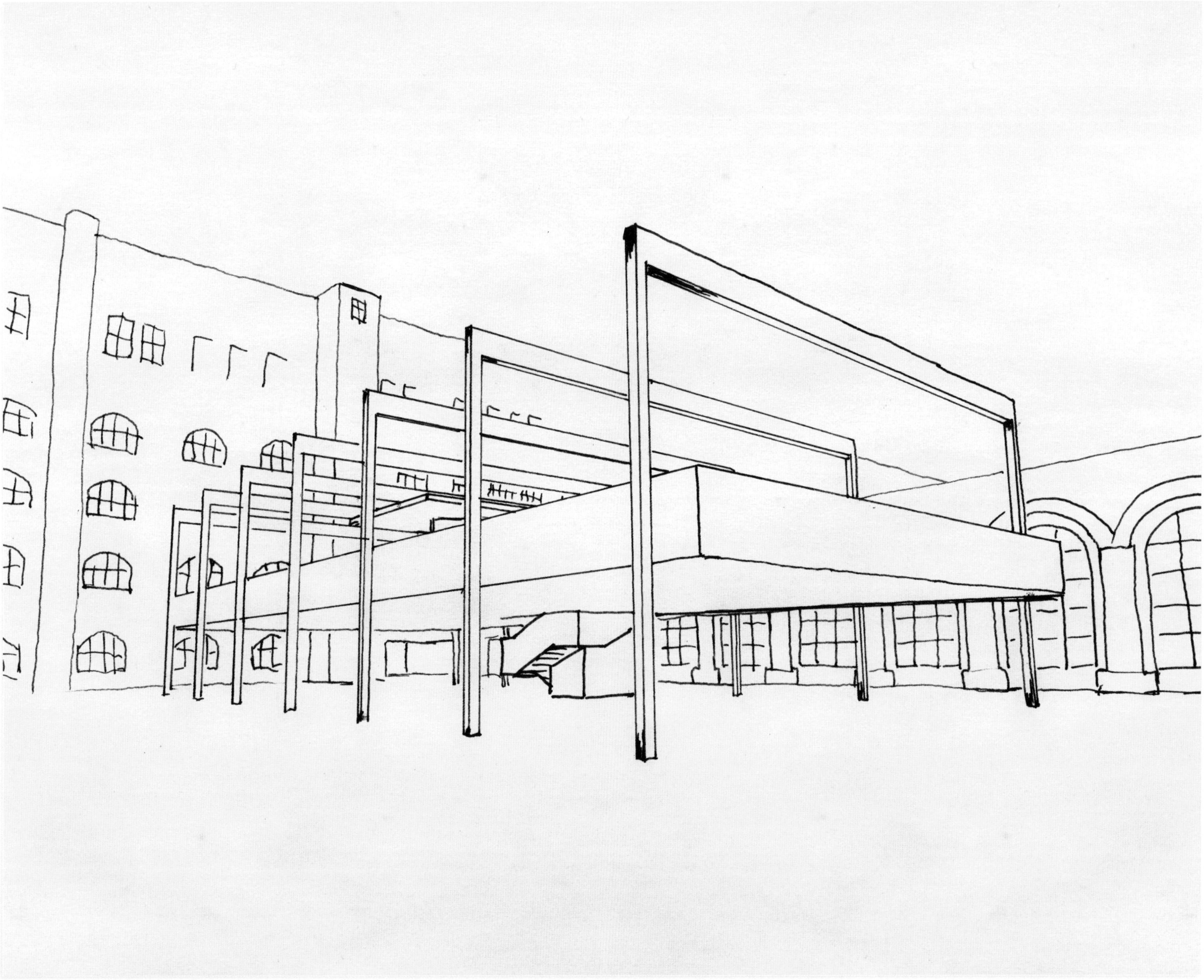

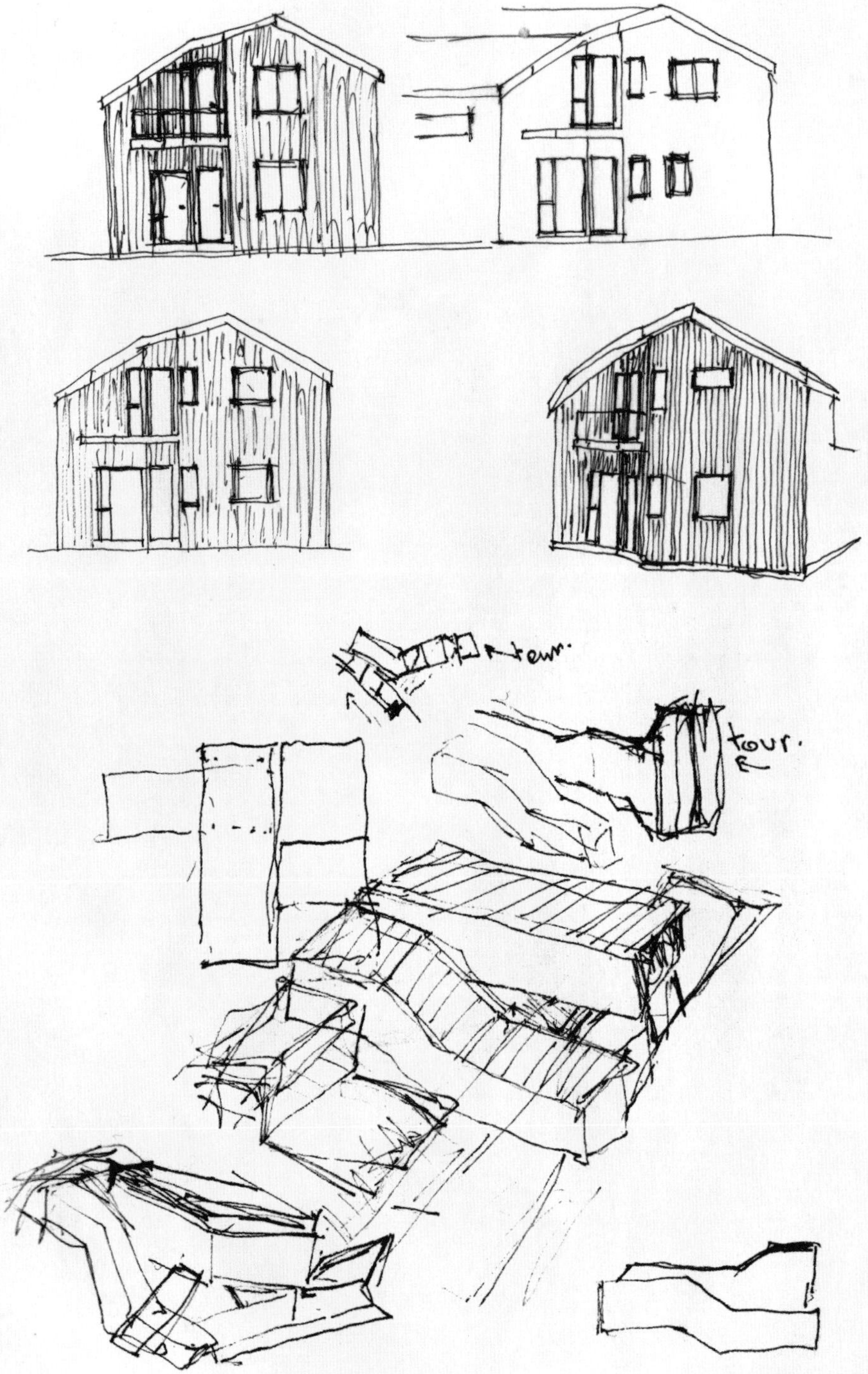

erskine - Gadelius Hus

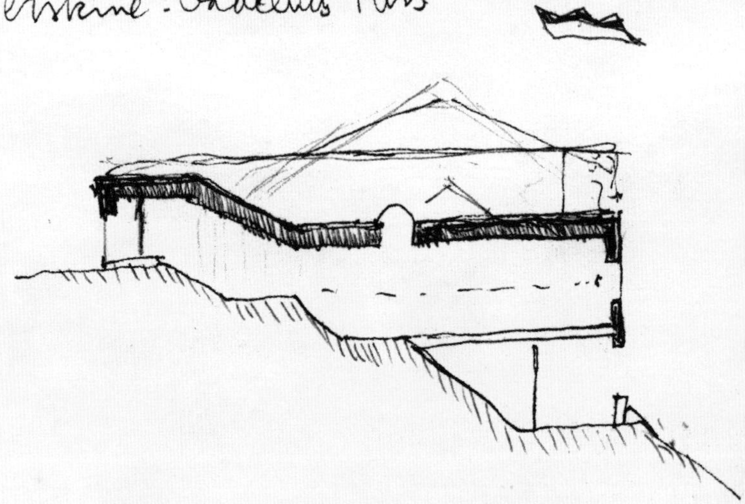

Koh Samui

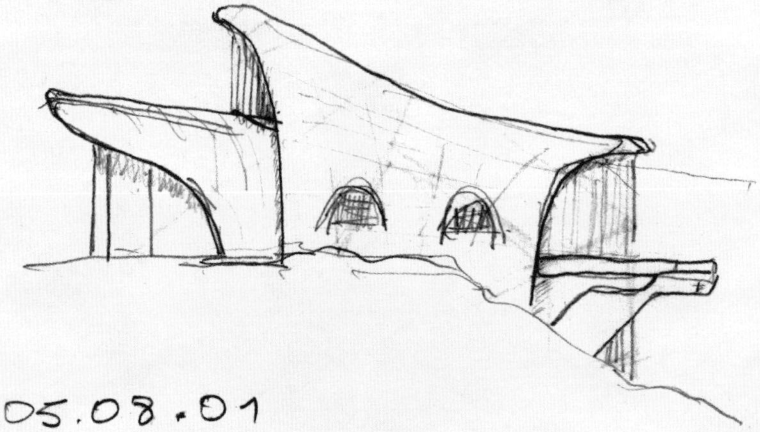

05.08.01

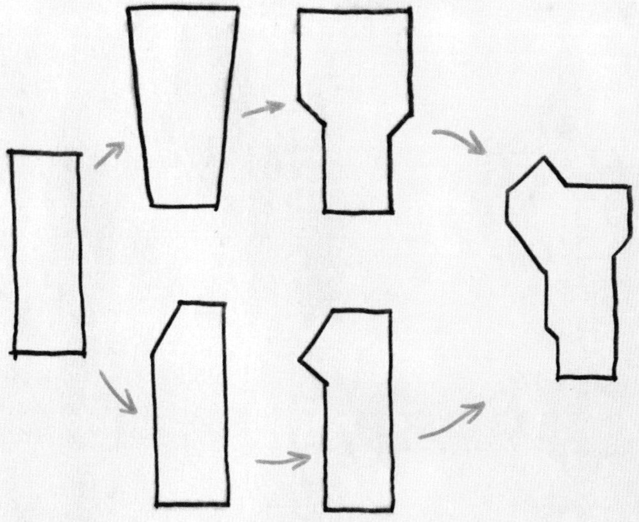

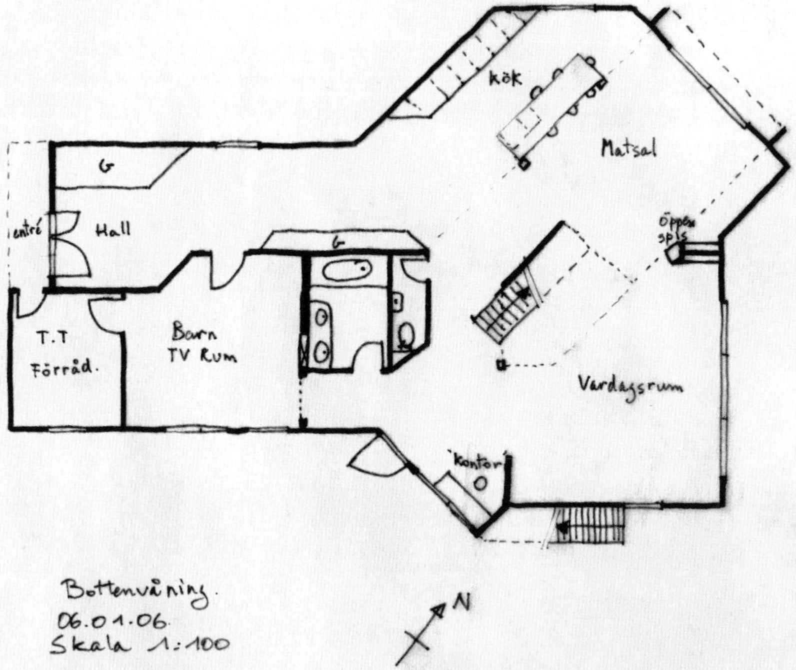
Kök
Matsal
G
entré
Hall
G
Öppen spis
T.T
Förråd.
Barn
TV Rum
Vardagsrum
Kontor
Bottenvåning.
06.01.06.
Skala 1:100
N

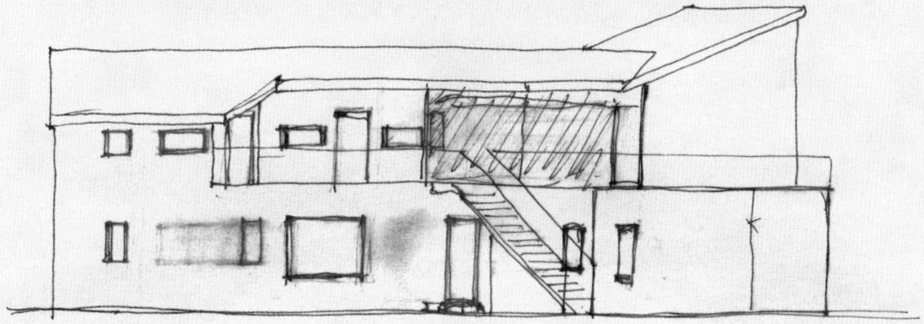

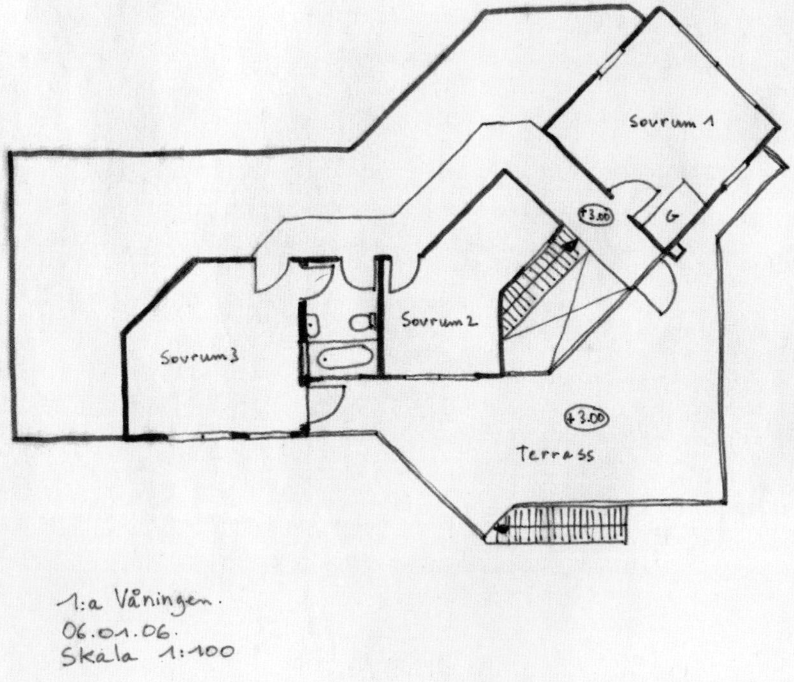
Sovrum 1
+3.00
G
Sovrum 2
Sovrum3
+3.00
Terrass
1:a Våningen.
06.01.06.
Skala 1:100

MASSIMILIANO FUKSAS

Studio Fuksas • Italy

Featured project: The Cloud [pp. 102–9]

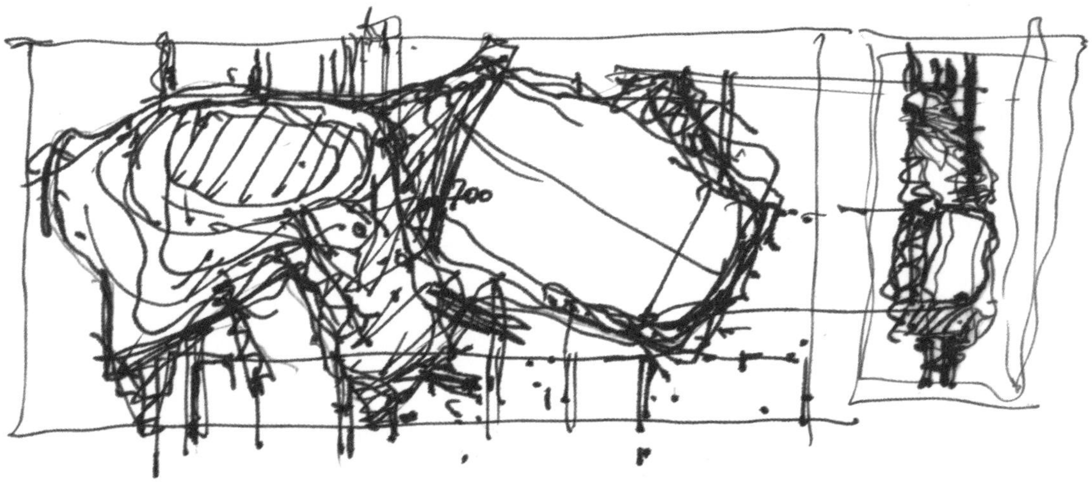

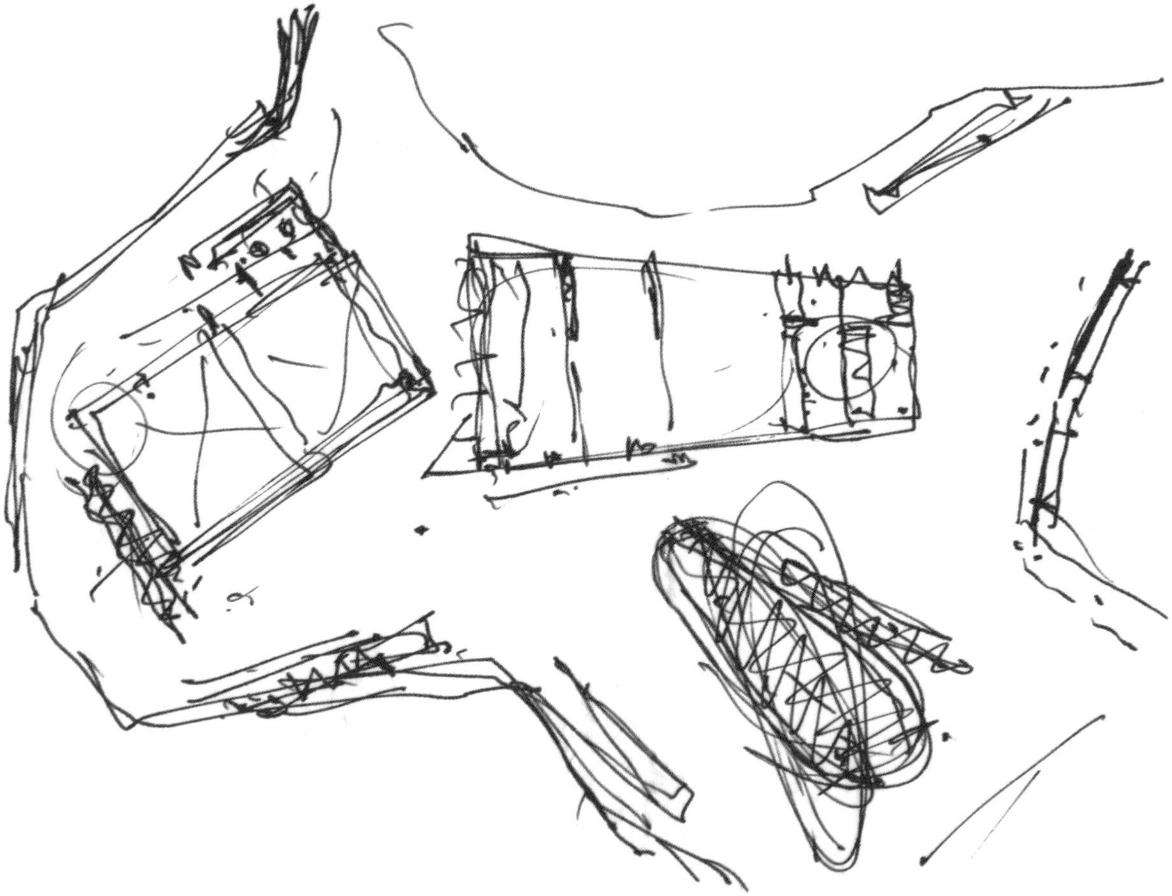

'In my view, a project arises from a drawing and a painting, then a model,' states architect Massimiliano Fuksas. 'These are the tools for increasing tension, without which you will never reach the emotions. Painting is a kind of incentive to achieve architecture. Architecture belongs to the world of art, art belongs to architecture, and vice versa.'

Led by Fuksas and his wife Doriana, Studio Fuksas has offices in Rome, Paris and Shenzhen, an international reputation for excellence, and over 600 completed projects to its name. The company's holistic approach across all scales has allowed it to devise completely integrated design solutions. The key to this, Fuksas believes, lies in research and in asking the right questions.

'I can control what I design through drawing and, later, the model,' he says. 'Thanks to those initial sketches, I can follow the process from the beginning, otherwise I wouldn't be able to articulate what is in my mind. The limitation of my method is that I cannot, and do not want to, delegate the creative phase to anyone else.'

Fuksas continues: 'Usually, I go from a drawing to a physical model. I like making large-scale models, such as 1:200 or 1:50, as I did for The Cloud. In that case, the model was 7 m (23 ft) long, made of wood, and is now exhibited in my studio. This is my way of taking control of the design process. The final phase comprises digital drawings, with my collaborators, organized into different groups, developing what has been decided.'

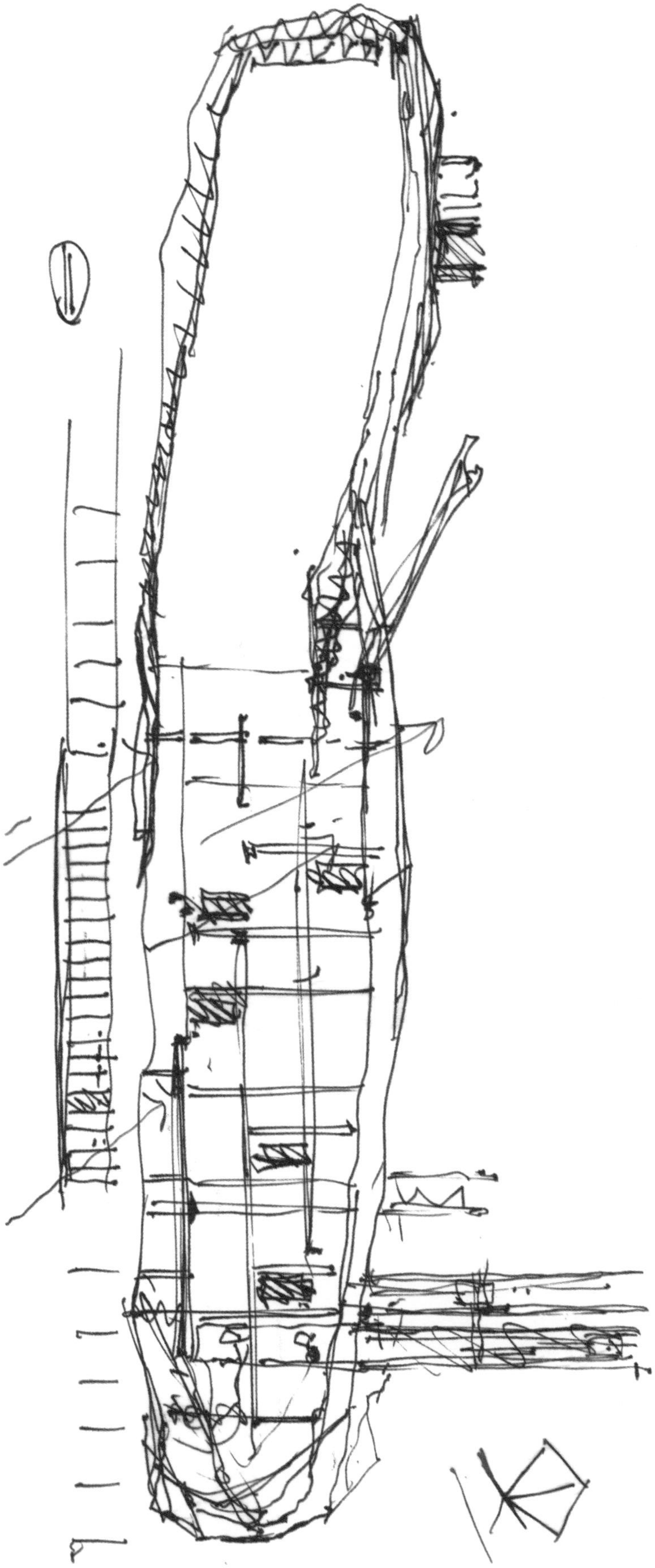

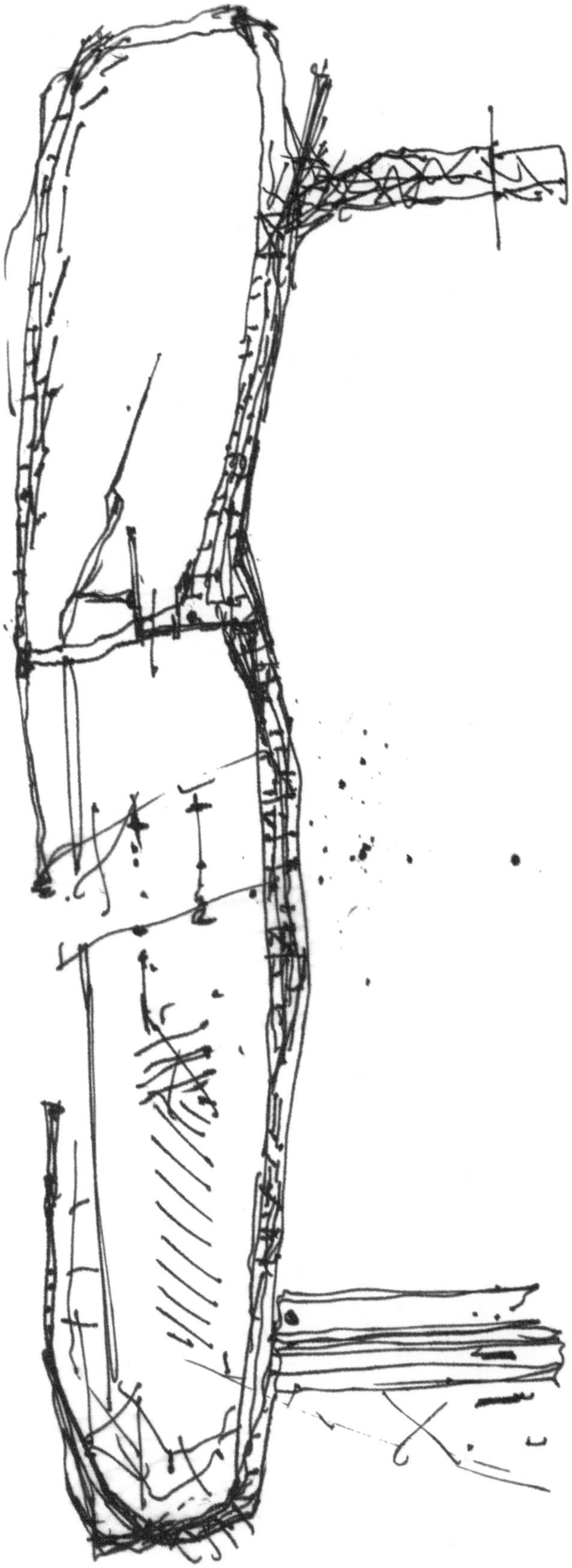

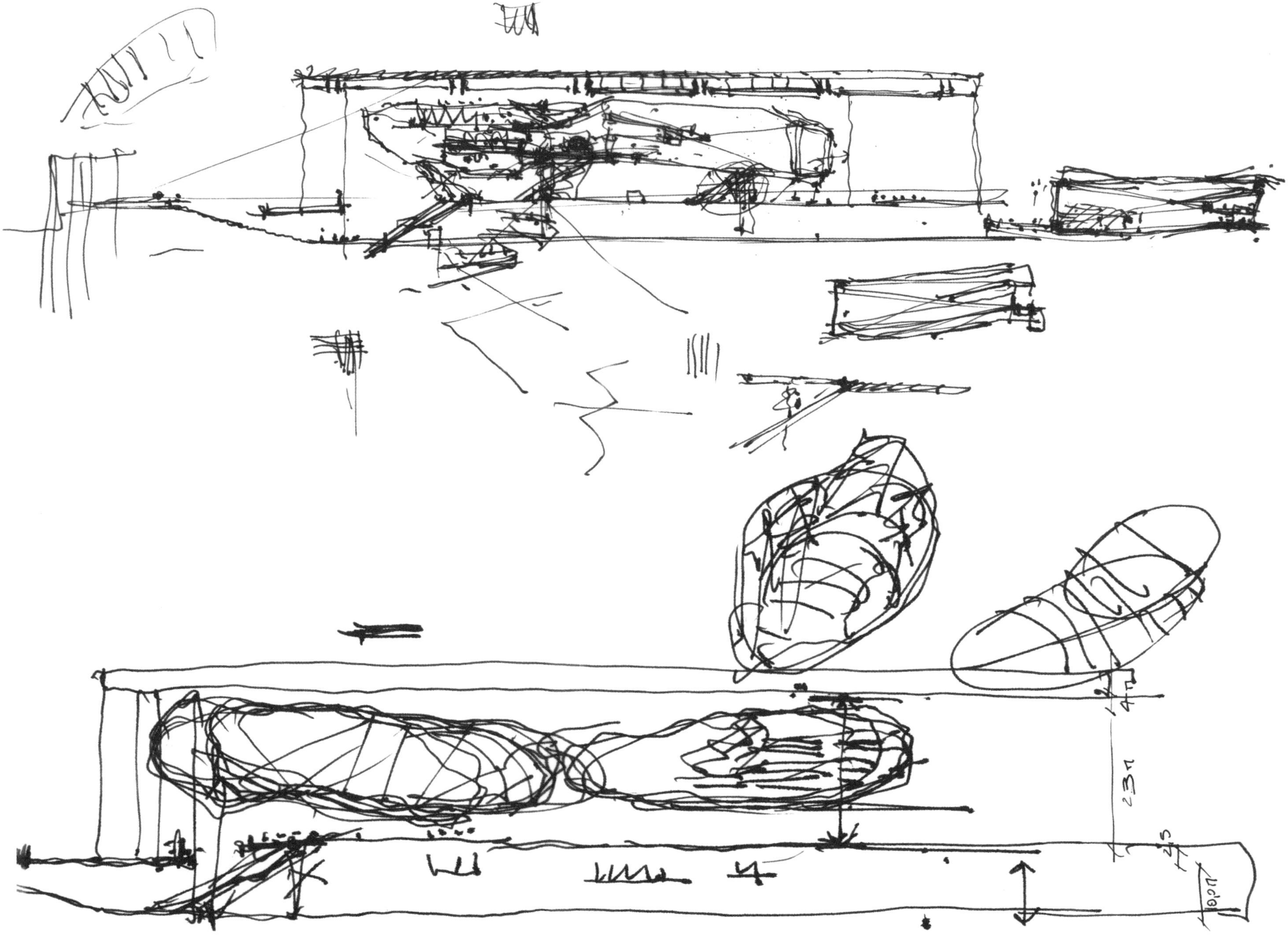

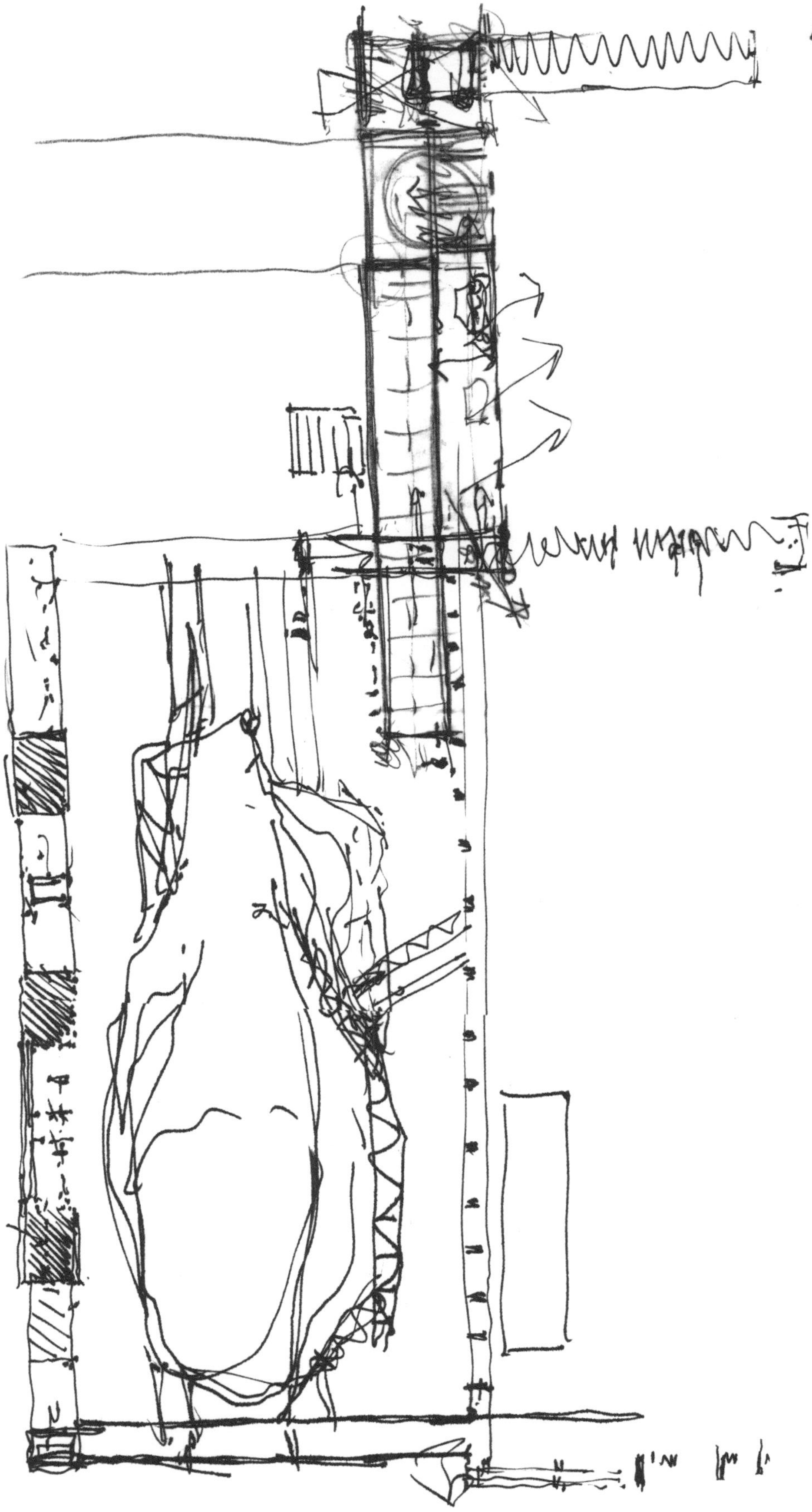

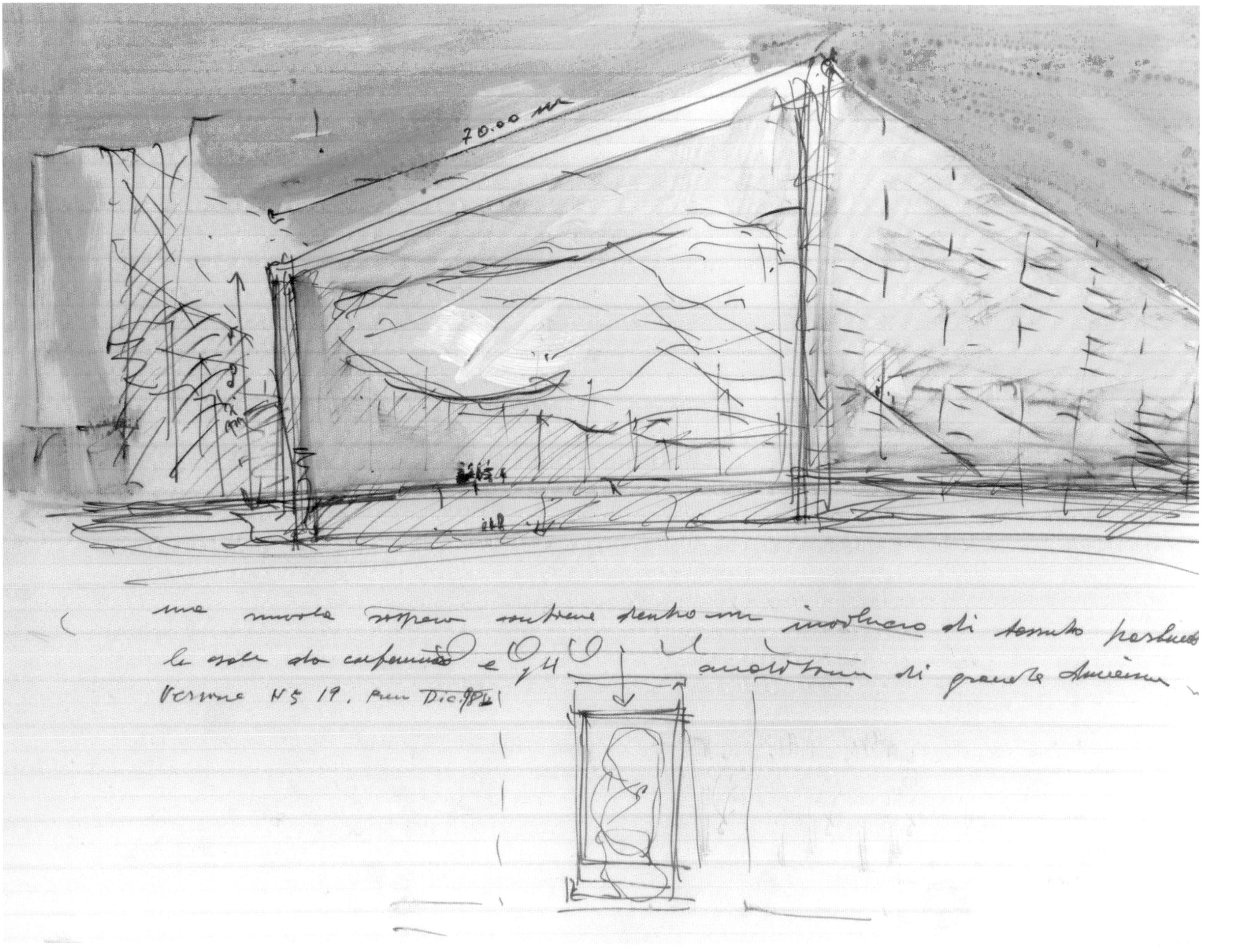
70.00 m
una nuvola sospesa contiene dentro un involucro di tessuto portante

7800 m

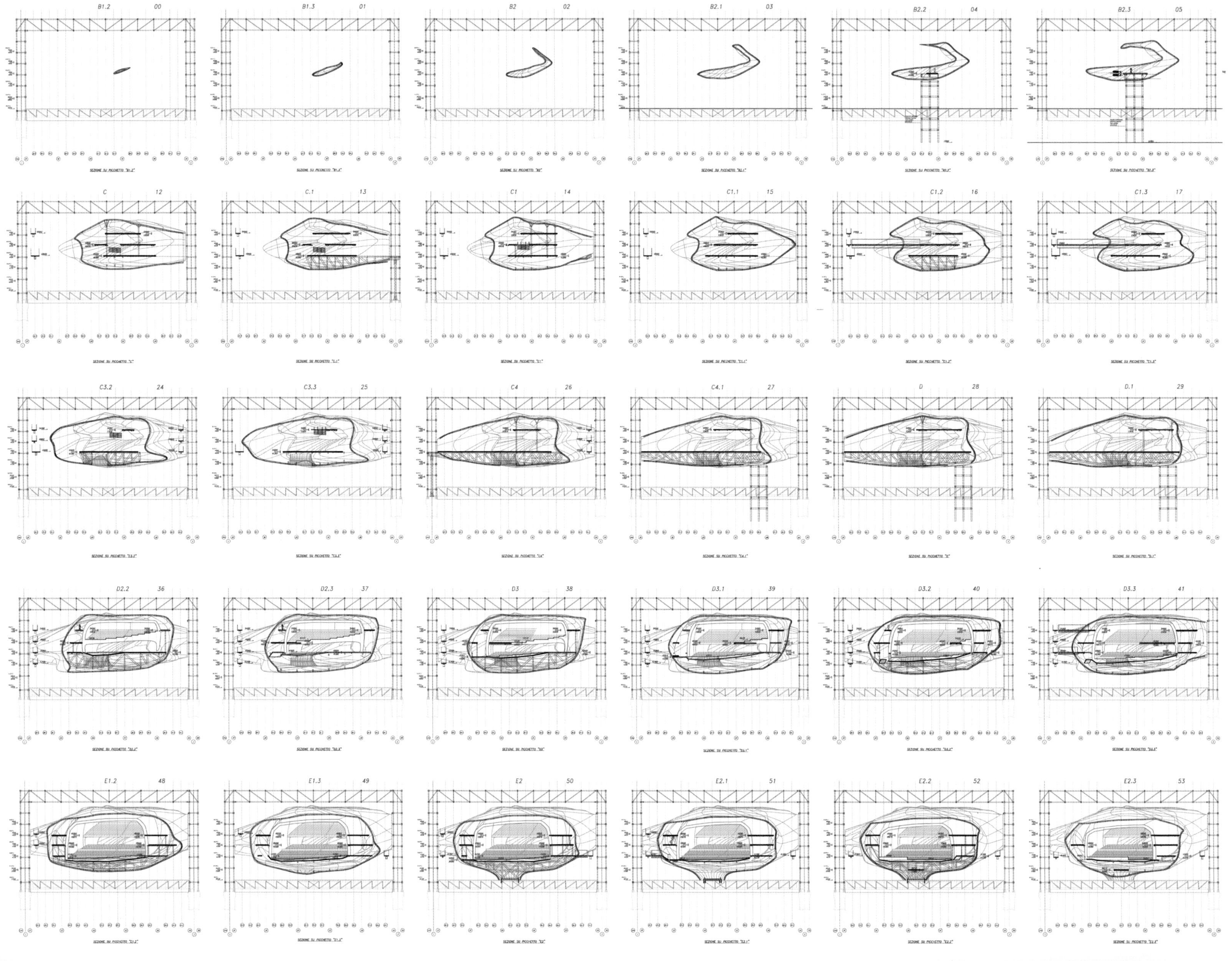

B1.2 00
SEZIONE SU PICCHETTO "B1.2"
B1.3 01
SEZIONE SU PICCHETTO "B1.3"
B2 02
SEZIONE SU PICCHETTO "B2"
B2.1 03
SEZIONE SU PICCHETTO "B2.1"
B2.2 04
SEZIONE SU PICCHETTO "B2.2"
B2.3 05
SEZIONE SU PICCHETTO "B2.3"
C 12
SEZIONE SU PICCHETTO "C"
C.1 13
SEZIONE SU PICCHETTO "C.1"
C1 14
SEZIONE SU PICCHETTO "C1"
C1.1 15
SEZIONE SU PICCHETTO "C1.1"
C1.2 16
SEZIONE SU PICCHETTO "C1.2"
C1.3 17
SEZIONE SU PICCHETTO "C1.3"
C3.2 24
SEZIONE SU PICCHETTO "C3.2"
C3.3 25
SEZIONE SU PICCHETTO "C3.3"
C4 26
SEZIONE SU PICCHETTO "C4"
C4.1 27
SEZIONE SU PICCHETTO "C4.1"
D 28
SEZIONE SU PICCHETTO "D"
D.1 29
SEZIONE SU PICCHETTO "D.1"
D2.2 36
SEZIONE SU PICCHETTO "D2.2"
D2.3 37
SEZIONE SU PICCHETTO "D2.3"
D3 38
SEZIONE SU PICCHETTO "D3"
D3.1 39
SEZIONE SU PICCHETTO "D3.1"
D3.2 40
SEZIONE SU PICCHETTO "D3.2"
D3.3 41
SEZIONE SU PICCHETTO "D3.3"
E1.2 48
SEZIONE SU PICCHETTO "E1.2"
E1.3 49
SEZIONE SU PICCHETTO "E1.3"
E2 50
SEZIONE SU PICCHETTO "E2"
E2.1 51
SEZIONE SU PICCHETTO "E2.1"
E2.2 52
SEZIONE SU PICCHETTO "E2.2"
E2.3 53
SEZIONE SU PICCHETTO "E2.3"

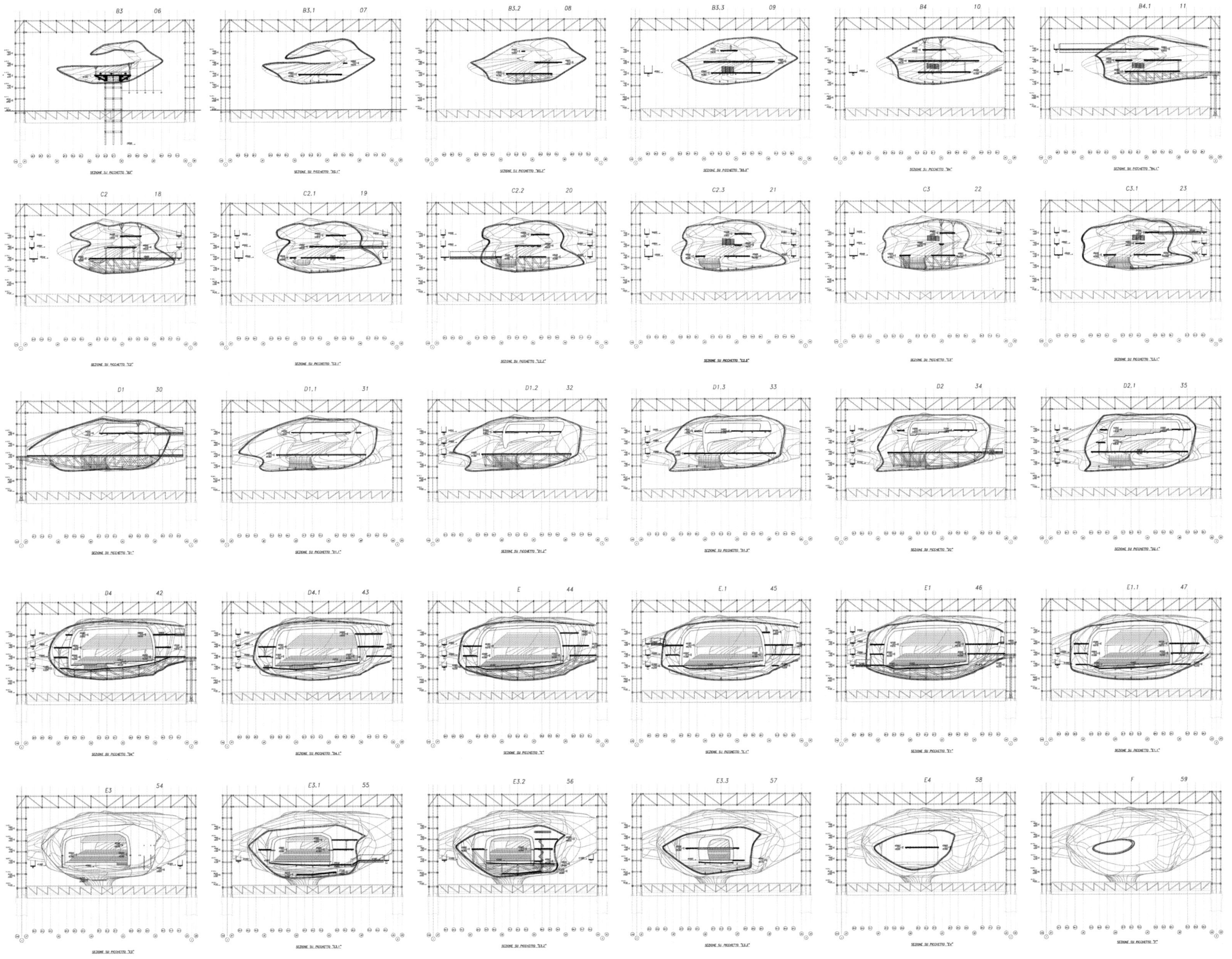
B3 06
SEZIONE SU PICCHETTO "B3"
B3.1 07
SEZIONE SU PICCHETTO "B3.1"
B3.2 08
SEZIONE SU PICCHETTO "B3.2"
B3.3 09
SEZIONE SU PICCHETTO "B3.3"
B4 10
SEZIONE SU PICCHETTO "B4"
B4.1 11
SEZIONE SU PICCHETTO "B4.1"
C2 18
SEZIONE SU PICCHETTO "C2"
C2.1 19
SEZIONE SU PICCHETTO "C2.1"
C2.2 20
SEZIONE SU PICCHETTO "C2.2"
C2.3 21
SEZIONE SU PICCHETTO "C2.3"
C3 22
SEZIONE SU PICCHETTO "C3"
C3.1 23
SEZIONE SU PICCHETTO "C3.1"
D1 30
SEZIONE SU PICCHETTO "D1"
D1.1 31
SEZIONE SU PICCHETTO "D1.1"
D1.2 32
SEZIONE SU PICCHETTO "D1.2"
D1.3 33
SEZIONE SU PICCHETTO "D1.3"
D2 34
SEZIONE SU PICCHETTO "D2"
D2.1 35
SEZIONE SU PICCHETTO "D2.1"
D4 42
SEZIONE SU PICCHETTO "D4"
D4.1 43
SEZIONE SU PICCHETTO "D4.1"
E 44
SEZIONE SU PICCHETTO "E"
E.1 45
SEZIONE SU PICCHETTO "E.1"
E1 46
SEZIONE SU PICCHETTO "E1"
E1.1 47
SEZIONE SU PICCHETTO "E1.1"
E3 54
SEZIONE SU PICCHETTO "E3"
E3.1 55
SEZIONE SU PICCHETTO "E3.1"
E3.2 56
SEZIONE SU PICCHETTO "E3.2"
E3.3 57
SEZIONE SU PICCHETTO "E3.3"
E4 58
SEZIONE SU PICCHETTO "E4"
F 59
SEZIONE SU PICCHETTO "F"

BENJAMIN GARCIA SAXE

Studio Saxe • Costa Rica

Featured project: A Forest for a Moon Dazzler [pp. 110–11]

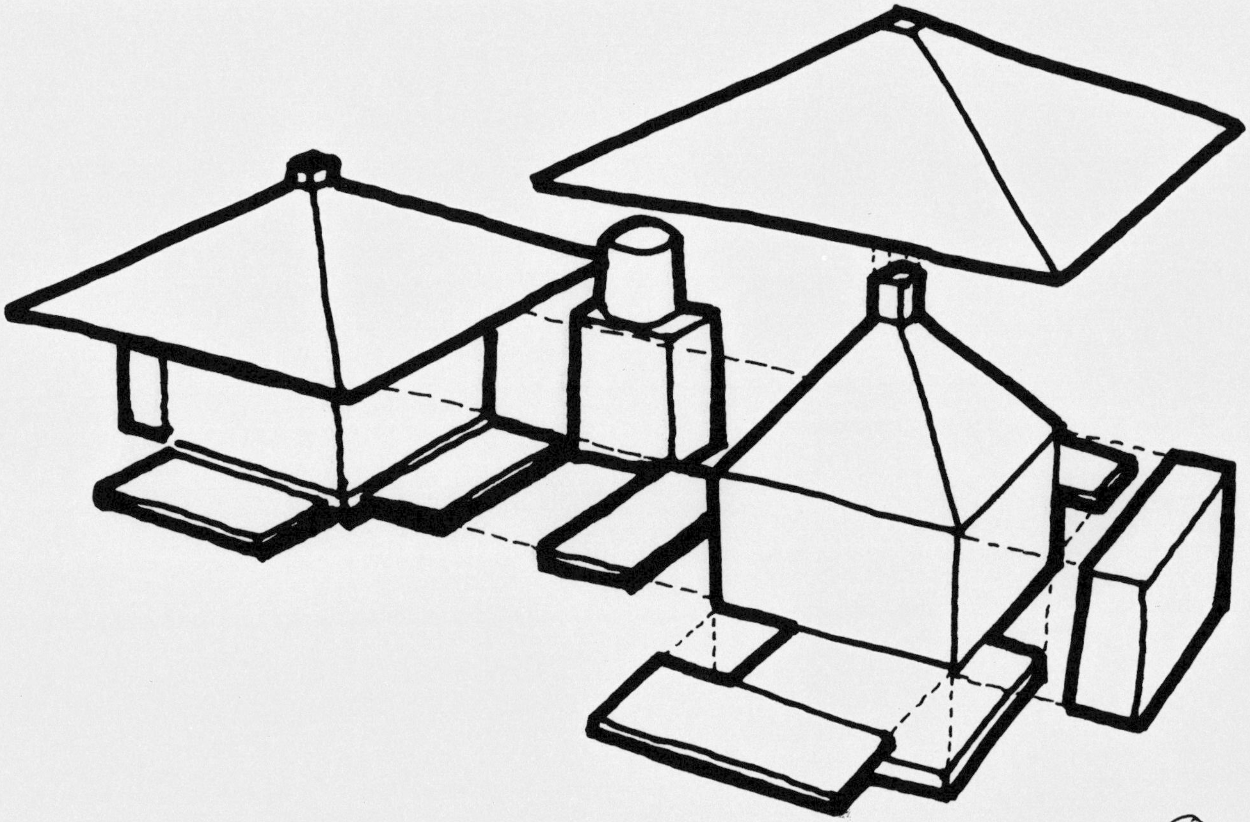

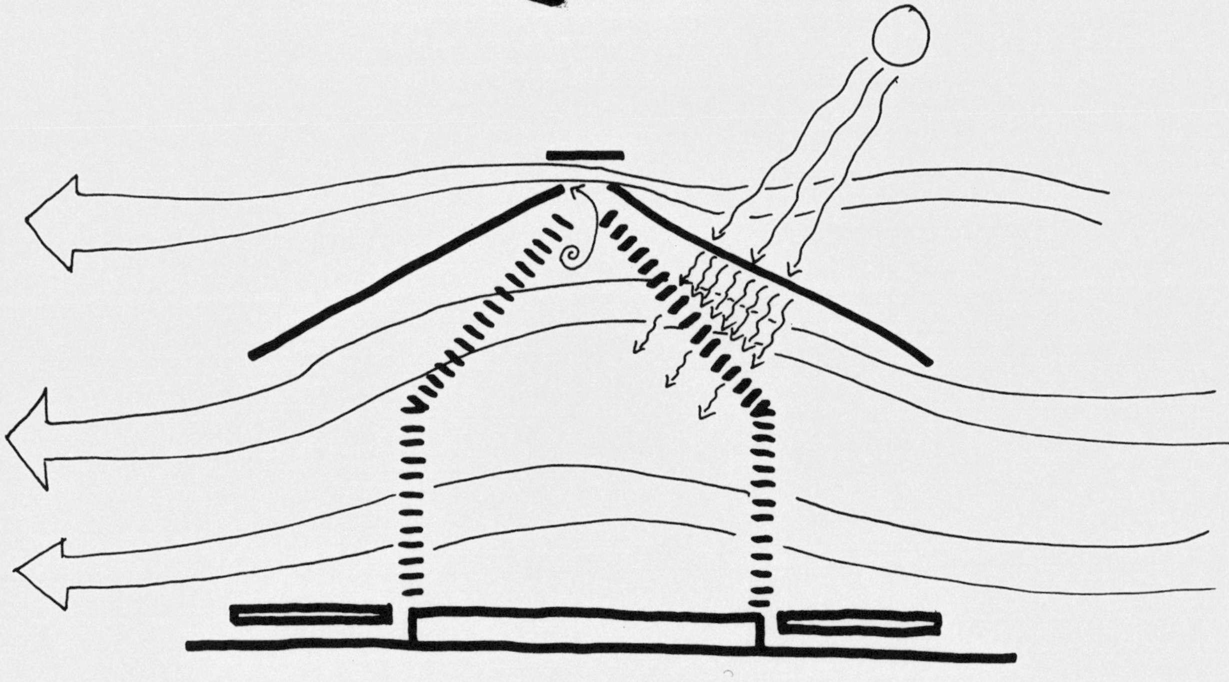

'My first sketches are very fluid and non-specific,' says Benjamin Garcia Saxe. 'As ideas become clearer, the drawings become simpler, until there might be just a few lines. I find that sketching helps me simplify ideas into basic components and forces me to condense complex thought into childlike diagrams that are easily understood. With the advent of computer-aided technology, we have lost the ability to create simple, timeless designs. Sketching is a more direct way of tapping into the instinctive notions of architecture.'

Garcia Saxe set up his practice in Costa Rica in 2004, with the aim of exploring our relationship with the natural environment through architecture. Since then, his team has grown to 10 and he has opened an office in London.

'In my personal design process, I use sketching in order to extract general concepts,' he says. 'Later on, I will use drawings to create details of a design. Finally, I use them to explain the ideas within a project. Throughout the process, I also use other means, including digital and physical models, to advance those same ideas. Often when I have an idea, I am eager to express it in any way possible. Sketching is usually quicker and more efficient, but it is the building of physical models that is perhaps the technique I am most drawn to.'

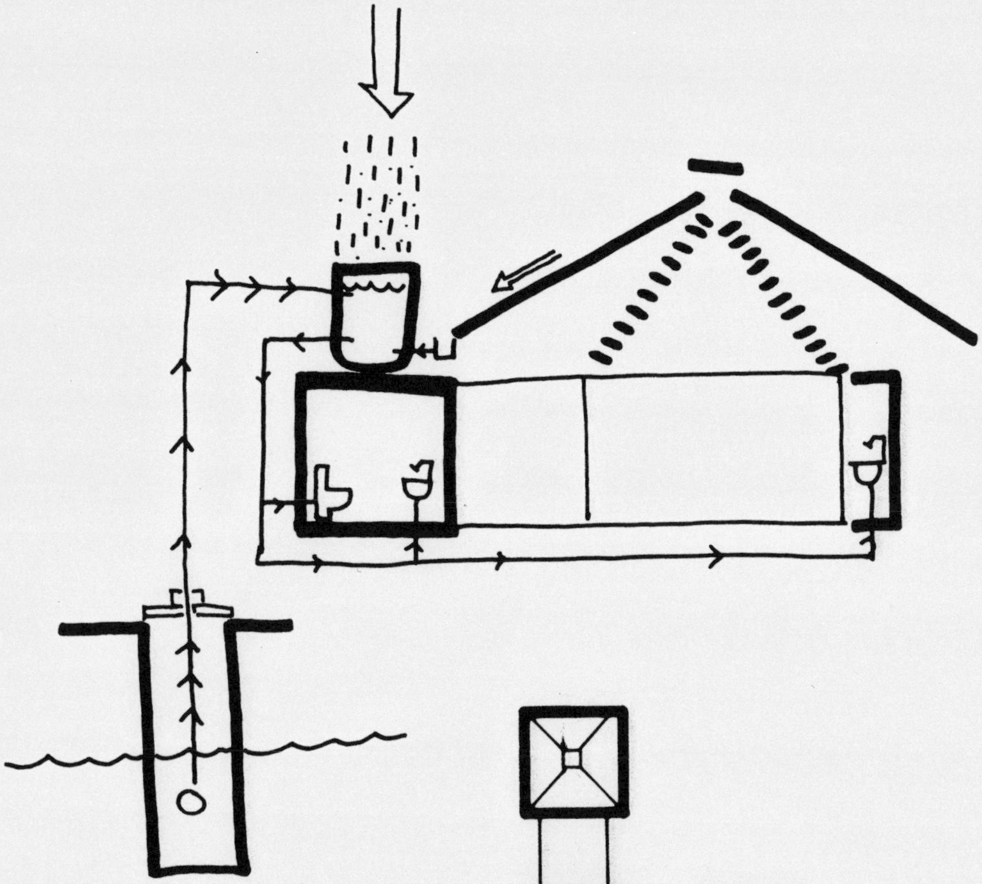

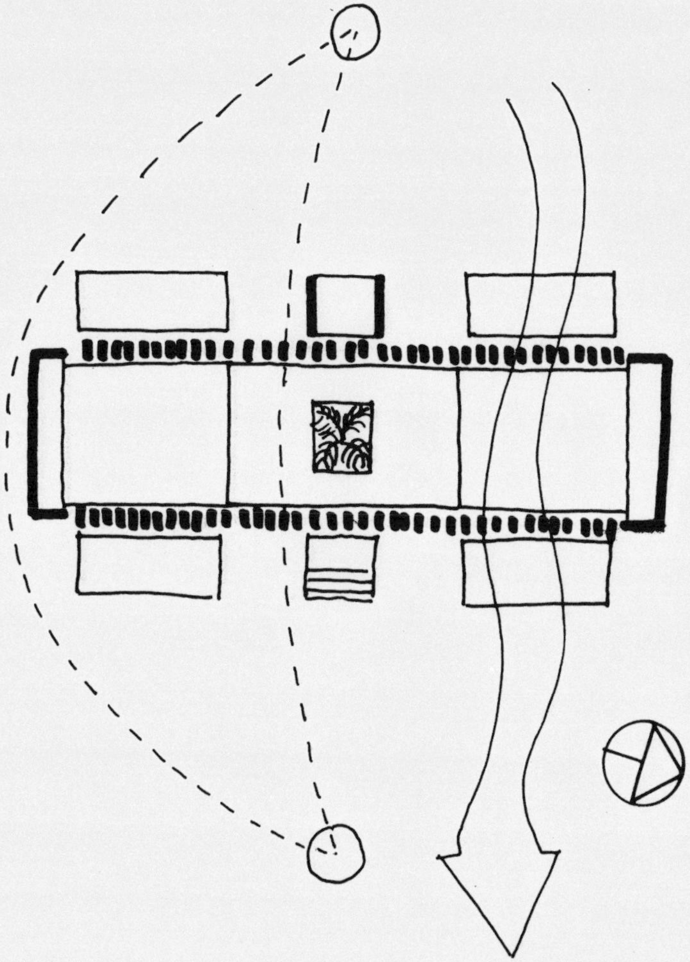

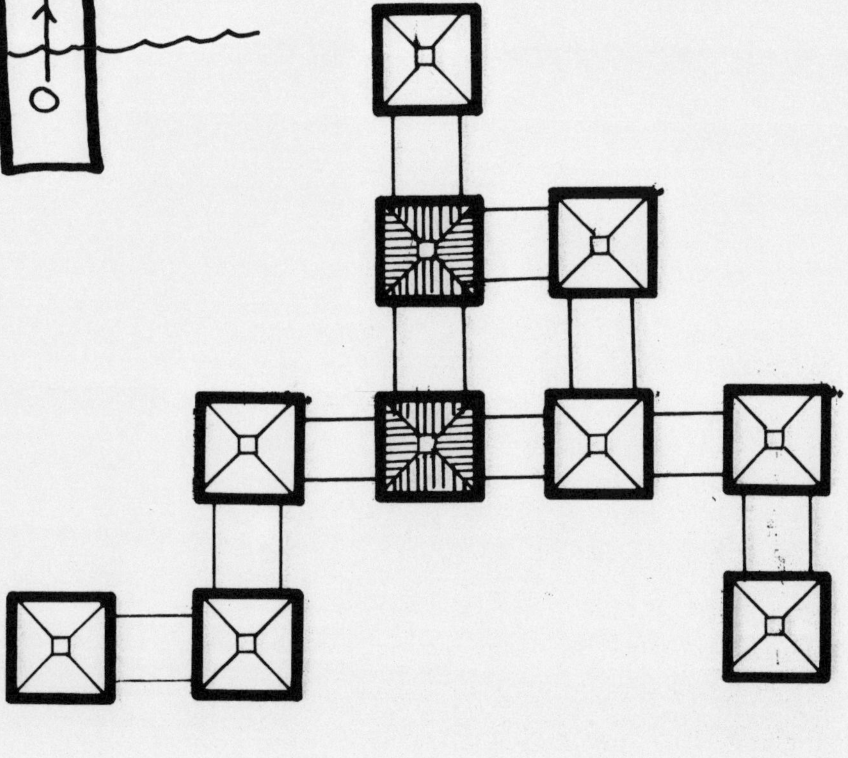

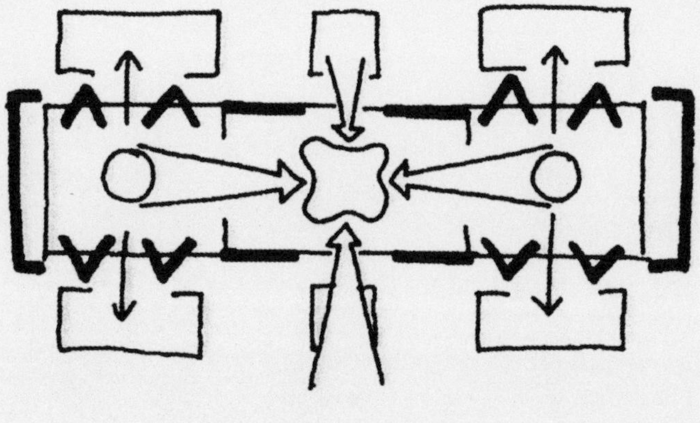

SASHA GEBLER

Gebler Tooth Architects • UK

Featured projects: Bassett Road [pp. 112, left; 113, right]
Regent's Park Road [pp. 112–13] · Hereford Road [p. 114]
Old Compton Street [p. 115] · Wapping High Street [pp. 116–17]
Holdhurst Manor [pp. 118–19]

'In my experience, architects trained entirely on AutoCAD and reliant on the Internet tend to be more editors than designers,' says Sasha Gebler of London-based firm Gebler Tooth Architects. 'Obviously, there are exceptions to this rule, but it does explain why much contemporary architecture is very bland and does not have many unique qualities or sense of place.'

He continues: 'I come from the last generation of the pre-digital design and construction world. In the 1970s, when I was training at Cambridge and then got my first job, computers were common, but not for producing drawings or designing with. There was no SketchUp and no Internet. I taught myself to draw by going to the Victoria & Albert Museum in the evenings and drawing the sculptures and bits of buildings in the collection there.'

As founding director and chairman of the company, Gebler has been instrumental in plotting a course that has seen it tackle all sectors of building, from airports to art spaces, restorations to multi-unit residential spaces. The key to its success, he believes, is versatility and good design.

'I have long held the view that art is an integral part of architecture, and is one of the few activities that combines the need for artistic, technical, communication and legal skills,' he says. 'The process of sketching or drawing is itself an artistic one, and enables direct communication from what is in one's mind to a third party. Despite the incredible power and ability to create new forms that digital devices offer, they also act as a barrier. Architects should be aware of that.'

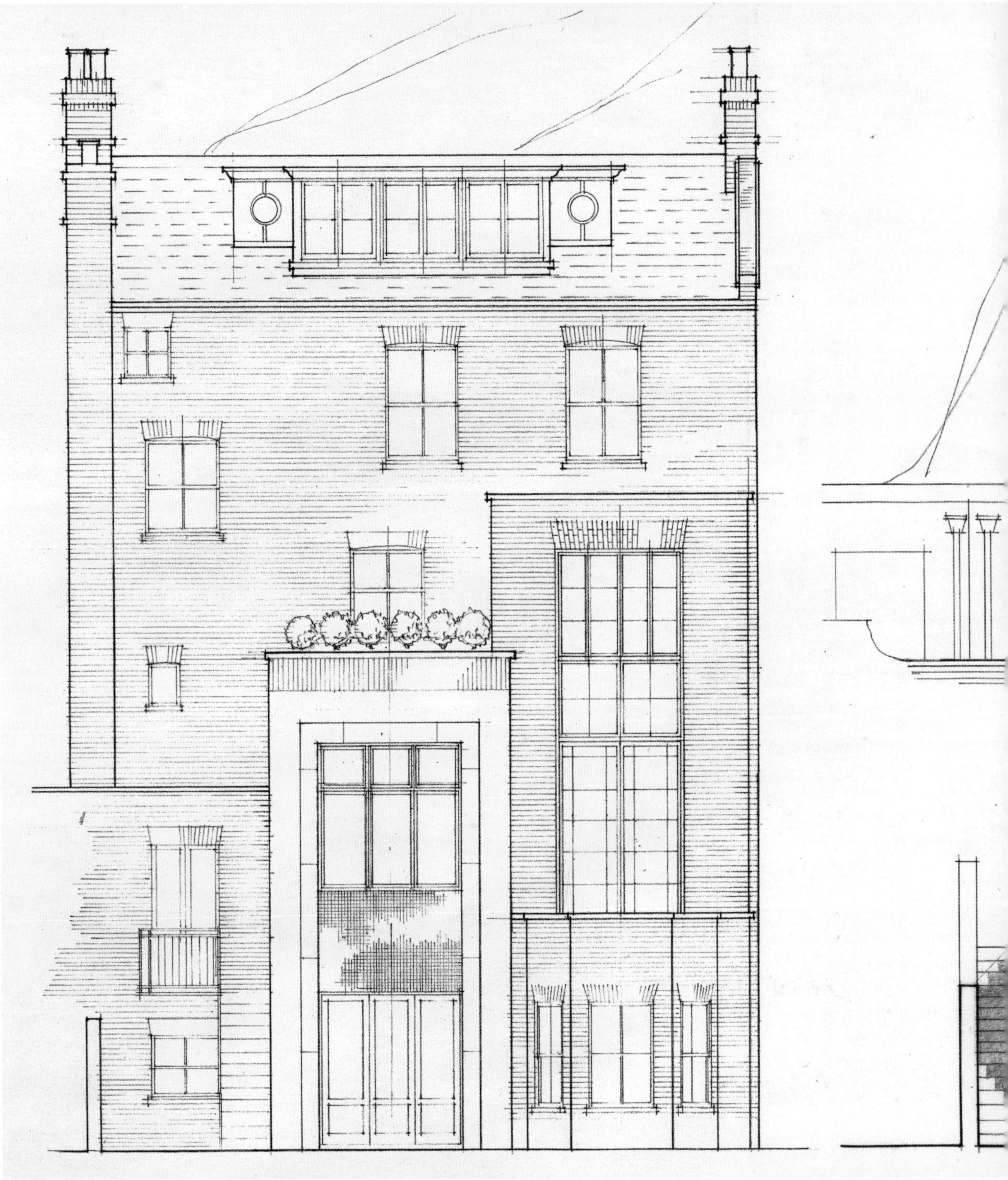

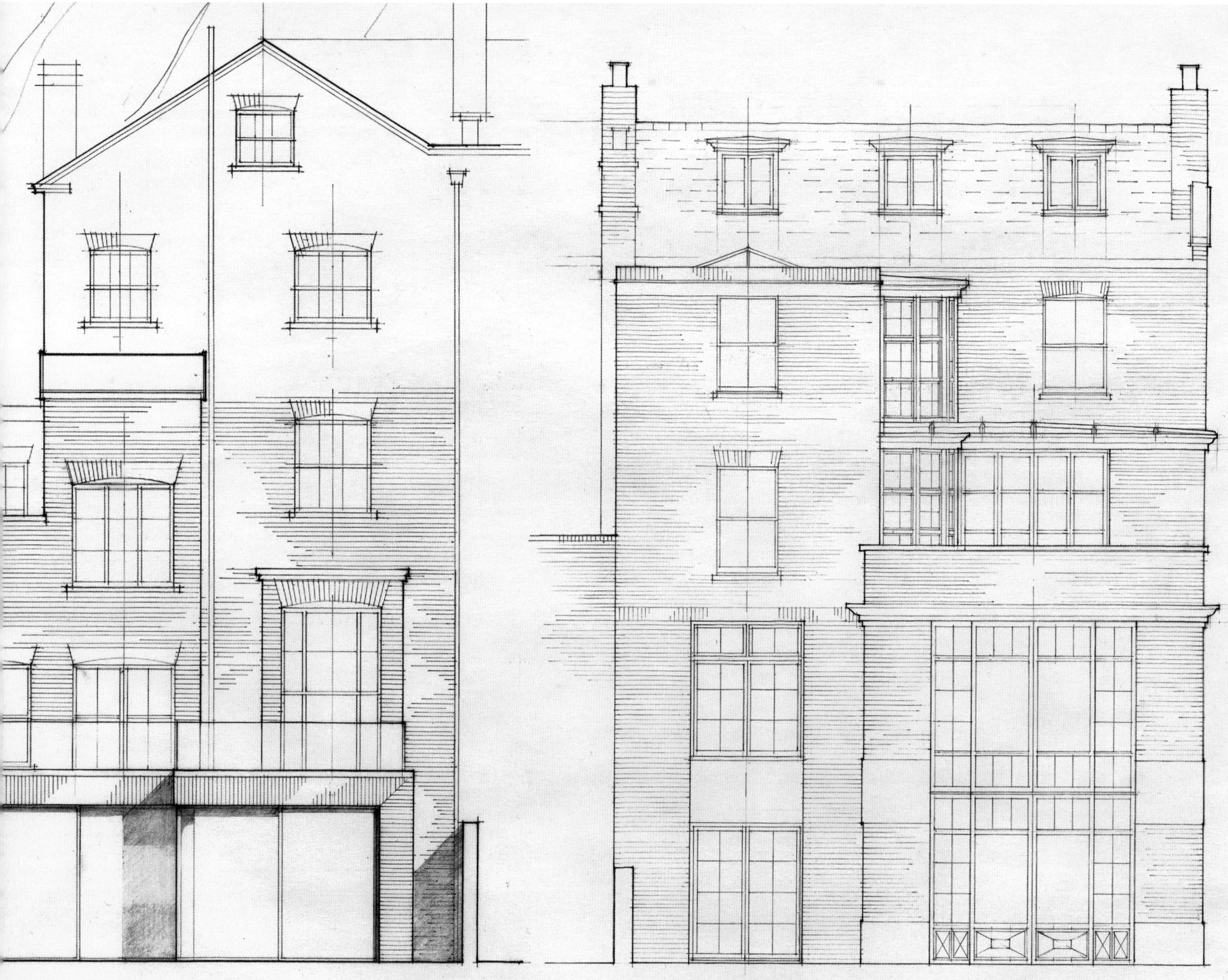

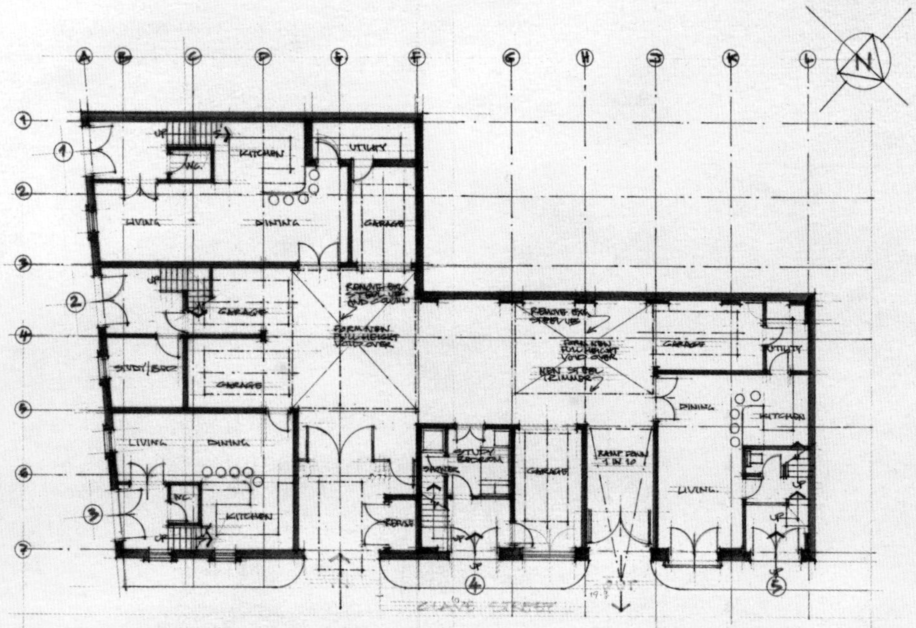

131 WAPPING HIGH ST. 5 UNIT SCHEME GROUND FLOOR PLAN, SCALE 1:100 246/

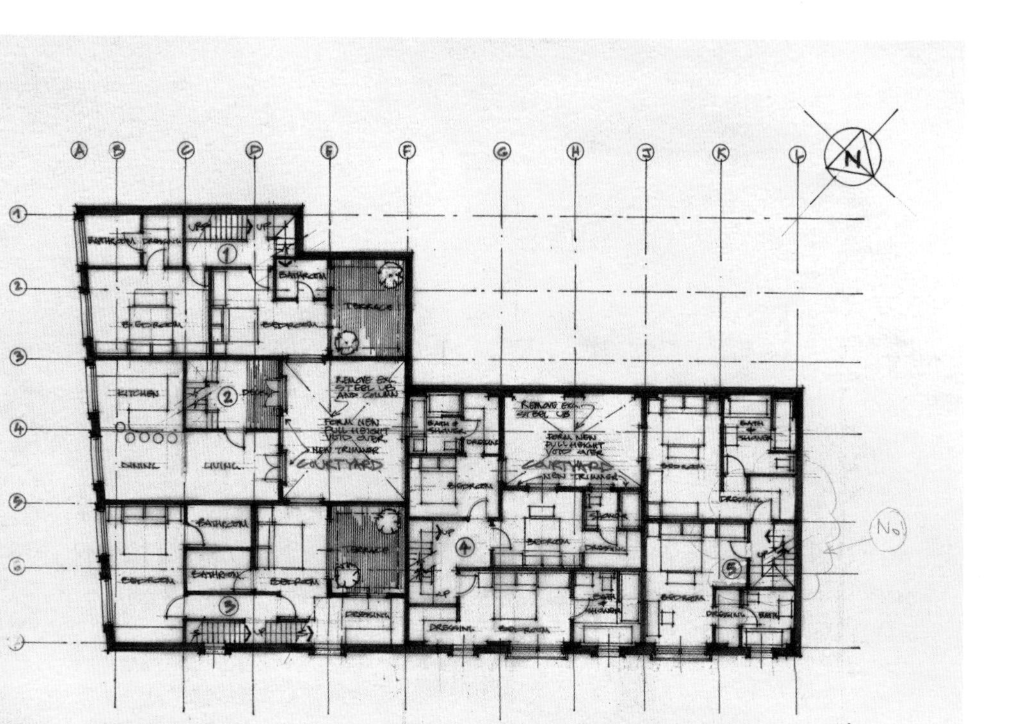

131 WAPPING HIGH ST. 5 UNIT SCHEME FIRST FLOOR PLAN, SCALE 1:100 246/

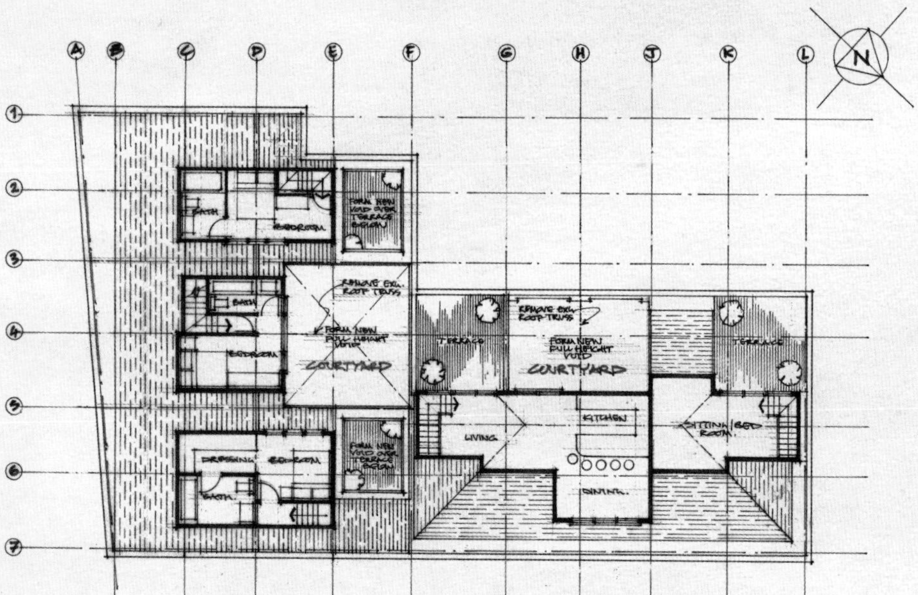

131 WAPPING HIGH ST. 5 UNIT SCHEME, SECOND FLOOR PLAN, SCALE 1:100 246/

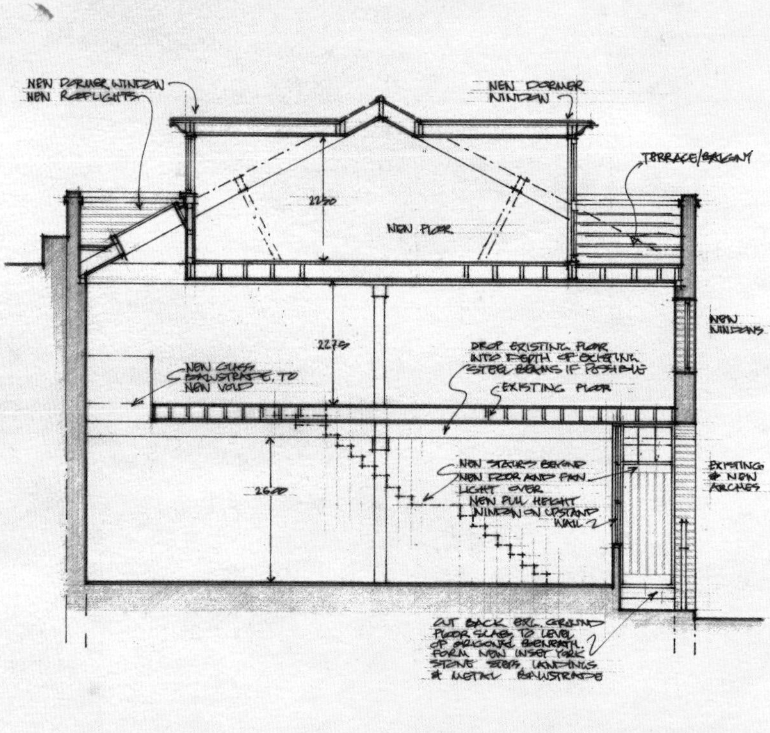

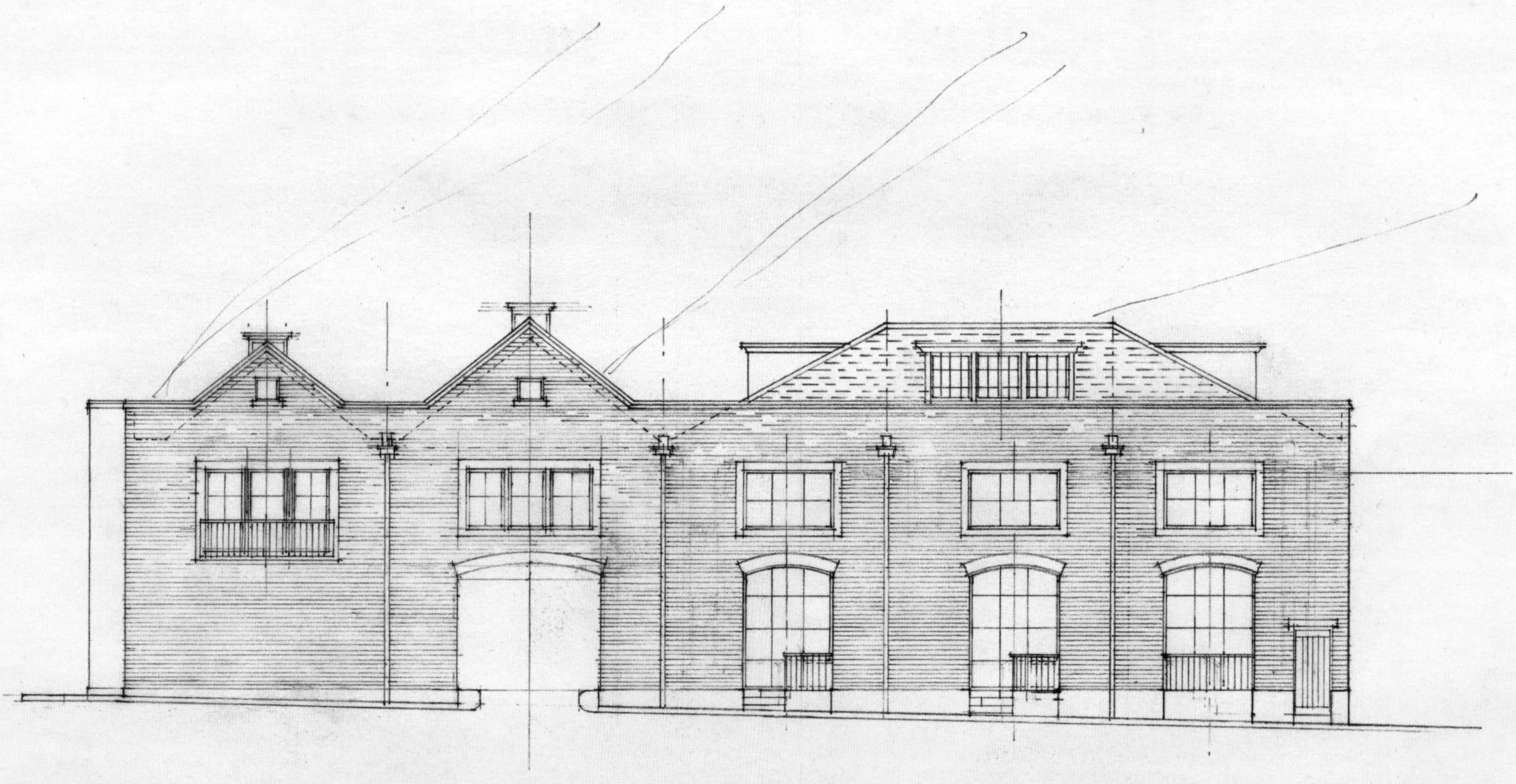

137 WAPPING HIGH STREET, PROPOSED ELEVATION TO CLAVE ST, SCALE 1:100

HOLDHURST FARM. CRANLEIGH, SURREY. WEST ELEVATION. SCALE 1:50.

HOLDHURST FARM. CRANLEIGH, SURREY, EAST ELEVATION, SCALE 1:50

HOLDHURST FARM. CRANLEIGH, SURREY, PROPOSED ELEVATION. GTA, MAY 2011.

CARLOS GÓMEZ

InN Arquitectura • Spain

Featured projects: Triana Civic Centre [pp. 120–1]
Castañuelo [pp. 122–3] · Madrid [p. 124] · Aachen [p. 125]

Having set up his small, innovative practice in Andalusia, Carlos Gómez specializes in the renovation and renewal of existing properties. 'The imprecision of the hand is an advantage in the early stages of a project, since it allows lines and ideas to interact in a sort of spontaneous dance,' he notes. 'This allows the subconscious to arise, as Alvar Aalto observed. After several attempts, some traces will gain prominence over others. These will become the master lines. From then on, there will be variations and adaptations, but the scheme is established.'

Gómez developed Vita Simplex, a model for managing self-build projects, especially for foreigners buying property in Spain. 'In the early stages, we use multiple drawings until we get to a satisfactory concept,' he explains. 'Roll paper is particularly useful at this point. We draw on metres of uncut paper, allowing us to keep the narrative of the project clear and clean. Later on, we will often sketch over and over again, with small variations, on thin paper that allows us to copy the previous drawing, somewhat like traditional animation. Up to this point, we use mostly soft lead pencils. It is not until we begin to reach a well-defined idea that we switch to freehand ink.'

For this architect, sketching is the most enjoyable part of the design process. 'The constant flow of ideas releases inner tension and lays down a mantle of calm,' he says. 'We architects must rebel against the frenetic production rhythm of our time. Good design can only arise from quiet observation, meditation and reflection.'

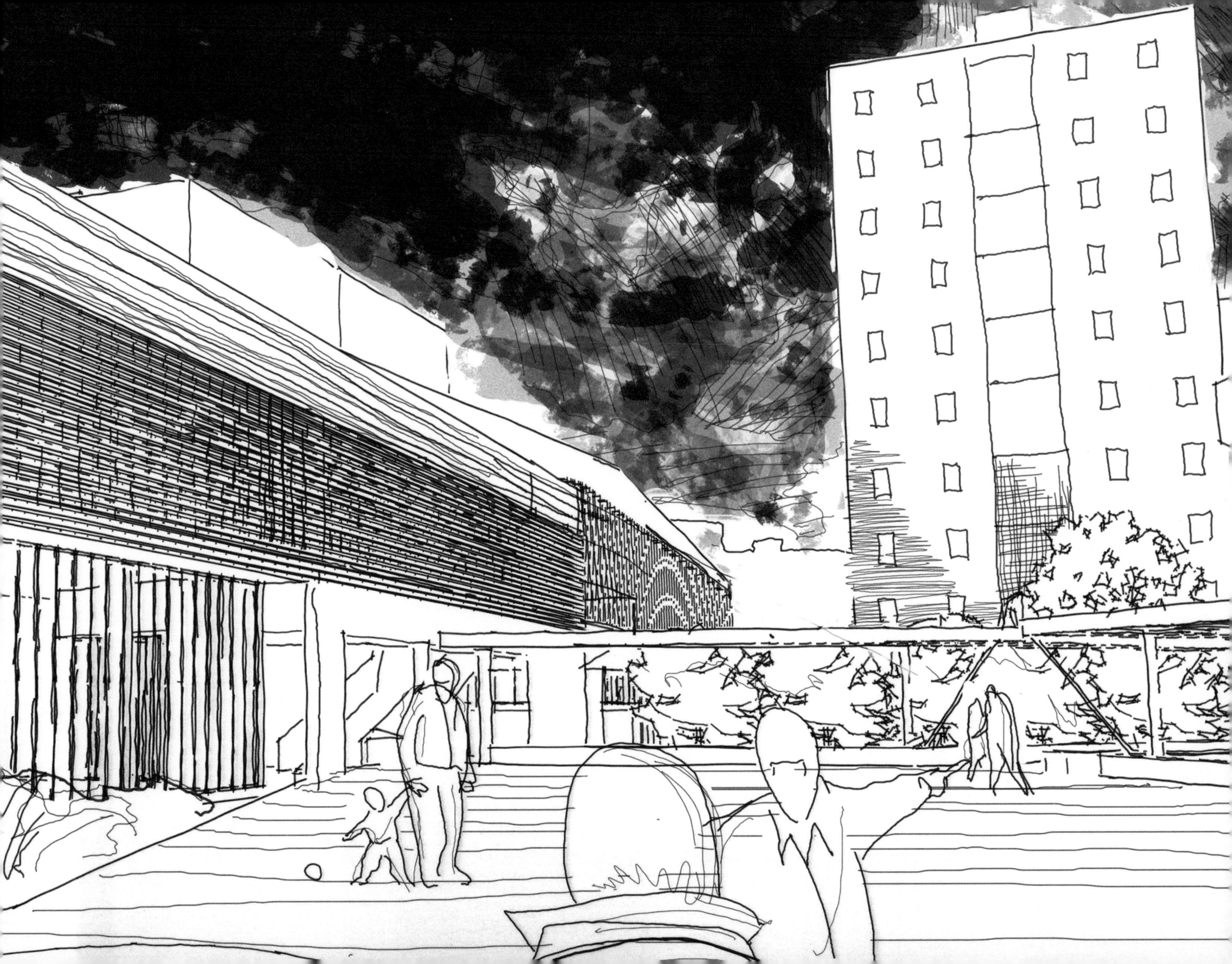

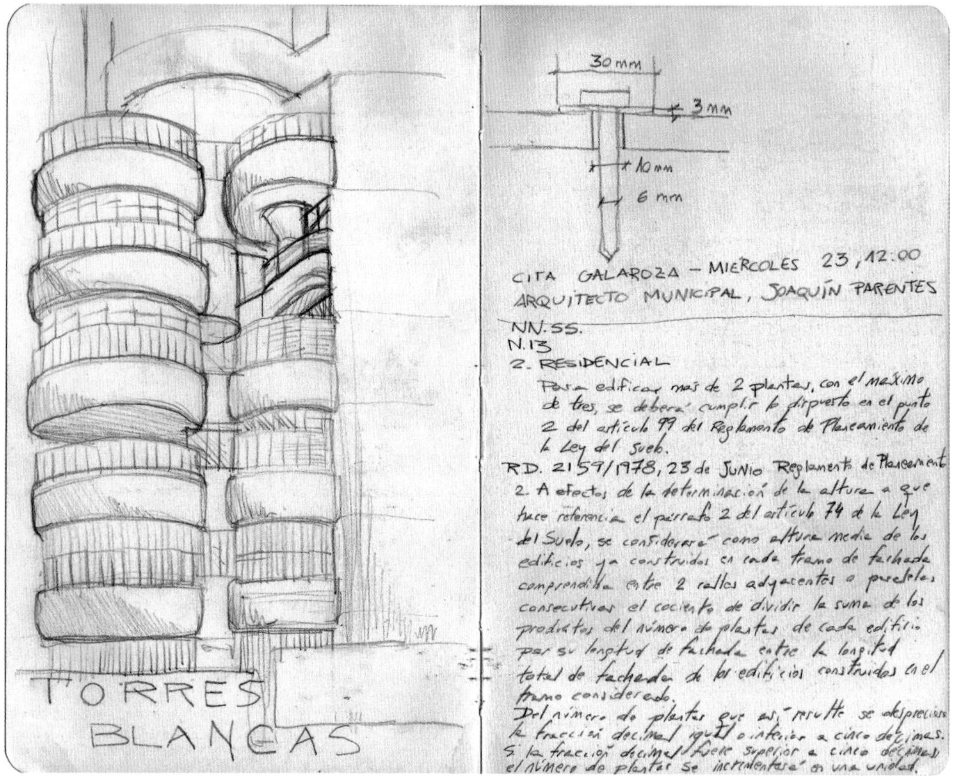
TORRES
BLANCAS
30 mm
3 mm
10 mm
6 mm
CITA GALAROZA – MIERCOLES 23, 12:00
ARQUITECTO MUNICIPAL, JOAQUÍN PARENTES
NN.SS.
N.13
2. RESIDENCIAL
Para edificar más de 2 plantas, con el máximo de tres, se deberá cumplir lo dispuesto en el punto 2 del artículo 99 del Reglamento de Planeamiento de la Ley del suelo.
RD. 2159/1978, 23 de JUNIO Reglamento de Planeamiento
2. A efectos de la determinación de la altura a que hace referencia el párrafo 2 del artículo 74 de la Ley del Suelo, se considerará como altura media de los edificios ya construidos en cada tramo de fachada comprendida entre 2 calles adyacentes o paralelas consecutivas el cociente de dividir la suma de los productos del número de plantas de cada edificio por su longitud de fachada entre la longitud total de fachadas de los edificios construidos en el tramo considerado.
Del número de plantas que así resulte se despreciará la fracción decimal igual o inferior a cinco décimas. Si la fracción decimal fuere superior a cinco décimas el número de plantas se incrementará en una unidad.

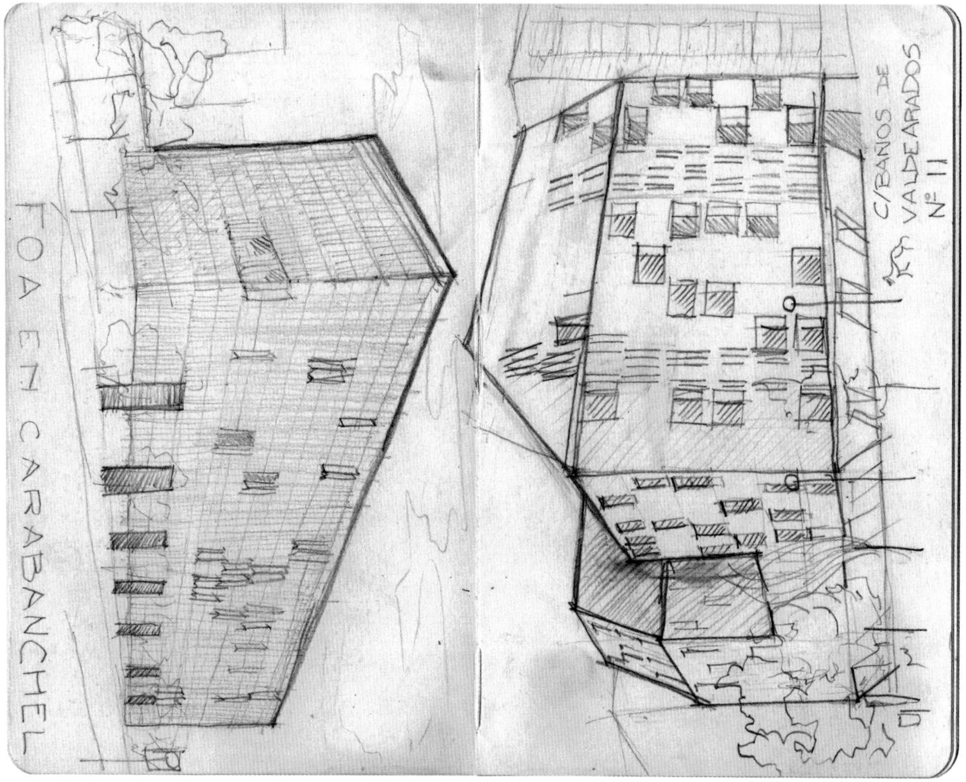
FOA EN CARABANCHEL
C/BAÑOS DE VALDEARADOS Nº 11

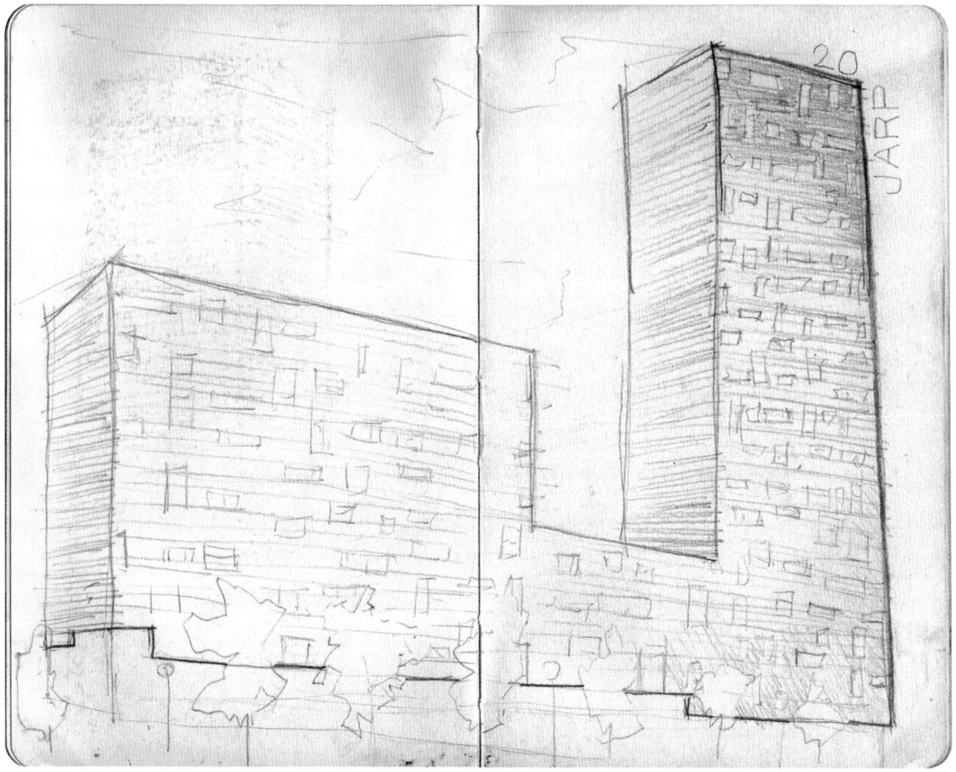
20
JARP

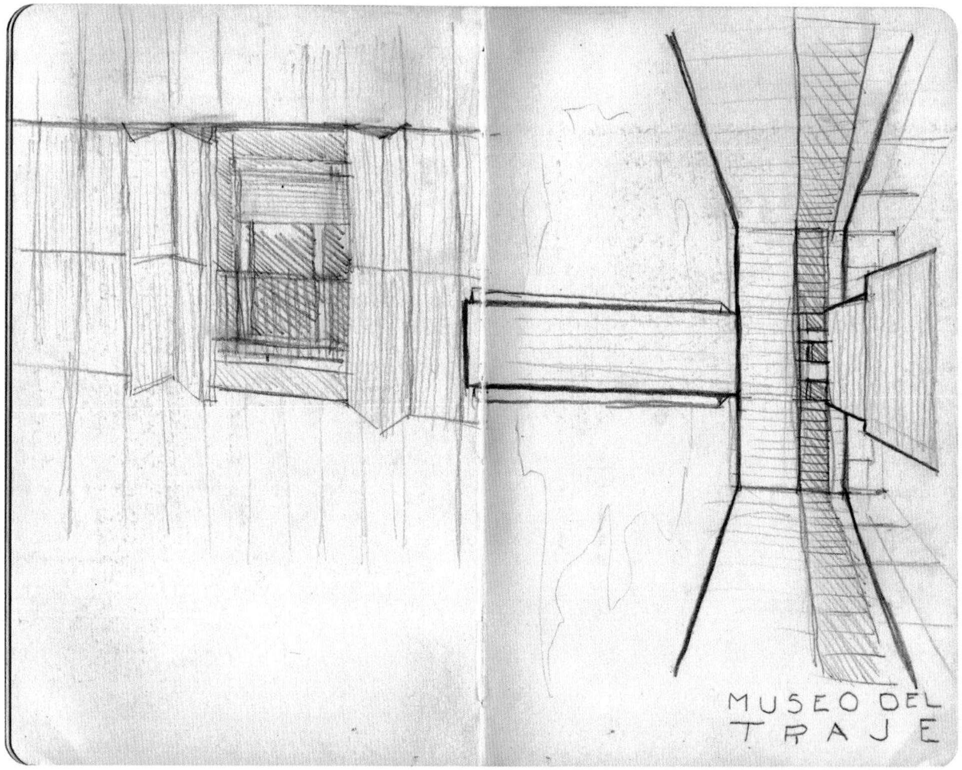
MUSEO DEL
TRAJE

MEG GRAHAM

Superkül • Canada

Featured projects: House on the Lake [p. 126, top]
Compass House [pp. 126–27] · +House [p. 127, right]

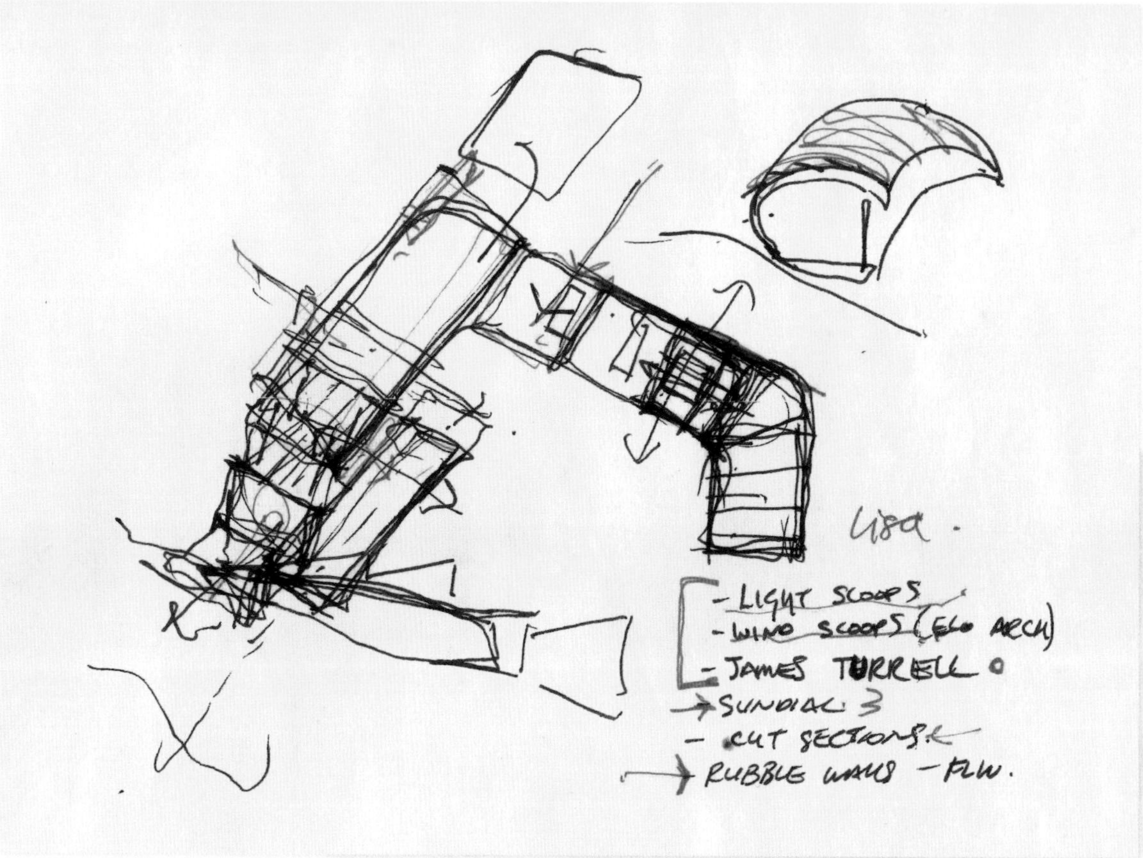

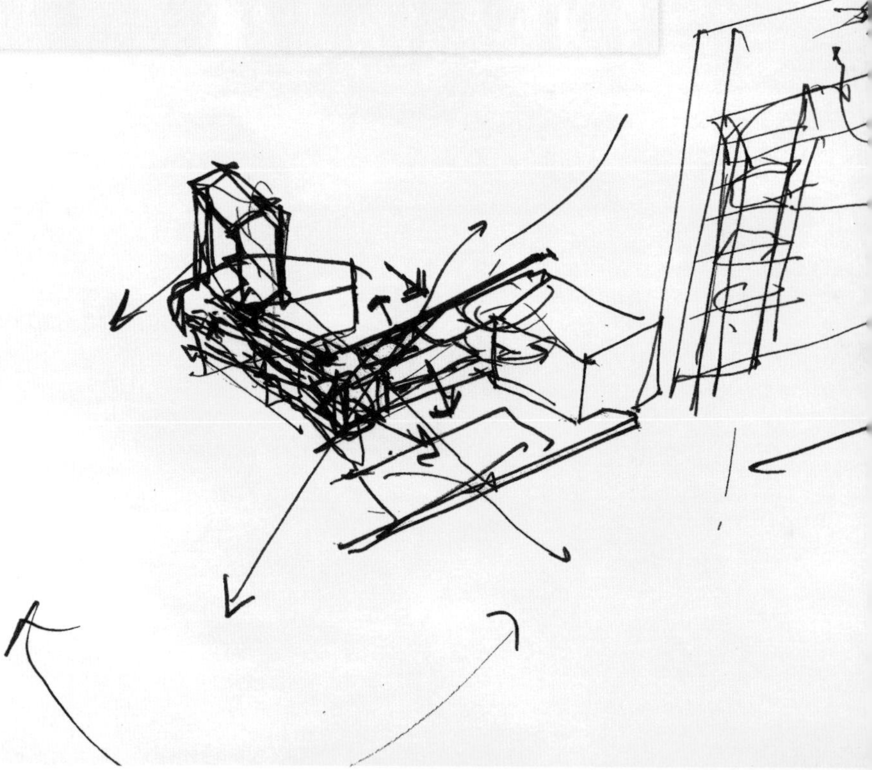

'We come to our projects with no preconceived notions of what they are going to look like, so for us, sketching is a multi-layered and iterative process,' says Meg Graham of Toronto-based practice Superkül. 'We sketch the site, the trees, the existing building; we sketch the program, the water, the land, and eventually the building emerges from those layered studies.'

Along with partner Andre D'Elia, Graham is principal of the practice, which was founded in 2002 and is now 19 strong. The list of awards bestowed on the company, both for architecture and interior design, is long.

'Some of our sketches are hard to read, because they can be layers upon layers of thought,' she continues. 'They are just part of our internal process. But in a meeting with a client, a sketch done right there at the table is essential to a collaborative and engaged design process.'

Graham believes that sketching gives her an almost visceral link to the construction of her designs. 'Sketching is such a foundational way of thinking for us, because it is so instinctive,' she says. 'There is no software between brain and hand, impeding the flow of information or jamming the signal. We sketch forms and places that are curious, interesting, beautiful or inspiring, which then enter our collective memory and become part of the flow of information.'

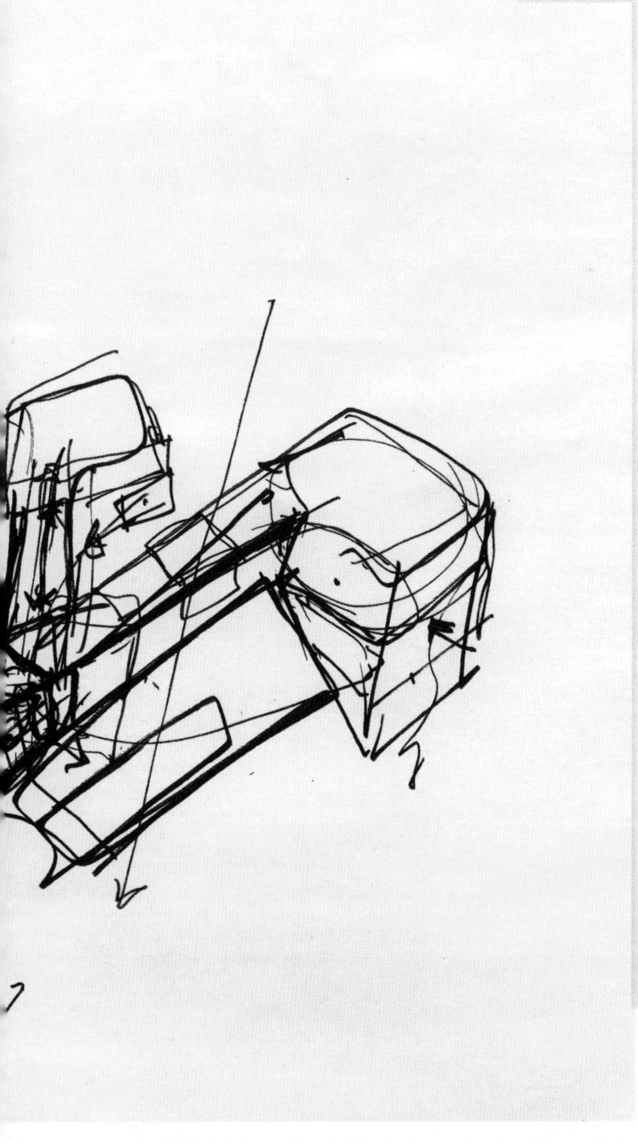

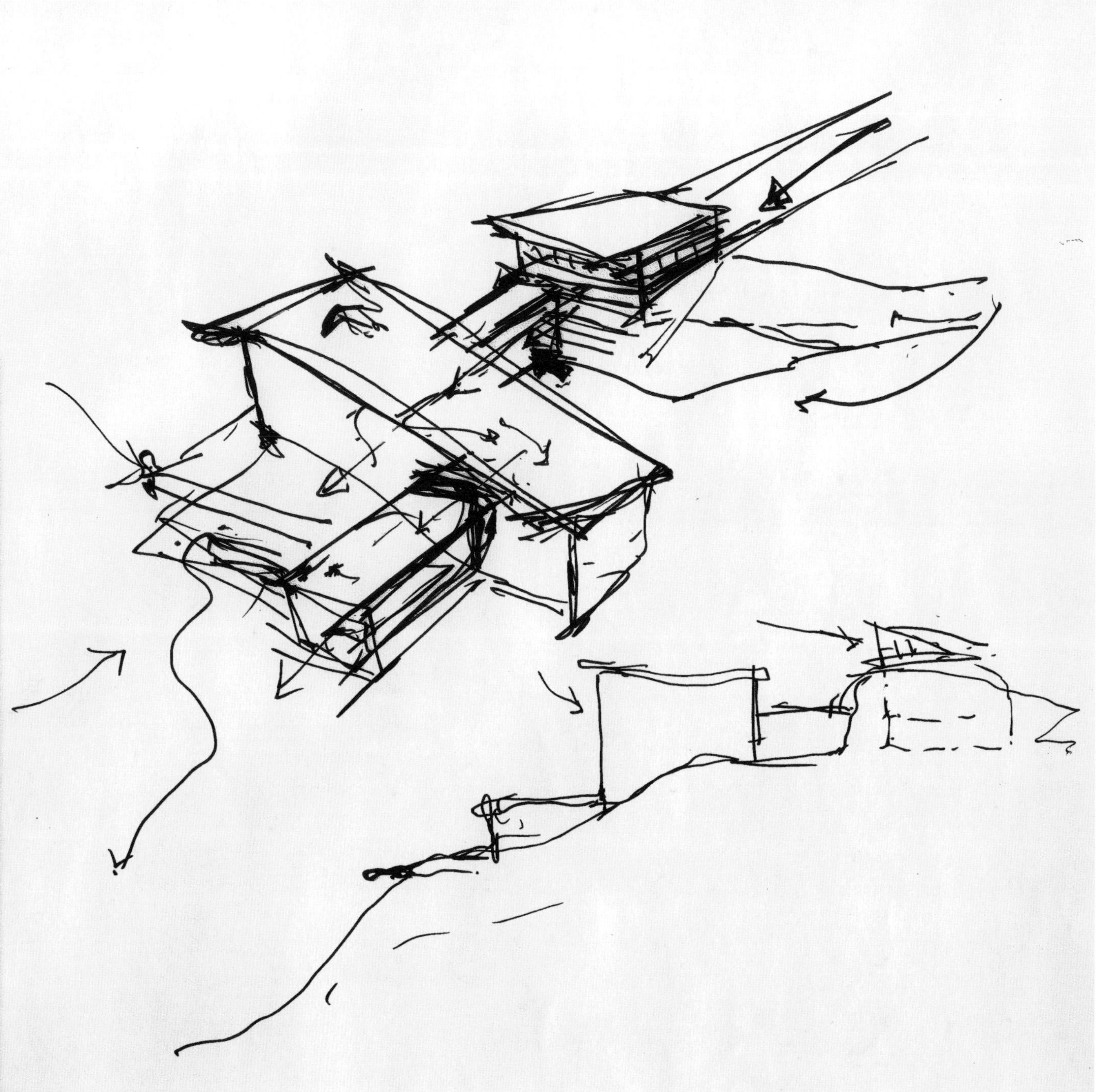

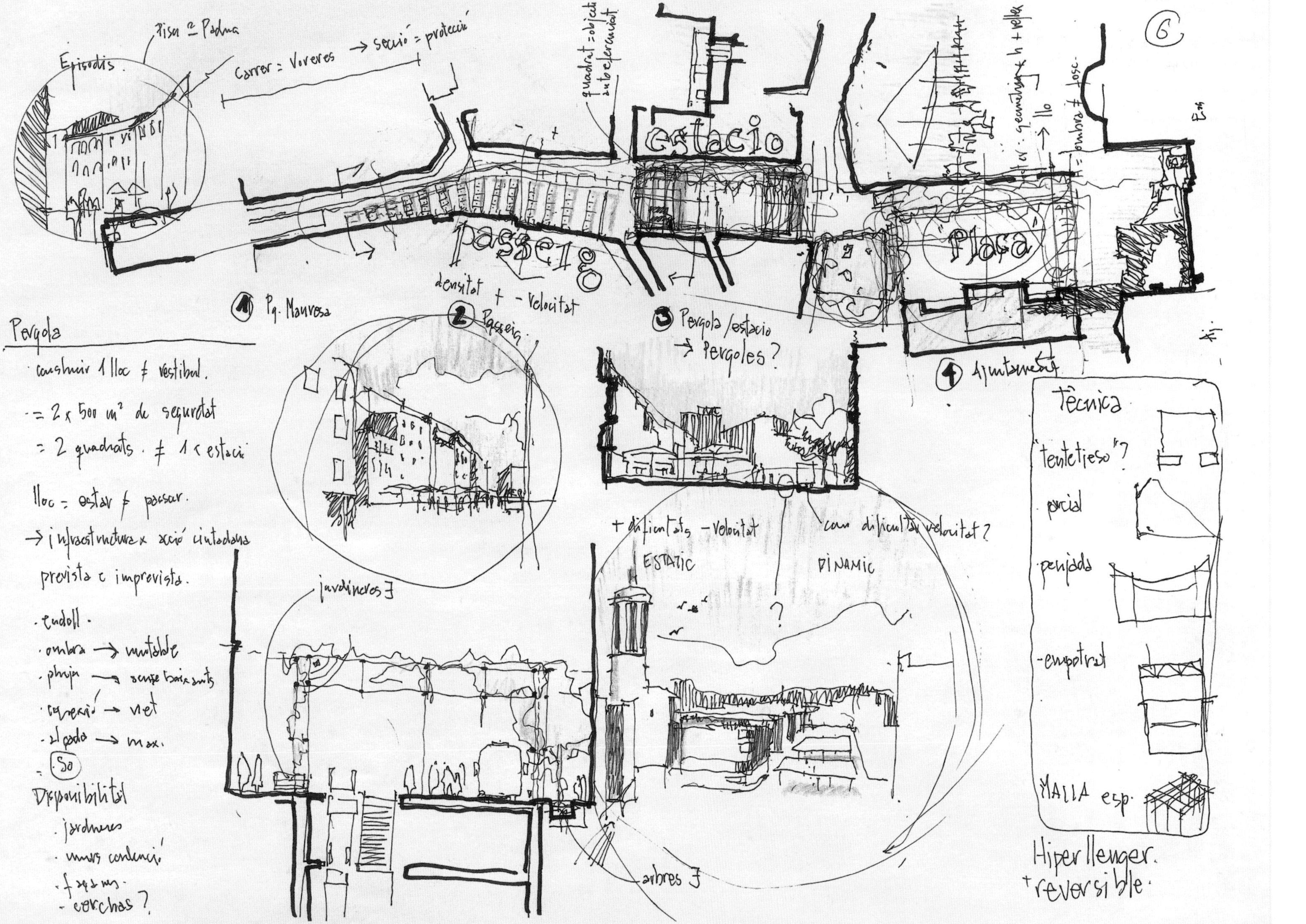
6
Episodis
Carrer = Voreres → secció = protecció
estacio
passeig
plaça
densitat + - velocitat
1 Pq. Manresa
2 Passeig
3 Pergola /estacio
→ Pergoles?
4 Ajuntament
Pergola
construir 1 lloc ≠ vestíbul.
= 2 x 500 m² de seguretat
= 2 quadrats ≠ 1 x estació
lloc = estar ≠ passar.
→ infraestructura x acció ciutadana
prevista i imprevista.
· endoll ·
· ombra → mutable
· pluja → sense baixants
· connexió → net
· il·luminació → max.
· So
Disponibilitat
· jardineres
· murs contenció
· fagames
· corchas?
+ dificultats - velocitat
com dificultar velocitat?
ESTATIC
DINAMIC
jardineres ∃
arbres ∃
Tècnica
"tentetieso"?
parcial
penjada
empotrat
MALLA esp.
Hiperllenger.
+ reversible.

HARQUITECTES

Spain

Featured projects: Main Square 1632 [p. 128]
House 1101 [p. 129, top; pp. 130–31]
House 905 [p. 129, bottom; p. 130, left]
House 1701 [pp. 132, 133]

'The sketch is a means of communication, as well as a good tool to use for analysis and creation, individually and collectively,' note the team at Spanish firm Harquitectes. 'Sketching is timeless, but not indispensable for architects who can communicate and design using other tools. Digital means are necessary to the whole design. Every work that needs precision is done by CAD, and at the end of a project, the digital work will have accounted for 90 per cent of the design time.'

Based in Barcelona, Harquitectes was set up in 2000 and is managed by four partners; David Lorente Ibáñez, Josep Ricart Ulldemolins, Xavier Ros Majó and Roger Tudó Galí. The quartet teach at various architectural schools, and are renowned for their pared-back style.

'Would we be able to work without sketching or other non-digital means?' they ask. 'Perhaps. To create the best design, it is necessary to be able to share knowledge with the entire team, and sketching is the perfect tool for that. On the other hand, models are almost always the best way to explain a project to those members of the team who are not specifically involved in it. Large models (1:20) are also used to show proposals to clients, as they can see at a glance the complexity involved. When a project is complete, the sketches go in the garbage, but a few – especially those drawn in our personal notebooks – survive.'

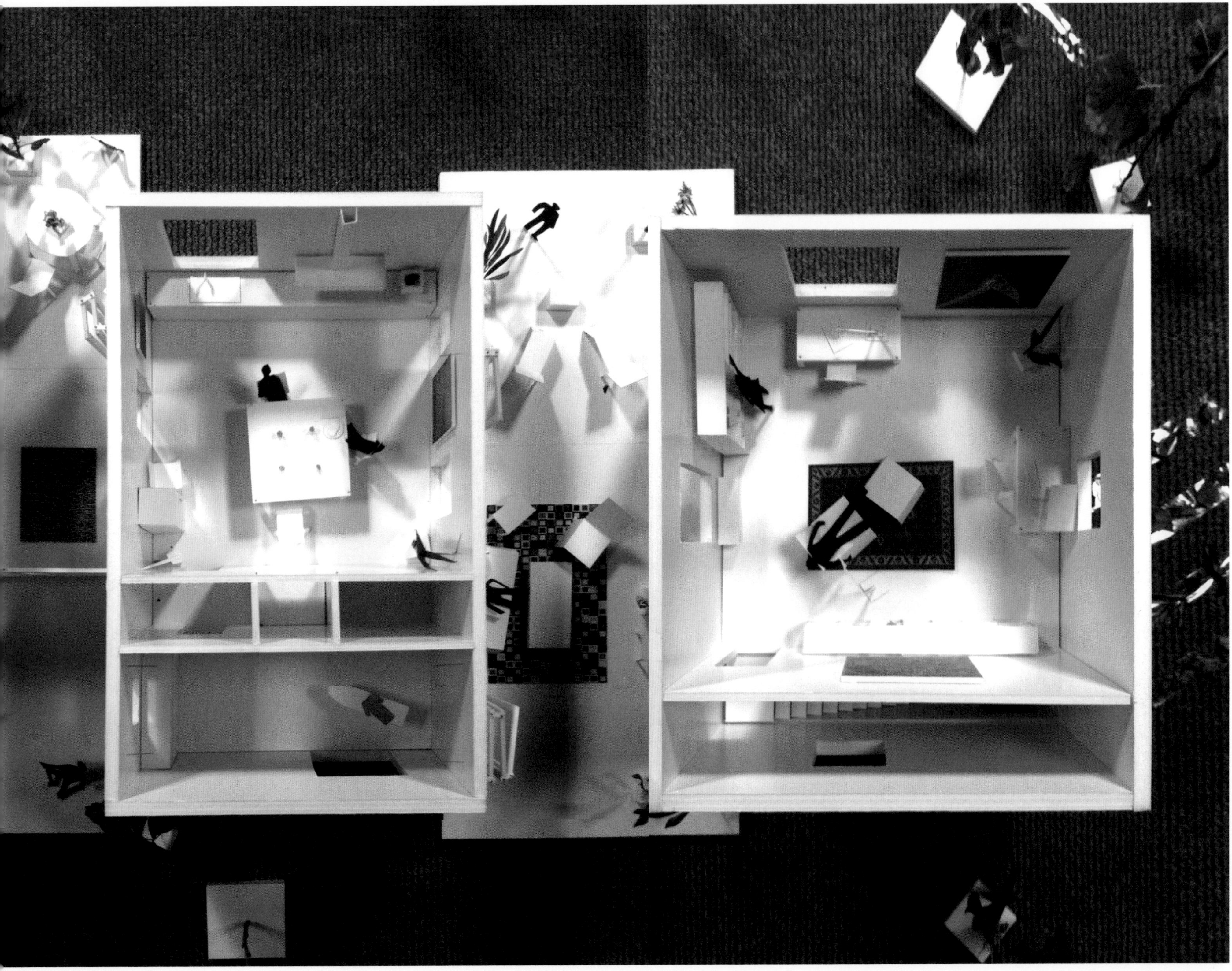

CARL-VIGGO HØLMEBAKK

Norway

Featured project: Torghatten footbridge [pp. 134–7]

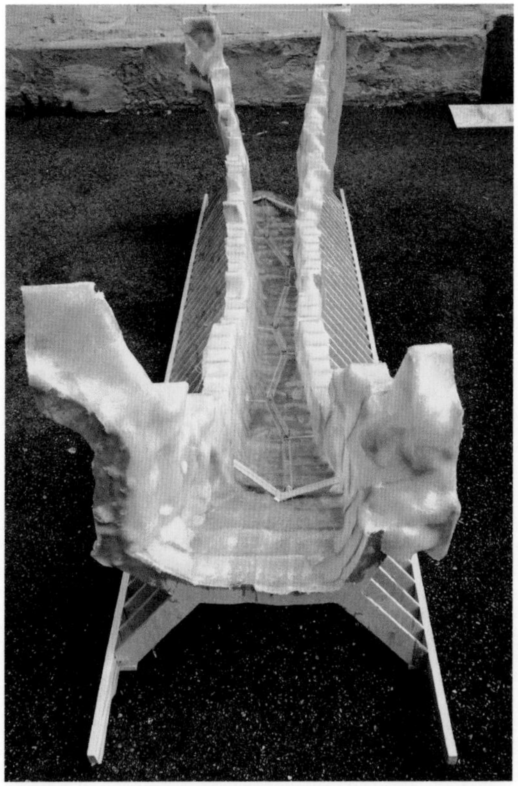

'Most of my sketches are thrown away during the design process,' says Norwegian architect Carl-Viggo Hølmebakk. 'This is OK when the ideas are incorporated into the project, but I can also be seduced by my own sketches and want to keep them. It is a little personal and sentimental, I suppose, to save them and look back at this fragile moment, when the process is over and the project is completed.'

Based in Oslo, Hølmebakk has taught at universities in Europe and the US. He has been nominated for the Mies van der Rohe Pavilion Award three times and honoured in Norway on a number of occasions. His work ranges from public-housing schemes to mountaintop sculptural installations. For the Torghatten footbridge in Brønnøy, he used a combination of design methods, including digital-mapping.

'We created a 3D model to illustrate some initial thoughts,' he says, 'but the tool didn't work, leaving the rock tunnel with no sense of materials, weight or structure. The act of building a physical model was an important door into the project. The wooden frames (still abstract, but with the rationality of the rock), the poisonous casting and hardening of polyester and fibreglass, the lead sheets (also toxic) and the sharp steel wires all gave the design process a particular attention and alertness that seemed important. The modelling somehow reminded us of the site – quite physically.'

When asked if he would be able to work without sketching or some other physical, non-digital means, Hølmebakk's reply sums up his passion for his craft. 'No,' he says. 'Not voluntarily.'

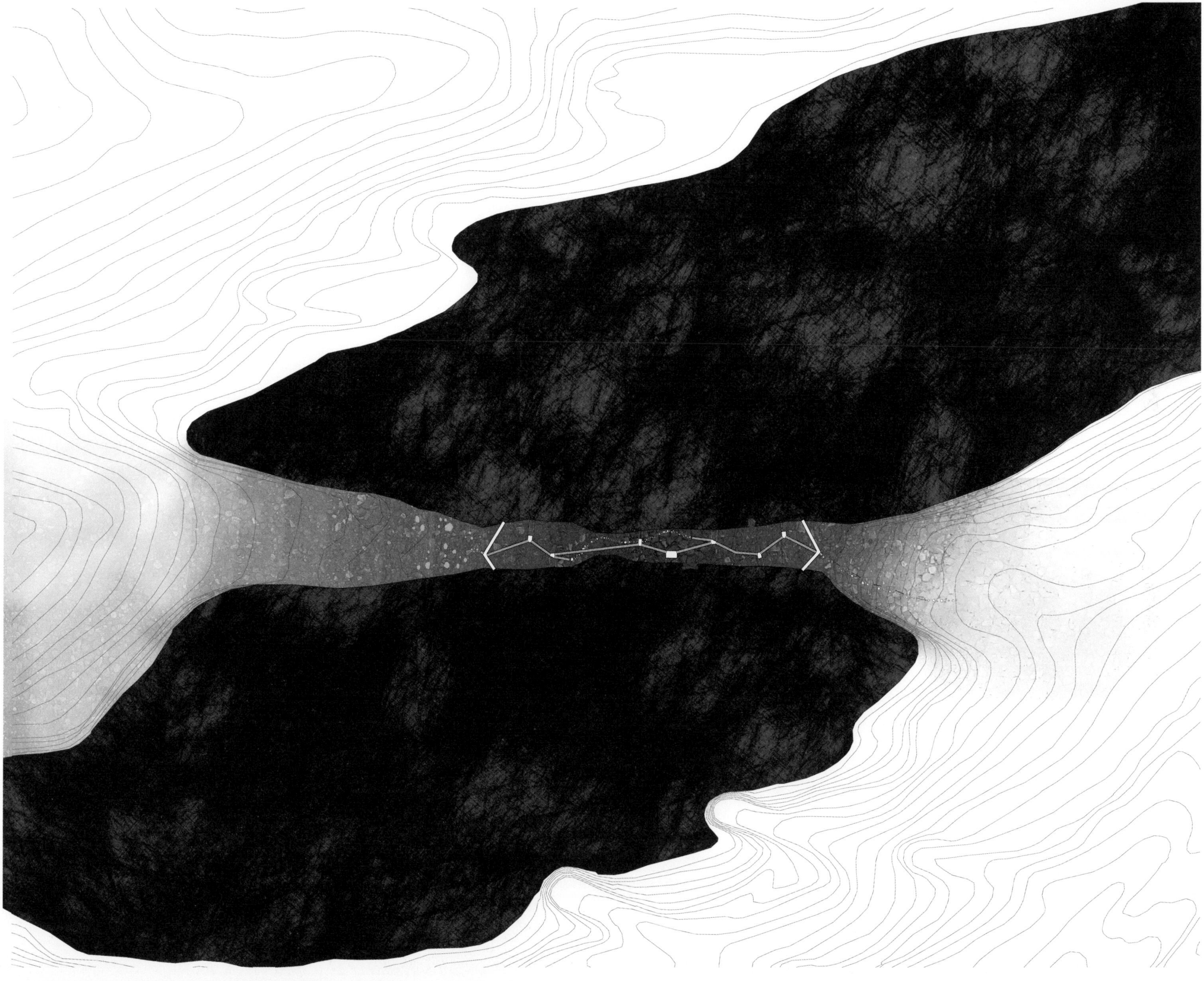

JOHANNA HURME, SASA RADULOVIC & KEN BORTON

5468796 Architecture • Canada

Featured projects: OMS Stage [p. 141]

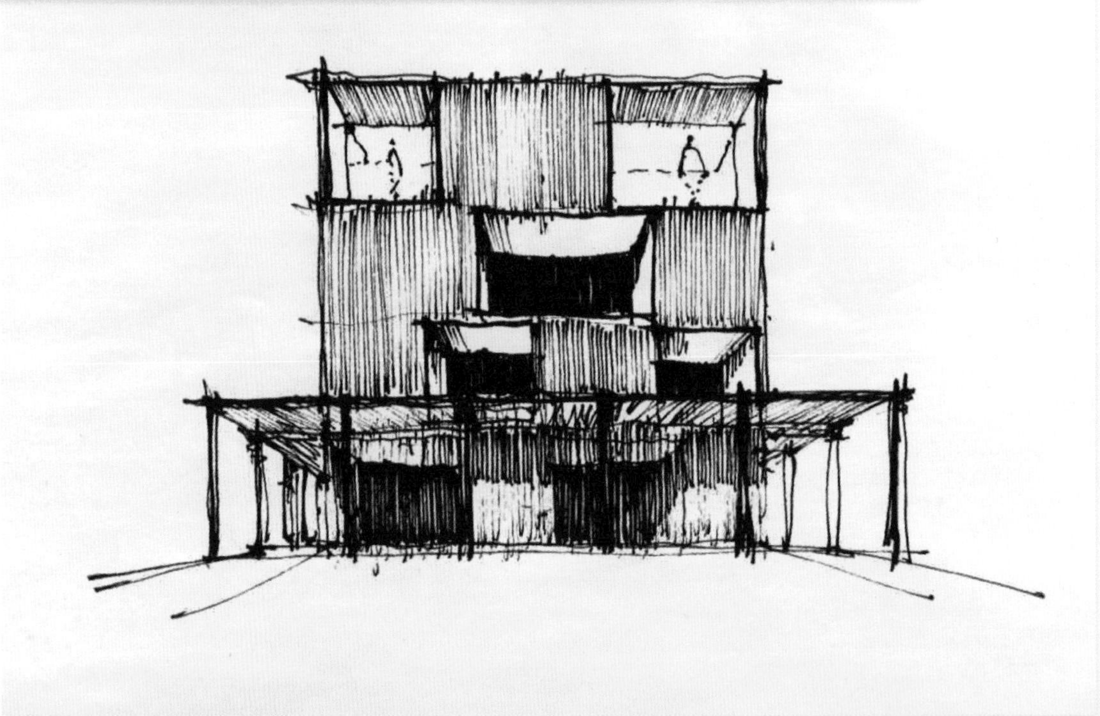

'Sketches aren't precious in our office,' say Johanna Hurme and Sasa Radulovic of 5468796 Architecture, who founded the company in 2007, later joined by Colin Neufeld. 'They are started on whatever scrap paper is available, and team members add to each other's drawings without a second thought. Ideas get layered on top, over and over, until a clarifying sketch is needed.'

Collaboration is the essence of design at this Manitoban firm. The practice – which goes by a series of numbers, rather than a name – has already won critical acclaim and awards in Canada and beyond. The secret of their success, Hurme and Radulovic believe, is their ability to work together: 'The team can work on a sketch simultaneously, and bounce visual and verbal ideas back and forth with instant feedback. There really is no digital equivalent to this that we know of. The physical nature of sketching improves our design work, because it allows us to design collaboratively; the sketch is a perfect companion to verbal communication, because it helps fill in the gaps where words fall short.'

The team uses sketches predominantly to communicate internally, but the pencil will be brandished on occasion in a meeting with clients. However, another physical design tool is king when explaining a project to outsiders: 'Because clients don't have much interaction with the sketches we produce, the physical model is our most important communication tool. Nothing helps them grasp their project like a model they can walk around and view from every angle.'

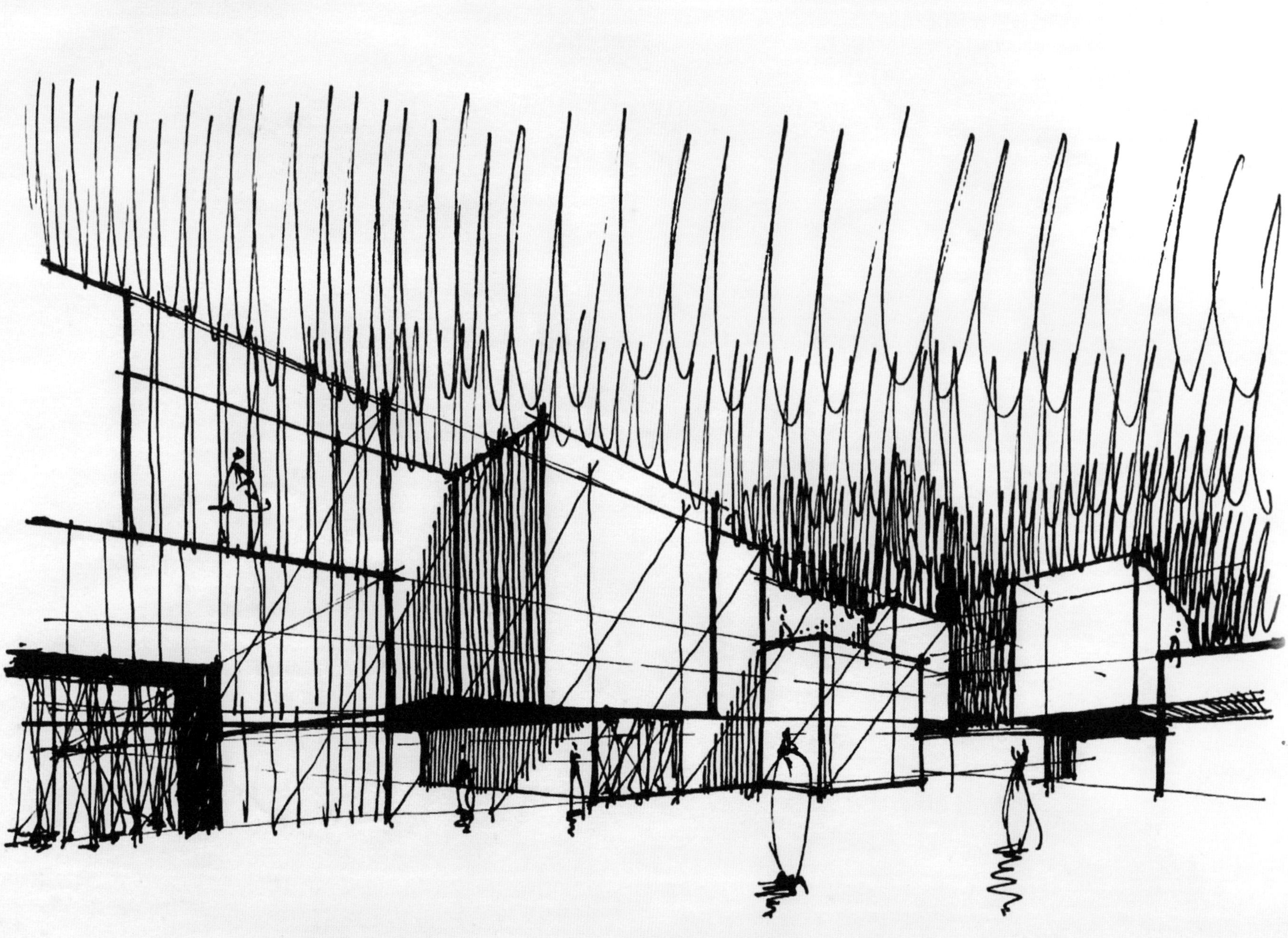

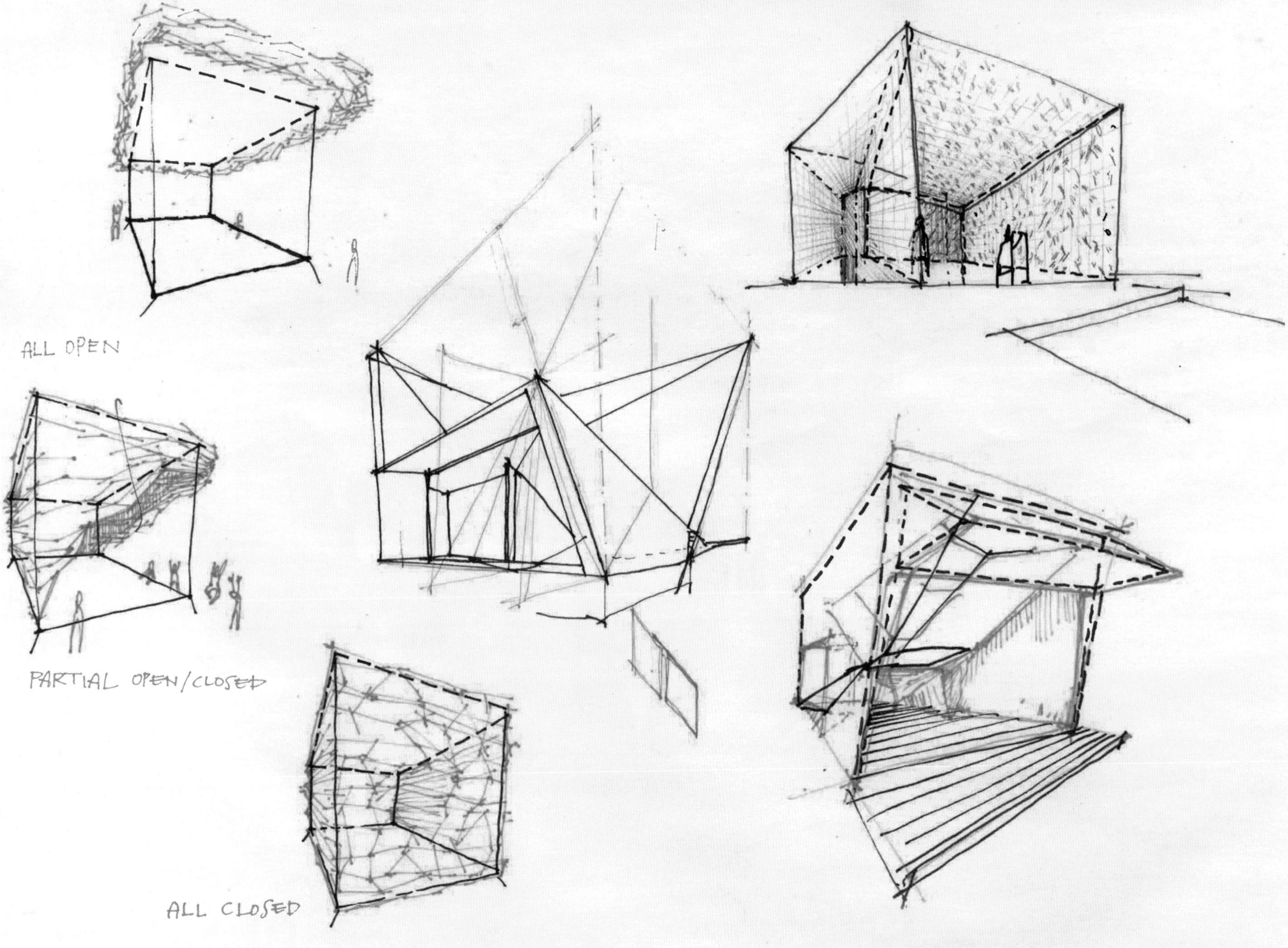
ALL OPEN
PARTIAL OPEN/CLOSED
ALL CLOSED

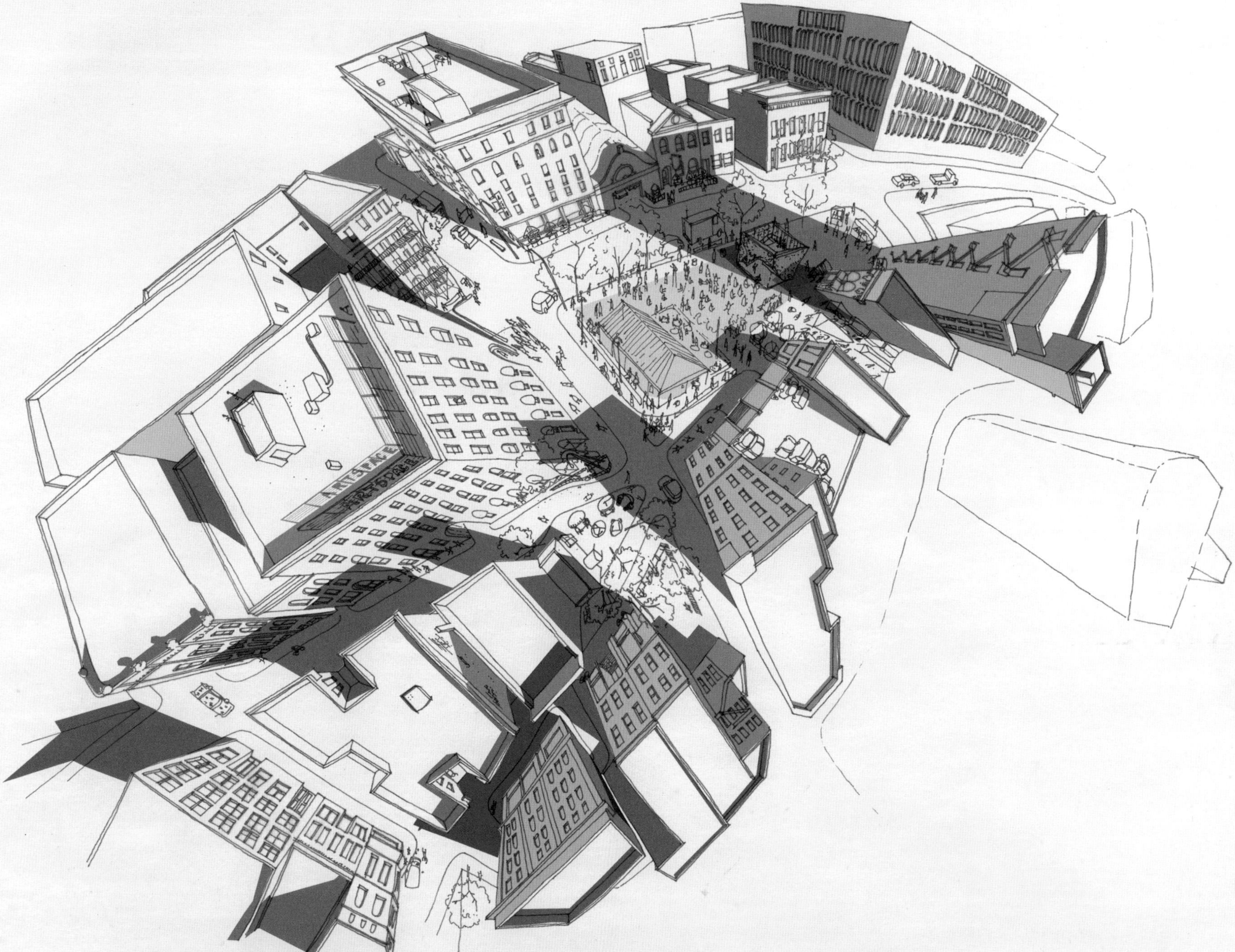
ARTSPACE

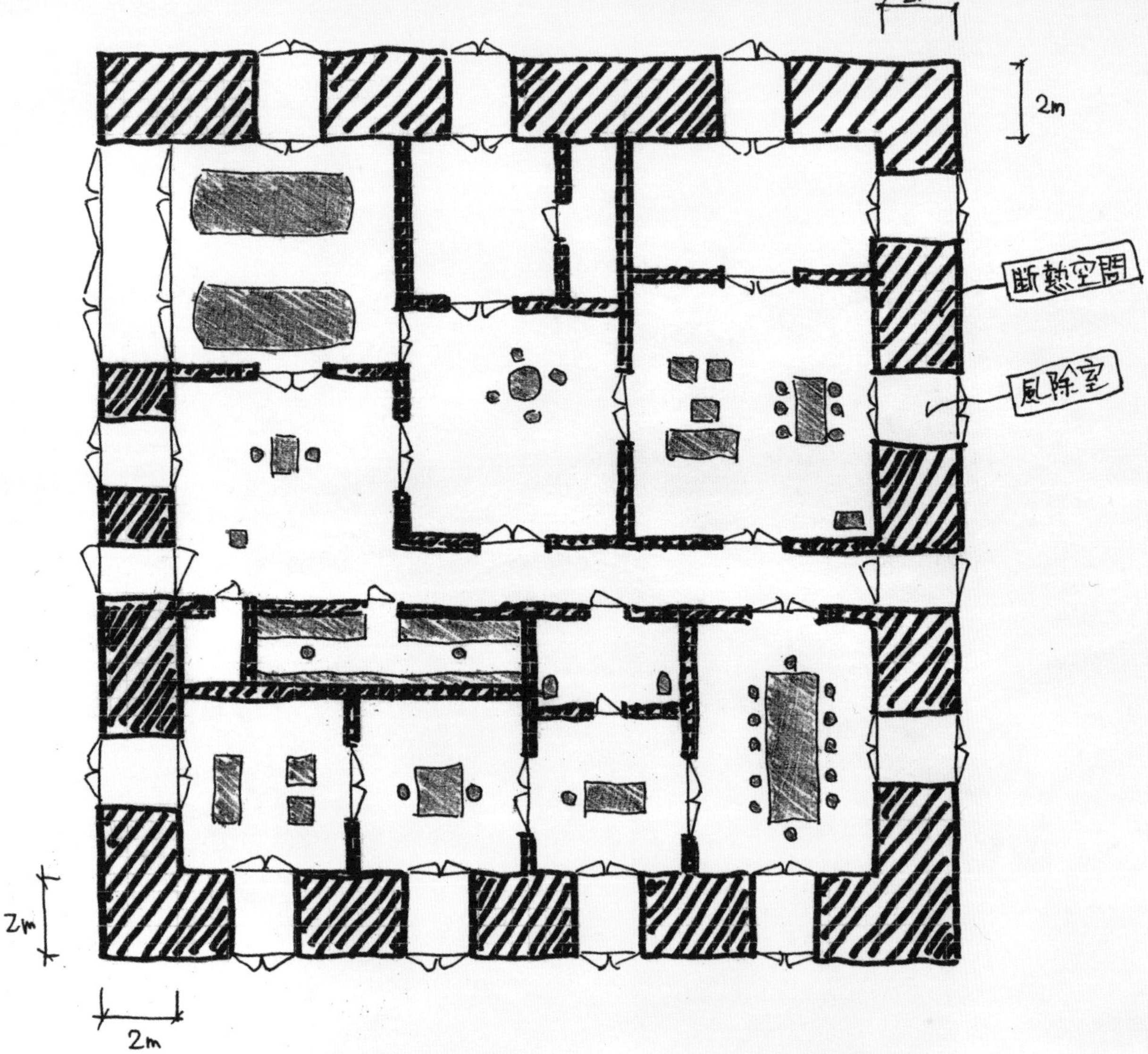
2m
2m
断熱空間
風除室
2m
2m

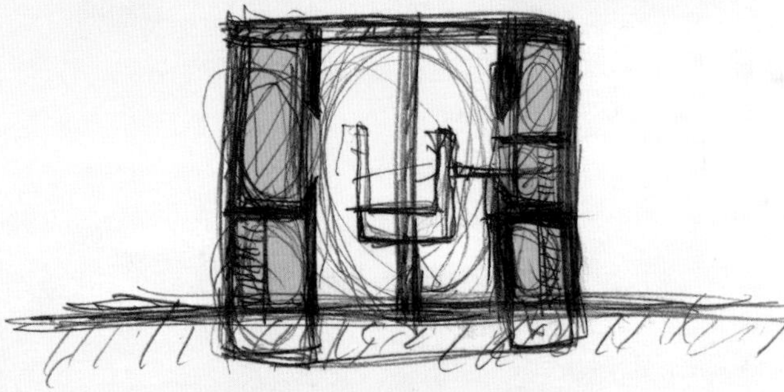

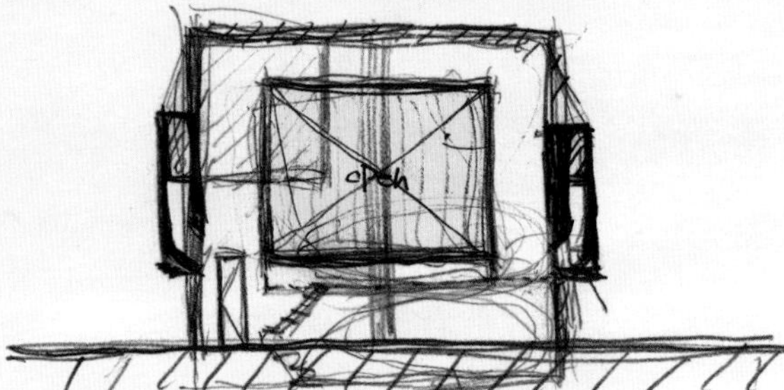
open

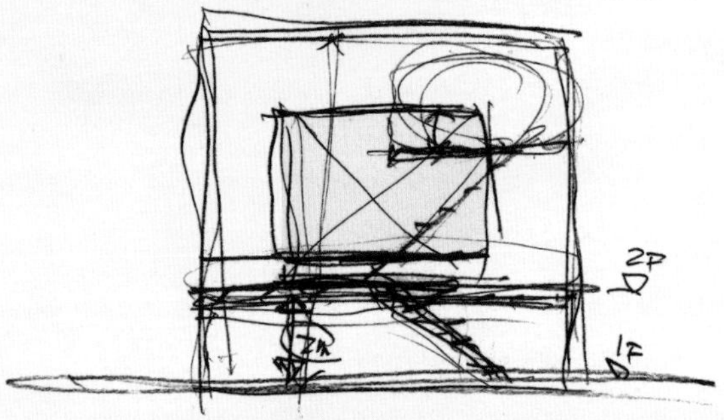
2F
1F

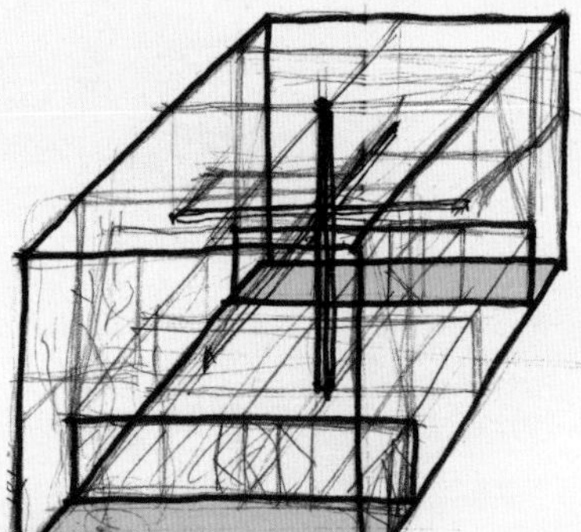

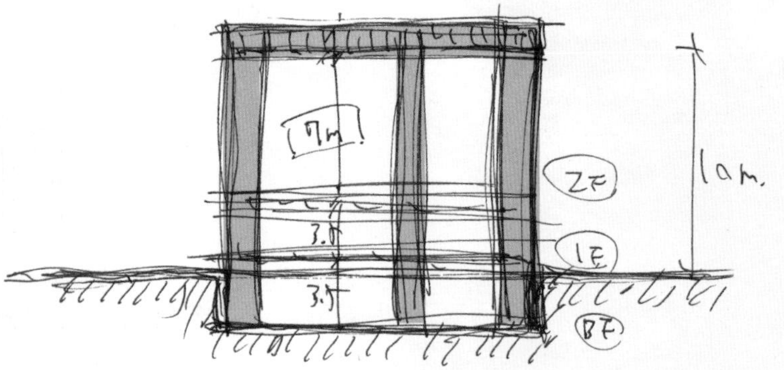
10m.
2F
1F
BF

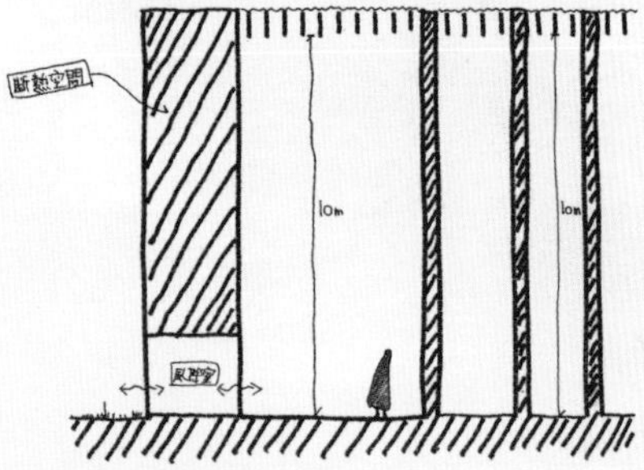
断熱空間
10m
10m
風除室

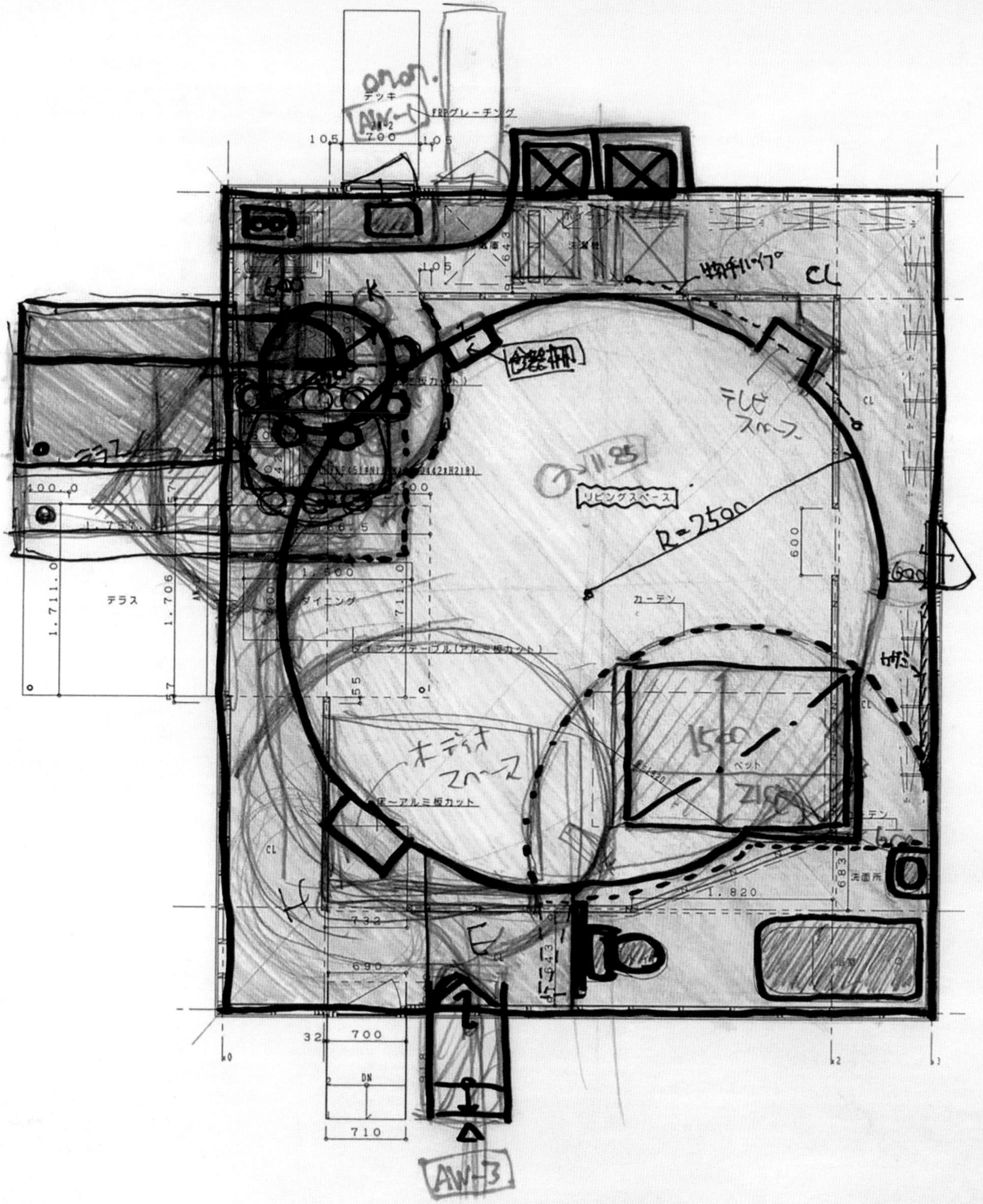

JUN IGARASHI

Jun Igarashi Architects • Japan

Featured projects: Ordos City [p. 142]
Rectangular Forest [pp. 143–45]

'There are times when I sketch a very hazy image, and there are others when I might draw the finished design in a flash,' says architect Jun Igarashi. 'Sketching is a very diverse and complicated task.'

Although still a youngster in the world of architecture (he was born in 1970), Igarashi has already amassed a serious collection of awards and accolades for his work. Marked out as one to watch by the Japan Institute of Architects and the *Architectural Review*, he is also passing on his skills to new designers as an instructor at the Nagoya Institute of Technology.

For Igarashi, sketching is at the crux of every building that he works on. 'Sketches are always the beginning of a design,' he says. 'I make a drawing based upon the sketch, and then sketch again, often directly onto the drawing. This way, I will be able to design and redesign over and over again.'

This architect can work anywhere, from his office to an aeroplane or café, and he sees his hand, and the pencil, as a direct link to his mind. 'The sketch is the perfect method for recording my thoughts,' he says. 'It is also possible to discover unconscious thinking and tap into ideas and inspirations that are not obvious at first. I think the sketch is the most important element or process in design.'

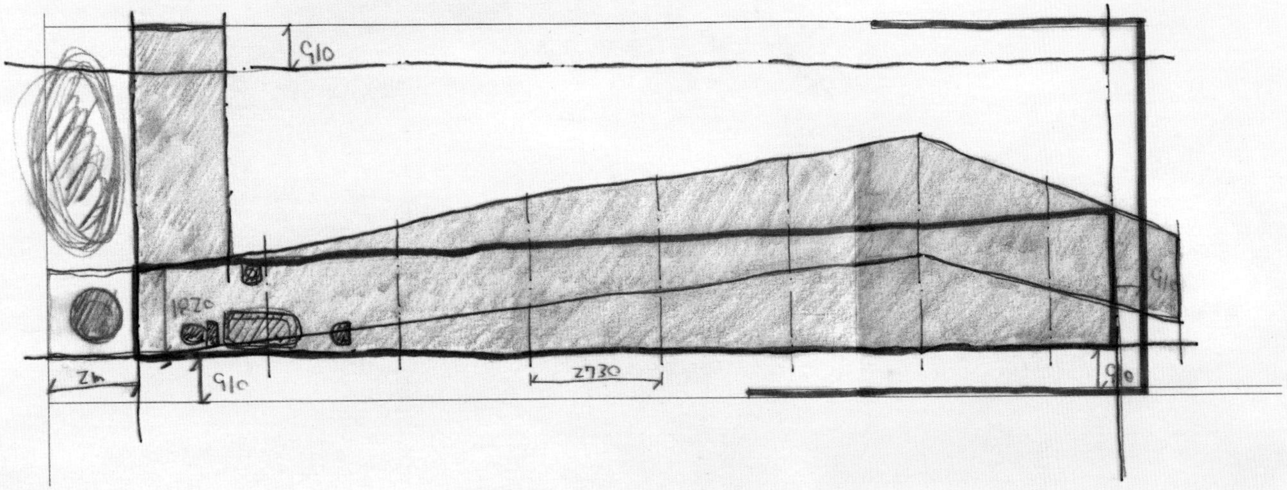
910
1820
2m
910
2730
910

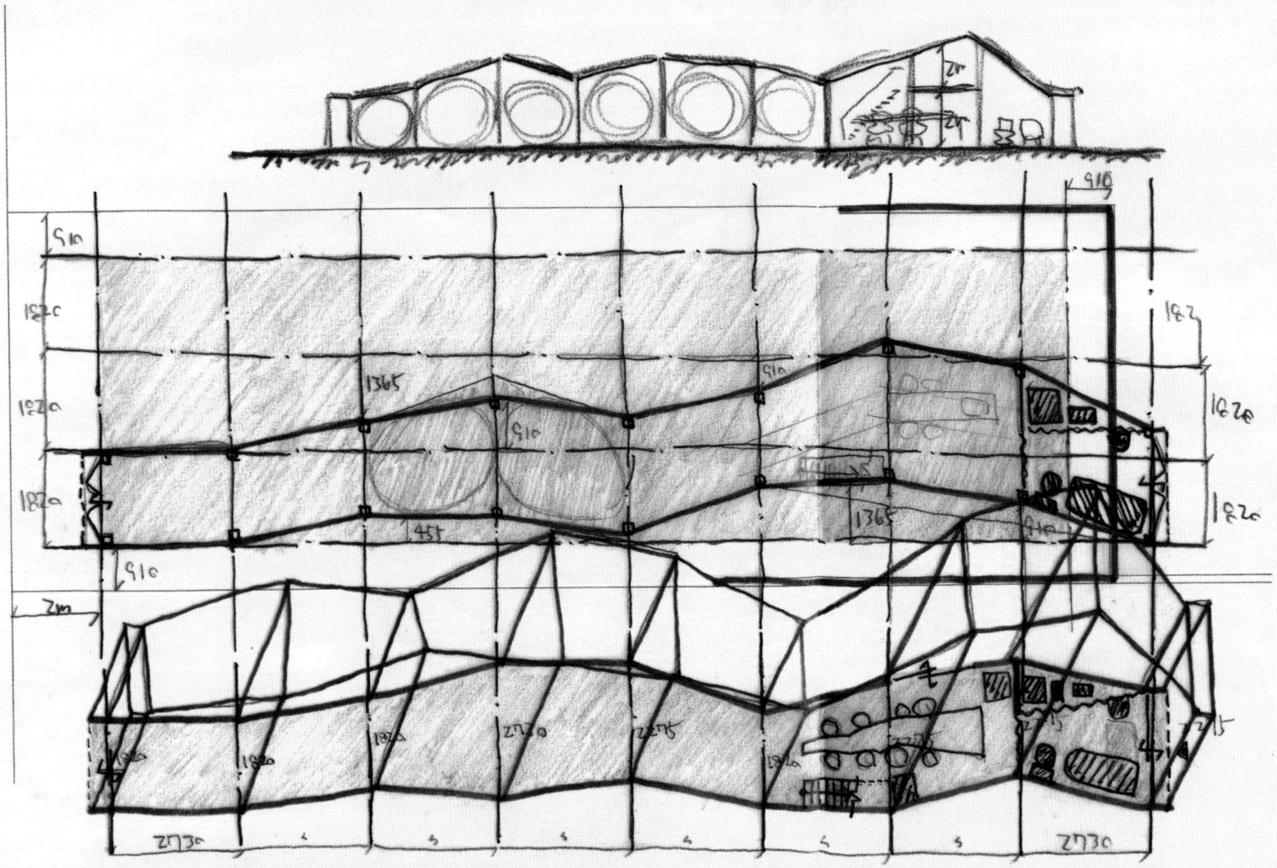
910
910
1820
1820
1820
1365
910
1820
1820
1365
910
2m
2730
2730

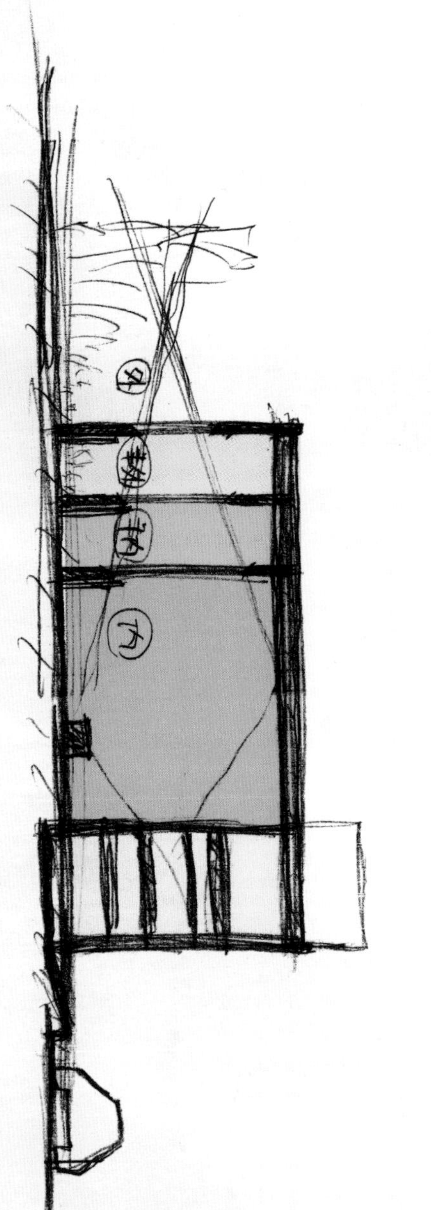

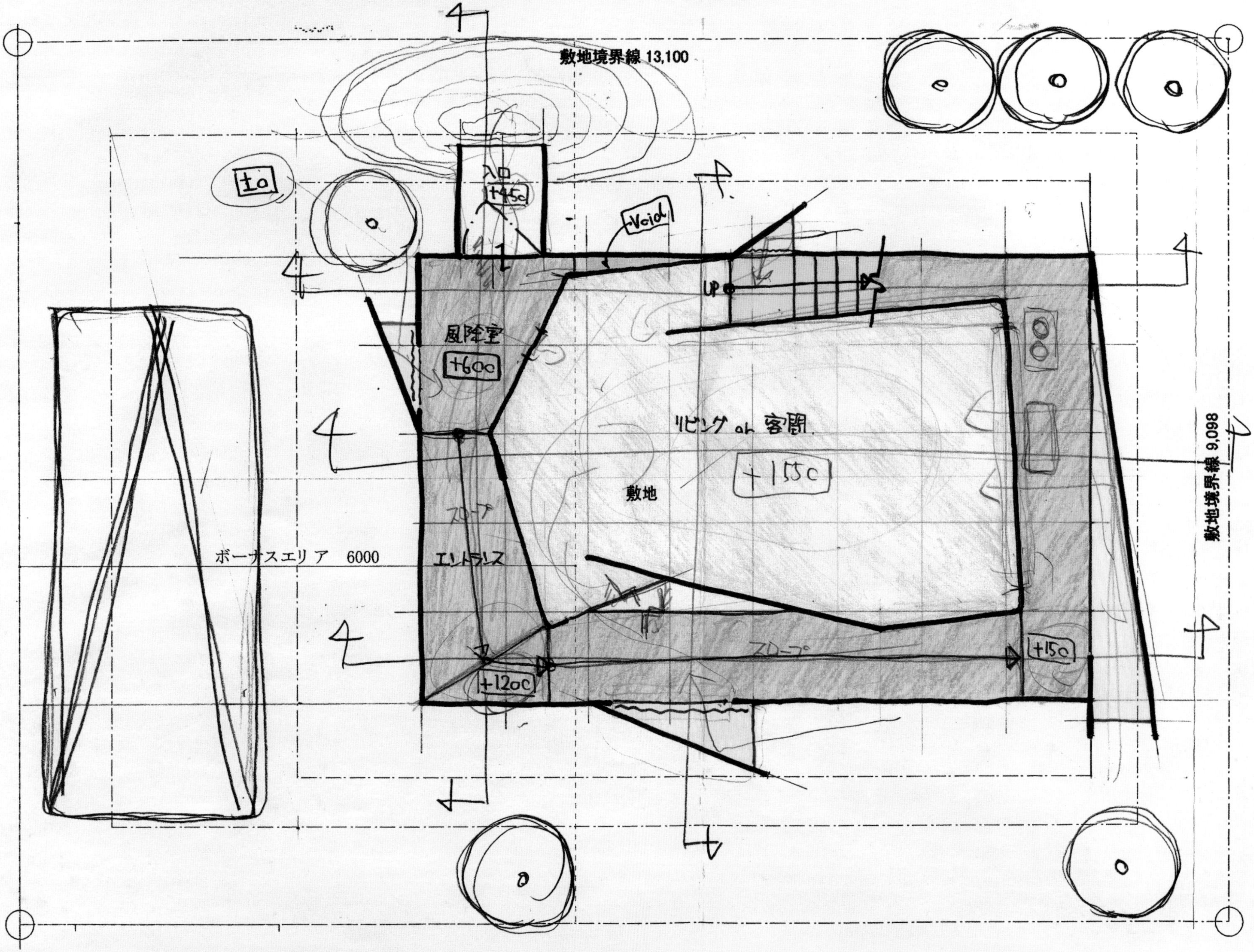
敷地境界線 13,100
敷地境界線 9,098
ボーナスエリア 6000
敷地
±0
入口
+450
Void
UP
風除室
+600
リビング or 客間
+155c
スロープ
エントランス
+120c
+150

ANDERSON INGE

Cambridge Architectural Research • UK

Featured projects: Southampton Row [p. 146]
Basham Park [pp. 146–7] · Mineral County Fairgrounds [pp. 148–49]

'The tool I mainly use for drawing is an all-graphite pencil,' says Anderson Inge of Cambridge Architectural Research. 'Imagine a pencil with the wood bit replaced with more graphite, and you've got it. I've grown dependent on this tool. If you hold it like a scalpel, you can instantly take advantage of the greater width of graphite to use it like a wide brush, allowing me to range freely back and forth between line and tonal stroke.'

Inge is a director at the company, an organization that aims to boost the contribution of research and analysis in the built environment. Trained as an architect, engineer and sculptor, he also lectures at the Architectural Association in London.

'The power of drawing by hand is that it can accommodate uncertainty, and out of the ambiguity and contradictions evolves the design,' he explains. 'Sometimes I draw a picture of something that is beginning to emerge in my mind's eye, but the design will still be gelling as I draw it. I sketch because it allows speculation. Sketching allows me to investigate physical possibilities that don't yet exist. Drawing by hand, in the moment, is the most important skill an architect can have.'

He continues: 'When I take a new group of students for our first drawing session at the British Museum, I pre-empt their anxiety by telling them straight out that strangers looking over their shoulders are going to be actively judging their sketches. I tell them that, like a bum note when singing, hit it with confidence and they'll think you're a pro.'

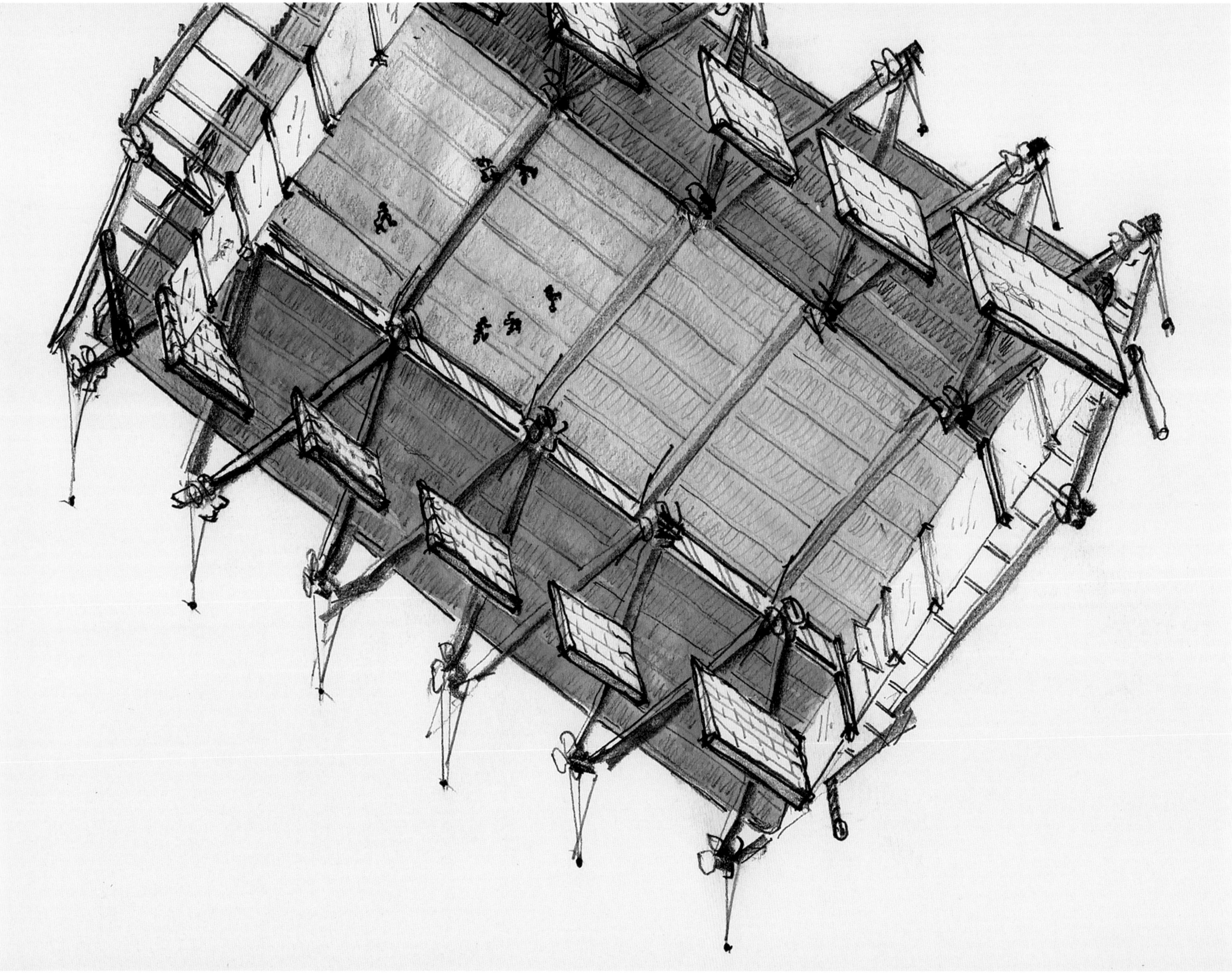

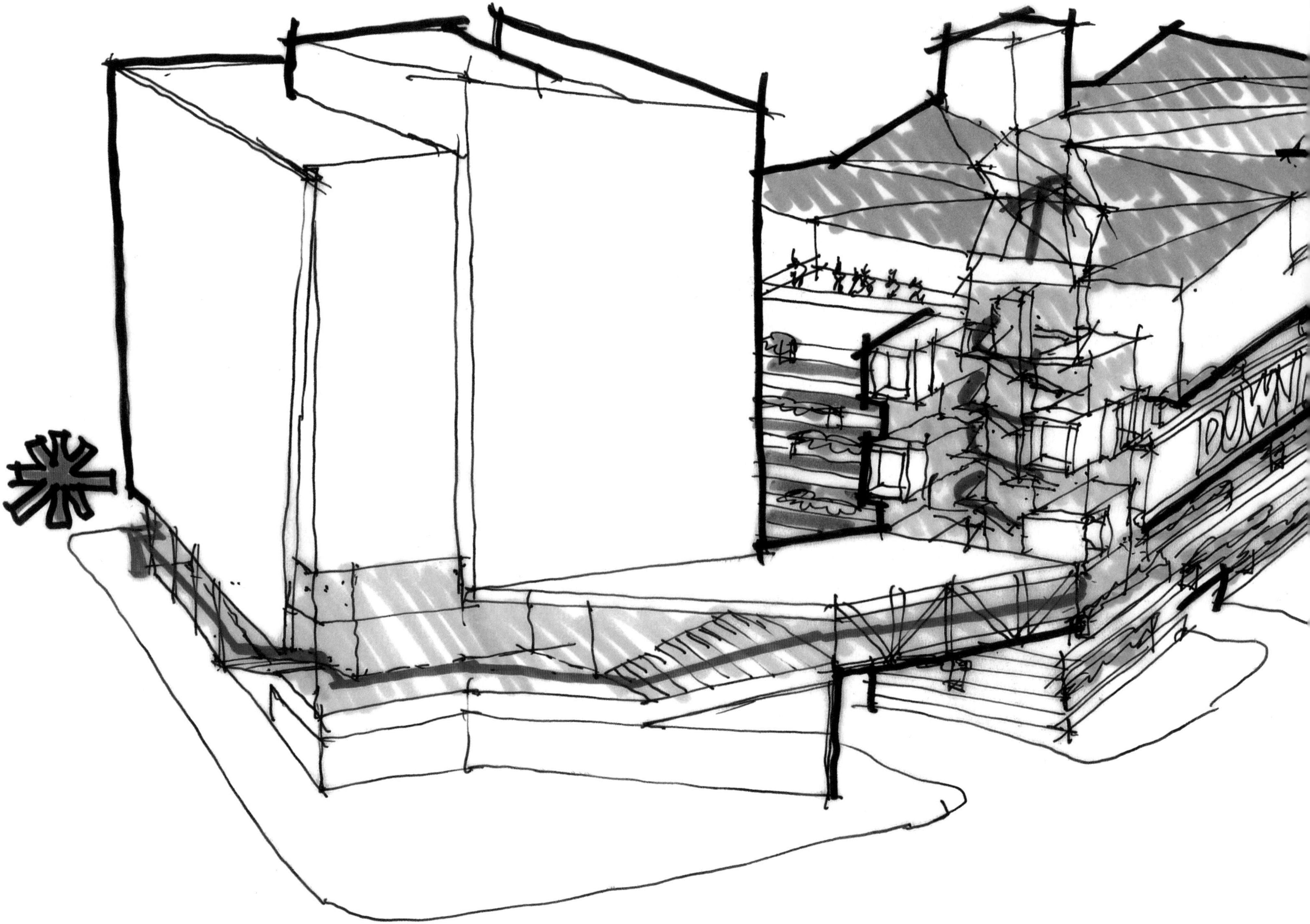

LES KLEIN
& CAROLINE ROBBIE

Quadrangle • Canada

'I sketch in layers,' says Les Klein, principal of Quadrangle, a Toronto-based practice that has won awards for new build, retrofit, domestic and international projects in a range of sectors, from multi-unit residential buildings to commercial headquarters.

'The sketches are almost always slower than my thoughts,' he continues, 'but they help determine the basic parameters of a project and form the germ of a design concept. The process of sketching engenders a higher level of understanding – there is a connection between the brain and the hand that is very palpable.'

Fellow principal and head of interiors Caroline Robbie agrees. 'The connection between what is in your head as you work your way through the design process and the act of drawing is fundamental to human creativity,' she explains. 'That hasn't changed with the digitization of the architectural process, as evidenced by the popularity of sketch-stylus/palette-digital hardware. I tend to sketch in a lateral-thinking, exploratory way. Initial thoughts on paper may be completely unrelated to the design problem, but at other times I use sketches to communicate a very linear process.'

Klein takes a different approach: 'The ideas arise out of a layering of sketches that explore the problem in higher and higher levels of detail. For me, this process works from the largest macro- to the smallest micro-scale.'

JAMES VON KLEMPERER

Kohn Pedersen Fox • USA

Featured projects: One Vanderbilt [p. 154]
One Nine Elms [pp. 154–5]

'You don't always know what you're going to draw when you pick up a pencil, so we repeat patterns we can barely discern,' says James von Klemperer. 'We make old mistakes in new ways. This inventive aspect of drawing, which almost goes beyond the mind of the artist, is a very important part of what sketching offers me.'

As president and design principal at Kohn Pedersen Fox, Von Klemperer has a strong influence over the way in which buildings are designed throughout this six-office, 550-employee firm with a global reach. 'At KPF, we work in teams with multiple people drawing by hand and by computer, and need to be able to combine both manual and digital media' he says.

'Often, I will sketch a very basic concept for a new project, which my colleagues will then develop into a specific shape or form,' he continues. 'This might come back as a carefully formulated computer drawing, which I rework until eventually we arrive at the ideal solution. It's a bit like a relay race, with different means of representation used in sequence to make a whole. Some of my most enjoyable drawings have been made with tracing paper over a computer drawing, because it provided a great 3D skeleton to embellish.'

He concludes: 'Depending on the kind of pencil you use, sketching can be pretty gutsy. I use China Markers, which are thick, waxy pencils. For me, they seem to draw out the big idea and make you commit yourself to the basic aspect of a building. It is important not to begin with decorative fussiness, but to think in these bold terms.'

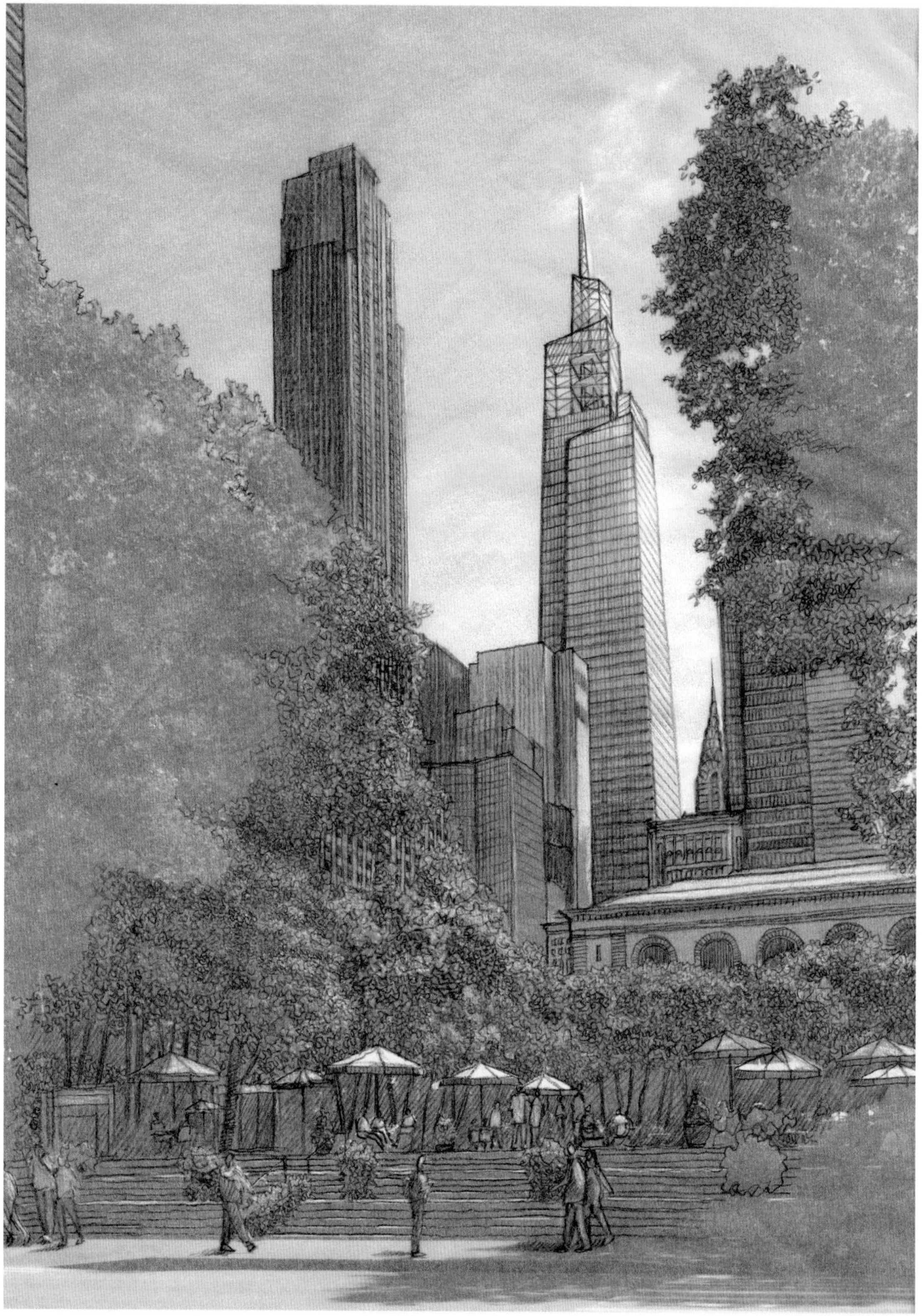

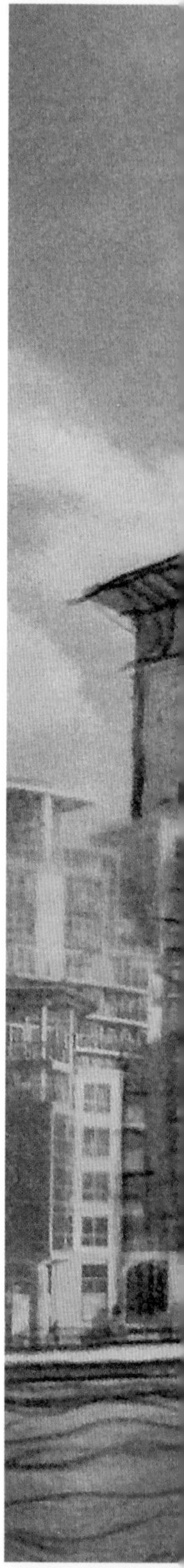

TIFFG

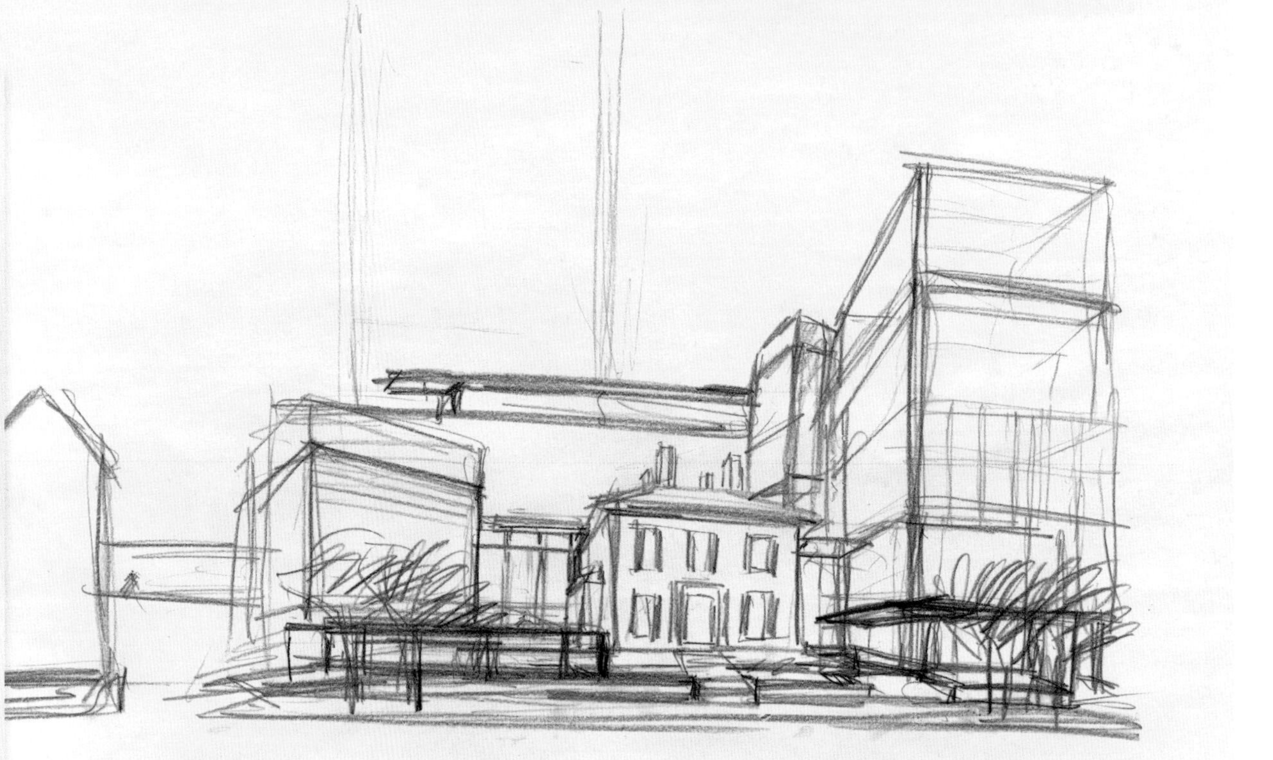

JARVIS ST.

NATIONAL BALLET SCHOOL

BRUCE KUWABARA

KPMB Architects • Canada

Featured projects: TIFF Bell Lightbox [pp. 156, left; 157]
National Ballet School of Canada [p. 156, top]
Kellogg School of Management [p. 156, bottom]

'Like the opening moves in a game of chess or the basic structure of a jazz composition, my sketches provide a generative idea and a formal direction that launch the project forward and form the basis for a series of ideas,' says Bruce Kuwabara, founding partner at the Toronto-based KPMB Architects.

'My drawings sometimes act as the opening to the greater development of a project, many of which are large and complex. The process of advancing the design goes back and forth between sketches, digital modelling and revisions, developing the ideas and the collateral spatial implications and potentials in our work.'

Along with two other partners – Marianne McKenna and Shirley Blumberg – Kuwabara leads the 100-strong firm, which has received over 250 awards. Each of the founding partners are recipients of the Order of Canada for their contribution to Canadian culture and society.

'The sketch launches an idea,' Kuwabara concludes. 'Few of my sketches are fully formulated ideas, but are part of an iterative process that moves towards greater design integration and expression of the construction and making of a building and landscape. My sketches are often reactive and very impulsive; some are drawn over other drawings as a way of editing and recording changes in the design direction. They are made for the design team, and only a select few are shown to clients and consultants.'

CHRISTOPHER LEE

Serie Architects • UK

Featured projects: Satsang Hall Complex [pp. 158–9]
Jameel Arts Centre [pp. 160–1]
Nodeul Dream Island Competition [pp. 162–3]
RCA Battersea Campus Competition [pp. 164–5]

'I often share my sketches with clients in the early phases of a project, and sometimes sketch in front of them during discussions,' notes Christopher Lee of Serie Architects. 'They genuinely enjoy this process, as they get involved in the project's conception. Sketches are a good way to show quickly what works and what doesn't.'

Founded in 2008 by Lee in London and Kapil Gupta in Mumbai, the company now also has offices in Singapore and Beijing. The practice sprang to prominence by winning international design competitions that included the Singapore State Courts Complex and the Jameel Arts Centre in Dubai.

Lee sketches in a way that is iterative, working out a problem over several scales and elements, and notes that a typical process will involve plans, sections, elevations and perspectives, all sketched out within the same few pages. He then goes on to model his designs in digital format, using Rhino software, but believes in the 'physical' of architectural design.

'The sketch has a certain looseness and ambiguity, and allows an idea to evolve as the same idea gets drawn over and over again,' he explains. 'I prefer pencil, as it allows different line weights, thicknesses, construction lines, shades. I sketch to clarify and to communicate my ideas. Sketching is very important, as the pencil is the only mediator between imagination and its formalization on paper. This process is liberating, as it is not reliant on a scripted digital command.'

SATSANG HALL

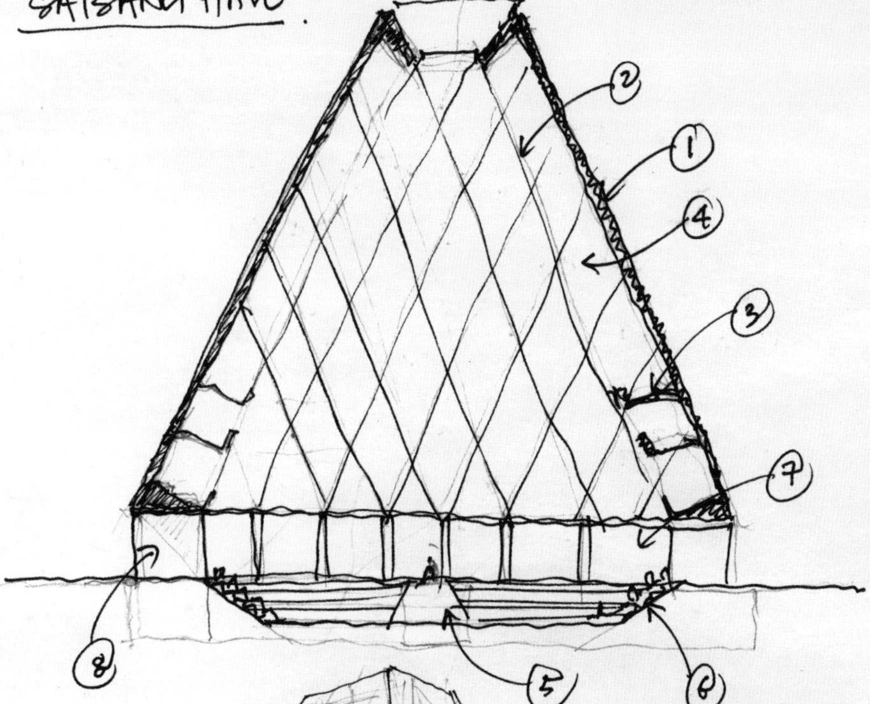

1. MARBLE CLADDING
2. CONCRETE FRAME EXPOSED
3. BALCONY SEATING

~~4. OPEN [illegible]~~

4. MARBLE INFILL
5. GURU'S PEDESTAL
6. TIERED SEATING
7. GLAZING OR OPEN
8. THIN FINS/ COLUMN

OTHER BUILDINGS

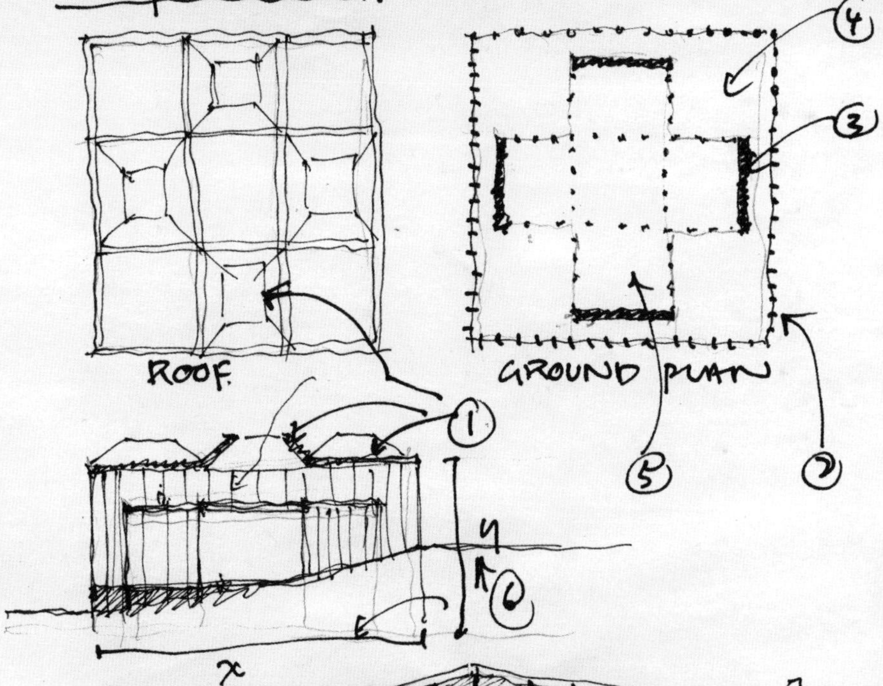

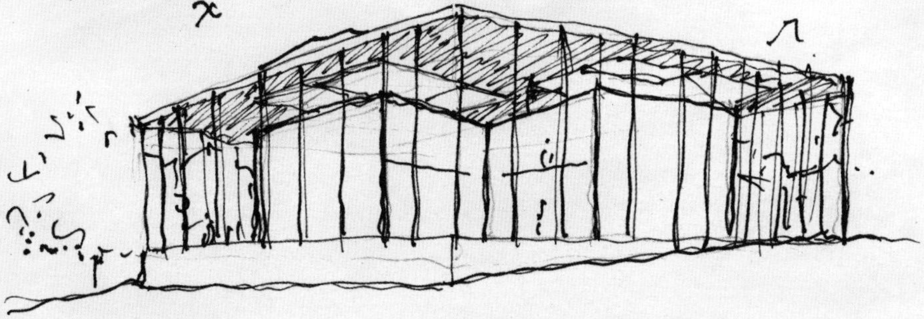

1. PYRAMIDAL ROOF (SLOPE ROOF PROFILE FOR CONSERVATIVES)
2. THIN/SLENDER COLUMNS
3. SOLID WALLS
4. SHELTERED COURT
5. INNER/PROGRAM SPACES
6. X/Y : CAN HAVE DIFF. PROPORTIONS FOR DIFF. BUILDINGS.

ASHRAM 2/2 9.8.12

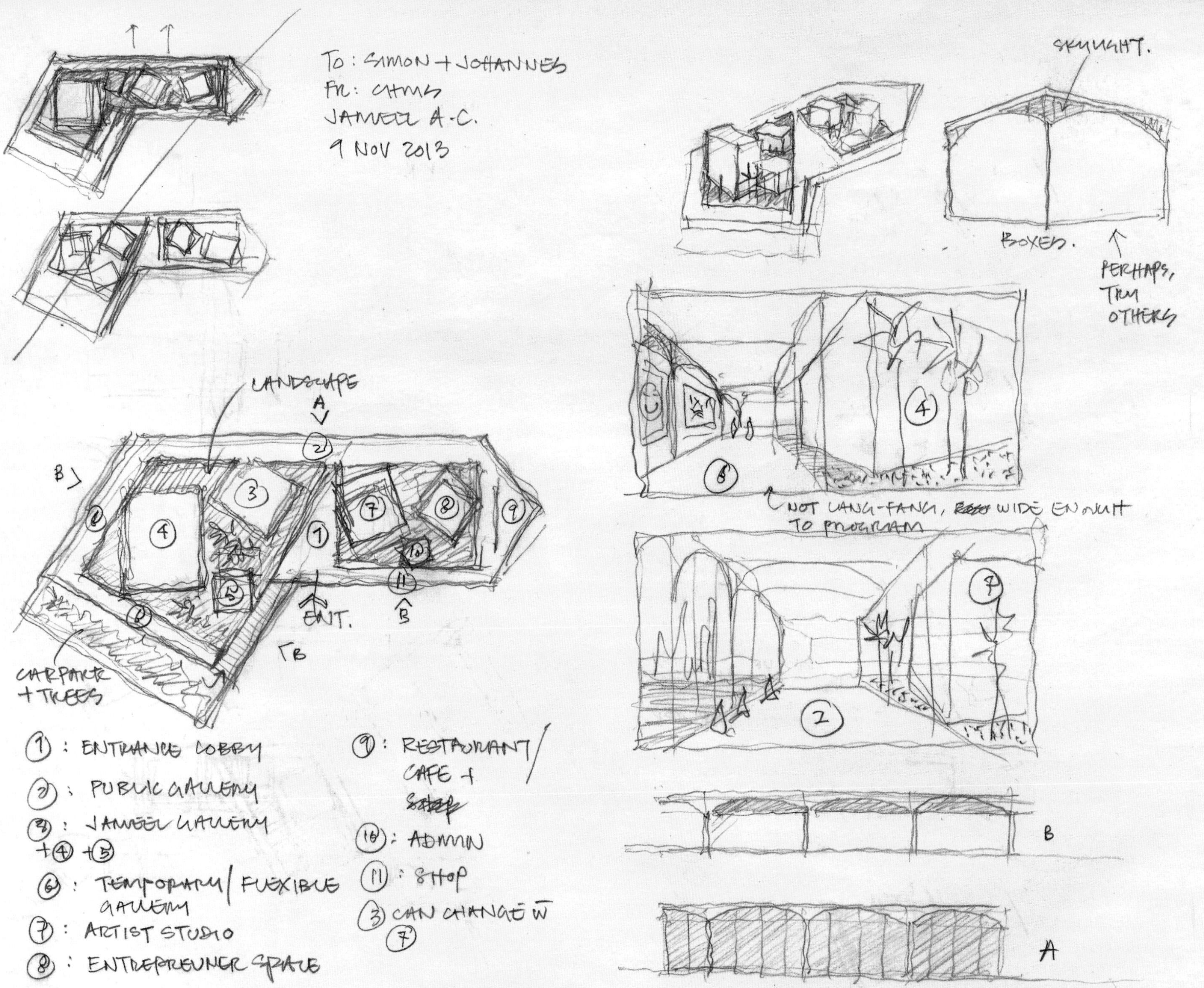
TO: SIMON + JOHANNES
FR: CHRIS
JAMEEL A.C.
9 NOV 2013
SKYLIGHT.
BOXES.
PERHAPS, TRIM OTHERS
LANDSCAPE
A
B
ENT.
CARPARK + TREES
NOT LANG-FANG, WIDE ENOUGH TO PROGRAM
1 : ENTRANCE LOBBY
2 : PUBLIC GALLERY
3 : JAMEEL GALLERY + 4 + 5
6 : TEMPORARY / FLEXIBLE GALLERY
7 : ARTIST STUDIO
8 : ENTREPREUNER SPACE
9 : RESTAURANT / CAFE + SHOP
10 : ADMIN
11 : SHOP
3 CAN CHANGE W 7

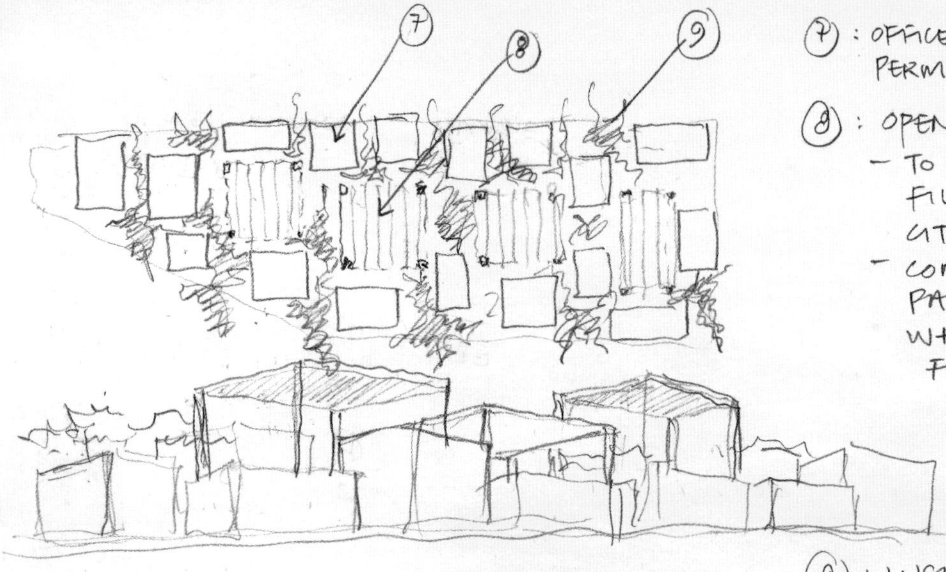

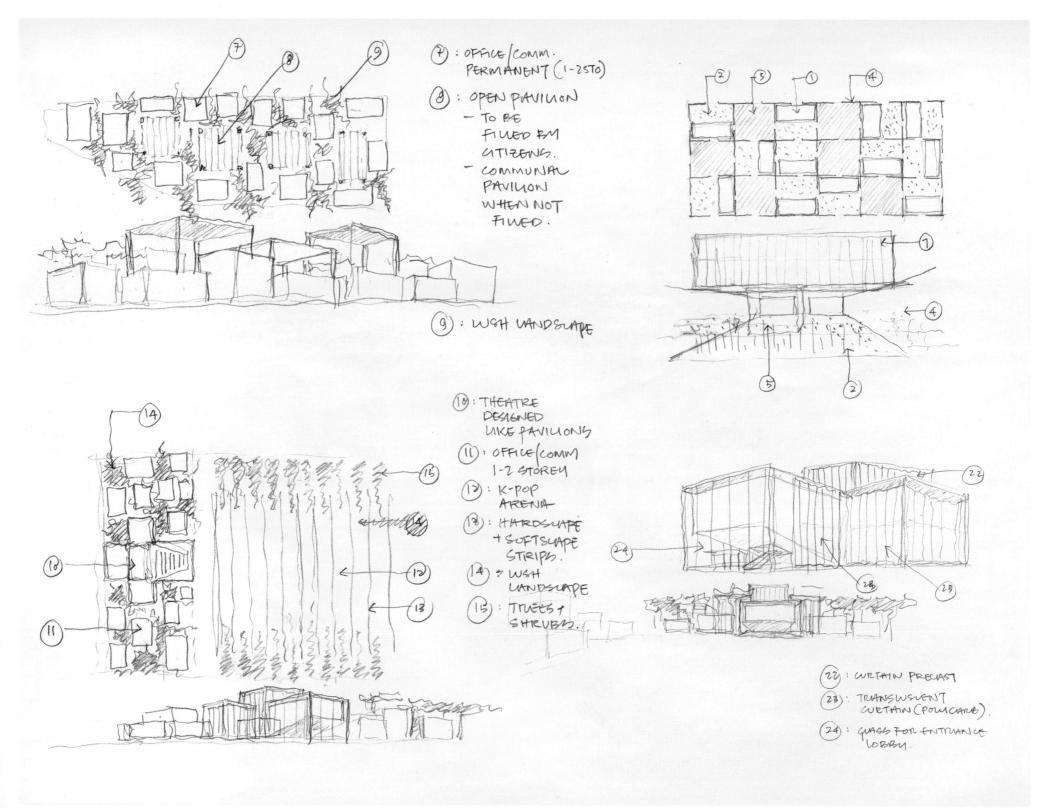

(7) : OFFICE/COMM. PERMANENT (1-2STO)

(8) : OPEN PAVILION
- TO BE FILLED BY CITIZENS.
- COMMUNAL PAVILION WHEN NOT FILLED.

(9) : LUSH LANDSCAPE

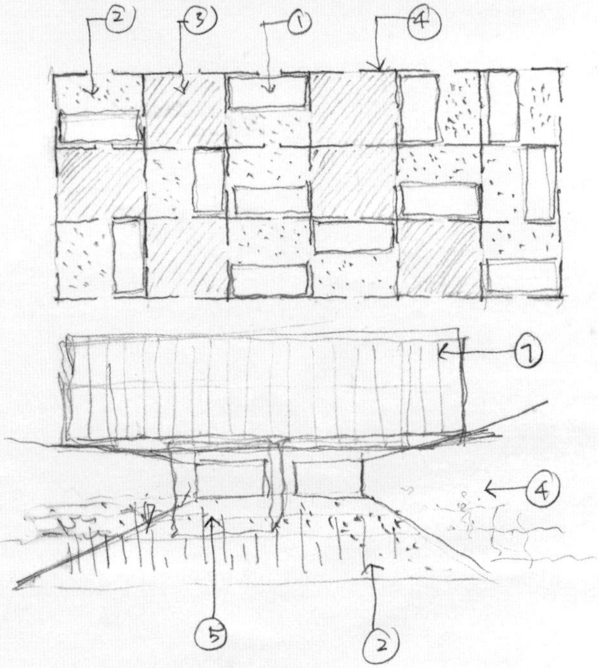

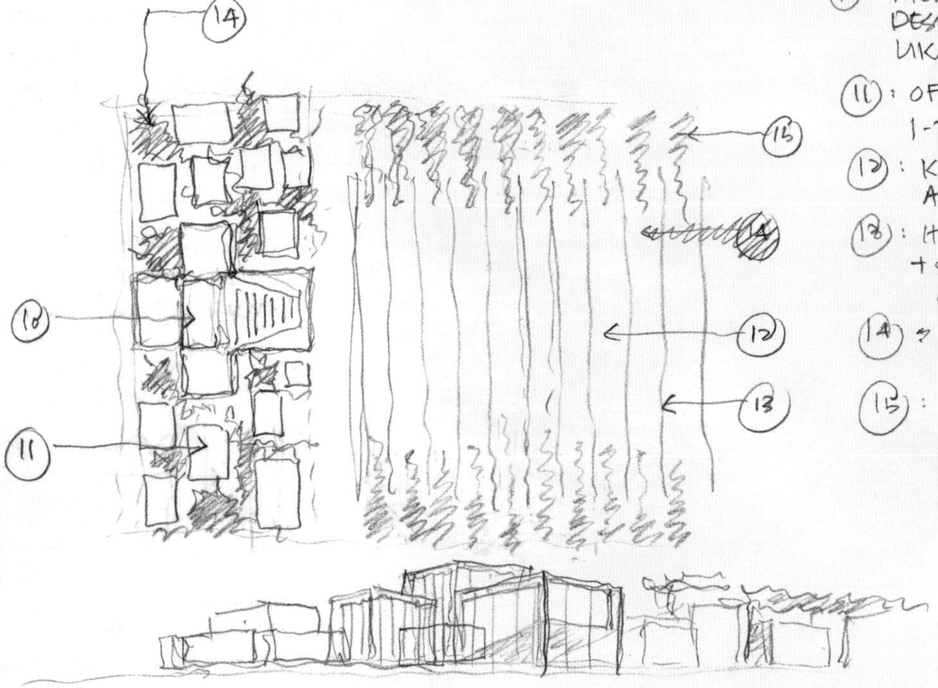

(10) : THEATRE DESIGNED LIKE PAVILIONS

(11) : OFFICE/COMM 1-2 STOREY

(12) : K-POP ARENA

(13) : HARDSCAPE + SOFTSCAPE STRIPS.

(14) : LUSH LANDSCAPE

(15) : TREES + SHRUBS.

(22) : CURTAIN PRECAST

(23) : TRANSLUCENT CURTAIN (POLYCARB).

(24) : GLASS FOR ENTRANCE LOBBY.

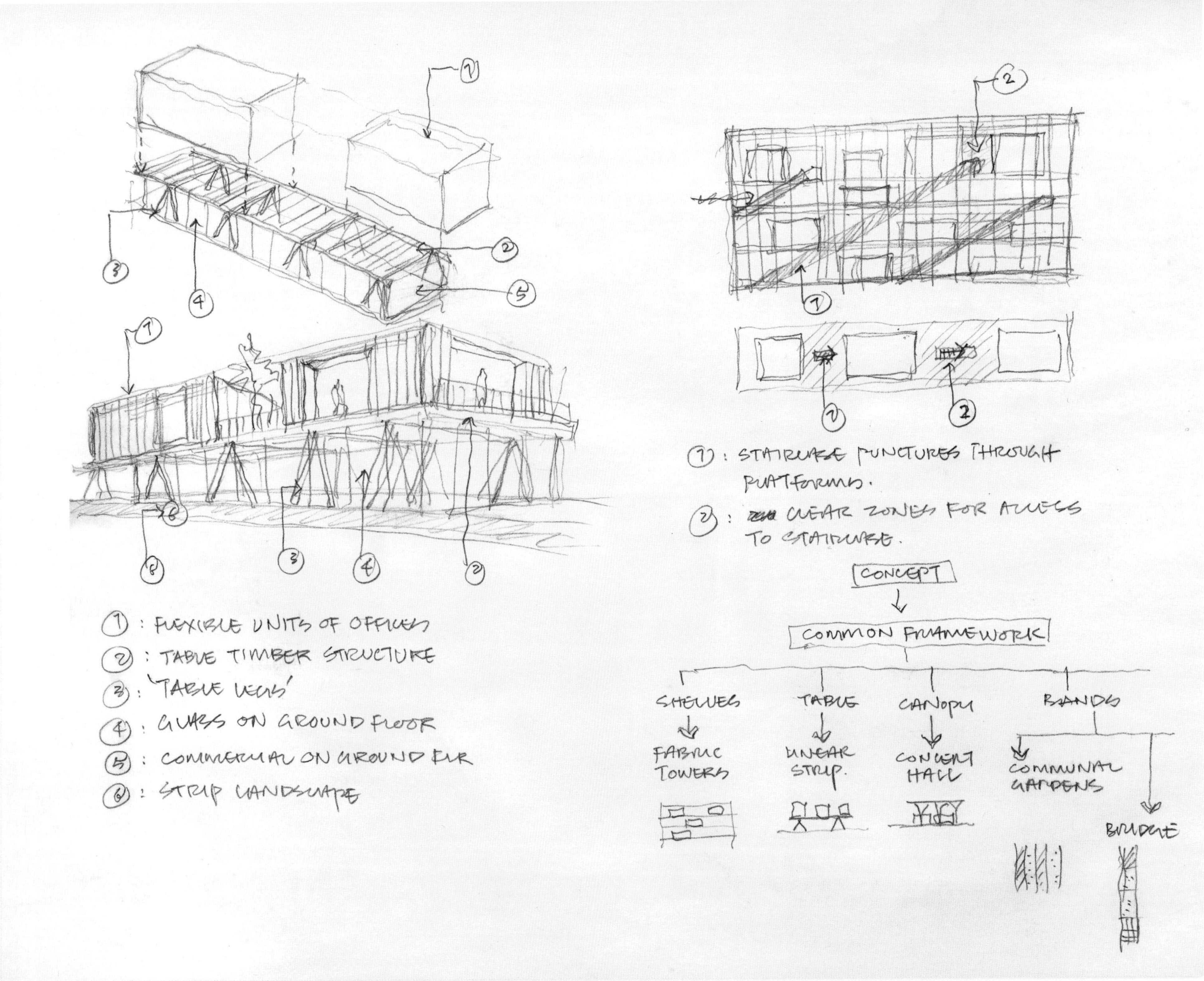
1 : FLEXIBLE UNITS OF OFFICES
2 : TABLE TIMBER STRUCTURE
3 : 'TABLE LEGS'
4 : GLASS ON GROUND FLOOR
5 : COMMERCIAL ON GROUND FLR
6 : STRIP LANDSCAPE
1 : STAIRCASE PUNCTURES THROUGH PLATFORMS.
2 : CLEAR ZONES FOR ACCESS TO STAIRCASE.
CONCEPT
COMMON FRAMEWORK
SHELVES
TABLE
CANOPY
BANDS
FABRIC TOWERS
LINEAR STRIP.
CONCERT HALL
COMMUNAL GARDENS
BRIDGE

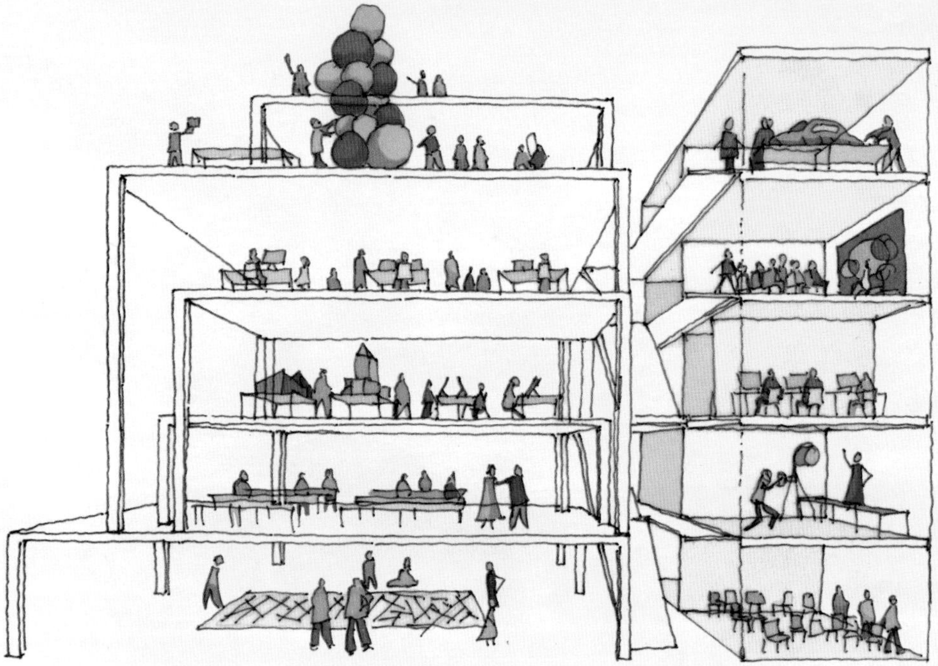
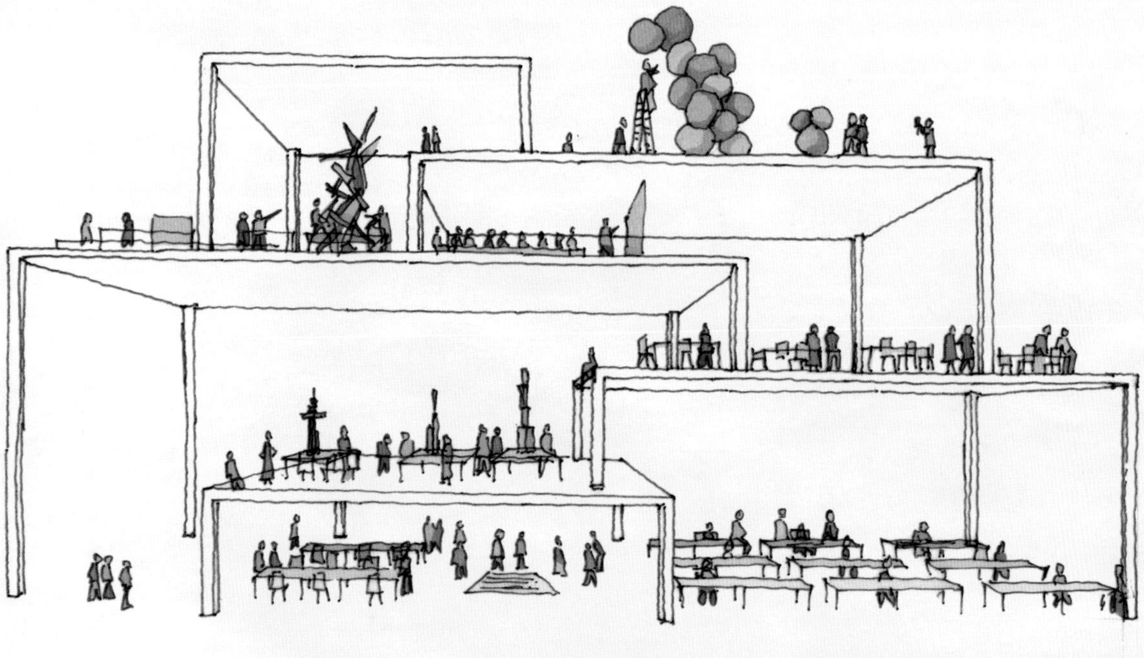

UFFE LETH

Leth & Gori • Denmark

Featured projects: Oluf Bagers Plads [p. 166, top] Christiansfeld [p. 166, bottom] Livsrum Herlev [p. 167, top left] Pulsen Community Centre [p. 167, top right] · Music Museum [p. 167, bottom left] · Dalsland House [p. 167, bottom right] Holtegaard Pavilion [p. 168] · Langvang Multifunctional Sports Building [p. 169]

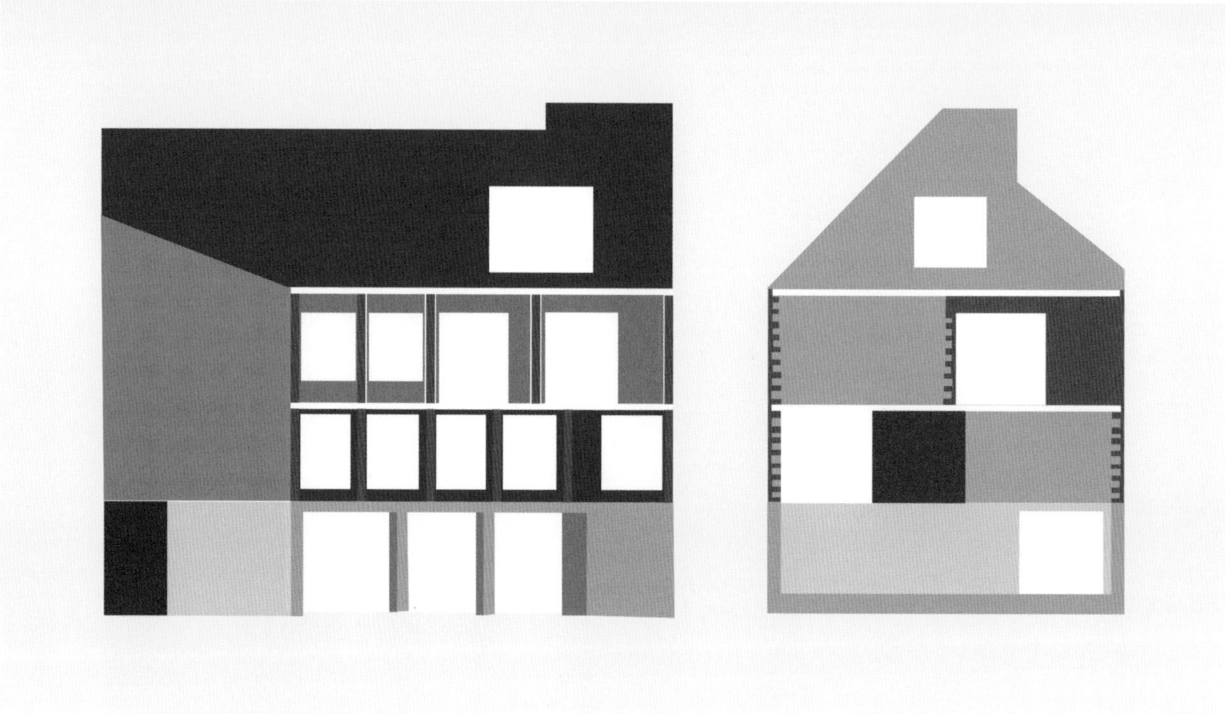

'Sketching improves our work in many different ways, most importantly by ensuring a dialogue between the projects and spaces we create and the human body,' says Uffe Leth of Danish firm Leth & Gori. Leth and his partner Karsten Gori, who both teach at the Royal Danish Academy of Fine Arts, School of Architecture, emphasize the importance of making the sketching process physical by getting the project out of the computer – 'to work with it, and look at and measure it with your own body', he adds. 'Something happens when you work with your hands and turn off your brain for a bit.'

This young team is renowned for its intelligent and uncomplicated designs, including Brick House, a home designed to last for five generations. The duo design architecture that is right for the human condition, so physical design methods suit it well.

'For us, the whole idea of the design process is to build, so we need to be sure that we understand the design, context and materials with our own bodies to ensure that the building works,' Leth continues. 'We would be able to work without sketching or other non-digital means, but the result, and process, would be less interesting. The ability, or courage, to sketch by hand is a huge advantage when it comes to a dialogue with clients. We often draw and sketch in meetings, and this ability to visualize ideas is a very important tool. We have not yet developed the skill to simultaneously draw different sketches with both hands, as Carlo Scarpa apparently did, but we are working on it!'

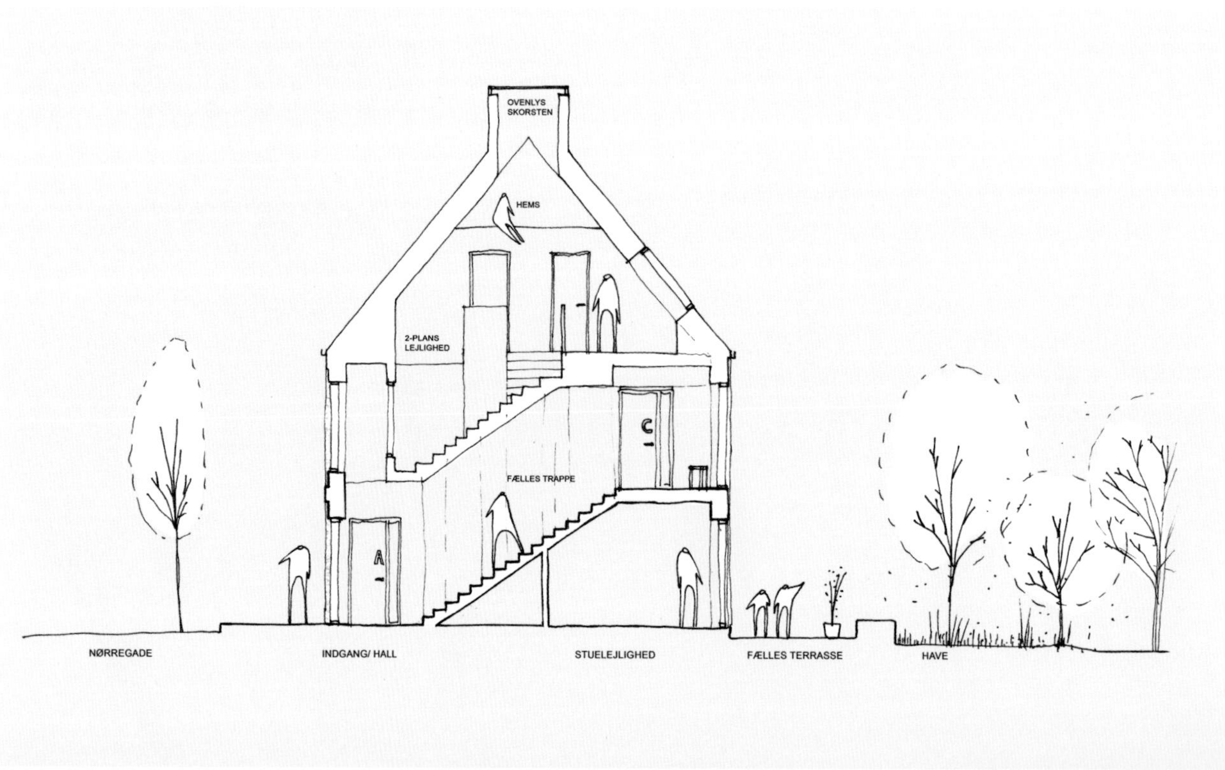

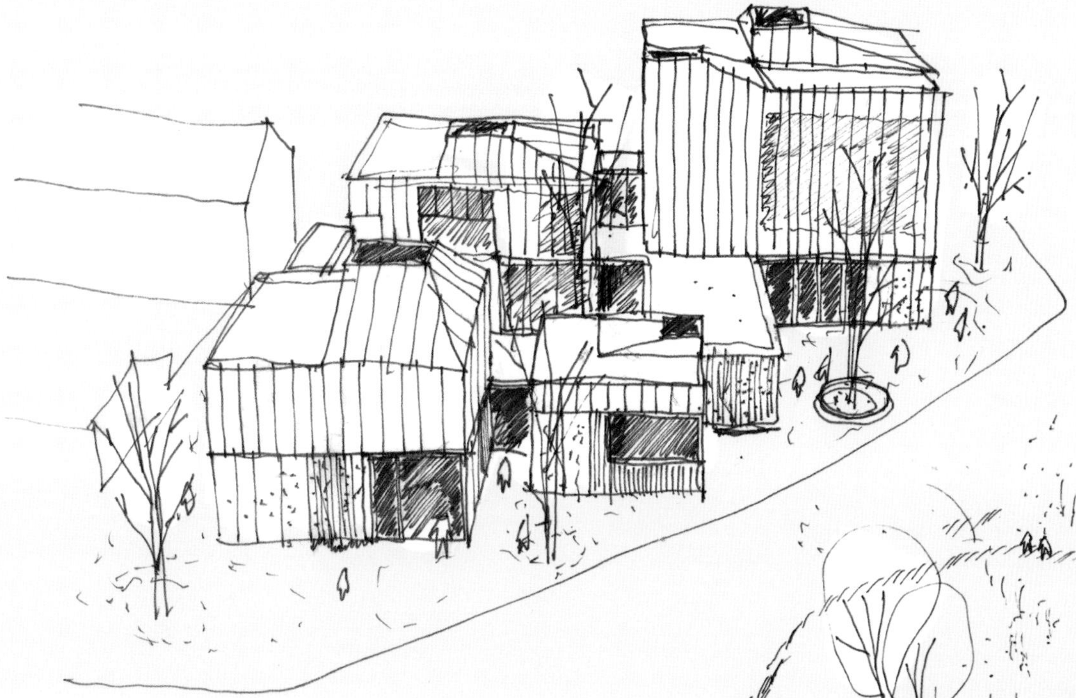

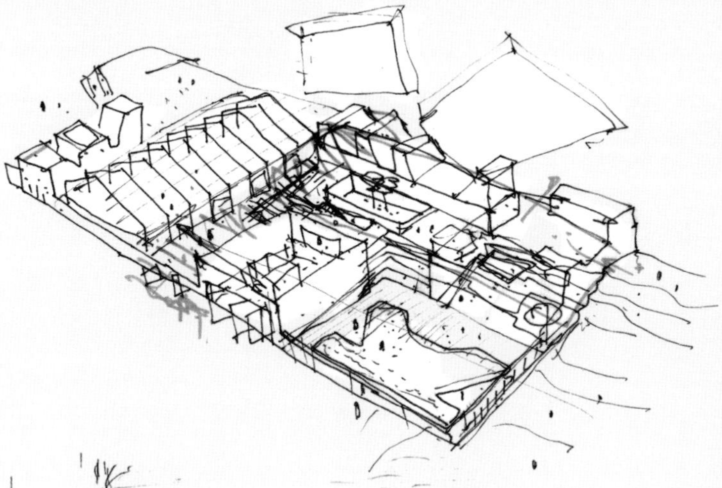

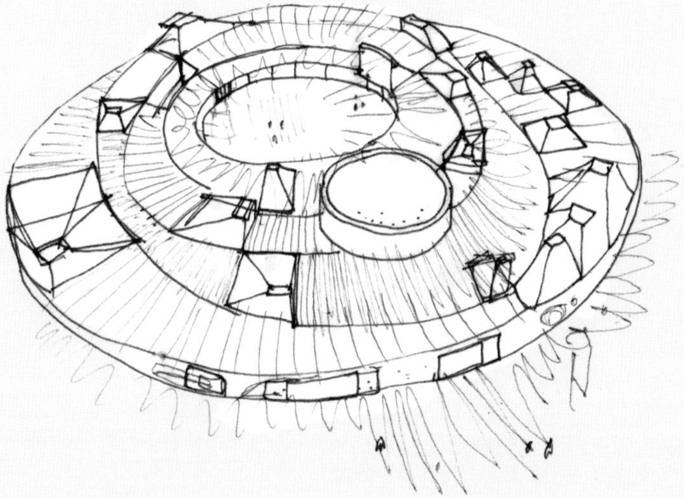

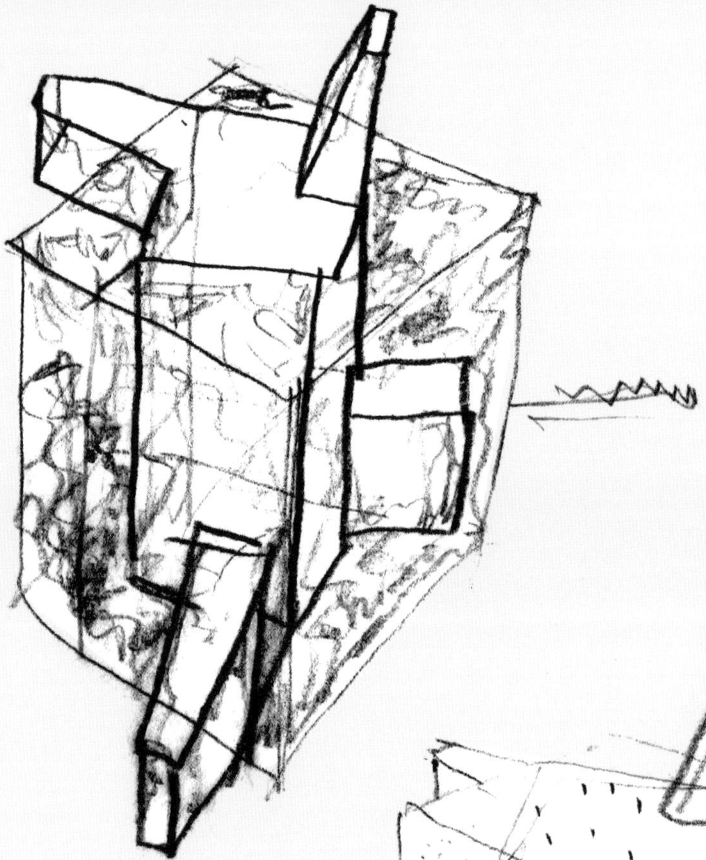

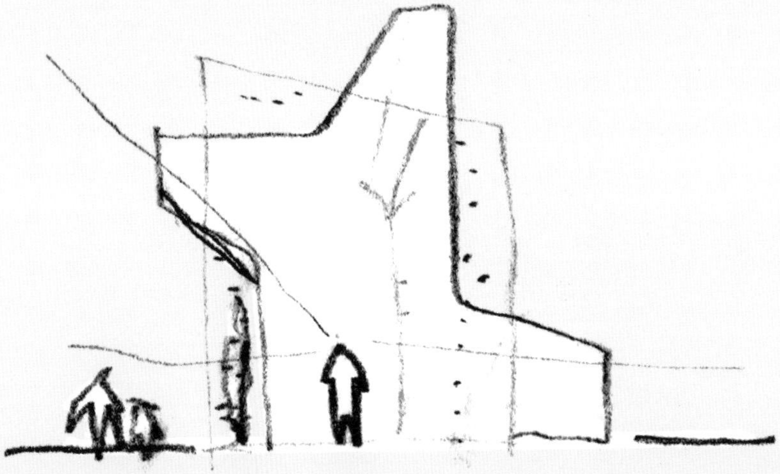

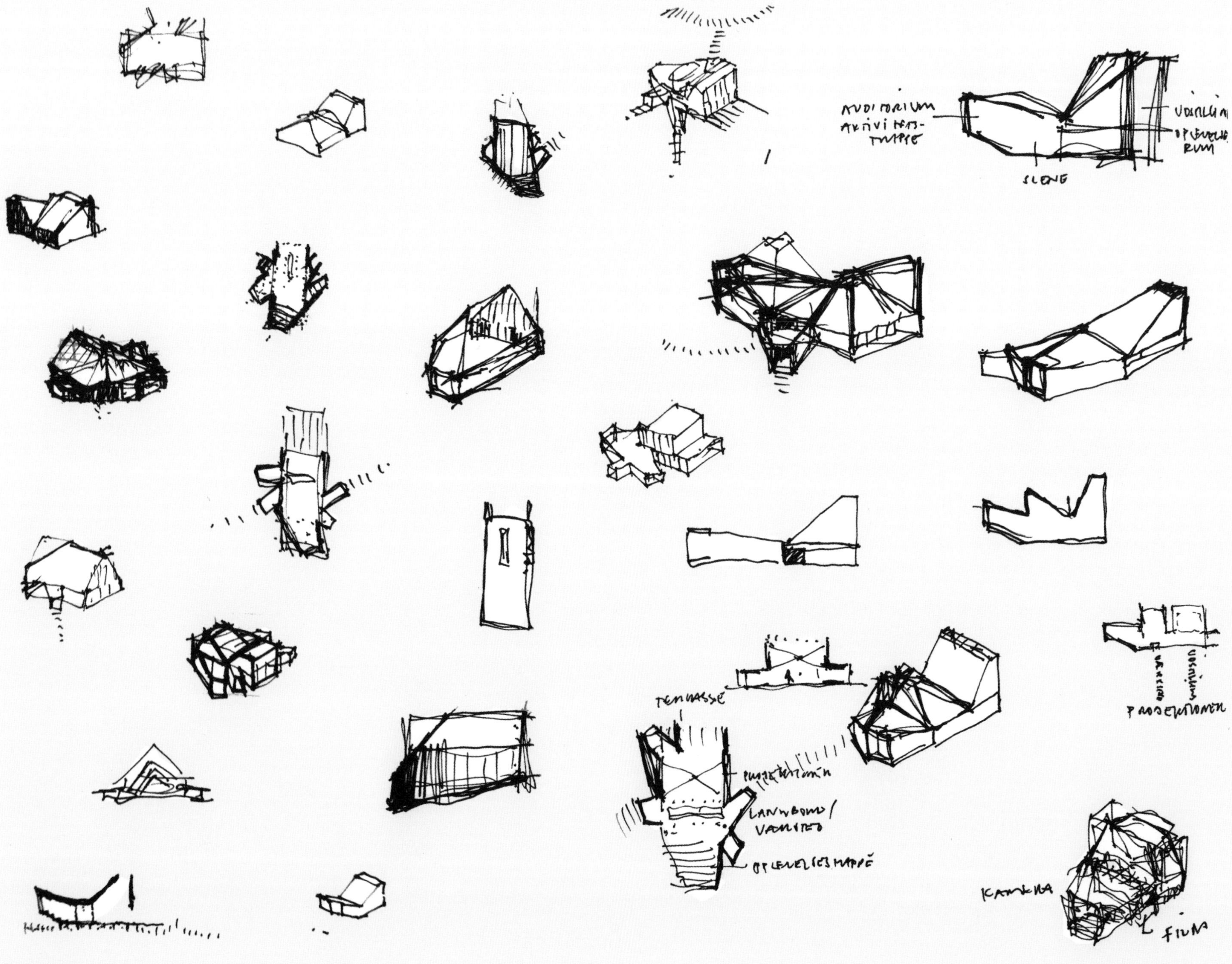
AUDITORIUM
RUM
KAMERA
FILM

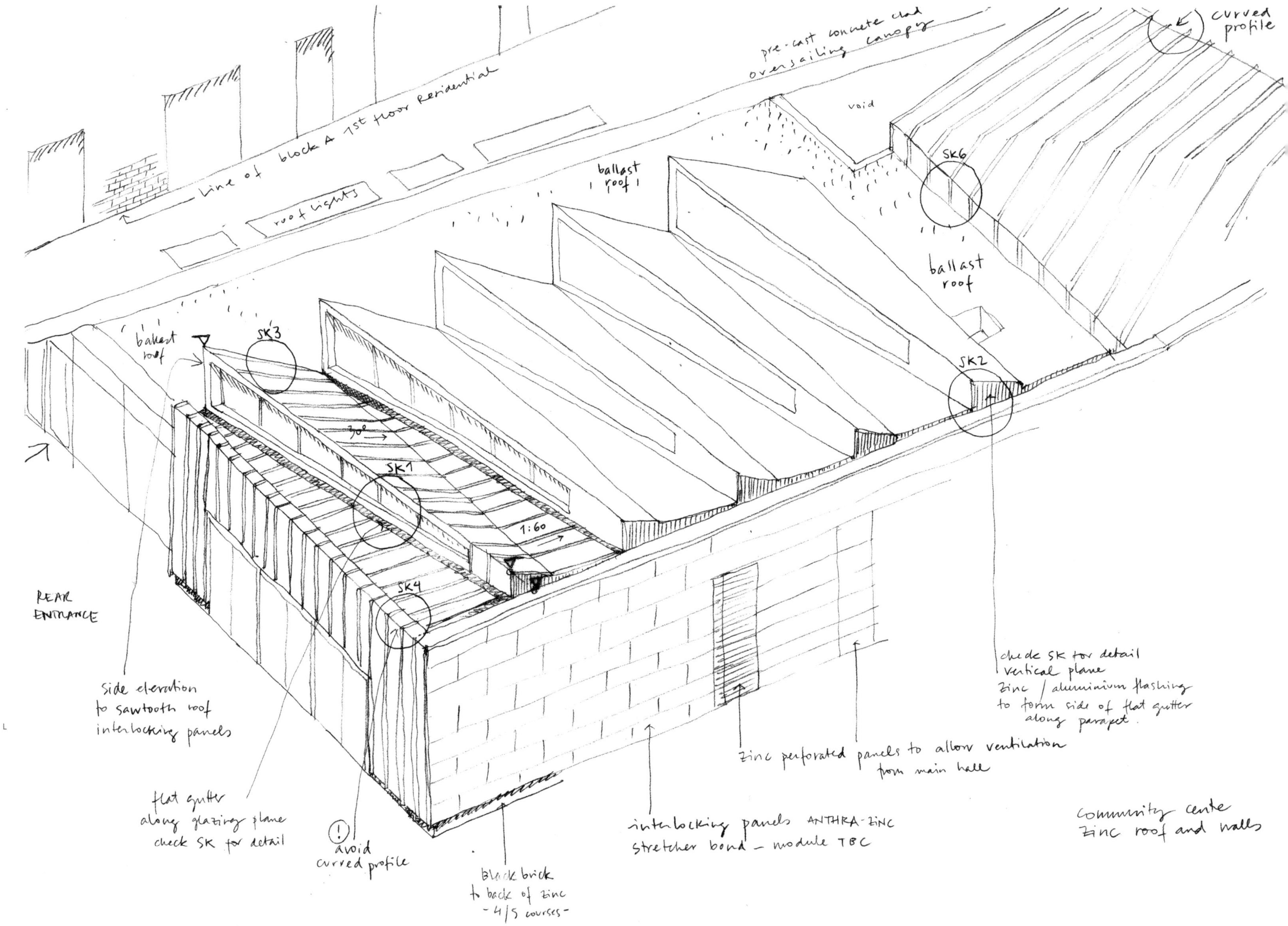
pre-cast concrete clad
oversailing canopy
curved
profile
void
Line of block A 1st floor Residential
roof lights
ballast
roof
SK6
ballast
roof
ballast
roof
SK3
30°
SK1
1:60
SK2
SK4
REAR
ENTRANCE
check SK for detail
vertical plane
Zinc / aluminium flashing
to form side of flat gutter
along parapet.
Side elevation
to sawtooth roof
interlocking panels
Zinc perforated panels to allow ventilation
from main hall
flat gutter
along glazing plane
check SK for detail
!
avoid
curved profile
interlocking panels ANTHRA-ZINC
stretcher bond - module TBC
Community centre
Zinc roof and walls
Black brick
to back of zinc
- 4/5 courses -

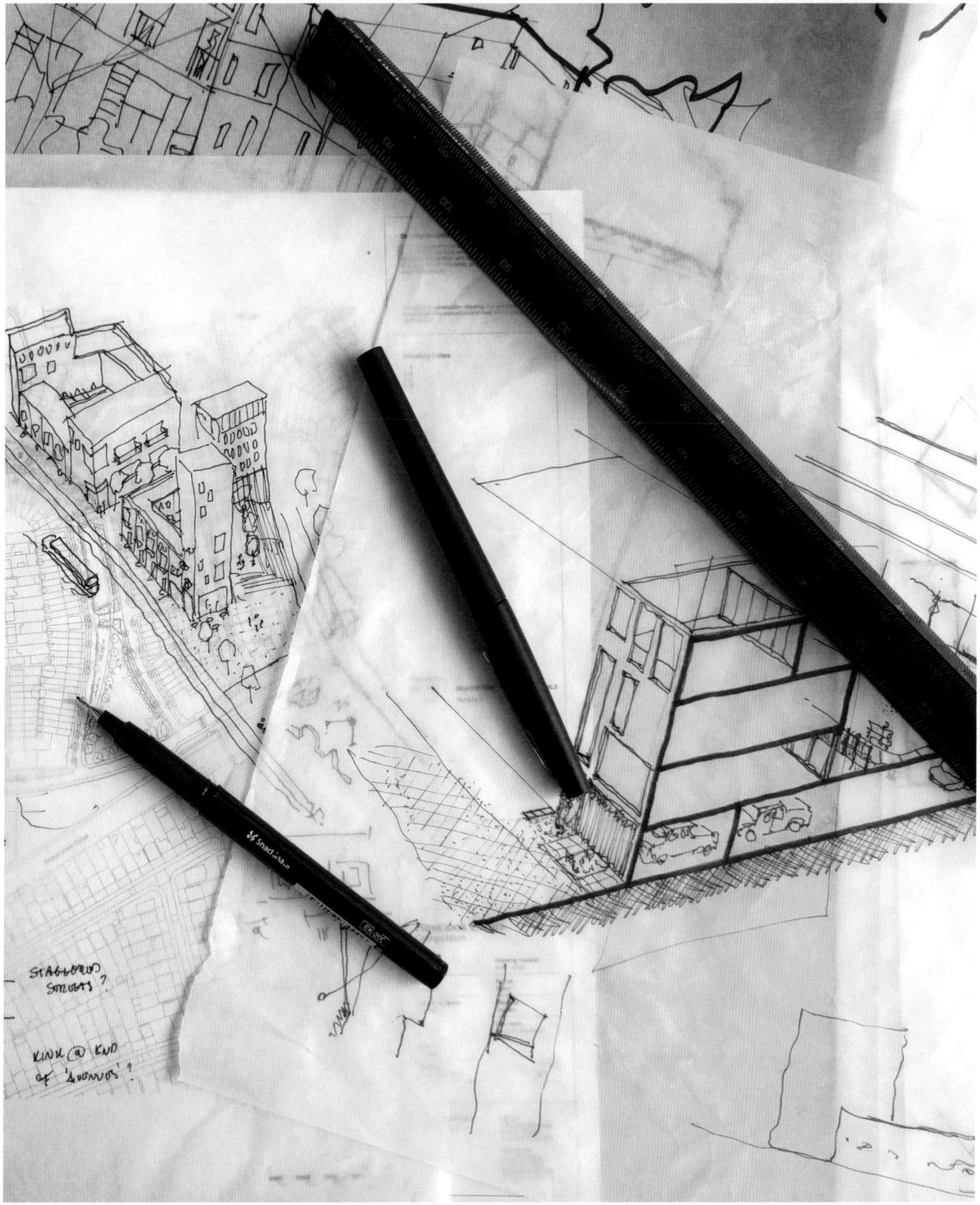

LEVITT BERNSTEIN

UK

Featured projects: Community centre [p. 170]
Residential sketches [pp. 171, 173] · Mews roof sketch [p. 172]
Colston Hall [pp. 174–5]

'Scanned and archived,' says project architect Clara Bailo. 'Added to the big pile on my desk,' notes her colleague Chris Gray. 'I keep some that have been translated into built work,' says associate director Mark Lewis, while project architect Dominic Cava-Simmons adds: 'Generally, they build up into a mound until they are recycled.'

The differing answers to the question of what architects at UK practice Levitt Bernstein do with their sketches hint, perhaps, at the mindset of each individual, but the overriding culture is one of physical design, where sketching and drawing plays a pivotal role. 'Sketching is an unhindered method of communicating ideas of all kinds, direct from the imagination to paper,' Lewis explains.

Senior associate Vinita Dhume adds: 'Design starts when you put your thoughts down on paper. Computer drawings become useful when designs are more fully formed and need to be explained technically, but drawing and sketching your thoughts is essential in the early stages of a design, and can help communicate your ideas very quickly.'

Bailo notes that teams on site are generally happy to see sketching used, 'because it is a quicker, more immediate way to relay information about a specific query'. Lewis agrees that clients like to see the architect sketch or draw, adding: 'They usually love to see a direct, hands-on approach. I was sketching a future phase of one of our own finished buildings, and the client thought that was great. Some clients are very disappointed when visiting the office to see no drawing boards.'

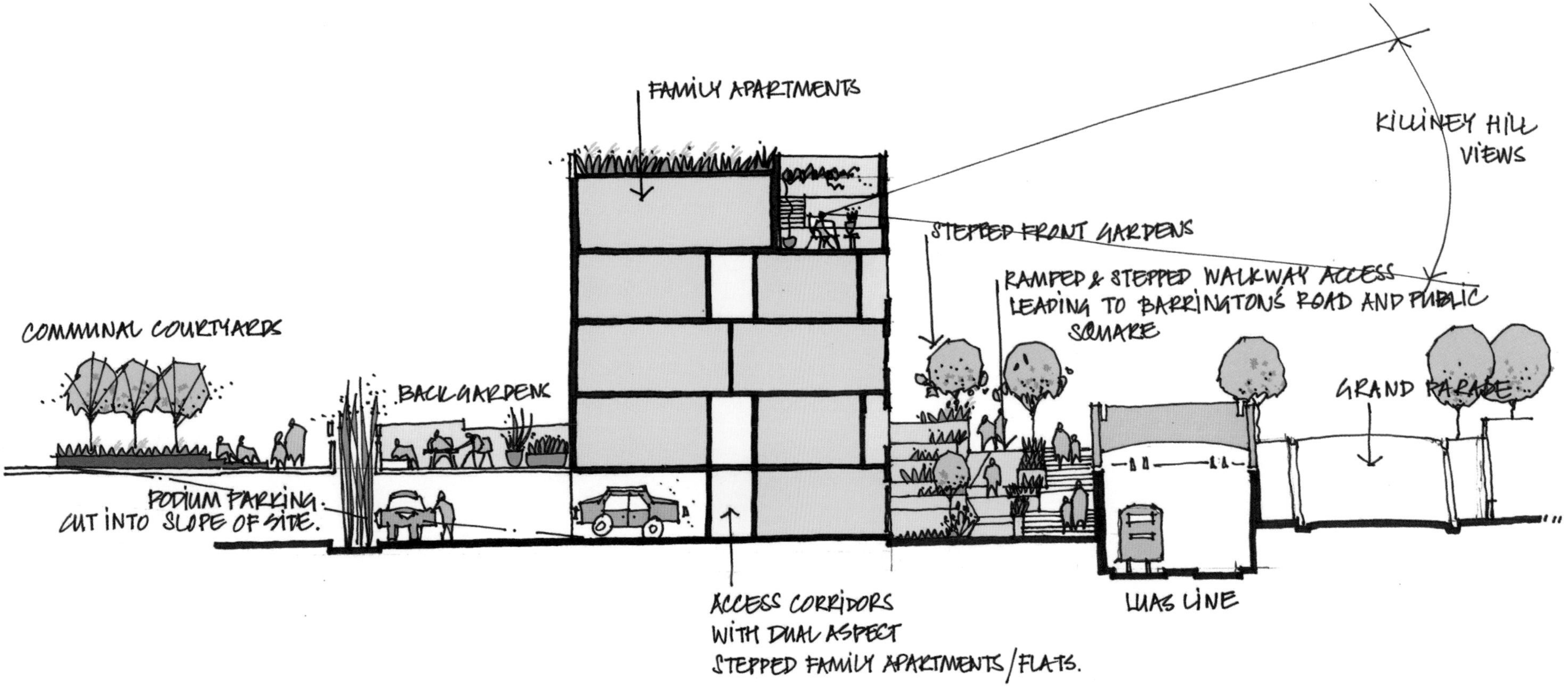
FAMILY APARTMENTS
KILLINEY HILL VIEWS
STEPPED FRONT GARDENS
RAMPED & STEPPED WALKWAY ACCESS LEADING TO BARRINGTON'S ROAD AND PUBLIC SQUARE
COMMUNAL COURTYARDS
BACK GARDENS
GRAND PARADE
PODIUM PARKING CUT INTO SLOPE OF SITE.
ACCESS CORRIDORS WITH DUAL ASPECT STEPPED FAMILY APARTMENTS/FLATS.
LUAS LINE

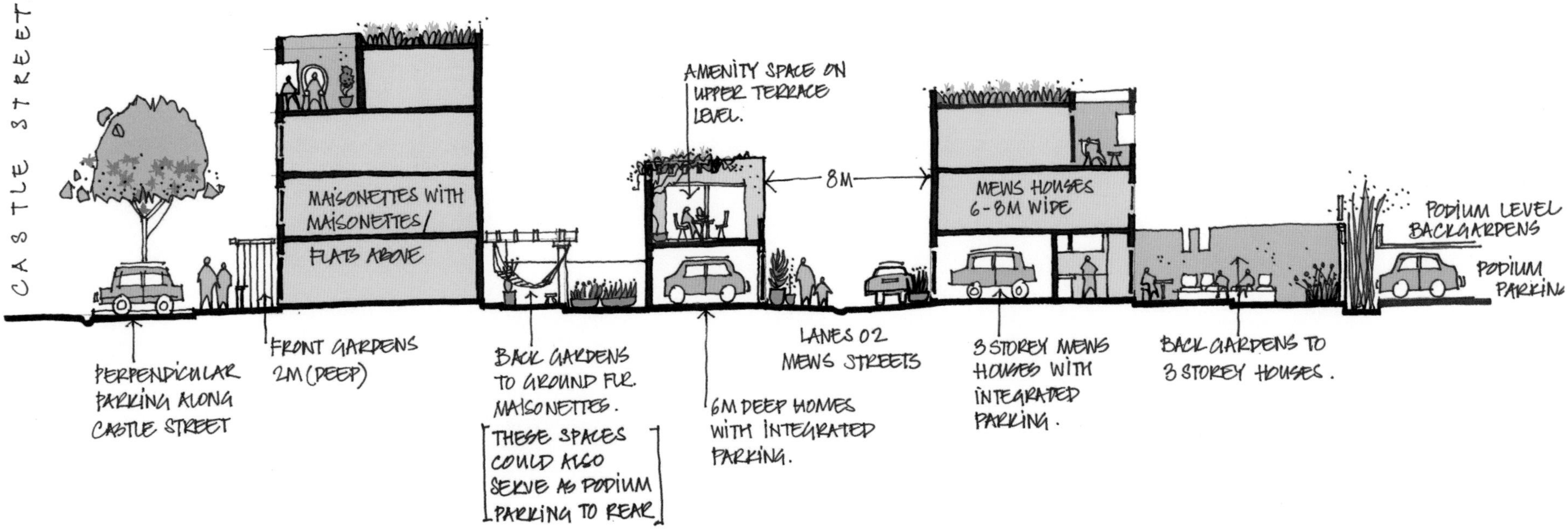
CASTLE STREET.
AMENITY SPACE ON UPPER TERRACE LEVEL.
8M
MAISONETTES WITH MAISONETTES/ FLATS ABOVE
MEWS HOUSES 6-8M WIDE
PODIUM LEVEL BACKGARDENS
PODIUM PARKING
PERPENDICULAR PARKING ALONG CASTLE STREET
FRONT GARDENS 2M (DEEP)
BACK GARDENS TO GROUND FLR. MAISONETTES.
THESE SPACES COULD ALSO SERVE AS PODIUM PARKING TO REAR
6M DEEP HOMES WITH INTEGRATED PARKING.
LANES OR MEWS STREETS
3 STOREY MEWS HOUSES WITH INTEGRATED PARKING.
BACK GARDENS TO 3 STOREY HOUSES.

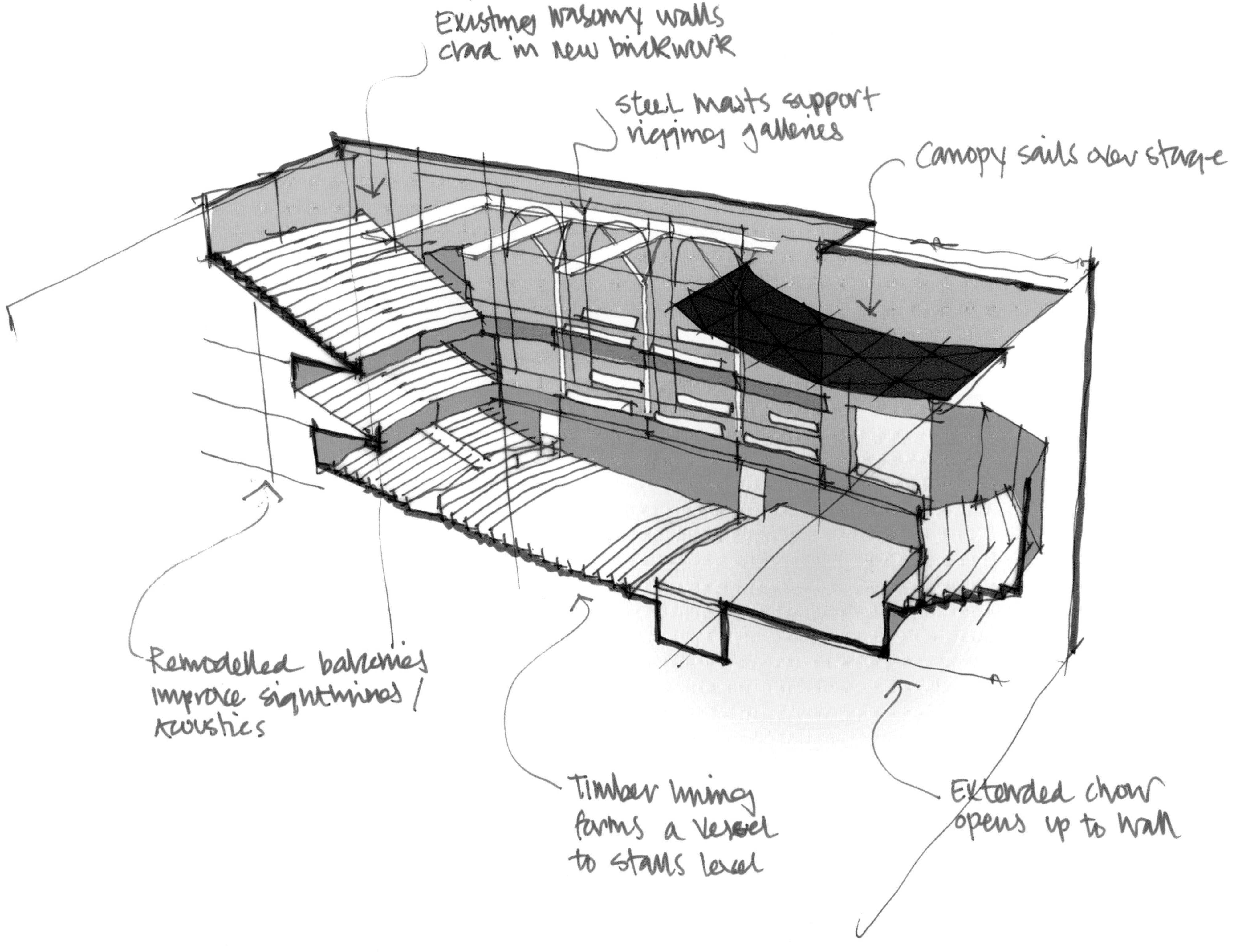
Existing masonry walls clad in new brickwork
Steel masts support rigging galleries
Canopy sails over stage
Remodelled balconies improve sightlines / acoustics
Timber lining forms a vessel to stalls level
Extended choir opens up to wall

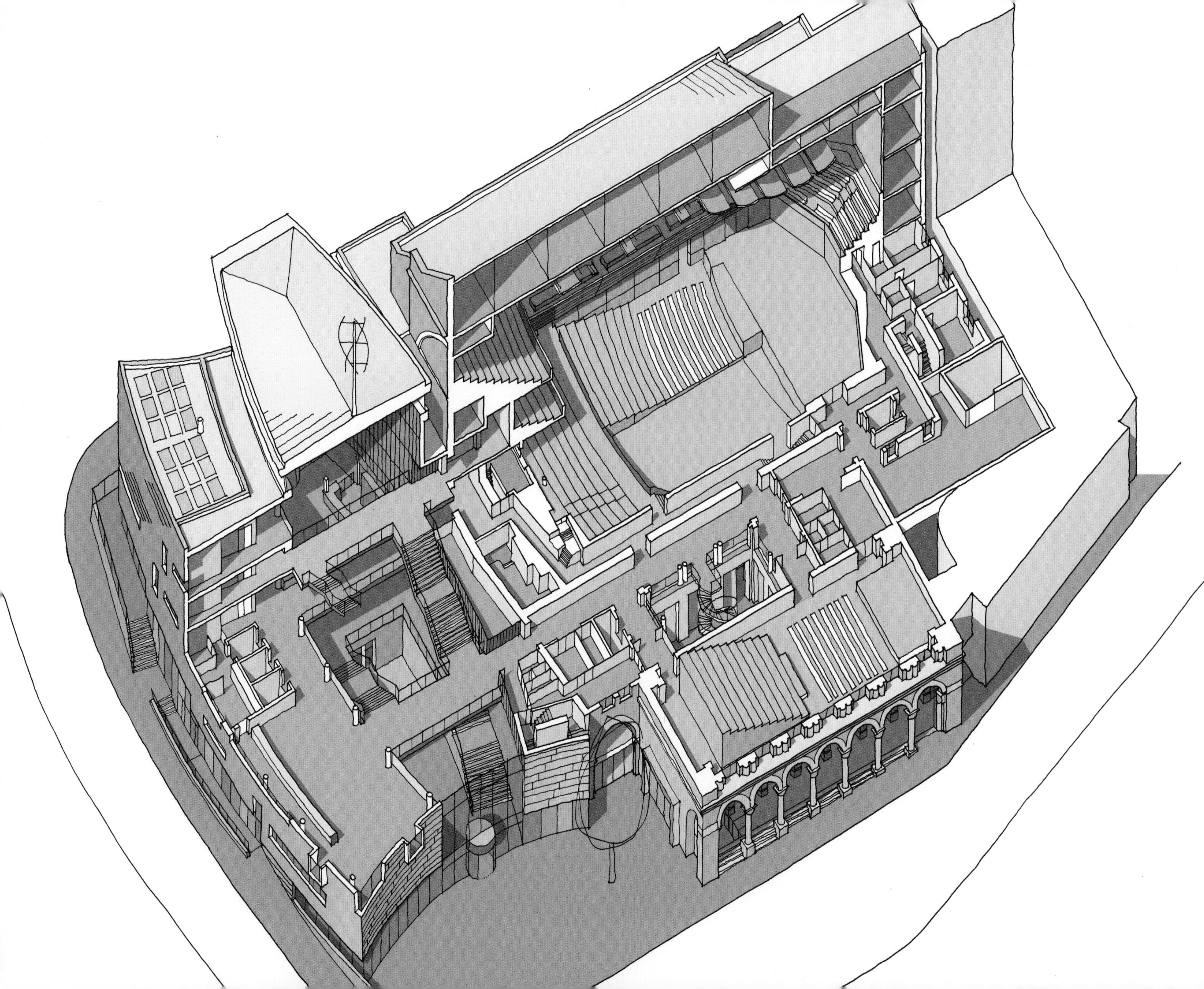

1776
10 28 AM SEPT. 11
HEART + SOUL MEMOR
SLURRY WALL
FOUDATI

DANIEL LIBESKIND

Studio Libeskind • USA

Featured projects: World Trade Center, New York [pp. 176–9]
Denver Art Museum [pp. 180–1] · Jewish Museum Berlin [pp. 182–3]

'Clients want to see an architect sketch,' notes Daniel Libeskind. 'They are too smart to be fooled by virtual reality, and always want to know what an architect can do with a piece of paper and a pencil. In my view, sketching is the key to architecture. It brings together the hand, eye and mind with the imagination and spirit. With new technology, incorporating ideas that are sketched out is actually a seamless process. I even have sketching programs on an iPad that are immediately available to my collaborators.'

One of the most famous architects working today, with offices in New York and Zurich, Libeskind is renowned for unique designs that often look as if they have fallen straight out of some digital otherworld. Looks can be deceiving, however, as the architect is firmly wedded to sketching as the foremost means of architectural design.

'I wouldn't know how sketching improves, alters or affects my designs, as opposed to using digital means, because I have always sketched,' he says. 'I would never dare undertake a project without it. When lightning strikes, I draw: outside, inside, on aeroplanes, on tablecloths, even sometimes on a blank wall. I sketch on whatever is to hand when inspiration strikes.'

What happens to these sketches afterwards is of no consequence. 'Sometimes they are lost,' Libeskind admits – but the design is now physical, and the process has begun.

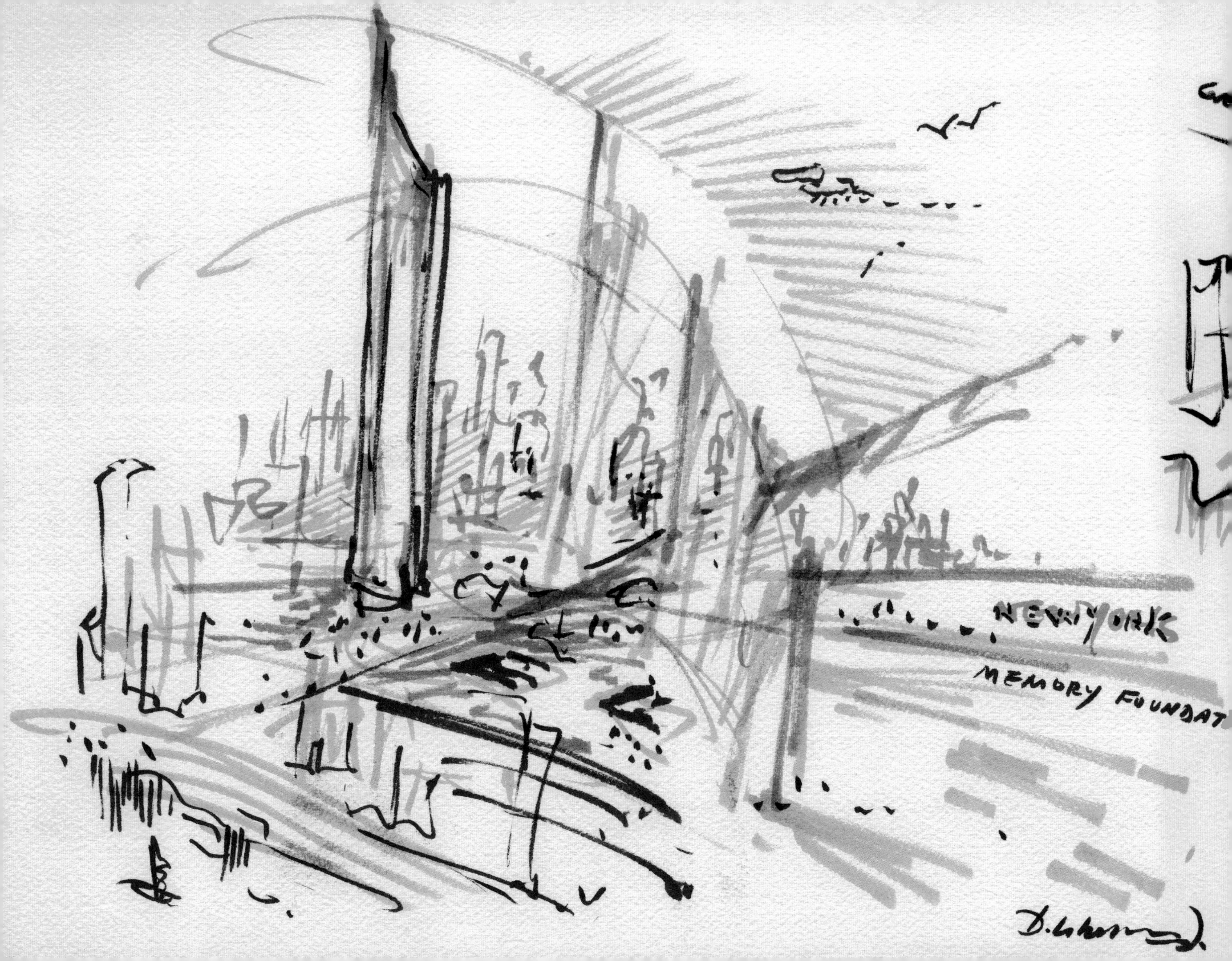
NEW YORK
MEMORY FOUNDAT

SEPT. 11. PLACE
CENTER
FULTON
HUDSON RIVER

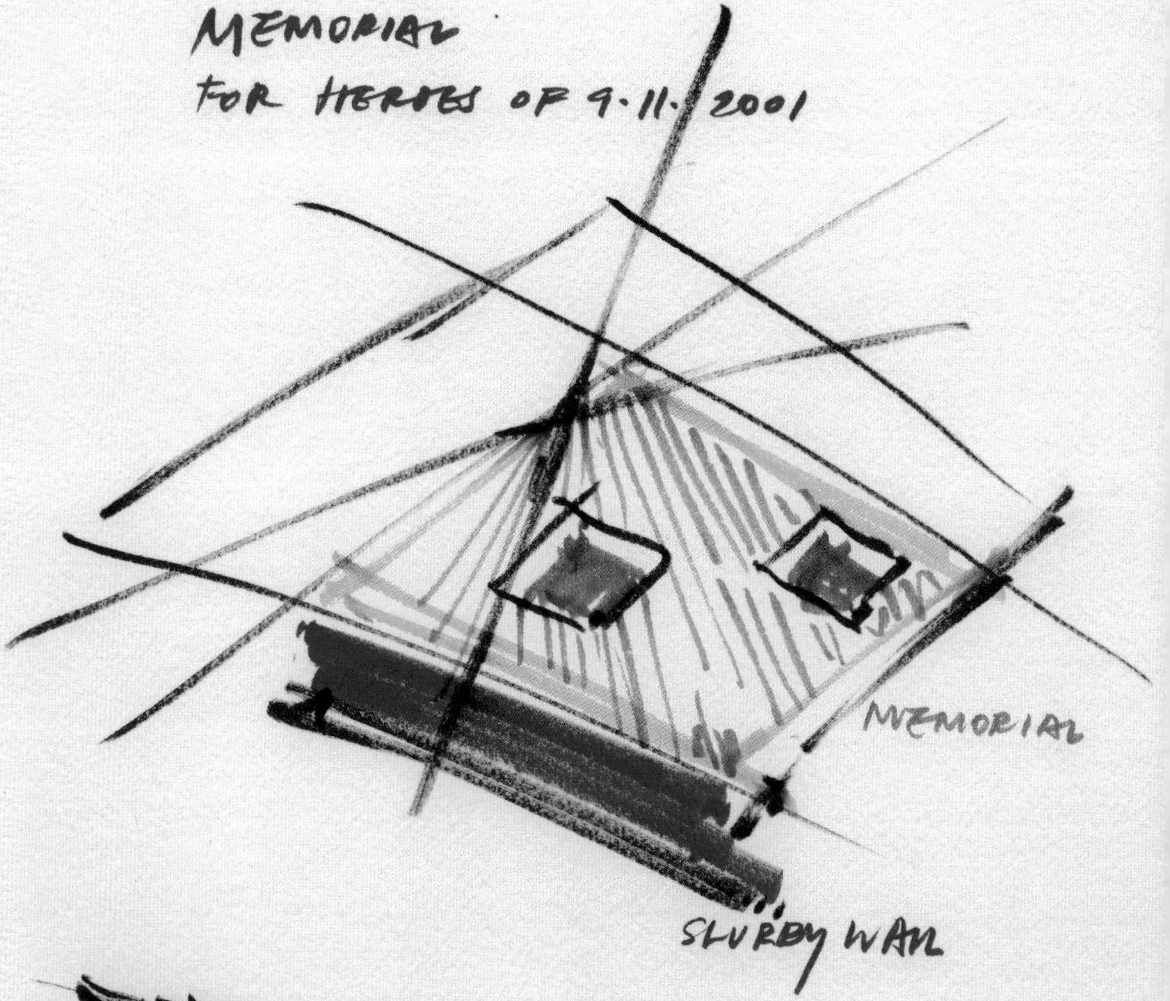
MEMORIAL
FOR HEROES OF 9.11.2001
MEMORIAL
SLURRY WALL

GROUND
SLURRY
FOUNDATION WALL

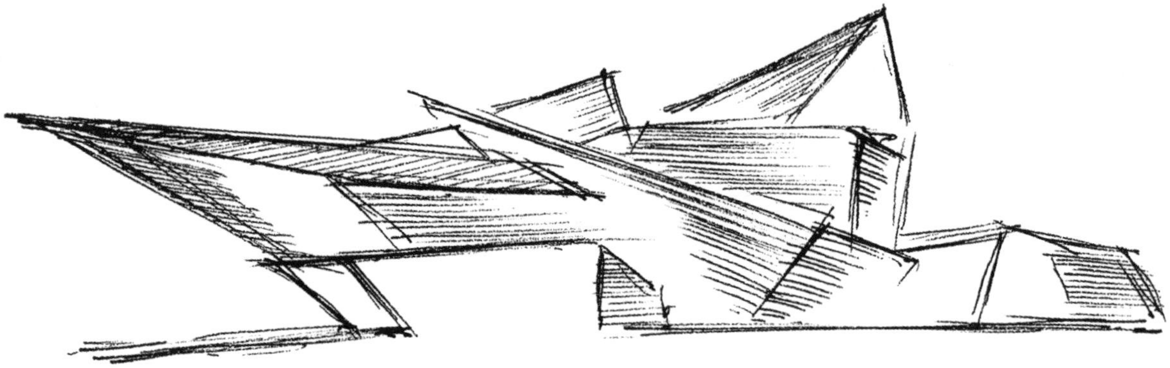

Jamie
KENNEDY
at the
Museum

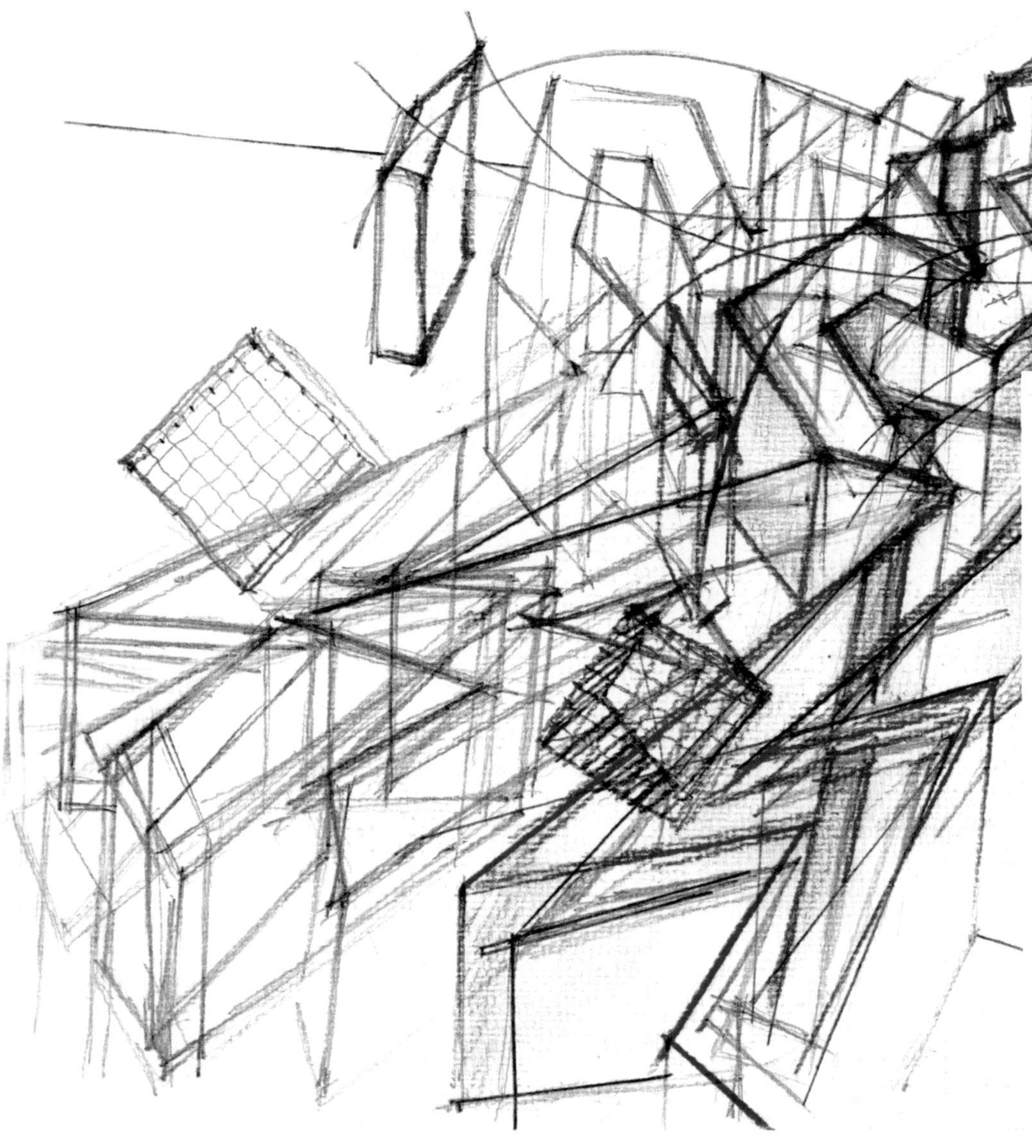

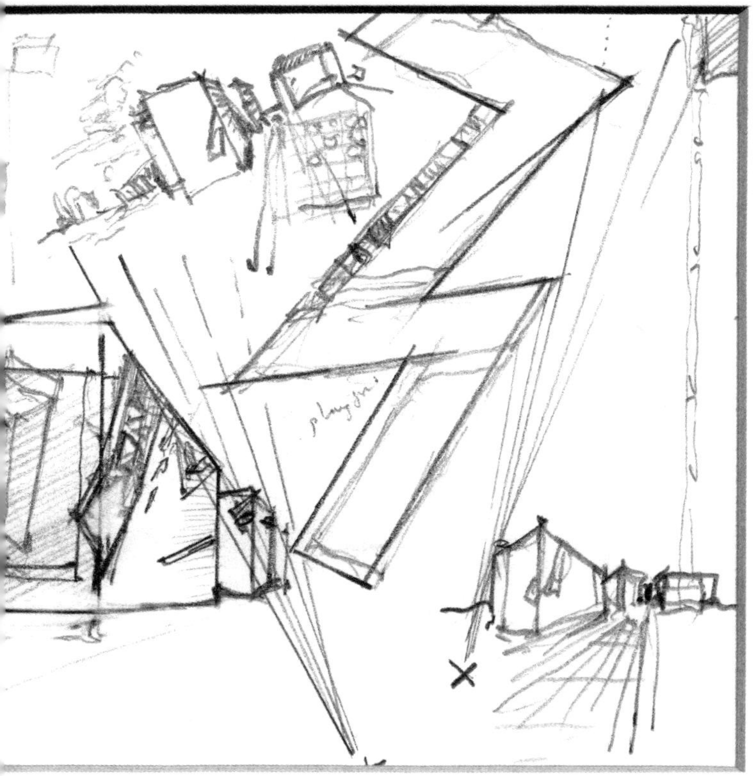

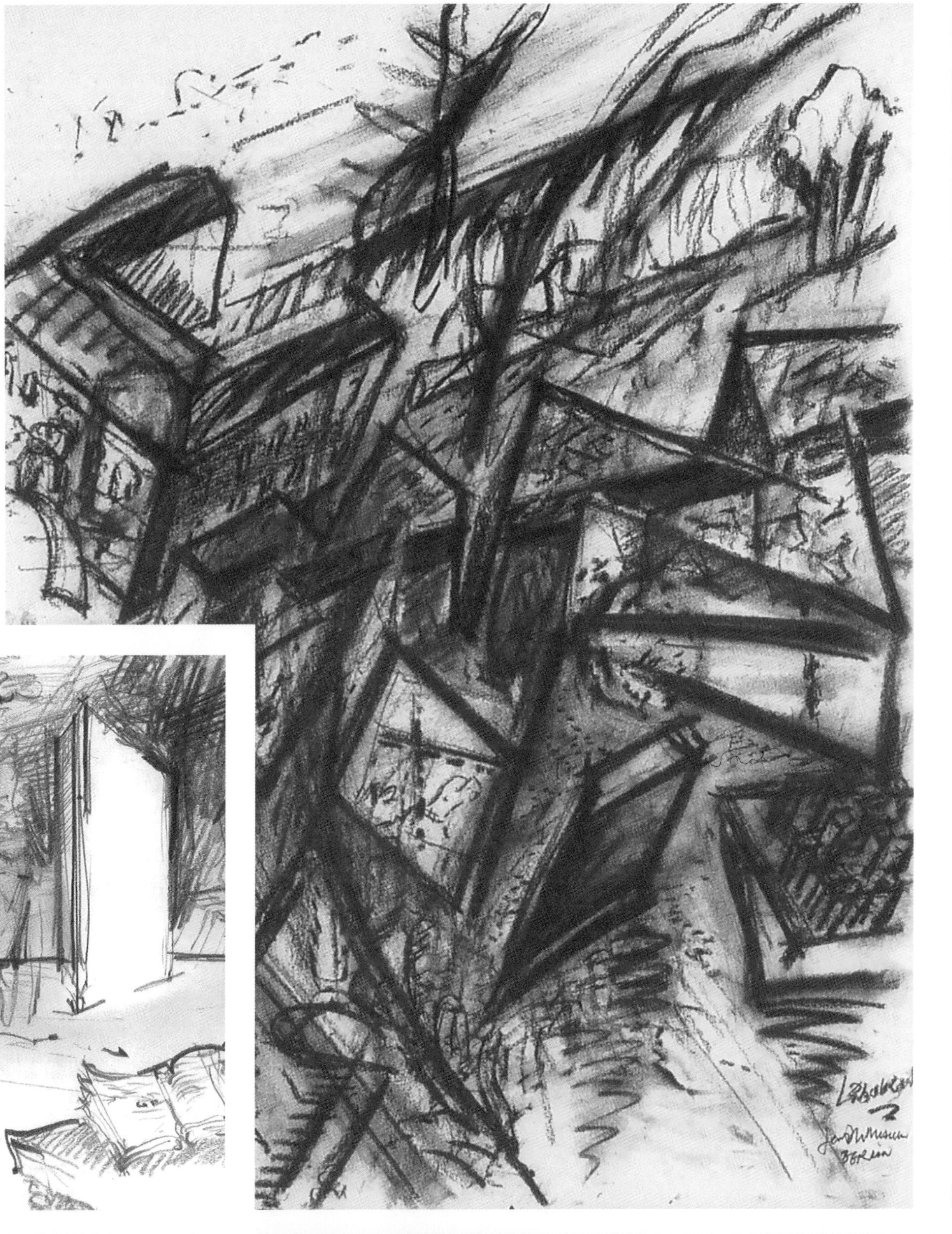

STEPHANIE MACDONALD & TOM EMERSON

6a architects • UK

Featured projects: Courtyard villa [p. 184, top]
House and studio in the park [p. 184, bottom]
Giardino Ibleo [p. 185] · Zingaro Inventory [p. 186]
Tonnara di Scopello [p. 187]

Stephanie Macdonald and Tom Emerson co-founded 6a architects in 2001, and today the company has over 40 employees. The firm is known for its art buildings, both exhibition spaces – such as the refurbishment of the textile and fashion galleries at the Victoria & Albert Museum – and studios for artists like photographer Juergen Teller.

'Hand-drawing is so important,' Macdonald states. 'It can take on different forms. Sometimes it is observational: by drawing a space – with all its objects or people – you see new aspects or qualities within it. This also gives you a chance to think about it, and for ideas to surface. At other times, sketching is a really good way of trying out a bunch of options quickly to see how it feels and to test what's working and what isn't.'

She continues: 'When drawing an idea for a building or a space, sketching helps me to understand what I like about it. It's usually quite fast and scribbly, working something out, before the computer process takes over for presentation.'

Emerson adds: 'Sketching is still the quickest and most direct route from idea to design, or from observation to document. It is like the lubricating oil in the complex digital-design production. There needs to be a bit of it everywhere.'

RAGUSA . IBLA

MILANO

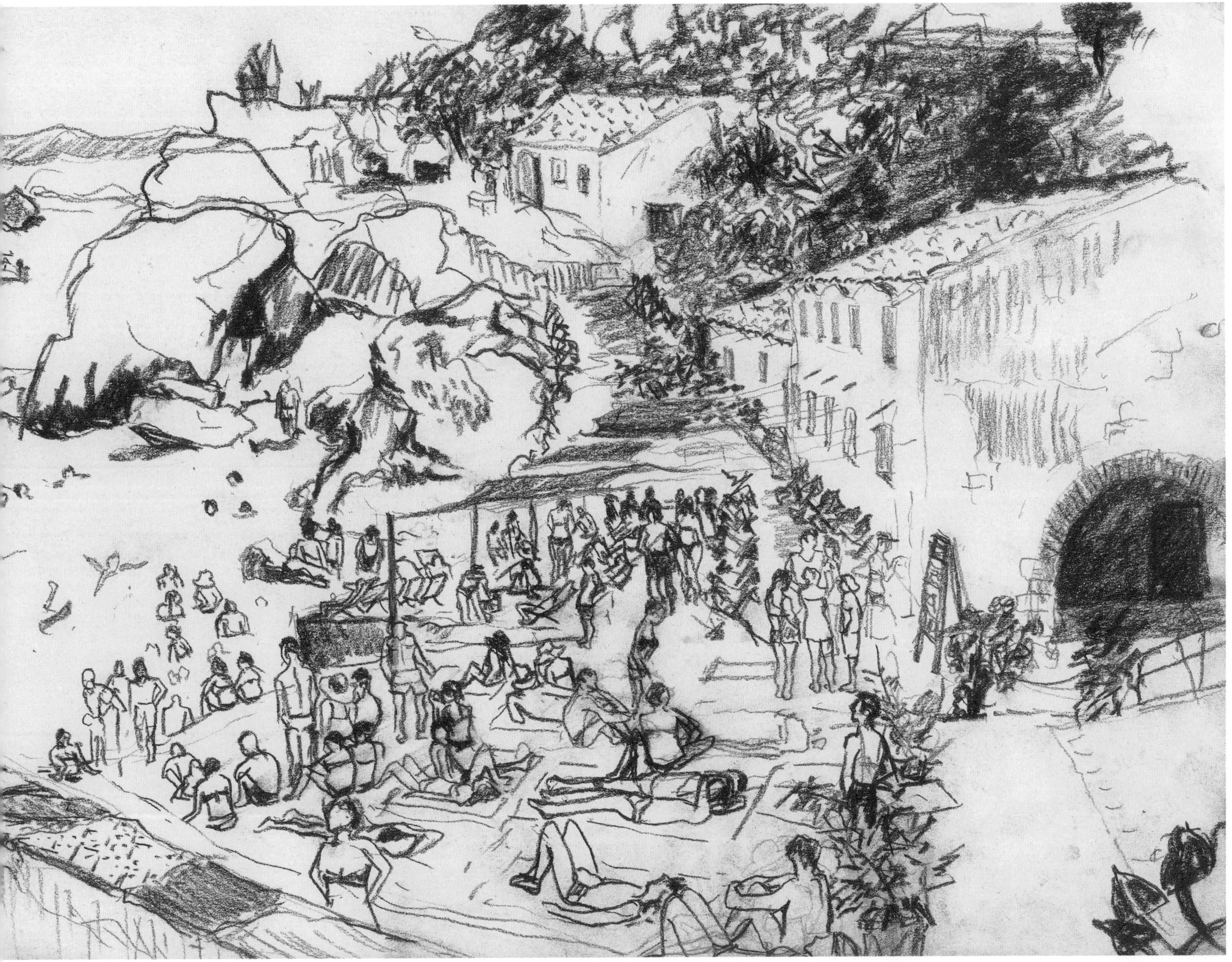

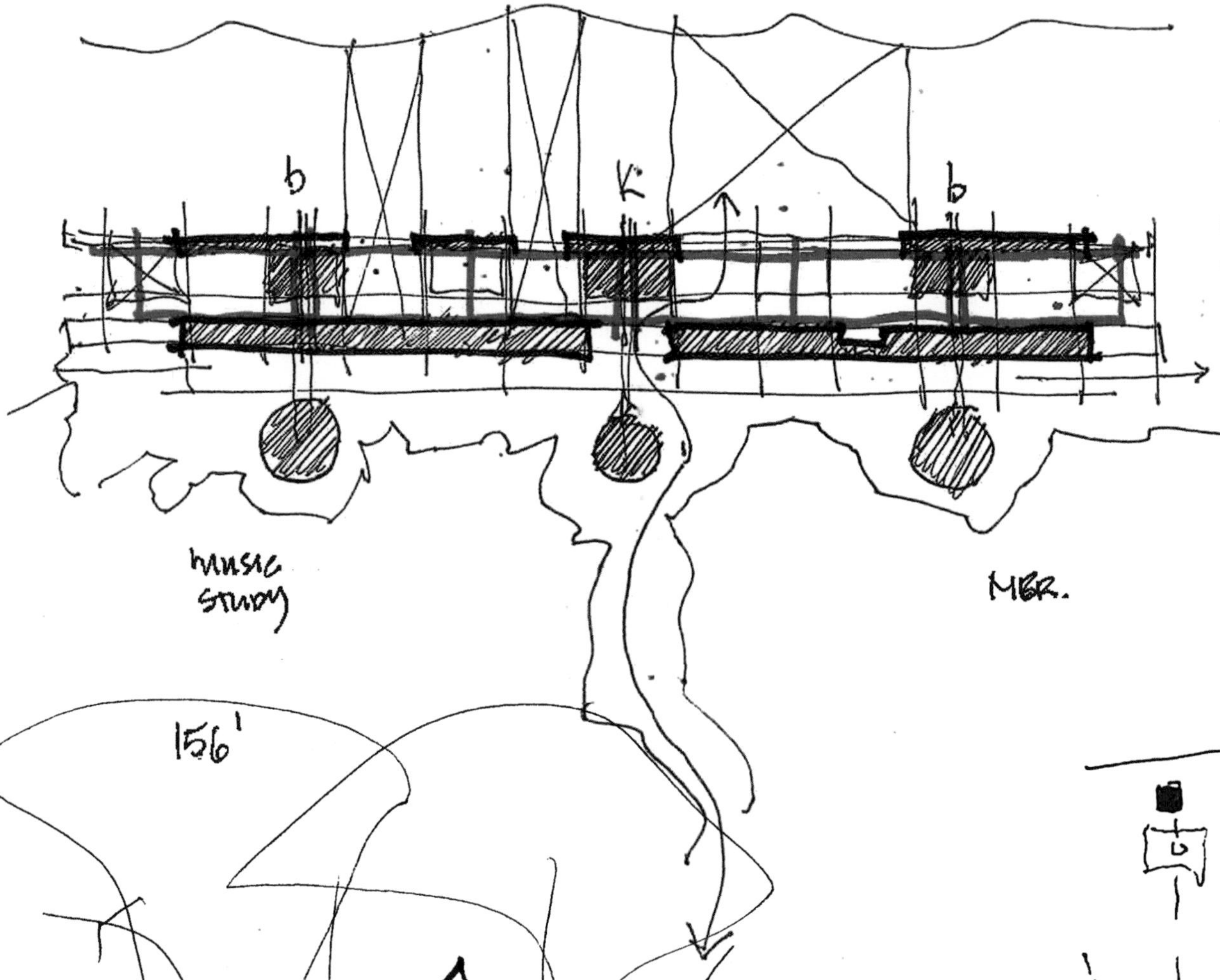
b
K
b
MUSIC STUDY
MBR.

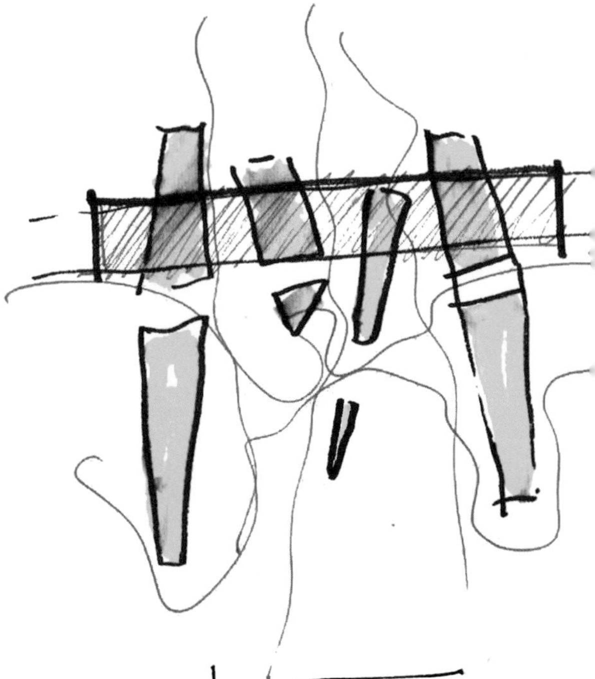

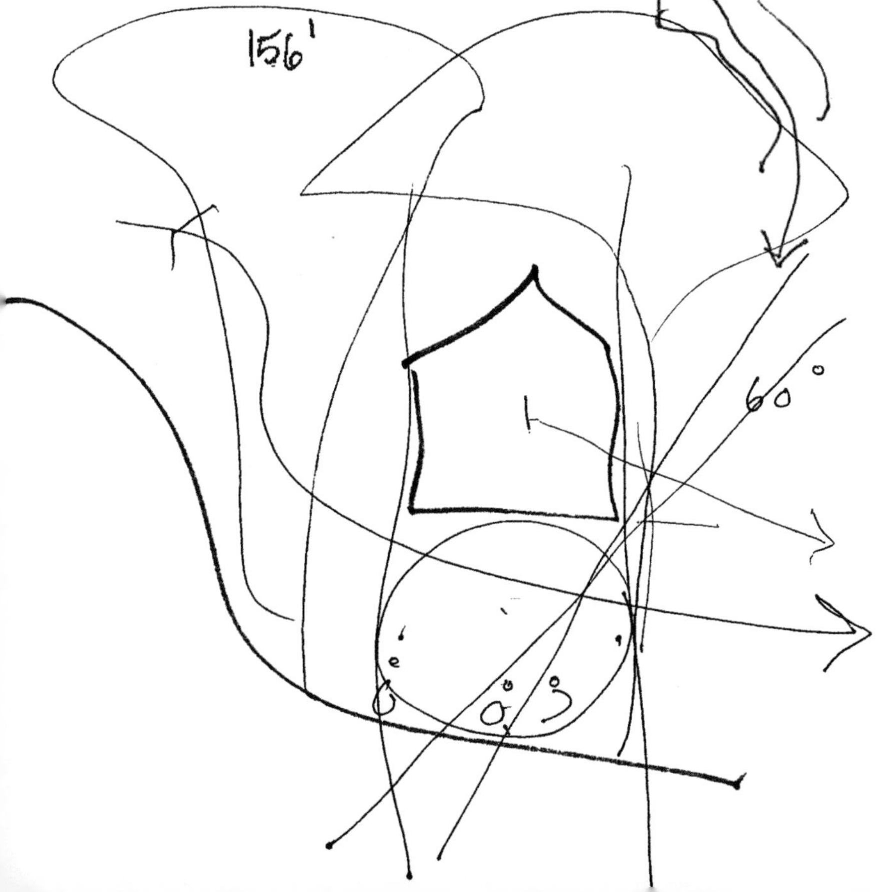
156'
60

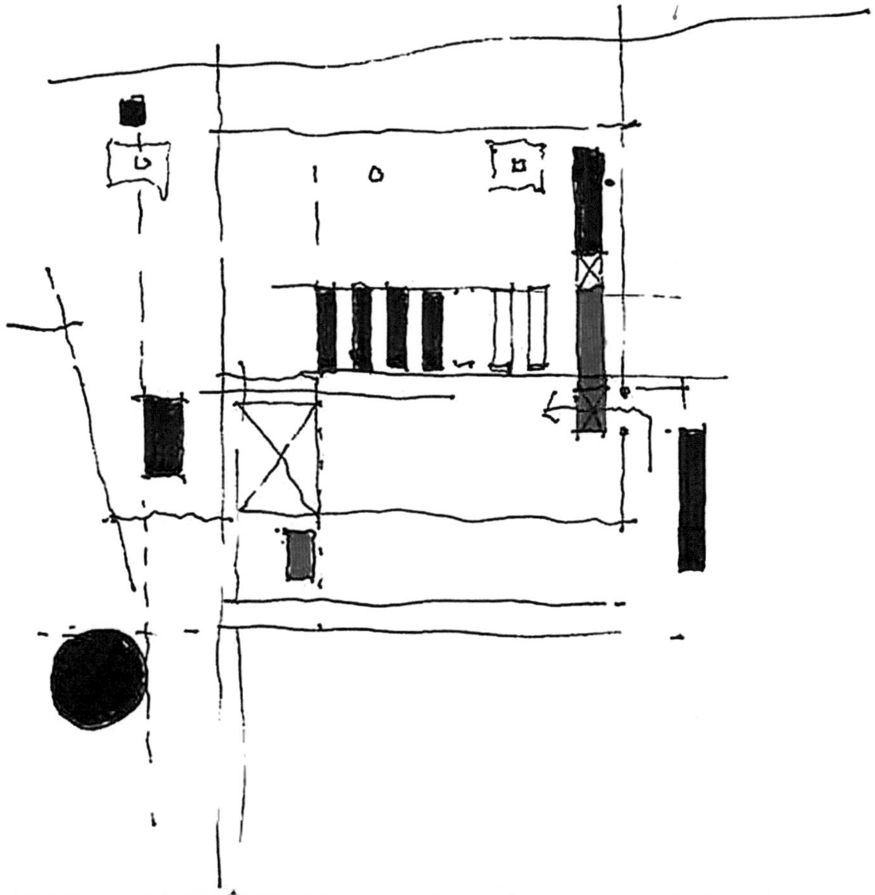

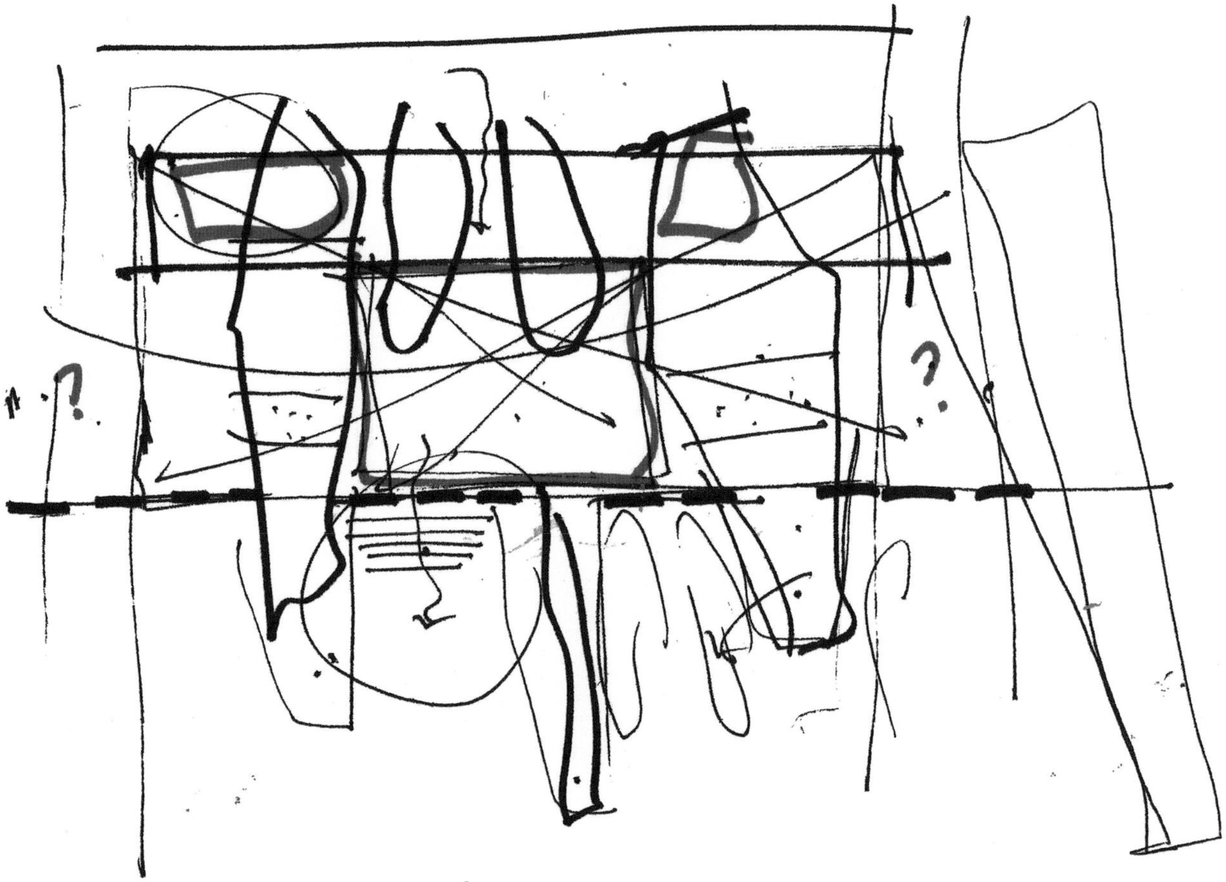

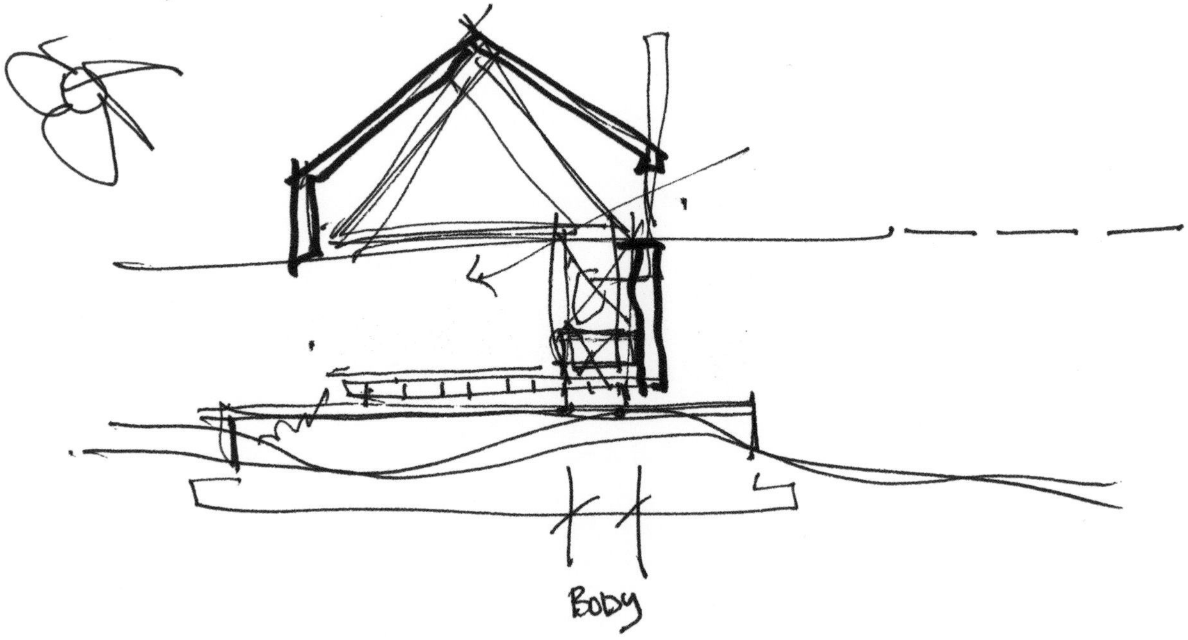

BRIAN MACKAY-LYONS

MacKay-Lyons Sweetapple Architects • Canada

The Nova Scotia firm of MacKay-Lyons Sweetapple, led by partners Brian MacKay-Lyons and Talbot Sweetapple, is relatively few in staff number but large in built presence. Its work includes ARC+ at the University of Toronto, the Canadian Chancery in Dhaka, Bangladesh, and a raft of critically acclaimed homes.

MacKay-Lyons believes that sketching is vitally important. 'A hand-sketch can entertain ambiguity or doubt through a mix of tentative or definitive lines, or show focus by leaving out less important information,' he explains. 'This makes it an interactive and tactile tool for design speculation. Sketching allows you to explore your intentions in a way that no other medium is able to do. It complements the digital tools.'

He continues: 'We use sketches to search for and clarify the parti for the whole project – sometimes in plan, sometimes in section, sometimes in 3D. The aim is to describe the total project from landscape scale to detail scale with maximum economy of line. Sketching collaboratively with clients brings them on an intellectual journey with you, which makes them feel respected and invested in. You feel the space through your fingertips in a live way, in real time, face to face with your client, consultants, staff and builders as a social art.'

MacKay-Lyons notes that 'the sketch tends to be a road map for a purposeful action by the design team, who are making digital drawings'. When asked if he would be able to work without non-digital means, he answers simply: 'No, not yet.'

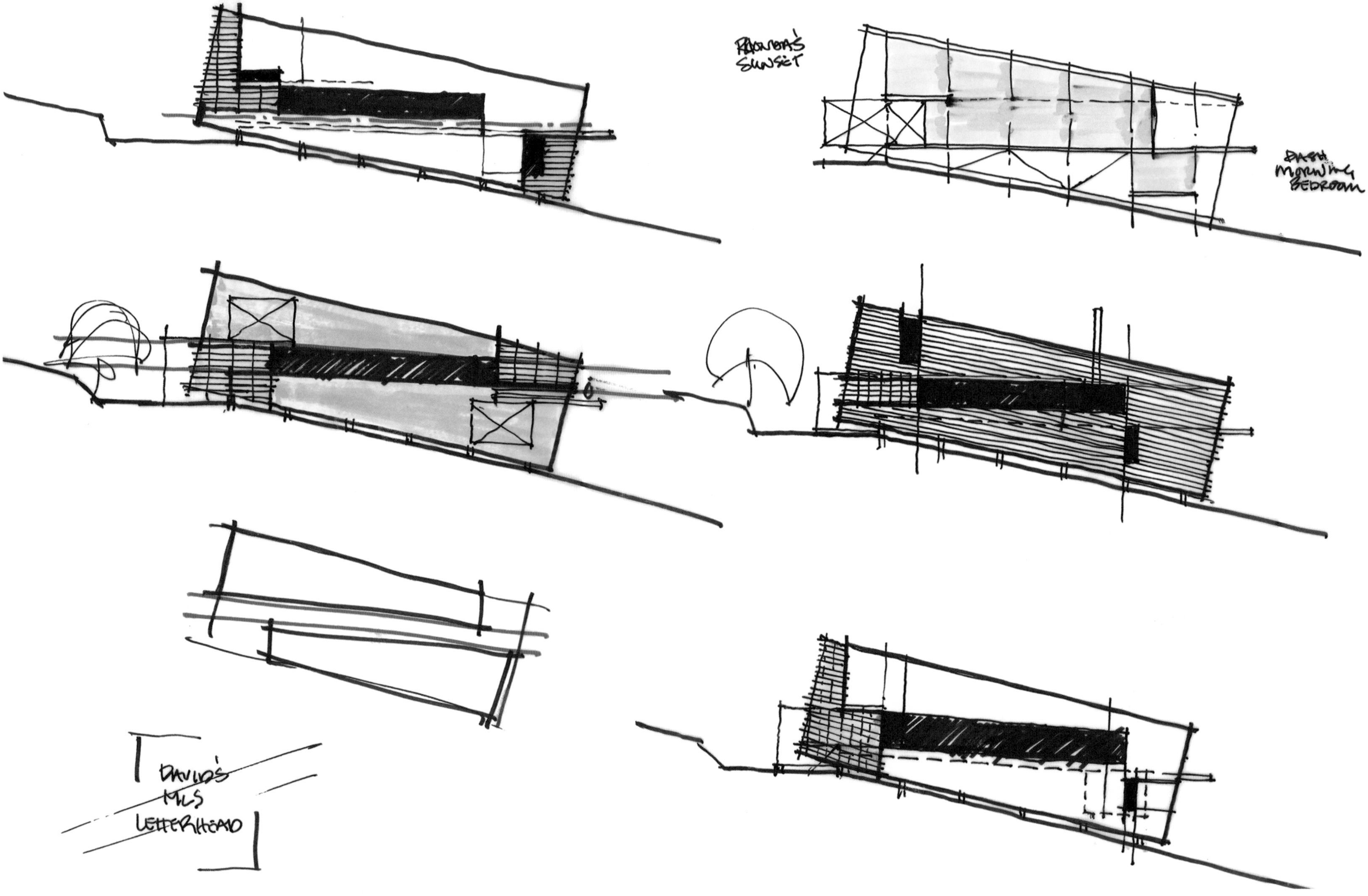
RHONDA'S SUNSET
DASH MORNING BEDROOM
DAVID'S MLS LETTERHEAD

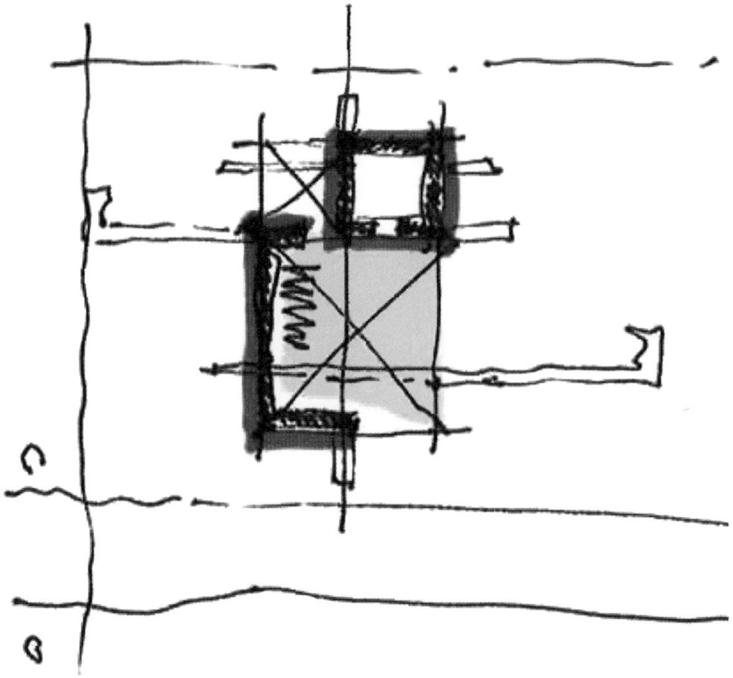
C
B

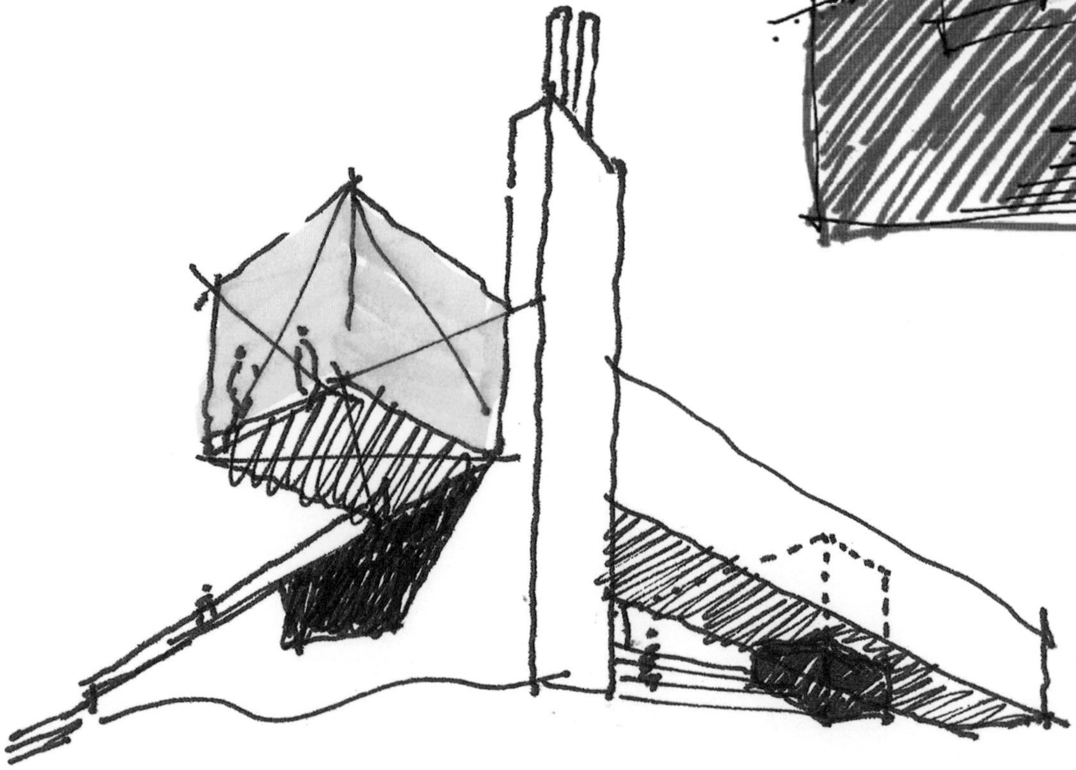

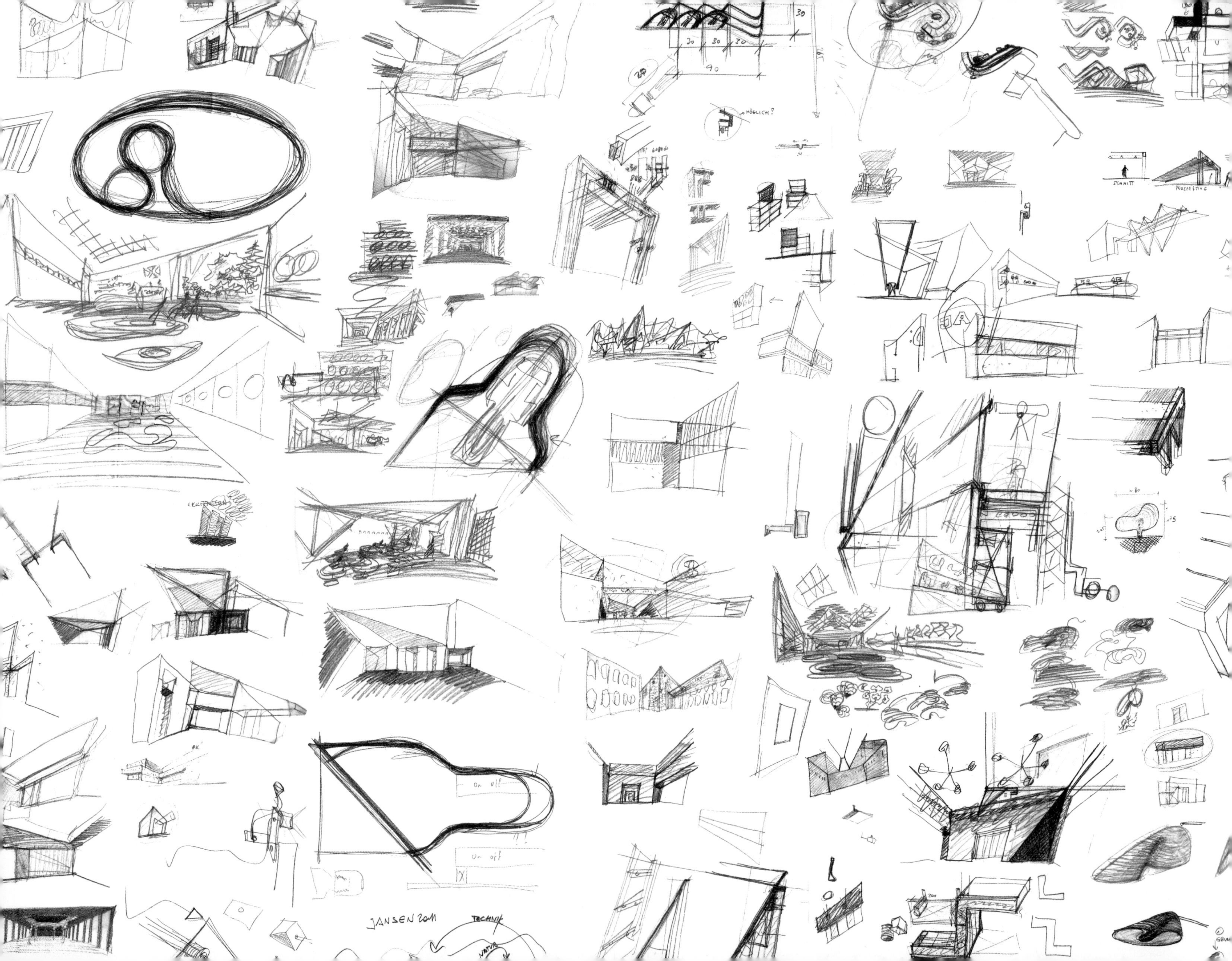
MÖGLICH?
SCHNITT
PERSPEKTIVE
on off
on off
JANSEN 2011
TECHNIK
NATUR

DAVIDE MACULLO

Davide Macullo Architects • Switzerland

Featured projects: Jansen Campus [pp. 192–5] · Tianjin Sales Centre [p. 196]
Yachting Club Villas [p. 197, top left] · Swiss House XXXII [p. 197, top right]
Residential Mountain Loft Apartments [p. 197, bottom left]
Recording Studio [p. 197, bottom right] · Swiss House XI [p. 198, top left]
Dongxiang Headquarters [p. 198, top right] · Swiss House XXXIV [p. 198, middle left]
Dubai Hotel and Spa [p. 198, middle right] · Swiss House III [p. 198, bottom left]
New Technical Centre [p. 198, bottom right] Guggenheim Museum [p. 199]

'The sketch is the soul of a project,' declares Swiss architect Davide Macullo. 'Any other media are just technical tools. That said, the model still belongs in the realm of the sketch. With a model, you can imagine a magical world. The mystery of designing is to begin without knowing what you want. Start without prejudices, and let the context tell you what is needed. New forms can arise only if you keep yourself free.'

Having worked in the Lugano-based atelier of Mario Botta for 20 years, Macullo has global experience and intuitive design skills. He established his own office in 2000, and has since gained international attention, winning awards and exhibiting at renowned furniture and design expos.

For Macullo, sketching is vital to everything that he does. His designs are drawn from the contexts in which they are inserted, and, he explains, 'only later is the unknown aesthetic revealed'. To achieve this, he and his colleagues sketch.

'First we present sketches, then models, then drawings,' he explains. 'The idea must be delivered with sketches to keep the attention focused on the reasons behind it. There are artists and architects who can barely draw a line, but they can use other media to transmit an idea of space. I can't: I need to sketch and imagine everything through the drawing.'

ECKE!
UNTERSICHT
RAUM GRAPHIK!

AUSSEN
INNEN
WD
INTERNE TRAGENDE STAHLBETON WAND
15
15
VORFABRIZIERTE BETON WAND
PRINZIP DETAIL STEIGZONEN
40 cm.
JAN
BETON

SWISS HOUSE ROSSA 2016

MASSIMO MARIANI

Massimo Mariani Architecture & Design • UK

Featured projects: Sketches for fantasy architecture [p. 200]
Architectural thoughts [pp. 201, 203] · Sketches for a carpet [p. 202]

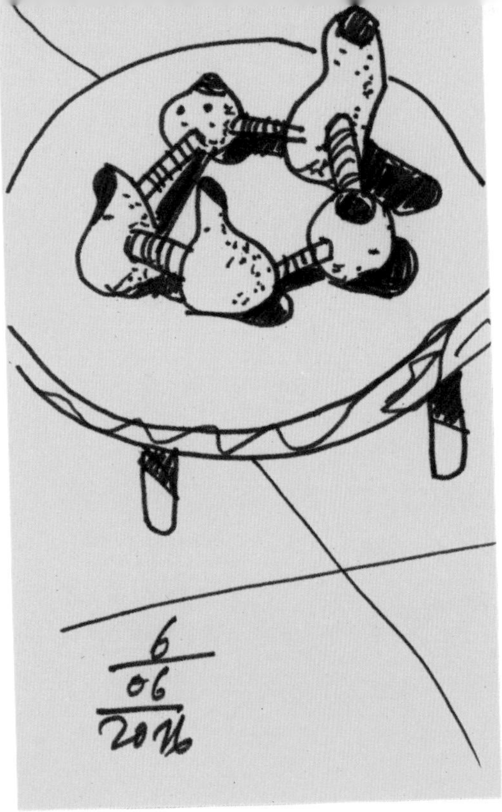

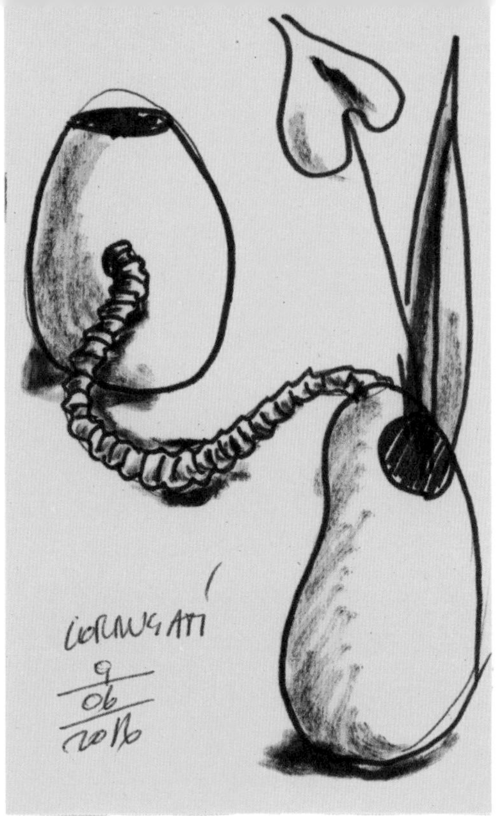

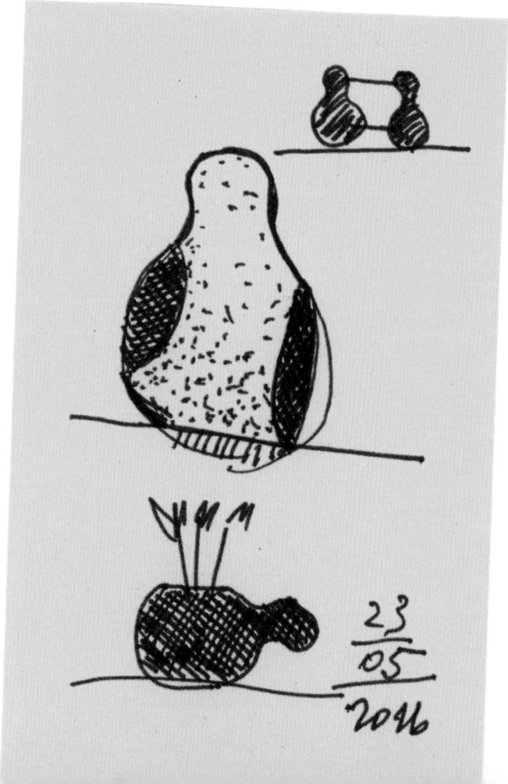

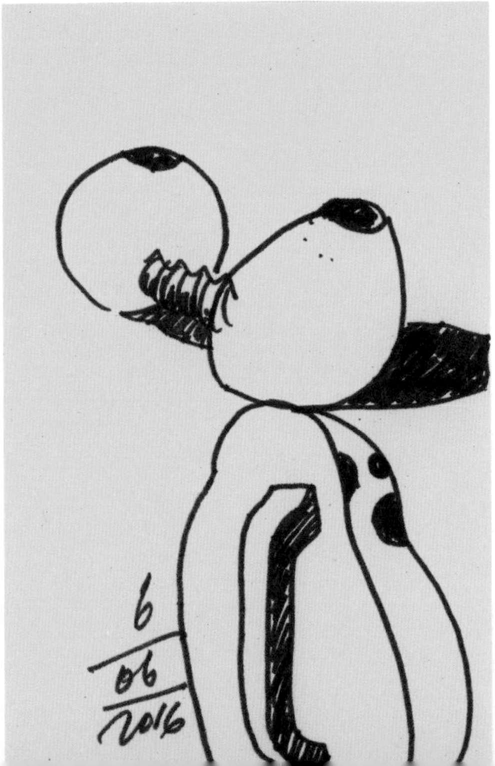

'For me,' says Italian architect Massimo Mariani, 'the sketch is thought and action, the fast materialization of an idea. Sketching is a necessity. It is of paramount importance to me, but I don't think there is a unique recipe for everyone. Sketching just happens to be my way to design. If I didn't sketch, I wouldn't have fun!'

Having studied with and worked for such architectural giants as Herman Hertzberger and Renzo Piano, Mariani moved from his native Florence to London in 1998. He set up his own practice six years later, and today is known for his designs for furniture companies such as Targa Italia and Danese Milano.

'The sketch is an evolving design process,' he explains. 'I start with one idea and finish with another. It's hard to know how the design will turn out, as the idea will change over time. The act of drawing is a process: when the sketch resembles the realization, it means that it was created later, not before. My clients almost always accept my work without much change. Generally, I will make a "beautiful" drawing and present it as such, but it will never be a carbon copy of what is eventually realized. It is a strategy, for prompting discussion.'

"TAX"

8/08/2011
"CASA

MACFARLANE HOUSE
NOV 8.10
EXTERIOR
(WINDOW)
ADDITION

INTERIOR
PERSPECTIVE
(STAIRS)

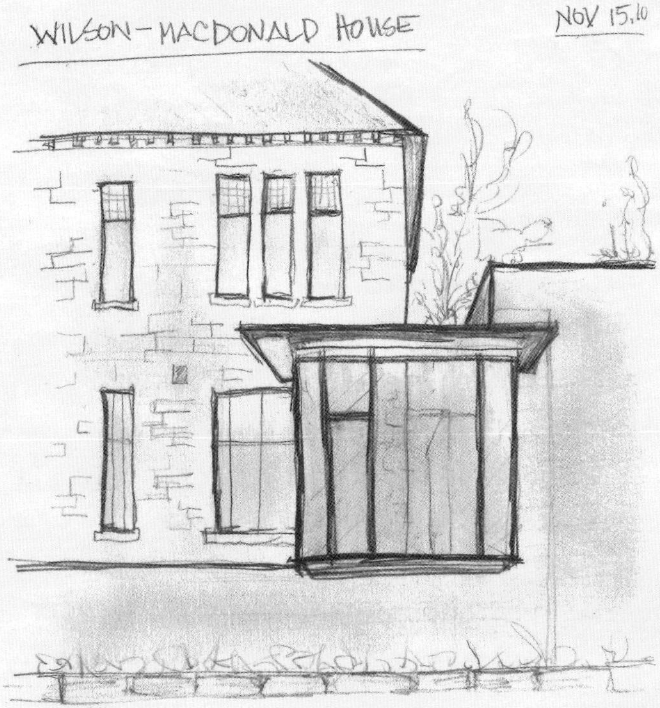
WILSON-MACDONALD HOUSE
NOV 15.10

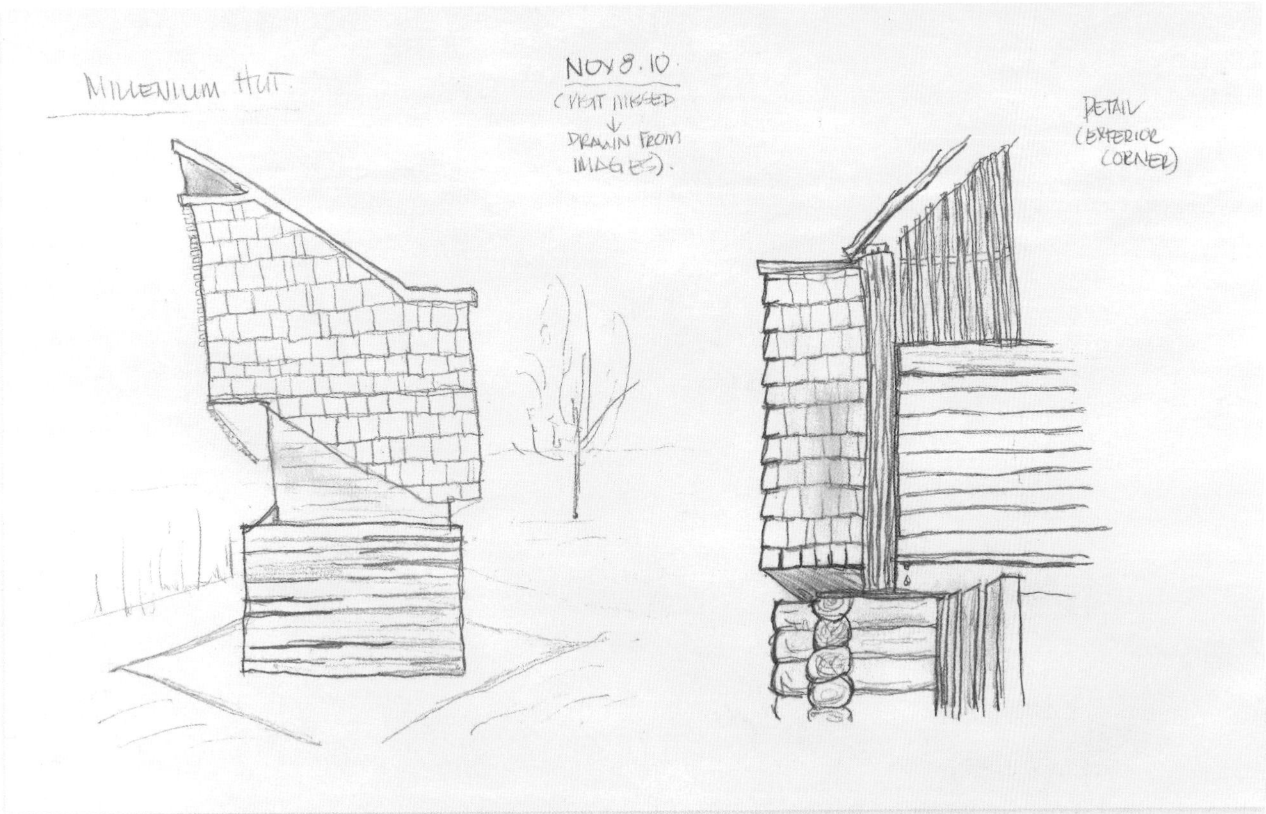

TARA McLAUGHLIN

+VG Architects • Canada

Featured projects: Broomhill [p. 204, top left] · Macfarlane House [p. 204, top right] · Millenium Hut [p. 204, bottom left; p. 205, top] Wilson MacDonald House [p. 204, bottom right; p. 205, bottom]

'Where do I sketch?' muses Tara McLaughlin of Canadian firm +VG (see also p. 36). 'It depends on what I am sketching. If I am doing a study, I'll go to site and sketch. If it is a new project, I'll develop the drawings further in the studio. Or I sketch in a notebook perched on the arm of my reading chair. It can be difficult when you are driving or standing in a queue and suddenly get an idea, but I simply have to stop what I am doing and sketch it out. Sometimes it is a drawing; sometimes it is a few words.'

Based in the company's Ottawa office, McLaughlin is part of a large multidisciplinary team that designs a wide range of projects, from residential homes to civic masterplans. 'Words are also an important part of sketching,' she says. 'I believe strongly in the relationship between drawing and reading. Sketching is a multi-layered process that begins with a few lines, and becomes something through thinking about an idea and allowing it to come to life on the page.'

In conclusion, she notes: 'Sketching has and always will be one of the most important parts of the design process for me. Digital means are used to develop the design once there is a clear idea of the concept, the scale and the relationship to the site, whether a pavilion in a field or an urban façade. Sketching is the first step towards establishing a relationship between what is initially conceived in the mind and what is actually produced.'

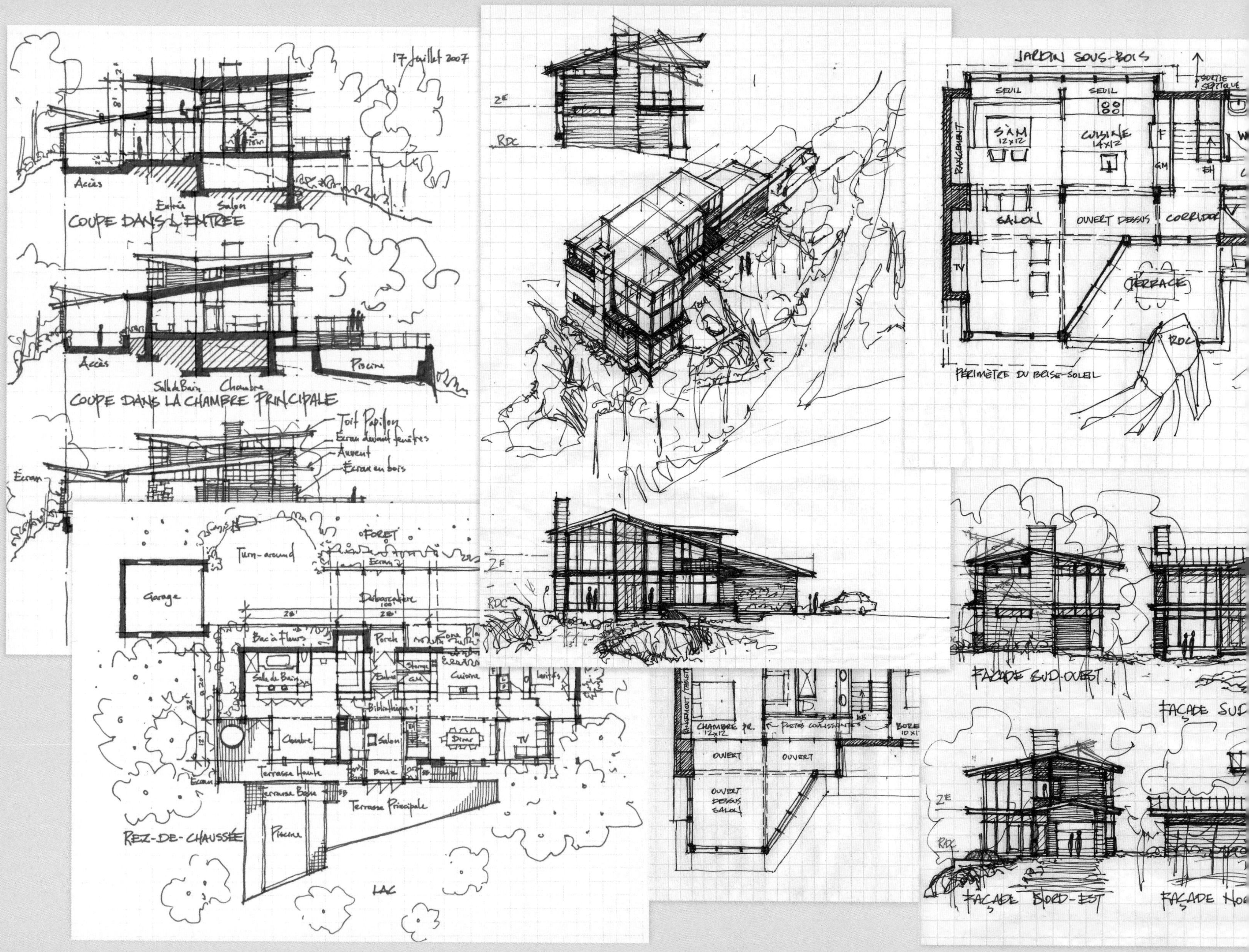
17 juillet 2007
Accès
Entrée
Salon
COUPE DANS L'ENTRÉE
Accès
Piscine
Salle de Bain
Chambre
COUPE DANS LA CHAMBRE PRINCIPALE
Toit Papillon
Écran devant fenêtres
Auvent
Écran en bois
Écran
FORÊT
Turn-around
Garage
Écran
Débarcadère
Bac à fleurs
Porch
Salle de Bain
Entrée
Storage
Cuisine
Chambre
Salon
Dîner
TV
Terrasse Haute
Baie
Terrasse Basse
Terrasse Principale
REZ-DE-CHAUSSÉE
Piscine
LAC
2E
RDC
JARDIN SOUS-BOIS
SEUIL
SEUIL
SÀM 12x12
CUISINE 14x12
RANGEMENT
SALON
OUVERT DESSUS
CORRIDOR
TERRASSE
ROC
PÉRIMÈTRE DU BRISE-SOLEIL
CHAMBRE PR. 12x12
PORTES COULISSANTES
OUVERT
OUVERT
OUVERT DESSUS SALON
FAÇADE SUD-OUEST
FAÇADE SUD
FAÇADE NORD-EST
FAÇADE NORD

ROB MINERS

Studio MMA • Canada

Featured projects: Ste-Adèle House [p. 206]
The Aerie [p. 207] • St-Faustin House [pp. 208–9]
Le Quai [p. 210] • Le Refuge [p. 211]

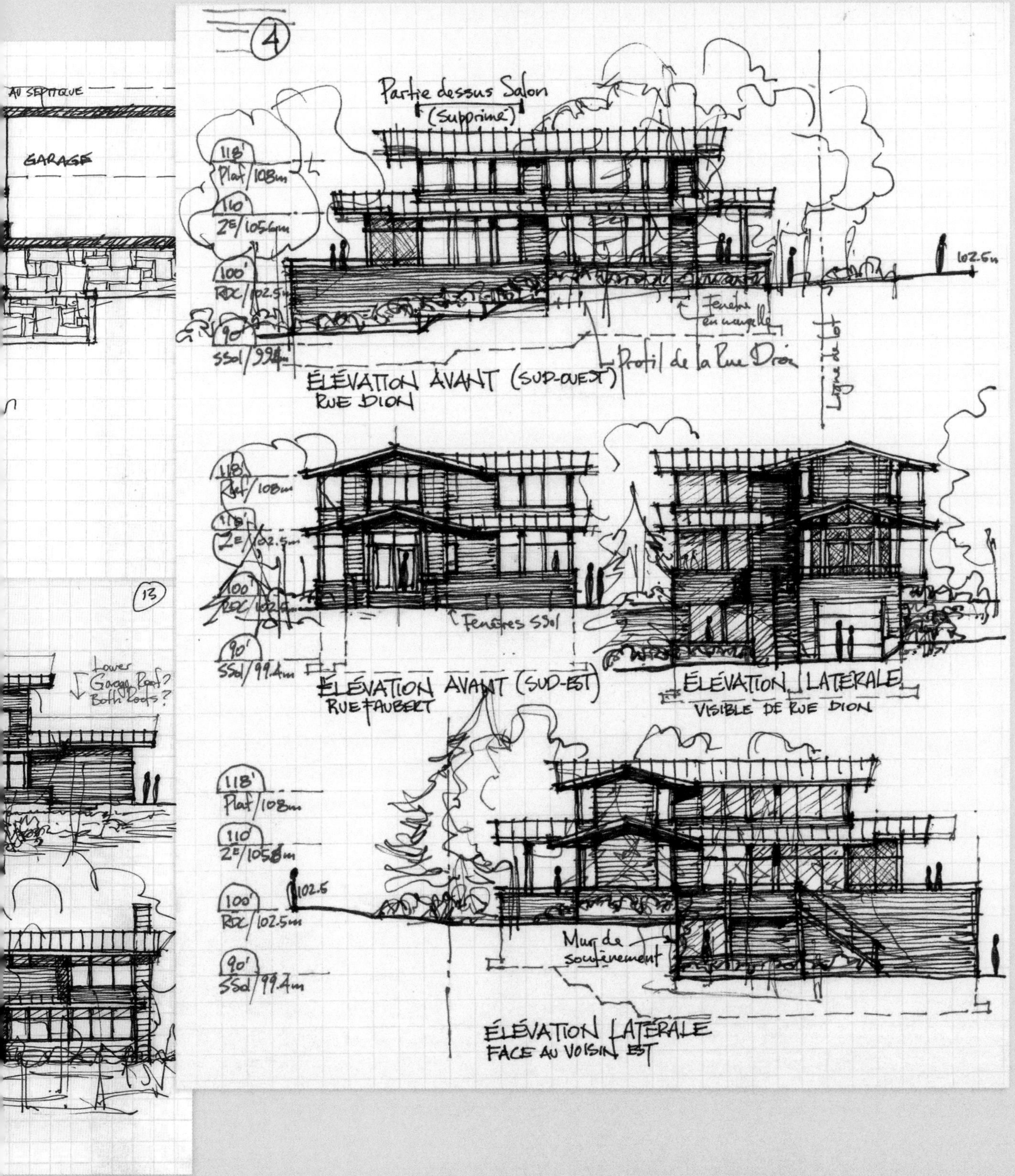

'Digital tools have advanced so much that I could design without sketching, as I see some of my younger colleagues doing,' notes Rob Miners of Canadian firm Studio MMA. 'But I would miss sketching terribly: it is a part of me and how I think. It allows for an instant, intuitive expression of my ideas in physical form, because I've been drawing since long before I knew my alphabet. I imagined a tree and it appeared on paper, and with each passing year, as my abilities improved, the drawing of the tree would satisfy me more.'

Miners, together with Vouli Mamfredis, founded Studio MMA in 1999. Based in Montreal, the company focuses on environmental design and has worked extensively with Mountain Equipment Co-op, a consumers' cooperative that sells outdoor recreation gear and clothing. It also built the first LEED-certified home for Habitat for Humanity in Canada.

'The best computer programs allow room for intuition and imprecision as a design advances,' he says. 'But they don't represent an innate skill developed over a lifetime, and have more barriers to expression and creativity. My sketching is a multi-layered process: initial thoughts have to be tested, and the design is informed by so many considerations that inevitably some solutions that seem perfect become flawed.'

Miners continues: 'A building needs to be designed in plan, in section and three-dimensionally, almost simultaneously, and each informing the others. Creating a building is like solving a puzzle, and sketching is the initial part of the process. The intuitive nature of it is perfect when ideas are forming, but when they need to be developed further, digital methods allow exploration to advance to the fine-tuning of ideas developed in sketch form.'

14 FACADE EST

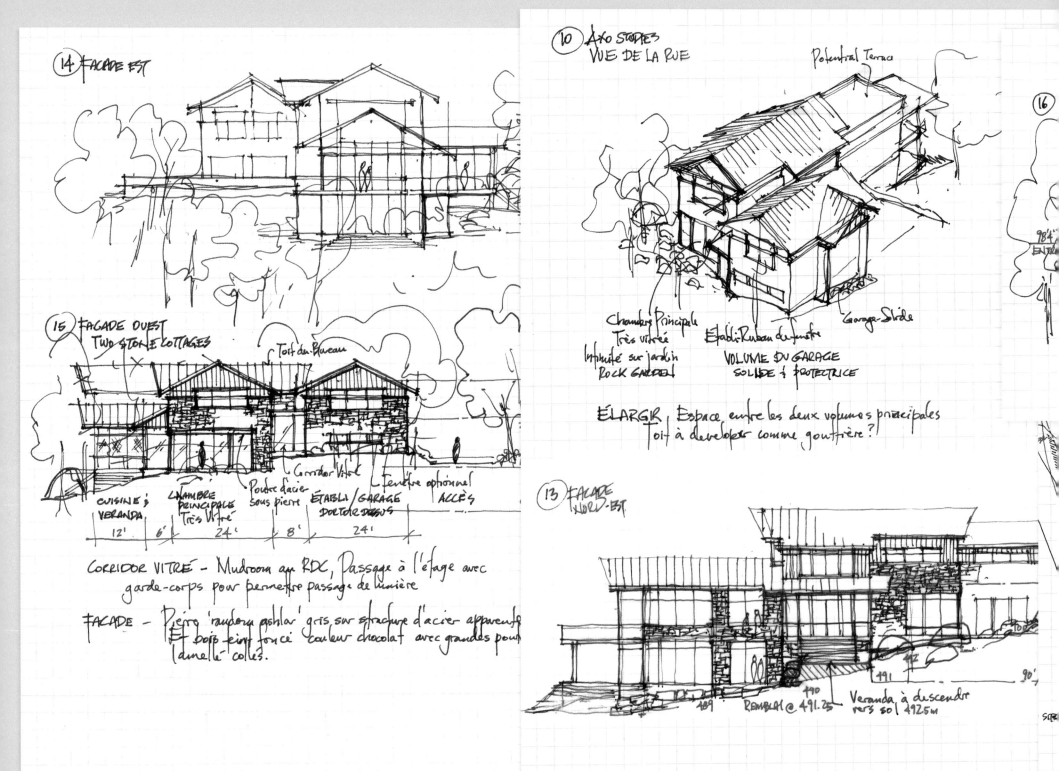

15 FACADE OUEST
TWO STONE COTTAGES

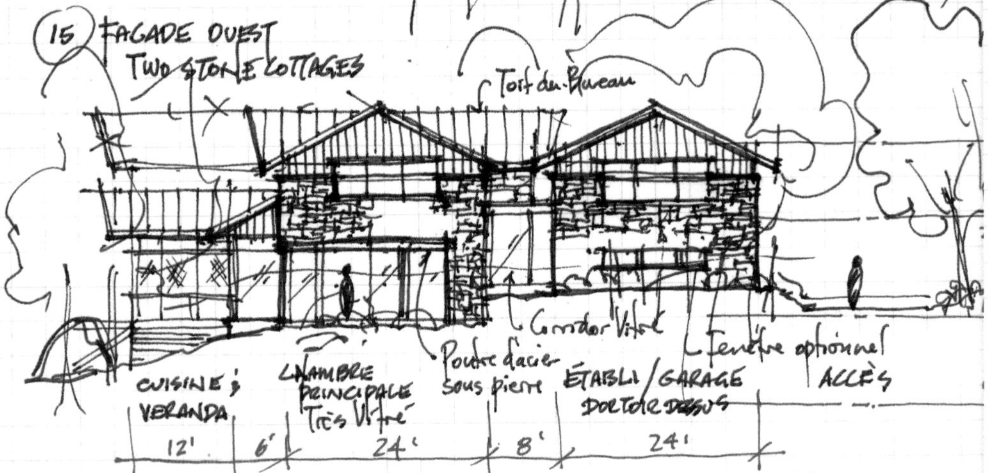

CORRIDOR VITRÉ – Mudroom au RDC, Passage à l'étage avec garde-corps pour permettre passage de lumière

FACADE – Pierre 'random ashlar' gris sur structure d'acier apparente Et bois teint foncé couleur chocolat avec grandes poutres lamellé collés.

10 AXO STUDIES
VUE DE LA RUE

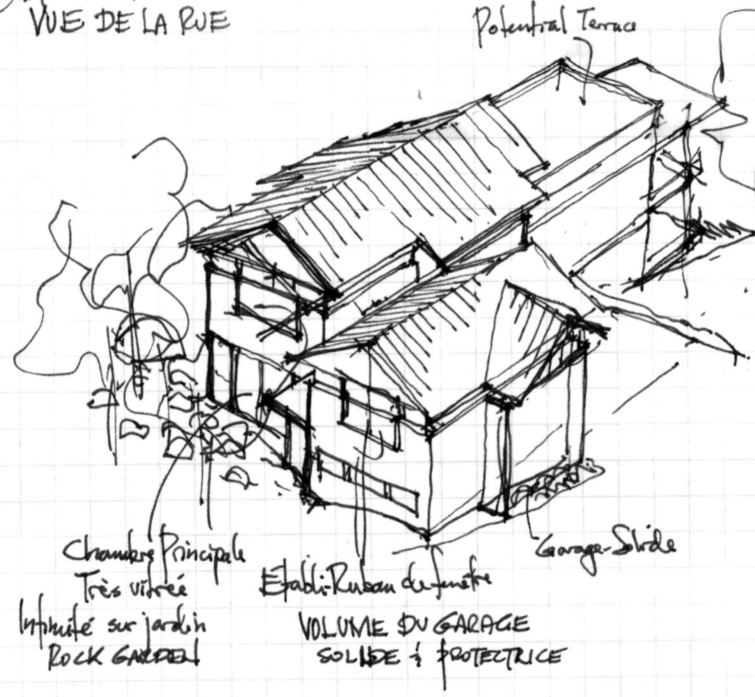

ÉLARGIR, Espace entre les deux volumes principales
Toit à développer comme gouttière?

13 FACADE NORD-EST

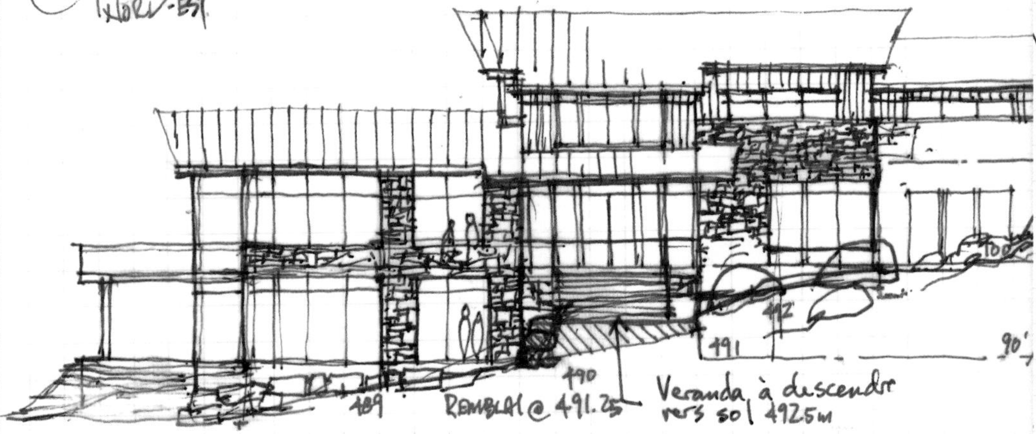

16

MUR DE PIERRES
ou béton teinté
EST
RDC
RDJ
Mur de pierres
pour soutennement.

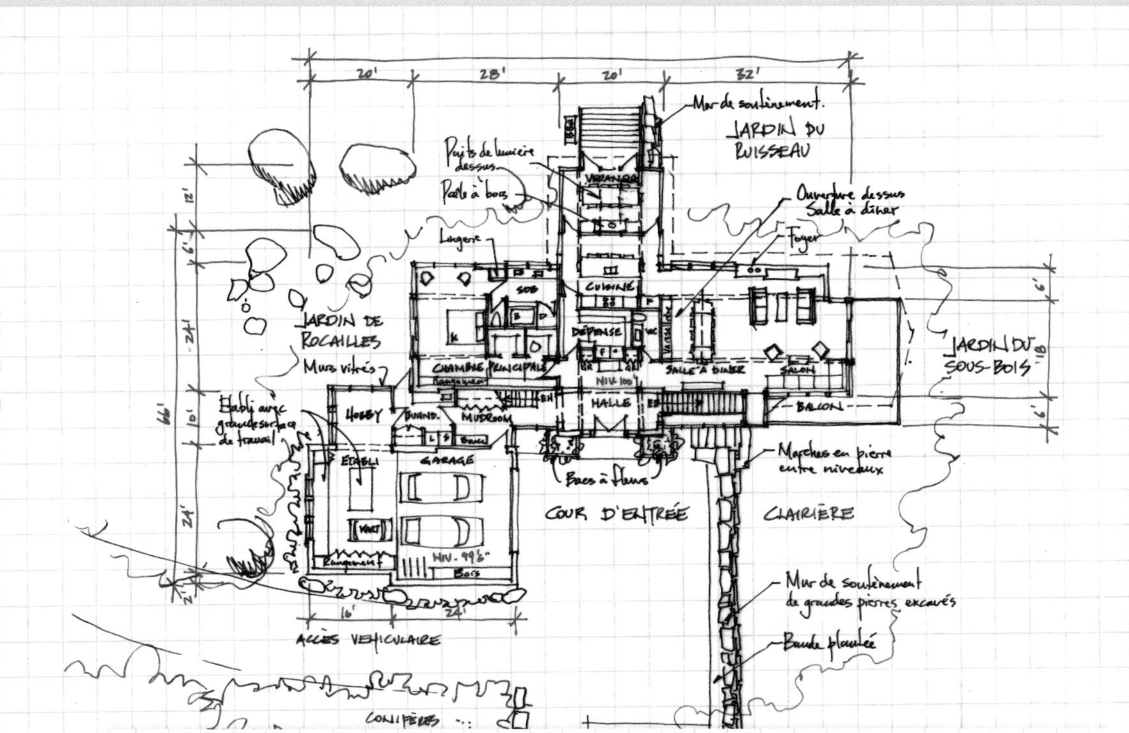
20'
28'
20'
32'
Mur de soutènement.
JARDIN DU
RUISSEAU
Puits de lumière
dessus
Poêle à bois
Ouverture dessus
Salle à dîner
Foyer
Lingerie
SDB
CUISINE
JARDIN DE
ROCAILLES
DÉPENSE
CHAMBRE PRINCIPALE
SALLE À DINER
SALON
JARDIN DU
SOUS-BOIS
Mur vitré
NIV. 100'
HALLE
BALCON
Établi avec
grande surface
de travail
HOBBY
MUDROOM
ÉTABLI
GARAGE
Bacs à fleurs
Marches en pierre
entre niveaux
COUR D'ENTRÉE
CLAIRIÈRE
NIV. 99'6"
Bois
Mur de soutènement
de grandes pierres excavés
16'
24'
ACCÈS VÉHICULAIRE
Bande plantée
CONIFÈRES

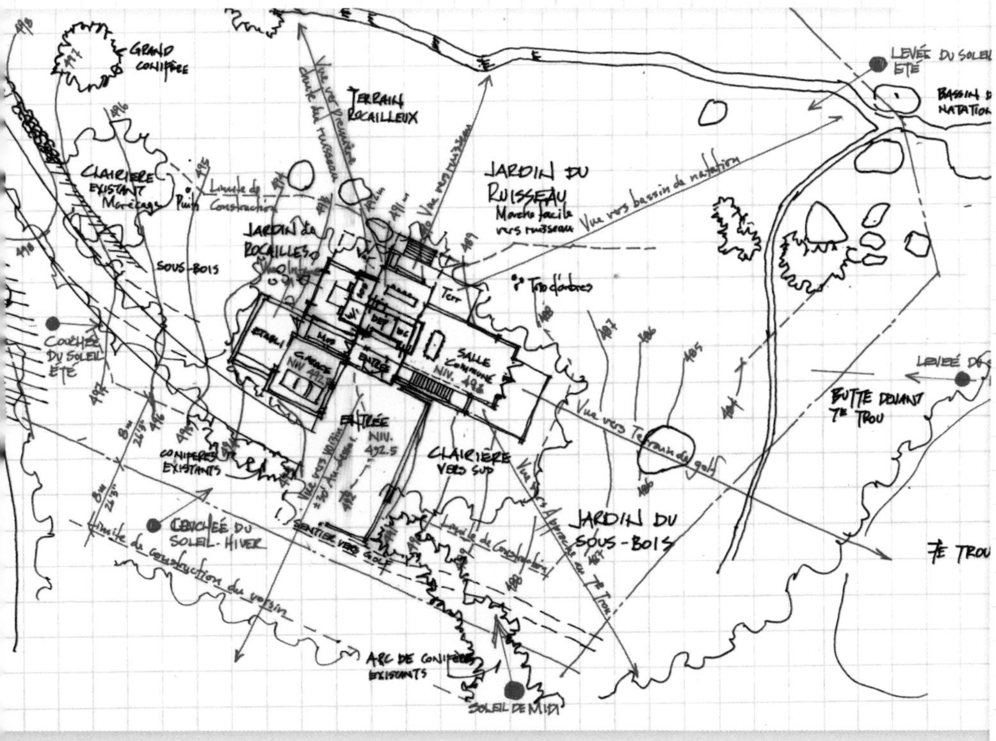
GRAND
CONIFÈRE
TERRAIN
ROCAILLEUX
LEVÉE DU SOLEIL
ÉTÉ
BASSIN DE
NATATION
JARDIN DU
RUISSEAU
Vue vers bassin de natation
CLAIRIÈRE
EXISTANT
Limite de
Construction
JARDIN de
ROCAILLES
SOUS-BOIS
COUCHER
DU SOLEIL
ÉTÉ
SALLE
COMMUNE
NIV. 493
GARAGE
ENTRÉE
NIV.
492.5
BUTTE DEVANT
7e TROU
LEVÉE DU
CONIFÈRES
EXISTANTS
CLAIRIÈRE
VERS SUD
Vue vers Terrain de golf
COUCHER DU
SOLEIL HIVER
JARDIN DU
SOUS-BOIS
7e TROU
ARC DE CONIFÈRES
EXISTANTS
SOLEIL DE MIDI

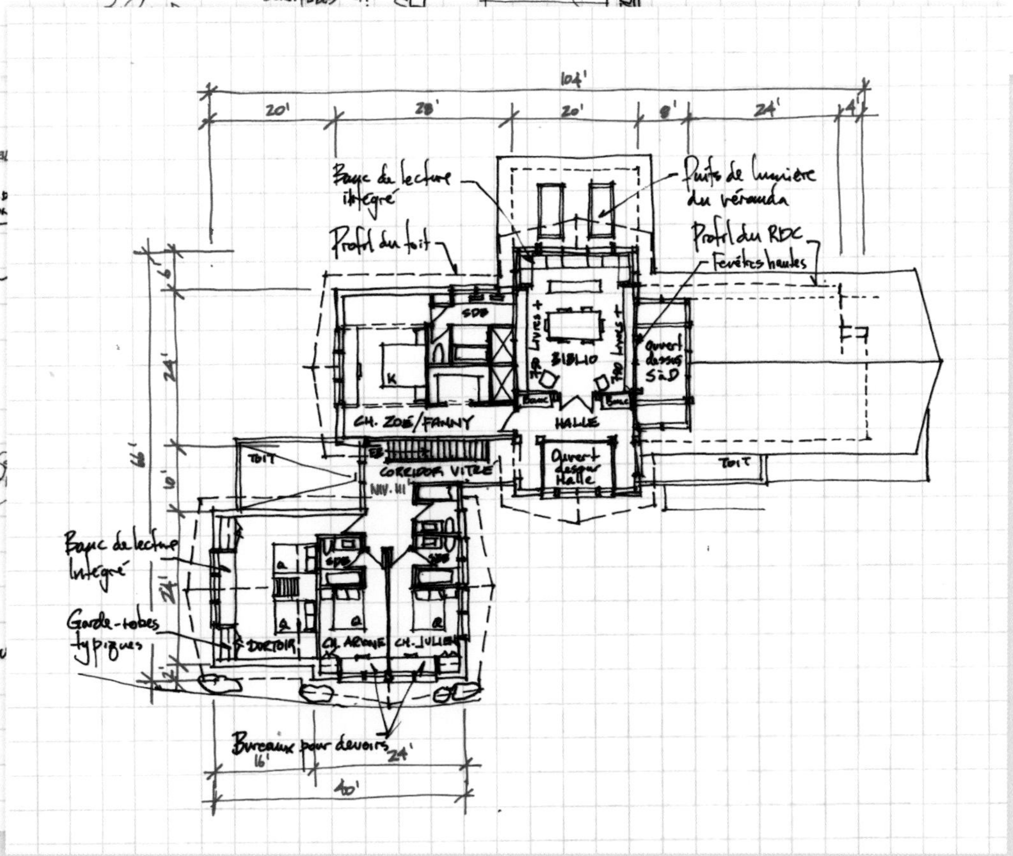
104'
20'
28'
20'
8'
24'
4'
Banc de lecture
intégré
Puits de lumière
du véranda
Profil du toit
Profil du RDC
Fenêtres hautes
SDB
BIBLIO
Ouvert
dessus
SàD
CH. ZOÉ/FANNY
HALLE
TOIT
Ouvert
dessus
Halle
CORRIDOR VITRÉ
NIV. 111
Banc de lecture
intégré
Garde-robes
typiques
DORTOIR
CH. ARIANE
CH. JULIEN
Bureaux pour devoirs
16'
24'
40'

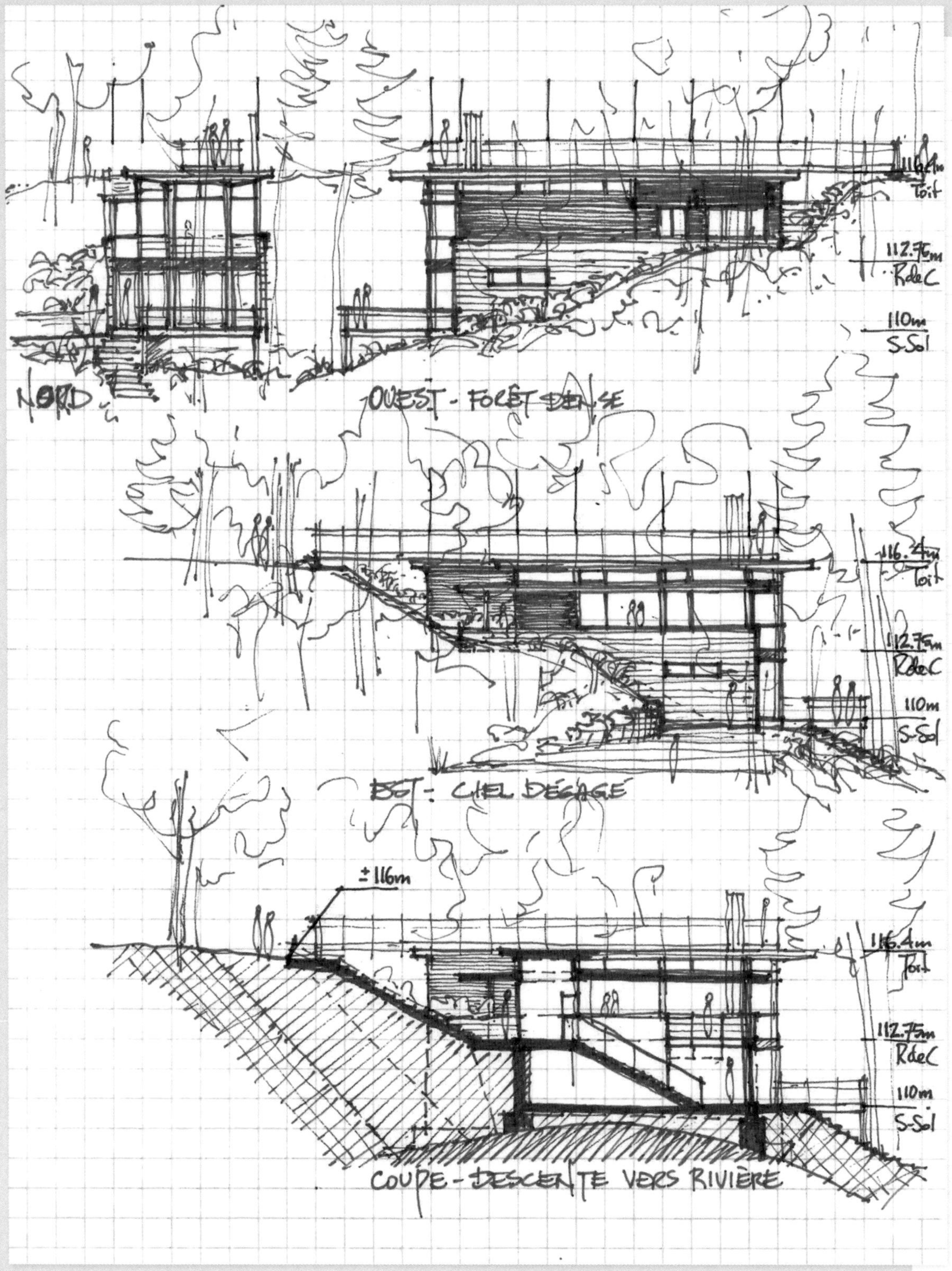
116.4m
Toit
112.75m
RdeC
110m
S-Sol
NORD
OUEST - FORÊT DENSE
116.4m
Toit
112.75m
RdeC
110m
S-Sol
EST - CIEL DÉGAGÉ
± 116m
116.4m
Toit
112.75m
RdeC
110m
S-Sol
COUPE - DESCENTE VERS RIVIÈRE

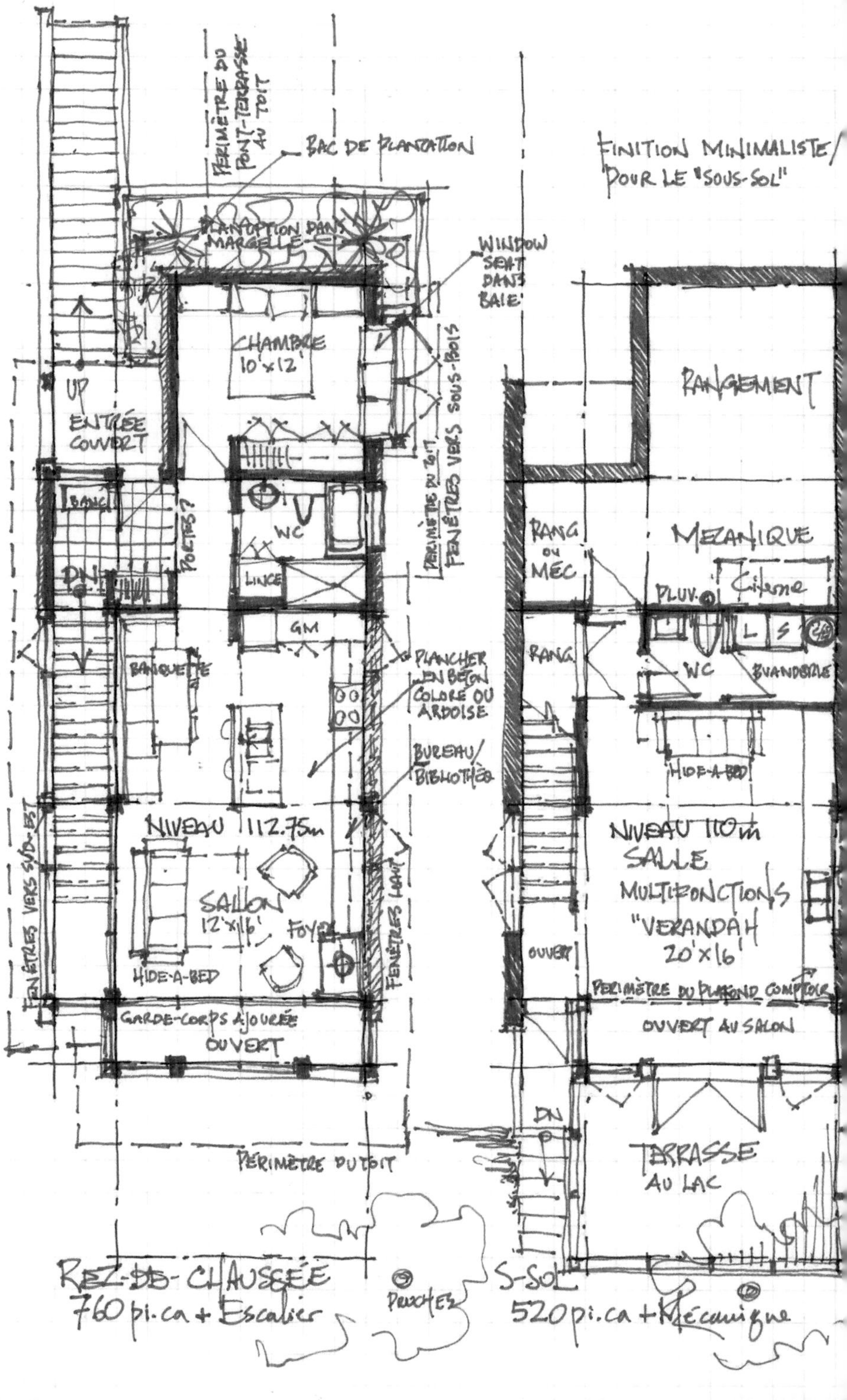
PÉRIMÈTRE DU PONT-TERRASSE AU TOIT
BAC DE PLANTATION
PLANTATION DANS MARGELLE
WINDOW SEAT DANS BAIE
CHAMBRE
10'x12'
UP
ENTRÉE COUVERT
BANC
DN
PORTES?
WC
LINGE
GM
PÉRIMÈTRE DU TOIT
FENÊTRES VERS SOUS-BOIS
BANQUETTE
PLANCHER EN BÉTON COLORÉ OU ARDOISE
BUREAU/ BIBLIOTHÈQUE
NIVEAU 112.75m
SALON
12'x16'
FOYER
HIDE-A-BED
FENÊTRES VERS SUD-EST
FENÊTRES LOFT
GARDE-CORPS AJOURÉE
OUVERT
PÉRIMÈTRE DU TOIT
REZ-DE-CHAUSSÉE
760 pi.ca + Escalier
FINITION MINIMALISTE/ POUR LE "SOUS-SOL"
RANGEMENT
RANG OU MÉC
MÉCANIQUE
PLUV.
Citerne
RANG
WC
BUANDERIE
HIDE-A-BED
NIVEAU 110m
SALLE MULTIFONCTIONS
"VERANDAH"
20'x16'
OUVERT
PÉRIMÈTRE DU PLAFOND COMPTOIR
OUVERT AU SALON
DN
TERRASSE AU LAC
S-SOL
520 pi.ca + Mécanique
PERCHES

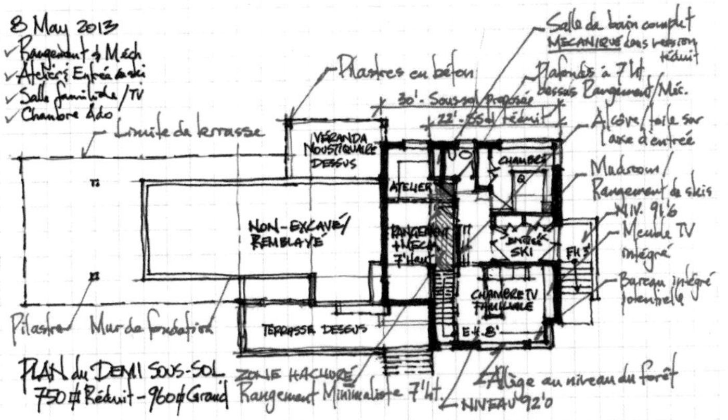
8 May 2013
Salle de bain complet
Plastres en béton
Limite de terrasse
VÉRANDA MOUSTIQUAIRE DESSUS
NON-EXCAVÉ/ REMBLAYÉ
ATELIER
CHAMBRE
Madroom/ Rangement de skis
Meuble TV intégré
Bureau intégré potentielle
CHAMBRE TV FAMILIALE
TERRASSE DESSUS
Pilastre
Mur de fondation
PLAN du DEMI SOUS-SOL
750 # Réduit - 960 # Grand
ZONE HACHURÉE
Rangement Minimaliste 7'ht.
Allège au niveau du forêt
NIVEAU 92'0

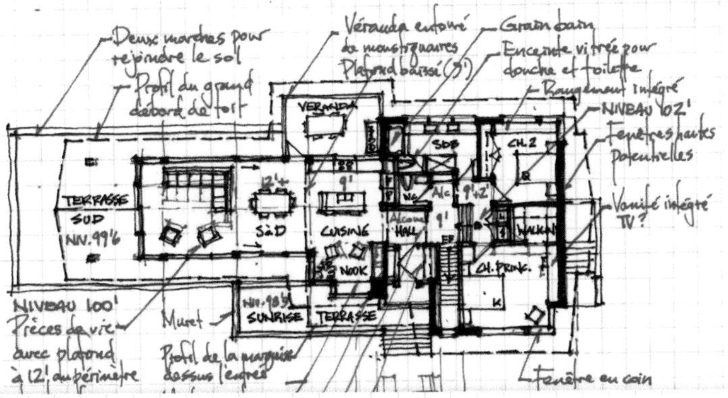
Deux marches pour rejoindre le sol
Profil du grand débord de toit
Véranda entouré de moustiquaires
Plafond baissé (9')
Grand bain
Enceinte vitrée pour douche et toilette
Rangement intégré
NIVEAU 102'
Fenêtres hautes potentielles
Vanité intégré TV?
TERRASSE SUD
NIV. 99'6
SAD
CUISINE
HALL
NOOK
WALK-IN
CH. PRINC.
SDB
CH. 2
VÉRANDA
SUNRISE
TERRASSE
NIVEAU 100'
Pièces de vie avec plafond à 12' au périmètre
Muret
Profil de la marquise dessus l'entrée
Fenêtre en coin

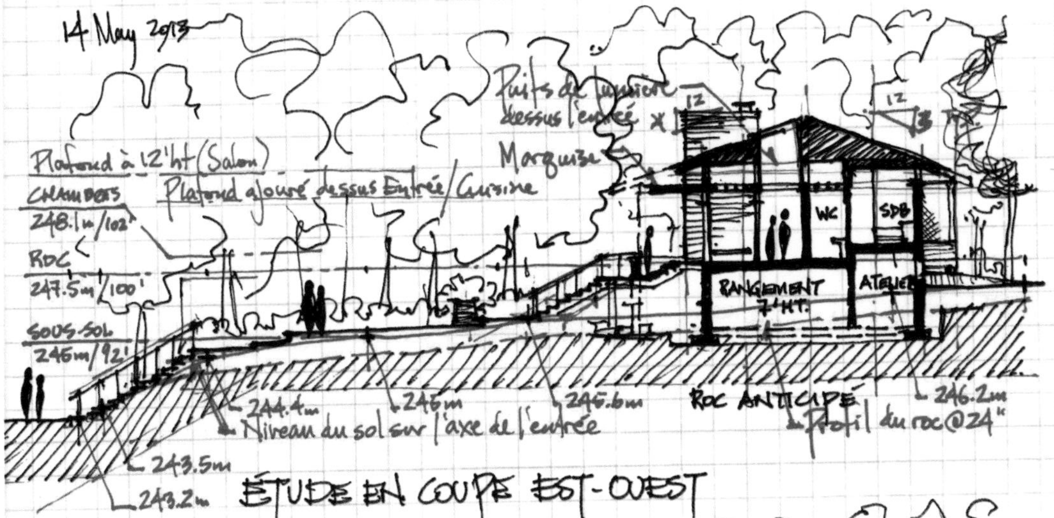
14 May 2013
Puits de lumière dessus l'entrée
Marquise
Plafond à 12'ht (Salon)
Plafond ajouré dessus Entrée/Cuisine
CHAMBRES
248.1m/102'
ROC
247.5m/100'
SOUS-SOL
245m/92'
WC
SDB
RANGEMENT 7'HT.
ATELIER
244.4m
245m
245.6m
ROC ANTICIPÉ
246.2m
Niveau du sol sur l'axe de l'entrée
Profil du roc @ 24"
243.5m
243.2m
ÉTUDE EN COUPE EST-OUEST

Fenêtres hautes potentielles
Plafond @ 12' (Salon)
CHAMBRES
248.1m/102'
Marches avec garde-corps
Entrée de ski avec marquise
FAÇADE OUEST

Toit prolongé dessus terrasse principale
Cheminée massif (maçonnerie/panneaux)
Window seat devant foyer
Terrasse basse derrière muret
12'ht (Salon)
Marches sans garde-corps
Roche au sud
FAÇADE EST

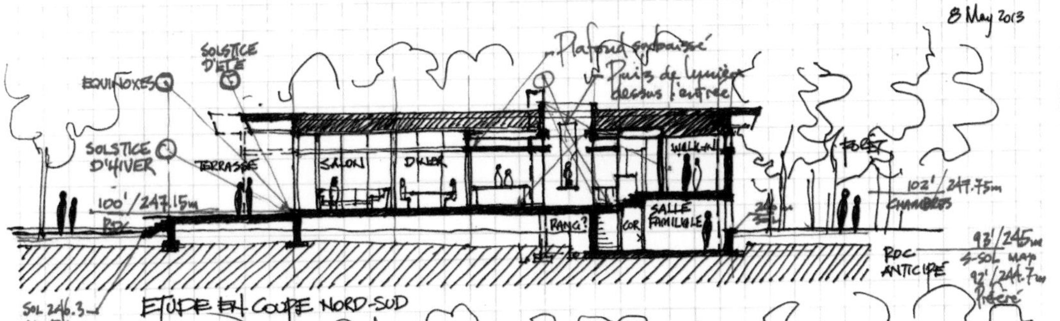
8 May 2013
SOLSTICE D'ÉTÉ
EQUINOXES
SOLSTICE D'HIVER
Plafond surbaissé
Puits de lumière dessus l'entrée
TERRASSE
SALON
DINER
WALK-IN
FORÊT
100'/247.15m
ROC
RANG?
COR
SALLE FAMILIALE
102'/247.75m
CHAMBRES
93'/245m
S-SOL
ROC ANTICIPÉ
SOL 246.3 MOYEN
ÉTUDE EN COUPE NORD-SUD

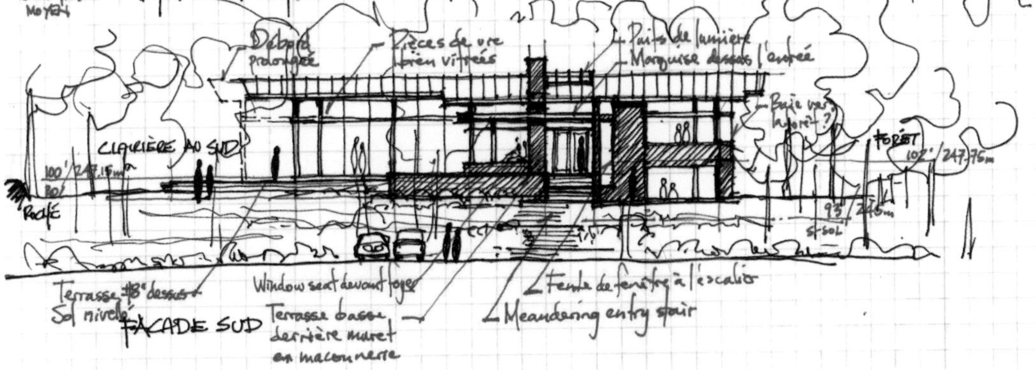
Débord prolongé
Pièces de vie bien vitrées
Puits de lumière
Marquise dessus l'entrée
CLAIRIÈRE AU SUD
FORÊT
102'/247.75m
100'/247.15m
ROCHE
93'/245m
S-SOL
Terrasse 18" dessus Sol nivelé
Window seat devant foyer
Fente de fenêtre à l'escalier
Meandering entry stair
FAÇADE SUD
Terrasse basse derrière muret en maçonnerie

PETER MORRIS

Peter Morris Architects • UK

Featured project: Vicars Road [pp. 212–15]

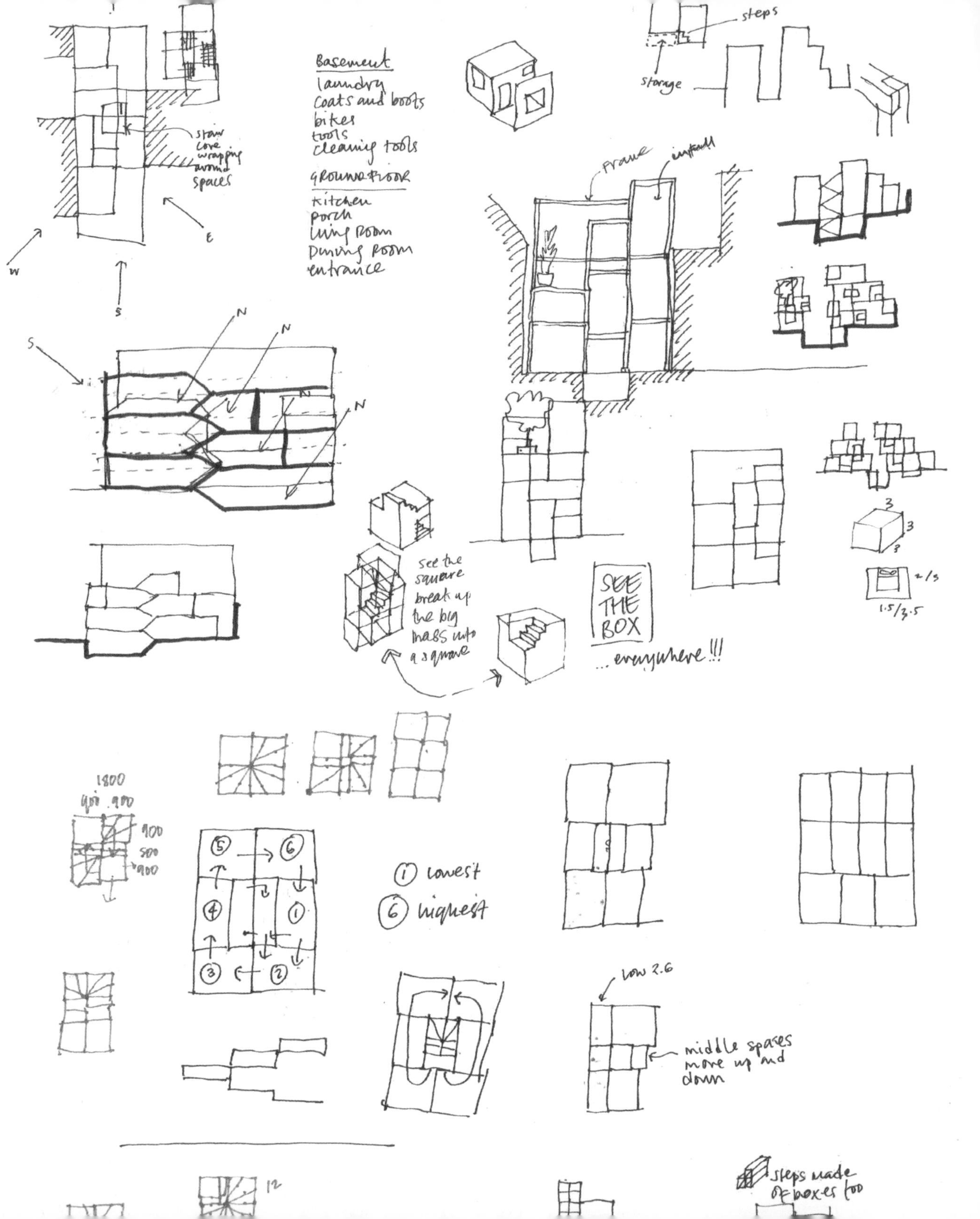

'I began sketching before I could walk,' says London-based architect Peter Morris. 'Sketching is intuitive. It requires very little thought, time, effort or resources, and gives me the freedom to explore my thoughts and ideas. Nothing can rival the act of sketching: the pen might be swapped with a gadget, the paper replaced by a tablet, but the act itself is unchangeable and unimprovable. In every building I've ever designed, sketching has been a vital part of the process.'

Morris and his team specialize in designing homes, predominantly within the densely populated urban centre of London. The challenges of weaving the new into the old make for exciting designs, always created physically by sketching. 'Sketches develop the story of a design through a strong visual narrative,' he says. 'Like a conversation, the destination is not always known at the start. It is a reactive practice: the way the first line is drawn influences the next, and so on. Clients often think design is a linear process, but that's because we explain things that way. In reality, design travels in tangents, loops and jumps, pulling in and spitting out all kinds of references. It is never linear.'

He continues: 'I have never been able to work without physically making something. Artists make their art. Designers don't make their designs, we instruct others to make them. We like to be control freaks, but we can't have complete control. Builders will always be interpreting our instructions, and so are part of the creative process. It would be an interesting exercise to use only words – no sketches – to explain our designs!'

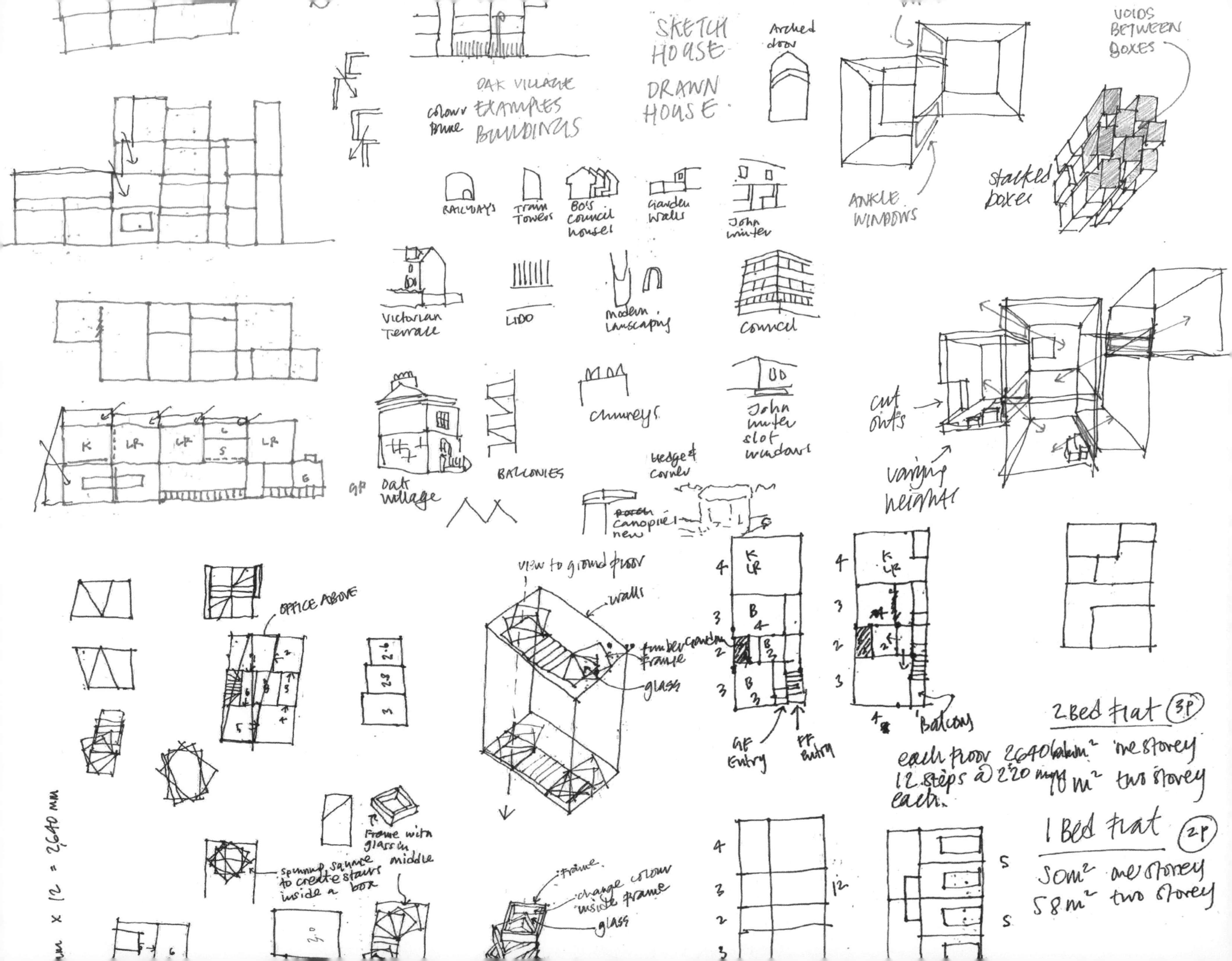
SKETCH HOUSE
DRAWN HOUSE
Arched door
OAK VILLAGE EXAMPLES BUILDINGS
colour frame
VOIDS BETWEEN BOXES
ANKLE WINDOWS
stacked boxes
RAILWAYS
Train Towers
Bo's council houses
Garden walls
John Winter
Victorian Terrace
LIDO
Modern Landscaping
Council
chimneys
John Winter slot windows
BALCONIES
GF Oak Village
hedge & corner
canopies new
cut outs
varying heights
view to ground floor
walls
timber/garden frame
glass
OFFICE ABOVE
GF Entry
FF Entry
Balcony
2 Bed Flat (3P)
each floor 2640mm² one storey
12 steps @ 220 mm each.
70m² two storey
1 Bed Flat (2P)
50m² one storey
58m² two storey
Frame with glass in middle
spinning square to create stairs inside a box
frame
change colour inside frame
glass
mm x 12 = 2640 mm

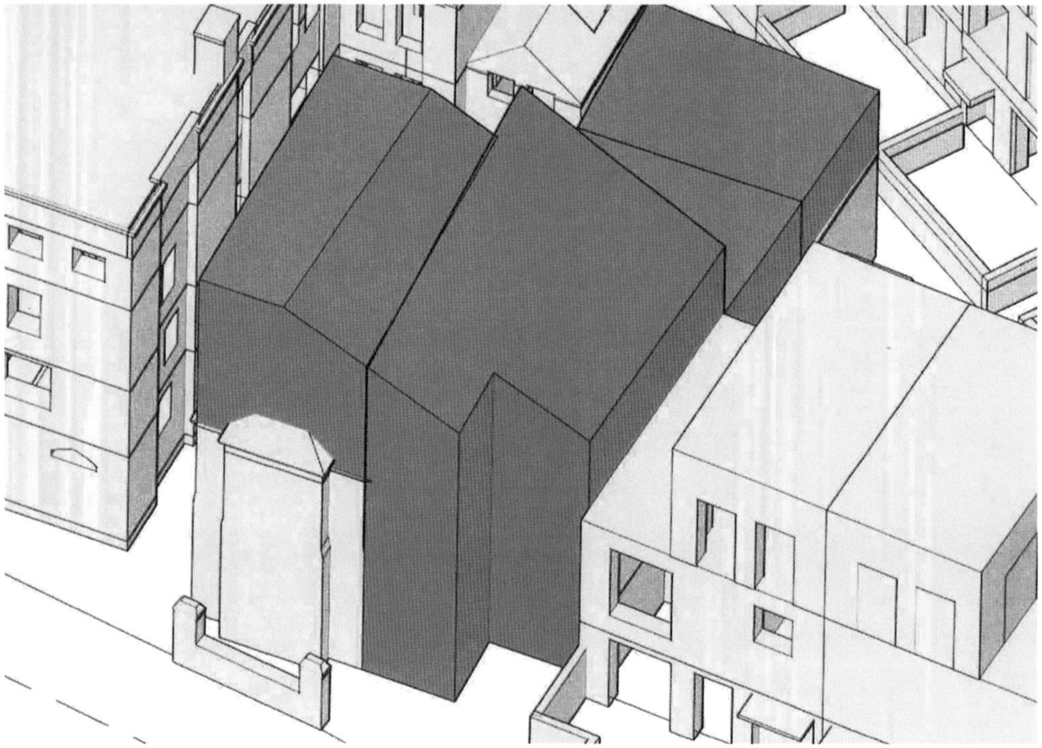
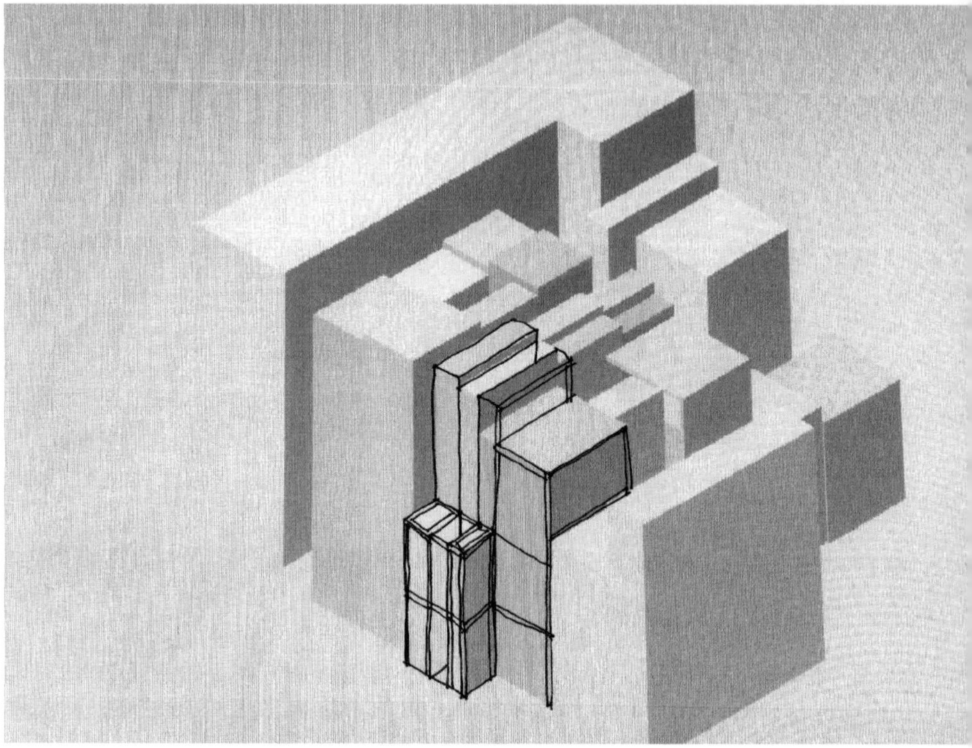
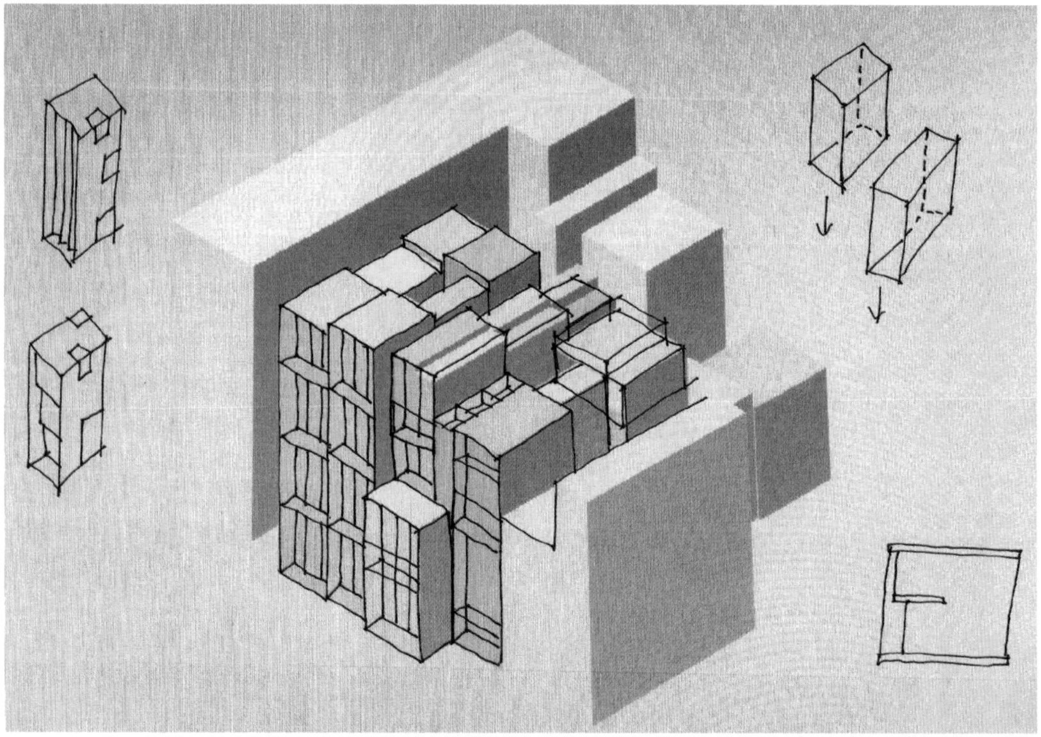
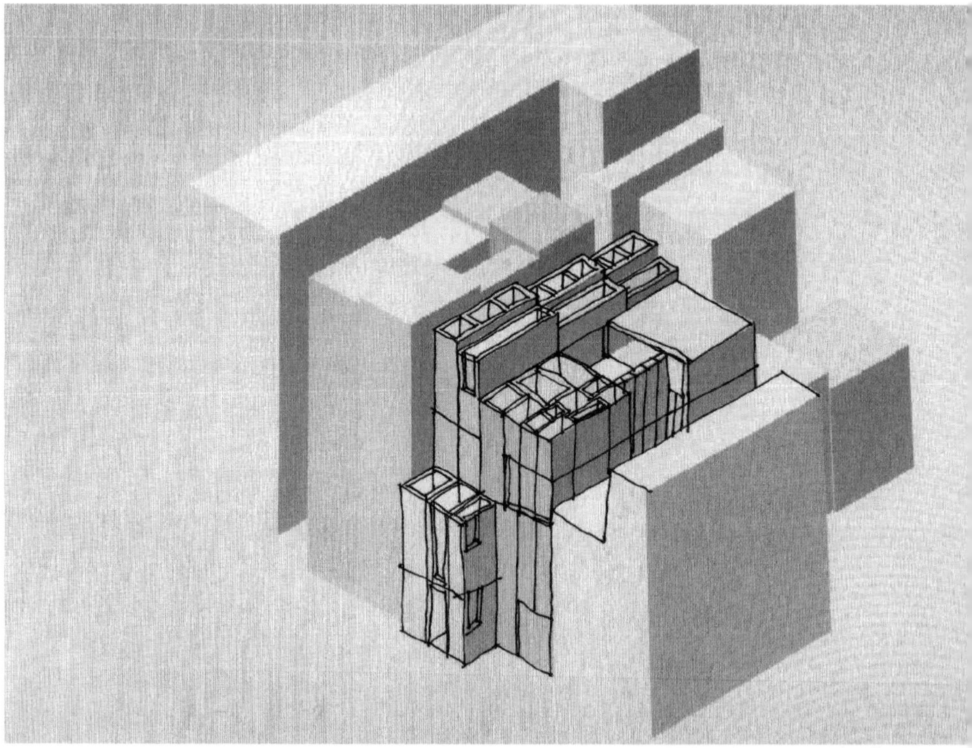

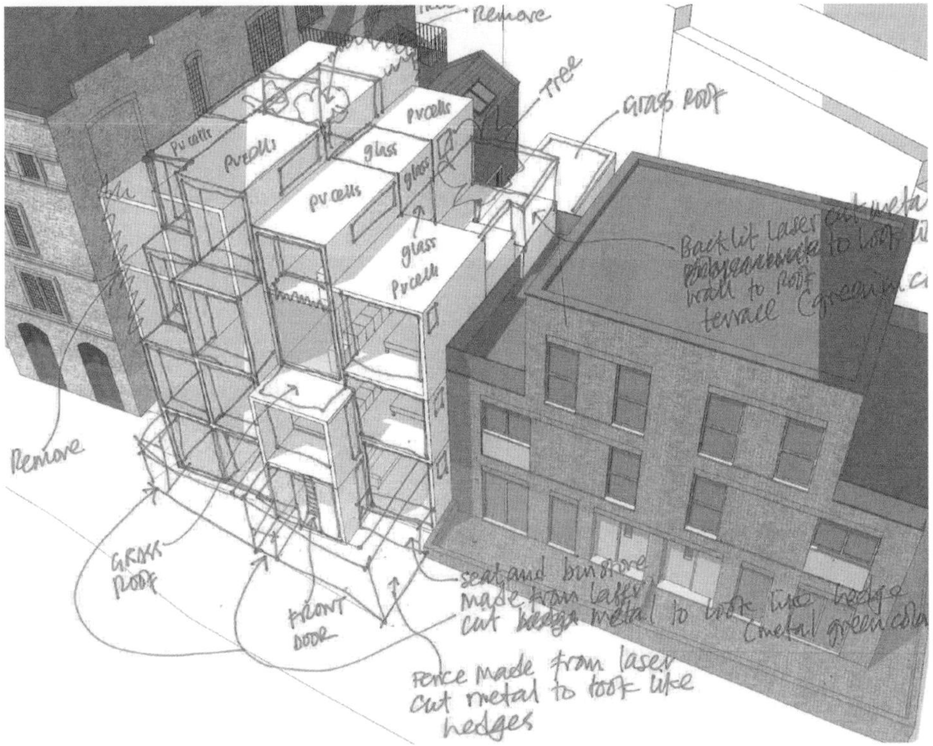
Remove
TREE
GRASS ROOF
PV cells
PVcells
PVcells
glass
PVcells
glass
glass
PVcells
Remove
GRASS ROOF
FRONT DOOR
seat and bin store made from laser cut metal to look like hedge
Fence made from laser cut metal to look like hedges

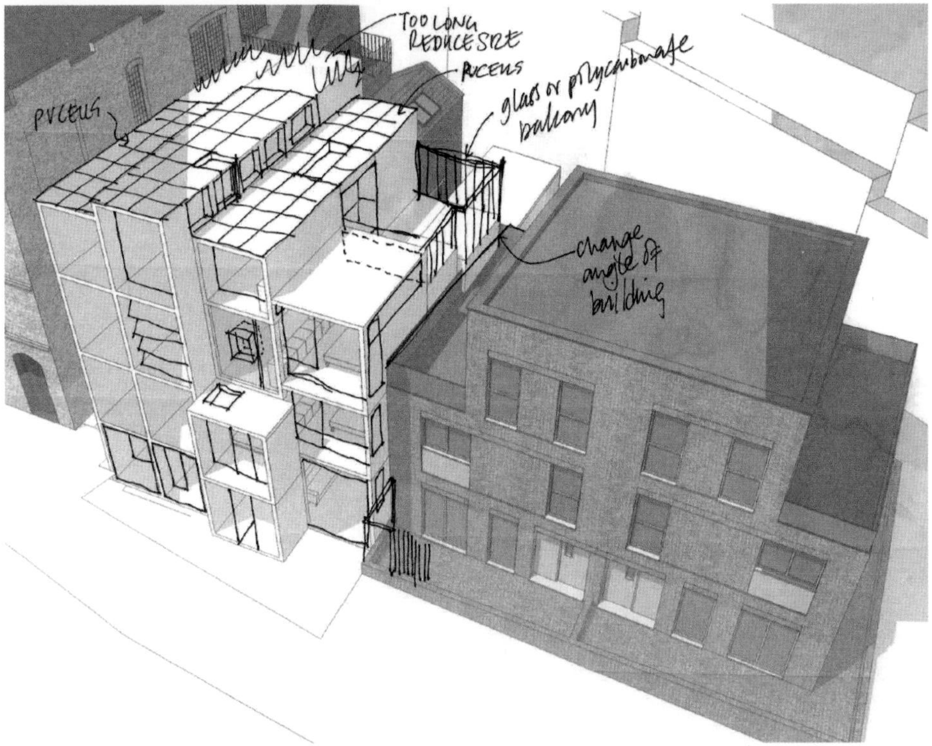
TOO LONG
REDUCE SIZE
PV CELLS
PV CELLS
glass or polycarbonate balcony
change angle of building

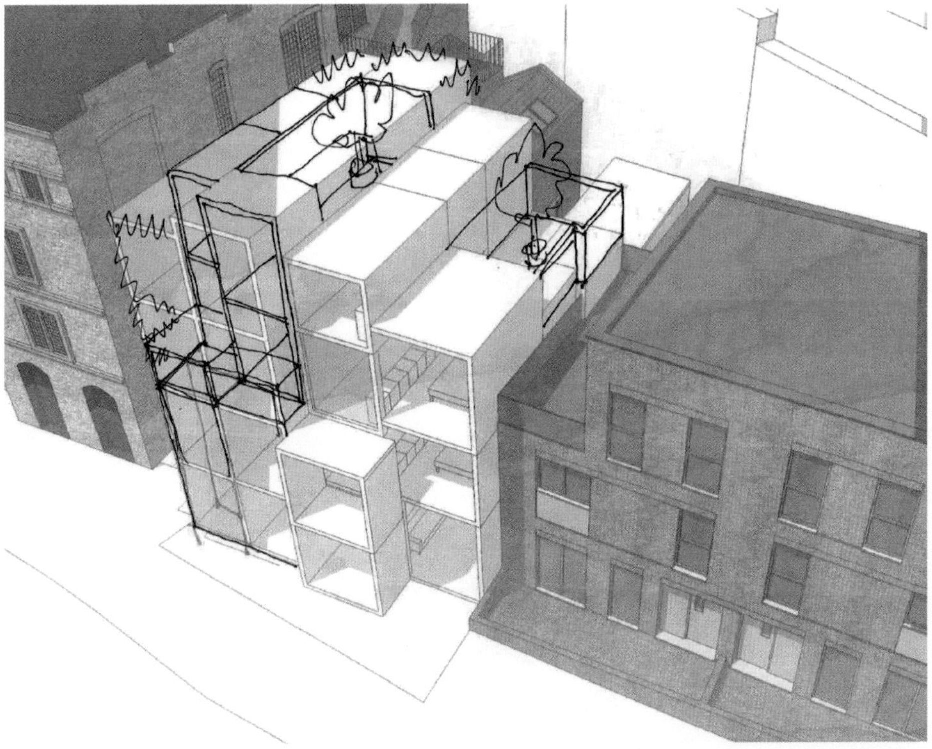

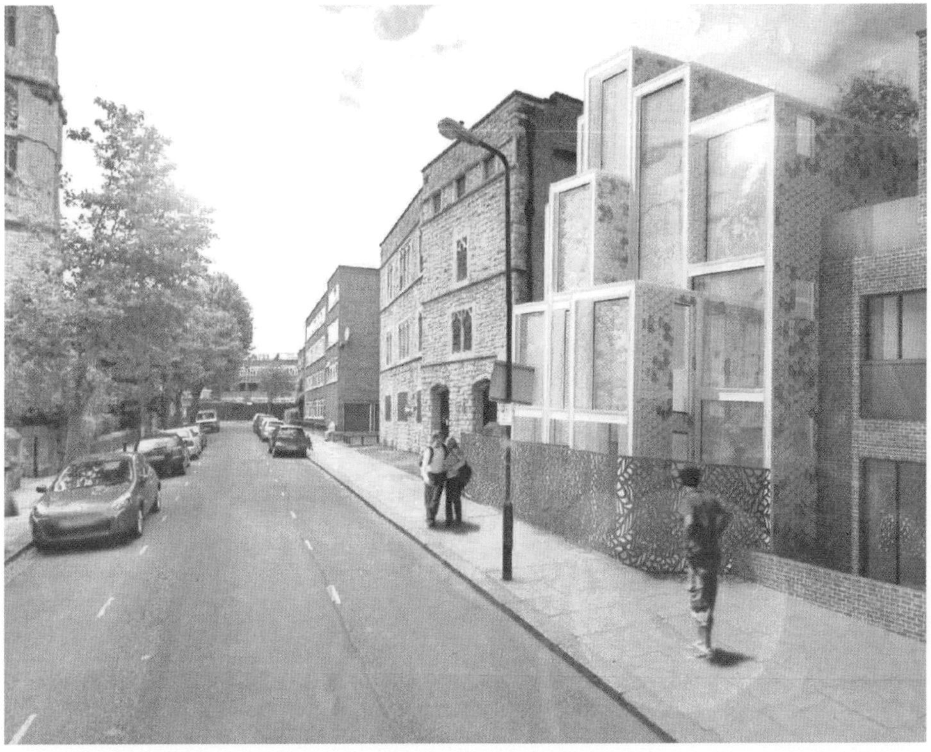

MVRDV

Netherlands

Featured projects: Museum of Rock [pp. 216–19]
Wai Yip Hong Kong [pp. 221–22] · KU.BE [p. 223]

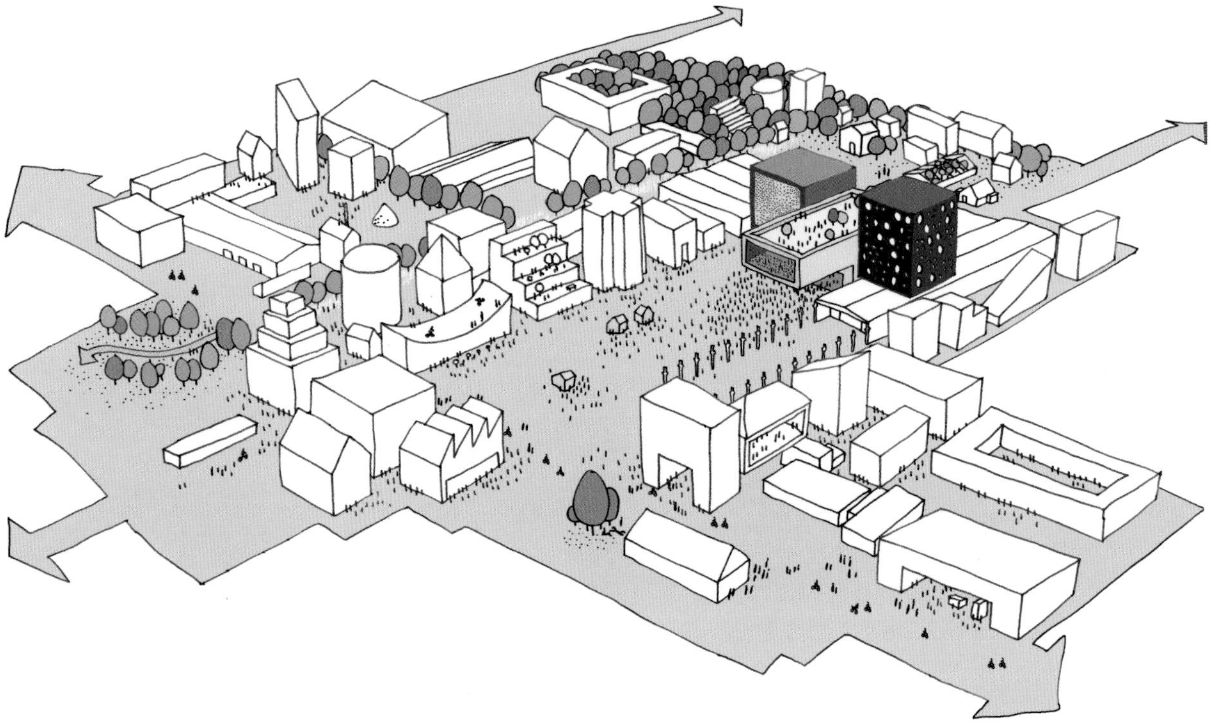

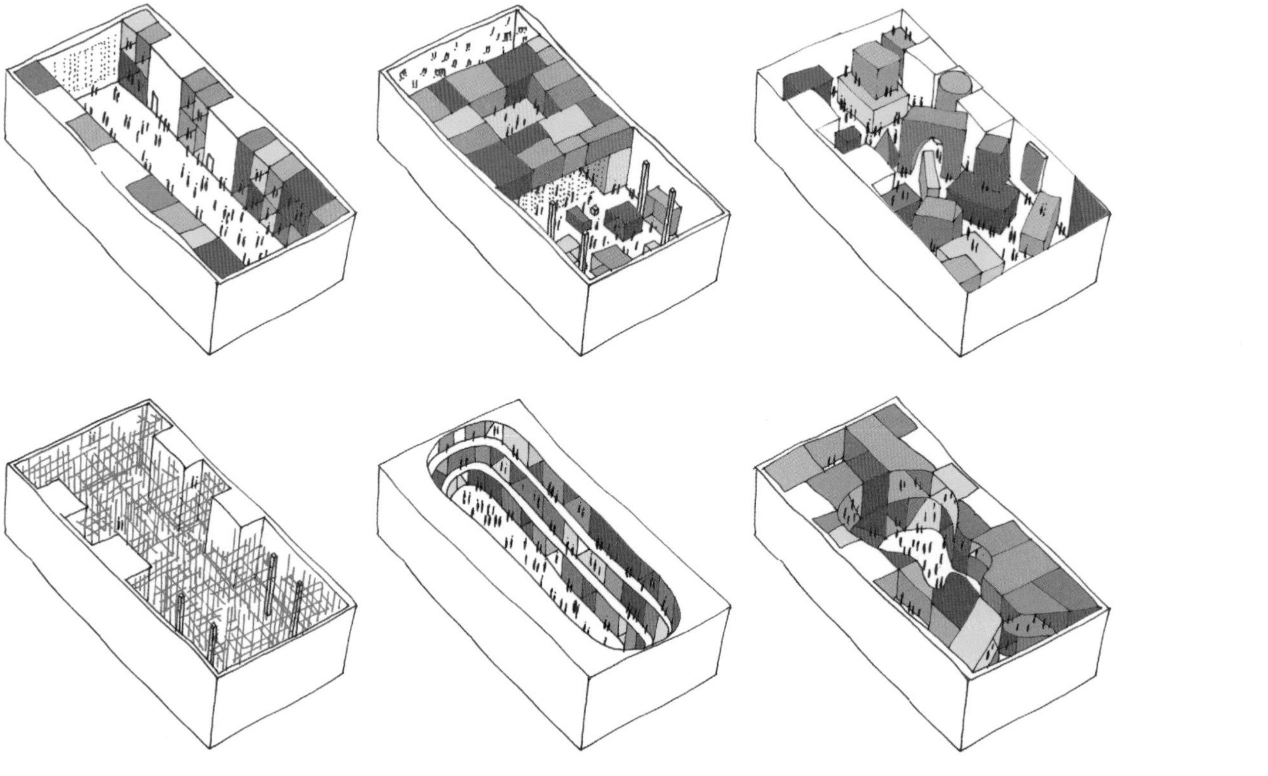

Dutch architectural firm MVRDV was founded in 1993 by Winy Maas, Jacob van Rijs and Nathalie de Vries. The company, which has offices in Rotterdam and Shanghai, relies on sketching, because it is an important method of communicating ideas between architects, engineers and clients.

'At MVRDV, sketching operates on multiple levels and for a variety of uses,' the founders explain. 'The "thinking", "talking", "humorous" or "render" sketch, even the "prescriptive" sketch. We often communicate ideas with clients using models and drawings, which allows them to be more actively involved in the design process. The use of unfinished, as yet undeveloped sketches helps to create a more interactive setting during design meetings.'

The trio describe the company's goal as the pursuit of radical, investigative spatial research, focusing on the urban landscape, the public realm and the influence of architecture on the everyday lives of its inhabitants and users. Each of their designs derives from in-depth analytical research, while challenging existing thinking and seeking exciting design solutions. Sketching is an integral part of this process, from start to finish.

'Sketching allows us to look at the project from a different perspective, sometimes discovering something that is hidden inside the computer,' they note. 'It mediates between being functional (generating, solving and communicating ideas more effectively) and being an aesthetic form of storytelling, from the initial idea to the final outcome, regardless of discipline.'

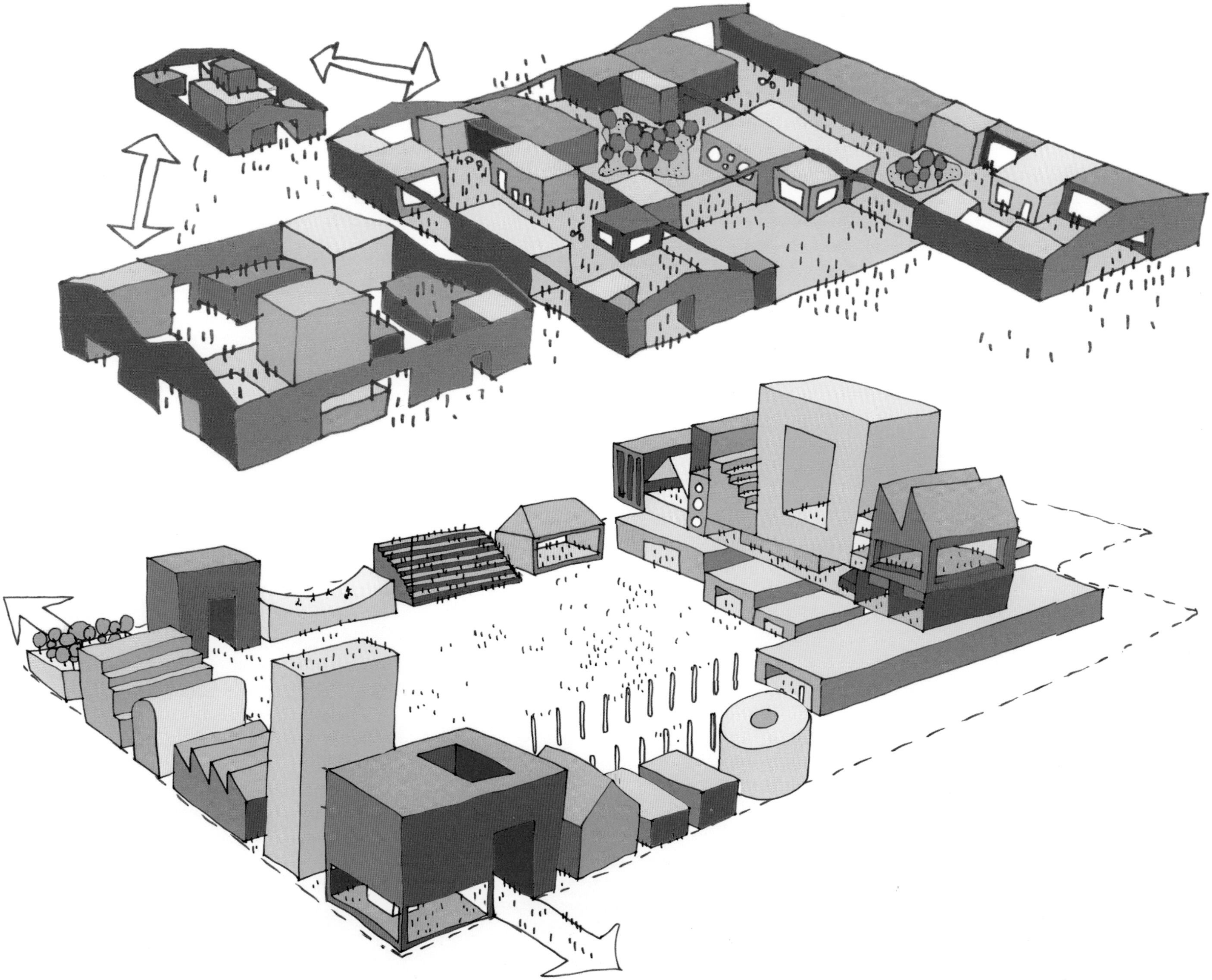

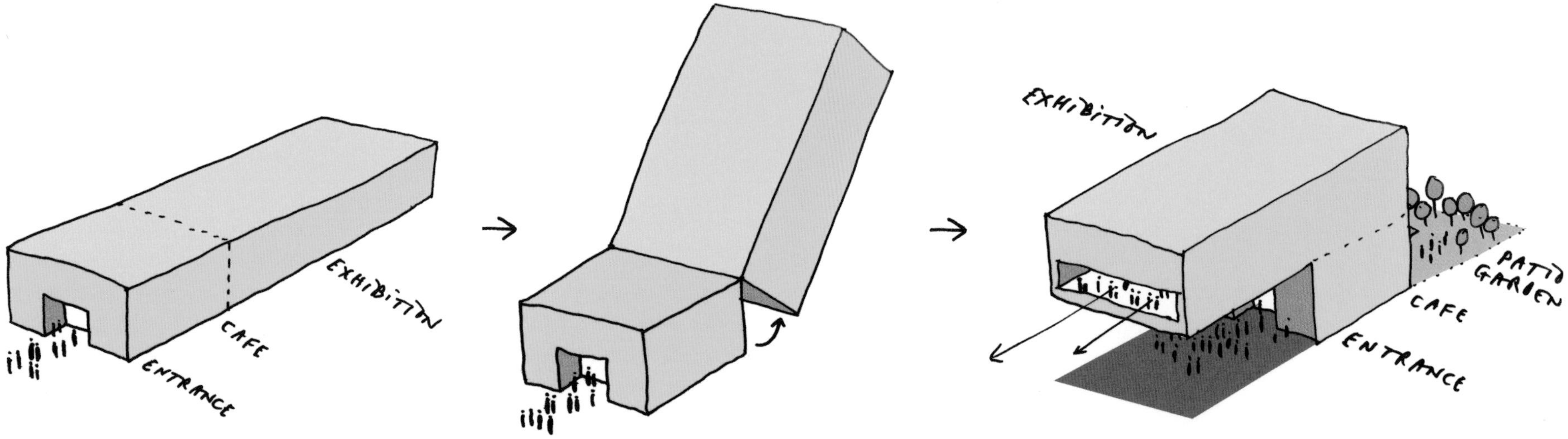
EXHIBITION
CAFE
ENTRANCE
EXHIBITION
PATIO
GARDEN
CAFE
ENTRANCE

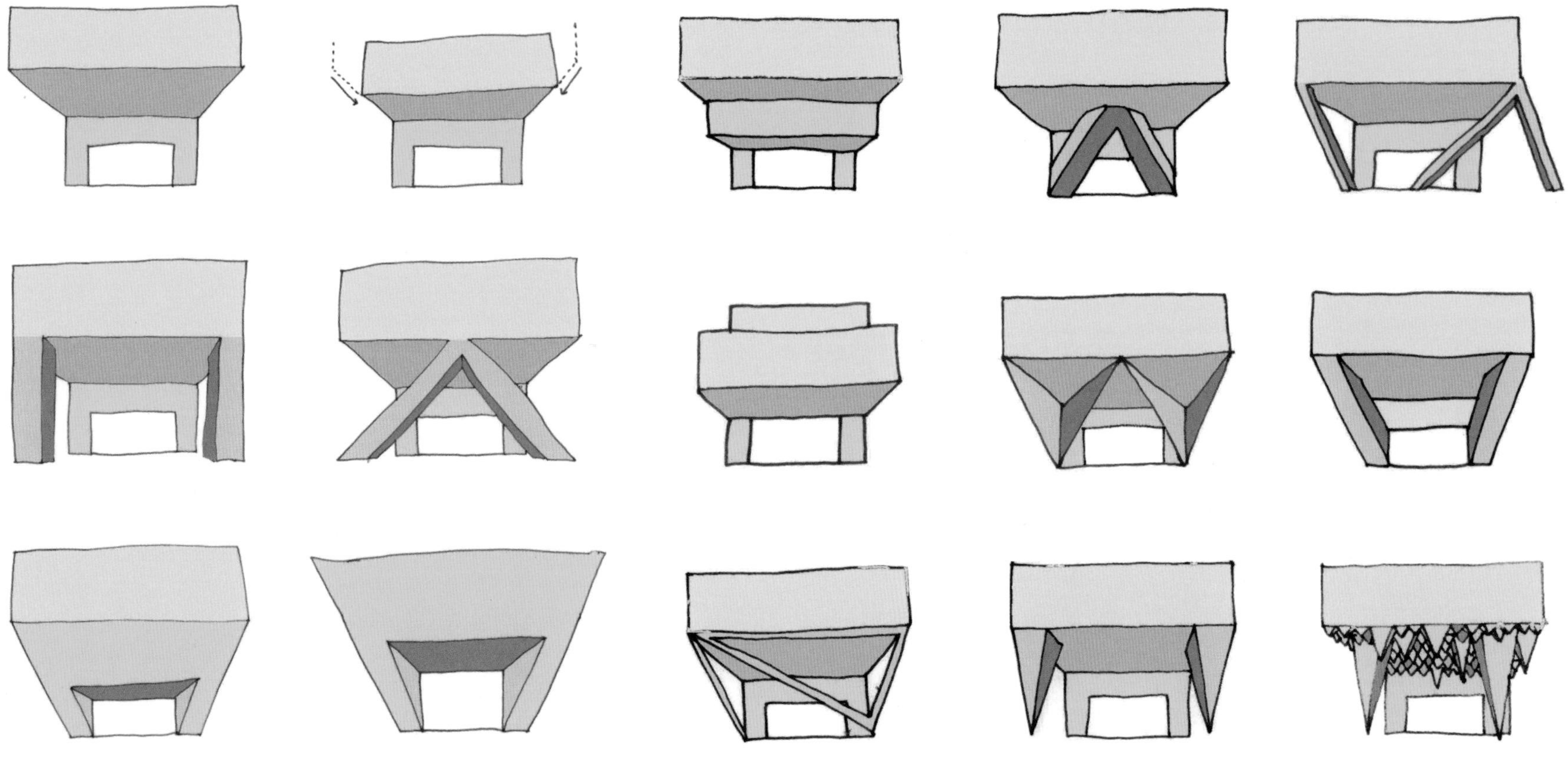

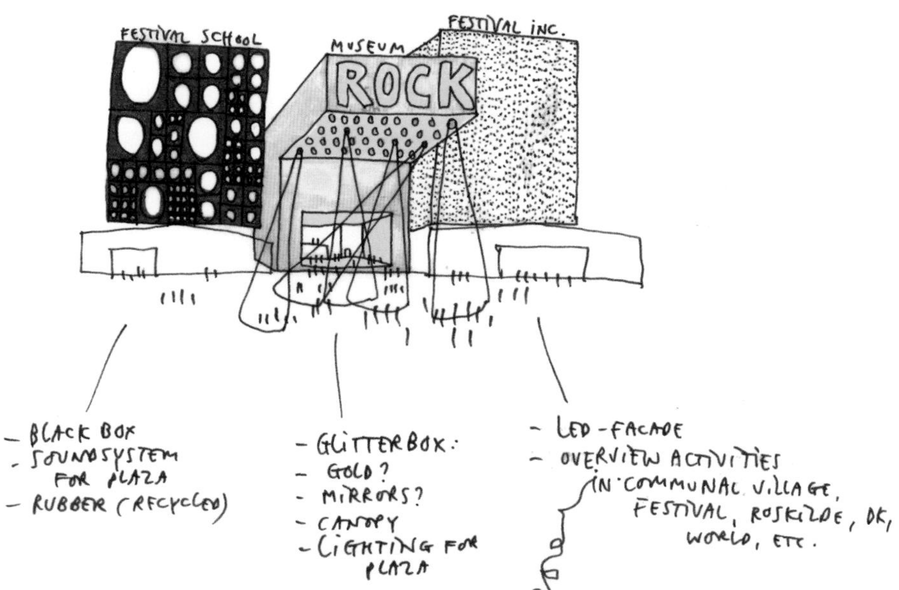
FESTIVAL SCHOOL
MUSEUM
FESTIVAL INC.
ROCK
- BLACK BOX
- SOUNDSYSTEM FOR PLAZA
- RUBBER (RECYCLED)
- GLITTERBOX:
- GOLD?
- MIRRORS?
- CANOPY
- LIGHTING FOR PLAZA
- LED-FACADE
- OVERVIEW ACTIVITIES IN COMMUNAL VILLAGE, FESTIVAL, ROSKILDE, DK, WORLD, ETC.

ROCK
MAGNET

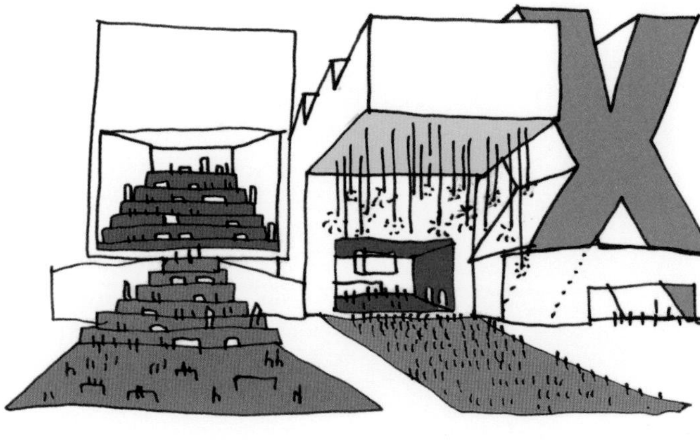
X

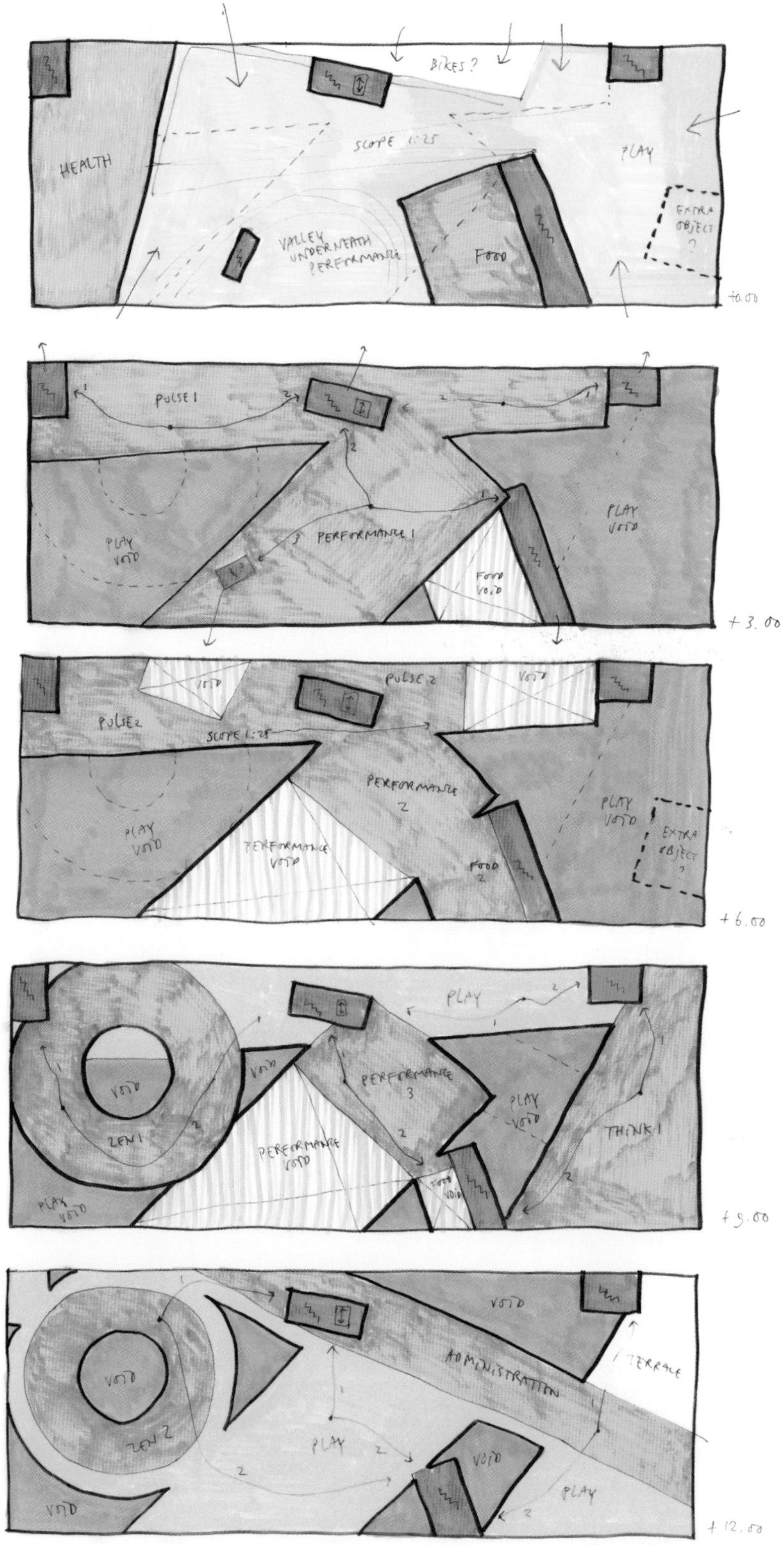
BIKES?
HEALTH
SCOPE 1:25
PLAY
EXTRA OBJECT ?
VALLEY UNDERNEATH PERFORMANCE
FOOD
±0.00
PULSE 1
PLAY VOID
PERFORMANCE 1
FOOD VOID
+3.00
VOID
PULSE 2
PULSE 2
SCOPE 1:25
PERFORMANCE 2
PLAY VOID
PERFORMANCE VOID
FOOD 2
EXTRA OBJECT ?
+6.00
PLAY
VOID
ZEN 1
PERFORMANCE 3
PERFORMANCE VOID
THINK 1
PLAY VOID
+9.00
VOID
ADMINISTRATION
TERRACE
ZEN 2
PLAY
+12.00

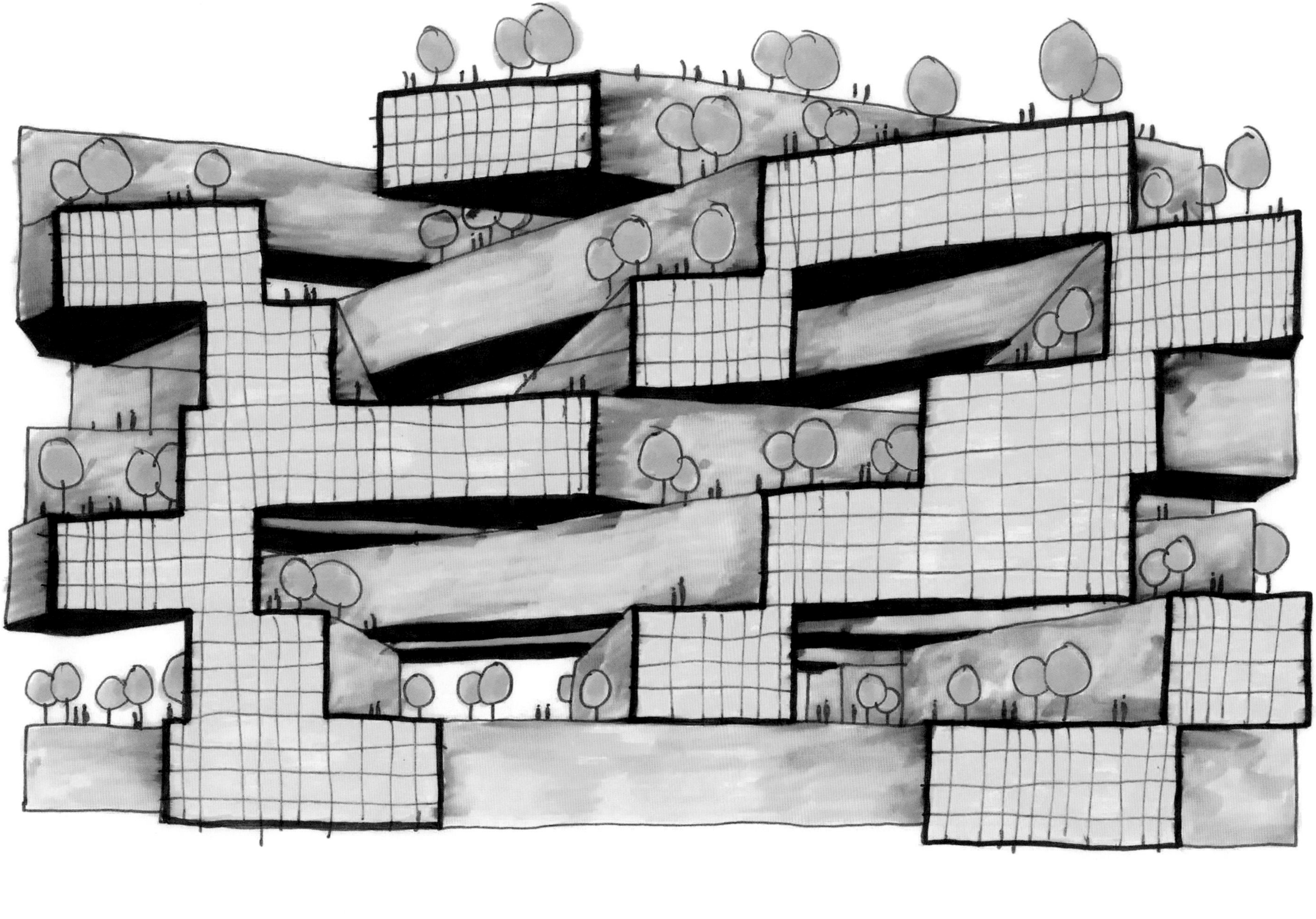

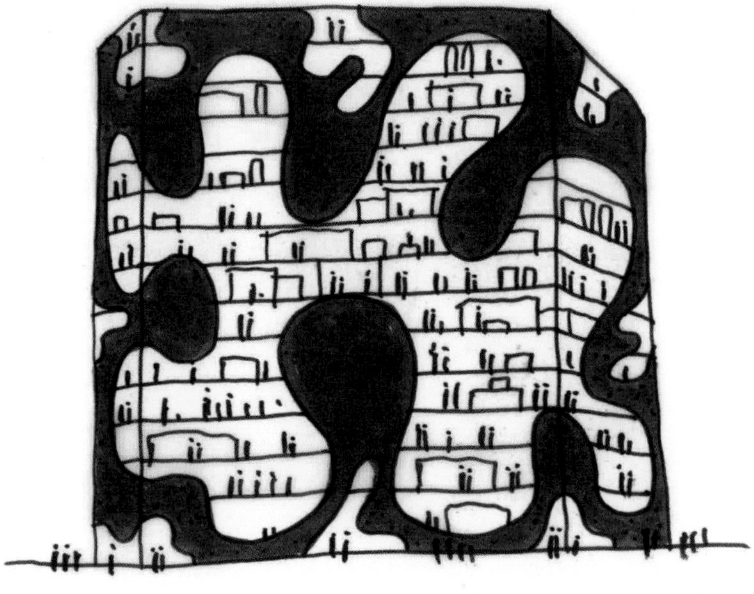

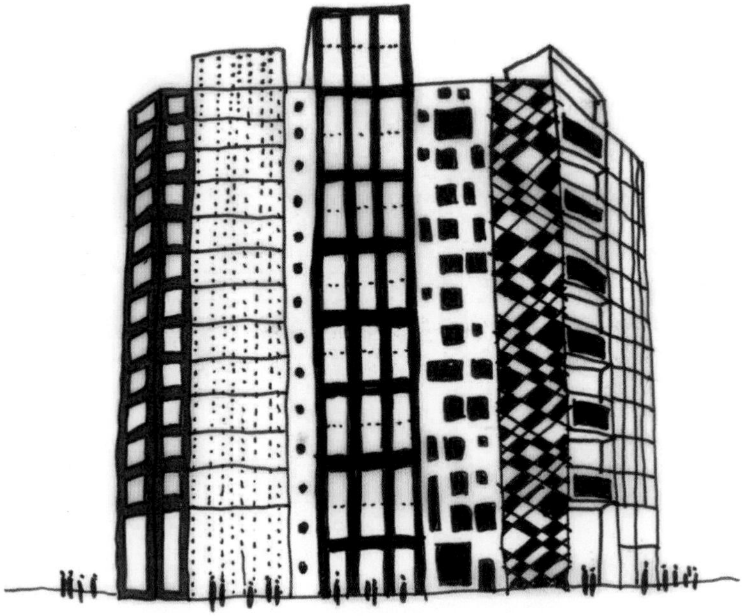

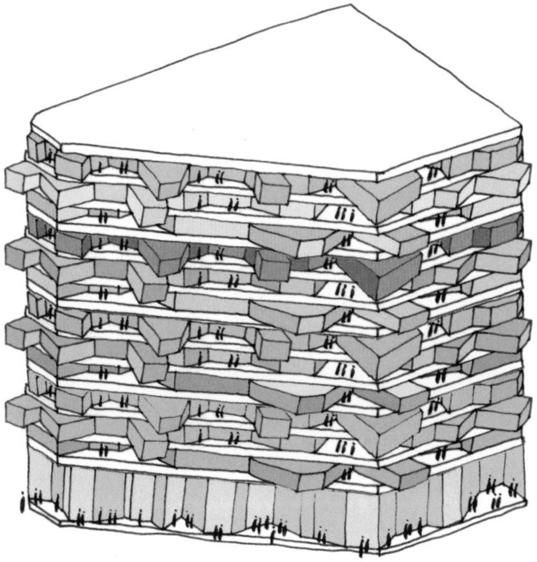
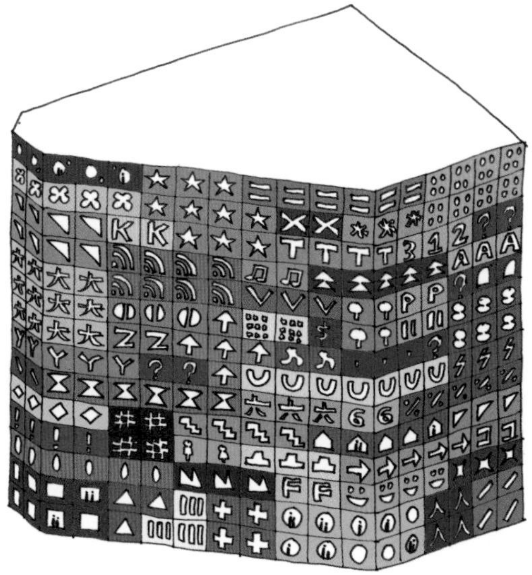

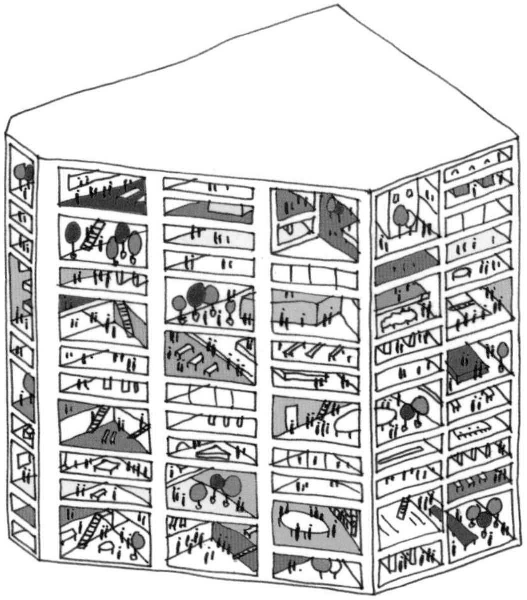
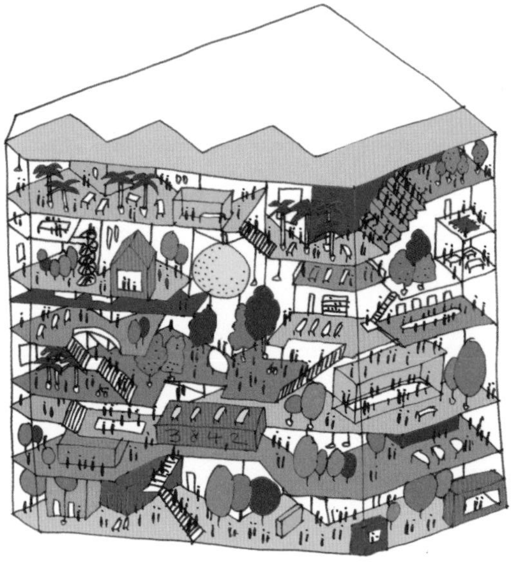
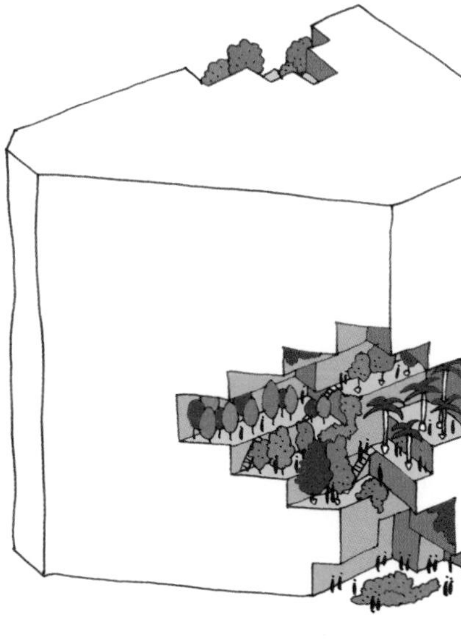

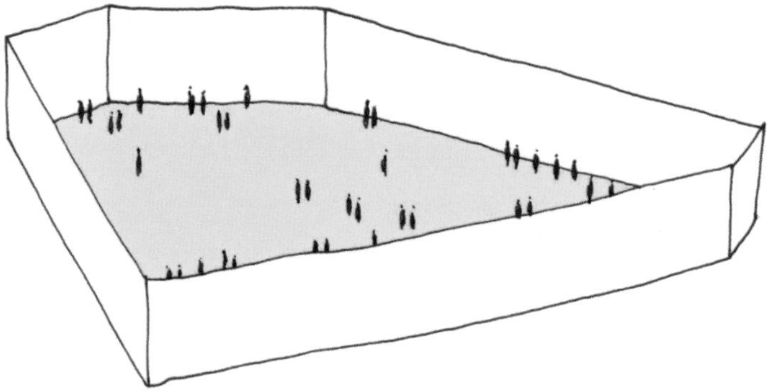

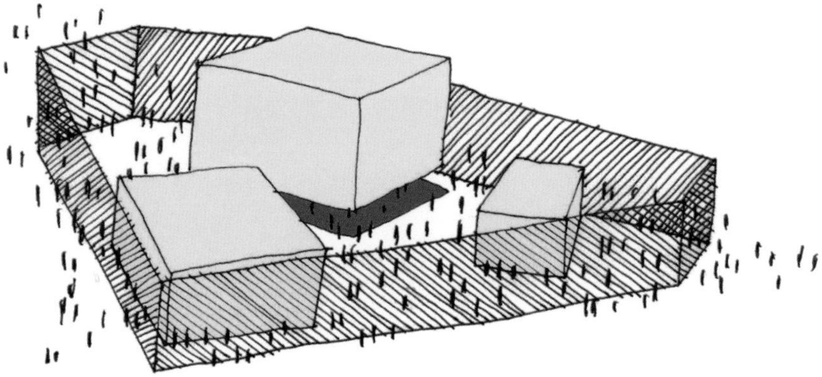

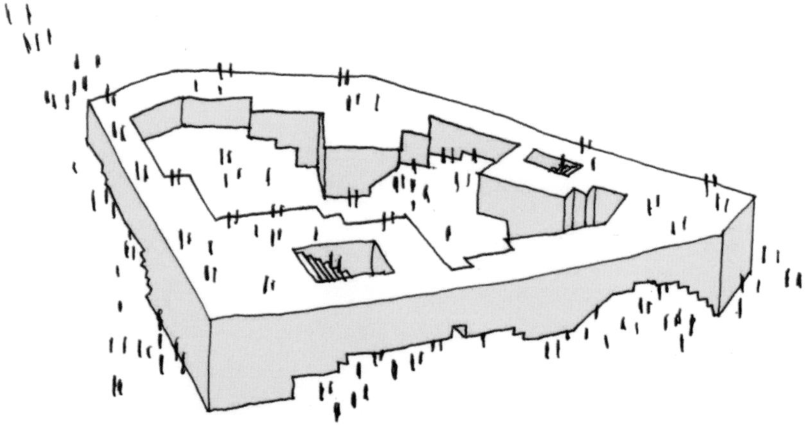

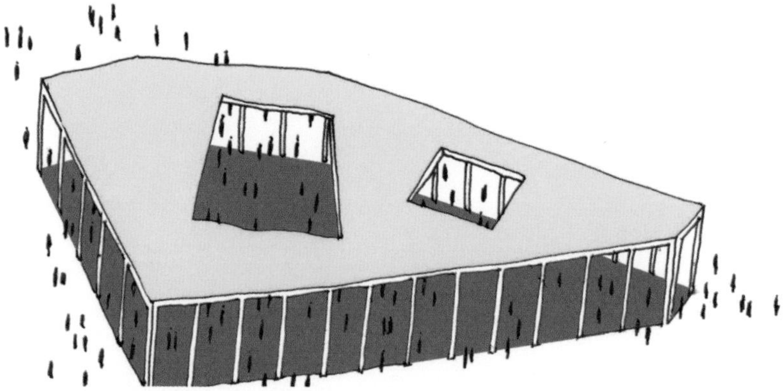

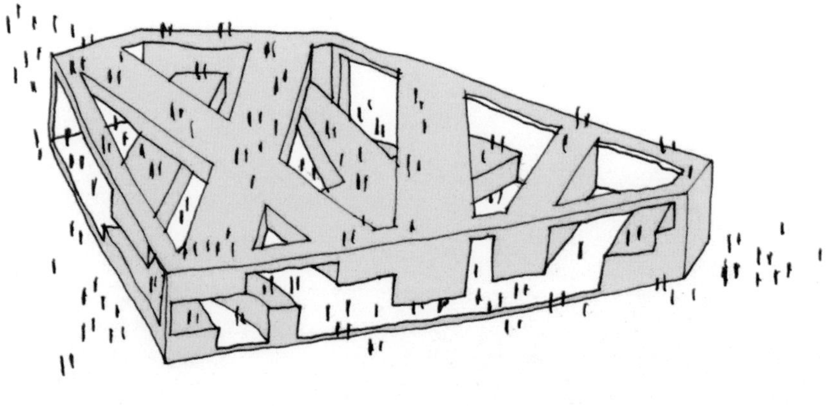

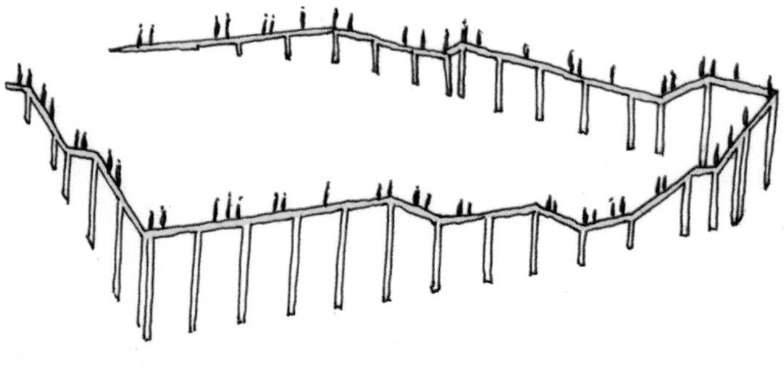

BRAD NETKIN

Stamp Architecture • Canada

Featured projects: Study for a screen porch [p. 224]
Strachan [p. 225, left and bottom right] · Thorndale [p. 225, top right]

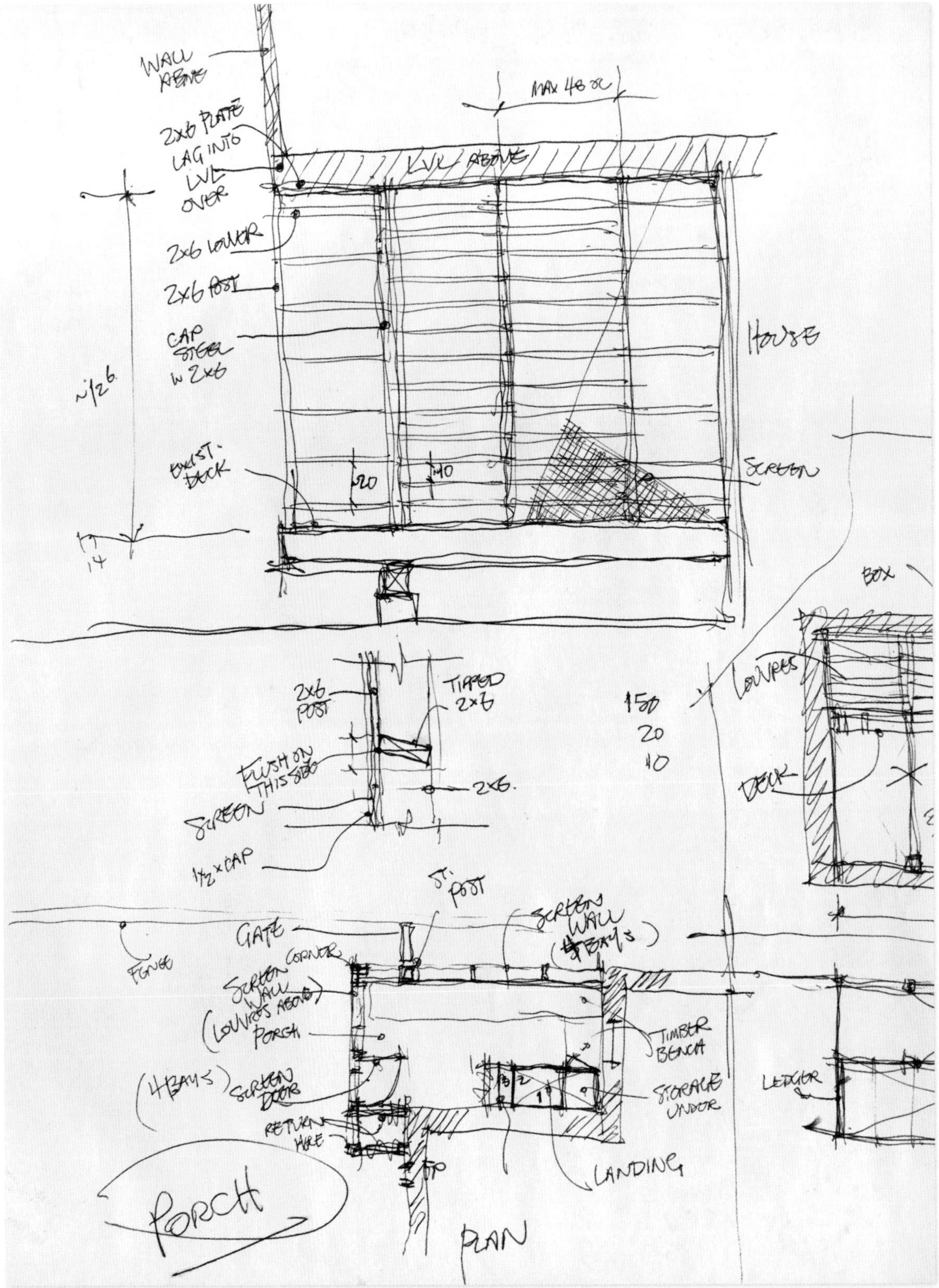

'For us, sketching is essential at all phases of design and construction, because we view the entire endeavour as an active process,' says Brad Netkin, principal at Toronto firm Stamp Architecture. 'Drawings act as a vehicle with which to communicate ideas, not an end in themselves. While there are always moments of clarity, design doesn't just happen. It involves working things out over time.'

Netkin graduated from the University of British Columbia School of Architecture in 1995, and has worked in the construction industry for over 25 years. 'Projects are messy, complicated things with many players, requiring continual communication and clarification,' he continues. 'By sketching "live" with the trade or the client, we can capture the momentum and refine our ideas before they are completed. This may be unconventional, but we think this improves the final product, because the pen is the most direct, immediate and fluid way of working out an idea.'

He adds: 'We could not communicate our ideas or execute our work without sketching. We constantly go back and forth with hand and digital design, but the computer is limited. It requires a table, a chair or a plug, input and output. This is a multi-step process, and along with the inherent "orthogonality" of CAD software, it creates a certain detachment. It also imposes a rigidity and sense of finality to the work that can limit the exploration and resolution of ideas.'

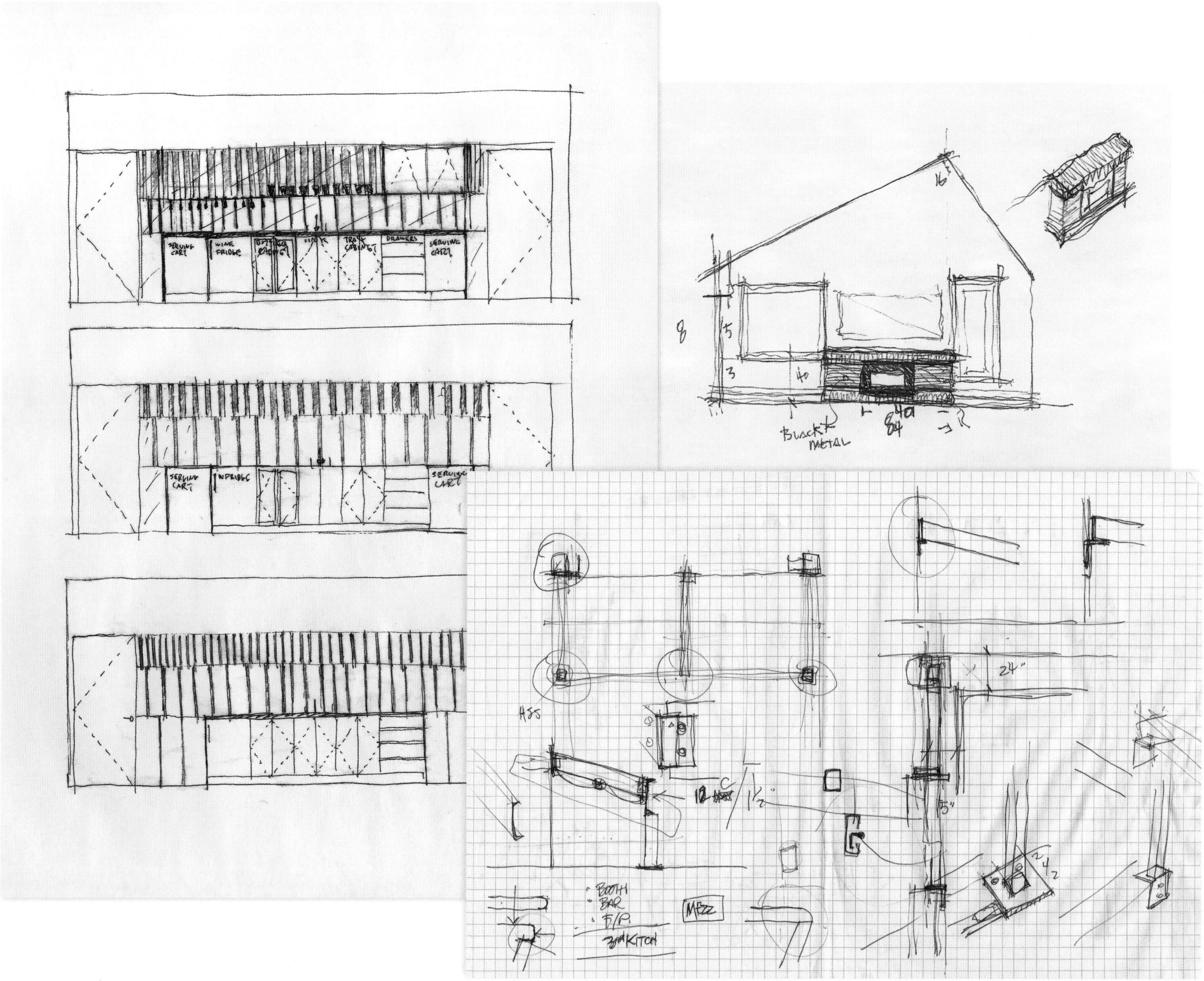
SERVING CART
WINE FRIDGE
DRAWERS
SERVING CART
SERVING CART
SERVING CART
BLACK METAL
24"
HSS
BOOTH
BAR
MEZZ

RICHARD NIGHTINGALE

Kilburn Nightingale Architects • UK

Featured project: St Paul's Cathedral School [pp. 226–9]

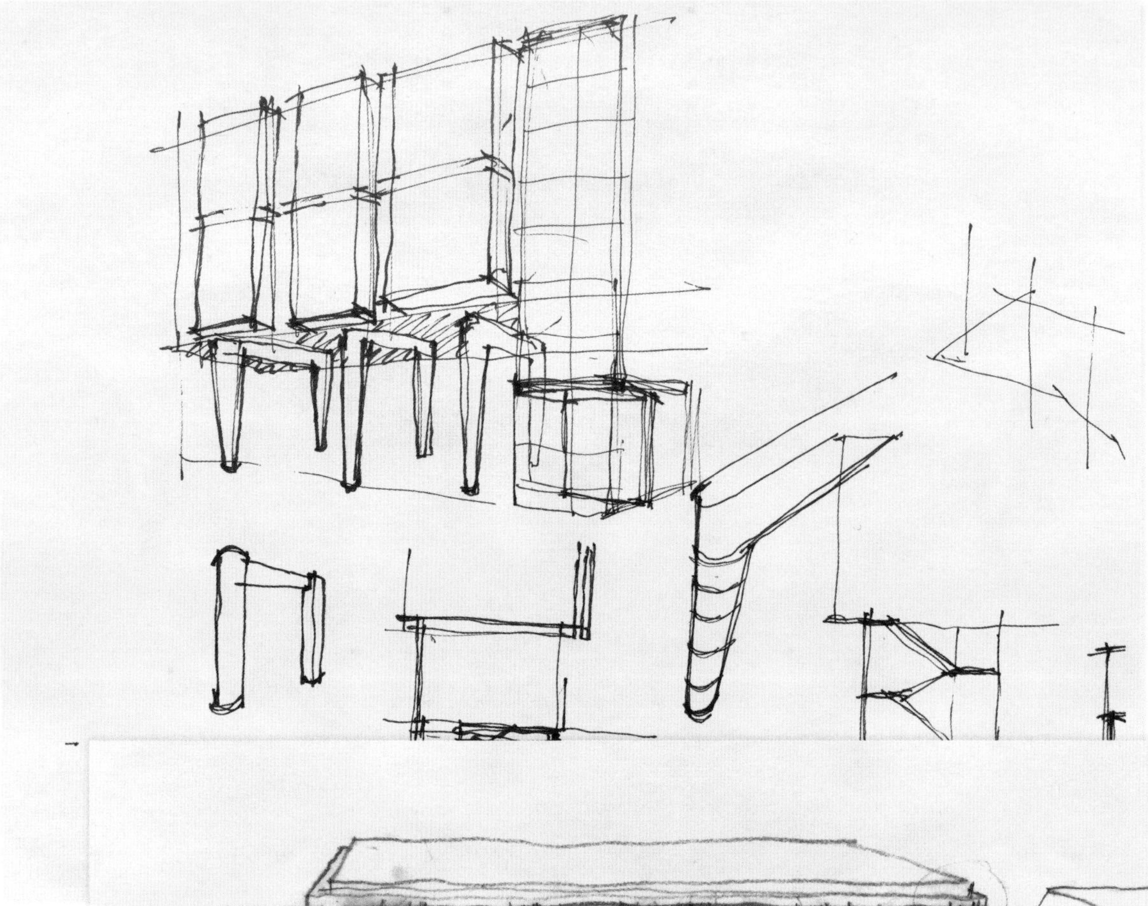

'I combine digital and hand-drawings throughout the design process,' says Richard Nightingale of Kilburn Nightingale Architects. 'Starting with CAD is often very useful: you can establish general principles, relationships and sizes, while avoiding the tyranny of a set scale or the expectation of a beautiful drawing. I then sketch over a very rough CAD drawing to develop the design in more detail, and often scan the sketch into a computer to add colour, texture and notes. The final drawings will usually be CAD, but are often supplemented by hand-sketches explaining details during construction.'

Nightingale is a founding partner of the London-based firm, which has a truly international portfolio: from houses in the Caribbean to a hotel in Argentina, eco-retreats in Zambia and Pakistan, and a high commission and arts foundry in Uganda.

'It is important with any type of project to investigate design options in a way that is exploratory and flexible, and to be able to transmit ideas effectively at all stages of the design process,' he explains. 'It doesn't really matter what means are used, but sketching is the most efficient and often the most accurate way of explaining a design in its unfinished state. This is frequently the case with detailed design, too: bricks, concrete and wood are not precise to the nearest millimetre, and so a slightly wobbly hand-drawn sketch can describe a construction detail more accurately than a computer drawing.'

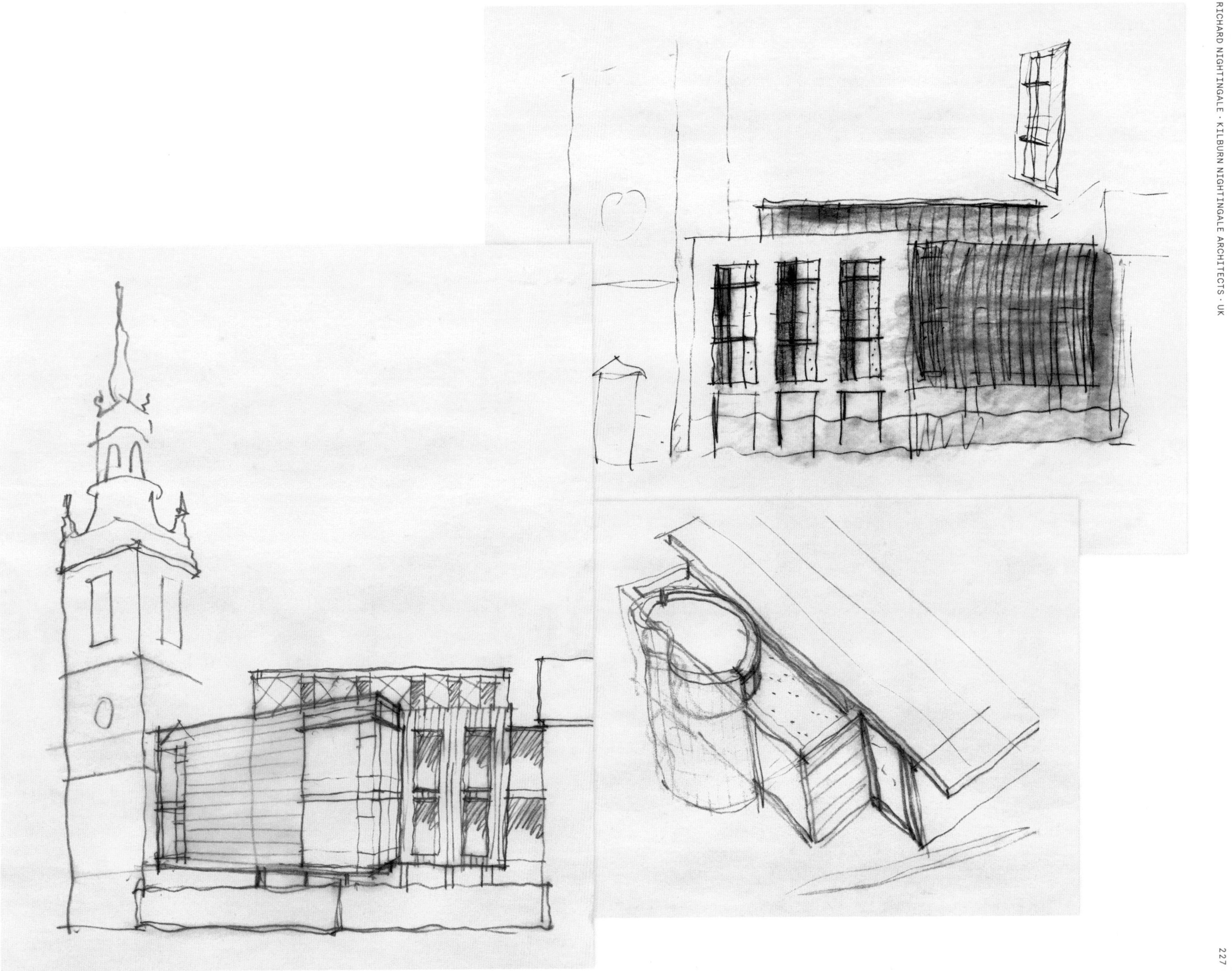

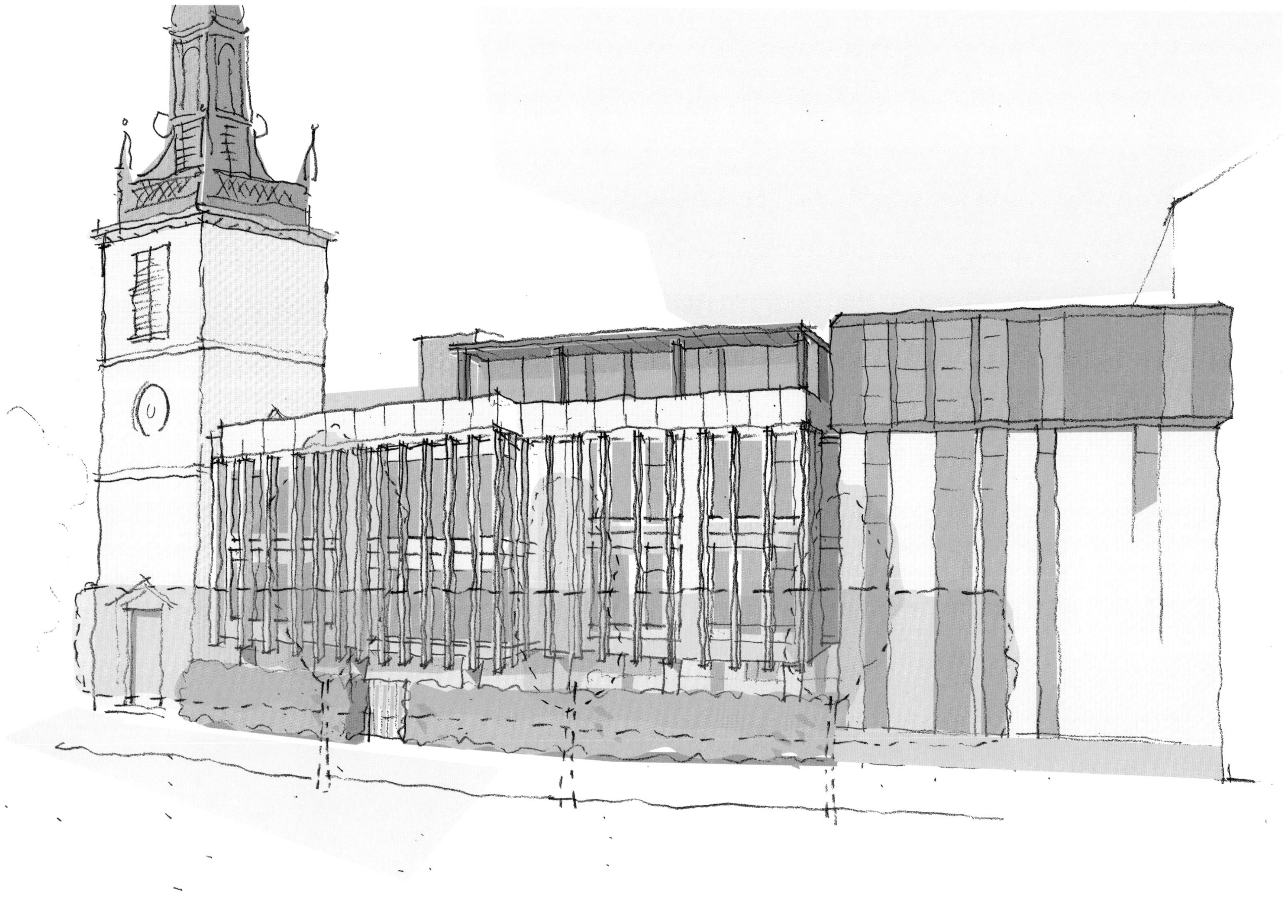

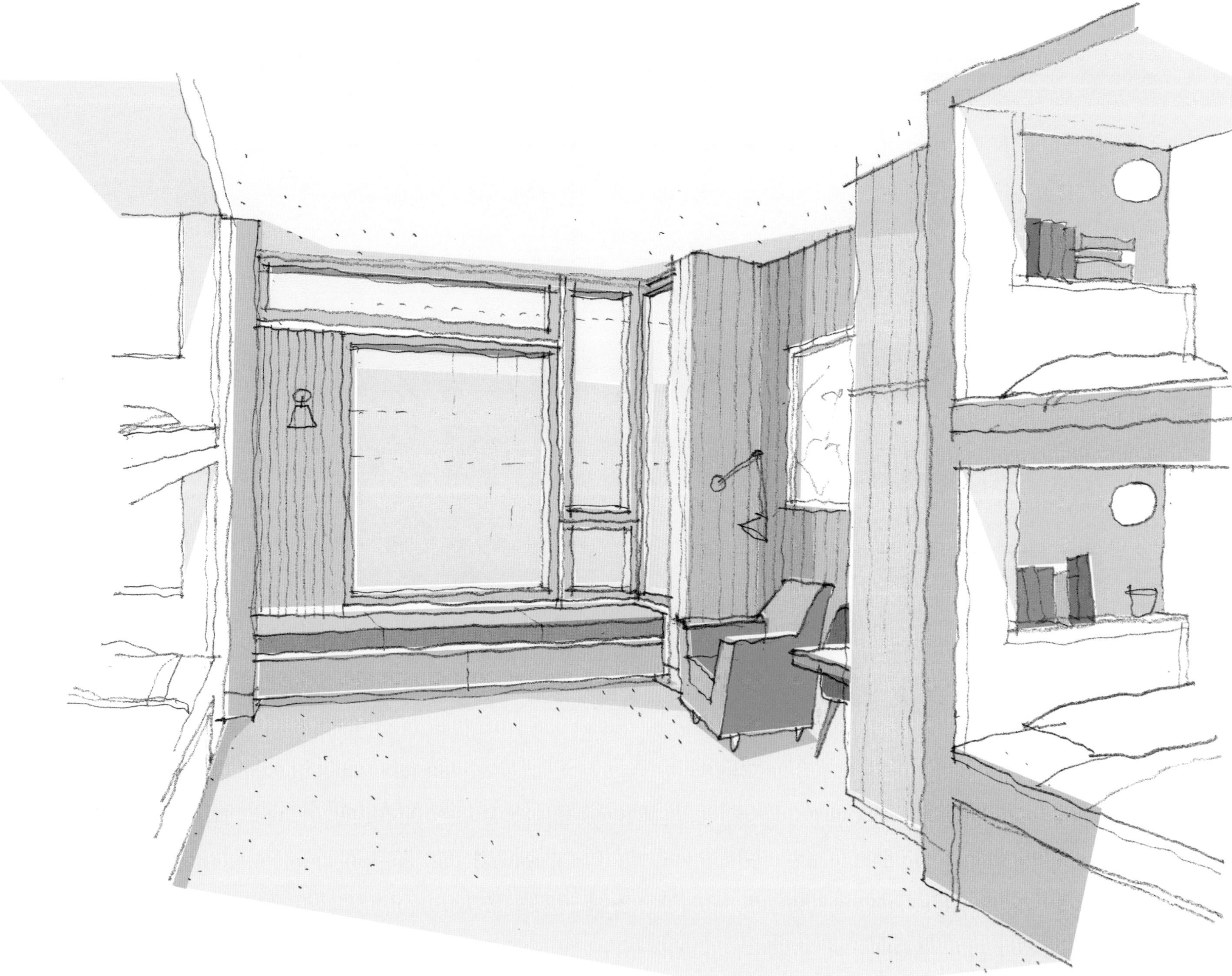

RICHARD OLCOTT

Ennead Architects • USA

Featured projects: Denning House [p. 230, top]
Stanford Law School [pp. 230, bottom; 231]
Bing Concert Hall [p. 232]
William J. Clinton Presidential Center [p. 233]

'The physical pleasure of sketching cannot be replicated in the digital world,' notes Richard Olcott, design partner at New York firm Ennead Architects. 'Whether you're using a soft pencil, watercolour or ink – all on good paper – it's the feel of moving across a blank page that is special.'

Olcott is viewed by his peers as an expert in the design of educational, cultural and civic architecture. His buildings are large and complex, subject to myriad design and economic constraints, and critiqued by a multitude of users and visitors. But through all of this, Olcott seems happy with his lot. 'Sketching gives you the freedom to try anything, without knowing how it will turn out,' he says. 'Building a drawing is an exciting, open-ended process, with no clear end. But knowing when to stop and move on to the next sketch is equally important.'

In its continual design quest, the company uses all manner of design tools, including 3D-printing, virtual reality, digital rendering, physical models and full-scale mock-ups, but Olcott knows what to fall back on when all else fails.

'Knowing how to sketch clearly, with the fewest lines possible, is important for conveying ideas, especially to those not well versed in the world of architecture,' he states. 'Doing so in front of a client forces you to get to the point. It remains the most immediate way of forming ideas and communicating them to others, but is by no means the only way.'

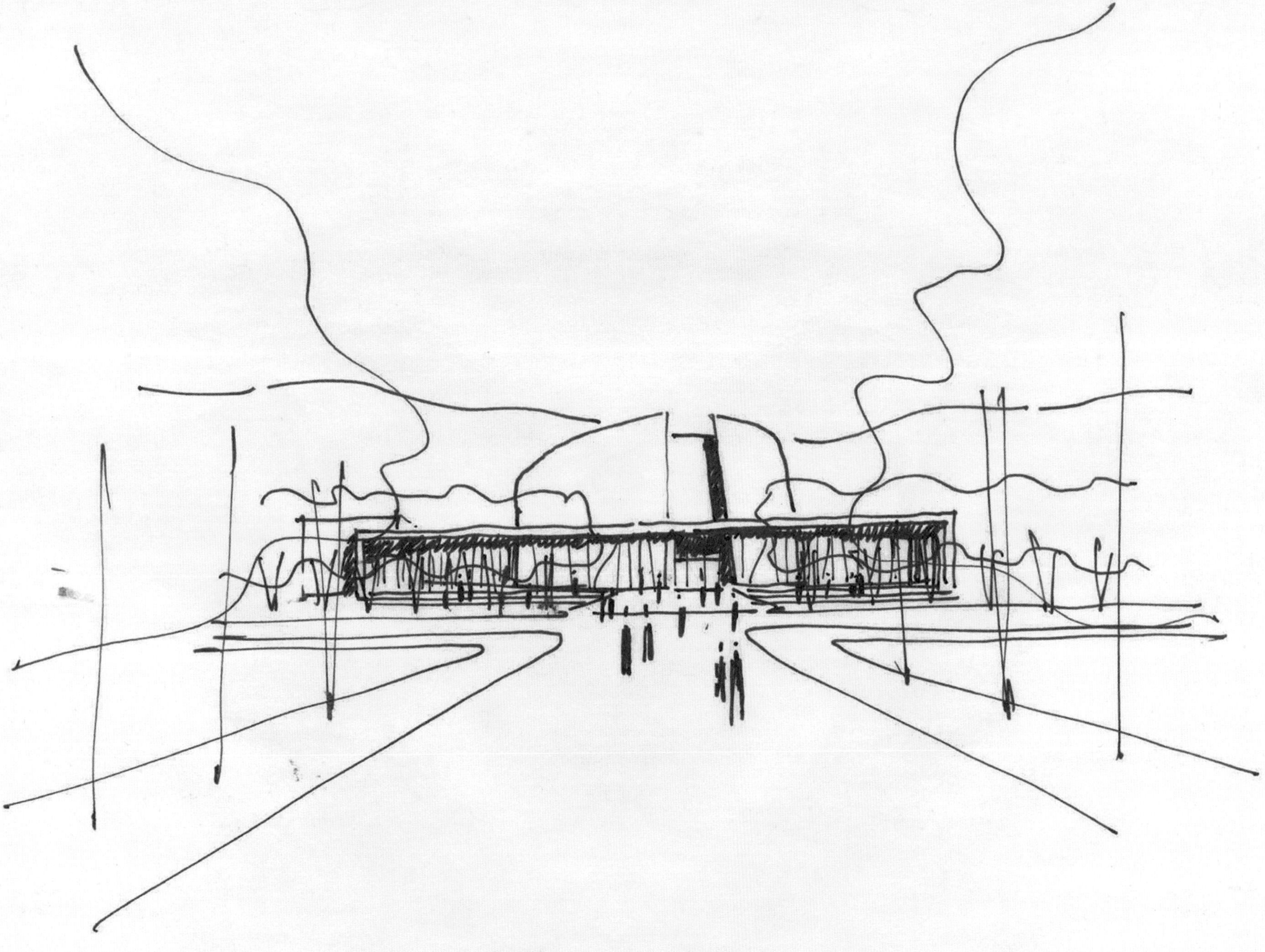

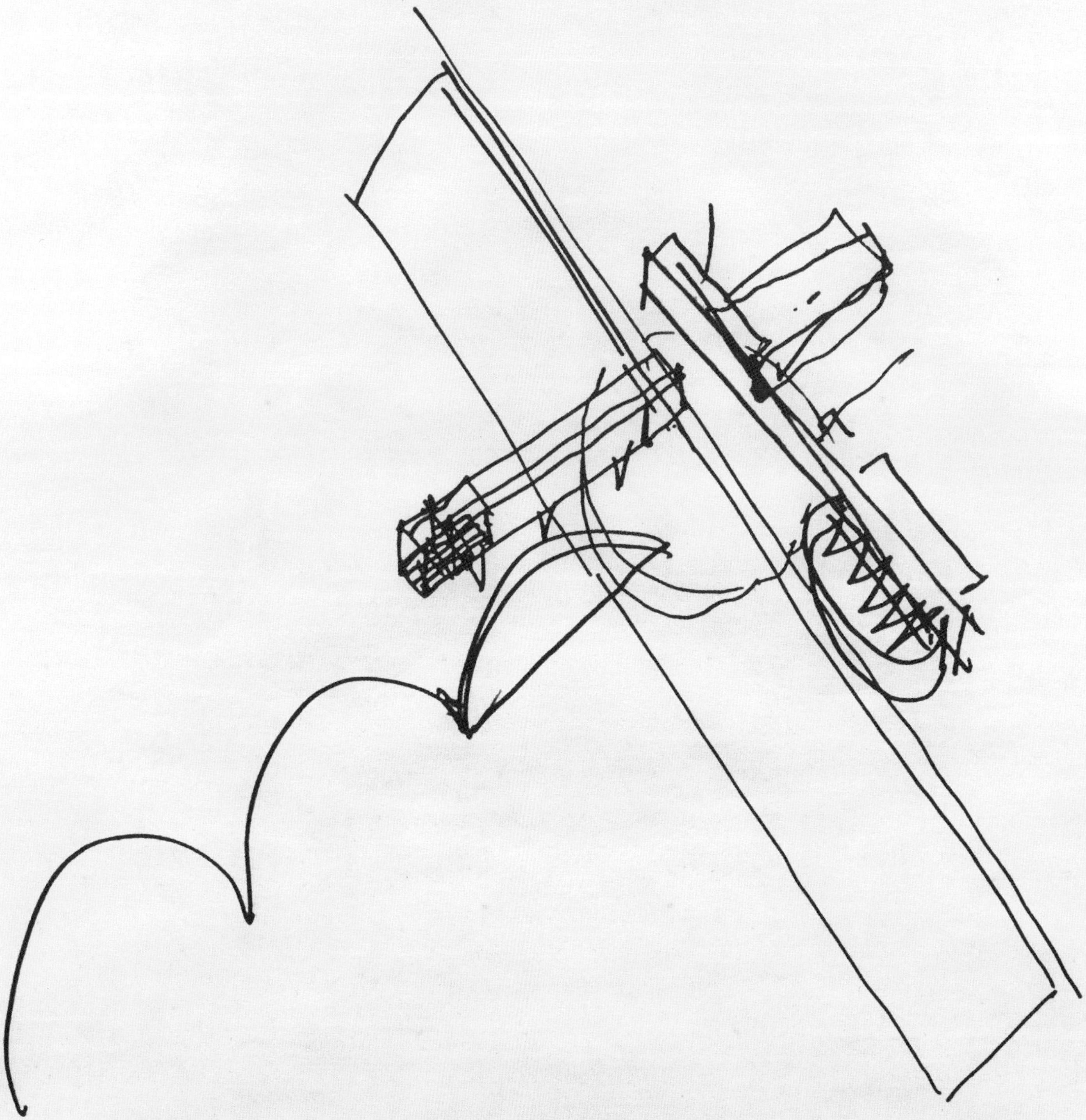

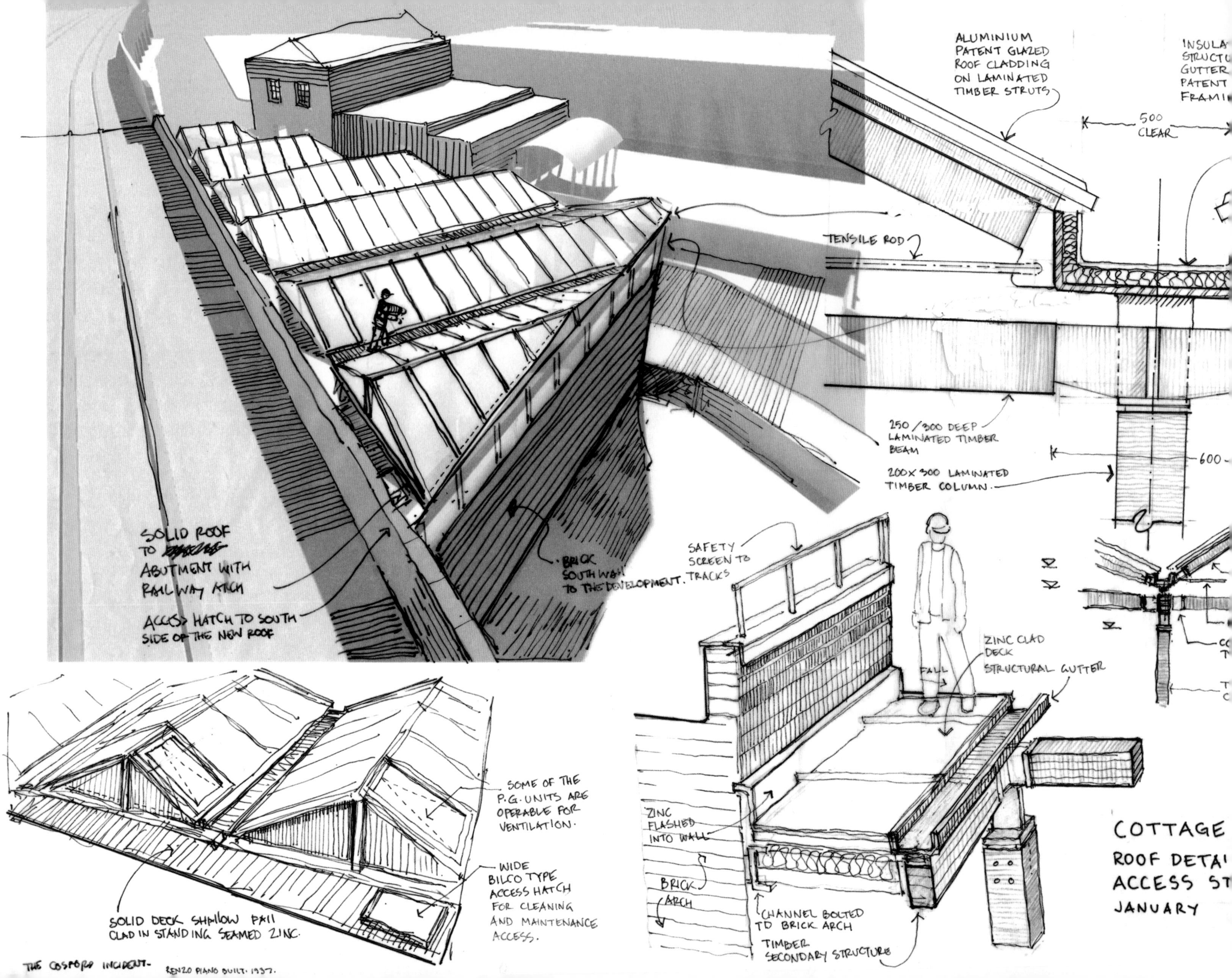
ALUMINIUM PATENT GLAZED ROOF CLADDING ON LAMINATED TIMBER STRUTS
INSULA
STRUCTU
GUTTER
PATENT
FRAMI
500 CLEAR
TENSILE ROD
250 / 300 DEEP LAMINATED TIMBER BEAM
200 X 300 LAMINATED TIMBER COLUMN.
600
SOLID ROOF TO ABUTMENT WITH RAILWAY ARCH
BRICK SOUTH WALL TO THE DEVELOPMENT.
ACCESS HATCH TO SOUTH SIDE OF THE NEW ROOF
SAFETY SCREEN TO TRACKS
ZINC CLAD DECK
FALL
STRUCTURAL GUTTER
ZINC FLASHED INTO WALL
BRICK ARCH
CHANNEL BOLTED TO BRICK ARCH
TIMBER SECONDARY STRUCTURE
SOME OF THE P.G. UNITS ARE OPERABLE FOR VENTILATION.
WIDE BILCO TYPE ACCESS HATCH FOR CLEANING AND MAINTENANCE ACCESS.
SOLID DECK SHALLOW FALL CLAD IN STANDING SEAMED ZINC.
COTTAGE
ROOF DETAI
ACCESS ST
JANUARY
THE COSFORD INCIDENT- RENZO PIANO BUILT. 1937.

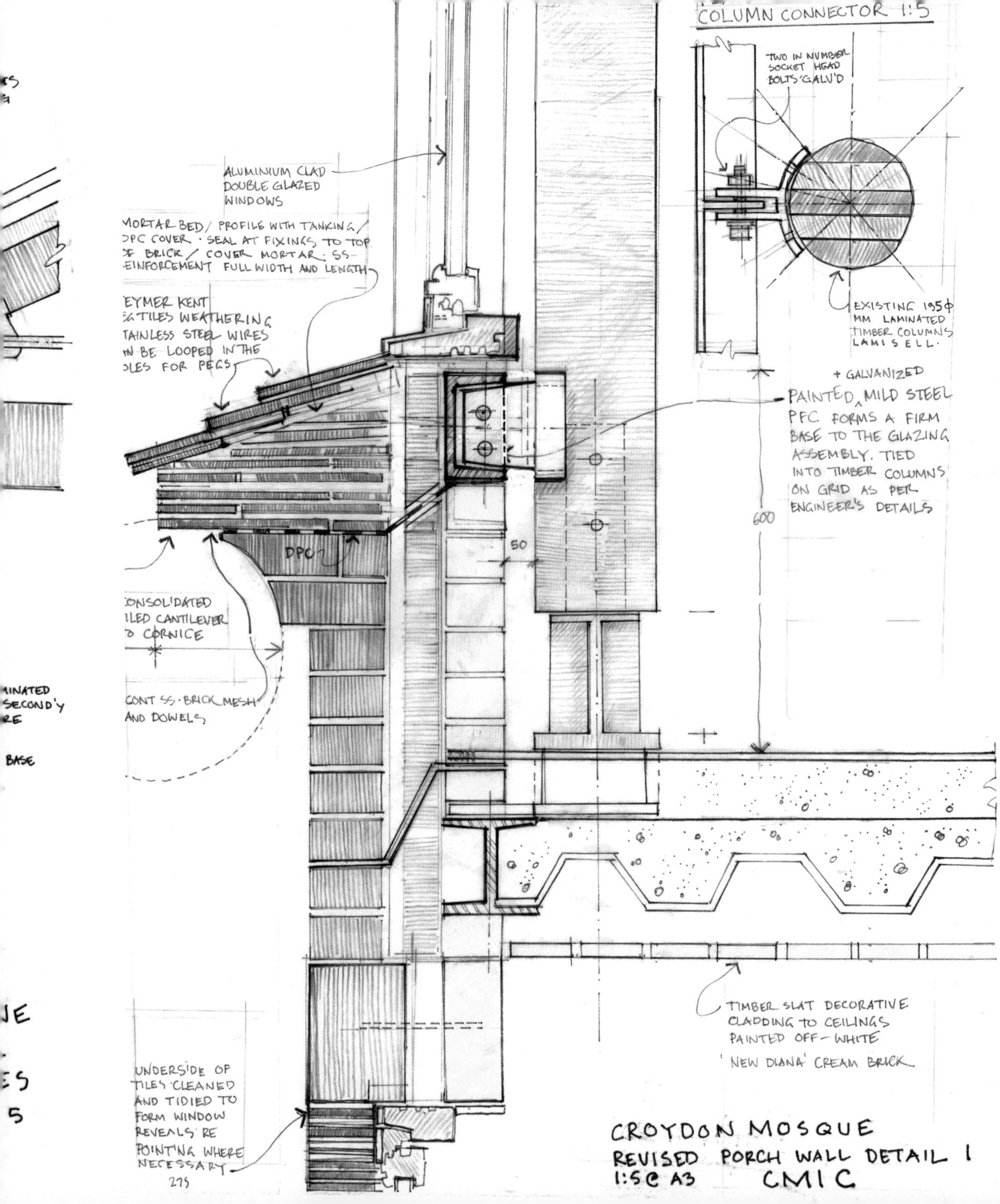

BENEDICT O'LOONEY

Benedict O'Looney Architects • UK

Featured projects: Cottage Grove [p. 234] · Croydon Mosque [p. 235]
Arch of Septimius Severus [p. 236] · Chandni Chowk [p. 237] · Chester [p. 238]
Salisbury [p. 239] · Yorkshire [p. 240] · Chipping Campden [p. 241]

'Before beginning any design work, I sketch to get to know the neighbourhood,' says London-based architect Benedict O'Looney. 'It is a fun part of the journey, and is key to familiarizing myself with the surrounding buildings and architectural context of the site.'

Like most of his colleagues, O'Looney readily admits that his studio makes extensive use of the computer, noting that it enables work to become easier and more productive. But he believes the machine is 'curiously resistant' to the free, unobstructed flow of ideas that hand-drawing offers.

'I really feel this when detailing,' he explains. 'When drawing at a close scale – 1:5 or 1:1, for example – you feel particularly connected to what you are drawing. I like to use coloured pencils or watercolours for details, so that the different materials are shown vividly and almost "felt". When a bricklayer or carpenter cannot speak or read English very well, small 3D studies of assemblies and hand-coloured details can successfully show how the completed thing should look.'

O'Looney sketches anywhere, but the kitchen table is a favoured place. 'It is a wide, very smooth wooden table from Heals,' he says. 'Its potential as a drawing surface was my principal criteria when choosing it. The townscape drawings I love doing are mostly drawn in situ, however. In the Atlantic climate of southern England, many layers of clothing and a wool beret are vital!'

IMP CAES AVRE
PR ET
PROPATVM
Q·R
LONDON DOCKS 1805 2ND OF LONDON'S ENCLOSED DOCKS
CORPORATION · LONDON DOCKS" CONVENIENTLY NEAR THE CITY
IN RICE, TOBACCO, WINE + BRANDY, EXCEPT THOSE SHIPS COMING FROM THE EAST AND

OF BETEL NUT GUYS AROUND WITH
LIGHTNING FAST JETS OF SPIT!
EMBER 27 2001. JAMA
IJD MOTOR PARTS BAZAAR.
E THE STRANGE TOUNGE-LIKE
ELLATION STRONGLY LINKING THE
ITECTURE OF THE RED FORT
RE GATE WITH THE SOUTH GATE
JAMA MASJID
EMBER 28th 2001. THICK THICK
DESCENDS UPON DELHI AT 7:00
ISIBILITY REDUCED TO 25/30 METRES
H HOUR. THICK FOG AND THE
FFIC PLOWS ON. HORNS AND THROTTLES
ING AWAY. THE GAURI SHANKAR MANDIR
FADED AWAY. DUNDOR CHORA - FOG.
ID - FOG. SHIVALA. A SCORE OF COOKS
NA WALLAHS ARE BUSY AROUND LAJ PAT
MARKET AROUND SUPPERTIME. MOST
ING A'TOP THE RAT HILL. HOT FRIED
D APPEARS TO BE BEING COOKED FOR
NEEDY HERE TOO ~ WHO ARE QUEUEING
OR SOME TASTY NAAN TREATS. WHAT
ZARRE SCENE. HERE FOOD HYGEINE
T NIL. BREAD, NAN-WALLA ON RAT
WIPES HIS HAND ON GROUND
ODICALLY. YIPES. RICKSHAW WALLAS
EXPERT NAN BREAD GUY WITH ROLLER.
ROLLS AND SHAPES BREAD-LETS
RECYCLING OF BOWLS OF HALF FINISHD
BACK INTO THE BIG POT SEEMS A
WORRYING HERE. I THINK I WILL
K TO A CUP OF CHAI. THE COOKER
CHED ABOVE MAY BE A COMMUNAL
VARIOUS FOLK GATHER AROUND
ALL INDIA RADIO NEWS AT 9:00PM.
CLOUDS GATHER BETWEEN PAK
INDIA. SHELLING CONTINUES AT
PUTED BORDER AREAS. WASHINGTON
IS FOR RAPPROACHMENT. RUMSFELD IS
TED. AKBAR...
COOK MEISTER WITH STICKS
KNEADING AND SHAPING
DAL GUY
CKS IN OVEN
DOORI OVEN UNDER THE TREE IN THE
MINUTES I HAVE BEEN SITTING HERE
WARDS OF 500 CHAPATIS HAVE BEEN
DE. IN BOTH THESE COOKING SCENES
VISION OF LABOUR IS KEY FOR MASS
ODUCTION. SMELLS GREAT. AND I AM
STAINED BY YUMMY CUPS OF TEA TO
LEFT. DAL HOTEL TO MY RIGHT.
L SORTS OF THINGS HANGING
ROM THE BIG TREE AT THIS PLEIN-AIR
TCHEN. PRESUMABLY TO KEEP THEM
F THE GROUND - THE RAT'S DOMAIN
ROTI
ODAY'S THICK FOG: THUNID: HAS
ROUNDED PLANES AT DELHI AIRPORT.
HAI GUY QUITS AT 11:00PM. FRIDAY
GHT. DAL HOTEL IS STILL GOING STRONG
HAI GUY IS A TEAM OF FOUR. DAL HOTEL
A TEAM OF SEVEN. FOUR OF WHOM ARE
EPICTED ABOVE. GAURI SHANKAR
ANDIR WAS SERIOUSLY WEIRD.
HOES OFF I CLIMBED THE MARBLE STEPS
THE FIRST FLOOR AND CONFRONTD
T A TEMPLE INTERIOR BUT WHAT LOOKED
GORE SANKAR MANDIR TWOA-TCHOW
BOLI. BABA. DESPITE THE UNRELE
THIS ENVIRONMENT. EVERYONE LIVE
IN HARMONY. TCHOW-TCHOWS. MACH
MONKEYS. HINDU'S. MOSLEMS. ALL SLE
ATOP ONE ANOTHER EASY-LIKE. IN
ALAM! DECEMBER 23RD ACE INDIAN
PLAYING ON PARADE ROAD. SERIOUSLY AC
SINGERS. SOME SORT OF INDIAN ACCORDIO
LOCKS TOGETHER AS THE MUSICIANS PU
MELODIES THE TUNES WORK AROUND A
THE COMPLEX RHYTHMIC UNDER WEAVE
THREAD OF SUNG MELODIC LINE. EA
A NUMBER OF DISTINCT SECTIONS
THE TUNES, OR COMPOSING FOR THIS MUSIC
ABSORB WESTERN FLAVOURS, MELODIC LINE
CHAMELEON LIKE FORMAT FOR SONG
LUCKNOW. U/P AGNIHOTRI BROTHERS.
LAJ PAT RAI

GILES GILBERT SCOTT "THE FINAL FLOWERING OF GOTHIC REVIVAL AS A VITAL, CREATIVE MOVEMEN[T] AND IS ONE OF THE GREAT BUILDINGS OF THE 20TH C[ENTURY]." CONSTRUCTION BEGAN IN 1904 AT THE HEIGHT OF [THE] CITY'S PROSPERITY AND FINISHED IN 1978 AS HER LONG ECONOMIC DECLINE REACHED ITS LOWEST POIN[T]. BOOK. JOHSEPH SHARPLES LIVERPOO[L] WITH HELP. SIMON BRADLEY. YALE. UNIVERSITY PRE[SS] WITH "FUNDED. (THE CATHEDRAL) LIVERPOOL. INSIGCANCE IN THE C17 TO BECOME COUNTRY'S 3RD PORT BY 1700. THEN 2ND TO LONDON EUROPE'S. I SURVIVED MY FEW NIGHTS WITH TADDIE ROOM 104. AT THE LIVERPOOL YHA.

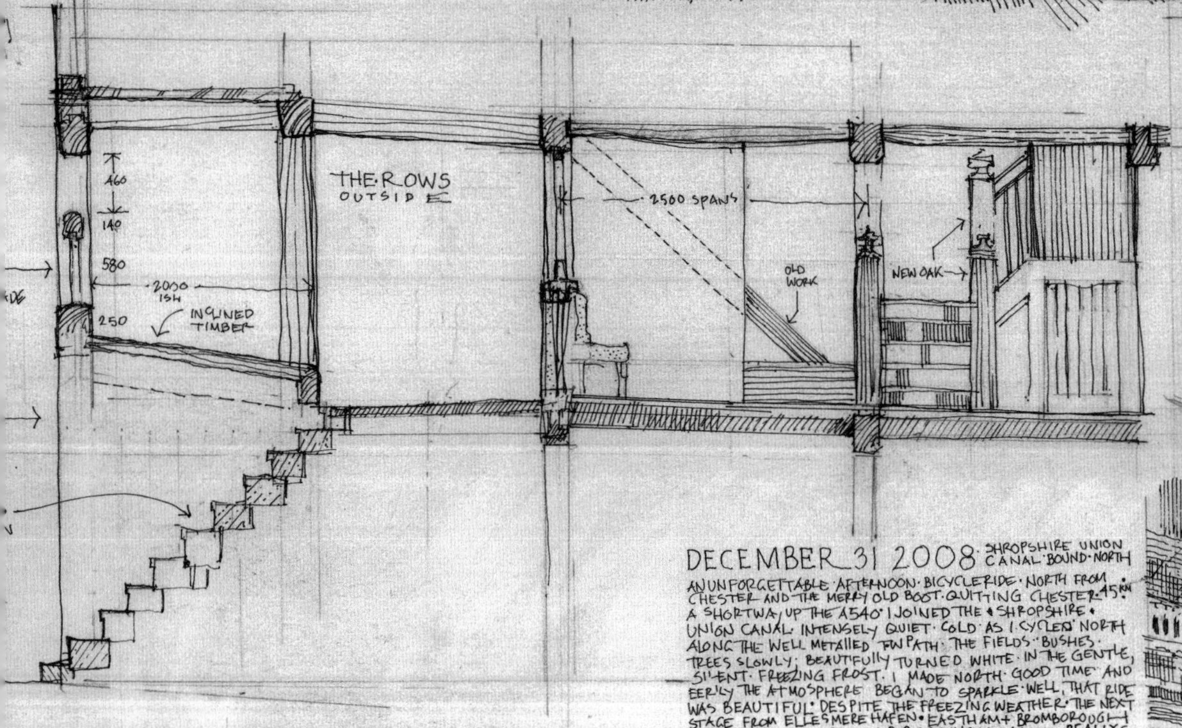

DECEMBER 31 2008. SHROPSHIRE UNION CANAL. BOUND. NORTH

AN UNFORGETTABLE. AFTERNOON. BICYCLERIDE. NORTH FROM CHESTER AND THE MERRY OLD BOOT. QUITTING CHESTER. 45KM. A SHORTWAY UP THE A540. I JOINED THE SHROPSHIRE UNION CANAL. INTENSELY QUIET. COLD. AS I CYCLED NORTH ALONG THE WELL METALLED TOWPATH. THE FIELDS.. BUSHES. TREES SLOWLY; BEAUTIFULLY TURNED WHITE. IN THE GENTLE, SILENT. FREEZING FROST. I MADE NORTH. GOOD TIME AND EERILY THE ATMOSPHERE BEGAN TO SPARKLE. WELL, THAT RIDE WAS BEAUTIFUL. DESPITE THE FREEZING WEATHER. THE NEXT STAGE FROM ELLESMERE HAFEN. EASTHAM + BROMBOROUGH TRANMERE. SUPER-PRETTY PORT SUNLIGHT. DARK. NOW REALLY COLD. MAN THOSE VIRGIN PENDOLINOS HAUL ASS ON THE NEWLY RESTORATED WEST COAST MAIN LINE. SEE NOTES ELSEWHERE. SOME FOLK HAVE BROAD ACCENTS HEREIN DEVA: OTHERS NOT SO. LOTS OF LAUGHING IN THE BOOT INN. VERY ANGLO. LOOKING FOLK HERE! WORDS OVERHEARD: "YOU MANKY BASTARD". THIS DRAWING SESSION REMINDS ME HOW DAMN POTENT THE ISOGRAPH CAN BE. QUITE FAIR, BLUE EYED AROUND THIS JOINT. IS THAT A CHESHIRE THING? LIKE ALSO THIS MUSICAL WAY OF TALKING. PINT OF BEST BITTER £1.51 IN THE BOOT SAMUEL SMITH'S.

ANGLICAN CATHEDRAL: VESTEY (331ft.) TALL. UK'S LARGEST [W]IDEST GOTHIC ARCHES [...]ALEY. ANOTHER PLACE [...]: FORMBY. POST PANAMAX [Q]UARRY SANDSTONE. VERY [...]Y STONE. SCOTT A CATHOLIC [...]. SO. SCOTT PLUS OLD BODLEY [...]K IS NO FLUKE" IT IS MANIFESTLY A MOST GIFTED MAN, OF COURSE

THE BOOT INN. CHESTER. C. 1640 ON THE "ROWS" WOW. ORIGINAL JOINT. FORMER MERCHANT'S HOUSE. FACADE. RESTORED IN THE 19TH C. THE ROWS ARE SO DAMN IMPRESSIVE HAVE FOUND I BIKE SHOP. ON THE ROAD TO THE STATION AND THE MAIN BOOKSHOP. OPPOSITE THE BOOT. WELL, THEY DEFINITELY SPEAK DIFFERENT HERE. BLUE BELLS. DIE ALTE CHESTER: DEVA" ROMAN LEGIONARY FORTRESS. MR. STARKEY. ROMAN WALLS + ROMAN AMPHITHEATRE... RIVER DEE AND A FINE RAILWAY JUNCTION. HEY! LOOK OUT FOR THE MIGHTY GAVIN FINNAN. DON'T GAVIN COME FROM HERE? I REMBER GETTING A GREAT POSTCARD [...] ROWS

HAUNCH OF VENISON · AN OLDENGLAND CHOP HOUSE · BISHOP POORE LAID THE FOUNDATION STONE FOR THE NEW CATHEDRAL IN 1220 · (ARCHBISHOP, STEPHEN LANGTON · CANTERBURY) "BUILDING CONTINUED AT THE UNCOMMONLY FAST RATE · LEADING OF THE ROOF IN 1266 ·

THE DESIGNER OF THE CATHEDRAL? MR · HARVEY PLEADS FOR NICHOLAS OF ELY. FIRST · MASTER MASON · NICHOLAS OF ELY · POSSIBLY THE DESIGNER WAS ELIAS DE DEREHAM CANNON OF SARUM · WHO WAS PRESENT AT RUNNYMEDE AN EXTREMELY ABLE CHURCHMAN AND ADMINISTRATOR,, ALSO AN ARTIST AND A MAN CLOSELY CONNECTED WITH ARCHITECTURE · DESIGNED THE SHRINE AT CANTERBURY FOR YOU KNOW WHO = FAGEBAT · FACIEBAT" HE WAS RESPONSIBLE FOR ·. NOT · HE DESIGNED · ELIAS DE DEREHAM · IN CHARGE OF KINGS WORKS AT WINCHESTER AND AT CLARENDON "AN INCOMPRABLE "ARTIFEX" ALSO RICHARD AND RICHARD OF FARLEIGH BUILT THE SPIRE · THE CATHEDRAL IS BUILT OF CHILMARK STONE · IE A STONE QUARRIED 12 MILES FROM THE SITE · 449 FT · LONG; 81 ft · tall · SPIRE 404 ft tall · (ONLY ULM taller · 19th C) 530 FEET TALL · THE PLAN OF THE SALISBURY CATHEDRAL IS THE BEAU IDEAL OF THE EARLY ENGLISH PLAN ·· ON A VIRGIN SITE THE DESIGNER COULD DO EXACTLY WHAT HE THOUGHT BEST · THE OUTCOME DIFFERS IN EVERY RESPECT FROM THE FRENCH IDEAL OF CHARTRES, REIMS, AND AMIENS; AT SALISBURY ALL IS RECTANGULAR · AND PARTS ARE KEPT NEATLY FROM PARTS ·· A SCREEN FACADE NOT ORGANICALLY GROWING OUT OF NAVE AND AISLES · FINISHES THE BUILDING TO THE WEST · "MOST UNIFIED IN APPEARANCE OF ALL ENGLISH CATHEDRAL

SPIRE" FAR TOO HIGH FROM THE E · E POINT OF VIEW · "IT HAPPENS TO BE A WORK OF A MASON OF THE HIGHEST GENIUS · WINDOWS ALL LANCETS MOSTLY IN PAIRS · THE INTERIOR OF SALISBURY CATHEDRAL IS AS UNIFIED AS IS THE EXTERIOR (THAT · AND WYATT'S · TIDYING UP GIVES IT IS PERFECTION ·

POULTRY CROSS

C15th CENTURY · WITH TOP PARTS OF 1853 THE ONE REMAINING OF FOUR MARKET CROSSES; CHEESE MARKET; WOOL CROSS · BARNEWELL'S CROSS · POULTRY CROSS "COUNTRY FOLK WOULD SE SELL THEIR PRODUCE BENEATH ITS ARCHES, AND ON OCCASION THEIR WOULD BE OPEN AIR SERMONS · THE CROSS IS FIRST MENTIONED IN 1335 · OPPOSITE, AND DATING TO THE SAME PERIOD ARE SEVERAL HALFTIMBERED BUILDINGS · MIKE'S SETTLING ACCOUNTS · INCLUDING · THE HAUNCH OF VENISON" BUSTLING WITH PILGRIMS · WHO VISITED ROY IS A GOOD FRIEND TO WILL · GRUNDIE · SALISBURY ST · OSMUND (CANNONISED 1457) WHO WAS CHANCELLOR OF ENGLAND 1074-1078 · BISHOP OF SALISBURY 1078 TO 1099 · THE GUILDHALL 1795 SIR ROBERT TAYLOR: NOTE RUSTICATED QUOINS; THE COLLEGE OF MATRONS 1682 · TO HOUSE 12 · CLERGY WIDOWS · FOUNDED BY BISHOP SETH WARD · PECKHAM FYE ON A WARTIME DRAMA · "STEVE" LIME LIGHT · LIME COALS 1879 · SWAN LIGHTBULB 20 MINUTES

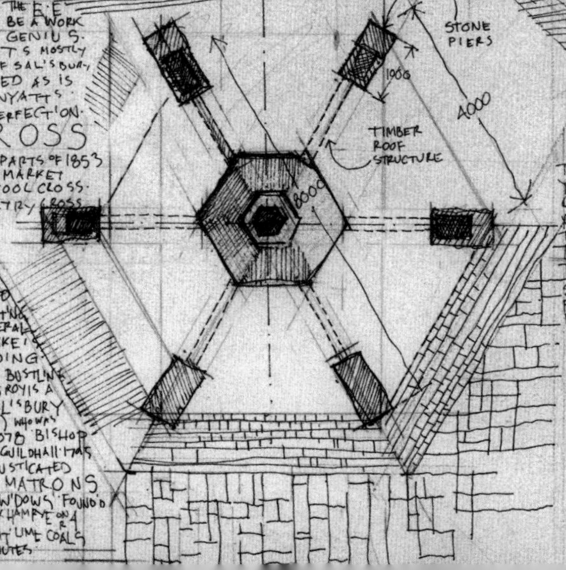

THOMAS ALVA EDISON · AFTER SWAN · ONE YEAR · 825 BULBS FOR D'OLY CARTE · 1885 CATHEDRAL ORIGINALLY AT OLD SARUM; NORMAN CATHEDRAL · SQUABBLES WITH THE MILITARY LED BISHOP POORE TO DECIDE TO REBUILD IN THE VALLEY BELOW · PEACE! THE PRESENT STREET "CHEQUERED STREET PLAN" · REG; ROWLAND, CHRIS PHIL; NIGEL · 1 OF 4 CROSSES · CHERRY · MIRANDA · MARYANN · BELINDA

HALIFAX TO ROCHDALE · I LIKED HALIFAX
BARRY AND SON'S HIGH VICTORIAN TOWN HALL
IS ABSOLUTELY FANTASTIC · VIBRANT · FULL OF
CRAZY WACKY HIGH VICTORIAN RENAISSANCE MADNESS
ALL IN SOME WONDERFUL BUFF STONE · CRISP, HIGHLY
DETAILED · THE GREAT LEEMING AND LEEMING WERE
IN EVIDENCE TOO · AS THE CITY'S MIGHTY 'BOROUGH
MARKET' WAS DESIGNED BY THEM TOO · ANOTHER
EXCITING LANDMARK IN HALIFAX IS THE MONUMENTAL
HALIFAX BUILDING SOCIETY HEADQUARTERS
AT THE TOP OF THE TOWN · FROM THE GOLDEN AGE OF
BDP · BUILDING DESIGN PARTNERSHIP · AT ABOUT
ONE I QUIT THE TOWN · HEADING NORTH AND UPHILL
PAST THE CITY PARK UP · UP AND OVER THEN A SHARP
DESCENT INTO SOWERBY BRIDGE · THE TALL SCARP
BETWEEN HALIFAX AND SOWERBY BRIDGE IS DOMINAT'
ED BY THIS IMMENSELY TALL FOLLY · WAINHOUSE TOWER
A CHIMNEY · OVERLOOKING CALDERDALE · OVER: →

CAN SEE MANY DIRECT LINKS BETWEEN THE ARCHITECT
RE OF THE EARLIER NATURAL HISTORY MUSEUM · THE S
ESOLUTION OF CURVED STONE · AND PLANAR ELEMENT.

UGTONIUS · AELECTUS.
GILLET AND JOHNSTON · LONDINIUM · AUGUSTA ·
JALLS · ABEL · 9 TON BELL · MANCHESTER TOWN HALL
80 ACRES: THE AREA ENCLOSED BY THE · OUR CITY
RIGINALLY BUILT BY ROMANS · DO
D 350?. CITY WALL · LONDON · 3½ MILES LONG ·
BRARY: ARCHITECT - CORSON · VERY GOOD.
Y THE 1950s 400 TRADERS
93–1904 · NEW HALL · LEEMING AND BAGSHAW + SONS
OF BATLEY.
PENCERS · AS A PENNY BAZAAR.
375; 1904; 1981 · FOUNDING LOCATION OF MARKS AND
NE IRON ARCHITECTURE · JOSEPH AND JOHN LEEMING ·
OMPLETELY FILLED WITH ACTIVITY AND ACTION · REALLY
ARKET · A HUGE SERIES OF CITY BLOCKS OF MARKET
WAS SO COMPLETELY TAKEN BY THE LEEDS KIRKGATE

WATERHOUSE · A TOTAL MASTER OF
SPACE AND ARCHITECTURE · AND AS
I AM FINDING HERE IN THE TOWN HALL ·
A GREAT DETAILER · FINE MOSAICS AND TILE
WORK · MANCHESTER · 1 ·
· 12: TOWN HALL
WATERHOUSE ·
1888 · LCC · MBW COUNTY · TESSELATED FLOORS ·
WONDERFUL COMBINATION OF CURVES AND
CURVED STONEWORK AND BEAUTIFUL
GLAZED PANELS ·
SUSAN · WAPPING HIGH STREET.
JANUARY 10TH 2015 · HALIFAX RIDE

LEEDS CITY LIBRARY
ALAN BENNETT SPENT LONG HOURS WORKING HERE
I WAS MUCH IMPRESSED WITH SIR GEORGE GILBERT SCO
LEEDS GENERAL INFIRMARY. 1869 · PLANNED AROUND
FLORENCE NIGHTINGALES PRINCIPALS · FOR SEPARATE
WINGS · LGI: LEEDS GENERAL INFIRMARY · WONDERFULLY

MY FIRST VISION OF THIS AMAZING COTSWOLD STONE. BROAD "OPENING" MARKET areas etc. ON OLD ROMAN WAY.
FOSS WAY
TO OXFORD A44
PLAN N.T.S.
MARKET HALL
FOSS WAY
SENSATIONAL Noctural ride SEZINCOTE – BLOCKLEY – BROAD CAMPDEN.
CHIPPING CAMPDEN WITH A VISITING SPANISH WINE AND SOME INTERESTING
historical programming on radio 4. SUNDAY night. TRIUMPHAL ARRIVAL INTO CHIPPING
CAMDEN @ 10:00 – FASCINATING. under a big pine tree in a terrace in
the Churchyard found a perfect place to sleep. slept a bit long 1:00 to
10:30 a brilliant, camoflaged – invisible – but welcoming corner of the
huge church grounds. In watching people use these spaces I can let them pace it
out for me, adjusting the count of strides based on the size and age of the walker.
The ground floor bay windows in stone really grow from the building and produce a really
distinctive footprint on to the ground surface. This village is so worthy of study
LIKE MORETON-IN-MARSH, CHIPPING CAMPDEN is a series of key
public buildings inflating, creating a public realm out at the high street.
MONDAY afternoon. AUSPICIOUS VISIT TO the "jubilee special" interview 5:30
FRIDAY @ SOM 4:30 FRIDAY WEEK @ Stanton Williams. An unfortunate week between
the two. WALLER AND SON, WALLER F.S. WALLER N.H.
WALLER AND Ashwell, Waller R. (of Bristol)
Waller + Wood, dominate the Artist's section
of the indexs of CLOUS. I PEVSNER. 11 LINES 31 REFS.
WIGAN dominating English rugby. "FAX" IT
ARCADED STOP raining built by Sir Baptist
possible exception MARKET HALL IN 1627 WAS
for the sale of cheese, butter and poultry.
bays, three gables on each side. Two bays and
on each side end TOWN HALL c.14
MONUMENTS IN CHIPPING CAMDEN CHU
of the highest order. ONE by sculptor to CHA
Marshall of Fleet Street. bizarre, closet-like
Tomb, too, Either Sir Baptist Hicks or son
fighting for the Royalist cause. A very lovley
with beautifully carved lace. Cool medieval
very rare. c.1500. Wooden plate set in to
inside creating a base for timber rafters.
SECTION 1:200
1 6 2 7
N
LOWER HIGH STREET
TOWER
SHEEP STREET

ANTHONY ORELOWITZ

Paragon Group • South Africa

Featured projects: Sanlam Santam [p. 242, top] • 140 West Street [p. 242, bottom] • Pan African Parliament Building [p. 243]

'Sketching is a mainstay of expression,' says Anthony Orelowitz, founder and director of Paragon Group, based in Johannesburg, South Africa. 'When I look back at the page, the process of sketching has often transferred what was happening in my mind's eye in a very fluid way. The connection between pen and paper is sensuous and expressive, and allows the design to develop fluidly, without breaking the connection between iteration.'

He continues: 'I sketch on paper, but use my iPad more and more. For me, sketching on the iPad offers an even more heightened experience, as pressure control is improved tenfold and toolsets are more comprehensive. It also allows for a number of different programs to be used, which in turn enables an increased range of expression.'

The firm, formed in 1997, has grown from four people to over 80 today, and takes on all types of projects in South Africa and beyond. 'As a team, we move continually between the sketch and computer modelling,' Orelowitz says. 'The one forms an overlay for the other. We never design in CAD: our 2D sketches lead to 3D models, which drive 3D sketches. This cycle runs until the design process is complete. Sketching is an integral part of it, and not just an initiator of the design development. For me, the concept is well imagined before I sketch, but it is only a point of departure. The beauty of sketching is that one can iterate very quickly and evolve the design fluidly, as a continual process.'

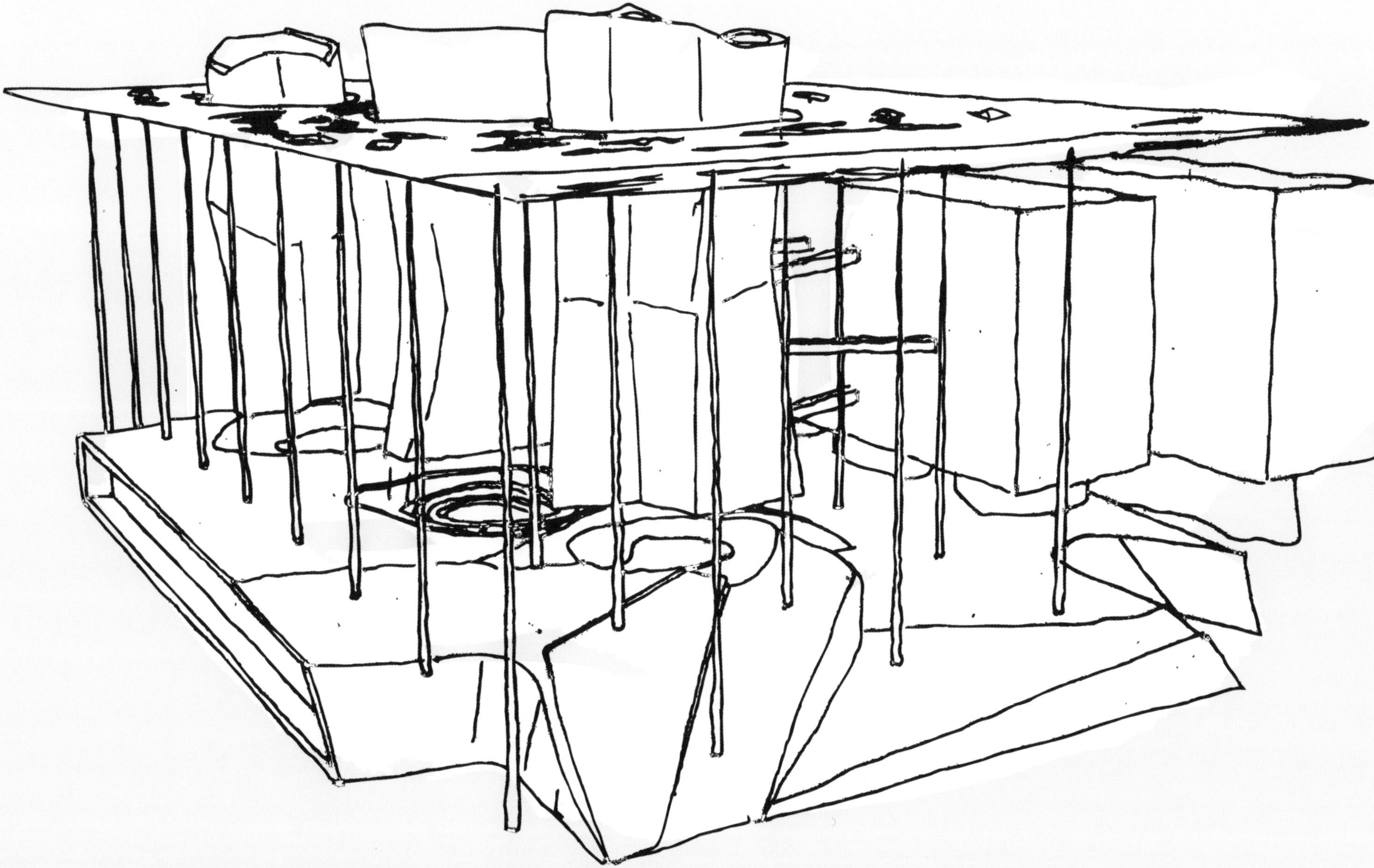

JOSEPH DI PASQUALE

JDP Architects • Italy

Featured projects: Tower concept [pp. 244–5]
Unitè concept [p. 246, left] · Guilin Hotel [p. 246, top right]
Vegetal skyscrapers [pp. 246, bottom right; 247, bottom]
Guangzhou Circle [p. 247, top]

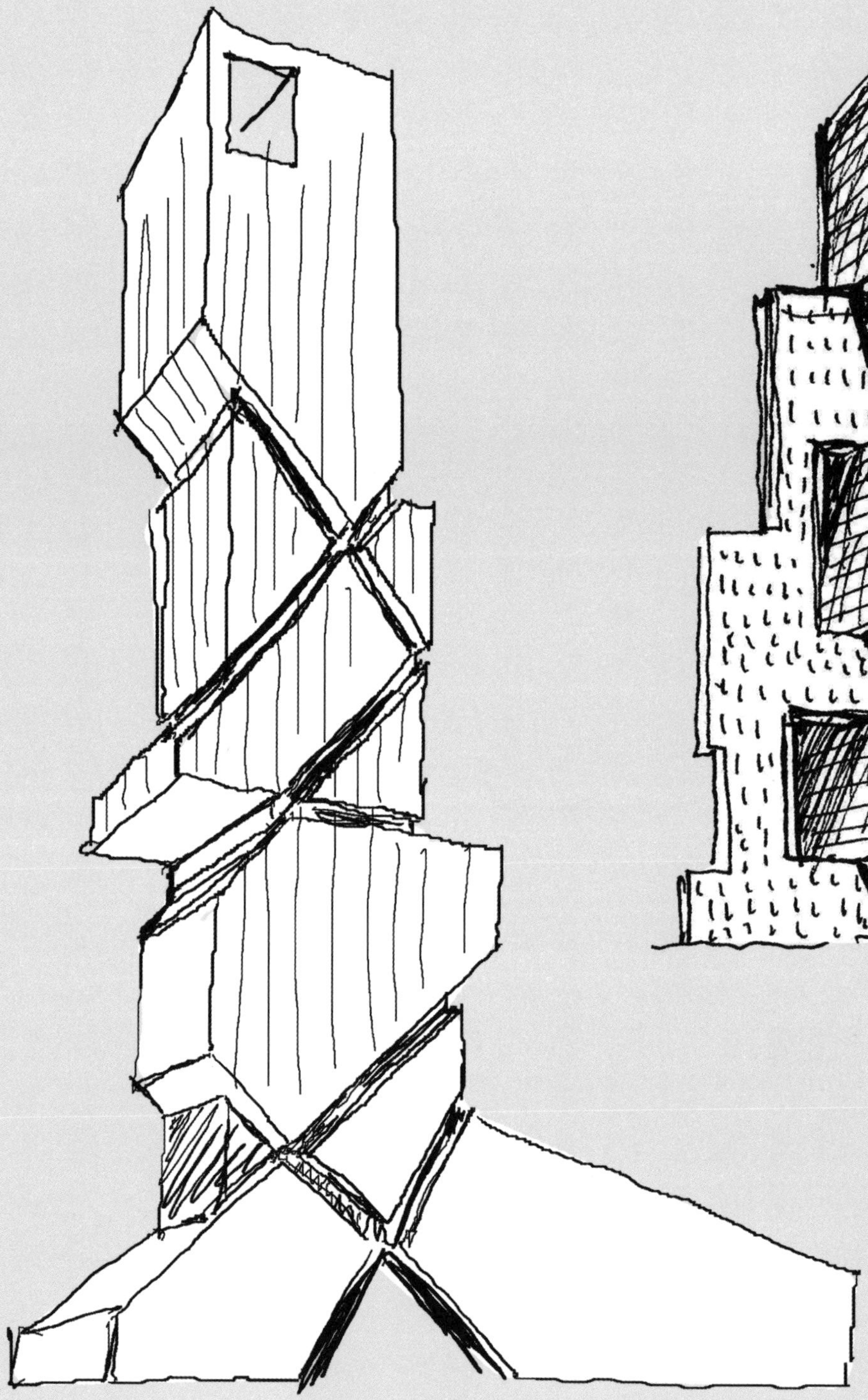

'Sketching directly into the digital world is something I couldn't manage without,' says Joseph di Pasquale of JDP Architects. 'My dream is to sketch directly onto the screen to communicate with the 3D software. I do use a notebook, but I prefer to sketch digitally, because I can edit the sketch "post-production" and combine my hand-sketching style with digital effects.'

Di Pasquale is among a new breed of architects keen to take their physical skills and use them in the digital realm, seeing digital methods as additions, rather than alternatives, to their arsenal. 'Sketching is a physical need,' he says. 'The more the design development becomes digital, the more I need to sketch to visualize ideas. Nowadays, sketching and maquettes are the only links with the physical world during the entire design process. Sketching is the most immediate way of visualizing emerging problems and the best method to start solving them.'

But while some architects communicate continuously with clients via sketches, di Pasquale uses them purely for research, starting with a big idea that is refined as the project unfolds. 'Normally I sketch to visualize the full idea at the beginning of the design process,' he says. 'I try to make it as detailed as possible. Only when I have found a sketch that fully convinces me can the design process start. Usually, my first sketch is the same view that becomes the main "photographic aspect" of the finished building.'

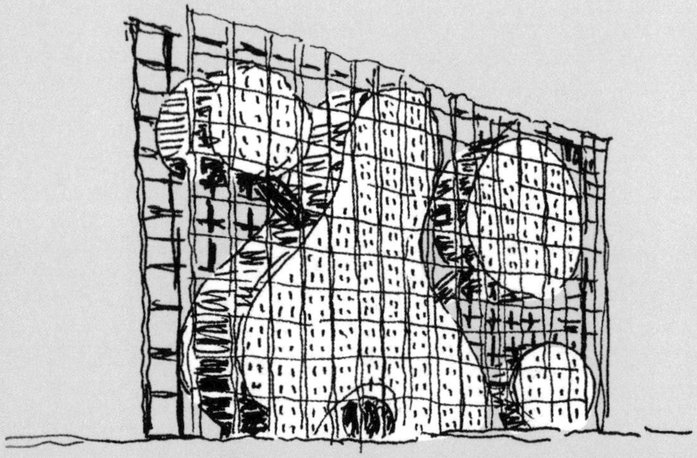
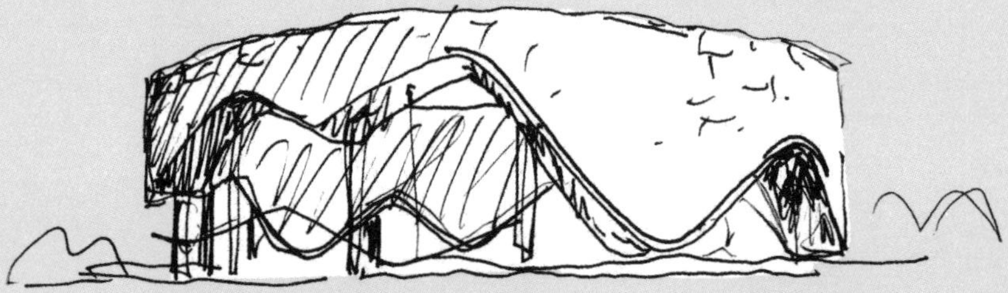
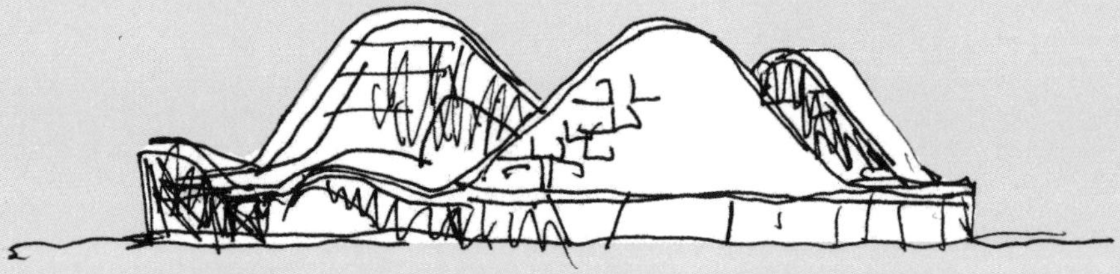

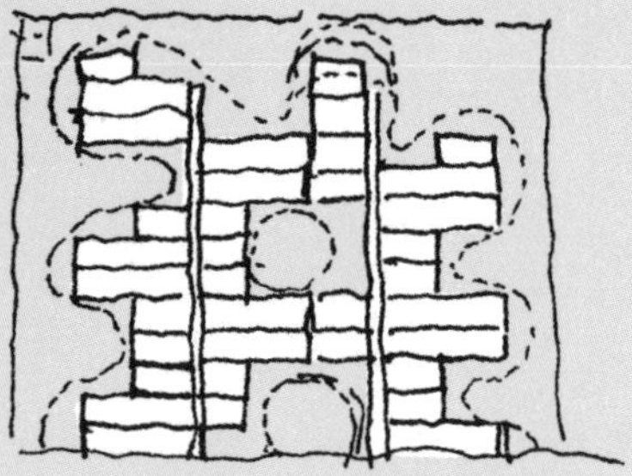
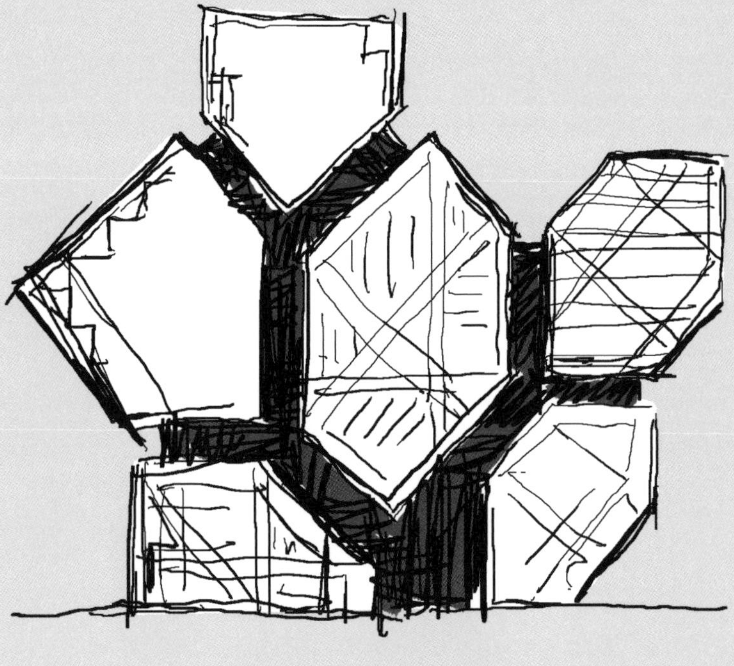

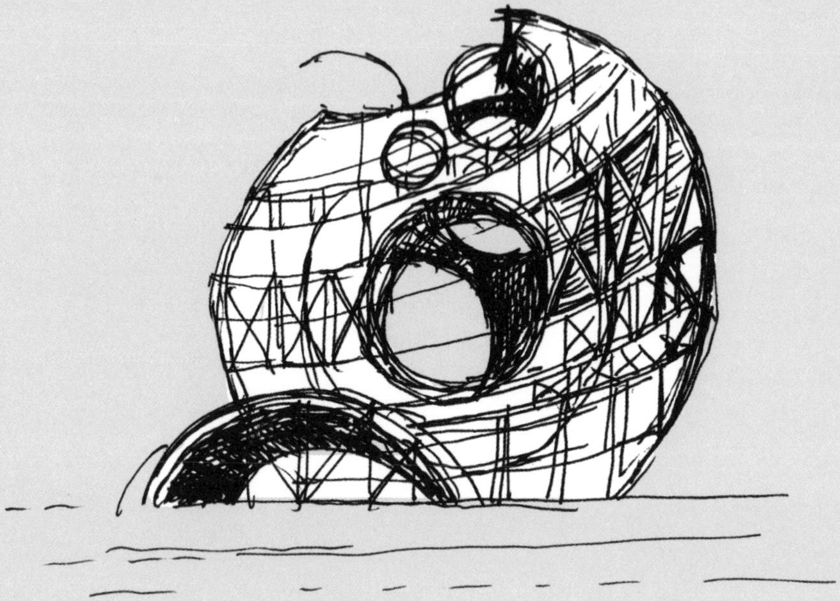

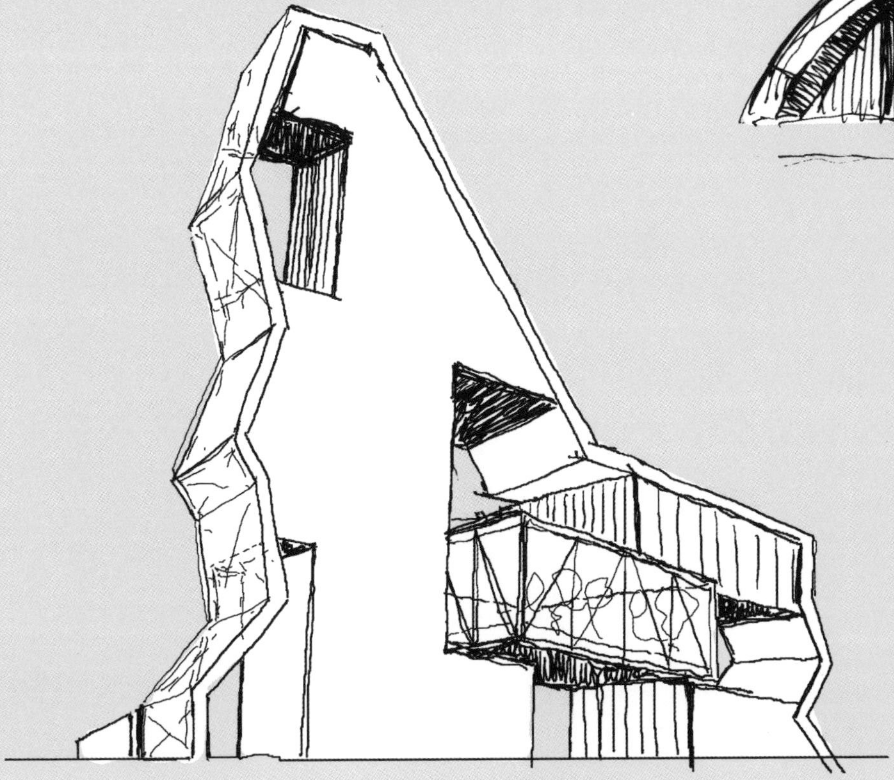

FELIPE PICH-AGUILERA

Pich Architects • Spain

Featured projects: Salvador de Bahia [p. 248, top]
La Colonia Rosa [p. 248, bottom] · Ampuries [p. 249]
San Bernabe [p. 250] · Gardeny [p. 251]

'Sketches allow you to deal with ambiguity,' states Felipe Pich-Aguilera. 'Architecture begins with intuitive ideas, which raise more questions than answers, and sketching is the only physical way I know of working with the precise and the imprecise at the same time. It would be impossible for me to work without sketching, as it is the most effective way to transmit and explain ideas in the process of fixing architecture and its development.'

In 1986 Pich-Aguilera became a founding partner of Pich-Aguilera Arquitectos, which he now heads with Teresa Batlle Pagès. In 2012 four new partners set up a spin-off called PiBarquitecturaSix, and today the two entities work under the umbrella Pich Architects, which is based in Barcelona.

'Drawings make it easier to present ideas and establish a dialogue, with clients and with my team,' Pich-Aguilera continues. He believes that sketching is a way of thinking – of 'developing ideas by projecting them outside your mind, to be tested through the eyes and then back inside again' – and sees it as an evolving process. And where does he sketch?

'I sketch anywhere – at the office, while I'm travelling, in a bar or a hotel room,' he says. 'There might be an urgent question to resolve in a project, a technical detail I'm worried about or the atmosphere of a particular city, which makes me stop and wonder what it is about this place that makes me feel good. There is always a reason to sketch.'

PAWEL PODWOJEWSKI

Motiv • Poland

Featured projects: Gdansk [pp. 252–5] · Qatar [pp. 256–7]
Finferries [pp. 258–9] · Dubai Blue [pp. 260–1]

'In the 21st century, young architects learn very quickly to work with digital tools,' says Pawel Podwojewski of Polish firm Motiv. 'Unfortunately, this makes the design process less creative. Digital tools should aid, rather than replace the traditional, more emotive approach.'

Podwojewski is himself a young architect, although he speaks like an old master. 'I hope that education will return to a focus on more traditional techniques, because the act of drawing is often accidental,' he says. 'These accidents bring beauty to life and uniqueness to design.'

His own Gdansk-based practice is by no means traditional, however, and is as adept at taking on graphic-design projects as it is at creating architecture. Podwojewski believes that he could design without sketching, but is not sure what kind of results he would get. 'It would be more difficult,' he explains, 'and in many ways more frustrating.'

Instead, the design process nearly always starts with a sketch. 'With the first sketches, it is easy to find a few directions that can be analysed to choose the best option,' Podwojewski notes. His sketches are then scanned, scaled and reworked in digital form using AutoCAD and 3ds Max, after which he returns to sketching directly onto the blueprints.

'Typical or standard solutions do not require sketching, and we solve them directly in digital space,' he says. 'The hard ones are solved on paper, sometimes during a meeting with engineers or sometimes travelling to and from the office. You do not need a battery or much space, just a pen and a notebook. That's the beauty of sketching.'

Wariant B.

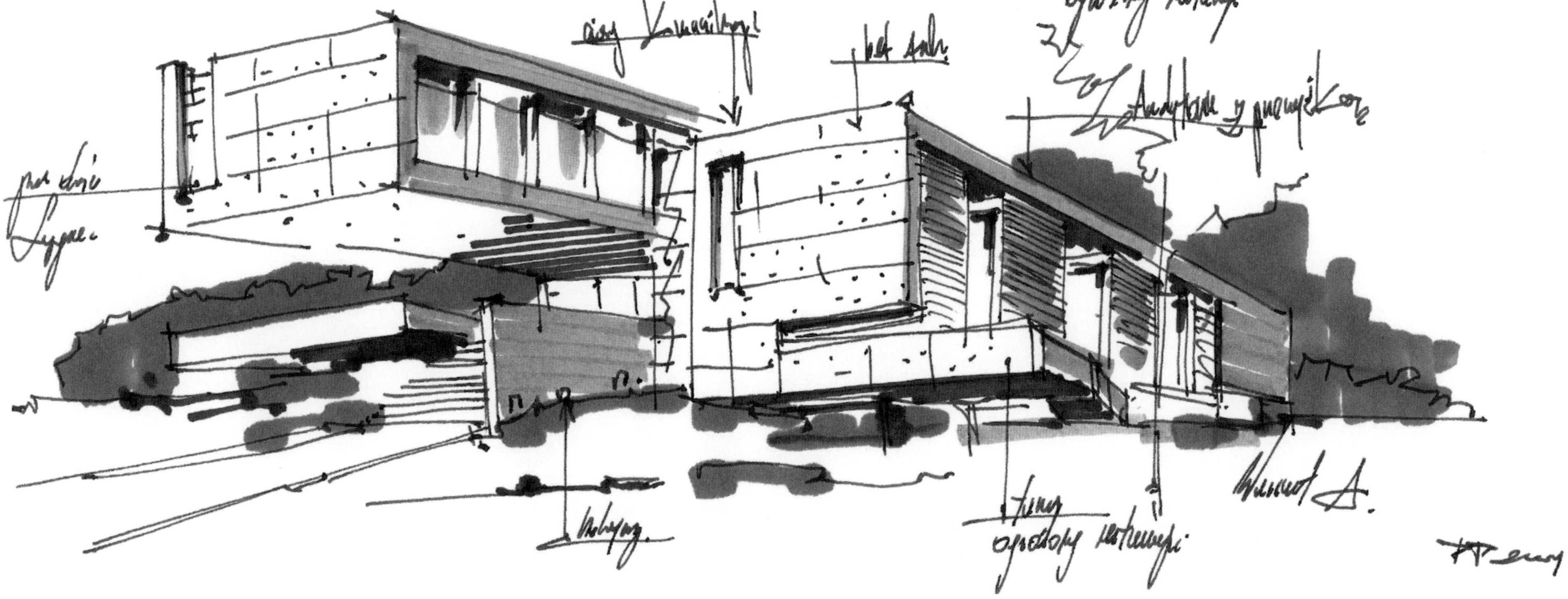
Wariant A.

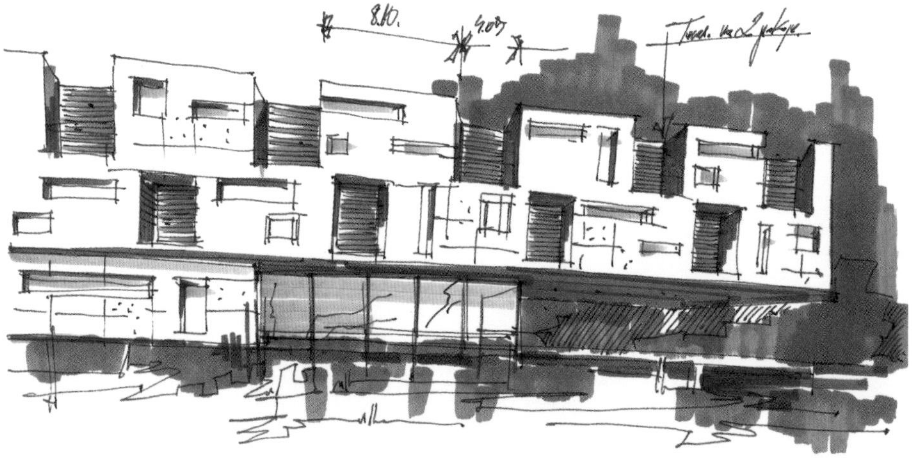

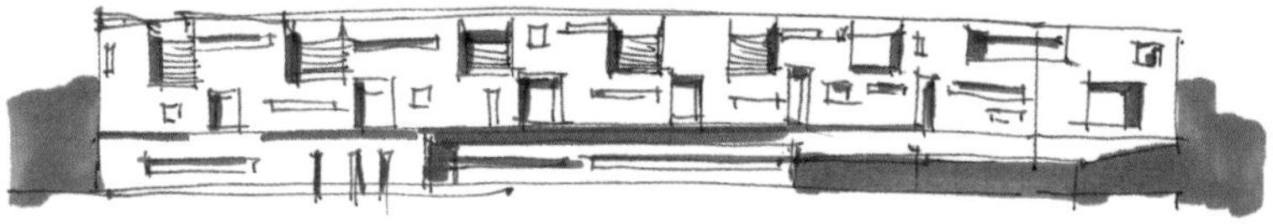

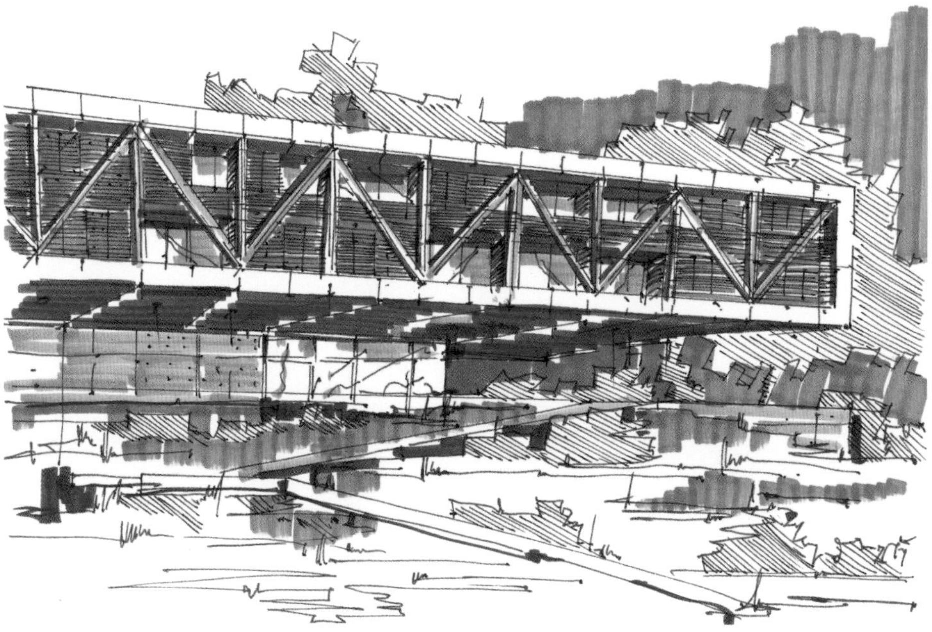

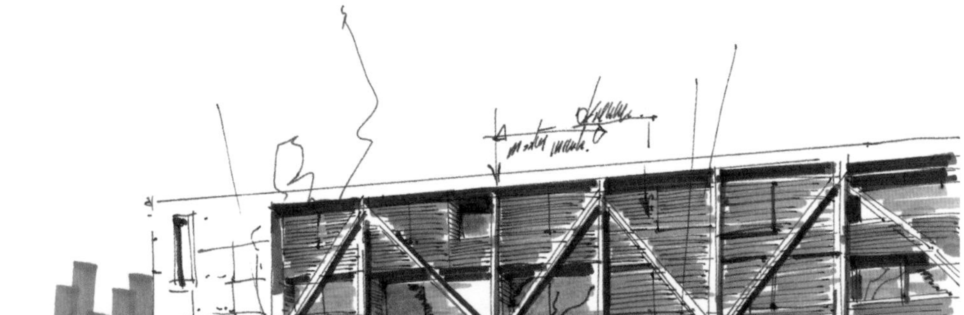

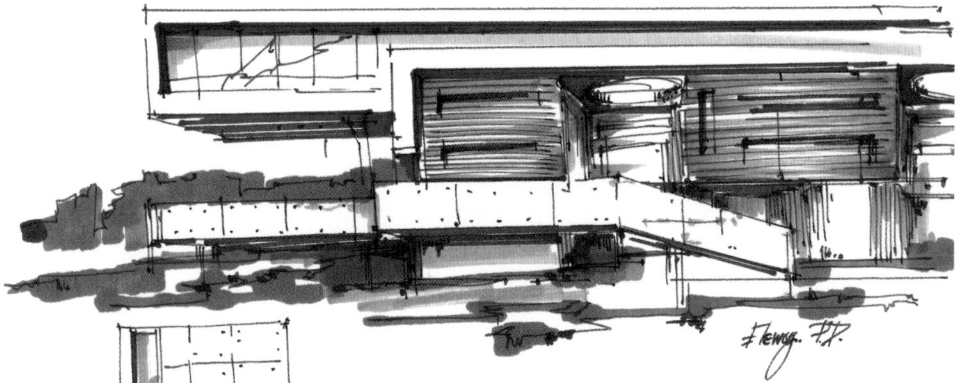

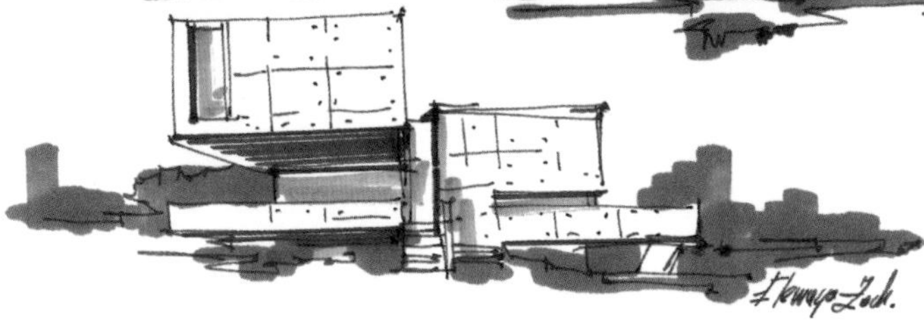

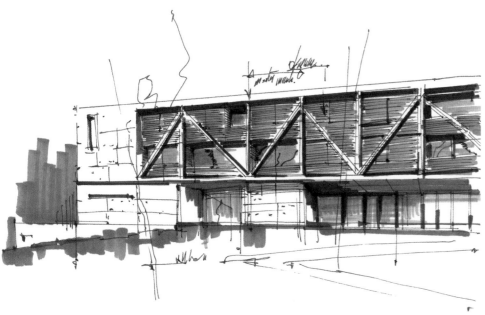

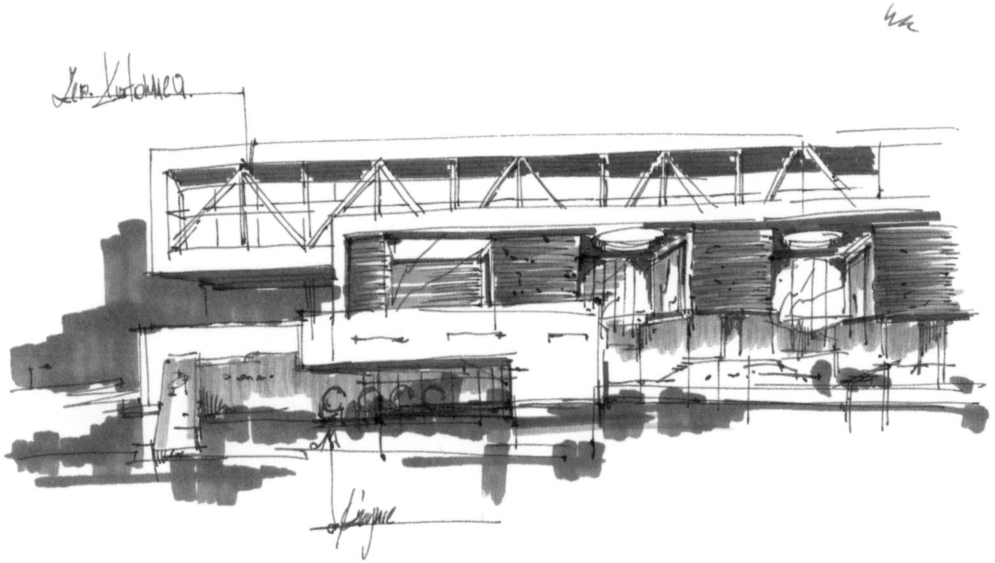

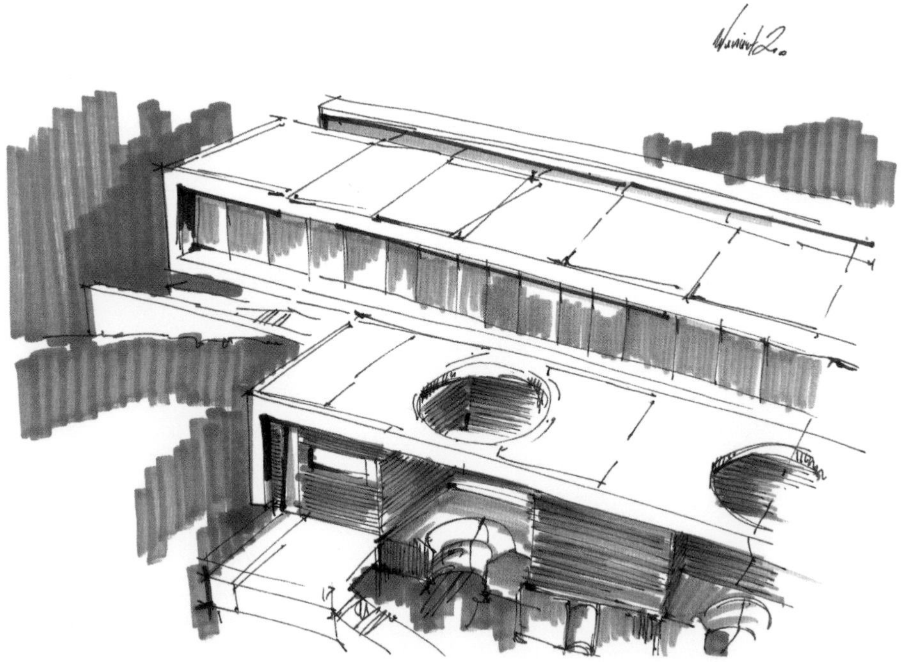

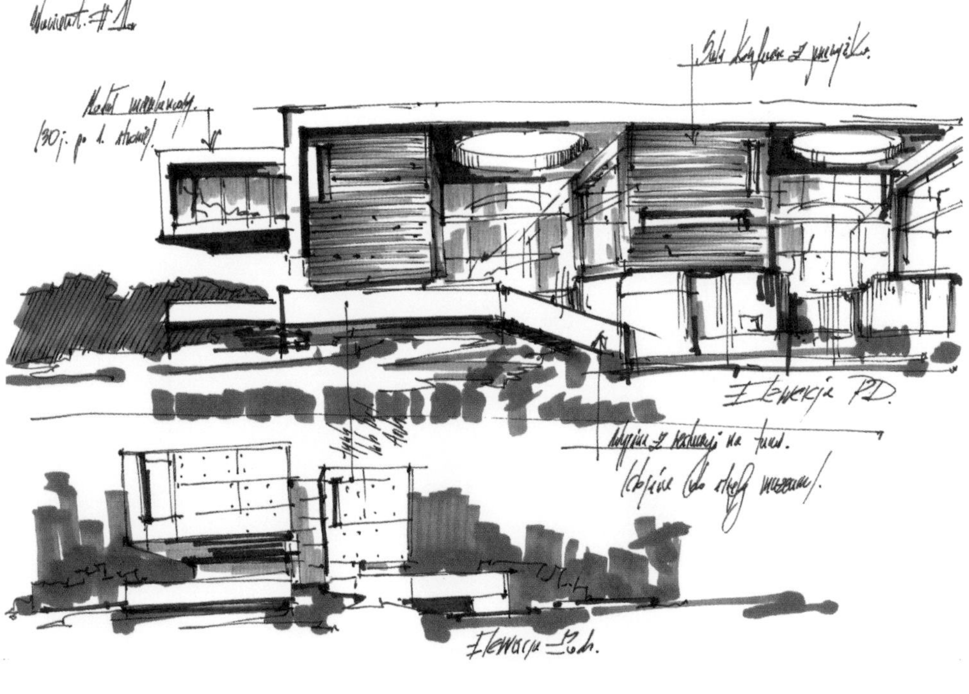

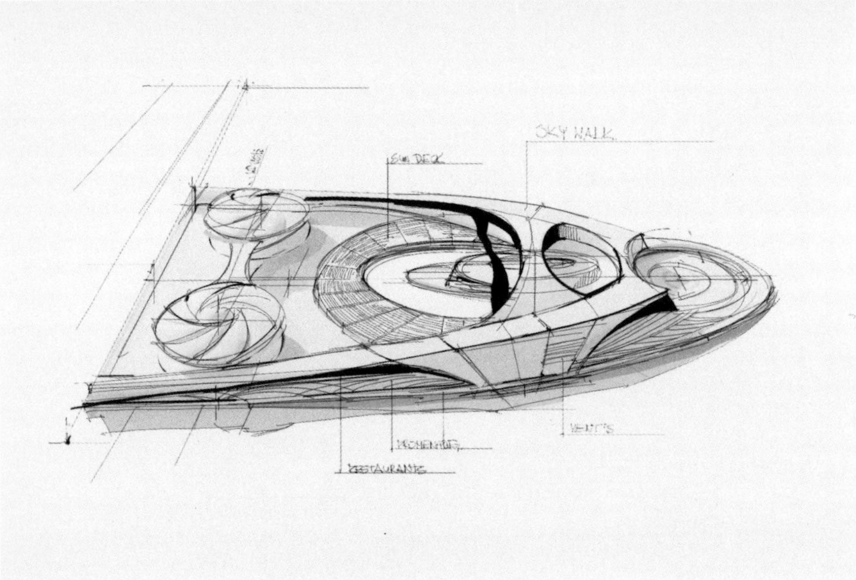
SKY WALK
SUN DECK
PROMENADE
RESTAURANTS
VENTS

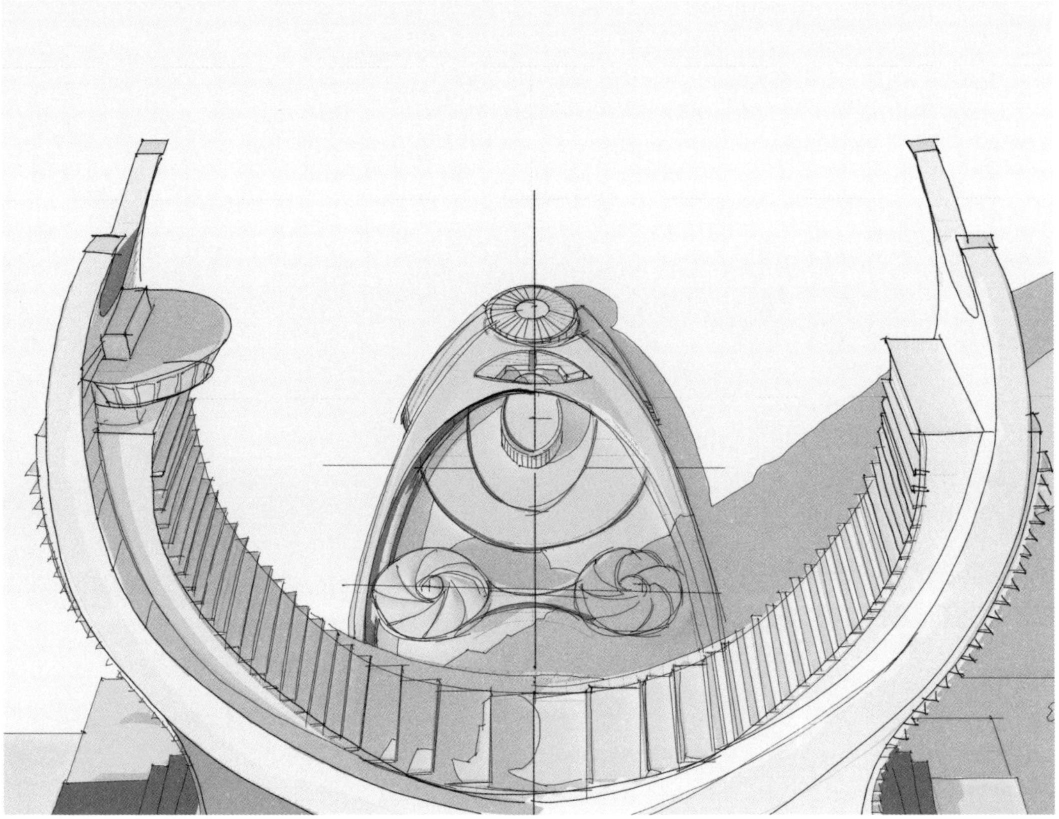

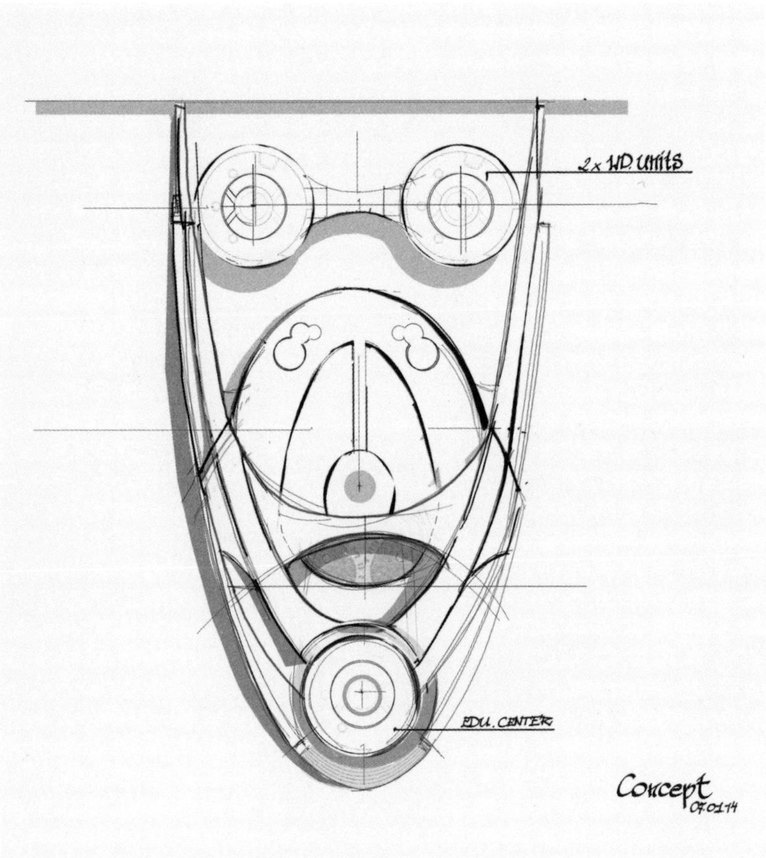
2x HD Units
EDU. CENTER
Concept
07.01.14

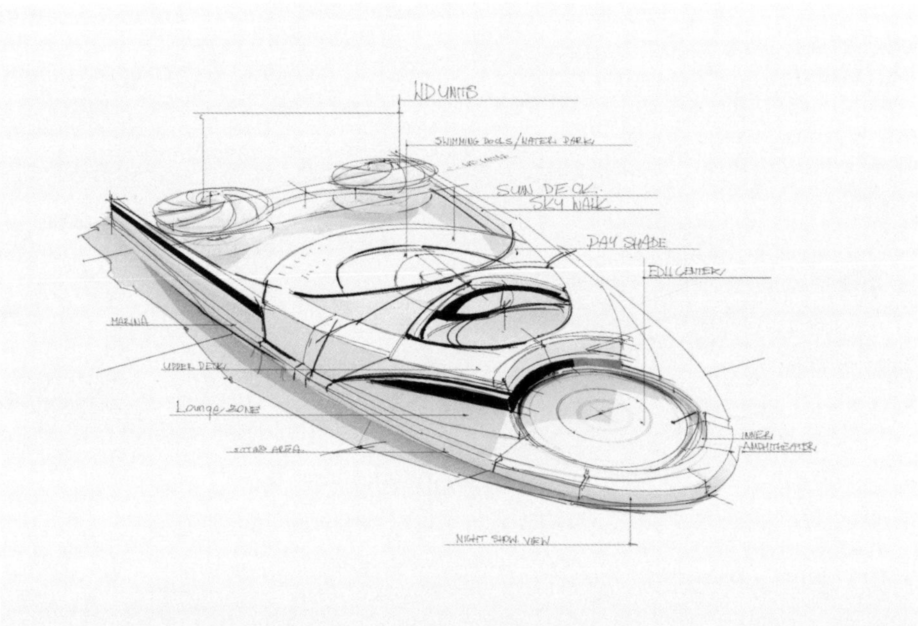
HD UNITS
SWIMMING POOLS/WATER PARK
SUN DECK.
SKY WALK.
DAY SHADE
EDU CENTER
MARINA
UPPER DECK
Lounge ZONE
SITTING AREA.
INNER AMPHITHEATER
NIGHT SHOW VIEW

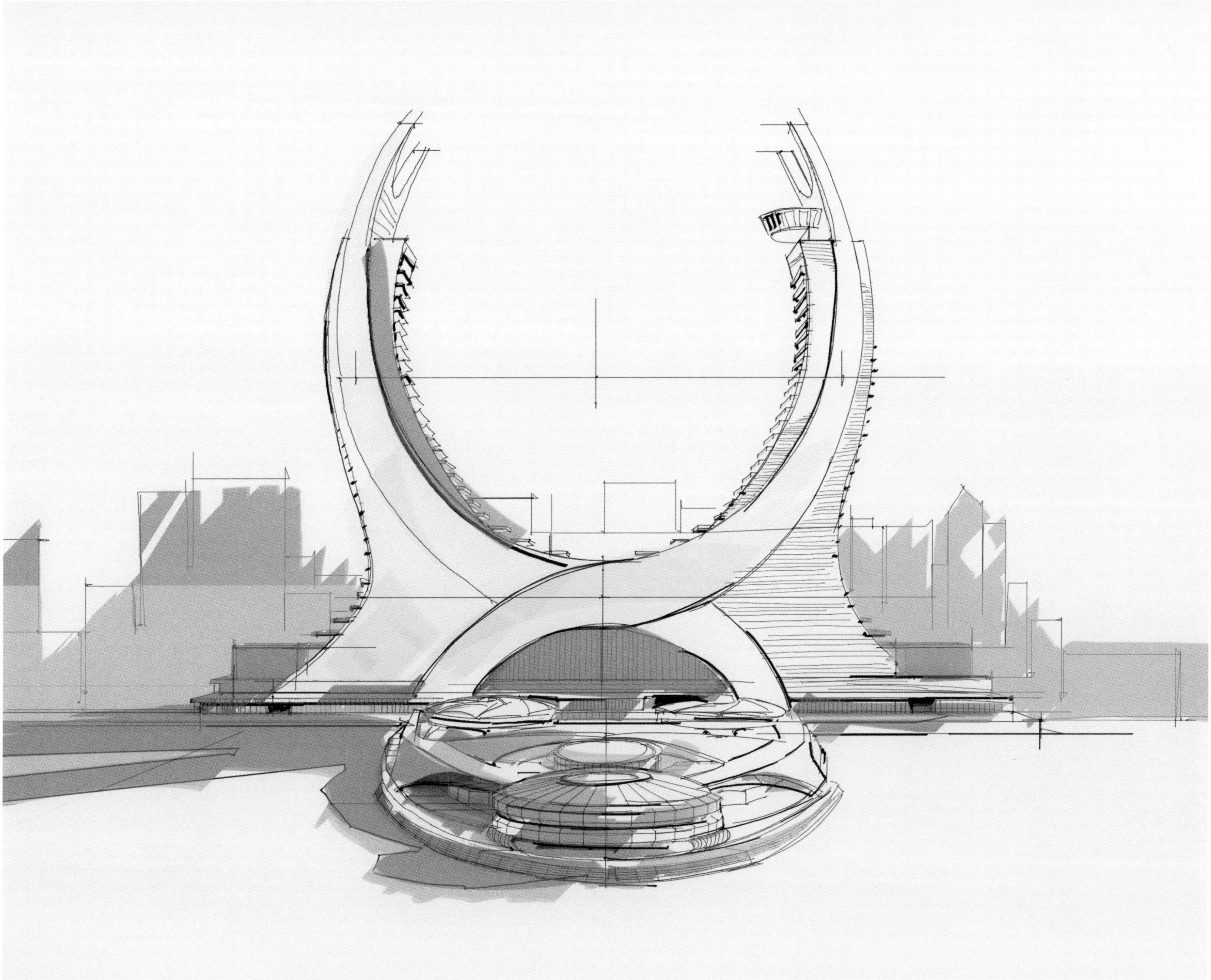

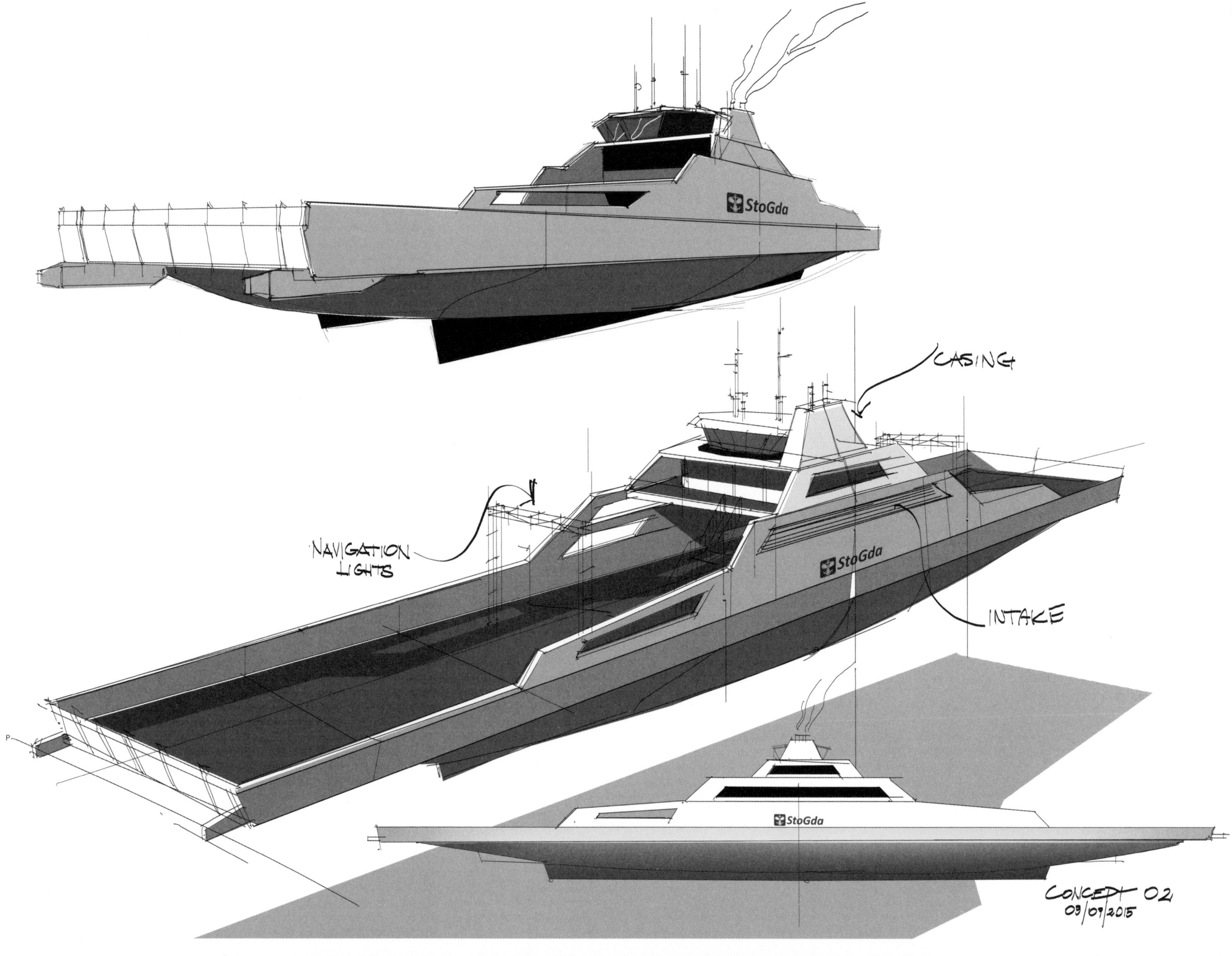
StoGda
CASING
NAVIGATION
LIGHTS
StoGda
INTAKE
StoGda
CONCEPT 02
03/09/2015

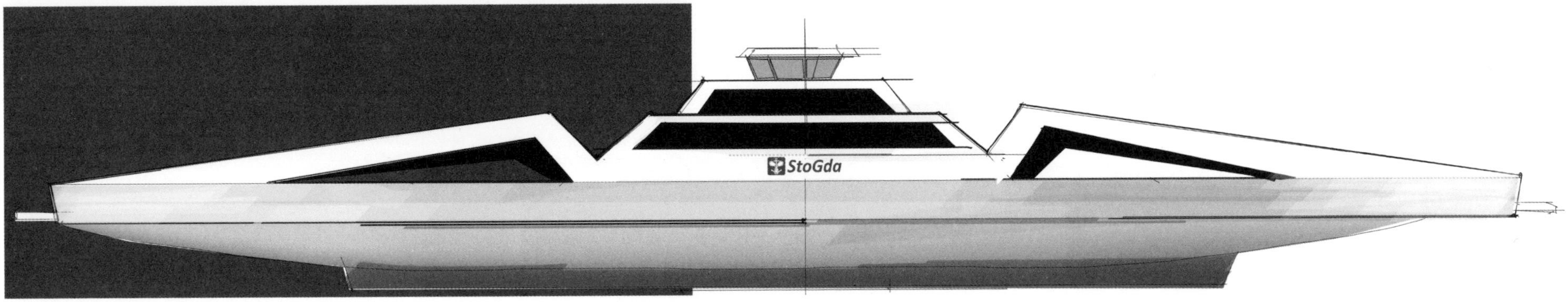
StoGda

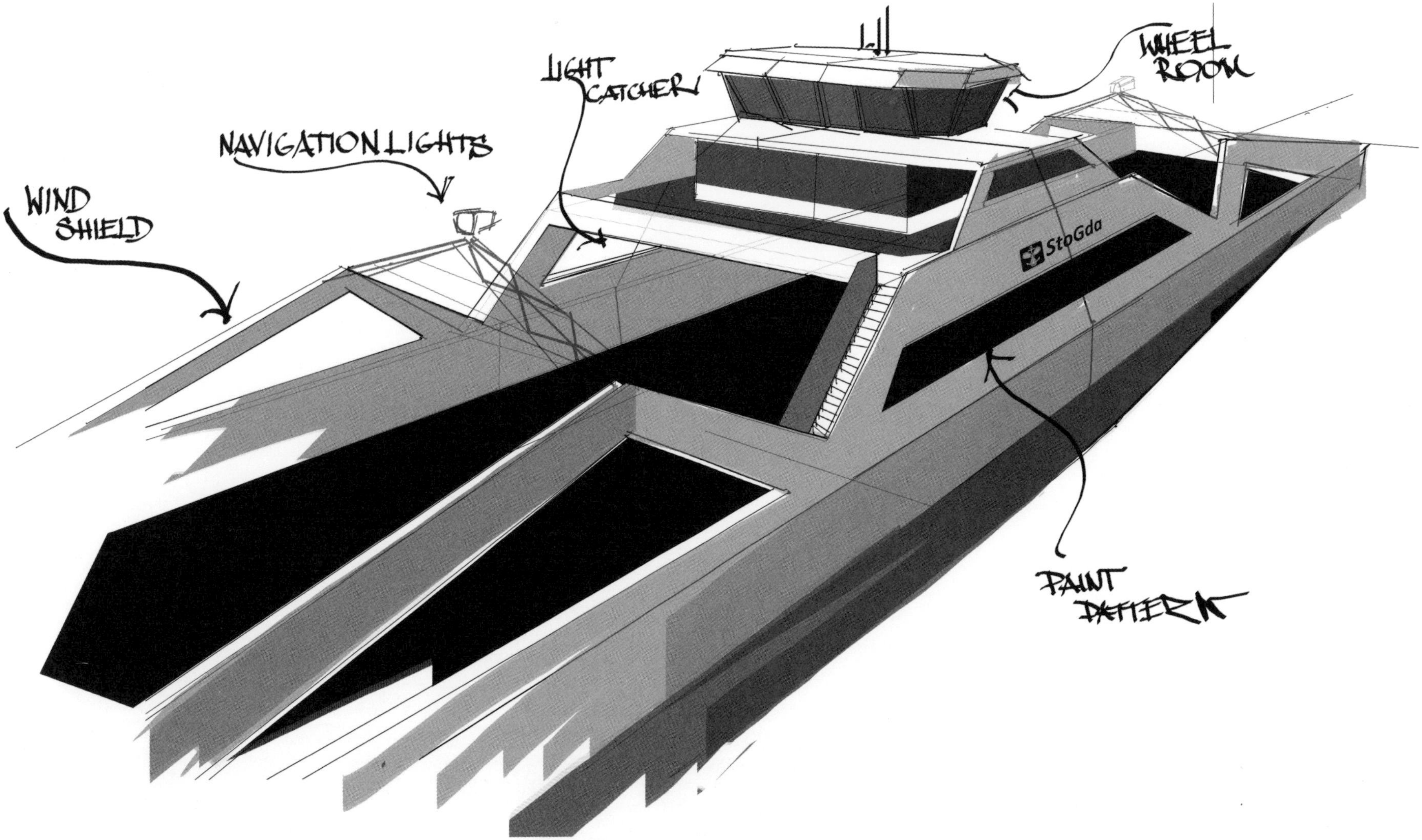
LIGHT CATCHER
WHEEL ROOM
NAVIGATION LIGHTS
WIND SHIELD
StoGda
PAINT PATTERN

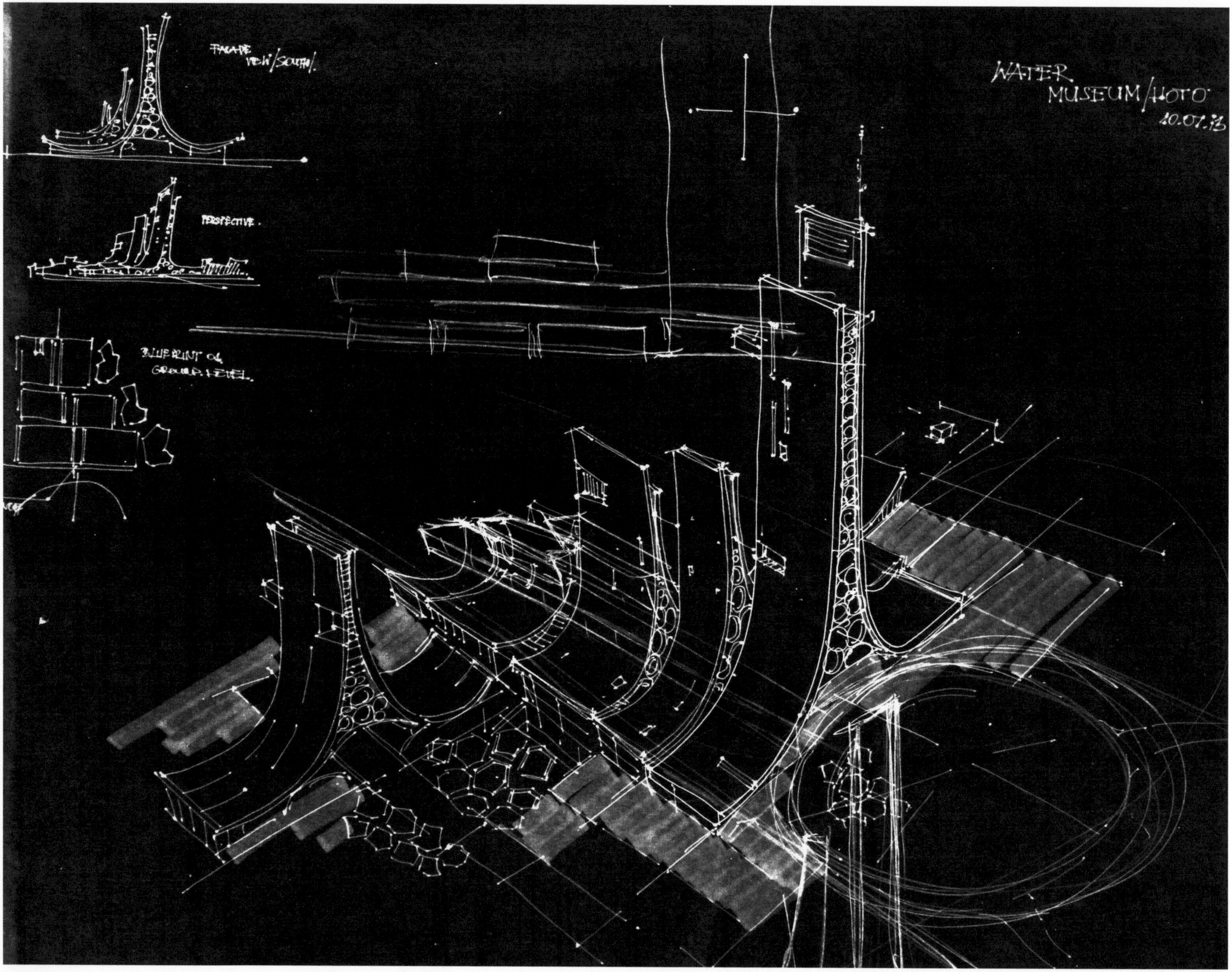
FAÇADE VIEW/SOUTH/.
PERSPECTIVE.
BLUEPRINT OF GROUND LEVEL.
WATER MUSEUM/HOTO
10.07.13

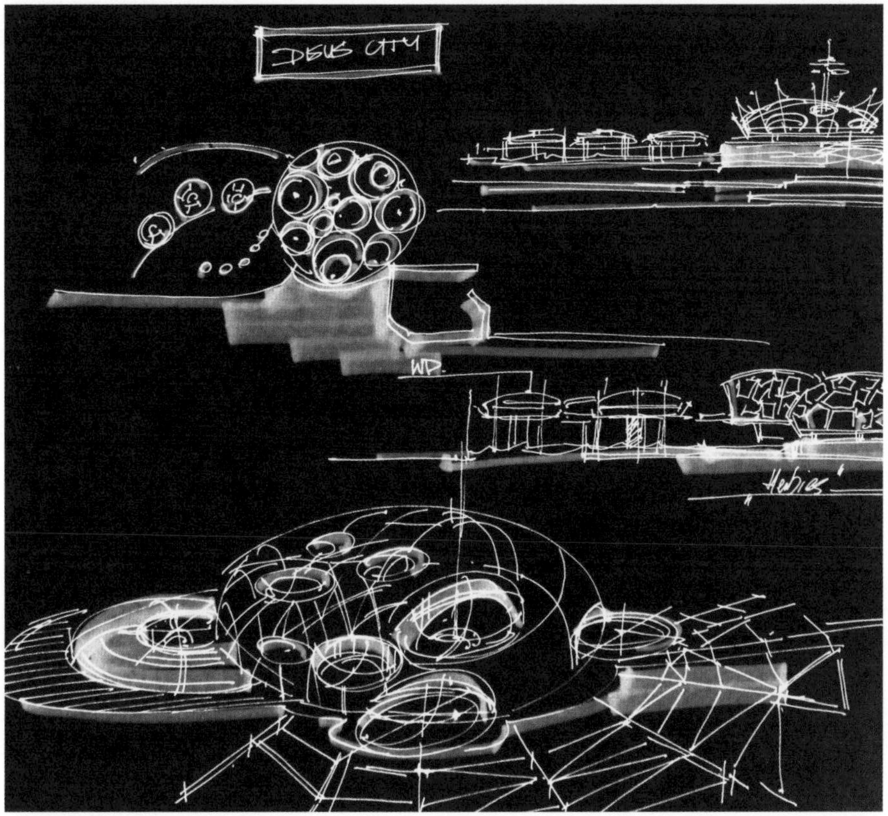

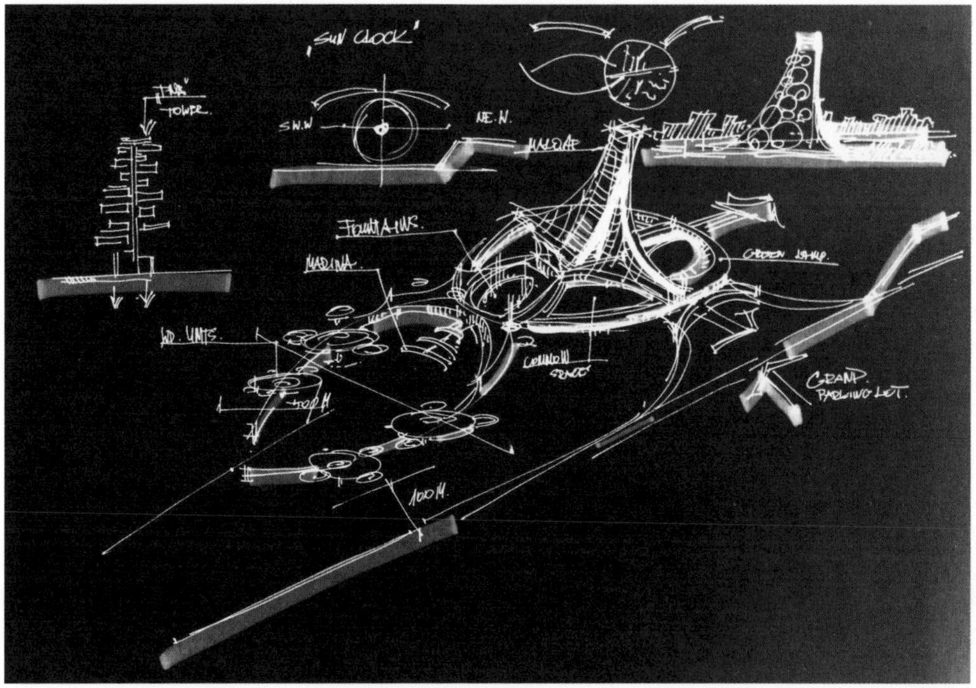
"SUN CLOCK"
TOWER
MARINA
GREEN LAKE
GRAND PARKING LOT.
100 M.

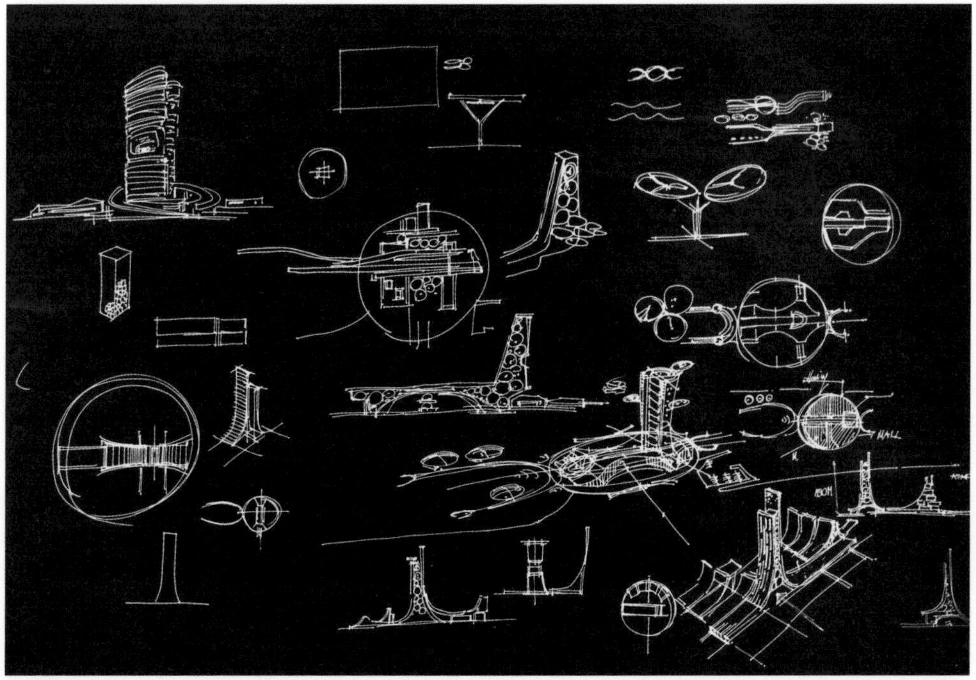

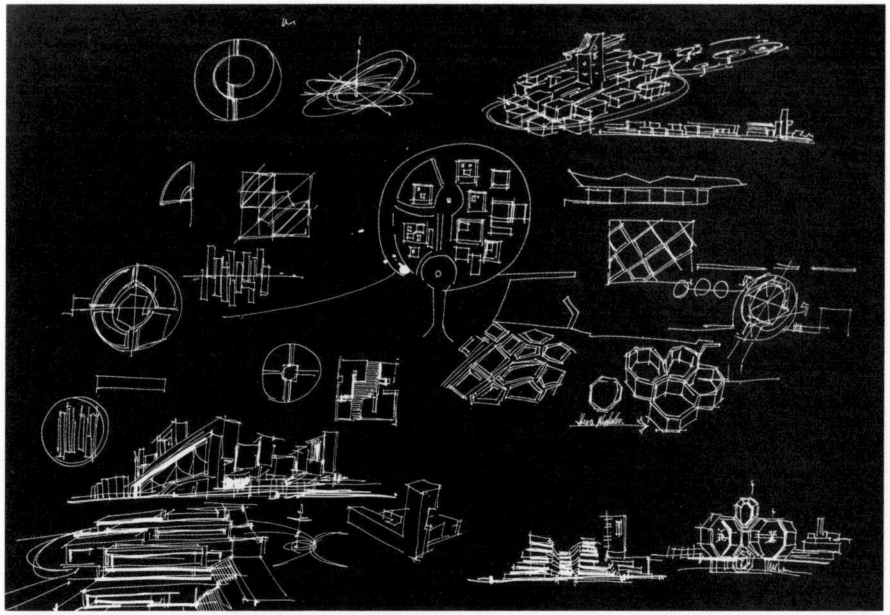

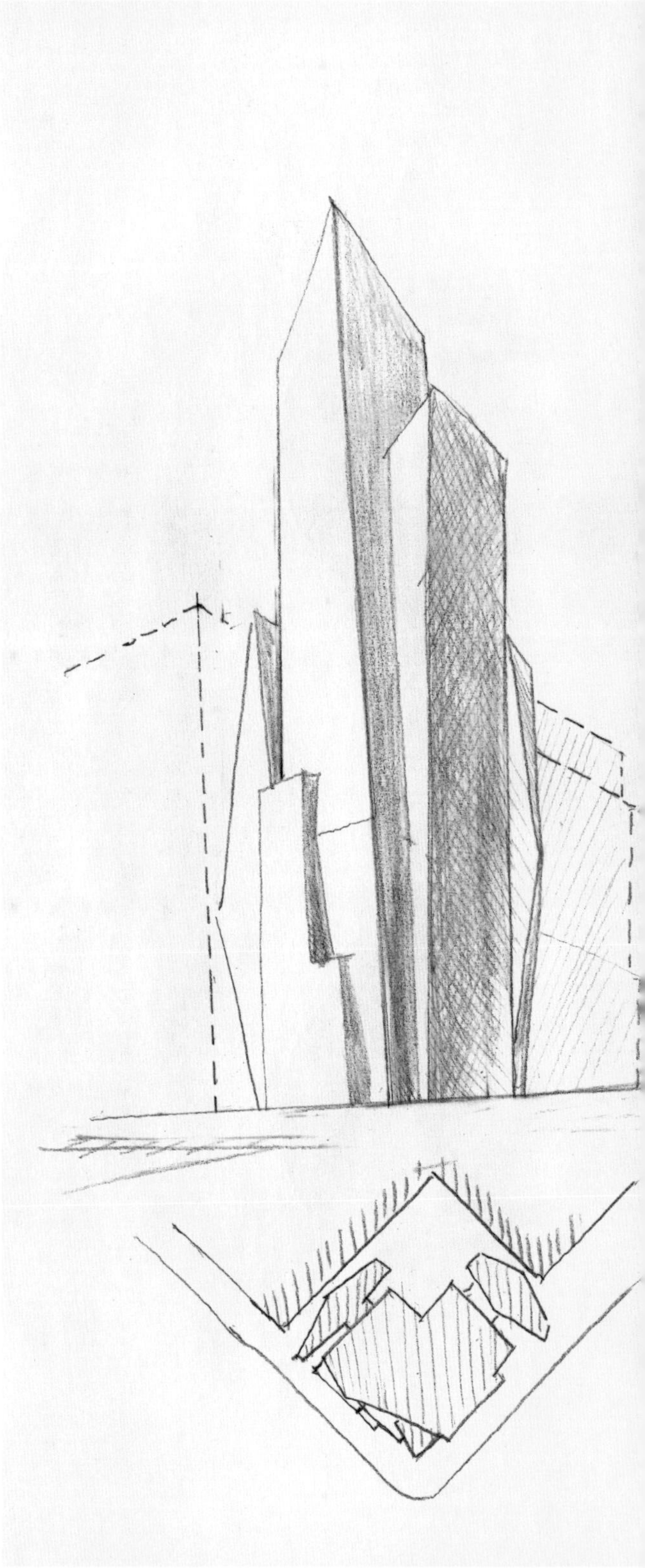

CHRISTIAN DE PORTZAMPARC

2Portzamparc • France

Featured projects: T1 Tower [p. 262, left] · LVMH Tower [p. 262, right]
Prism Tower [pp. 262–63] · New York City Opera [p. 263, right]
House of Dior Seoul [p. 264, left] · Tongzhou · [pp. 264–65]
Cidade Das Artes [p. 265, top right] · Musée Hergé [p. 265, bottom right]

'Architecture and town planning are concerned with space,' says Christian de Portzamparc of Parisian firm 2Portzamparc. 'It is impossible to imagine and render space without representing it, so we need figures and drawings, techniques that allow us to pass from three dimensions to something transmissible in two dimensions.'

De Portzamparc is one of Europe's best-known and decorated architects. In 1994, at the age of 50, he became the first French architect to receive the prestigious Pritzker Prize. He has been made Commandeur des Arts et des Lettres, Officier de l'Ordre du Mérite and Chevalier de l'Ordre de la Légion d'Honneur, and has been appointed an Honorary Fellow of the American Institute of Architects.

'Sketches and more elaborate drawings are created in tandem, and translated early on into numerical modelling and physical models to prevent errors in dimensions, scale, light and colours,' he says. 'I find that a model can act like a sketch. We strive to make the design readable to our clients: sometimes we show them the first sketches, sometimes we don't need to. You learn quickly to be wary of the pretty drawing for the sake of it.'

He continues: 'A sketch is a way of verifying the idea in one's mind. It can also be a process that makes thought happen. The drawing creates thought, while also making it possible to check the validity of an idea. One is constantly in the "architectural essay" with the drawing.'

SANJAY PURI

Sanjay Puri Architects • India

Featured projects: The Bridge [p. 266, top] · Destination [p. 266, bottom]
Stellar [p. 267, top] · The Street [p. 267, bottom, left]
Hill House [p. 267, bottom right]

'Sketching is the most important tool for design,' insists architect Sanjay Puri. 'Using software to generate an idea seems mechanical and takes longer when compared to a sketch, which is an extension of your thoughts in graphic form.' He believes that sketches are the most fluid transportation of ideas to paper: 'In just a few minutes one can sketch, revise and work out a design in all planes with views.'

As head of one of India's most successful firms, Puri has built an office that is 72 strong, and has worked in the US and Europe, as well as Asia. The practice has won over 100 international awards, from organizations including the World Architecture Festival and the Chicago Athenaeum Museum of Architecture and Design.

'I begin with rough sketches, sometimes overlaying them with different colours,' he says. 'It starts with a very rough idea, which is transformed into a final design sketch, or series of sketches. It is a very fast process. I sketch plans and sections and lay them out, so that all of the options are visible when creating the final set of drawings. This needs space, which a large table provides – as opposed to a computer screen, when you have to close one drawing before looking at another. The sketching process is also more inclusive, and is the fastest and clearest way for me to design.'

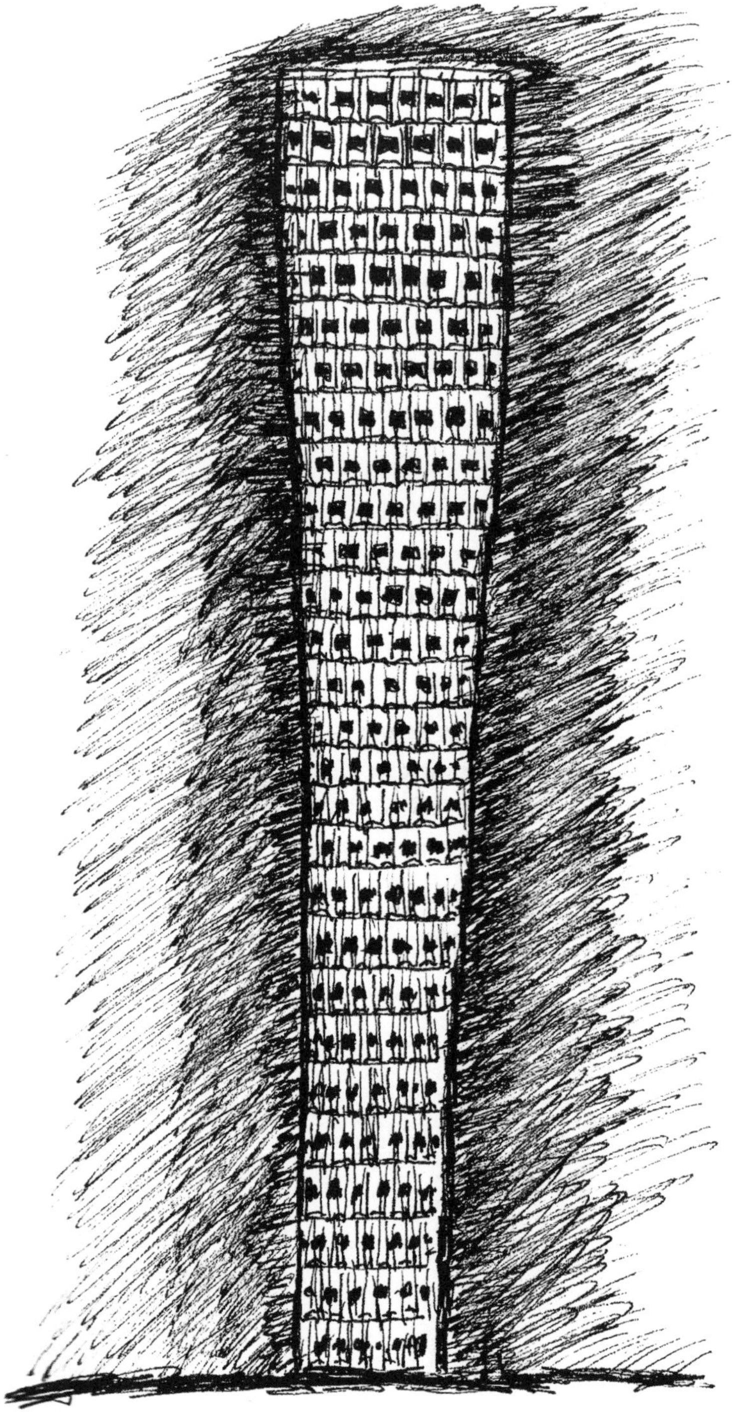

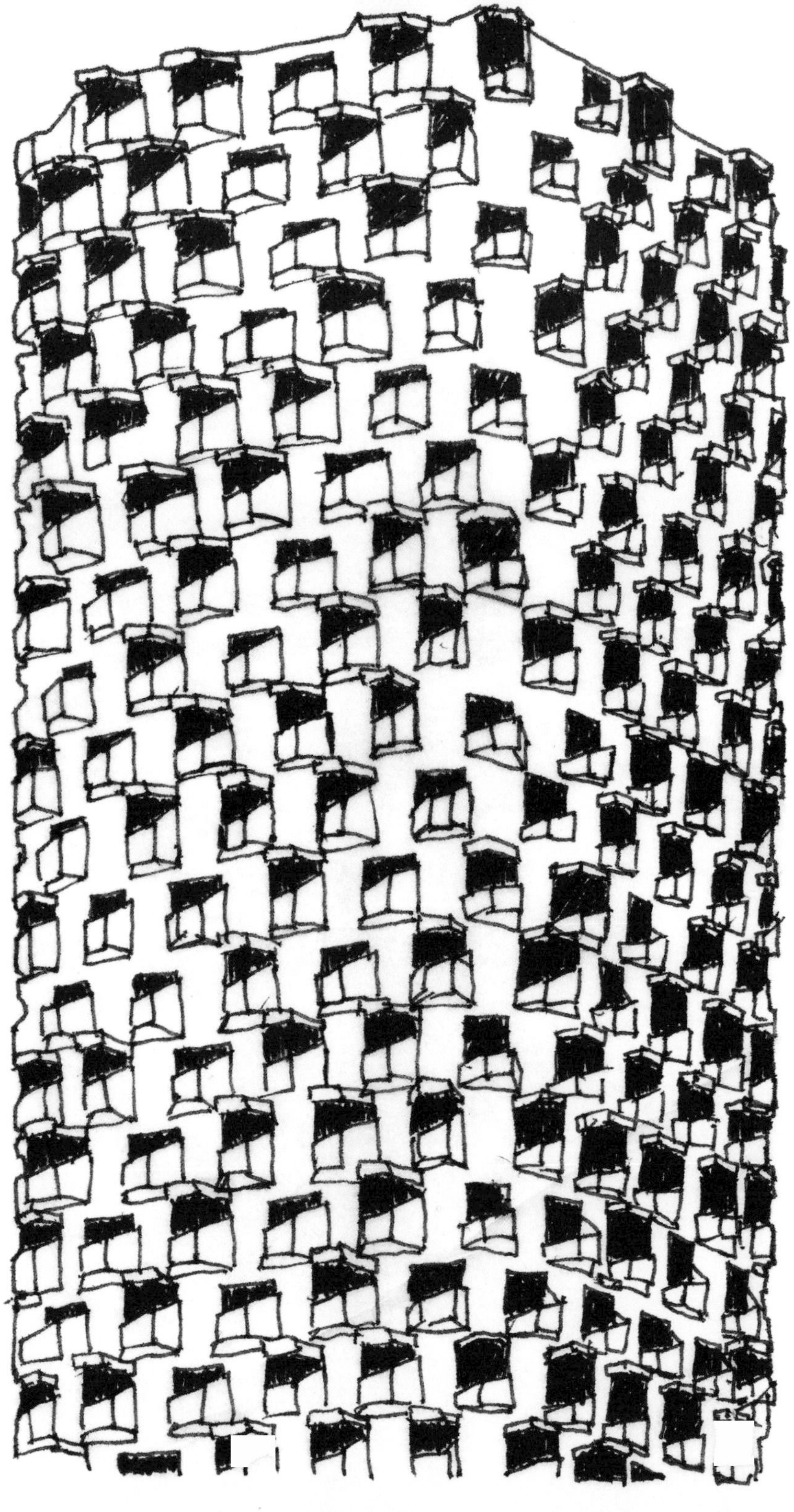

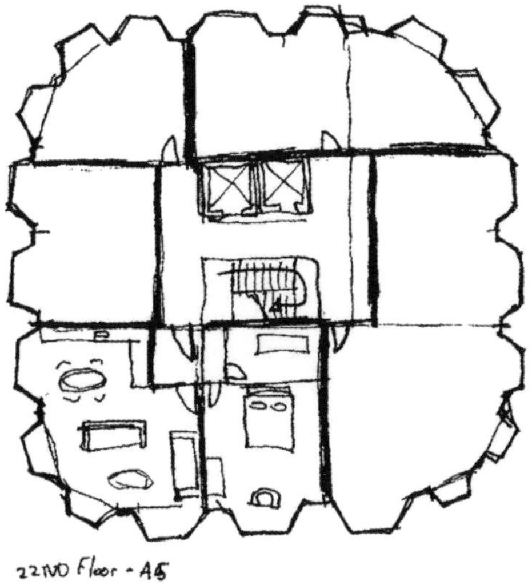

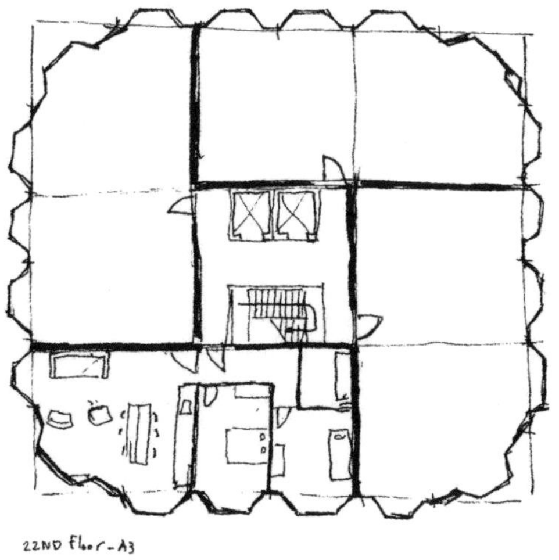

MATTHIJS LA ROI

Matthijs la Roi Architects • UK

Featured project: Conradstraat Tower [pp. 268–71]

'I foresee a future in which the differences between analogue and digital will blur with the improvement of augmented reality,' says Dutch-born, UK-based architect Matthijs la Roi. 'There are already software packages that allow you to draw in 3D with the use of VR, a process that is intuitively closer to drawing by hand than with a mouse. As long as your brain and body are using the same creative processes to explore design ideas, the distinction between analogue and digital becomes less important.'

Still in his thirties, la Roi is a forerunner of the next generation of architects, those for whom digital techniques are as conventional as physical ones. From his office in London, he fuses the latest technologies and ideas with the traditional to design award-winning architecture, including the Museum of Hospitality in the Netherlands, which opens in 2019.

'I use sketches to find solutions for specific, localized design problems,' he says. 'It often takes a couple of iterations to arrive at a final solution, switching back and forth between a computer and sketching. Sketching helps us discuss ideas, but our studio is also interested in the time dimension of our work. We use simulations and generative algorithms, which are digital and time-based. As a medium, drawing deals mainly with a frozen state of a design. From that perspective, some of our design methods cannot be replaced by purely analogue ones. Sketching is used mainly as a direct, face-to-face communication tool.'

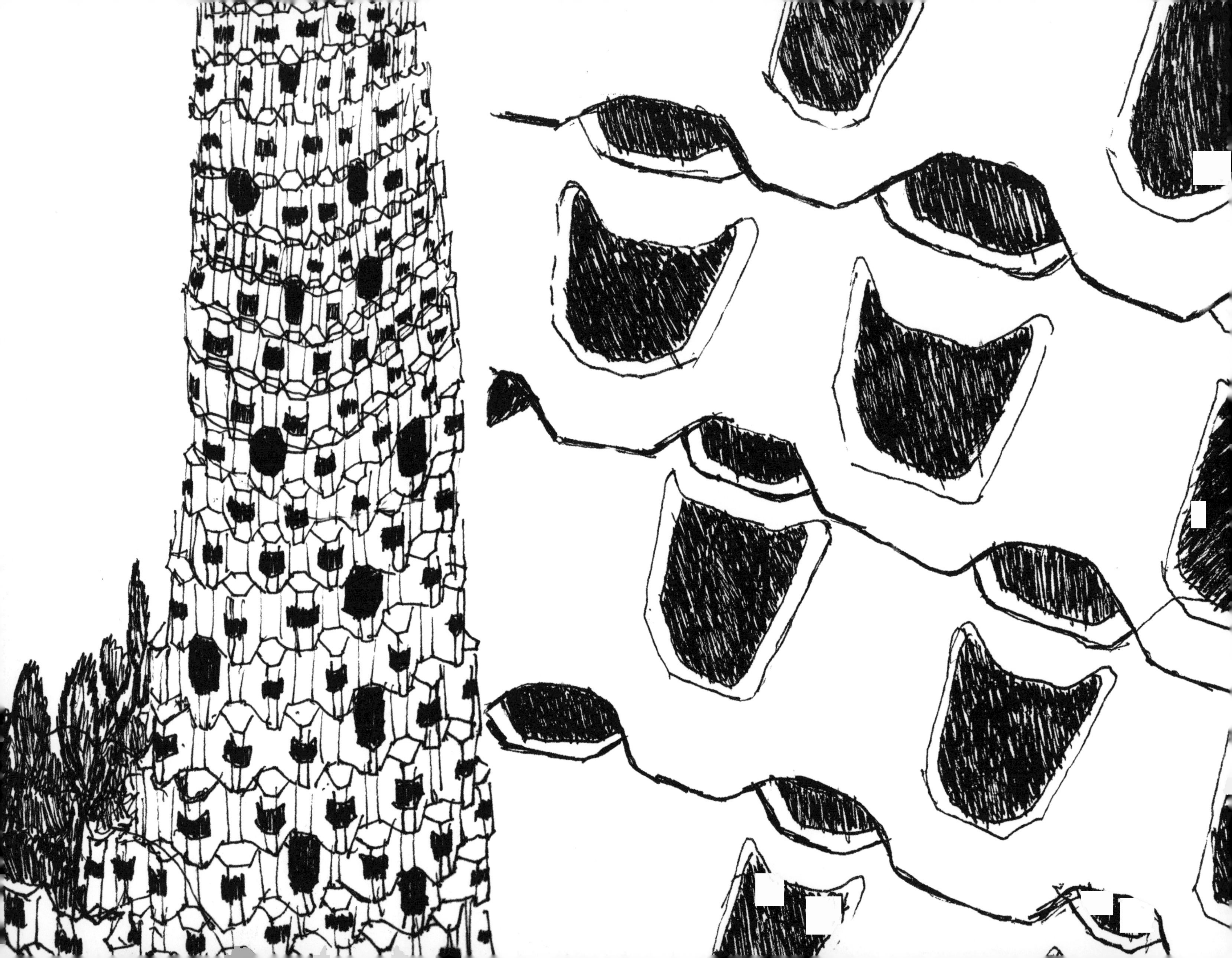

MOSHE SAFDIE

Safdie Architects • USA

Featured projects: National Gallery of Canada [pp. 272–5]
Khalsa Heritage Centre [pp. 276–7] · Holocaust History Museum [pp. 278–9]

'For me, sketching is the basic tool for evolving design concepts and, in later phases of the work, developing details and examining particular issues in the overall scheme,' says Moshe Safdie of Boston-based Safdie Architects. 'I have two modes of sketching. The first is large-format, working on trace, sometimes over base drawings or site plans, using charcoal and CarbOthello pastel pencils, which are smudgeable and soluble. Charcoal can be rubbed away, is malleable and lends itself to the evolution of an idea, while colours enhance elements within the design and its organization. I am indebted to Louis I. Kahn, with whom I apprenticed, for this technique.'

He continues: 'The second method is working with pen, ink and my sketchbook, all of which are always with me. I can sink into them at work, on aeroplanes, in cars, even in waiting rooms. I've worked in sketchbooks for the past 50 years. Since I am constantly working on three or four projects at the same time, they are a mélange of project studies at different phases.'

Ink drawings are most effective, Safdie says, when it comes to 'thinking through building sections, construction details and 3D spaces'. He adds: 'I tend to annotate drawings, photographing and sending them to the office for further digital development. In recent years, the design process has been enriched by the cross-fertilization of my own hand-sketches with 3D computer studies produced in the office, which are then developed into models at various scales. I cannot conceive of the design process without this triangulation. I depend on my sketches for thinking through ideas, on the 3D studies for evolving those sketches into tangible geometries, and on the models for understanding the spatial implications of what we are doing.'

calm down space
get scale right
can be smaller!?

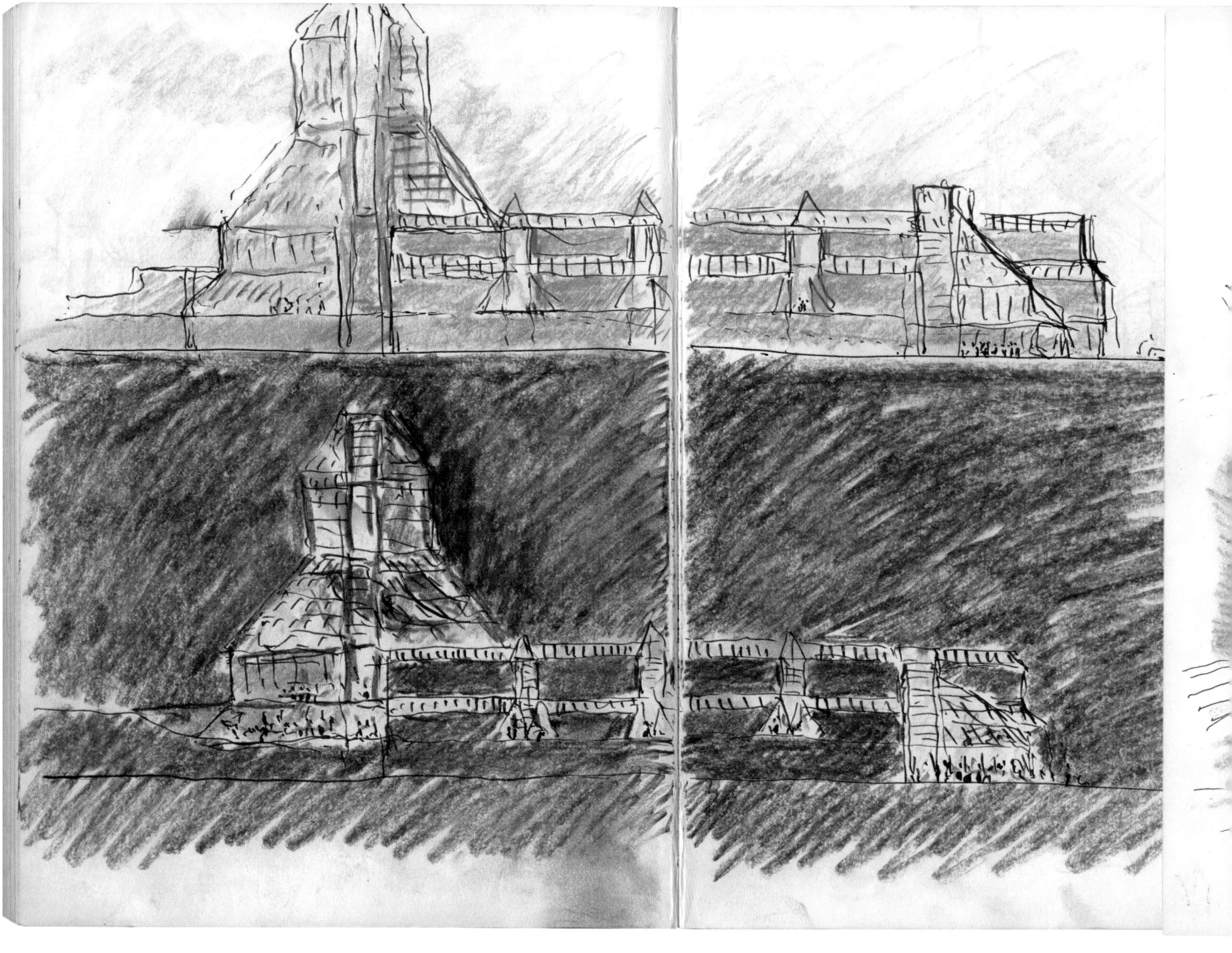

glass roof

Jassalmer
from the
magazine
get calmer!

get more
space in

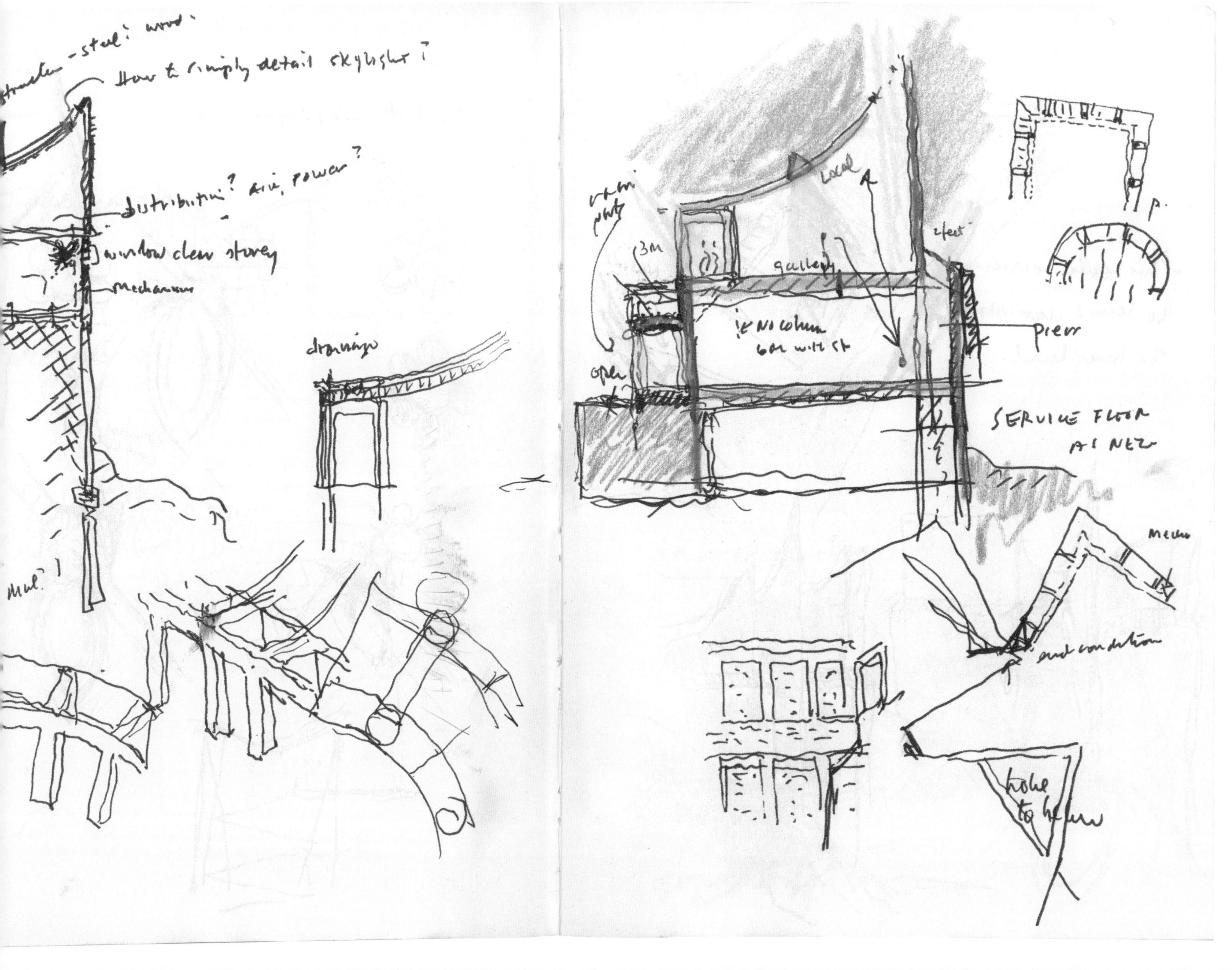
How to simply detail skylight ?
distribution ? air, power ?
window clear storey
drainage
gallery
pier
SERVICE FLOOR
end condition
hole to below

yad v

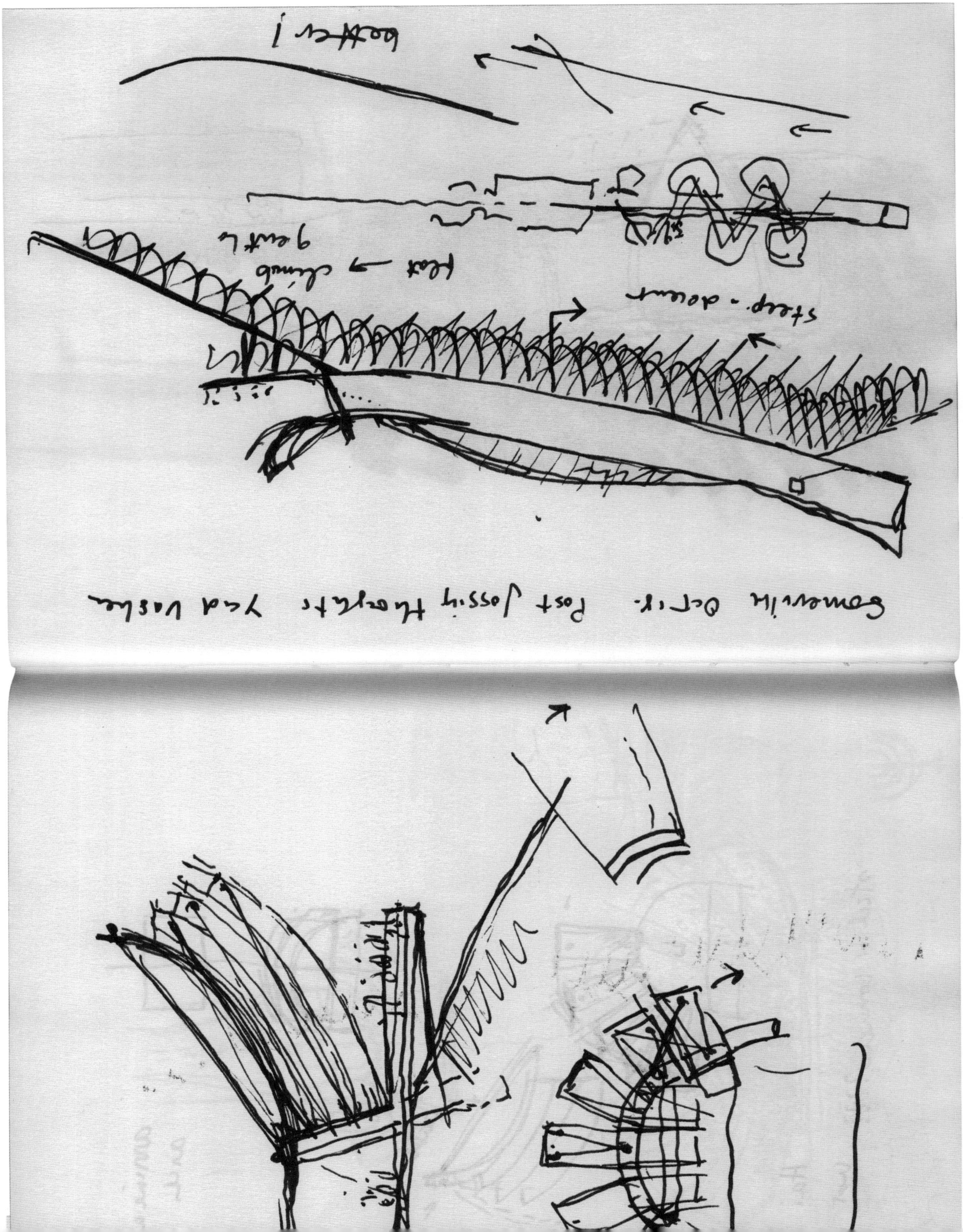
Somerville Oct 18. Post Jogging thoughts Yad Vashem
steep - down
flat → climb gentle
better!

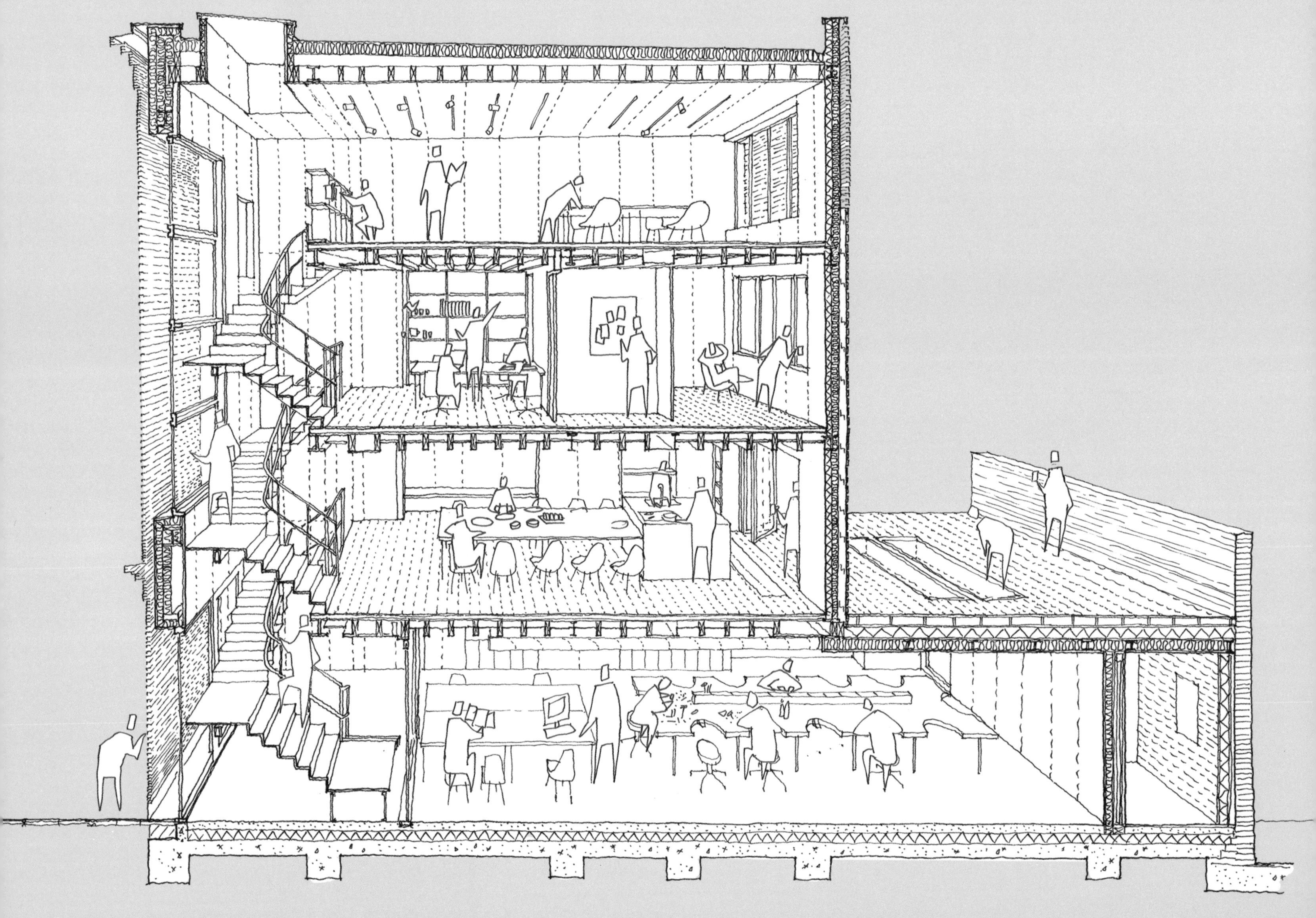

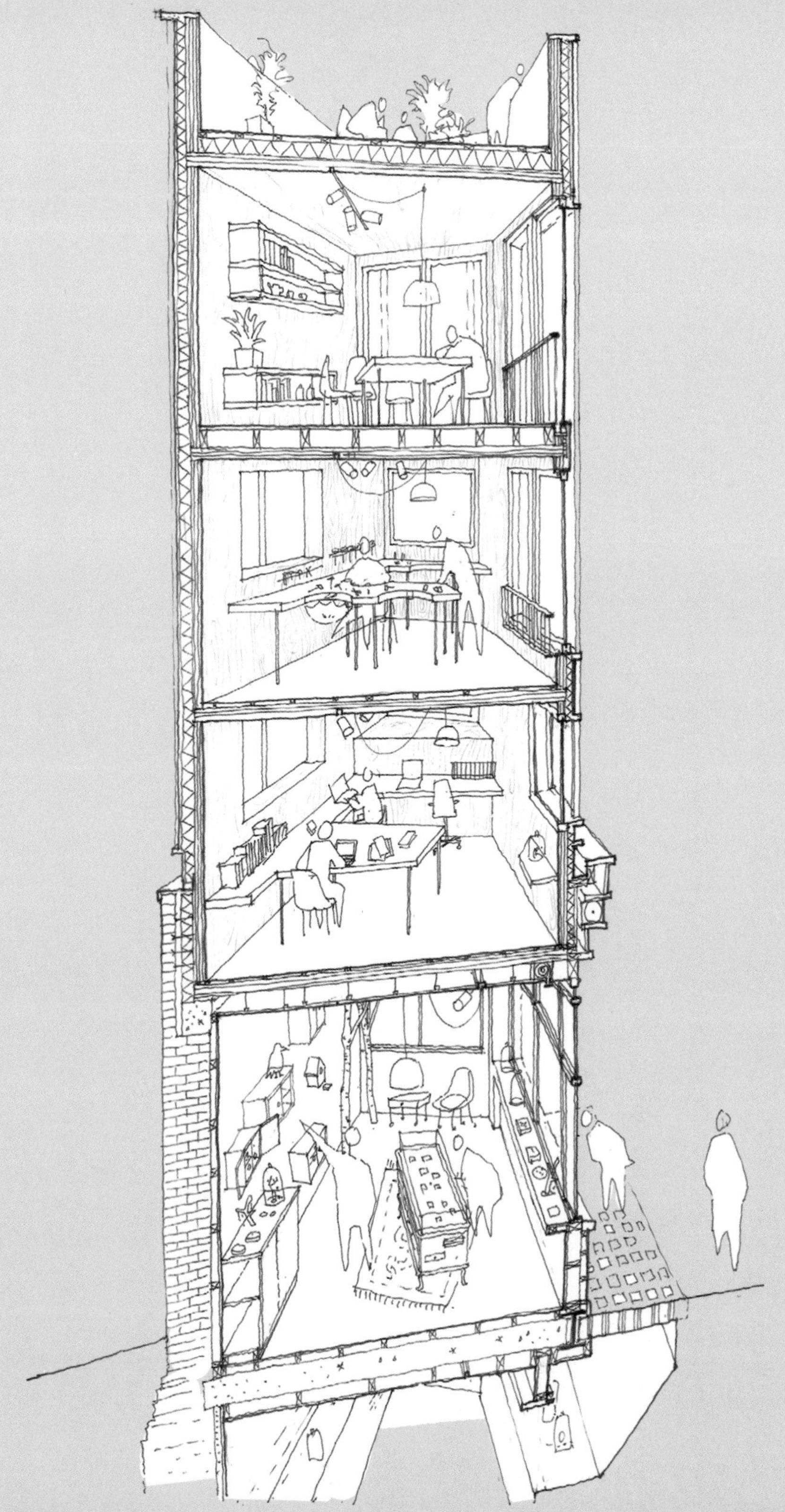

DEBORAH SAUNT

DSDHA • UK

Featured projects: Caxton Walk [p. 282]
Cambridge Circus [pp. 282–3]

'Sketching takes time, and in this space thoughts can develop and mature,' explains Deborah Saunt, co-founder of DSDHA. 'The duration of a sketch enables layers of unspoken histories, influences and hopes to coalesce as a proposition. Equally, an urgent sketch can liberate an embodied energy from within the project. We use sketching as a tool to develop ideas, rather than fixing them on paper, which is why we often sketch on photos, CGIs, and so on.'

Saunt formed the London-based practice with David Hills, and their work has been recognized with 17 awards from the Royal Institute of British Architects in the last decade, and twice-nominated for the EU Prize for Contemporary Architecture – Mies van der Rohe Award. The studio is heavily involved in education, with Saunt currently teaching at a number of universities.

'Sketching enables us to present ideas in a less definitive manner, to open them up for discussion with the studio, with clients, the public and stakeholders,' she says. 'It allows them to contribute and have their say in the final design. We are honest in our methods and tend not to move towards an architecture of the "finished object", so we use models and sketches for as long as possible in the design process. Our clients enjoy the open-ended nature of a sketch as a point of encounter or exchange, so they can be present in the process.'

Saunt concludes: 'Sometimes we redraw our sketches to see what a project reveals when it is completed and occupied. The dialogue between the original sketch and the end result is a curious one: it shows the collective nature of authoring architecture. As a designer, one leads the song, but the sound is unique as its own presence.'

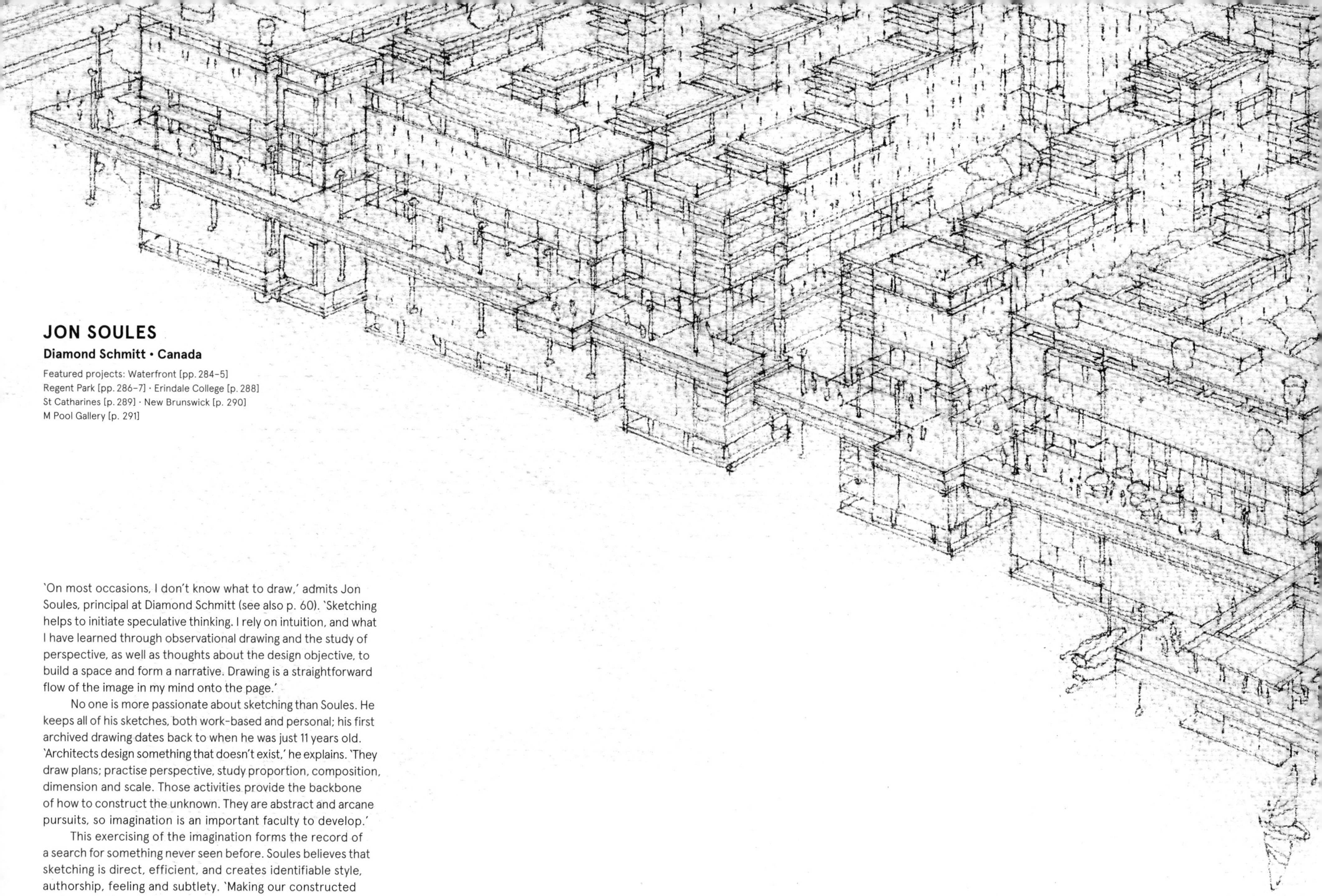

JON SOULES

Diamond Schmitt • Canada

Featured projects: Waterfront [pp. 284–5]
Regent Park [pp. 286–7] · Erindale College [p. 288]
St Catharines [p. 289] · New Brunswick [p. 290]
M Pool Gallery [p. 291]

'On most occasions, I don't know what to draw,' admits Jon Soules, principal at Diamond Schmitt (see also p. 60). 'Sketching helps to initiate speculative thinking. I rely on intuition, and what I have learned through observational drawing and the study of perspective, as well as thoughts about the design objective, to build a space and form a narrative. Drawing is a straightforward flow of the image in my mind onto the page.'

No one is more passionate about sketching than Soules. He keeps all of his sketches, both work-based and personal; his first archived drawing dates back to when he was just 11 years old. 'Architects design something that doesn't exist,' he explains. 'They draw plans; practise perspective, study proportion, composition, dimension and scale. Those activities provide the backbone of how to construct the unknown. They are abstract and arcane pursuits, so imagination is an important faculty to develop.'

This exercising of the imagination forms the record of a search for something never seen before. Soules believes that sketching is direct, efficient, and creates identifiable style, authorship, feeling and subtlety. 'Making our constructed environment is an important cultural process,' he says. 'Sketches and drawings express the ideas behind the genesis of our cultural realm. A mediocre design can leave an audience apathetic, but a great design can create excitement about the making of a new place and pride in the ultimate accomplishment.'

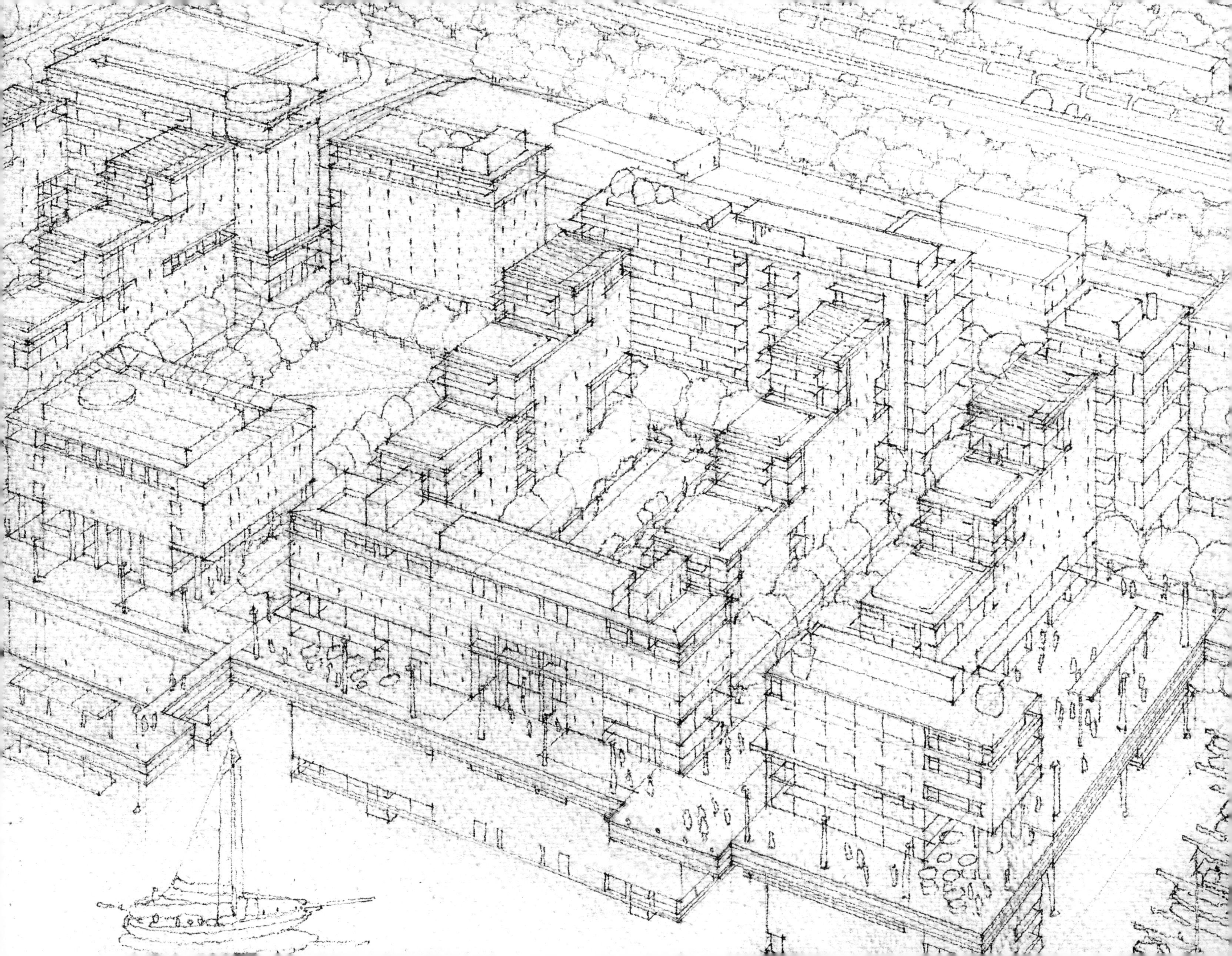

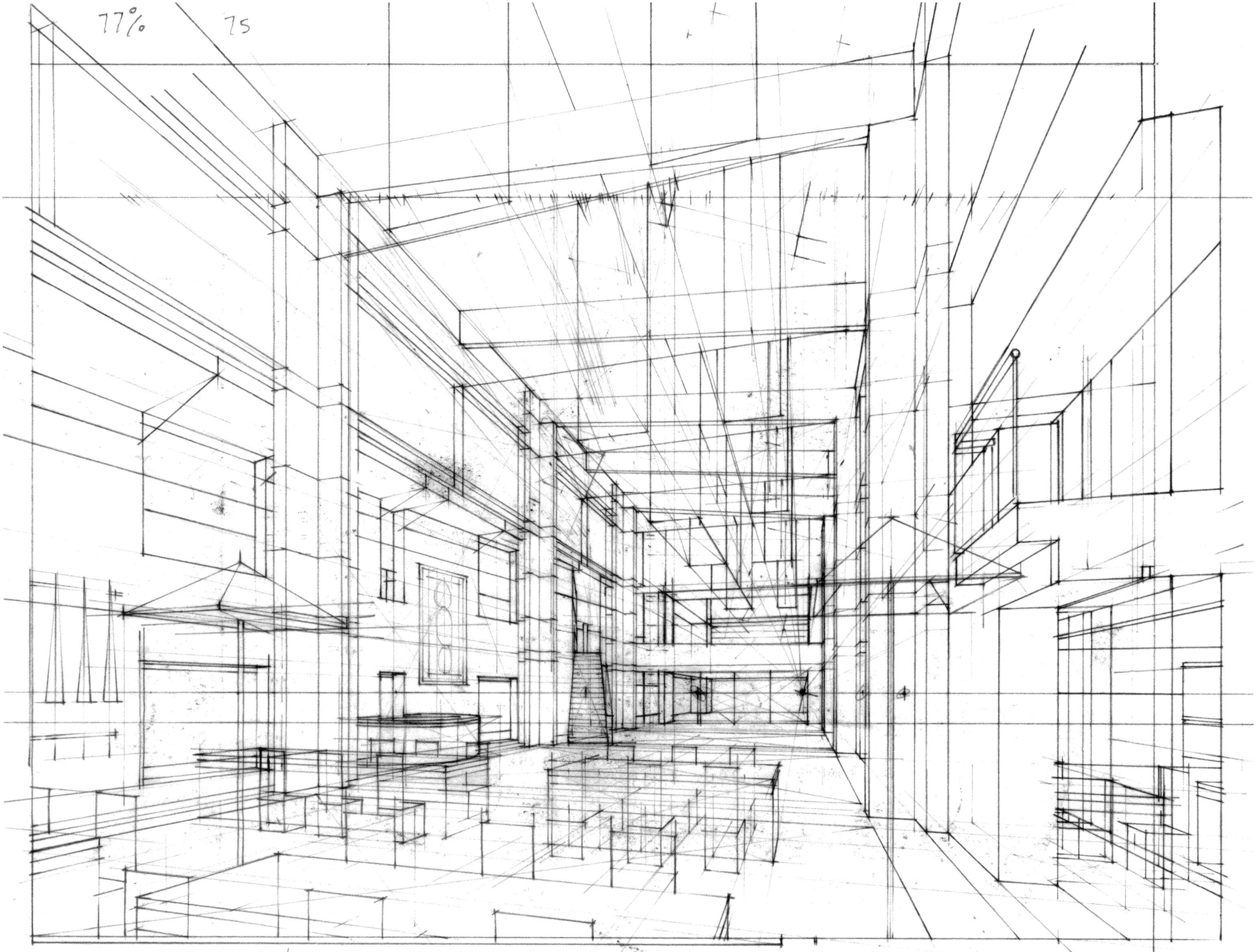

ERINDALE COLLEGE DECEMBER 1996

KENTARO TAKEGUCHI & ASAKO YAMAMOTO

Alphaville Architects • Japan

Featured projects: Catholic Suzuka Church [pp. 292–3]
Dig in the Sky [pp. 294–5] · House Folded [p. 296, left and top right]
House Twisted [p. 296, bottom right] · Koyasan Guest House [p. 297]
Skyhole [pp. 298–9]

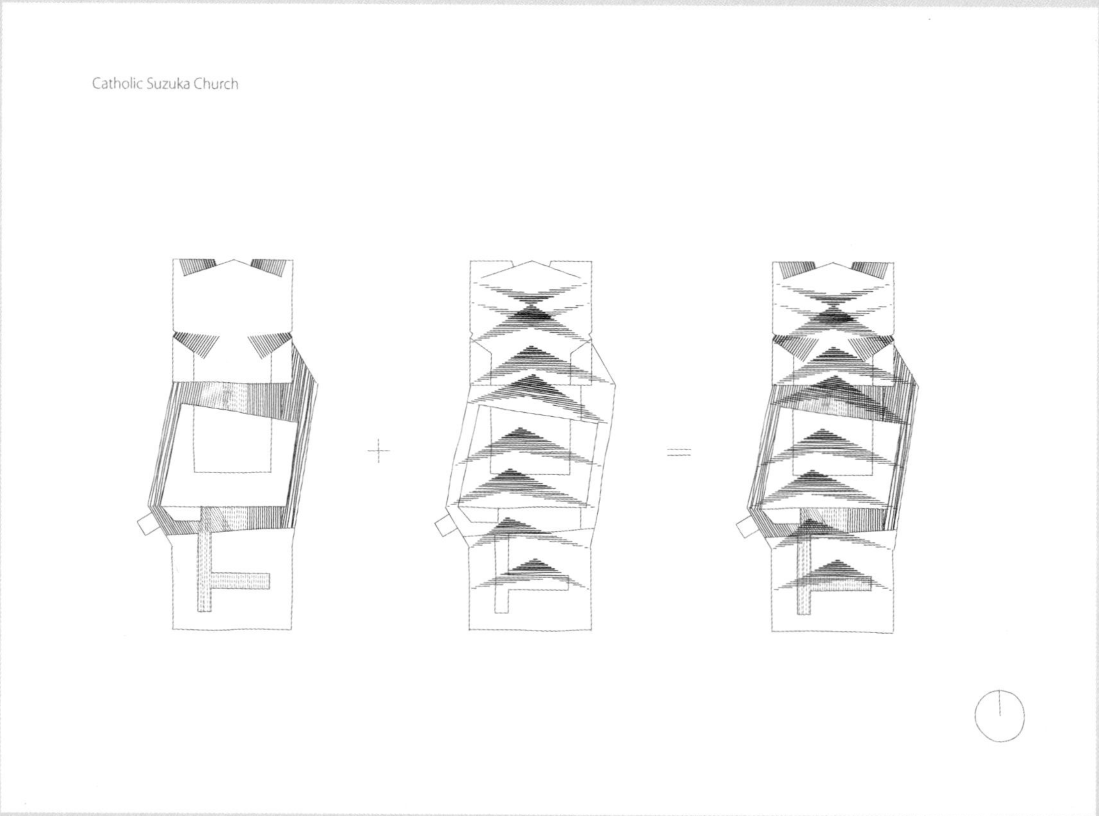

'We find that drawing in front of our clients is the quickest and easiest way of conveying our thoughts to them,' say Kentaro Takeguchi and Asako Yamamoto, founding partners of Alphaville Architects. 'We draw directly onto the basic CAD drawings, developing and expressing the digital concept. We believe there is no big difference between analogue and digital drawings, apart, perhaps, from some difference in resolution. But with technological developments, in future this will disappear.'

Since graduating from Kyoto University in 1994, the pair have been prolific designers, even while studying at the Architectural Association in London (Kentaro) and the National School of Architecture in Paris (Asako). They formed the company in 1998, and have gone on to build a host of exciting, challenging buildings, from private residences to churches.

'Sketching is a profound way to study architecture,' they note, 'because it is a way to be connected directly to the minds of architects, and therefore to the study of architects of the past. It is a means of considering the design, and the most important in making the idea concrete and expressing it to another person. We could design without sketching, but it would take more time and the critical resolution would be lost. We can respond to a theme most accurately with a clear and concrete sketch.'

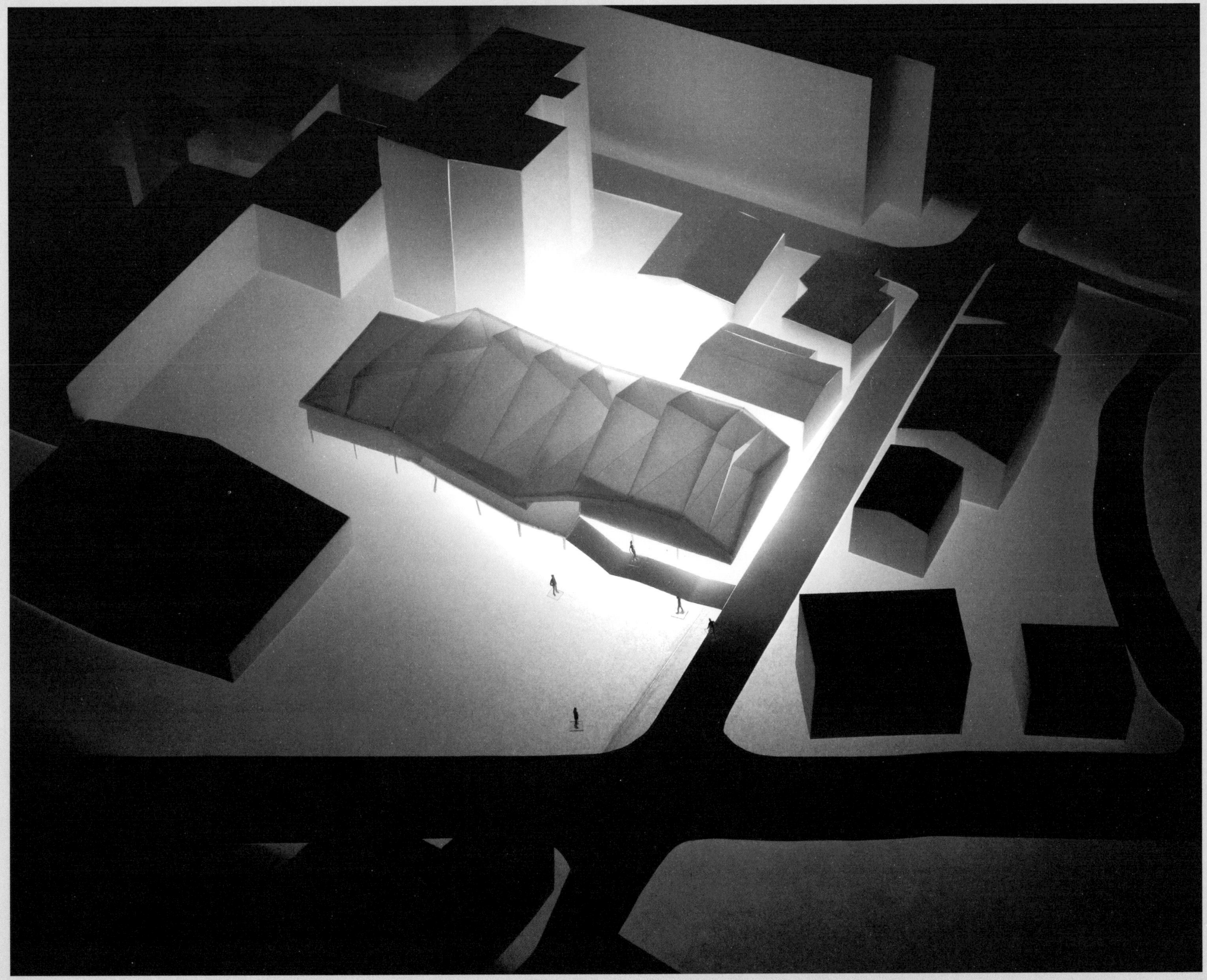

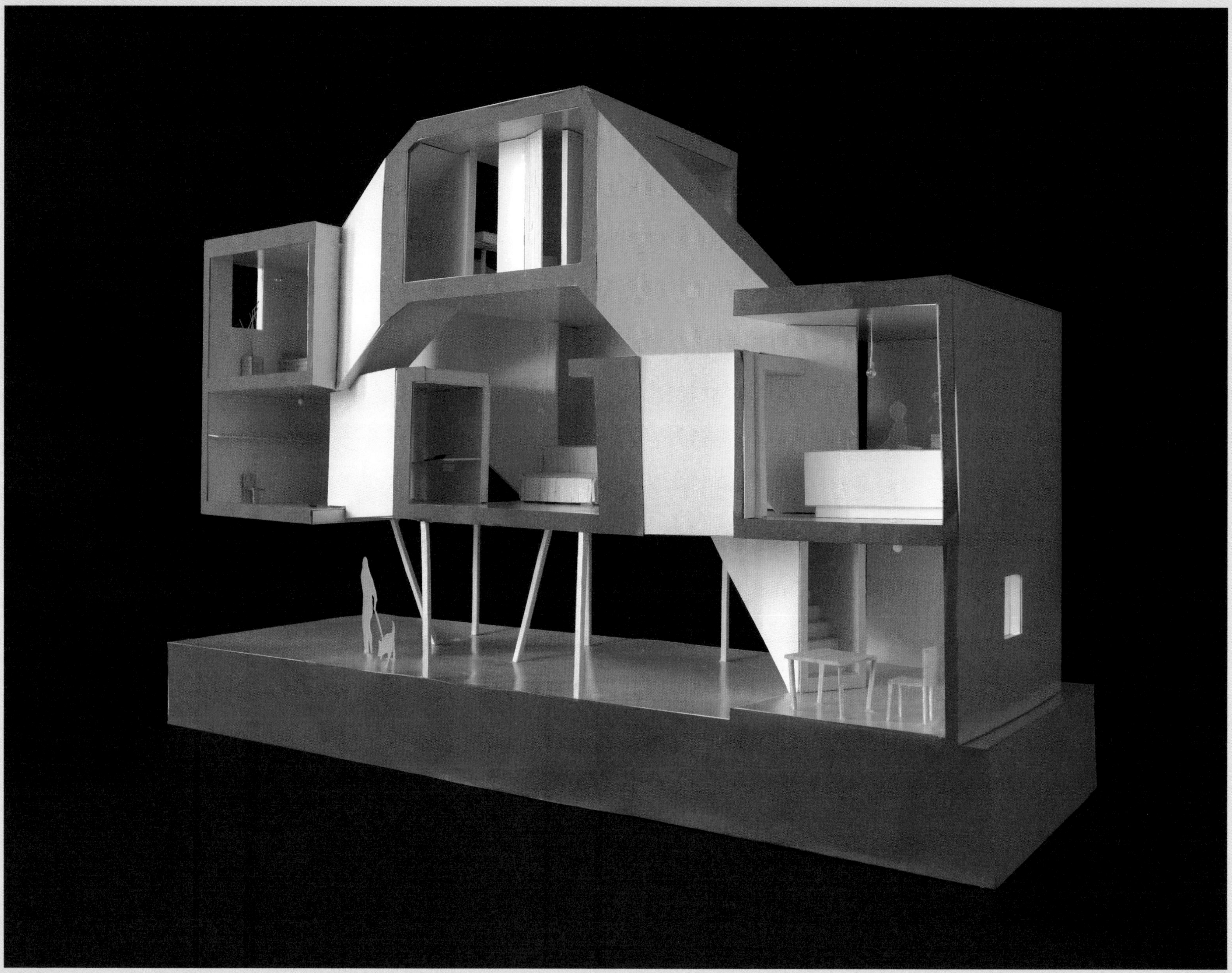

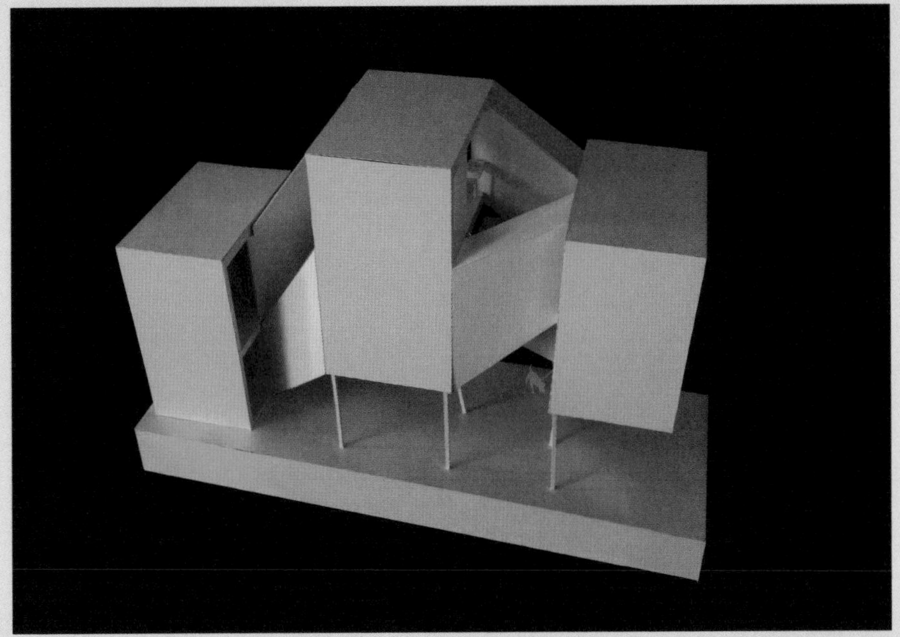

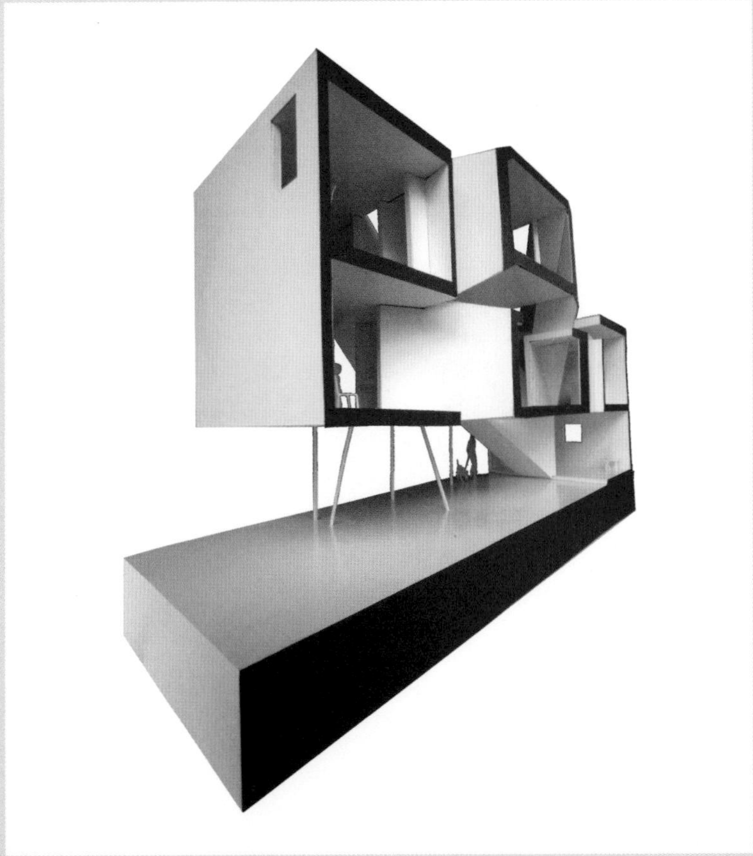

Dig In the Sky

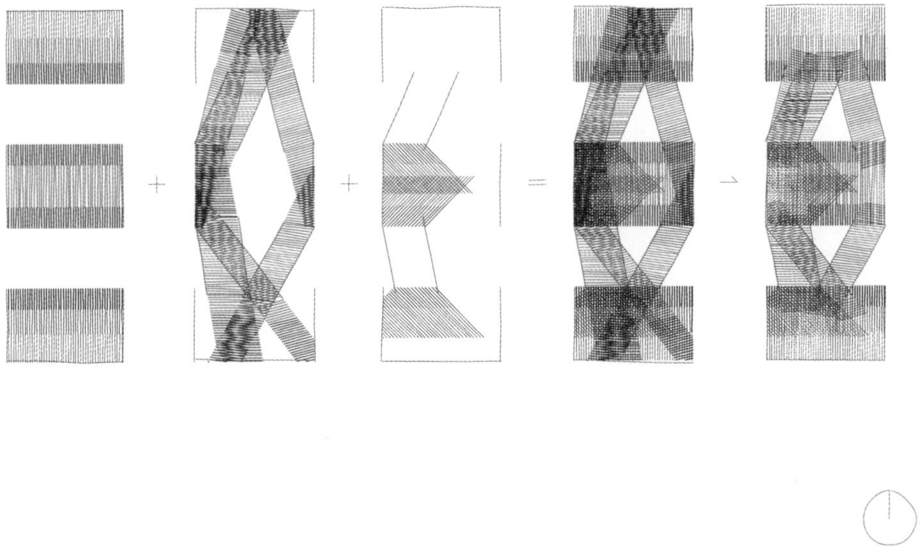

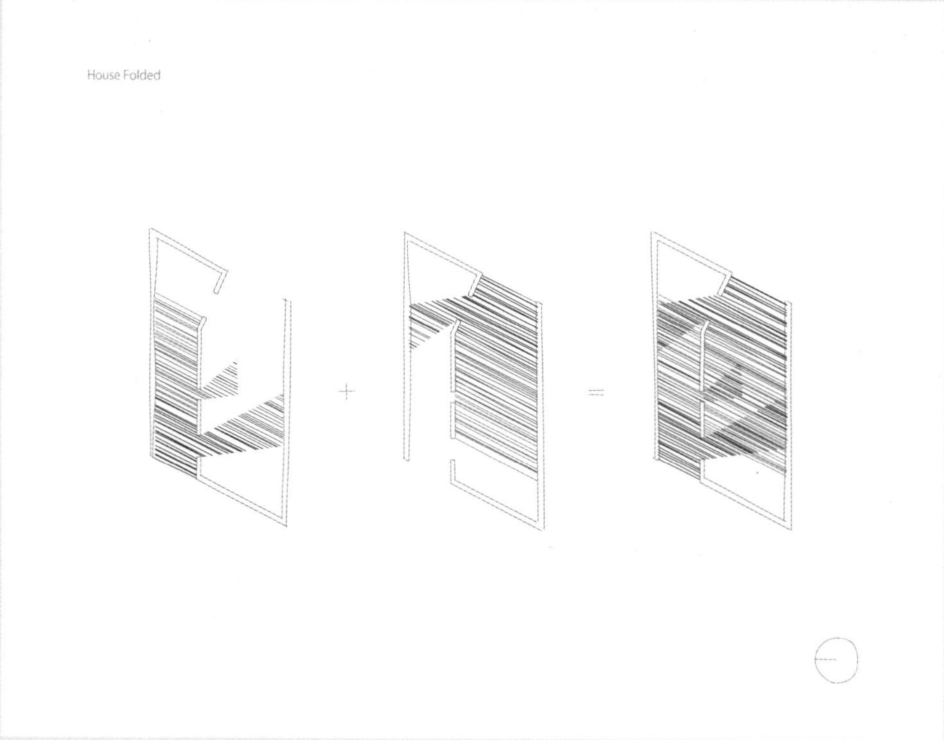
House Folded

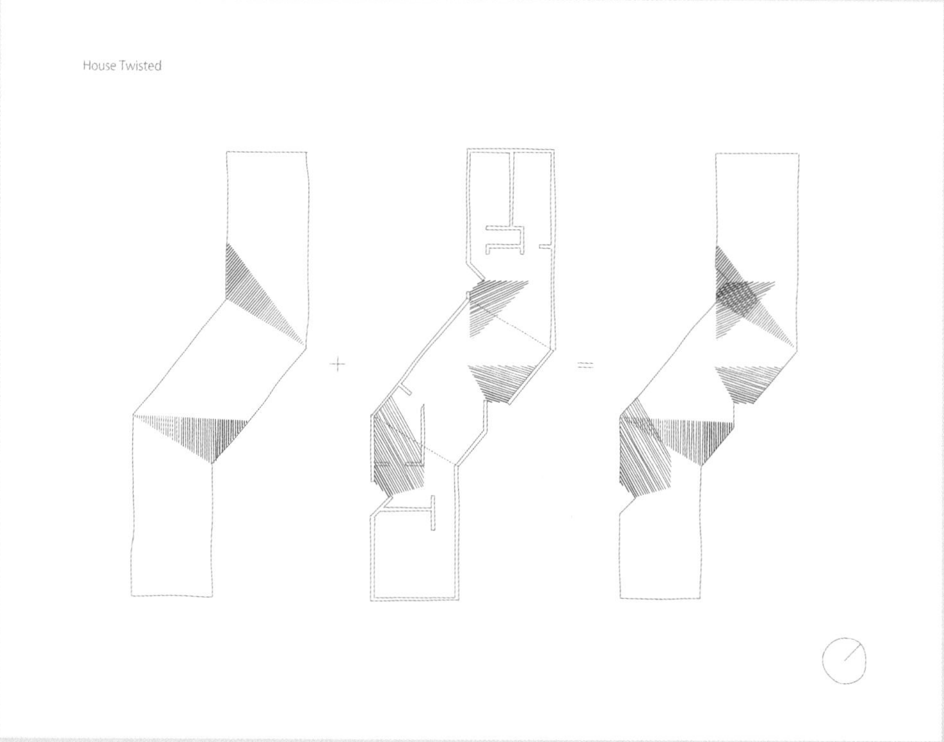
House Twisted

2段ベッドと屋根を支えるだけの
軽快な架構が、家具であり同時に
ているね。

Koyasan Guest House

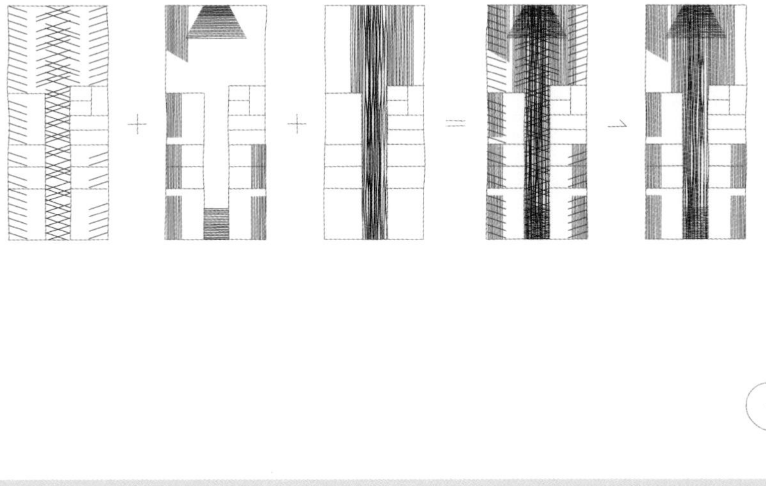

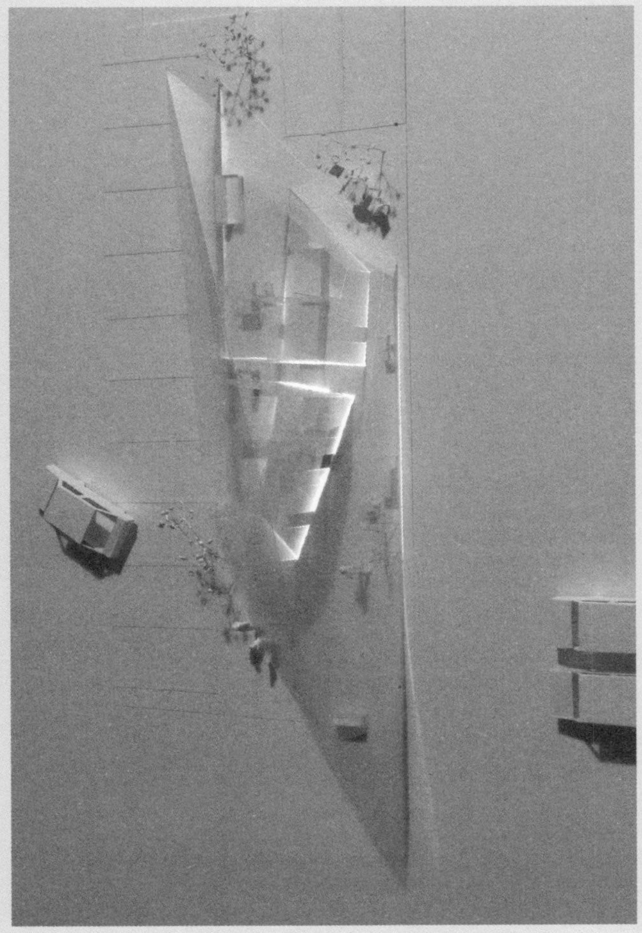

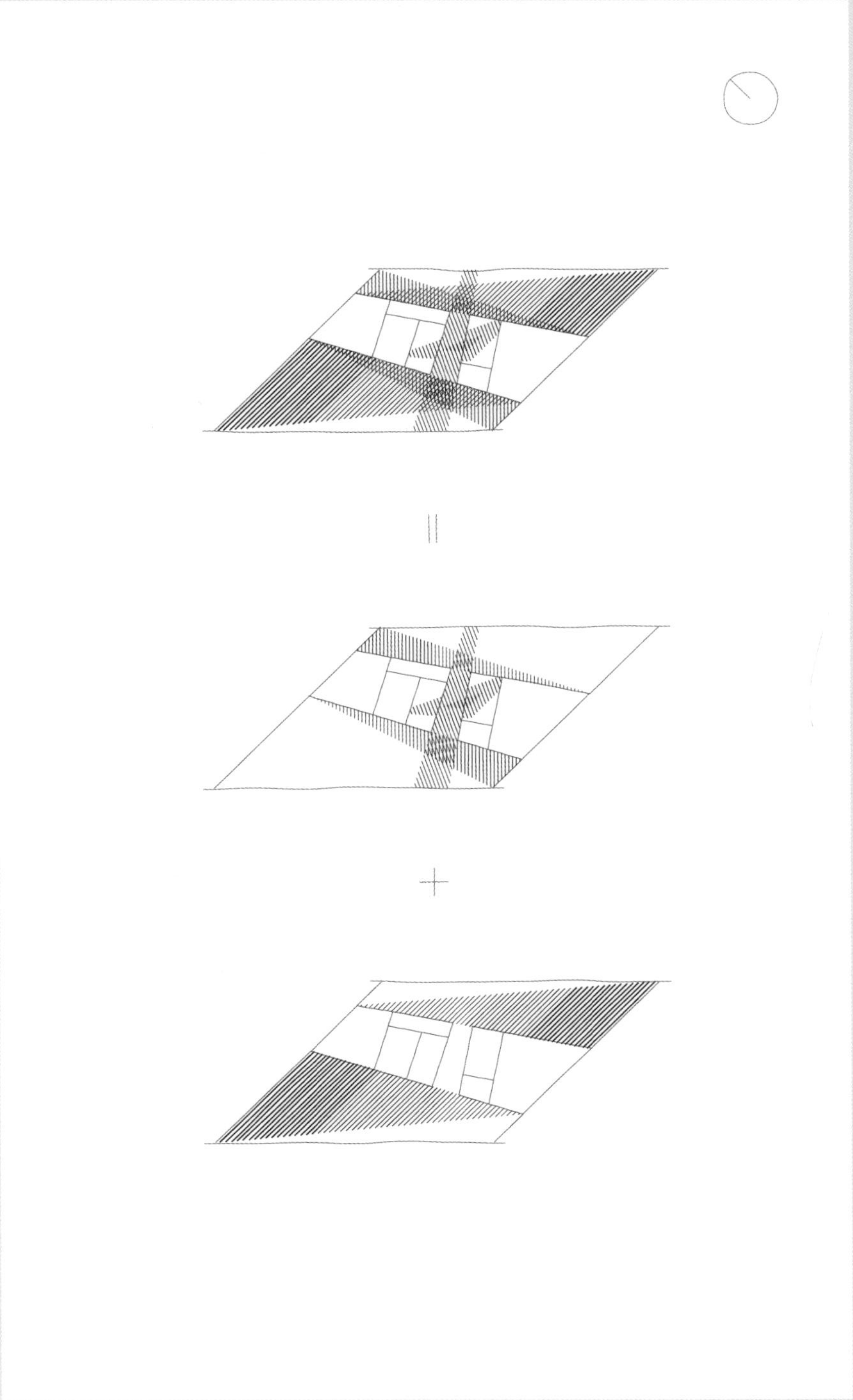

ANDERS TYRRESTRUP

AART Architects • Denmark

Featured project: Viking Age Museum [pp. 300–5]

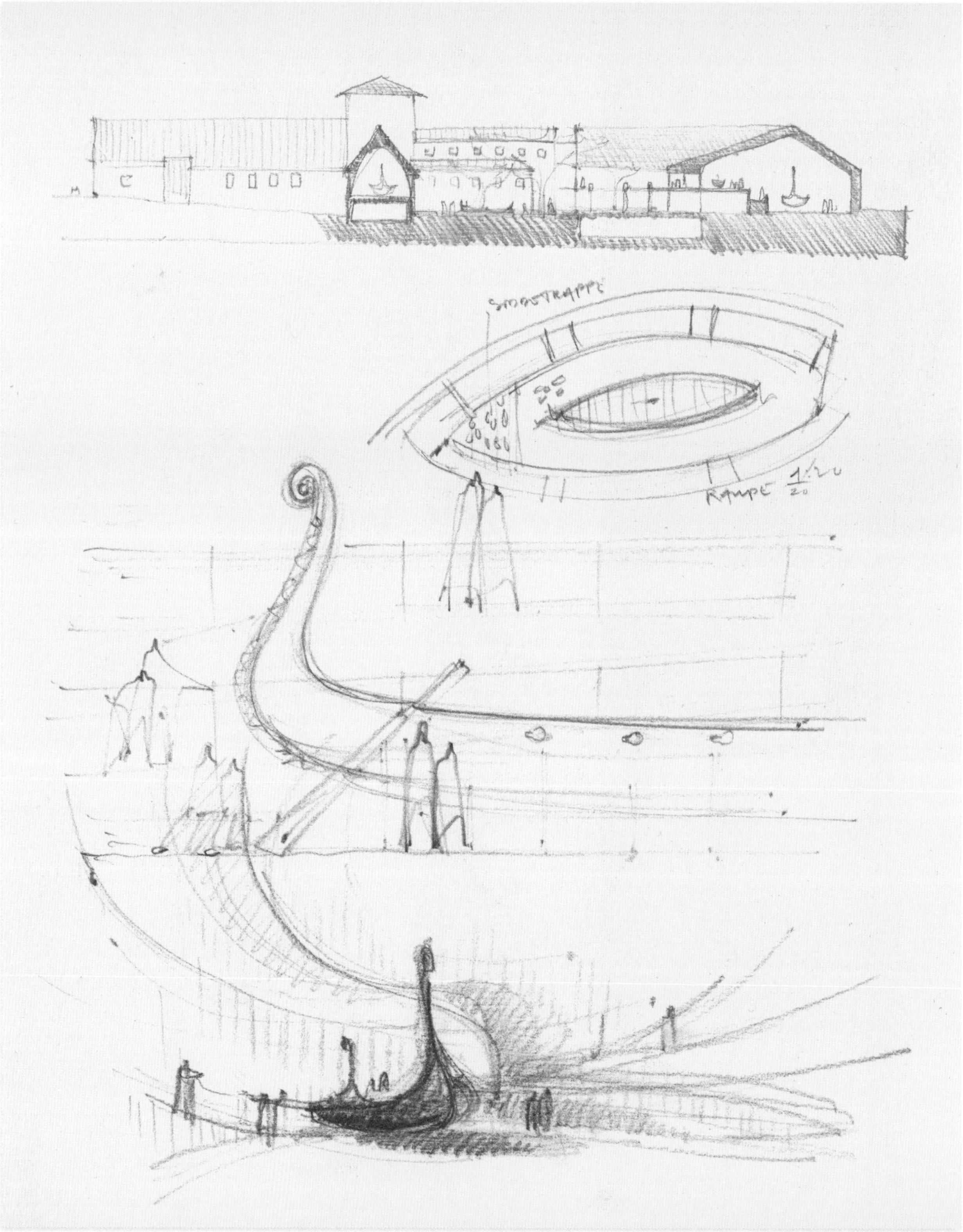

'In this digital age, there is something liberating about sketching,' says Anders Tyrrestrup of AART Architects. 'It is an analogue conceptual working method, which gives you the freedom to come up with an idea and explore it further, whether individually or with team members. The physical nature of it allows for spontaneous reflection, as well as a natural intuition and curiosity.'

Tyrrestrup is a founding partner at AART, which has locations in Aarhus, Copenhagen and Oslo, and is an influential partner in Sustainia, the world's largest platform for sustainable solutions. 'Sketching has the power to bring people together and convey potential ideas,' he says. 'Drawing ideas on site brings the design process closer to the clients. It is very hard to imagine designing without sketching. In fact, I have developed a handicap of sorts, because I now find it difficult to communicate a project without having a pen in my hand!'

He concludes: 'Sketching is a multi-layered process. Instead of formulating a conclusion, it takes you and other members of the team on a creative journey, in which you constantly reflect on a concept, explore its possibilities and create the perfect setting to bring it to life. It is an iterative process, from the first reflections of a concept to the final detailing.'

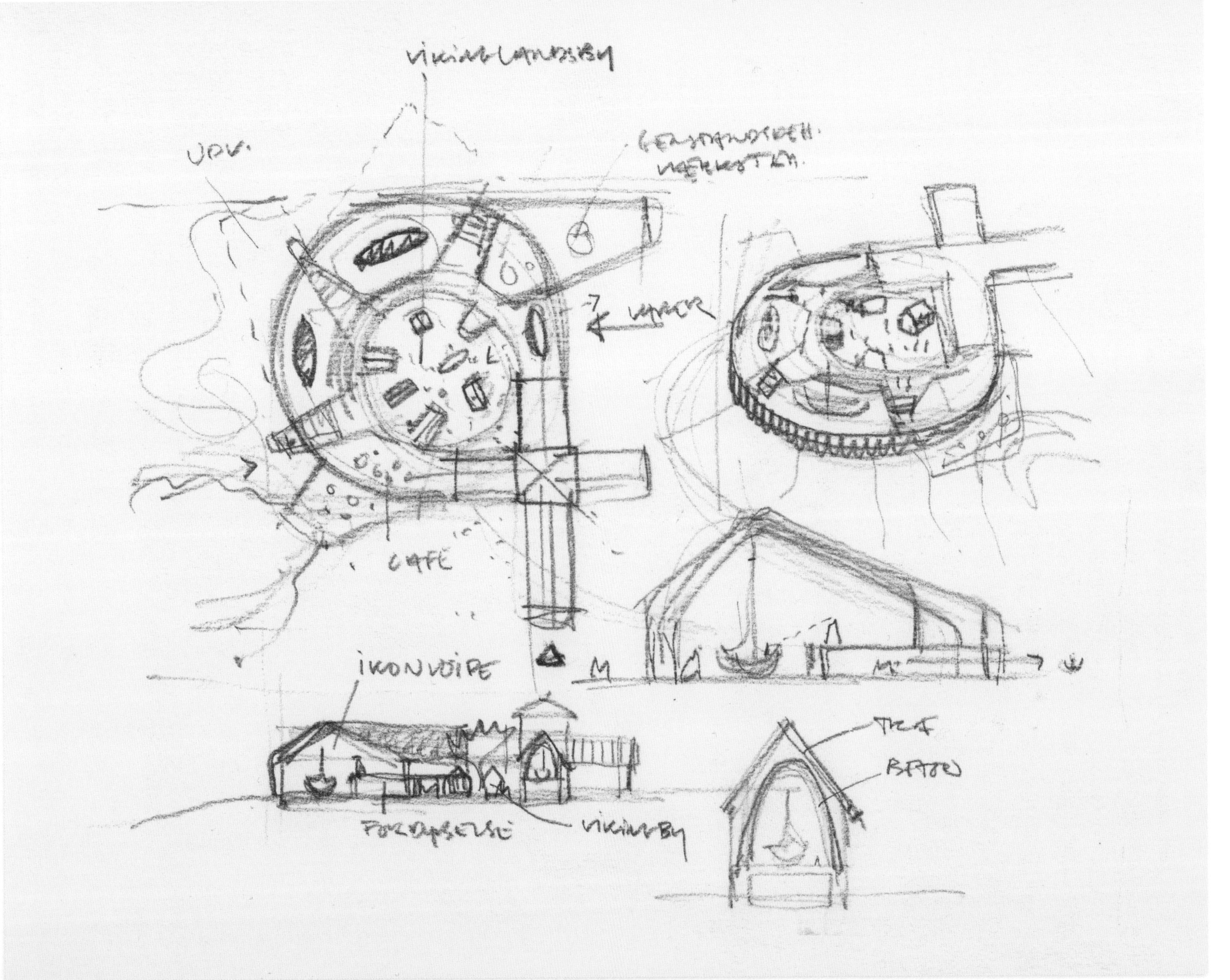
UDV.
CAFE
TRÆ
BETON
FORDYBELSE
VIKINGBY

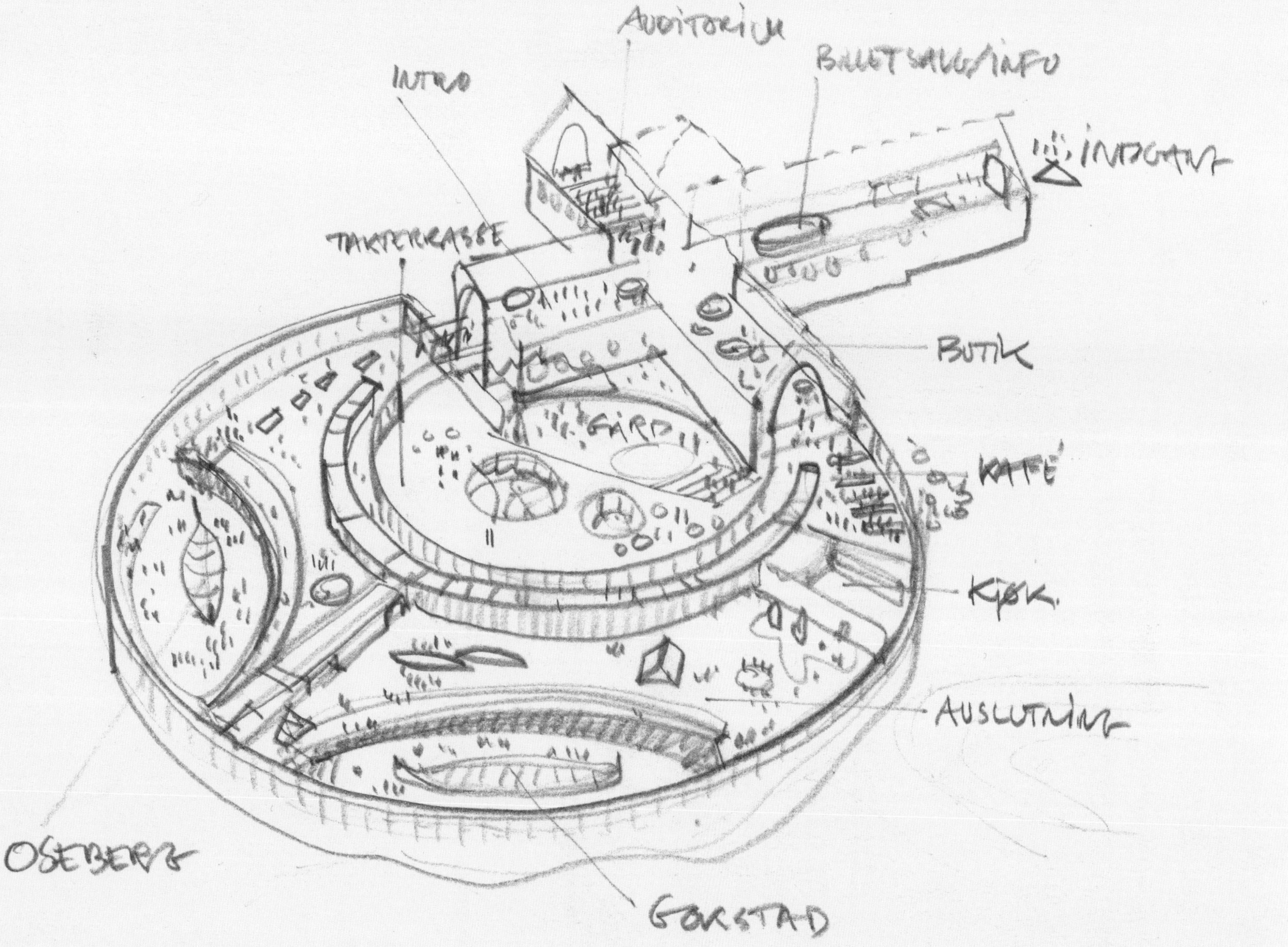
AUDITORIUM
BILLETSALG/INFO
INTRO
INNGANG
TAKTERRASSE
BUTIK
GÅRD
KAFÉ
KIOSK
AVSLUTNING
OSEBERG
GOKSTAD

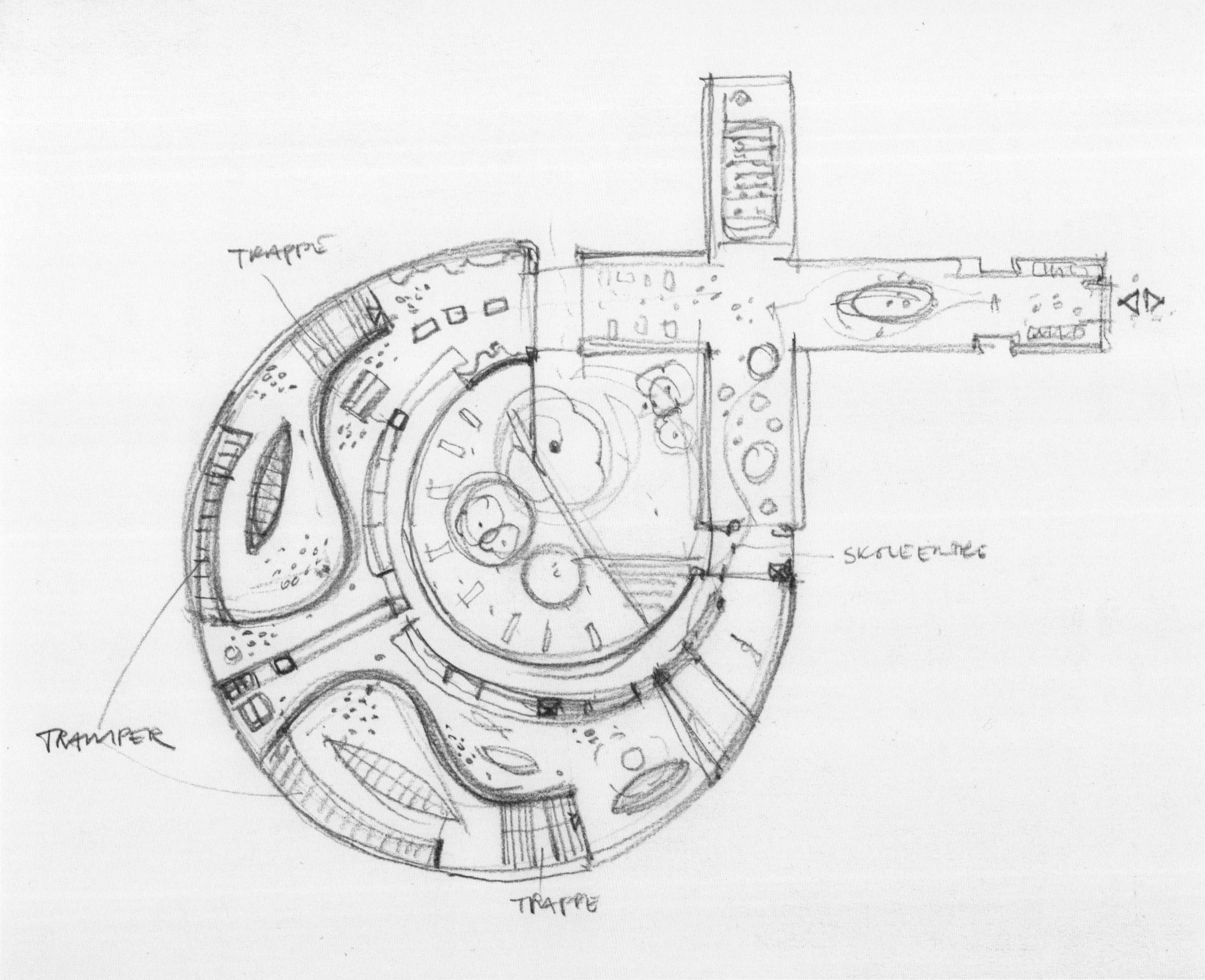
TRAPPE
TRAPPER
TRAPPE
SKOLEENTRE

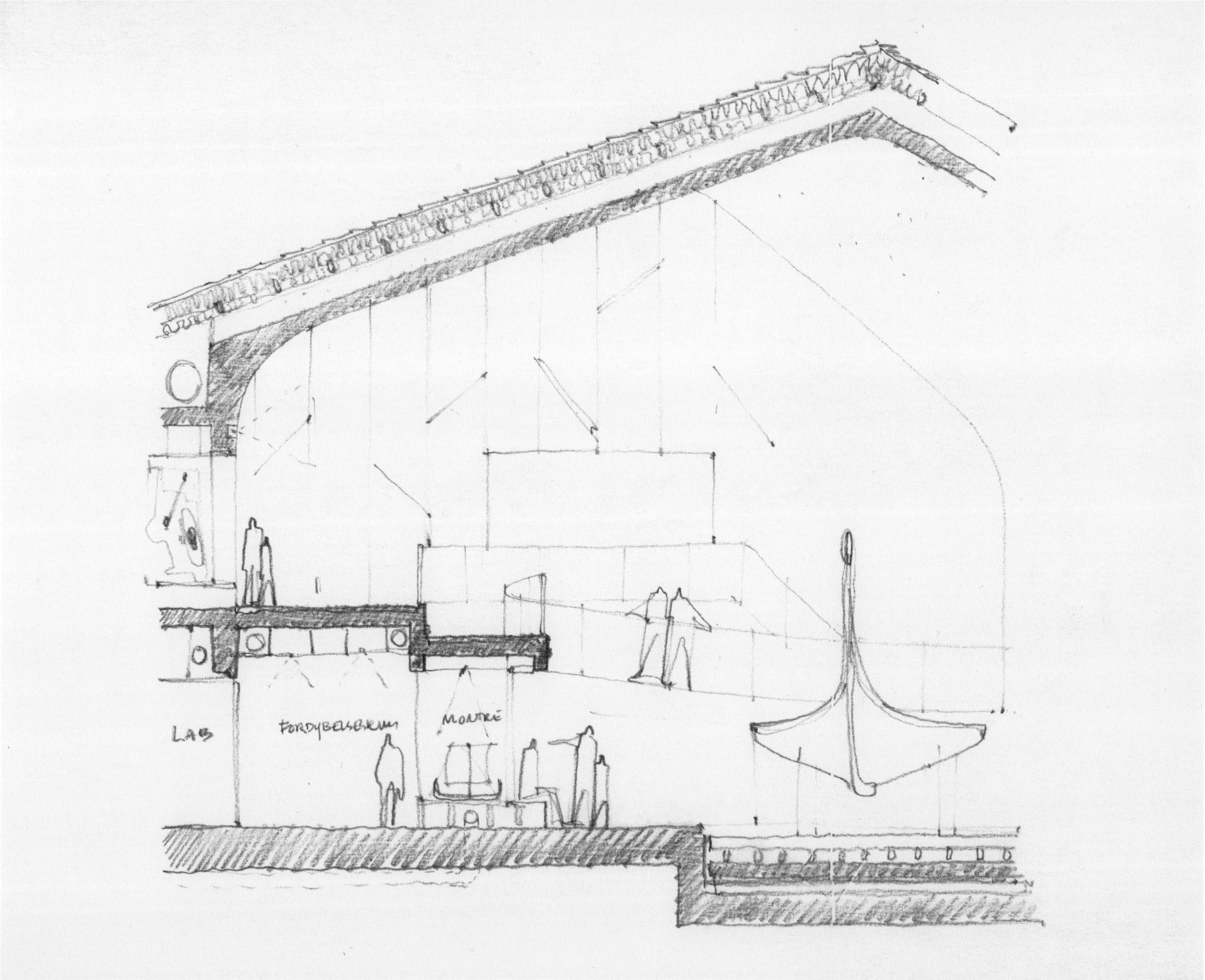
LAB
FORDYBELSESRUM
MONTRÉ

NIJS DE VRIES

Netherlands

Featured project: Hotel Salvation [pp. 306–11]

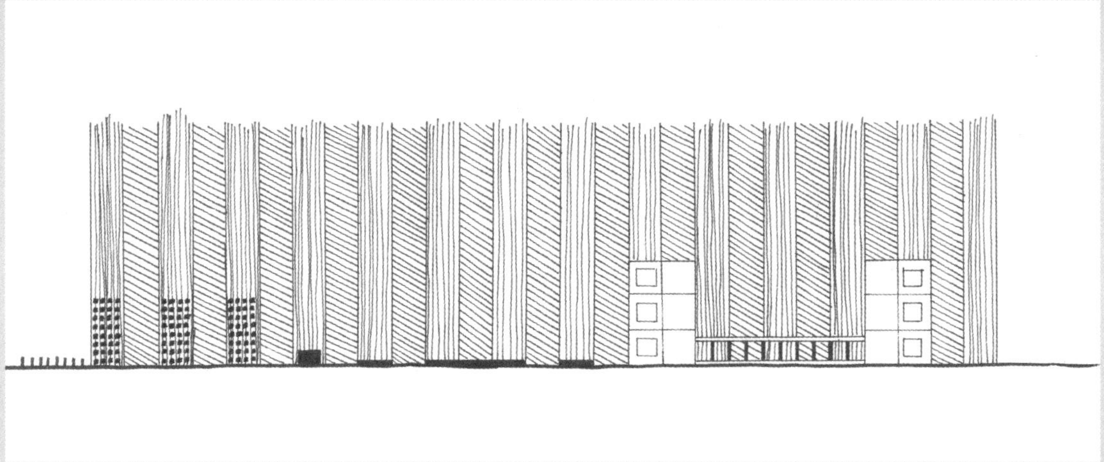

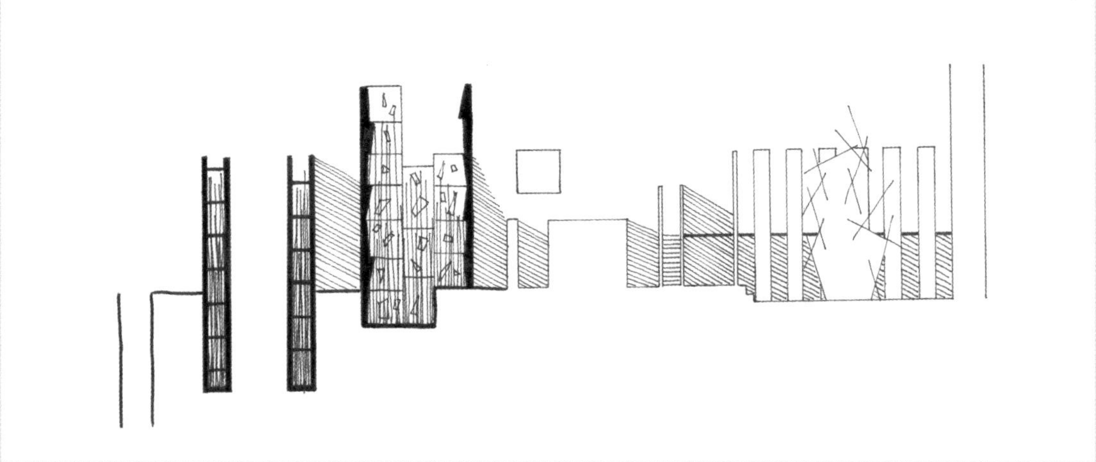

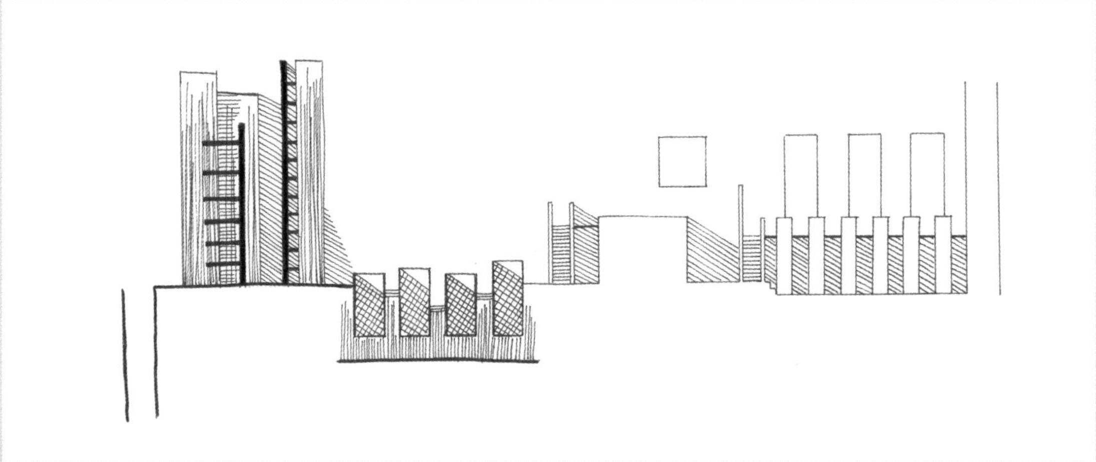

'I usually produce drawings on a roll of sketching paper,' says Dutch architect Nijs de Vries. 'These sketches can be seen as a sequence through the design process, helping to structure it. Whenever I get stuck or need to think something over, I look back at my drawings to retrace the process. Quick sketches help to visualize ideas and serve as an explanatory medium in making a concept clear.'

Having graduated from the Eindhoven University of Technology in 2017 with a Masters in Architecture, Building and Planning, De Vries notes that his goal is to 'create spaces that make people wonder why they are there and experience emotions they did not expect to feel'.

Of the Hotel Salvation project, he says: 'I made many sketches to help get the concept and process straight, before translating them into line drawings with the aid of a 3D model, so that they functioned as an underlayer for the final digital collage. Because I was striving for a particular atmosphere for each image, I used a large number of textures that, when put together using Photoshop, would portray the feeling I had in mind.'

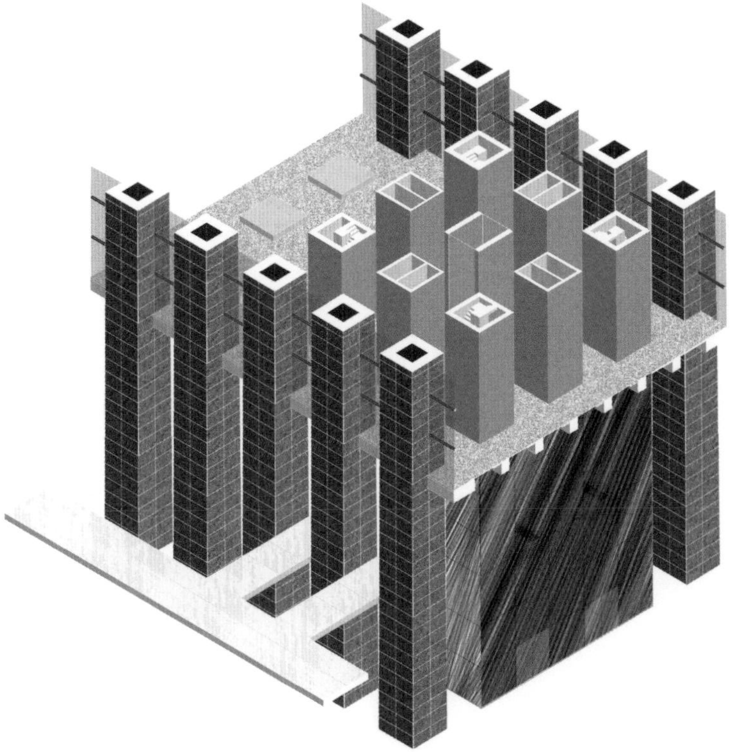

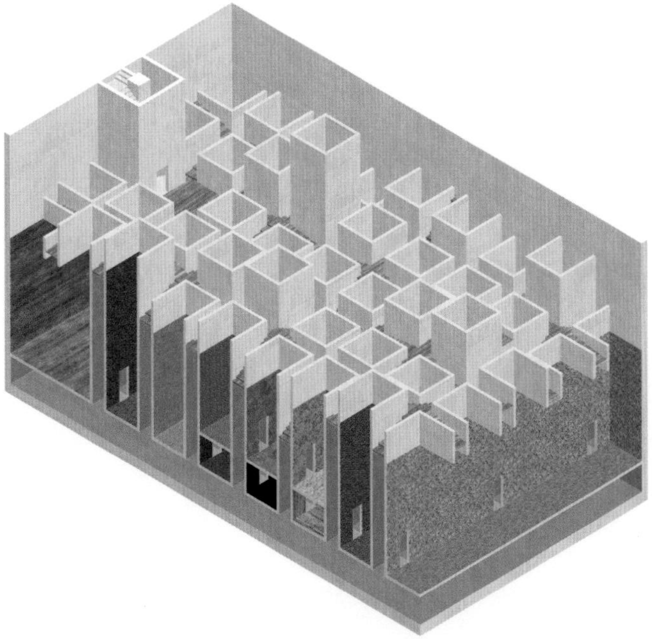

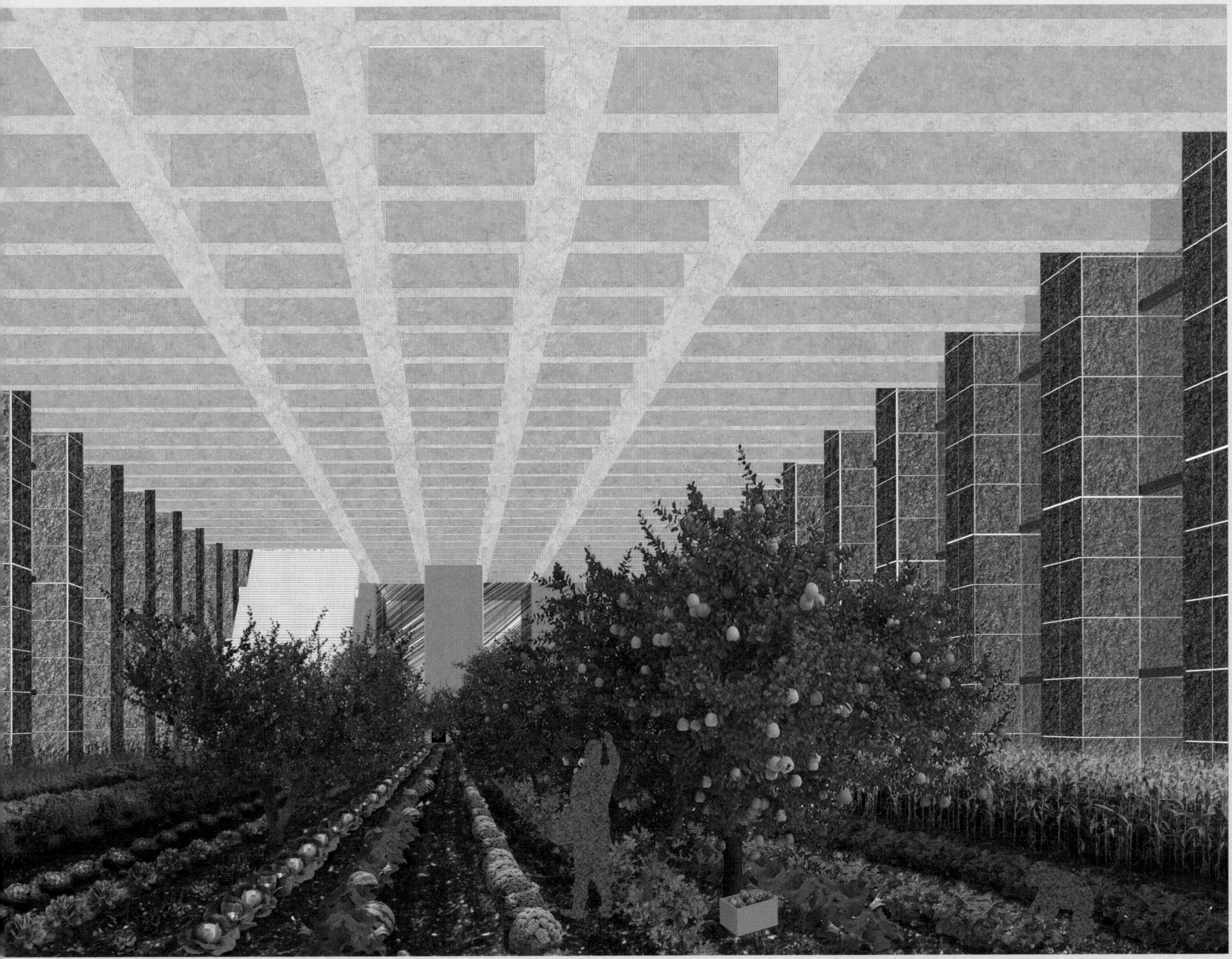

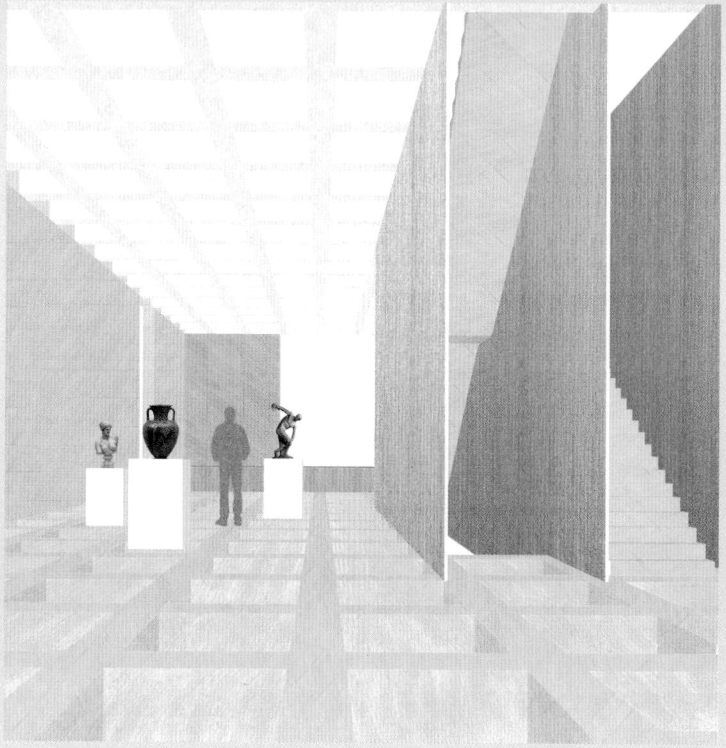

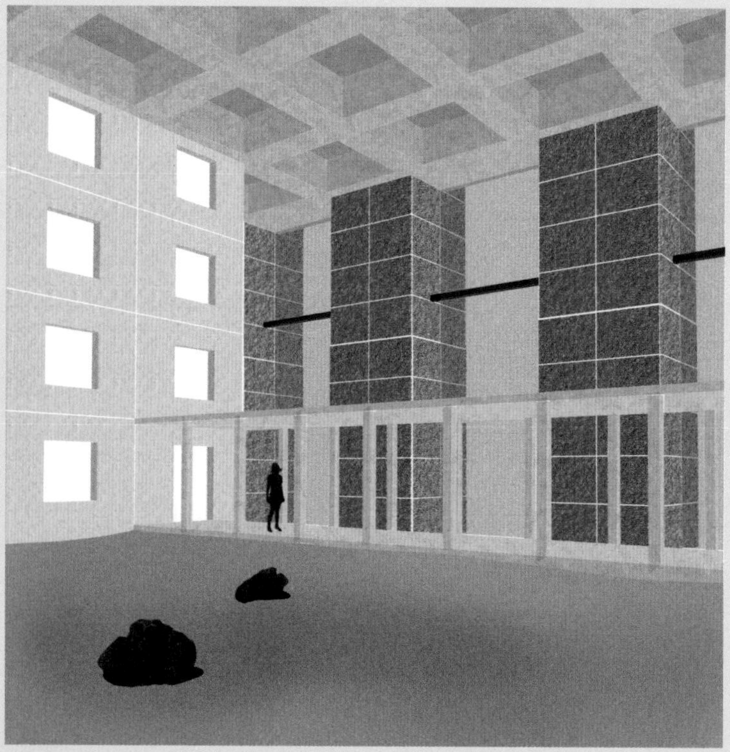

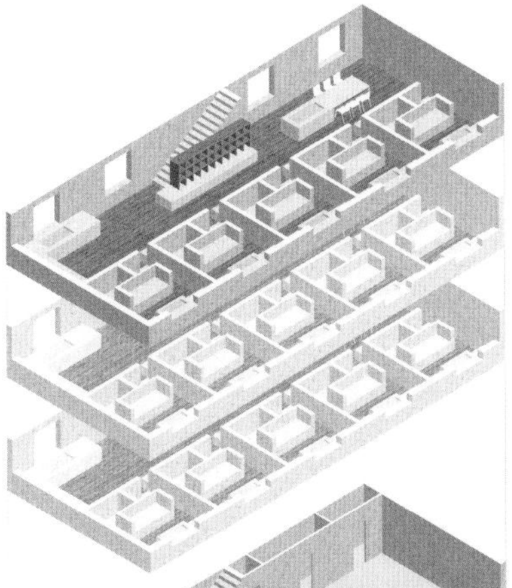

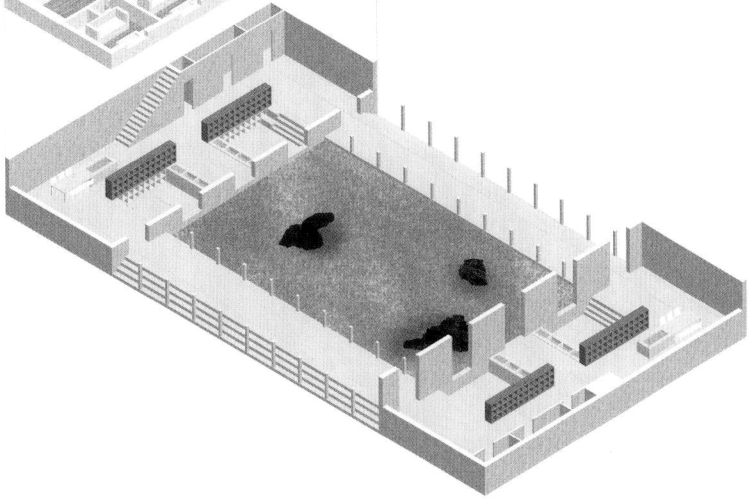

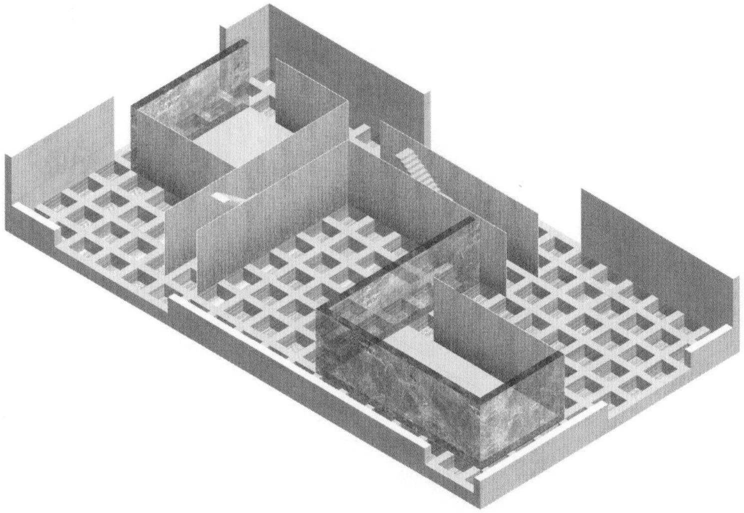

KRISTEN WHITTLE

Bates Smart • Australia

Featured projects: Australian Embassy [pp. 312–13]
Royal Children's Hospital [pp. 314–15]

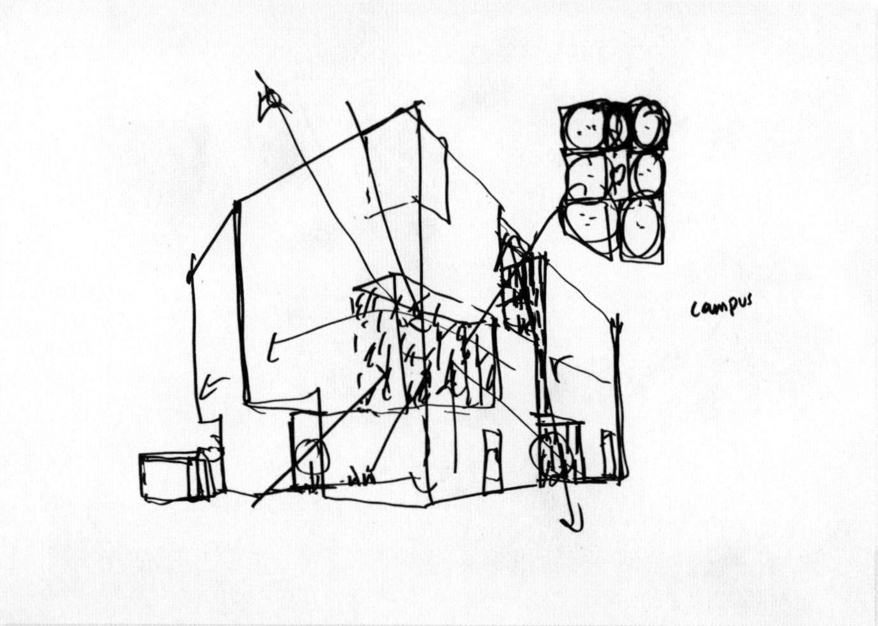

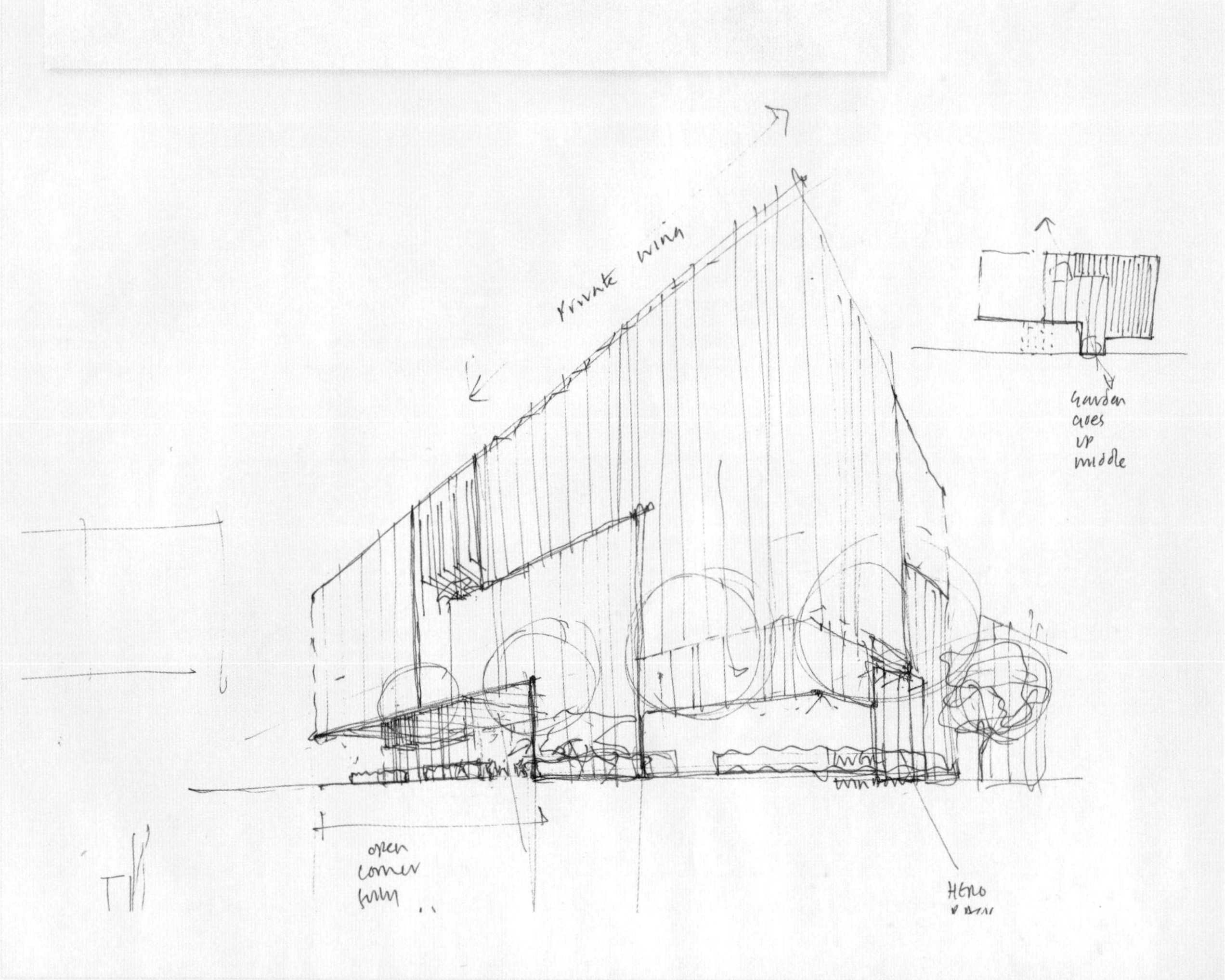

'From what I can see, a computer cannot manifest the whole essence of a project,' says Kristen Whittle, a director at Australian firm Bates Smart. 'It can document geometry or capture light, but cannot encapsulate thinking, concept and materiality instantaneously, all in one hit.'

Whittle believes that sketching is critically important in the 21st century, and that its underlying value lies in how the medium enables practitioners to maintain a human connection with architecture. 'A physically sketched design means that a humanist sentiment is embodied in a building,' he says. 'I think that people are seeking that from architecture. Sketching is thinking: the more you sketch, the more you put your feelings and ideas together. In my case, I can feel the manifestation of an architectural idea through a drawing.'

He also believes that sketching is the fastest and most capable tool for understanding the 'rapid prototyping of an idea', reflecting 'the quickest, most immersive way to enter into and develop a project'. Whittle also sees sketches as highly complex and nuanced, and emotive in nature. 'The reason people love looking at sketches is that they get a lot from them,' he says. 'It is not just the person who has created the sketch, it is the person who is seeing it. You can read a million things into a drawing.'

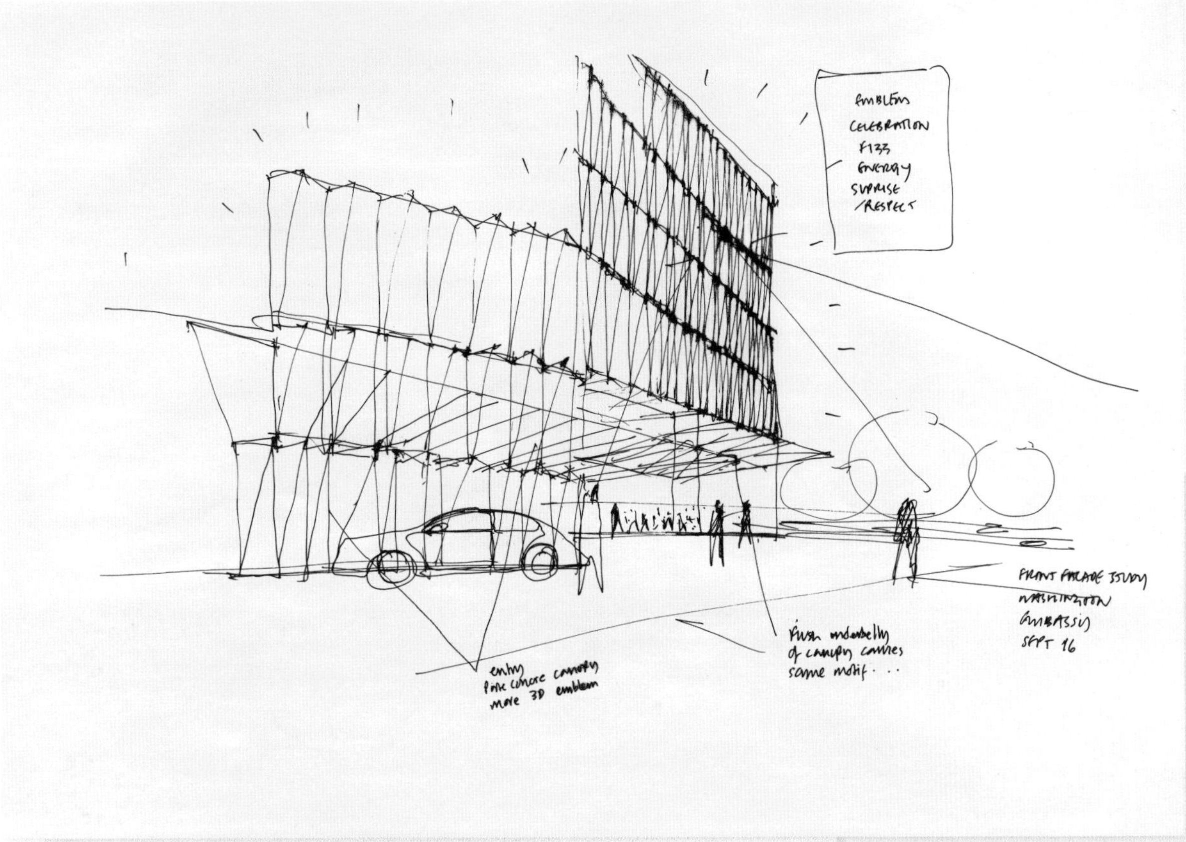
EMBLEM
CELEBRATION
FIZZ
ENERGY
SURPRISE
/RESPECT
entry
more 3D emblem
same motif . . .
FRONT FACADE STUDY
SEPT 16

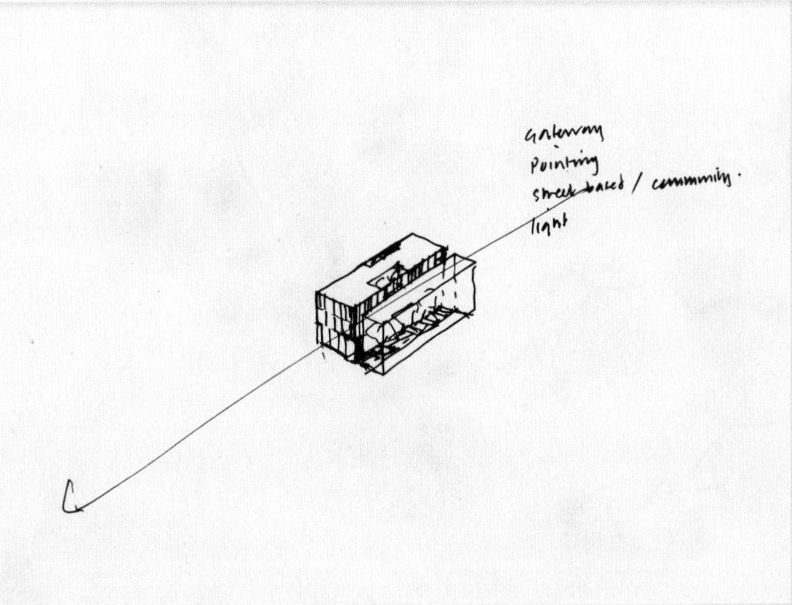
Gateway
Pointing
street based / community.
light

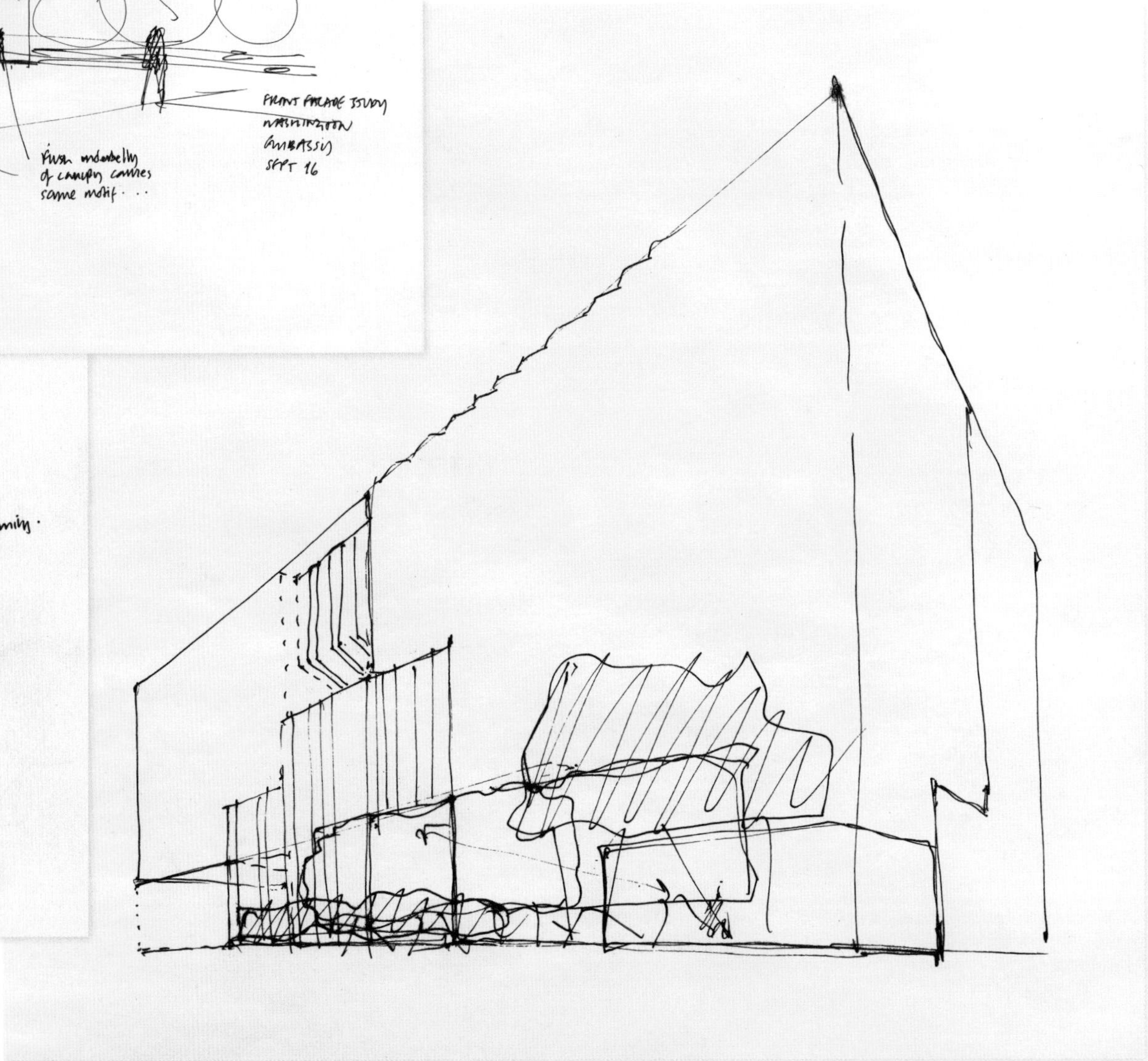

touch ground
RCH
MCRI

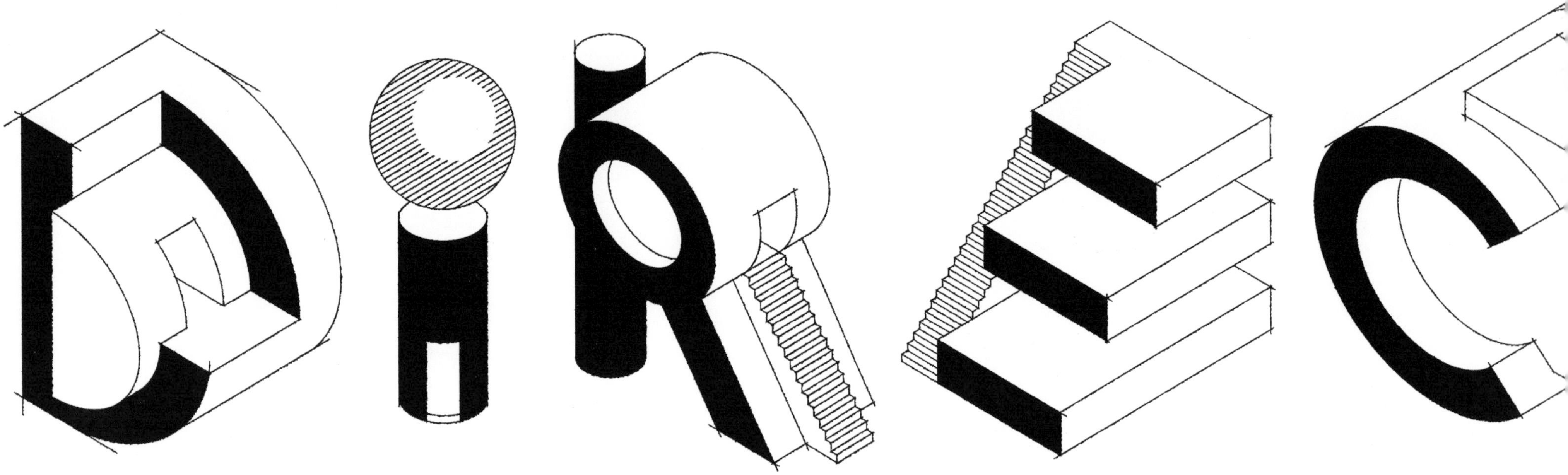
DIREC

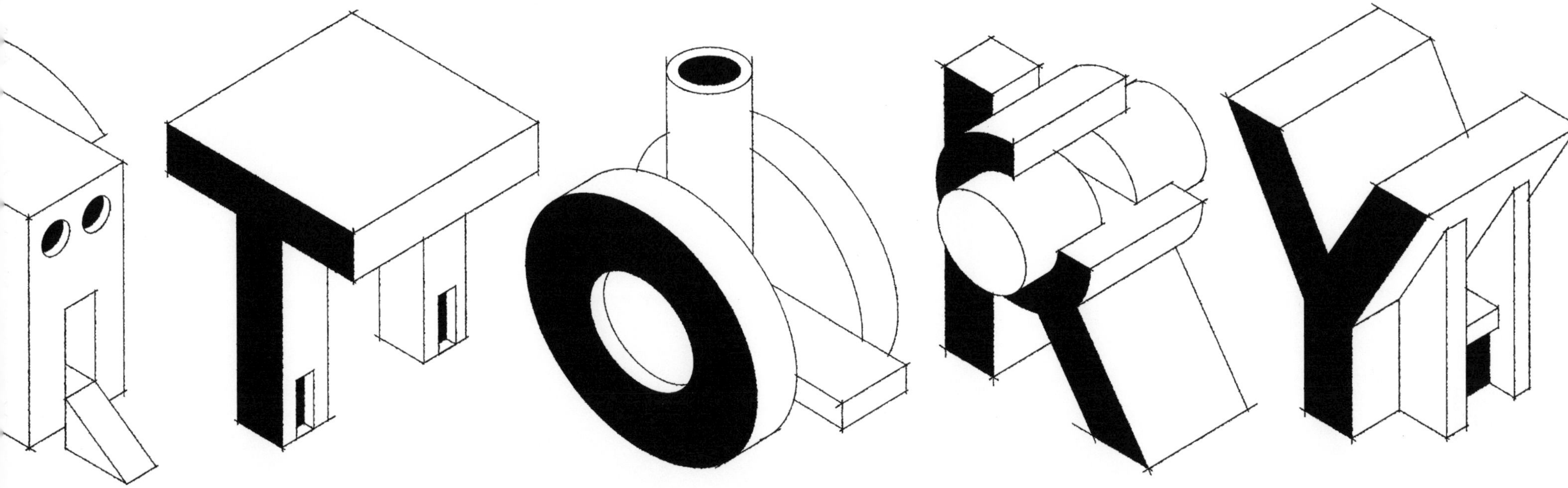
TORY

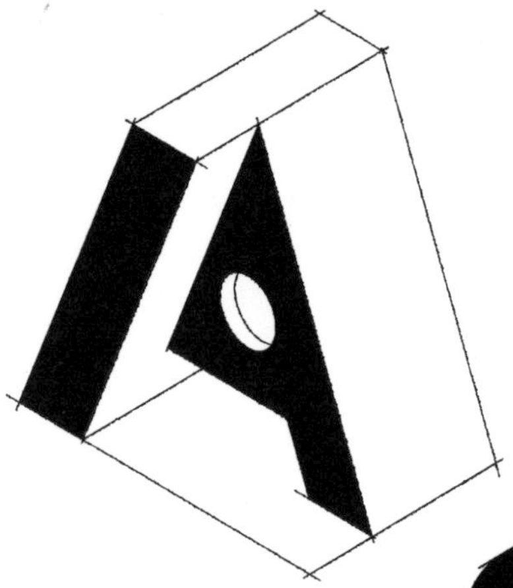

Ben Adams [018]
Ben Adams Architects
London, UK
benadamsarchitects.co.uk

Manuel Aires Mateus [024]
Aires Mateus e Associados
Lisbon, Portugal
airesmateus.com

Wiel Arets [026]
Wiel Arets Architects
Amsterdam, Netherlands
wielaretsarchitects.com

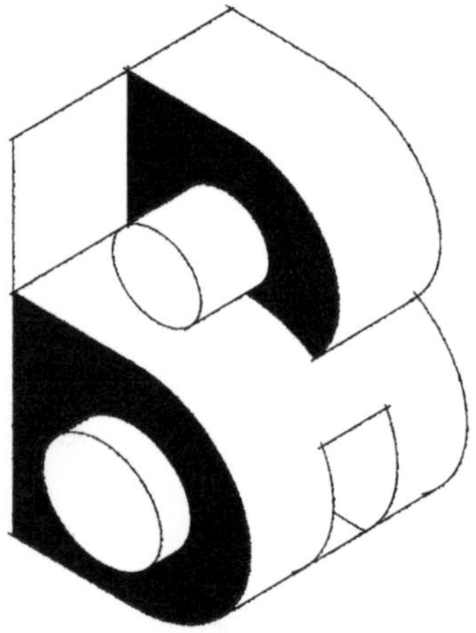

Cecil Balmond [028]
Balmond Studio
London, UK
balmondstudio.com

Ben van Berkel [032]
UNStudio
Amsterdam, Netherlands
unstudio.com

Peter Berton [036]
+VG Architects
Toronto, Canada
ventingroup.com

Adam Brady [038]
Lett Architects
Peterborough, Canada
lett.ca

Jacob Brillhart [040]
Brillhart Architecture
Miami, USA
brillhartarchitecture.com

Will Burges [042]
31/44 Architects
London, UK
3144architects.com

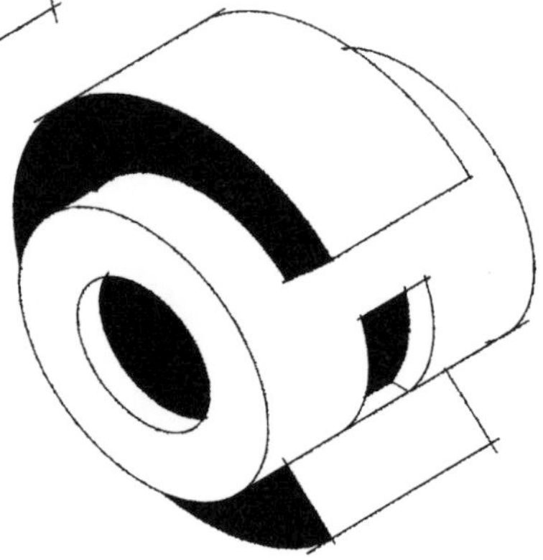

Alberto Campo Baeza [050]
Studio Alberto Campo Baeza
Madrid, Spain
campobaeza.com

Jo Coenen [056]
The Hague, Netherlands
jocoenen.com

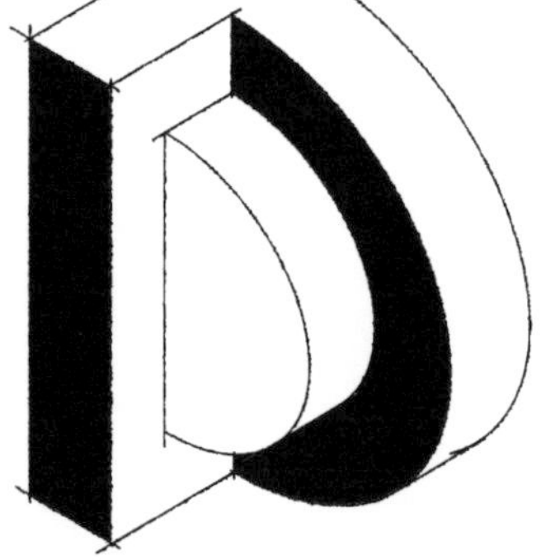

Jack Diamond [060]
Diamond Schmitt
Toronto, Canada
dsai.ca

Heather Dubbeldam [066]
Dubbeldam Architecture & Design
Toronto, Canada
dubbeldam.ca

Duggan Morris Architects [72]
London, UK
dugganmorrisarchitects.com

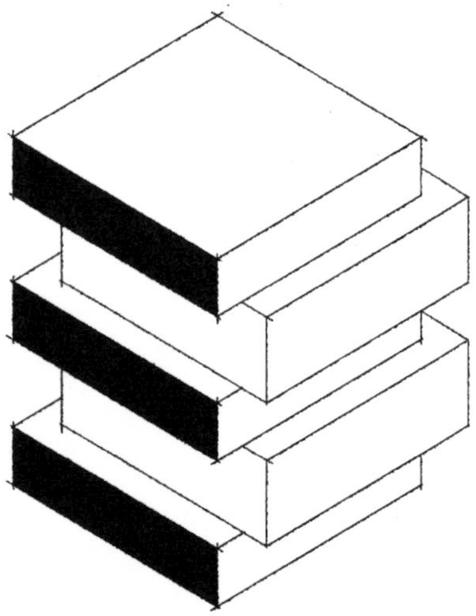

Piet Hein Eek & Iggie Dekkers [080]
Eek en Dekkers
Eindhoven, Netherlands
pietheineek.nl

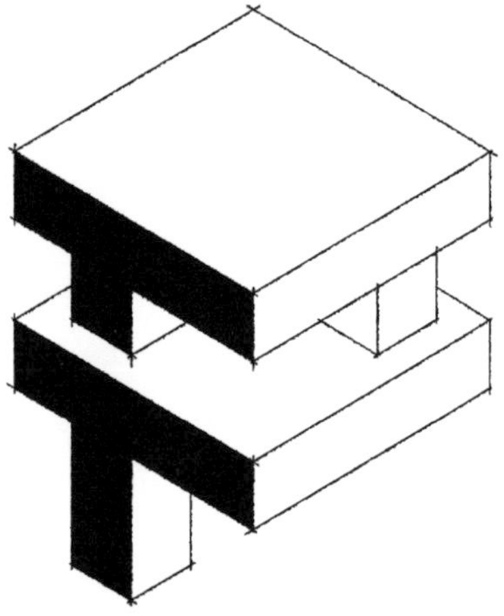

Ricardo Flores & Eva Prats [090]
Flores & Prats Arquitectes
Barcelona, Spain
floresprats.com

Albert France-Lanord [098]
AF-LA
Stockholm, Sweden
af-la.com

Massimiliano Fuksas [102]
Studio Fuksas
Rome, Italy
fuksas.it

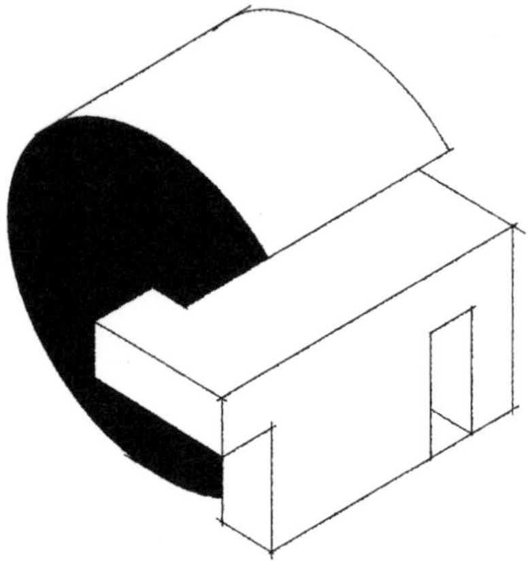

Benjamin Garcia Saxe [110]
Studio Saxe
San Jose, Costa Rica
studiosaxe.com

Sasha Gebler [112]
Gebler Tooth Architects
London, UK
geblertooth.co.uk

Carlos Gómez [120]
InN Arquitectura
Galaroza, Spain
gogoarq.com

Meg Graham [126]
Superkül
Toronto, Canada
superkul.ca

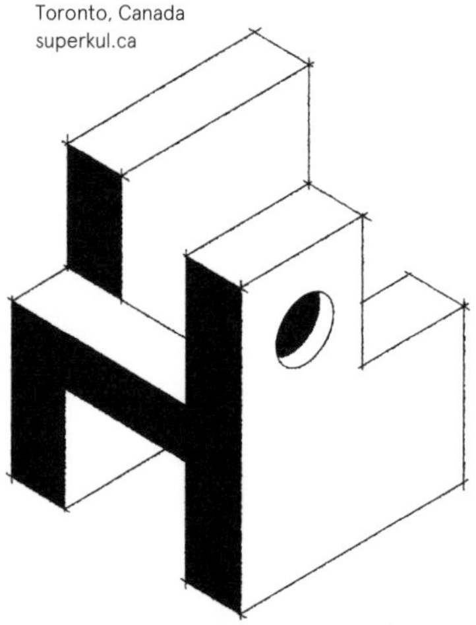

Harquitectes [128]
Sabadell, Spain
harquitectes.com

Carl-Viggo Hølmebakk [134]
Horten, Norway
holmebakk.no

Johanna Hurme, Sasa Radulovic & Ken Borton [138]
5468796 Architecture
Winnipeg, Canada
5468796.ca

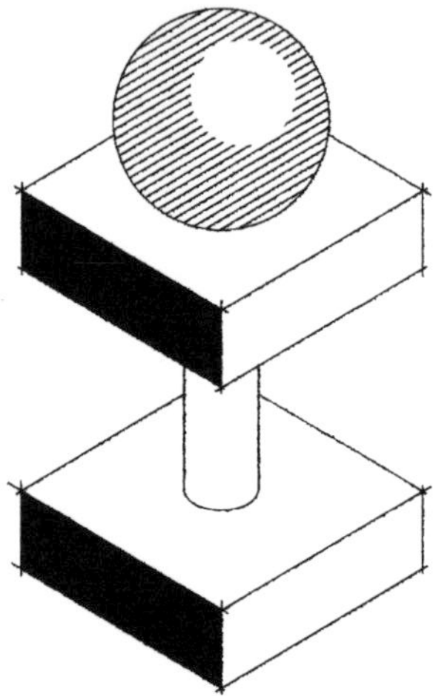

Jun Igarashi [142]
Jun Igarashi Architects
Sapporo, Japan
jun-igarashi.com

Anderson Inge [146]
Cambridge Architectural Research
Cambridge, UK
carltd.com

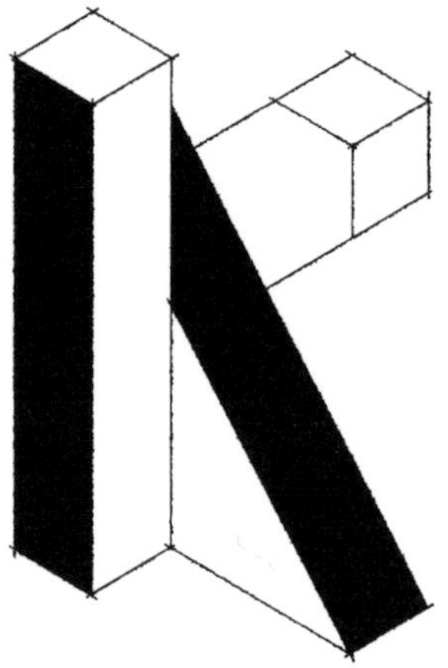

Les Klein & Caroline Robbie
Quadrangle [150]
Toronto, Canada
quadrangle.ca

James von Klemperer [154]
Kohn Pedersen Fox
New York, USA
kpf.com

Bruce Kuwabara [156]
KPMB Architects
Toronto, Canada
kpmb.com

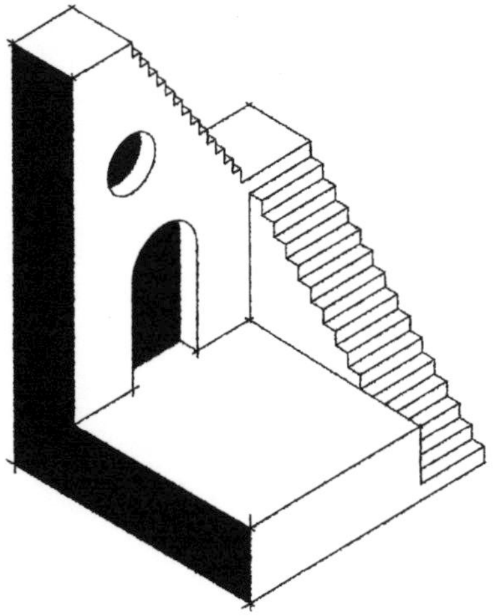

Christopher Lee [158]
Serie Architects
London, UK
serie.co.uk

Uffe Leth [166]
Leth & Gori
Copenhagen, Denmark
lethgori.dk

Levitt Bernstein [170]
London, UK
levittbernstein.co.uk

Daniel Libeskind [176]
Studio Libeskind
New York, USA
libeskind.com

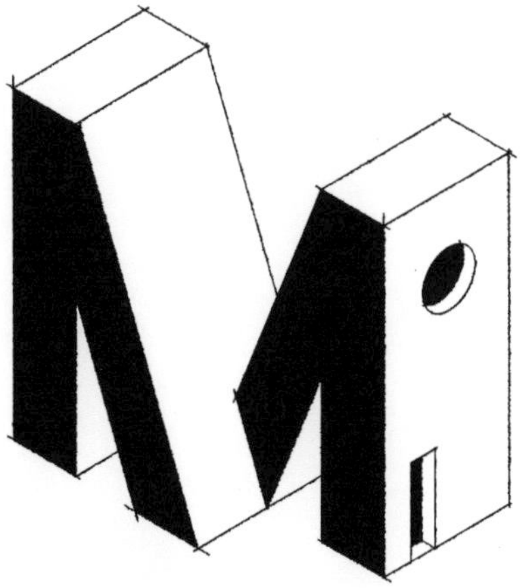

Stephanie Macdonald
& Tom Emerson [184]
6a architects
London, UK
6a.co.uk

Brian MacKay-Lyons [188]
MacKay-Lyons Sweetapple Architects
Halifax, Canada
mlsarchitects.ca

Davide Macullo [192]
Davide Macullo Architects
Lugano, Switzerland
macullo.com

Massimo Mariani [200]
Massimo Mariani
Architecture & Design
London, UK
massimomariani.co.uk

Tara McLaughlin [204]
+VG Architects
Ottawa, Canada
ventingroup.com

Rob Miners [206]
Studio MMA
Montreal, Canada
studiomma.ca

Peter Morris [212]
Peter Morris Architects
London, UK
petermorrisarchitects.com

MVRDV [216]
Rotterdam, Netherlands
mvrdv.nl

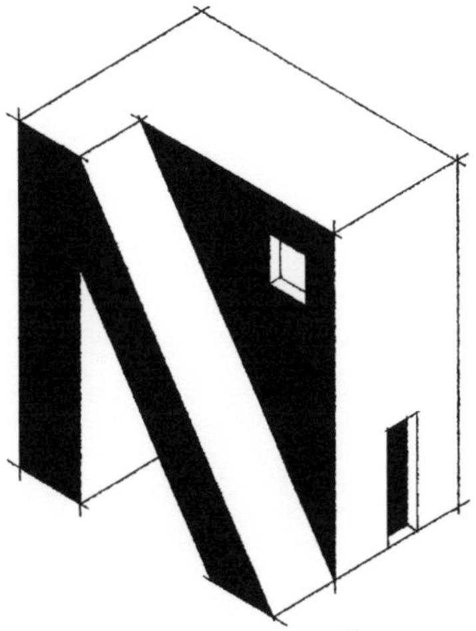

Brad Netkin [224]
Stamp Architecture
Toronto, Canada
stamparchitecture.net

Richard Nightingale [226]
Kilburn Nightingale Architects
London, UK
kilburnnightingale.com

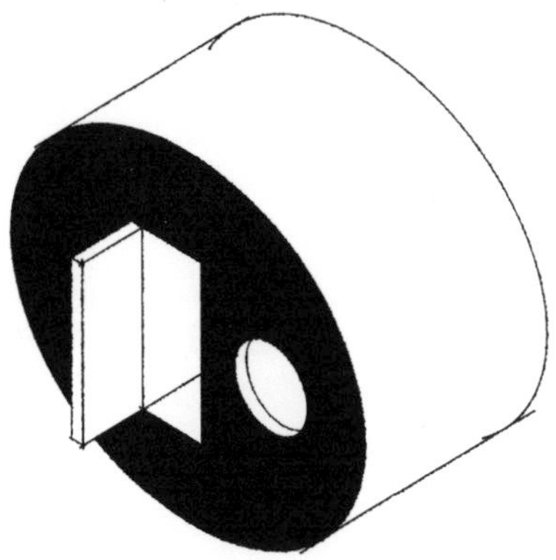

Richard Olcott [230]
Ennead Architects
New York, USA
ennead.com

Benedict O'Looney [234]
Benedict O'Looney Architects
London, UK
benedictolooney.co.uk

Anthony Orelowitz [242]
Paragon Group
Johannesburg, South Africa
paragon.co.za

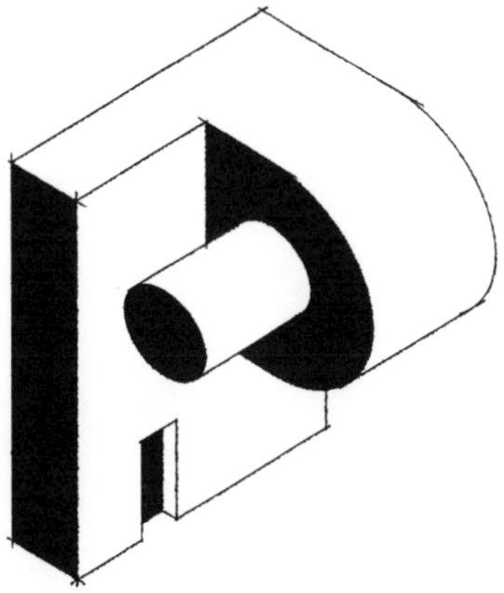

Joseph di Pasquale [244]
JDP Architects
Milan, Italy
amprogetti.it

Felipe Pich-Aguilera [248]
Pich Architects
Barcelona, Spain
picharchitects.com

Pawel Podwojewski [252]
Motiv
Gdansk, Poland
motiv-studio.com

Christian de Portzamparc [262]
2Portzamparc
Paris, France
christiandeportzamparc.com

Sanjay Puri [266]
Sanjay Puri Architects
Mumbai, India
sanjaypuriarchitects.com

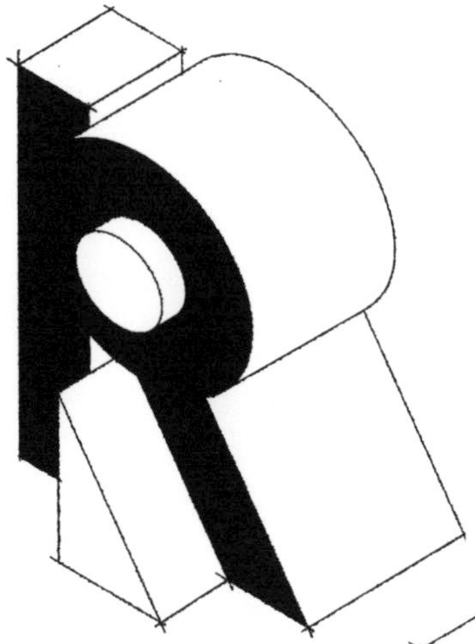

Matthijs la Roi [268]
Matthijs la Roi Architects
London, UK
matthijslaroi.nl

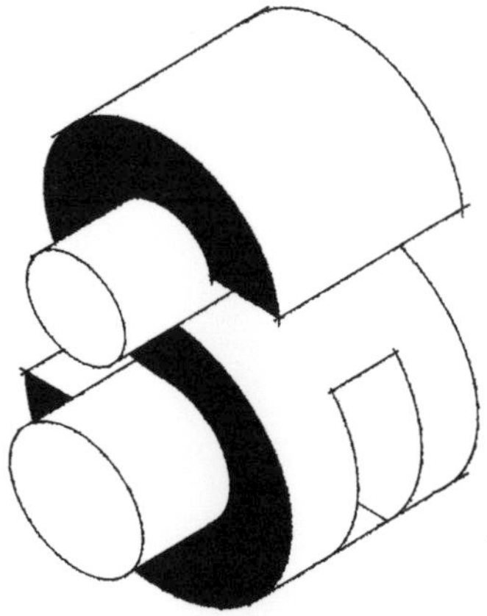

Moshe Safdie [272]
Safdie Architects
Boston, USA
safdiearchitects.com

Deborah Saunt [280]
DSDHA
London, UK
dsdha.co.uk

Jon Soules [284]
Diamond Schmitt
Toronto, Canada
dsai.ca

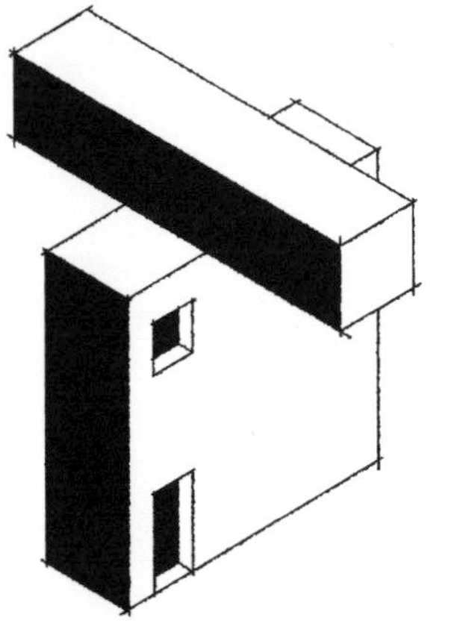

Kentaro Takeguchi
& Asako Yamamoto [292]
Alphaville Architects
Kyoto, Japan
a-ville.net

Anders Tyrrestrup [300]
AART Architects
Aarhus, Denmark
aart.dk

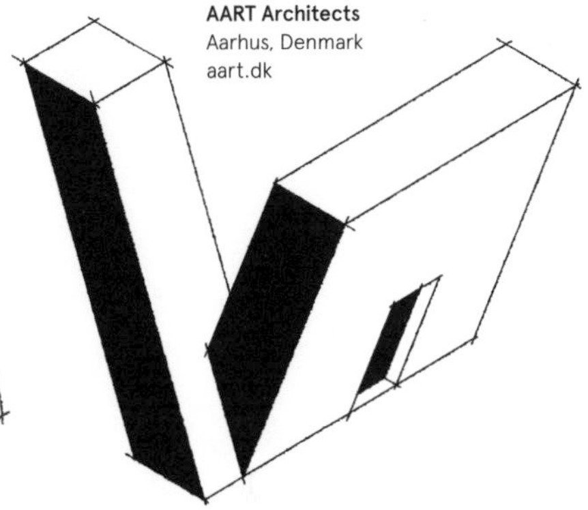

Nijs de Vries [306]
Eindhoven, Netherlands
nijsdevries.com

Kristen Whittle [312]
Bates Smart
Melbourne, Australia
batessmart.com

For my dad, a quiet inspiration

Making Marks: New Architects' Sketchbooks

First published in 2019 in the United States of America by
Thames & Hudson Inc., 500 Fifth Avenue, New York, New York 10110

www.thamesandhudsonusa.com

Library of Congress Control Number 2018945289

ISBN 978-0-500-02131-6

Printed and bound in China by Reliance Printing (Shenzhen) Co. Ltd.